वनज्योत्स्ना–सहस्रसौमनसी

FLORA & PLANT KINGDOM

IN

SANSKRIT LITERATURE

JYOTSNAMOY CHATTERJEE FESTSCHRIFT

Published by
EASTERN BOOK LINKERS
(Indological Publishers and Book Sellers)
5825, New Chandrawal
Jawahar Nagar, Delhi-10007
Phone : 3970287
E-mail : easternbook@mantraonline.com

Phones : 7143397, 7466139, 7120287

Kalidasa Academy of Sanskrit Music & Fine Arts Series No. 10

First Edition : 2003

Price : Rs. 2,000.00

ISBN : 81-7854-027-4

Printed at : R. K. Offset Process
Naveen Shahdara, Delhi-110032

KALIDASA ACADEMY OF SANSKRIT MUSIC & FINE ARTS SERIES NO. 10

वनज्योत्स्ना–सहस्त्रसौमनसी

VANAJYOTSNĀ-SAHASRASAUMANASĪ

FLORA & PLANT KINGDOM IN SANSKRIT LITERATURE

JYOTSNAMOY CHATTERJEE FESTSCHRIFT

Editor
ABHA KULSHRESHTHA
M.A., LL.M., D.LL., M.B.I.M. (London)
Advocate, Delhi High Court;
Former Visiting Faculty
Faculty of Law
Jamia Millia Islamia & University of Delhi

Asstt. Editor
ANJU BALA
M.A., Ph.D.
Publication Secretary
Kalidasa Academy of Sanskrit
Music & Fine Arts
Delhi

Managing Editor
JAGAN NATH
News Editor, World News Service (N.D.)
Depthnews Asia, New Delhi Bureau
(Manila, Philippins);
D.A.V. Centenary Public School
New Delhi

EASTERN BOOK LINKERS
DELHI :: (INDIA)

KALIDASA ACADEMY OF SANSKRIT MUSIC & FINE ARTS SERIES NO. 10

VANAJYOTSNĀ-SAHASRASAUMANASĪ

FLORA & PLANT KINGDOM IN SANSKRIT LITERATURE

JYOTSNAMOY CHATTERJEE FESTSCHRIFT

Principal Investigators & Editors

PROF. SUSHMA KULSHRESHTHA
D. Phil., D. Litt., F.R.A.S. (London)
Member, Faculty of Arts
University of Delhi;
Hony. Director
Kalidasa Academy of Sanskrit
Music & Fine Arts, Delhi

ACHARYA DR. JAGDISH SAHAI
M. Mus., M. Dip., D. Mus.
Ex. Principal, Institute of Music &
Fine Arts, Jammu (J.&K.);
Director, Cultural Deptt.
The Indian Public School
Rajawala, Dehradun

EASTERN BOOK LINKERS
DELHI :: (INDIA)

PRESENTED TO OUR ESTEEMED

JYOTISHMAN JYOTSNAMOY CHATTERJEE

A GREAT LOVER OF FLORA & PLANT KINGDOM &
INDOLOGY & MUSICOLOGY

ON THE AUSPICIOUS OCCASION OF HIS

75TH

BIRTH ANNIVERSARY

(25TH NOVEMBER, 2002)

AMṚTAMAHOTSAVA

❖JAGDISH SAHAI KULSHRESHTHA

❖SUSHMA KULSHRESHTHA

❖ABHA KULSHRESHTHA

❖ARUNA MOHAN

❖ANJU BALA

FOREWORD

I have immense pleasure in introducing to the world of scholars the present volume *Vanajyotsnā-Sahasrasaumanasī* brought out in honour of Shri Jyotsnamoy Chatterjee, an ardent devotee and lover of *Sāhitya-Saṅgīta-Kalā,* literature, music and arts. Indeed, it is a laudable venture of his numerous colleagues, friends and admirers to honour him, a savant of rare distinction with the presentation of a Festschrift on his 75th birth anniversary, his *Amṛtamahotsava*.

This Festschrift comprises eleven panegyrics and poetic compositions by renowned composers and sixty-four research papers by eminent scholars touching many aspects of the theme entitled *Flora and Plant Kingdom in Sanskrit Literature.* They are all original studies on an area of their specialization. I am sure, this volume will be received as an inspiring cascade of Indology with fervour, zeal and freshness by veteran scholars, budding penmen and young researchers alike.

I take this opportunity to congratulate the two distinguished principal editors Prof. Dr. Jagdish Sahai Kulshreshtha and Prof. Sushma Kulshreshtha, both felicitated in Limca Book of Records-2002, for bringing out an epitome of *Sāhitya, Sangīta* and *Kalā* in the form of this illustrious volume presented in honour of our dear friend Shri Jyotsnamoy Chatterjee. Our other editors Ms. Abha Kulshreshtha, Dr. Anju Bala and Shri Jagan Nath also deserve high applause for their meticulous job. The distinguished contributors equally deserve our heartiest congratulations for their distinct contributions.

This volume is a befitting tribute to Shri Jyotsnamoy Chatterjee's life long devotion and dedication to literature, music and arts and his selfless service to humanity. Shri Chatterjee has carved a rare niche for himself in the field of literature and arts and is known for his simplicity, suavity and civility.

UNIVERSITY OF CALIFORNIA
BERKELEY, USA
Devaprabodhinī Ekādaśī
15th November, 2002

RAM KARAN SHARMA
Ex.Vice-Chancellor
Sanskrit Universities, Darbhanga & Varanasi
President, World Association for Sanskrit Studies

卐 卐 卐

EDITORIAL

जयन्ति ते सुकृतिनः रससिद्धाः महोदयाः।
नास्ति येषां यशःकाये जरामरणजं भयम्।।

Today, on the auspicious occasion of *Mārgaśīrṣa Kṛṣṇa Pañcamī,* it is our proud privilege to offer our adorations and felicitations to our esteemed Jyotishman Jyotsnamoy Chatterjee, an ardent devotee and lover of *Sāhitya-Saṅgīta-Kalā:* Literature, Music and Arts in the form of this *Abhivandana-pañcasaptati-patrapuṣpāñjaligrantha, Vanajyotsnā-sahasrasaumanasī,* a volume in his honour on his 75th birth anniversary, his *Amṛtamahotsava.*

We are happy to present this volume *Flora & Plant Kingdom in Sanskrit Literature* comprising seventyfive panegyrics, poetic compositions, articles and research papers, that have been included to serve as a *floral felicitation of vāk* to the genius of the grand savant Shri Jyotsnamoy Chatterjee who is a rare blend of a great connoisseur of literature, music and arts, an ardent lover of devotional pencraft and Kālidāsa, a strict disciplinarian and a humanist, a loving father and a sincere friend, an adept astrologer and an expert photographer, a pilgrim and a world tourist and an ardent lover of world flora and fauna. This *Amṛtamahotsava* Festschrift *Vanajyotsnā-sahasrasaumanasī* is divided into the following four cascades and sixteen sections symbolising sixteen *Puruṣottamakalās* :

Cascade I	:	Kālidasa- Sumanojharī Suṣamā Kalāśrīḥ (comprising four sections)
Cascade II	:	Vanaspati-Kalā-Rasajharī Flora & Floral Arts Ilā-Kalāśrīḥ (comprising seven sections)
Cascade III	:	Surabhāratī- Sumanojharī (comprising three sections)
Cascade IV	:	Sumanomālā: Florilegium (comprising two sections)

This *amṛtamahotsava* volume *Flora & Plant Kingdom in Sanskrit Literature* comprises a beautiful garland, a *vaijayantīmālā* of sixty four flowers in the form of sixty four learned papers and a charming bouquet, *puṣpastabaka* of eleven colourful varied flowers in the form of eleven poetic compositions consisting of hundreds of select poems on flora from renowned Indologists and poets of India (few maiden papers from our researchers too) covering diverse aspects of Indology mainly centring upon Flora and Plant Kingdom in Sanskrit Literature.

The volume opens with cascade I : *Kālidāsa-sumanojharī: Suṣamā-Kalāśrīḥ* comprising four sections in English. The first three sections of this Festschrift comprise ten papers by the writer of these lines, some singly by her and some jointly. *Ṛtusaṁhāra,* being the maiden composition of our Kavikulaguru, the first paper of this volume is entitled Floral decoration ornamentation and cosmetics in *Ṛtusaṁhāra*. The section I:*Kālidāsakṛtinirjharī* comprises three papers presenting plant kingdom in *Ṛtusaṁhāra, Kumārasaṁbhava* and *Vikramorvaśīya* respectively. Section II:Flora in collective works of Kālidāsa presents a beautiful panorama of sixty four lotus blossoms, forty images of mango blossoms, miraculous ten longing trees, *dohadavṛkṣas* and, mango blossoms and male cuckoo in Kālidāsa. Section III : *Saṁskṛtasāhityāmṛtanirjharī* opens with 'Līlākamala in Sanskrit Literature' jointy penned by the composer of these lines and Prof. Ila Ghosh. Then follows a paper 'Eroticism and flower blossoms in *Gāthāsaptaśatī'* jointly written by Dr. Sushma and Ms. Abha Kulshreshtha. The concluding paper of this section is entitled 'Contribution of Pt. Jagannātha Miśra to Rāga - Iconification in *Rasakalpadruma* with special reference to flora' by an eminent musicologist Prof. Jagdish Sahai Kulshreshtha and Ms. Sushma.

The section IV : Flora : Scientific Perspective opens with an informative and analytical paper 'Vedic Flora : A Study' by Dr. Bidyut Lata Ray followed by an equally learned paper 'The concept of plant science in ancient Indian literature' by Dr. Mukta Biswas. Then follows a paper presenting at length scientifically the classification of plants and plant substances in Sanskrit literature by Dr. Nirmal Trikha. Shri S.K. Singhal and Dr. Vandana Gupta discuss scientifically, flora and defence mechanism in plants in their papers respectively. Then comes a wonderful paper 'Mango Mian !!!' by an eminent journalist Shri Jagan Nath. He presents all the aspects concerning mango, the king of fruits in his highly informative and learned paper. The last paper of this section is by a famous horticulturist Dr. Darshananand wherein he presents *Yajña*, yoga and fruits in wasteland and environment.

Cascade II : Flora & Floral Arts divided into seven sections comprises thirty four papers in Hindi and three collections of poetic compositions in Sanskrit by renowned scholars. The section V : Introduction & Floral Arts opens with the key-note paper on 'Flora & Plant Kingdom in Sanskrit Literature' presented by Prof. Shridhar Vasishtha. He has initiated the theme mentioning thereby the main features, aspects and dimensions related to it. In the next paper entitled '*Vaṭabījaśrī*, a senior scholar Dr. Kaushalya Gupta initiates and elaborates the theme of flora in her peculiar style mentioning numerous areas of research related to it. Then follow four very interesting and lively papers on four *kalās* : *mālyagrathana, śekharakāpīdayojana, gandhayukti* and *vṛkṣāyurveda,* all related to flora by Dr. Ila Ghosh, a versatile writer working on arts for the last many years. The last paper of this section entitled *Prācīna bhāratīya prasādhana* is an artistic presentation by a talented budding scholar Dr. Shailesh Kumar Mishra.

In the section VI : Flora in Vedic Epic and Purāṇic Literature is presented a variety of papers on Vedic Literature, *Rāmāyaṇa, Mahābhārata* and *Śrīmadbhāgavatapurāṇa*. A paper entitled *Kālidāsa-sāhitya evaṁ pādapapuṣpaphalasamṛddhi* by Prof. Prabhu Dayalu Agnihotri, an authority on Kālidāsa and a doyen of Indology adorns section VII : Flora in poetic works of Kālidāsa. Then follow four papers on *Raghuvaṁśa, Kumārasambhava, Meghadūta* and *Ṛtusaṁhāra* by Dr. Sushma, Dr. Lata, Dr. Anand Kumar and Dr. Sachchidanand Pathak, all dealing at length with different aspects of plant kingdom. *Kālidāsa kā karṇikāra* is the marvellous last paper of this section penned down by an eminent scholar Dr. Kaushal Gupta having expertise in plants.

The section VIII entitled *Kālidāsanāṭyāmṛtanirjharī* opens with a paper *Mālavikāgnimitra men vṛkṣapuṣpasaundarya* by Dr. Urmi Bhushan Gupta followed by an article on *Abhijñānaśākuntala* and a collection of floral verses from *Vikramorvaśīya.* 'Flora in *Bṛhattrayī* and individual poets, the section IX comprises four papers on *Kirātārjunīya, Śiśupālavadha* and *Naiṣadhīyacarita* dealing with flora. Then are included three papers on Bhāsa, Jayadeva and Paṇḍitarāja Jagannātha presenting plant kingdom in their respective works.

Five informative and interesting papers on different plants and trees, *viz., Tulasī, Aśvattha, kuśa,* magnificence of flora in rainy season and the five arrows of Cupid adorn the section X entitled *Vṛkṣāyurvedakāmaśāstranirjharī*. *Jyotiṣasmṛtinirjharī,* the section XI opens with a learned paper entitled *Jyotiṣaśāstra men vanaspativijñāna*' by famous Jyotirvid Dr. Nagendra Pandeya. Then follow two papers on plant science in *Manusmṛti* and *Āṅgirasasmṛti* by Dr. Urmila Rustagi and Dr. Mina Kumari respectively.

Cascade III : *Surabhāratī-Sumanojharī* comprises three sections and ten papers in Sanskrit. Section XII : *Vedāmṛtanirjharī* opens with a learned paper entitled *Atharvavede vānaspatikaṁ cintanam* by an eminent scholar Prof. Chandrakant Shukla. Then are included two papers on *Śukla Yajurveda* and *Kṛṣṇa Yajurveda* respectively. The section XIII entitled *Kālidāsasāhityāmṛtanirjharī* begins with a paper on the dramatic works of Kālidāsa by Dr. Amita Sharma. She presents in her paper a picturesque scenario of plants depicted as *Uddīpanavibhāva*. Dr. Shashi Tiwari brings forth the grandeur of plants as found in Kālidāsa's plays. In the next paper is described the beauty of *Aśoka* tree by Dr. Anju Bala. The last paper of this section presents the environmental grandeur and fragrance as found in *Raghuvaṁśa,* section XIV entitled *Saṁskṛtasāhityajyotiṣanirjharī* comprises three papers on different aspects of flora. The last learned paper of this section is *Jyotiṣaśāstre vanaspatiḥ* by an eminent astrologer Pt. Ramdev Jha.

Cascade IV : Florilegium : *Sumanomālā* consists of two sections. Section XV is divided into two parts : Panegyricon and Modern Hindi Literature. The first part of this section opens with two benedictory poems by a famous poet and scholar Pt. Shivji Upadhyay. Then follow two panegyrics and one small poem penned down by Padmashri Prof. Sumati Mutatkar. The second part of this section begins with a philosophical poem in Hindi by Mrs. S. Mutatkar. Then follows a benedictory poem by Pt. Ramdev Jha. *Sīkho taruon se śīśa navānā* is the next marvellous poem by Ms. Pallavi Mohan who is the youngest poetess finding place in this volume. The following poem of this section is by a famous ophthalmologist Dr. Pradeep Sharma. Numerous poems on different plants and trees composed by Dr. Kaushalya Gupta adorn this section. The concluding entry of this section is song-verses composed by Smt. Kamlesh Kumari Kulshreshtha compiled by Prof. Shakuntala Mullick and Ms. Meena Chandra.

The last section XVI : Flora in *Anyokti* Literature is a beautiful florilegium made of colourful fragrant flowers. The first collection consists of *anyokti* verses on different flowers composed by Paṇḍitarāja Jagannātha and compiled by Shri Ravindra Kishore Sinha and Smt. Rita Sinha. The second collection which adorns this section comprises *anyokti* verses on different trees penned down by Paṇḍitarāja Jagannātha and assembled by Padmashri Sumati Mutatkar and Dr. Chandrakant Dwivedi. The last collection of *anyokti* verses is from the famous work *Subhāṣitaratnabhāṇḍāgāra*. This is a rare compilatory adornment by Shri Jyotsnamoy Chatterjee and Dr. Raman Kumar Sharma, both enjoying the divine beauty of the *Nandanakānana* of Lord Indra. Here comes to an end the present volume.

We with to put on record our deep sense of gratitude to the contributors all of whom are eminent scholars in their respective fields. The ready response of veteran scholars such as Prof. Prabhu Dayalu Agnihotri, Padmashri Prof. Sumati Mutatkar, Prof. Shridhar Vasishtha, Prof. Chandikaprasad Shukla, Prof. Shakuntala Mullick, Prof. Shivji Upadhyay, Prof. Chandrakant Shukla, Shri Ravindra Kishore Sinha, Smt. Rita Sinha, Prof. Ila Ghosh, Pt. Ramdev Jha, Dr. Nagendra Pandeya, Dr. Sachchidanand Pathak, Dr. Kaushalya Gupta, Dr. Bidyut Lata Ray, Dr. Urmi Bhushan Gupta, Dr. Urmila Rustagi, Dr. Shashi Tiwari, Dr. Kamal Anand, Dr Amita Sharma, Dr. Darshananand, Dr. Mukta Biswas, Mrs. Shashiprabha Goel, Dr. Pravesh Saxena, Dr. Aruna Mohan, Dr. N. Balakrishnan, Dr. Pushpa Gupta and Ms. Abha Kulshreshtha to name only a few, has been extremely rewarding. The learned contributions made by them have justified the idea of this *Amṛtamahotsava* volume that comprises gems of pencraft on Flora & Plant Kingdom in Sanskrit Literature.

We wish to mention here with delight that to celebrate Kālidāsa Mahotsava, Kalidasa Academy of Sanskrit Music & Fine Arts organised a two-day National Research Seminar on Flora & Plant Kingdom in Sanskrit Literature on 26th and 27th November, 2001 in D.A.V. Centenary Public School, Paschim Enclave and S.G.T.B. Khalsa College, University of Delhi respectively. About thirty scholars presented their papers on different aspects of the theme of the seminar.

Kālidāsa Mahotsava and the National Research Seminar were a grand success. Besides famous poets and eminent scholars who presented their poetic compositions and research papers, host of veteran scholars and dignitaries of the Sanskrit and Indology world graced the occasion with their presence as Inaugurators, Presidents, Chief guests, Sectional Presidents and Guests of Honour etc. A few of them deserve special mention. They are Prof. R.K. Sharma, Ex. Vice-Chancellor, Sanskrit Universities, Darbhanga and Varanasi, Dr. K.P.A. Menon, Chancellor, S.L.B.S. Rashtriya Sanskrit Vidyapeeth, New Delhi, Shri Kulanand Bharatiya, Chairman, Delhi Sanskrit Akademi, Shri R.K. Sinha, President and Director General, International Institute of Security and Safety Management, New Delhi, Dr. Lalita Gupta, renowned astrologer, Prof. Krishna Lal, Ex. Prof. and Head, Deptt. of Sanskrit, University of Delhi, Pt. Ramdev Jha, Ex. Prof. and Head of Jyotiṣa Vibhāga, S.L.B.S.R. Sanskrit Vidyapeeth, New Delhi, Prof. Y.D. Sharma, Ex. Professor and Head, Gurukul Kangri Vishvavidyalaya, Haridwar, Kaviratna Shrikrishna Semwal, Dr. T.R. Sharma, Convenor, Sanskrit Deptt., Khalsa College, Dr. Urmila Rustagi, Principal, Miranda House, University of Delhi, Dr. Saraswati Bali, Vice-Principal, Kalindi College, Dr. Ichcharam Dwivedi, Head, Puranetihasa Vibhaga, S.L.B.S.R. Sanskrit Vidyapeeth, Shri Chand Kiran Saluja of Central Institute of Education, Dr. D.S. Clair, Principal, S.G.T.B. Khalsa College, University of Delhi and Shri S.C. Anand, Principal, D.A.V. Centenary Public School, New Delhi and many others.

Learned papers presented at the National Seminar held in D.A.V. Centenary Public School and S.G.T.B. Khalsa College and many other papers which on request were written and sent by scholars afterwards have been included in this volume to paint a colourful picture of Flora and Plant Kingdom in Sanskrit Literature.

Vanajyotsnā-sahasrasaumanasī comprises fifty one contributions by the pencraft of women scholars and twenty four contributions authored by men scholars. This is a splendid scenario indeed! We have only pointed out here some of the special features of this volume and leave the rest to the connoisseurs and discerning readers of Sanskrit and Indology.

We wish to express our gratitude to the venerable Prof. R.K. Sharma for recording the Foreword to *Vanajyotsnā-sahasrasaumanasī* : Flora & Plant Kingdom in Sanskrit Literature.

We wish to record our sincere thanks and gratitude to all the scholars, composers, poets, Shri J. Chatterjee's friends and admirers who spontaneously responded to our invitation enabling us to succeed in the venture of this *Amṛtamahotsava* volume through their learned papers and compositions sent well in time.

We wish to place on record our gratitude and indebtedness to all our friends, colleagues, disciples and Shri Chatterjee's friends who spontaneously offered their valuable services and made themselves available to us in the preparation and printing of this volume. Some of them are Shri Jagan Nath, Dr. Kamal Anand, Dr. Urmi Bhushan Gupta, Dr. Pravesh Saxena, Dr. Pushpa Gupta and Dr. Manju Rawal.

We are extremely thankful to the Editor, Asstt. Editor and Managing Editor : Ms. Abha Kulshreshtha, Dr. Anju Bala and Shri Jagan Nath respectively and to all the members of the publication committee who have successfully performed their meticulous job. We extend our affectionate blessings to our dear disciples Dr. Anju, Ms. Subhadra and Ms. Meena. May God bless them! We wish to express our gratitude to Prof. R.K. Sharma, Padmashri Prof. Sumati Mutatkar and Pt. Ramdev Jha who have been the inspiration and guiding force throughout.

We express our sincere thanks to Shri Sham Lal Malhotra, Proprietor, Eastern Book Linkers, who undertook the publication of this work and brought it out with beautiful presentation in record time. For beautiful computer composing, our thanks are due to Shri Kanwar Chand. Shri Ravi Malhotra and his associates have worked hard and through their careful efficiency, this volume consisting of 512 pages in Double Demy size (23" × 36"/8) could be published in a period of 125 days from 24.7.2002 to 25.11.2002.

In the end, through this commemorative Festschrift *Vanajyotsnā-sahasrasaumanasī,* on the occasion of his *Amṛtamahotsava,* his 75th birth anniversary, we wish that our revered Jyotishman Jyotsnamoy Chatterjee who imbibed in himself unfathomable depths of knowledge and was endowed with remarkable human qualities, a gem himself indeed, always remain alive in the hearts of all who loved, respected and adored him :

ज्योतिष्मान् ज्योत्स्नामयो जीव्यादनन्तं समाः।

JAGDISH SAHAI KULSHRESHTHA
DEHRADUN
Mārgaśīrṣa Kṛṣṇa Pañcamī
25th November, 2002

SUSHMA KULSHRESHTHA
Hony. Director
Kalidasa Academy of
Sanskrit Music & Fine Arts, Delhi

卐 卐 卐

CONTENTS

卐 卐 卐

CASCADE I
(ENGLISH)

KĀLIDĀSA-SUMANOJHARĪ

SUṢAMĀ-KALĀŚRĪḤ

कालिदास-सुमनोझरी

सुषमा-कलाश्रीः

जायन्ते कति जज्ञिरे कति जनिष्यन्ते कतीह क्षितौ
स्त्रष्टारो नितरामिदं तु कविभिर्निर्मत्सरैः कथ्यताम्।
आपूर्वापरदक्षिणोत्तरहरित्साहित्यसिंहासन-
स्वैरारोहपराक्रमं भजतु कः श्रीकालिदासात्परः।।

पुरा कवीनां गणनाप्रसङ्गे कनिष्ठिकाधिष्ठितकालिदासा।
अद्यापि तत्तुल्यकवेरभावादनामिका सार्थवती बभूव।।

चूताङ्कुरास्वादकषायकण्ठः पुंस्कोकिलो यन्मधुरं चुकूज।
मनस्विनीमानविघातदक्षं तदेव जातं वचनं स्मरस्य।।

Section I - Flora in Individual Works of Kālidāsa
Section II - Flora in Collective Works of Kālidāsa

CASCADE-I
(ENGLISH)

KĀLIDĀSA-SUMANOJHARĪ

SUṢAMĀ-KALĀŚRĪḤ

कालिदास-सुमनोझरी

सुषमा-कलाश्रीः

स्त्रीणां स्पर्शात्प्रियङ्गुर्विकसति बकुलः सीधुगण्डूषसेकात्
पादाघातादशोकस्तिलककुरबकौ वीक्षणालिङ्गनाभ्याम्।
मन्दारो नर्मवाक्यात्पटुमृदुहसनाच्चम्पको वक्त्रवाता-
च्चूतो गीतान्नमेरुर्विकसति च पुरोनर्तनात्कर्णिकारः।।

अस्पृष्टदोषा नलिनीव दृष्टा हारावलीव ग्रथिता गुणौघैः।
प्रियाङ्कपालीव विमर्दहृद्या न कालिदासादपरस्य वाणी।।

शंभुस्वयंभुहरयो हरिणेक्षणानां येनाक्रियन्त सततं गृहकर्मदासाः।
वाचामगोचरचरित्रविचित्रिताय तस्मै नमो भगवते कुसुमायुधाय।।

Section III - Flora in Sanskrit Literature
Section IV - Flora : Scientific Perspective

Section I

FLORA IN INDIVIDUAL WORKS OF KĀLIDĀSA

कालिदासकृतिनिर्झरी

FLORAL DECORATION ORNAMENTATION & COSMETICS IN ṚTUSAṀHĀRA

Sushma Kulshreshtha

Kālidāsa was a peerless poet *par excellence* in many *Śāstras* and arts. He excelled all other poets, including Vālmīki, in Plant Science. He has presented beautiful paintings of trees, plants, creepers, blossoms, flowers and fruits. He has referred to more than 65 plants and trees in *Ṛtusaṁhāra* alone. Plants and trees referred to in *Ṛtusaṁhāra* along with their botanical names are as follows :

1. Abja - Nymphaea alba Linn
2. Aguru - Aquilaria agallocha Roxb
3. Ambuja - Nymphaea alba Linn
4. Amburuha Nymphaea alba Linn
5. Āmra - Mangifera Indica Linn
6. Aravinda - Nymphaea alba Linn
7. Arjuna - Terminalia Arjuna W. & A.
8. Aśoka - Saraca Indica Linn
9. Atimukta - Hiptage Benghalensis Kurz
10. Bakulu - Mimusops Elengi Linn
11. Bandhūka - Pentapetes Phoenicea W. & A.
12. Bandhujīva - Pentapetes Phoenicea W. & A.
13. Campaka - Michelia Champaca
14. Candana - Santalum Album Linn
15. Cūta - Mangifera Indica Linn
16. Ikṣu - Saccharum Officinarum Linn
17. Indīvara - Nymphaea Stellata Walld
18. Kadamba - Anthocephalus Indicus A. Rich.
19. Kakubha - Terminalia Arjuna
20. Kālāguru - Aquilaria agallocha Roxb
21. Kalhāra - Nelumbo Nuciferra Garten (Red Lotus)
22. Kālīyaka - Santalum Album Linn (Yellow Sandal)

23. Kamala - Nelumbo Nuciferra Garten
24. Kaṅkeli
25. Kandalī - Musa Sapinetum Linn
26. Karṇikāra - Cassia Fistula Linn (Amalatasa)
27. Kāśa - Saccharum sponatum Linn
28. Kesara - Mimusops Elengi Linn
29. Ketakī - Pandanus Tectorius Soland
30. Kiṁśuka - Buttea Monosparma (Linn) Kurz
31. Kovidāra - Bauhinia Verigata Linn
32. Kumuda - Nymphaea Esculenta
33. Kunda - Jasminum Pubescens Willd
34. Kuṅkuma - Corcus Sativus Linn
35. Kuravaka - Rhododendron Arborium
36. Kusumbha - Carthamus Tinctorius Linn
37. Kuṭaja - Holarrhena Antidysenterica
38. Kuvalaya - Nymphaeaceae
39. Lodhra - Symplocos Paniculaṭa wall
40. Mālatī - Jasminum Grandiflorum Linn
41. Mṛṇāla - Nelumbo Nuciferra Garten
42. Mustā - Cyperus Rotundus Linn
43. Nalinī - Nelumbo Nuciferra Garten
44. Navamallikā - Jasminum Arborescens Roxb
45. Navamālikā - Jasminum Arborescens Roxb
46. Nīlotpala - Nymphaea Stellata Willd
47. Nīpa - Anthocephalus Indicus A.Rich
48. Padma - Nelumbo Nuciferra Garten
49. Paṅkaja - Nelumbo Nuciferra Garten
50. Pāṭala - Stereospermum Suaveolens
51. Priyaṅgu - Callicarpa Maczophylla
52. Śaileya - Parmelia Perlata Ach
53. Śāli - Oryza Sativa
54. Śālmali - Bomban Heptaphyllumar Salmalia Malabarica
55. Śaṣpa - (Sprouting Grass)
56. Śephālikā - Vitex Trifolia Linn.
57. Śyāmā - Echnocar Pus Frutascens
58. Sahakāra - Mangifera Indica Linn
59. Saptacchada - Alostonia Scholaris.
60. Sarja - Vateria Indica Linn

61. Tāmbūla - Piper Betle Linn
62. Utpala - Nymphaea Stellata
63. Vakula - Mimusops Elengi Linn
64. Vaṁśa - Bambusa Arundinacea
65. Yūthikā - Jasminum Auriculatum Vlol

Kālidāsa has referred to these plants, trees, creepers, blossoms and flowers to describe the six seasons in *Ṛtusaṁhāra*. With each reference he has some motive. Sometimes he uses trees, plants and flowers to bring forth the beauty of a paticular season. Sometimes he describes flowers as standard of comparison. Sometimes he describes his heroines using these flowers as decoration. Women are very fond of flowers. They decorate their person in various ways. They adorn their bosom with flower-garlands. They decorate their tresses with flowers, blossoms and flower-garlands. They wear flowers or petals or tree-leaves as ear-ornaments too. In the present paper, an attempt is made to show the expertise of Kālidāsa in plant science with reference to floral decoration, ornamentation and cosmetics in *Ṛtusaṁhāra* only.

Mālyagrathana[1] or the making of the flower garlands was a very popular art fondly loved by amorous maidens. They used to pluck or collect flowers and make the garlands. They used to make garlands themselves and then adorn their bosoms with these garlands. Here are some beautiful illustrations :

1. नितम्बबिम्बैः सदुकूलमेखलैः स्तनैः सहाराभरणैः सचन्दनैः।
शिरोरुहैः स्नानकषायवासितैः स्त्रियो निदाघं शमयन्ति कामिनाम्।।

2. पयोधराश्चन्दनपङ्कचर्चितास्तुषारगौरार्पितहारशेखराः ।
नितम्बदेशाश्च सहेममेखलाः प्रकुर्वते कस्य मनो न सोत्सुकम्।।

3. सचन्दनाम्बुव्यजनोद्भवानिलैः सहारयष्टिस्तनमण्डलार्पणैः।
सवल्लकीकाकलिगीतनिःस्वनैः प्रबोध्यते सुप्त इवाद्य मन्मथः।।[2]

Beautiful damsels remove the heat (summer sufferings) felt by their lovers by their round hips covered with silk-cloths and having waist bands, by their breasts pasted with sandal and bedecked with flower-garlands and other ornaments and by their tresses perfumed with the cosmetics used in bathing. Rising breasts of damsels smeared with thick sandal-paste and wearing at their tops snow-white flower-garlands and hips bedecked with girdles made of gold—whose calm mind is not agitated with sentiments of love by these ? In the summer season, even the sleeping sentiment of love is awakened like a sleeping lover by means of the breezes of fans soaked with sandal-water, by means of placing the round breasts covered with flower-necklaces of women and by the sweet songs sung in accompaniment of *Vīṇā*.

In all these illustrations, the breasts of beautiful damsels are described as smeared with thick sandal-paste and adorned with flower-garlands. Their tresses are perfumed with the cosmetics used in bathing.

4. शिरोरुहैः श्रोणितटावलम्बिभिः
कृतावतंसैः कुसुमैः सुगन्धिभिः।
स्तनैः सहारैर्वदनैः ससीधुभिः
स्त्रियो रतिं संजनयन्ति कामिनाम्।।

5. हारैः सचन्दनरसैः स्तनमण्डलानि
श्रोणीतटं सुविपुलं रसनाकलापैः।
पादाम्बुजानि वरनूपुरशेखरैश्च
नार्यः प्रहृष्टमनसोऽद्य विभूषयन्ति।।[3]

By their tresses hanging down over their broad hips, by sweet- odoured flowers made up into ear-ornaments, by breasts adorned with flower-garlands and by mouths smelling liquor, the womn are inflaming love in their lovers. Filled with great delight, the ladies are decorating their round breasts with flower-garlands soaked in sandal-paste, their broad hips with girdle strings and their lotus-like feet with sweet sounding anklets.

Here also damsels are adorning their breasts with flower-garlands soaked in sandal-paste. They are wearing flowers as ear-ornaments.

Women are very fond of different varieties of hair-do and hair-styles. They perfume their hair with a variety of objects which will be discussed in this paper later. Women decorate their tresses with flower-garlands and different flowers and blossoms. The flowers used for hair-decoration are : *Bakula (Kesara)*, *Mālatī*, *Yūthikā*, *Kadamba*, *Ketakī*, *Aśoka* and *Navamallikā*. A brief description of these flowers is presented herewith.

1. BAKULA (KESARA) (Mimusops Elengi Linn)

Kālidāsa has used *kesara* to denote *bakula* flower which is one of the most fragrant white flowers known as *Maulaśrī* or *Maulasirī*. *Bakula* or *kesara* is a *dohadavṛkṣa*, longing tree which requires *Sīdhugaṇḍiṣaseka-mukhamadirā* or pouring of wine through the mouth of a beautiful damsel:

स्त्रीणां स्पर्शात्प्रियङ्गुर्विकसति बकुलः सीधुगण्डूषसेकात्।[4]

Bakula's other name is *kesara*-के जले सरति इति केसरः. Its foliage floats on the surface of water. Hence, it is called *kesara*. Kālidāsa and his heroines are very fond of this fragrant flower. His heroines wear girdle-strings composed of this flower as is described :

स्रस्तां नितम्बादवलम्बमाना पुनः पुनः केसरदामकाञ्चीम्।
न्यासीकृता स्थानविदा स्मरेण मौर्वीं द्वितीयामिव कार्मुकस्य।।[5]

× × × × ×

तव निःश्वसितानुकारिभिः बकुलैरर्धचितां समं मया।
असमाप्य विलासमेखलां किमिदं किन्नरकण्ठि! सुप्यते।।[6]

2. MĀLATĪ (Jasminum Grandiflorum)

Mālatī is jasmine flower. *Mālatī* bears fragrant white flowers which open towards evening. It is a very fragrant and delicate flower. Its sweet-smelling odour and delicacy are often described by Sanskrit poets as is seen in the following verses though negatively :

अविदितगुणापि सत्कविभणितिः कर्णेषु वमति मधुधाराम्।
अनधिगतपरिमलापि हि हरति दृशं मालतीमाला।।[7]

तदङ्गमार्दवं द्रष्टुः कस्य चिते न भासते।
मालतीशशभल्लेखा कदलीनां कठोरता।।[8]

Mālatī-मलते शोभां धारयति, मल + अतिच् + ङीष् + or मां लाति इति मालः विष्णुः तम् अतति, माल + अत्+ इन्[9] is a beautiful white flower which whitens the garden :

काशैर्मही शिशिरदीधितिना रजन्यो
हंसैर्जलानि सरितां कुमुदैः सरांसि।
सप्तच्छदैः कुसुमभारनतैर्वनान्ताः
शुक्लीकृतान्युपवनानि च मालतीभिः।।[10]

Mālatī blossoms in rainy season :

वर्षासु जाता नवयौवनश्रीराशावधूः प्रौढपयोधराभूत्।
पुष्पोद्गमोऽजायत मालतीनां बभूवुरस्पृश्यतमास्तटिन्यः।।[11]

This verse is a beautiful illustration of *Asaṅgati* alaṁkāra too. Poets have composed lovely *Anyoktī*-verses centring *Mālatī* flower. For example, the following verses can be relished :

किं मालतीकुसुम ताम्यसि निष्ठुरेण
केनापि यत्किल विलूनगितो लताग्रात्।
लोकोत्तरेण विलसद्गुणगौरवेण
को नामुना शिरसि नाम करिष्यति त्वाम्।।
म्रदीयस्त्वाधिक्यान्न भवति विमर्दक्षममिदं
न चान्येभ्यो रूपं भवति कुसुमेभ्योऽधिकतरम्।
प्रसूनं मालत्यास्तदपि हृदयाह्लादकरणं
प्रवीणैरामोदैर्भवति जगतो मौलिनिलयम्।।[12]

3. YŪTHIKĀ (Jasminum Auriculatum Vlol)

Yūthikā or *Yūthī*-यूथं पुष्पवृन्दमस्ति अस्याः, यूथ + ठन् + टाप्, यूथ + अच् + ङीष् is a creeper that blossoms in rainy season. Its flowers are creamish white and fragrant. Women adorn their tresses with *Yūthikā* flowers. Urvaśī used to decorate her hair with *Yūthikā* blossoms as is described in the following verse :

मदकल युवतिशशिकला गजयूथप यूथिकाशबलकेशी।
स्थितयौवना स्थिता ते दूरालोके सुखालोका।।[13]

Yūthikā's other names are *Gaṇikā, Pītā* and *Hemapuṣpikā* too. It is called *Gaṇikā* as it attracts like a courtesan-गणिकेव चित्ताकर्षकत्वात्.[14] It has several varieties. One of its varieties produces yellow blossoms; hence the names *Pītā* and *Hemapuṣpikā*. This variety is called *Svarṇayūthikā* too. *Mālatī, Mallikā* and *Kunda* flowers are different varieties of *Yūthikā*. *Yūthikā* blossoms in clusters.

4. KADAMBA (Anthocephalus Indicus A. Rich)

Kadamba is a tree with orange-coloured fragrant blossoms (M. Williams). *Kadamba* flowers bloom at the advent of rainy season. Women use these flowers to adorn their tresses especially in the parting of their hair.

It is said that *Kadamba*-कद् + अम्बच् (कदति हिनस्ति बद्धकोष्ठताम्)[15] blossoms at the thundering of clouds in rainy season :

महीमण्डलीमण्डपीभूतपाथोधरारब्धहर्षासु वर्षासु सद्यः।
कदम्बे प्रसूनं प्रसूने मरन्दो मरन्दे मिलिन्दो मिलिन्दे मदोऽभूत्।।[16]

Kadamba trees are abundantly found in the Himālayas :

पृथुकदम्बकदम्बकराजितं ग्रथितमालतमालवनाकुलम्।
लघुतुषारतुषारजलश्च्युतं धृतसदानसदाननदन्तिनम्।।[17]

Breezes rendered fragrant by *Kadamba*-blossoms are often described by our poets :

अभिभवति मनः कदम्बवायौ मदमधुरे च शिखण्डिनां निनादे।
जल इव न धृतेश्चचाल जिष्णुर्नहि महतां सुकरः समाधिभङ्गः।।[18]

× × × × ×

नवकदम्बरजोरुणिताम्बरैरधिपुरन्ध्रि शिलीन्ध्रसुगन्धिभिः।
मनसि रागवतामनुरागिता नवनवा वनवायुभिरादधे।।[19]

× × × × ×

ते चोन्मीलितमालतीसुरभयः प्रौढाः कदम्बानिलाः।[20]

5. KETAKĪ (Pandanus Tectorius Soland)

Katekī (कित् + ण्वुल् + ङीष्) is a tree in the form of a shrub. Its flowers are white which blossom in rainy season. Its shrubs are abundantly found in coastal regions. It is a very fragrant flower. Pollens of *Ketakī* flowers are described as being carried by the breeze :

वेलारुणः केतकरेणुभिस्ते सम्भावयत्याननमायताक्षि।
मामक्षमः मण्डनकालहानेर्वेत्रीव बिम्बाधरबद्धतृष्णम्।।[21]

Returning from Laṅkā, Śrīrāma addresses his sweet-heart thus: O long-eyed lady, the breeze blowing over the sea-coast decorates thy face with the pollen of *Ketaka*-flower. It knows as it were, that I who have fixed my longing upon thy *bimba*-like lips, cannot brook the delay caused by decorations.

Women are very fond of decorating themselves with flower-ornaments. They wear petals or leaves of *Ketaka*-flower as ear-ornaments as can be seen is this verse :

विलासिनीविभ्रमदन्तपत्रमापाण्डुरं केतकबर्हमन्यः।
प्रियानितम्बोचितसंनिवेशैर्विपाटयामास युवा नखाग्रैः।।[22]

Ketakī-leaves are surrounded by thorns as is described in the following verses :

पत्राणि कण्टकशतैः परिवेष्टितानि
वार्तापि नास्ति मधुनो रजसान्धकारः।
आमोदमात्ररसिकेन मधुव्रतेन
नालोकितानि तव केतकि दूषणानि।।

× × × × ×

एतासु केतकिलतासु विकासिनीषु
सौभाग्यमद्भुततरं भवती बिभर्ति।
यत्कण्टकैर्व्यथितमात्मवपुर्न जानं-
स्त्वामेव सेवितुमुपक्रमते द्विरेफः।।[23]

According to poetic convention, *Ketakī* flower is not offered to Lord Maheśvara in worship as can be seen in the following verse :

एकेन चेत्परिहृतोऽसि महेश्वरेण
किं तेन केतक विषादमुरीकरोषि।
अन्ये न किं जगति सन्ति महागुणज्ञा
ये त्वां वहन्ति शिरसा नरदेवदेवाः।।[24]

6. AŚOKA (Saraca Indica Linn)

Jonesia Asoka Roxb or *Saraca Indica Linn* is a tree of moderate size belonging to the leguminous class with magnificent red flowers (Monier Williams). *Aśoka* is a *dohadavṛkṣa*- longing (wishing) tree. It's a poetic convention that the *aśoka* requires to be struck by beautiful damsels with their feet adorned by tinkling anklet bells, so that it is able to put forth blossoms :

सनूपुररवेण स्त्रीचरणेनाभिताडनम्।
दोहदं यदशोकस्य ततः पुष्पोद्गमो भवेत्।।[25]

This tree puts forth its flowers in spring season. *Aśoka*-flowers are one of the five arrows of Cupid :[26]

अरविन्दमशोकश्च चूतश्च नवमल्लिका।
नीलोत्पलञ्च (कुरबकञ्च) पञ्चैते पुष्पवाणस्य सायकाः।।

Women are very fond of adorning themselves is various ways. *Aśoka*- leaves are described to have been used by women for decorating their ears. *Aśoka*-flowers are creamish white and red. *Aśoka*-tree does not bear fruits as is described in the following verse :

किं ते नम्रतया किमुन्नततया किं वा घनच्छायया
किं वा पल्लवलीलया किमनया चाशोक पुष्पश्रिया।
यत्त्वन्मूलनिषण्णखिन्नपथिकस्तोमः स्तुवन्नन्वहं
न स्वादूनि मृदूनि खादति फलान्याकण्ठमुत्कण्ठितः।।

श्रीभोजदेवस्य[27]

A number of *anyokti*-verses have been composed centring *Aśoka*-tree referring to its high fortune of being a *dohadavṛkṣa* and having its wish fulfilled by pretty dames :

गर्वायसे विकचकोरक मञ्जुगुञ्ज-
दुद्वृत्तषट्पदघटाविभवेन किं नु।
वामभ्रुवां चरणताडनदोहदानि
किं नाम न स्मरसि तावदशोक तानि।।
उन्मीलयन्ति कुसुमानि मनोरमाणि
के नाम नात्र तरवाः समयोचितानि।
कस्येदृशं कथय दोह दमस्ति तस्य
यादृग्विनिर्मितमशोकमहीरुहस्य ।।[28]

7. NAVAMALLIKĀ OR MALLIKĀ (NAVAMĀLIKĀ) (Jasminum Sambac)

Navamallikā or *Navamālikā* or *Mallikā* or *Mallī* is a variety of jasmine flower. *Navamallikā* flowers bloom in the evening. These flowers are white in colour. *Śuklābhisārikās* are very fond of decorating themselves with white *Mallikā*-flowers :

मल्लिकामाल्यभारिण्यः सर्वाङ्गीणार्द्रचन्दनाः।
क्षौमवत्यो न लक्ष्यन्ते ज्योत्स्नायामभिसारिकाः।।[29]

This verse is a marvellous illustration of *Mīlita* figure of speech. *Navamālikā* flowers are very delicate and extremely odorous. The *Navamālikā*-creeper is described as entwining the mango tree. *Navamālikā* creepers appear to have constituted pleasure-bowers.[30]

Our poets are very fond of describing *mithunabhāva* between a creeper and a tree which can be relished in the following verse :

अमदयन्मधुगन्धसनाथया किसलयाधरसंततया मनः।
कुसुमसंभृतया नवमल्लिका स्मितरुचा तरुचारुविलासिनी।।[31]

The creeper *Navamāllikā,* the pretty consort of trees, gladdened the mind of beholders with her smiling beauty put forth by the blossoming flowers, spreading over the sprouts as her lower lip and accompanied by the fragrance of honey as her wine.

Mallikā-flowers bloom in the evening. They are extremely fragrant. Beautiful damsels adorn their hair with *mallikā* flowers as described by Kavikulaguru thus:

वनेषु सायन्तनमल्लिकानां
विजृम्भणोद्गन्धिषु कुड्मलेषु।
प्रत्येकनिक्षिप्तपदः सशब्दं
संख्यामिवैषां भ्रमरश्चकार।।

स्नानार्द्रमुक्तेष्वनुधूपवासं
विन्यस्तसायन्तनमल्लिकेषु।
कामो वसन्तात्ययमन्दवीर्यः
केशेषु लेभे बलमङ्गनानाम्।।[32]

In the forests the bee, with its humming placed its foot on each of the buds of the evening-blooming-jasmine-creepers emitting fragrance through its opening folds and began to count as it were their number. The God of love whose strength was diminished due to the departure of Vasanta, the spring, again acquired it in the hair of the young ladies, which were unbraided on account of their being wet by bathing and in which evening-jasmine-flowers were woven after making them perfumed. This reveals that women were very fond of perfuming their hair too.

Navamallikā blooms at the advent of summer season :

रवितुरङ्गतनूरुहतुल्यतां
दधति यत्र शिरीषरजोरुचः।
उपययौ विदधन्नवमल्लिकाः
शुचिरसौ चिरसौरभसम्पदः।।[33]

× × × ×

रेजे पुष्पैर्ग्रीष्ममासाद्य मल्ली
मल्लीं सद्यः संश्रयन्तो स्म भृङ्गाः।
भृङ्गैस्तत्रारम्भि हर्षेण गानं
गाने लौल्यं लेभिरे योगिनोऽपि।।[34]

Amorous damsels adorn their person with garlands made of *mallikā* flowers during evenings and arouse love :

तदात्वस्नातानां दरदलितमल्लीमुकुलिताः
स्रजो बिभ्राणानां मलयजरसार्द्रद्रवपुषाम्।
निदाघाग्निप्लोषग्लपितमभिसायं मृगदृशां
परिष्वङ्गोऽनङ्गः पुनरपि शनैरङ्कुरयति।।[35]

Navamallikā is one of the five arrows of Cupid, the God of Love. Hence, damsels decorate their hair with *Navamallikā* flowers to kindlle love in and beget love of their sweet- hearts. The following verse (describing *puruṣāyita)* presents a *nāyikā* whose tresses are adorned with *Navamallikā* flowers :

पततु तवोरसि सततं दयिताधम्मिल्लमल्लिकानिकरः।
रतरसरभसकचग्रहलुलितालकवल्लरीगलितः ।।[36]

Now are presented herewith the flowers as hair-decoration and ear-ornamentation in *Ṛtusaṁhāra :*

Illustrations :

1. शिरसि बकुलमालां मालतीभिः समेतां
विकसितनवपुष्पैर्यूथिकाकुड्मलैश्च ।
विकचनवकदम्बैः कर्णपूरं वधूनां
रचयति जलदौघः कान्तवत् काल एषः।।[37]

This rainy season arranges like a lover, on the heads of beloveds, a garland of *bakula*-flowers together with the blossoms of *mālatī,* newly bloomed flowers and the buds of *yūthikā* and arranges ear-ornaments of newly-blossomed *kadambas*. This is a marvellous description of rainy season which has been personified in a magnificent manner. He is a lover decorating the tresses of his beloveds with *bakula*-garlands woven with newly bloomed varied flowers, including *mālatī* blossoms and *yūthikā*-buds. He is decorating the ears of his beloveds with newly-blossomed *kadambas*.

Here, the rainy season is acting like an experienced lover. The amorous sports of lovers are multifaceted. One of the love-sports popular amongst the lovers is that the lover prepares different hair-styles and adorns the tresses of his beloved with fresh flowers, new blossoms and flower-garlands. Lord Śiva was well-versed in hair-dressing and hair-decoration :

तां पुलोमतनयालकोचितैः पारिजातकुसुमैः प्रसाधयन्।
नन्दने चिरमयुग्मलोचनः सस्पृहं सुरवधूभिरीक्षितः।।[38]
रतिश्लथं तत्कबरीकलापमंसावसक्तं विगलत्प्रसूनम्।
स पारिजातोद्भवपुष्पमय्या स्रजा बबन्धामृतमूर्तिमौलिः।।[39]

Celestial damsels gazed long with longing at the Odd-Eyed Lord Śiva as He decorated Umā's tresses in the Nandana groves with *Pārijāta*-blossoms that were usually worn in her hair by Śacī, the daughter of Puloman. With a wealth of *Pārijāta*-flowers, the Moon-Crested Lord Śiva wreathed Pārvatī's beautiful hair that lay loose clinging to her shoulders, its knot undone as they were engrossed in passionate love and all the flowers in it slipping down.

Prince Aja, along with his sweet darling Indumatī, used to prepare an amorous girdle-string with *bakula*-flowers for her.[40] Pārvatī's tresses were adorned with *madhūka*-garland by a female beautician as bridal make-up :

धूपोष्मणा त्याजितमार्द्रभावं केशान्तमन्तःकुसुमं तदीयम्।
पर्याक्षिपत्काचिदुदारबन्धं दूर्ववता पाण्डुमधूकदाम्ना।।[41]

One of the ladies tied the beautiful mass of her hair, the moisture of which was removed by the smoke of incense and which had flowers inside it, with a garland of yellow *Madhūka* flowers intermixed with *dūrvā* grass, so as to form a charming knot. This beautiful description paints before us the bridal picture of Pārvatī with a very lovely hair-do with a yellow *Madhūka*-flower-garland interwoven with green *dūrvā* grass.

In *Pārvatīpariṇaya*, Pārvatī's tresses are adorned with *mandāra* flowers :

आगुल्फलम्बमस्याः कुन्तलमन्तर्निगूढमन्दारम्।
संयम्य चतुरबन्धं सखीजनः स्तिमितनेत्रमास चित्रम्।।[42]

Bakula, Mālatī, Yūthikā and *Kadamba*-all these flowers bloom in rainy season. These flowers are fondly loved by amorous women. Not only do they use these flowers as hair-decoration or ear-ornament but they use them as proper names too for maidens. Bakulāvalikā is Mālavikā's female friend. Mālatī is the heroine of the drama *Mālatīmādhava*. Similarly, Yuthikā or its Hindi version Jūhī are also popular proper names.

2. मालाः कदम्बनवकेसरकेतकीभि-
रायोजिताः शिरसि बिभ्रति योषितोऽद्य।
कर्णान्तरेषु ककुभद्रुममञ्जरीभिः
श्रोत्रानुकूलरचितानवतंसकाँश्च ।।[43]

These days (in rainy season) pleasure-seeking amorous women wear on their heads garlands made of new flowers of *kadamba (nīpa) kesara (bakula)* and *ketakī* and in their ear-spaces (they wear) ear ornaments made of *kakubha (arjuna)-manjarīs* that suit their ears.

Here also women are decorating their tresses with garlands composed of fresh flowers of *kadamba, bakula* and *ketakī. Kadamba* and *bakula* are very delicate flowers often used for hair-decoration. Women are wearing *kakubha mañjarīs*-fresh *kakubha* sprouts as their ear ornaments.

3. केशान्नितान्तघननीलविकुञ्चिताग्रा-
नापूरयन्ति वनिता नवमालतीभिः।
कर्णेषु च प्रचलकाञ्चनकुण्डलेषु
नीलोत्पलानि विकचानि निवेशयन्ति।।[44]

The women are decorating their dark and thick tresses with curly ends with the fresh *mālatī*-flowers and they are placing bloomed blue lotuses in their ears which were previously adorned with golden ear-rings. Darkenss, thickness and curliness are the three praiseworthy qualities of the tresses of beautiful women. They are well-versed in making different hair styles and decorating their tresses with fresh *mālatī*-flowers. They are wearing blossoming blue lotuses as their ear-ornaments.

4. कर्णेषु योग्यं नवकर्णिकारं
स्तनेषु हारा अलकेष्वशोकम्।
शिखासु फुल्ला नवमालिकाश्च
प्रयान्ति कान्तिं प्रमदाजनस्य।।[45]

The amorous damsels put on befitting new *karṇikāra*-blossoms in their ears, wear garlands on their bosom, decorate their curly tresses with *aśoka*-flowers and put on a garland *(gajarā)* made of opened buds of *navamālikā* on their *veṇī*-hair-do. This verse brings forth a beautiful description of amorous dames wearing charming hair-do with floral decoration and ear-ornamentation. This is truly a feast to the eye of the connoisseur. Such beautiful scenes are available these days in Beauty Contests or Fashion shows or Film Award ceremonies.

5. मनोज्ञकूर्पासकपीडितस्तनाः सरागकौषेयविभूषितोरवः।
निवेशितान्तःकुसमैः शिरोरुहैर्विभूषयन्तीव हिमागमं स्त्रियः।।[46]

With their breasts pressed by pretty brassieres, thighs adorned with coloured silken garments and tresses bedecked with flowers, the damsels are, as it were, beautifying the winter season. Here also the women are decorating their hair with flowers.

HAIR COSMETICS AND CONDITIONERS

Kavikulaguru was well-versed in the art of cosmeticism too. Cosmetics are being used by men and women to improve their beauty. Cosmetics are used to improve the quality and shining of hair and also to improve complexion. Kālidāsa has referred to numerous cosmetics in *Ṛtusaṁhāra*. For want of space, here we will limit ourselves to hair cosmetics only. Some illustrations referring to hair cosmetics are cited here :

1. नितम्बबिम्बैः सदुकूलमेखलैः
स्तनैः सहाराभरणैः सचन्दनैः।
शिरोरुहैः स्नानकषायवासितैः
स्त्रियो निदाघं शमयन्ति कामिनाम्।।[47]

Beautiful damsels remove the heat (summer sufferings) felt by their lovers by their round hips covered with silk-cloths and having waist-bands, by their breasts pasted with sandal and bedecked with flower-garlands and other ornaments and by their tresses perfumed with the cosmetics used in bathing. Women used a variety of cosmetics while bathing. Some of these were used by them to perfume and condition their tresses.

2. गात्राणि कालीयकचर्चितानि
सपत्रलेखानि मुखाम्बुजानि।
शिरांसि कालागुरुधूपितानि
कुर्वन्ति नार्यः सुरतोत्सवार्थम्।।[48]

For celebrating the festival of *samprayoga* (sexual union), ladies rub their limbs with yellow sandal past, decorate their lotus-like faces with leafy lines and perfume their tresses with the incense of black *aguru*. It was prevalent among the amorous damsels that they used to perfume their hair with different cosmetics particularly with the incense of black *aguru*. *Kālīyaka* is yellow sandal :

अथ जायकम्। कालीयकं च कालानुसार्यं च।[49]

All these three denote yellow sandal which is extremely fragrant. *Aguru* is an incense. Its six names are :अथ समार्थकम्। वंशकागुरुराजार्हलोहं कृमिजजोङ्गकम्।[50]

The black variety of this *aguru* is called *aguru* or *kālāguru* :

3. अगुरुसुरभिधूपामोदितं केशपाशं
गलितकुसुममालं कुञ्चिताग्रं वहन्ती।
त्यजति गुरुनितम्बा निम्ननाभिः सुमध्या
उषसि शयनमन्या कामिनी चारुशोभा।।[52]

Another woman of heavy hips, deep navel, slender waist and charming beauty, is leaving her bed-chamber, in the morning having her abundant tresses, curled at ends, scented with the fragrant smoke of *aguru* and without flower-garlands. Here also, a damsel has perfumed her thick tresses with the incense of *aguru*.

Amorous men and women used to get their bed-chambers scented with the incense of black *aguru* :

गृहीतताम्बूलविलेपनस्त्रजः पुष्पासवामोदितवक्त्रपङ्कजाः।
प्रकामकालागुरुधूपवासितं विशन्ति शय्यागृहमुत्सुकाः स्त्रियः।।[53]

In conclusion, it can be said with affirmity that Kālidāsa was well-versed in numerous *kalās viz., puṣpāstaraṇa, aṅgarāga, mālyagrathana, nepathyaprayoga, gandhayukti, bhūṣaṇayojana, vṛkṣāyurveda* and many others which find an appropriate place in *Ṛtusaṁhāra*. I have tried in this paper to present a picture of flower-garlands, floral hair decoration, ear-ornamentation and cosmetics as found in *Ṛtusaṁhāra*. At the same time, the expertise of our Kavikulaguru in other arts can also be relished here. It would be proper if modern researchers analytically go through the works of Kālidāsa with reference to sixty-four arts propounded by sage Vātsyāyana in his *Kāmasūtra*[54] and present exhaustive study. 'Sixty - four arts in Kālidāsa' is still an untouched and untrodden field of research. The writer of these lines has brought out five volumes pertaining to *Music in Kālidāsa*[55] and three volumes pertaining to *Erotics in Kālidāsa*.[56]

REFERENCES & NOTES

1. *Kamasutra* - 1.3.15
2. *Ṛtusaṁhāra* - 1.4,6,8
3. *Ṛtusaṁhāra* - 2.18; 3.20
4. *Kumārasambhava* (Kale Edition)-Quoted in Notes on 3.26
5. *Kumārasambhava* - 3.55
6. *Raghuvaṁśa* - 8.64
7. *Vāsavadattā* - verse 11
8. *Sāhityadarpaṇa* - Illustration of *Tulyayogitā* given after 10.48
9. *Saṁskṛta-Śabdārtha-Kaustubha* - p. 919
10. *Ṛtusaṁhāra* - 3.2
11. *Alaṁkārakaustubha* - Illustation 1 of *Asaṅgati Alaṁkāra*
12. *Śārṅgadharapaddhati* - 1006-1007
13. *Vikramovaaśīya* - 4.24
14. *Prayogātmaka Abhinava Dravyaguṇavijñānam* - p. 253

15. *Prayogātmaka Abhinava Dravyaguṇavijñānam* - p. 226
16. *Subhāṣitaratnabhāṇḍāgāra-Prakaraṇa* 6, *Varṣāvarṇanam* - 47, p. 356
17. *Kirātārjunīya* - 5.9
18. *Kirātārjunīya* - 10.23
19. *Śiśupālavdha* - 6.32
20. *Sāhityadarpaṇa* - 1.2
21. *Raghuvaṁśa* - 13.16
22. *Raghuvaṁśa* - 6.17
23. *Śārṅgadharapaddhati* - 1012,1013
24. *Subhāṣitaratnabhāṇḍāgāra-Prakaraṇa* 5, *Vṛkṣānyoktayaḥ* 92, p. 250
25. *Kumārasambhava*-quoted in Mallinātha's commentary on 3.26
26. *Flora and Plant Kingdom in Sanskrit Literature*-For details please see Papers entitled *Longing Trees in Kālidāsa* and *Kālidāsapraṇīta Raghuvaṁśa men dohadataruśrī* by Prof. Sushma Kulshreshtha
27. *Śārṅgadharapaddhati* - 1004
28. *Subhāṣitaratnabhāṇḍāgāra* - *Prakaraṇa* 5, *Vṛkṣānyoktayaḥ* 74,75, P.250
29. *Kuvalayānanda* - 146
30. *Kālidāsa-Kośa* (Sures Chandra Banerji) - p. 9
31. *Raghuvaṁśa* - 9.42
32. *Raghuvaṁśa* - 16.47,50
33. *Śiśupālavadha* - 6.22
34. *Subhāṣitaratnabhāṇḍāgāra* - *Prakaraṇa* 6, *Grīṣmavarṇana*-1, p. 350
35. *Śārṅgadharapaddhati* - 3834
36. *Subhāṣitāvalī* - 2120
37. *Ṛtusaṁhāra* - 2.24
38. *Kumārasambhava* - 8.27
39. *Kumārasambhava* - 9.21
40. *Raghuvaṁśa* - 8.64
41. *Kumārasambhava* - 7.14
42. *Kumārasambhava* - verse from *Pārvatīpariṇaya* quoted in Notes on 7.14, p. 346
43. *Ṛtusaṁhāra* - 2.20
44. *Ṛtusaṁhāra* - 3.19
45. *Ṛtusaṁhāra* - 6.5
46. *Ṛtusaṁhāra* - 5.8
47. *Ṛtusaṁhāra* - 1.4
48. *Ṛtusaṁhāra* - 4.5
49. *Amarakoṣa* - 2.6.25-26
50. *Amarakoṣa* - 2.6.26
51. *Amarakoṣa* - 2.6.27
52. *Ṛtusaṁhāra* - 5.12

53. *Ṛtusaṁhāra* - 5.5

54. *Kāmasūtra* - 2.13

55. (i) *Instrumental Music in Kālidāsa* - 1986

(ii) *Music in Kālidāsa* - 1988

(iii) *Music of Birds and Animals in Kālidāsa* - 1989

(iv) *Meghadūta-Saṅgīta-Pallavī* - 1990

(v) *Ṛtusaṁhāra-Saṅgīta-Surabhi* - 1992

56. (i) *Etotics in Kālidāsa* - Vol. I *Nāyakanāyikāguṇālaṅkāra*-1995

(ii) *Erotics in Sanskrit and English Literature*-Vol. I *Kālidāsa and Shakespeare* - 1996

(iii) *Etotics in Kālidāsa* - Vol. II *Carnal Conditions - Types of Love - Stages of Love* - 1998

(iv) *Etotics in Kālidāsa* - Vol. III *Samprayoga* (under print)

卐 卐 卐

EROTICISM & PLANT KINGDOM IN KUMĀRASAMBHAVA

Sushma Kulshreshtha

Dīpaśikhā Kālidāsa, a peerless poet *par excellence,* was acquainted with and affluent in various systems of Philosophy, several schools of religious beliefs, Politics, Economics, Dramaturgy, Erotology, Music and Fine Arts and Plant Science too. Just as the works of Kālidāsa abound in numerous references to Philosophy, Musicology, Erotics etc., in the same way multiple references to more than 120 plants and trees adorn his works. In *Kumārasambhava* only, there are references to more than 50 plants and trees. They along with their botanical names are as follows :

1. Akṣa (Terminalia Belerica Roxb)
2. Aravinda (Nymphaea Stellata Willd)
3. Alaktaka (Laccifer Lacca)
4. Ambhoja (Nymphaea Alba Linn)
5. Araṇi (Agnimantha) (Premna Latifalia Roxb)
6. Aśoka (Saraca Indica Linn)
7. Āmra (Mangifera Indica Linn)
8. Utpala (Nymphaea Stellata Willd)
9. Kamala (Nelumb Nucifera Garten)
10. Kadalī (Musa Sapinetum Linn)
11. Karṇikāra (Amalatāsa) (Cassia Fistula Linn)
12. Kalpavṛkṣa (Santānavṛkṣa)
13. Kāliyaka (Pītacandana) (Santalum Album Linn)
14. Kāśa (Tṛṇaviśeṣa) (Saccharum Sponatum Linn)
15. Kunda (Camelī) (Jasminum Pubececses Willd)
16. Kuśa (Darbha) (Desmostachya Bipinnata Linn)
17. Kesara (Bakula) (Mimusops Elengi Linn)
18. Kīcaka (Vaṁśa) (Bambusa Bambos Durce)
19. Candana (Santalum Album Linn)
20. Tamāla (Tejapāta) (Cinnamomum Tamal Nees)
21. Tāla (Borassus Falbelefer Linn)
22. Tilaka (Wendlandia Exerta Pers)
23. Darbha (Desmostachya Bipinnata Stapf)
24. Dūrvā (Dūba) (Cynodon Doctylon Roxb)
25. Devadāru (Cedrus Deodara Roxb)
26. Nameru (Punnāga) (Calophyllum Inophylla)

27. Navamallikā (Camelī) (Jasminum Arborescens)
28. Nīlotpala (Nymphaea Stellata Willd)
29. Padminī (Nelumb Nucifera Garten)
30. Pārijāta (Nyctanthes Arbortristis Linn)
31. Puṣkarabīja (Kamalagaṭṭā)
32. Priyāla (Cirauñjī) (Bachanania Lanzan Spreng)
33. Phalinī (Priyaṅgu) (Callicarpa Macrobhylla Vahul)
34. Bimba (Coccinia Indica)
35. Bhūrja (Bhojapatra) (Betula Utilis D. Don)
36. Madhūka (Mahuā) (Madhuca Indica J.F.)
37. Mandāra (Erythrina Suberosa Roxb)
38. Mṛṇāla (Nelumb Nucifera Garten)
39. Yava (Hordeum Vulgare Linn)
40. Raktapalāśa
41. Lavaṅga (Syzygium Aromaticum (Linn) Merr)
42. Lodhra (Symplocos Piniculata Wall)
43. Vetra (Calamus Tenuits Roxb)
44. Śāla (Shorea Robusta Garten)
45. Śirīṣa (Albizia Lebbeck Benth)
46. Śaileya (Parmelia Perlata Ach)
47. Sarala (Pinus Longifolia Roxb)
48. Sahakāra (Mangifera Indica Linn)
49. Siddhārtha (Brassica Campestris Linn)
50. Sindhuvāra (Vitex Negundo Linn)
51. Haricandana (Santalum Album Linn)

Kavikulaguru Kālidāsa has referred to all the aforesaid plants and trees at a number of places in his works in the course of his narratives and descriptions as well as in the usage of similes, metaphors and *utprekṣās*. At places, the poet has referred to these plants and trees drawing references to some other *Śāstra* or Science, *viz.*, *Āyurveda* (Science of Medicine), *Saṅgītaśāstra* (Musicology) and *Kamaśāstra* (Erotics or Erotology) also. The blend of Plant Science or *Vṛkṣāyurveda* with that of musicology and erotology has lent additional charm to these references.

In the present paper, an attempt has been made to show the expertise of Kālidāsa in Plant Science or *Vṛkṣāyurveda* discussing at length the following six trees citing all concerned references found in *Kumārasambhava*. The medicinal (Āyurvedic) qualities and values of these trees have also been given :

1. Āmra
2. Aśoka
3. Kesara

4. Kīcaka
5. Karṇikāra
6. Pārijāta

1. ĀMRA (CŪTA) (Mangifera Indica Linn)

Āmra or mango is the king of Indian fruits. Not only in India, mango is loved by many all over the world. It has hundreds of varieties. Its other names are : *Kāmaśara, Cūta, Rasāla, Kāmavallabha, Vāmāṅga, Sahakāra, Kīreṣṭa* and *Mādhavadruma* :

आम्रः कामशरश्चूतः रसालः कामवल्लभः।
वामाङ्गः सहकारश्च कीरेष्टो माधवद्रुमः।।

Kālidāsa has referred to *Āmra* or *Cūta* at a number of places in the *Kumārasambhava* and almost every time he has blent his description with some other *Śāstra* or *Vidyā* which brings forth his vast erudition. Some examples are presented herewith :

Examples :

1. चूताङ्कुरास्वादकषायकण्ठः पुंस्कोकिलो यन्मधुरं चुकूज।
मनस्विनीमानविघातदक्षं तदेव जातं वचनं स्मरस्य।।[1]

Among the birds, the male and the female cuckoo are the luckiest and the most famous ones for singing. The poetic eulogy showered on the sweet notes of music is that of male cuckoo which is a zoologically proved fact and was known to our magnificent poet. For the music of the male cuckoo, he very adeptly uses the term 'पुंस्कोकिलकूजित'. पञ्चम, the fifth note of music is generated from the throat of कोकिल[2]. In spring, the king of seasons, mango trees are full of mango sprouts. The male cuckoo feasts on these and by sipping the fresh juice of these sprouts, he sings sweetly with an impassioned throat. This is his melodious music which becomes Cupid's eloquent mandate empowered to break down the pride of the high-minded damsels.

Here the word कषाय denotes various meanings—(i) a throat tinged with passion; (ii) a throat clear on account of the astringency of the mango sprout; (iii) a throat which has become reddish brown by the juice of mango sprouts; (iv) a throat which is सुरभित (fragrant) and hence capable of producing sweet sounds.[3]

Ladies having a proper sense of their honour are called मनस्विनी (high-minded lady). When a lady's lover is attracted towards another woman, the wrath generated out of jealousy is called 'मान' :

स्त्रीणामीर्ष्याकृतः कोपो मानोऽन्यासङ्गिनि प्रिये।[4]

As soon as the high-minded ladies listen to the sweet notes uttered by the male cuckoo, they at once give up their मान with regard to their sweet hearts as if they have been directed by the eloquent command of the God of Love :

कोकिलकूजितश्रवणानन्तरं स्मराज्ञप्ता इव मानं जहुरित्यर्थः।[5]

Now in a single verse, we come across the poet's high expertise in the science of love, science of seasons, science of trees, science of birds and science of music.

The picturesque idea of the above verse has been brought out in other works too. Some illustrations are cited here :

(i) त्यजत मानमलं बत विग्रहैर्न पुनरेति गतं चतुरं वयः।
परभृताभिरितीव निवेदिते स्मरमते रमते स्म वधूजनः।।[6]

(ii) प्रियसखीसदृशं प्रतिबोधिताः किमपि काम्यगिरा परपुष्टया।
प्रियतमाय वपुर्गुरुमत्सरच्छिदुरयाऽदुरयाचितमङ्गनाः।।[7]

(iii) दत्तं प्रियाभिर्बहुमानपूर्वमासाद्य चूतासवमन्यपुष्टाः।
आमोदिभिः पञ्चमरागभेदैः प्राबोधयन्पञ्चशरावलेपम्।।[8]

2. हरितारुणचारुबन्धनः कलपुंस्कोकिलशब्दसूचितः।
वद सम्प्रति कस्य बाणतां नवचूतप्रसवो गमिष्यति।।[9]

The voice of the cuckoo becomes clear and sweet when it tastes the mango sprouts. Hence, the melodious voice of the cuckoo indicates the presence of mango blossoms. When Kāma was reduced to ashes by the fire of Śiva's fury, Rati lamented thus : 'Say, by whom the fresh blossom of the mango tree, the beautiful stem of which is reddish green and the sprouting of which is proclaimed by the notes of the male cuckoo, will now be employed as his arrow?' Here also Kālidāsa refers to the music of पुंस्कोकिल.

3. पार्वती तदुपयोगसम्भवां
विक्रियामपि सतीं मनोहराम्।
अप्रतर्क्यविधियोगकारिता-
माम्रतेव सहकारतां ययौ।।[10]

During their love-sports, Śiva asks Pārvatī to drink the wine brought for her by the presiding deity of the Gandhamādana. When Pārvatī drank the wine, she underwent a *vikriyā,* a change, which made her even more attractive and enchanting as a common mango tree is changed by some indefinable power in Nature into the special and fragrant kind of *sahakāra.* The *vikriyā,* the change, is generally for the worse (न हि विक्रिया क्वापि मनोहरा भवति-नारायणः) but the change made Pārvatī more beautiful. *Āmra* and *sahakāra* both signify a mango tree but the latter refers to a particular species whose blossoms are exceedingly fragrant (सहकारोऽतिसौरभ इत्यमरः). This verse poses before us a big question. An ordinary mango tree cannot be transformed into one of the *sahakāra* species unless it is treated with some magical charms which is expressed by अप्रतर्क्यविधियोग or the inscrutable power of the Creator. अप्रतर्क्यविधियोग may refer to मणिमन्त्रौषधकालादियोग too as is explained by commentator Nārāyaṇa. It means an ordinary mango tree can be transformed into the fragrant species of *sahakāra* by the magical usage of jewels, gems, *mantras* or verses of sacred texts and medicinal herbs during a particular time. Such treatment can definitely bring radical changes in a tree. Pārvatī too underwent just a similar magical change after drinking the wine. Those who are well versed in Plant Science and Agricultural Science know very well that trees and plants are given varied types of treatment which bring forth amazing improvements resulting in a better quality and variety of flowers and fruits. This very fact was known to

Kālidāsa.

While commenting on this verse, Vallabhadeva also expresses his surprise that *āmra* can contain *āmratā* only and *sahakāra* can contain *sahakāratā* only. How is it possible that *āmratā* can be changed into *sahakāratā* :

अप्रतर्क्यो दुर्ज्ञेयो यो विधियोगो दैवव्यापारस्तेन विनिर्मितां कृताम्। आम्रता हि केनचिद् दैवभावात् सहकारतां सम्पद्यते वयं न विद्मः (जानीमः)। कस्मिन् देशे कविना आम्रसहकारयोः प्रकृतिविकारभावो दृष्टोऽस्माभिर्हि सामान्यविशेषभावस्तयोरुपलब्धः। तथा चोक्तम्—

अपुष्पफलवानाम्रः पुष्पितश्चूत उच्यते।
पुष्पैः फलैस्तु संयुक्तः सहकार उदाहृतः।।[11]

Kālidāsa has answers for this query with the appropriate inclusion of अप्रतर्क्यविधियोग. A poet of high calibre alone can make such wonderful remarks. On the one hand, he is describing the amorous sports of Śiva and Pārvatī while on the other, he describes Pārvatī's beauty, which has been enhanced by the magical charm rendered to her by the divine wine provided by the wish-giving trees and brought by the presiding deity of the Gandhamādana forest. Here, we find *Pārvatīgata rūpotpannā* and *gandhotpannā vaiṣayikī rati* very beautifully painted by Dīpaśikhā Kālidāsa.

4. परलोकविधौ च माधव स्मरमुद्दिश्य विलोलपल्लवाः।
निवपेः सहकारमञ्जरीः प्रियचूतप्रसवो हि ते सखा।।[12]

O Mādhava (Vasanta), in the memorial rites for Kāma, offer the spray of fragrant mango blossoms with trembling young leaves as your friend was very fond of mango flowers. Here, Kālidāsa once again uses *sahakāra* and *cūta* in one verse. He blends here the Plant Science with the *nivāpa* ceremony, a rite performed after death.

5. सद्यः प्रवालोद्गमचारुपत्रे नीते समाप्तिं नवचूतबाणे।
निवेशयामास मधुर्द्विरेफान्नामाक्षराणीव मनोभवस्य।।[13]

Madhu, the Spring season, having fitted up the arrow of Kāma in the shape of young mango blossoms with fresh leaves as its beautiful feathers, immediately inscribed on it the letters, as it were, of the name of the Mind-born (Cupid), in the shape of the bees.

The mango blossom is one of the five floral arrows of Cupid :

अरविन्दमशोकश्च चूताश्च नवमल्लिका।
नीलोत्पलश्च पञ्चैते पुष्पबाणस्य सायकाः।।

It was usual with great warriors to have their names inscribed on their arrows :

बाणाक्षरैरेव परस्परस्य नामोर्जितं चापभृतः शशंसुः।[14]

Here, Kālidāsa has blent Plant Science with War Science and erotology.

अथ स ललितयोषिद्भ्रूलताचारुशृङ्गं
रतिवलयपदाङ्के चापमासज्य कण्ठे।
सहचरमधुहस्तन्यस्तचूताङ्कुरास्त्रः
शतमखमुपतस्थे प्राञ्जलिः पुष्पधन्वा।।[15]

Then the God of the Flower Bow, having his bow with its ends curved beautiful as the arching eyebrows of graceful women, slung over his neck bearing the marks of Rati's bracelets and having his arrow of young sprouts of mango tree deposited in the hands of his bosom friend Madhu (Spring), approached with folded hands the God of a Hundred Sacrifices (Indra). Here, the imprint of Rati's bracelets over the neck of Kāma indicates their amorous embrace.

7. महीभृतः पुत्रवतोऽपि दृष्टि-
स्तस्मिन्नपत्ये न जगाम तृप्तिम्।
अनन्तपुष्पस्य मधोर्हि चूते
द्विरेफमाला सविशेषसङ्गा।।[16]

The eyes of the Mountain-lord, though blessed with a son, were never satiated by the sight of this child of his (Pārvatī); the circling bees are specially drawn to the mango blossoms though the spring season blooms with countless flowers. In the midst of an endless shower of beautiful flowers in vernal season, the fresh mango sprouts excel all.

8. लग्नद्विरेफाञ्जनभक्तिचित्रं
मुखे मधुश्रीस्तिलकं प्रकाश्य।
रागेण बालारुणकोमलेन
चूतप्रवालोष्ठमलञ्चकार ।।[17]

The Vernal Beauty, having displayed on her forehead a *tilaka* (the *tilaka* flower) artistically painted with black pigment in the shape of the bees that clinged to it, ornamented her lip in the form of the tender mango shoots with a red tint (red lac) mellow like dawn's first light. Here, Plant Science is beautifully mingled with Seasonology and the art of make-up

Medicinal Values

पक्वं तु मधुरं वृष्यं स्निग्धं बलसुखप्रदम्।
गुरुवातहरं हृद्यं वर्ण्यं शीतमपित्तलम्।।
कषायानुरसं वह्निश्लेष्मशुक्रविवर्धनम्।। भावप्रकाशनिघण्टौ।

2. AŚOKA (Saraca Indica Linn)

Jonesia Aśoka Roxb is a tree of moderate size belonging to the leguminous class with magnificent red flowers. Aśoka is a *dohadavṛkṣa*-longing (wishing) tree. The longing of a pregnant woman for particular objects is called *dohada*. These are some *dohadavṛkṣas* which at budding time long to be touched by the foot or the mouth of a lovely woman. It's a poetic convention (*kavisamaya*) that the *Aśoka* requires to be struck by beautiful females with their feet adorned with tinkling anklet bells, so that it is able to bring forth flowers :

सनूपुररवेण स्त्रीचरणेनाभिताडनम्।
दोहदं यदशोकस्य ततः पुष्पोद्गमो भवेत्।।[18]

The jingling anklet bells worn by women produce musical sounds. Music, be it of human beings or birds or animals, encompasses and influences the whole world. Music is three-fold : Vocal, Instrumental and Dance. The splendour of music is to be witnessed in our poetic conventions too that are related to the yearning (longing) trees.

The Aśoka tree becomes laden with blossoming flowers when kicked by the beautiful damsels whose feet are adorned with tinkling anklet bells. The sounds of anklet bells resemble the sounds of idiophones or *ghanavādyas*. The *Nameru* tree blossoms listening to the music and the *Karṇikāra* tree blooms seeing a dance performed before it. Hence, in poetic convention too, music has its significant place where the vocal, instrumental and dance recitals performed by beautiful ladies enable the *Nameru, Aśoka* and *Karṇikāra* trees to blossom :

नूपुरान्वितपादेन तरुण्या ताडितो भृशम्।
अशोकः केसरो वक्त्रसीधुसिक्तश्च फुल्लति।। प्रयोगरत्नावल्याम्।

स्त्रीणां स्पर्शात्प्रियङ्गुर्विकसति बकुलः सीधुगण्डूषसेकात्
पादाघातादशोकस्तिलककुरबकौ वीक्षणालिङ्गनाभ्याम्।
मन्दारो नर्मवाक्यात्पटुमृदुहसनाच्चम्पको वक्त्रवाता-
च्चूतो गीतान्नमेरुर्विकसति च पुरोनर्तनात्कर्णिकारः।।[19]

Examples :

1. असूत सद्यः कुसुमान्यशोकः
स्कन्धात्प्रभृत्येव सपल्लवानि।
पादेन नापैक्षत सुन्दरीणां
सम्पर्कमासिञ्जितनूपुरेण ।।[20]

Madhu (the vernal season), Kāma's bosom friend unfolded in that forest assuming his true form, where Śiva was practising *Samādhi*. At once, the *Aśoka* tree showered sprays of flowers and fresh leaves blooming straight from the trunk without waiting for the delicate touch of a pretty woman's foot adorned with jingling anklet bells for blossoming. This is the only verse where Aśoka tree blooms without its longing fulfilled by the touch of beautiful dames. This verse proves that Kālidāsa was aware of the poetic conventions, different types of *dohadas* of different trees and various fine arts, *viz.*, music and dance. The word *āsiñjitanūpureṇa* denotes instrumental music and dance.

2. अशोकनिर्भर्त्सितपद्मराग-
माकृष्टहेमद्युतिकर्णिकारम्।
मुक्ताकलापीकृतसिन्धुवारं
वसन्तपुष्पाभरणं वहन्ती।।[21]

In Spring season, Pārvatī wore a decoration of spring flowers. The *Aśoka* blossoms put the rubies into shame, the *Karṇikāra* sprays stole the lustre from gold and the *Sindhuvāra* buds shone like a necklace of pearls. Hence, the red *Aśoka* flowers, the yellow *Karṇikāra* flowers and the white *Sindhuvāra* flowers worn by Pārvatī enhanced her natural charm. Here, Kālidāsa has fully utilized the flower kingdom to decorate his heroine. *Karṇikāra* is also a *dohada* tree which requires dancing by a damsel for its blooming.

Medicinal Values

अशोकः शीतलस्तिक्तो ग्राही वर्ण्यकषायकः।
दोषापची तृषादाहकृमिशोषविशास्त्रजित्।।
अशोकस्य त्वचा रक्तप्रदरस्य विनाशिनी।। शालिग्रामनिघण्टौ।

3. KESARA (Bakula) (Mimusops Elengi Linn)

Kesara denotes three different plants, viz., Minmusops Elengi Linn, Rottleria Tenctoria and Mesua Ferrea. In *Saṁhitā* and *Nighaṇṭugranthas, Kesara* has been used to denote *Nāgakesara, Padmakesara* and *Bakula*. Most of the scholars are of the view that *Kesara* is cultivated and found in Kashmir. Kālidāa has used *Kesara* to donote *Bakula* flower which is one of the most fragrant white flowers known as *Maulaśrī* or *Maulasirī*. In Sanskrit literature, *Kesara* is used in the sense of *Puṣpaparāga* or filament of a lotus or of any flower or vegetable too. *Kesara* or *Bakula* is a *dohadavṛkṣa* that requires *Śīdhugaṇḍuṣaseka-mukhamadirā* or pouring of wine through the mouth of a beautiful dame.

Examples :

1. स्रस्तां नितम्बादवलम्बमाना पुनः पुनः केसरदामकाञ्चीम्।
न्यासीकृतां स्थानविदा स्मरेण मौर्वीं द्वितीयामिव कार्मुकस्य।।[22]

When Pārvatī was coming to the *āśrama* of Śiva to serve Him, she was again and again drawing up with her hand her girdle-string composed of *Bakula*-flowers, slipping off her hips, which was, as it were, a second string for his bow deposited there by Cupid who knew the proper place for it. The girdle-string made of fragrant *Bakula* flowers was adding to the charm of Pārvatī.

2. आर्द्रकेसरसुगन्धि ते मुखं
मत्तरक्तनयनं स्वभावतः ।
अत्र लब्धवसतिर्गुणान्तरं
किं विलासिनि! मधुः (मदः) करिष्यति।।[23]

The presiding deity of the Gandhamādana forest brought wine for Pārvatī to honour her. Śiva said—O sportive lady! Since your mouth possesses the fragrance of fresh *Bakula* flowers and the corners of your eyes are naturally rose-red, then, what other grace can a mouthful of wine impart to you? The intoxication of wine brings two changes: it renders the mouth fragrant and colours the eyes red making them look more attractive. Since, Pārvatī already possessed these two things, there was nothing more that wine could accomplish in her case. Pārvatī was a *padminī nāyikā* so naturally her mouth was fragrant like fresh *Bakula* flowers and she was *vilāsinī,* hence, the corners of her eyes were red. This verse is a beautiful illustration of *Pārvatīgata rūpotapannā* and *gandhotpannā vaiṣayikī rati*. Here Kālidāsa has blent Plant Science with erotology very successfully.

3. तस्य जातु मलयस्थलीरते-
धूतचन्दनलतः प्रियाक्लमम्।
आचचाम सलवङ्गकेसर-
श्चाटुकार इव दक्षिणानिलः।।[24]

Once, when Śiva was sporting with his beloved Pārvatī on the grounds of the Malaya mountain, the southern breeze that had been rustling through sandalwood-groves and blowing through clove-orchards came wafting their pollen and like a sweet-spoken lover or adulator removed the tiresomeness of Pārvatī born of sexual sports (pleasure-sports). Here, *kesara* has been used in the sense of the filaments of *Lavaṅga* flower. सलवङ्गकेसरः and धूतचन्दनलतः— these two epithets indicate fragrance and coolness of the breeze. The southern breeze acted as a चाटुकार— an adept adulator or flatterer who drank (dried) up the sex-fatigue of Pārvatī. Here, the usage आचचाम (drank up) is wonderful. In today's world, we come across this word चाटुकार many times. If a person wishes to be a real चाटुकार, he should be able to drink up the fatigue of his lord or beloved. Then only he can succeed in his ventures. This fact was known to Kālidāsa two thousand years ago. Thus, in this verse, we find a blend of Plant Science, erotology and sociology too.

Medicinal Values

(i) बकुलः शीतलोहृद्यो विषदोषविनाशनः।
मधुरश्च कषायश्च मदाढ्यो हर्षदायकः।। राजनिघण्टौ।

(ii) पुष्पं कषायं शीतं पित्तकफास्त्रजित्। राजनिघण्टौ।

(iii) बकुलस्य फलं रुक्षं विशदं स्तम्भनं गुरु।
कषायं मधुरं शीतं लेखनं कफपित्तहृत्।
दन्तदार्ढ्यकरं ग्राहि विबन्धाध्मानवातकृत्।
तद्बीजं दन्तचालघ्नं न स्याच्छीर्षरुजापहम्।। शालिग्रामनिघण्टौ।

4. KĪCAKA (Vaṁśa) (Bambusa Bambos Durce)

Kīcaka (Vaṁśa) is a hollow bamboo whistling or rattling in the wind. *Kīcakas* are found everywhere mostly in Orissa, Assam, East Bengal etc. We get *Vaṁśalocana,* a precious medicinal item from the hollow of the female *Kīcaka* plant. There are many varieties of bamboos in India but the variety which is hollow and produces musical sound when filled with wind is called *Kīcaka*. *Vaṁśī* or *veṇu* or flute is made of *Kīcaka* bamboo only. While describing the beauty of mountain Himālaya, Kālidāsa refers to the music of the Kinnaras where in musical accompaniment on aerophone *Vaṁśī* is being provided by the Himālaya Himself :

यः पूरयन्कीचकरन्ध्रभागा-
न्दरीमुखोत्थेन समीरणेन।
उद्गास्यतामिच्छति किन्नराणां
तानप्रदायित्वमिवोपगन्तुम्।।[25]

Himālaya, the king of mountains, fills the hollow bamboo stems with breeze he exhales through his cave-mouths as if aspiring to accompany on flutes, note by note the sweet melodies of the fauns sung in a very high pitch that is in *Gāndhāra grāma*. This verse for the first time indicates the origin of *vaṁśī* and is very significant with regard to its musical content. Kālidāsa was well versed in a music. That is why he could describe the minutest details regarding *Kinnaras, udgāna* and *tānapradāyitva*. Hence, this verse brings forth our poet's excellent expertise in the field of Plant Science, musicology and anthropology too.

Medicinal Values

वंशोम्लः तुवरस्तिक्तः शीतलः सारको मतः।
वस्तिशुद्धिकरः स्वादुश्छेदनो भेदको मतः।।
कफं रक्तं रुजं पित्तं कुष्ठं शोथं व्रणं तथा।
मूत्रकृच्छ्रप्रमेहार्शान् हन्ति चैव विनाशयेत्।। निघण्टुरत्नाकरे।

5. KARṆIKĀRA (AMALATĀSA) (Cassia Fistula Linn)

Karṇikāra blossoms in spring season. In Sanskrit literature, *Karṇikāra* is used in the sense of golden *Campā, Kaṭhacampā, Mandāra* or *Amalatāsa*. It seems, Kālidāsa has used *Karṇikāra* in the sense of golden *Campā* and at places in the sense of *Amalatāsa* too.

Examples :

1. उमापि नीलालकमध्यशोभि विस्रंसयन्ती नवकर्णिकारम्।
चकार कर्णच्युतपल्लवेन मूर्ध्ना प्रणामं वृषभध्वजाय।।
अथोपनिन्ये गिरिशाय गौरी तपस्विने ताम्ररुचा करेण।
विशोषितां भानुमतो मयूखैर्मन्दाकिनीपुष्करबीजमालाम्।।[26]

Uma bowed so low to the Bull-emblemed God that the tender young leaf shoot at her ear slipped and fell. The fresh *Karṇikāra* flowers shining in the midst of her blue-black tresses got loosened. Then, Pārvatī offered to Śiva, given to asceticism, a rosary of the seeds of lotuses grown in the Mandākinī and dried up by the rays of the Sun, with her hand which had a rosy complexion. Here, Plant Science is mingled with erotology as Pārvatī's *Nāyikālaṅkāra Bhāva* is found in these verses.

2. अशोकनिर्भर्त्सितपद्मरागमाकृष्टहेमद्युतिकर्णिकारम्।
मुक्ताकलापीकृतसिन्धुवारं वसन्तपुष्पाभरणं वहन्ती।।[27]

For critical comments on this verse, please see the heading '*Aśoka*'.

3. वर्णप्रकर्षे सति कर्णिकारं दुनोति निर्गन्धतया स्म चेतः।
प्रायेण सामग्र्यविधौ गुणानां पराङ्मुखी विश्वसृजः प्रवृत्तिः।।[28]

The *Karṇikāra* flower, though of gorgeous colour, pained the mind by its odourlessness. Generally, the mind of the Creator is averse to bestowing the entirety of excellence on any one thing. It appears that *Karṇikāra* here denotes *Amalatāsa*.

Medicinal Values

कर्णिकारो दीर्घफलः स्वर्णाङ्गः स्वर्णभूषणः।
आरग्वधो गुरुः स्वादुः शीतलस्रंसनोत्तमः।।
तत्फलस्रंसनं रुच्यं कुष्ठपित्तकफापहम्।
ज्वरे तु सततं पथ्यं कोष्ठशुद्धिकरं परम्।। भावप्रकाशनिघण्टौ।

6. PĀRIJĀTA (HARAŚṚṄGĀRA) (Nyctanthes Arbortristis Linn)

Pārijāta is one of the five trees of paradise produced at the churning of the ocean and taken possession of by Indra, from whom it was afterwards taken by Kṛṣṇa. It is a tree with beautiful flowers known as *Haraśṛṅgāra* or *Harasiṅgāra* also :

Examples :

1. तां पुलोमतनयालकोचितैः पारिजातकुसुमैः प्रसाधयन्।
नन्दने चिरमयुग्मलोचनः सस्पृहं सुरवधूभिरीक्षितः।।[29]

2. रतिश्लथं तत्कबरीकलापमंसावसक्तं विगलत्प्रसूनम्।
स पारिजातोद्भवपुष्पमय्या स्रजा बबन्धामृतमूर्तिमौलिः।।[30]

3. स्वर्वाहिनीवारिविहारचारी रतान्तनारीश्रमशान्तिकारी।
तौ पारिजातप्रसवप्रसङ्गो मरुत्सिषेवे गिरिजागिरीशौ।।[31]

Celestial damsels gazed long with longing at the Odd-Eyed Lord Śiva as He decorated Umā's tresses in the Nandana groves with *Pārijāta* blossoms that were usually worn in her hair by Śacī, the daughter of Puloman. With a wealth of *Pārijāta* flowers, the Moon-Crested Lord Śiva wreathed Pārvatī's beautiful hair that lay loose clinging to her shoulders, its knot undone as they were engrossed in passionate love and all the flowers in it slipping down. The Mountain-Lord (Śiva) and the Mountain's daughter (Pārvatī) enjoyed the breeze cool from playing on the celestial river's waters, fragrant from blowing through groves of blooming *Pārijāta* trees and bringing welcome relief to ladies fatigued by love's passionate sports.

In all these examples, Plant Science is interwoven with *Cāṭu Nāyakālaṅkāra, Prasādhanakalā*-the art of make-up by a male beautician Lord Śiva and erotology also.

4. किरीटकोटिच्युतपारिजातपुष्पोत्करेणानमितेन मूर्ध्ना।
स्वर्गैकवन्द्यो जगदेकवन्द्यं तं देवदेवं प्रणनाम देवः।।[32]

The Luminous Lord (Indra), the one lord adored in Heaven, now bowed his head low before the Lord of Lords (Śiva) adored by the whole Universe. Clusters of *Pārijāta* blossoms fell down from the corners of his crown. *Pārijāta* flowers were used to decorate the crown of Indra.

5. निसर्गकल्पद्रुमतोरणं तं स पारिजातप्रसवस्रगाढ्यम्।
दिव्यैः कृतस्वस्त्ययनं मुनीन्द्रैरन्तःप्रविष्टप्रमदं प्रपेदे।।[33]

Coming to that *Vaijanyanta* palace festooned with leaves and flowers of the *Pārijāta* tree, where the trees of paradise formed a natural archway, where celestial damsels had already entered, Kumāra Kārttikeya was welcomed by the divine sages, luminous with benedictions. In the above two examples, Plant Science is mixed with the art of decoration.

Medicinal Values

(i) प्राग्रक्तः पारिजातश्च हरशृङ्गारपुष्पकः।
नालकुङ्कुमको रागपुष्पोऽयं खरपत्रकः।। निघण्टुसंग्रहे।

(ii) रसः प्राग्रक्तपत्रस्य ज्वरघ्नस्तिक्तकः स्मृतः।
पर्णखण्डसमायुक्तः त्वचा कासविनाशनः।। शालिग्रामनिघण्टौ।

Thus, Kālidāsa has magnificently blent Plant Science, musicology and erotology in many references to these six trees, enabling us to acquaint ourselves with these sciences. A poet with unique erudition like Kālidāsa can alone bring together too many *vidyās* and *śāstras* at one place. Perhaps, this is one of the aspects of his *sarvātiśāyinī pratibhā* and his everlasting fame for the last 20 centuries.

I conclude this paper with a verse from *Kumārasambhava* which comprises the *Trayī* of Plant Science, musicology and erotology :

गीतान्तरेषु श्रमवारिलेशैः
किञ्चित्समुच्छ्वासितपत्रलेखम्।
पुष्पासवाघूर्णितनेत्रशोभि
प्रियामुखं किंपुरुषश्चुचुम्ब।।[34]

The Kimpuruṣa, in the intervals of musical songs kissed his beloved's face, having its eyes rendered attractive as they rolled with intoxication caused by the flower-wine and having its floral paintings a little marred by the drops of perspiration brought on by exertion.

REFERENCES & NOTES

1. *Kumārasambhava* (Kale Edition) - 3.32
2. *Saṅgītadarpaṇa* -
षड्जं वदति मयूरः पुनः स्वरमृषभं चातको ब्रूते।
गान्धाराख्यं छागो निगदति च मध्यमं क्रौञ्चः।।
गदति पञ्चममञ्चितवाक् पिको रटति धैवतमुन्मददर्दुरः।
शृणि समाहतमस्तककुञ्जरो गदति नासिकया स्वरमन्तिमम्।। 170-171
3. *Kumārasambhava* - Mallinātha's commentary on 3.32 -
चूताङ्कुराणामास्वादेन कषायकण्ठो रक्तकण्ठः। 'सुरभावपथे रक्ते कषायः' इति केशवः।
4. *Kumārasambhava* - 3.32, Notes, p. 62
5. *Kumārasambhava*-Mallinātha's commentary on 3.32
6. *Raghuvaṁśa* - 9.47
7. *Śiśupālavadha* - 7.8

8. *Pārvatīpariṇaya* - 3.3
9. *Kumārasambhava* - 4.14
10. *Kumārasambhava* - 8.78
11. *Kumārasambhava* - Vallabhadeva's commentary on 8.78
12. *Kumārasambhava* - 4.38
13. *Kumārasambhava* - 3.27
14. *Raghuvaṁśa* - 7.38
15. *Kumārasambhava* - 2.64
16. *Kumārasambhava* - 1.27
17. *Kumārasambhava* - 3.30
18. *Kumārasambhava* - quoted in Mallinātha's commentary on 3.26
19. *Kumārasambhava* - quoted in Notes on 3.26
20. *Kumārasambhava* - 3.26
21. *Kumārasambhava* - 3.53
22. *Kumārasambhava* - 3.55
23. *Kumārasambhava* - 8.76
24. *Kumārasambhava* - 8.25
25. *Kumārasambhava* - 1.8
26. *Kumārasambhava* - 3.62, 65
27. *Kumārasambhava* - 3.53
28. *Kumārasambhava* - 3.28
29. *Kumārasambhava* - 8.27
30. *Kumārasambhava* - 9.21
31. *Kumārasambhava* - 9.38
32. *Kumārasambhava* - 12.29
33. *Kumārasambhava* - 12.43
34. *Kumārasambhava* - 3.38

卐 卐 卐

PLANT KINGDOM IN VIKRAMORVAŚĪYA

Sushma Kulshreshtha

Kālidāsa was well-versed in plant science. Multiple references to more than 120 plants and trees, flowers and fruits adorn his works. In *Vikramorvaśīya* only, there are references to more than 30 plants and trees. They along with their botanical names are :

1. Aśoka (Saraca Indica Linn)
2. Atimukta (Mādhavī) (Hiptage Benghalensis Kurz)
3. Bhūrja (Bhojapatra) (Betula Utilis D. Don)
4. Bisa (Lotus-stalk)
5. Cūta (Mango) (Mangifera Indica Linn)
6. Haricandana (Santalum Album Linn)
7. Jambū (Syzygium Cumini Skeel)
8. Kadamba (Anthocephalus Indicus A. Rich)
9. Kalpataru (Celestial Tree)
10. Kamala (Nelumb Nucifera Garten)
11. Kandalī (Crinum Delixum Ker)
12. Karṇikāra (Amalatāsa) (Cassia Fistula Linn)
13. Kumuda (Nymphia)
14. Kunda (Kaundīlatā) (Camelī) (Jasminum Pubececes Willd)
15. Kurabaka (Rhododendron Arborium)
16. Lavalī (Cicca Acida (L.) Merr)
17. Mandāra (Erythrina Suberosa Roxb)
18. Mādhavī (Hiptage Bengholensis Kurz)
19. Mṛṇāla (Nelumb Nucifera Garten)
20. Nalinī (Lotus)
21. Nicula (Barringtonia Acutangula Garten)
22. Nīpa (Anthocephalus Indicus A. Rich)
23. Padminī (Nelumb Nucifera Garten)
24. Puṇḍarīka (White Lotus)
25. Rājajambū (Syzygium Cumini Skeel)
26. Śādvala (A kind of grass)

27. Sahakāra (Mangifera Indica Linn)
28. Sallakī (Boswellia Serrata Roxb)
29. Śaṣpa (Sprouting grass)
30. Tāla (Borassus Falbelefer Linn)
31. Yūthikā (Jasminum Auriclatum Vlol)

Dīpaśikhā Kālidāsa has referred to all the aforesaid plants and trees in *Vikramorvaśīya* in the course of his narratives and descriptions as well as in the usage of similer, metaphors and *utprekṣās*. At some places, the poet has referred to these plants and trees drawing references to some other *Śāstra* or *Vidyā viz., Āyurveda* (Science of Medicine), *Saṅgītaśāstra* (Musicology) and *Kāmaśāstra* (Erotics or Erotology) also. The blend of plant science or *Vṛkṣāyurveda* with that of some other *Śāstra* has lent additional charm to these references.

In the present paper, an attempt is made to show the expertise of Kālidāsa in plant science discussing at length the following 20 plants and tree citing concerned references found in *Vikramorvaśīya.*

1. AŚOKA 2. CŪTA 3. KURABAKA

Aśoka, Cūta and *Kurabaka,* all these three are longing trees.[1] According to poetic convention (*Kavisamaya*), *Aśoka* requires to be strucks by beautiful females with their feet adorned with tinkling anklet bells to bring forth flowers :

सनूपुररवेण स्त्रीचरणेनाभिताडनम्।
दोहदं यदशोकस्य ततः पुष्पोद्गमो भवेत्।।

At being greeted with the mouth-breeze of beautiful damsels, the *Cūta,* mango tree puts forth its blossoms : वक्त्रवाताच्चूतः. At being embraced by pretty women, the *Kurabaka* tree puts forth its blossoms : तिलककुरबकौ वीक्षणालिङ्गनाभ्याम्. *Aśoka* is a tree of moderate size belonging to the leguminous class with magnificent red flowers (Monier Williams). Its leaves are stated to have been used by women for adorning their ears. Mango blossoms are described as being used in the worship of Kāmadeva, Cupid one of whose five arrows is supposed to be made of these blossoms. Mango blossoms are very fragrant.[3] *Kurabaka* blooms in spring. It is used by women to decorate the top-knot of their hair.

Illustrations

(1) अग्रे स्त्रीनखपाटलं कुरबकं श्यामं द्वयोर्भागयो-
र्बालाशोकमुपोढरागसुभगं भेदोन्मुखं तिष्ठति।
ईषद्बद्धरजःकणाग्रकपिशा चूते नवा वल्लरी
मुग्धत्वस्य च यौवनस्य च सखे मध्ये मधुश्रीः स्थिता।[4]

King Purūravas beholding the beauty of the *Pramadavana* which is suggestive of the advent of spring says thus :

Here is the *Kurabaka* flower, towards its tip whitish-red like the nail of a lady's finger and at its sides black; the new *Aśoka* blossom stands ready to burst, charming on account of its accumulated redness, and on the mango-tree, the new blossom appears greyish towards its tips on account of the pollen being but slightly formed. So my friend, Vernal Beauty stands between infancy and youth. The first two lines of this verse describes youth in a concealed state (*mugdhatva* or the state immediately preceding youth), and the third line describes the first manifestation of youth. The three words *Kurabaka*, *rāga* and *rajaḥ* may respectively refer to their secondary sense of childhood (*Kurabaka,* primarily implying scantiness of honey), feeling of love (the precursor of youth) and puberty (the first manifestation of youth).[5]

4. KARṆIKĀRA 5. NALINĪ

Karṇikāra is also a longing tree. At being greeted with a dance-performance in front of it by beautiful damsels, it puts forth its blossoms : पुरोनर्तनात्कर्णिकारः. *Nalinī* is a lotus plant.

(2) उष्णालुः शिशिरे निषीदति तरोर्मूलालवाले शिखी
निर्भिद्योपरि कर्णिकारमुकुलान्यालीयते षट्पदः।
तप्तं वारि विहाय तीरनलिनीं कारण्डवः सेवते
क्रीडावेश्मनि चैव पञ्जरशुकः क्लान्तो जलं याचते।।[6]

Oppressed by heat the peacock sits in the cool basin round the root of a tree; the bee breaks open the *Karṇikāra* bud and lies in it; leaving the heated water, the flamingo resorts to the lotus-creeper on the bank; and the encaged parrot in the pleasure-house, being exhausted, begs for water. Here is a beautiful description of a hot midday. Two flowers and four birds are mentioned in a very natural style. An illustration of a beautiful blend of flora and fauna.

(3) परिजनवनिताकरार्पिताभिः
परिवृत एष विभाति दीपिकाभिः।
गिरिरिव गतिमानपक्षलोपा-
दनुतटपुष्पितकर्णिकारयष्टिः।।[7]

Surrounded by the torches in the hands of his attendant maids, His Majesty Purūravas appears like a mountain possessed of motion on account of its wings not being cut off, with the *Karṇikāra* trees in blossom along its slopes. Here, we find a picturesque simile presented by Kālidāsa.The king appears like a moving mountain and the torches are like the yellow blossoms of the *Karṇikāra* tree. This verse has partial resemblance with the verse in *Raghuvaṁśa,* सञ्चारिणी दीपशिखेव रात्रौ.[8] Indumatī was *sañcāriṇī dīpaśikha* and the king is *gatimān giriḥ*.

(4) सरसि नलिनीपत्रेणापि त्वमावृतविग्रहां
ननु सहचरीं दूरे मत्वा विरौषि समुत्सुकः।
इति च भवतो जायास्नेहात् पृथक्स्थितिभीरुता
मयि च विधुरे भावः कोऽयं प्रवृत्तिपराङ्मुखः।।[9]

King Purūravas chides a *cakravāka* thus: When the person of your mate is concealed from your sight even by a lotus-leaf in the lake, you consider her to be at a great distance from you, and wail anxiously; such is your fear of separation out of the love you have to your mate;

whereas, for me who am actually bereaved of my beloved sweet-heart, your sympathy is such that you refuse even to give me any information regarding her! The *cakravāka* bird is represented as a type of constancy and connubial love. He cannot brook the least separation from his mate. Even a leaf separating him from his beloved is enough to make him cry piteously for her. The same is the case with the female bird. Sanskrit poets believe that an inevitable decree of fate separates them in the night-time, when their cries are heart-piercing, *c.f.* नलिनीपत्रान्तरितमपि सहचरमपश्यन्ती चक्रवाक्यारटति।[10]

6. KUMUDA

Kumuda is the esculent white water-lily (Monier Williams). This flower blossoms at night. Extremely white objects are compared with *Kumuda*.

(5) अङ्गमनङ्गक्लिष्टं सुखयेदन्या न मे करस्पर्शात्।
नोच्छ्वसिति तपनकिरणैश्चन्द्रस्यैवांशुभिः कुमुदम्।।[11]

Purūravas expresses his joy thus : My body, tormented by the pangs of love, none else would be able to gladden with the touch of her (Urvaśī's) hand, the moon-lotus does not blossom by the rays of the sun, but only by those of the moon. A similar idea is found in *Abhijñānaśākuntala* also :

कुमुदान्येव शशाङ्कः सविता बोधयति पङ्कजान्येव।[12]

7. MĀDHAVĪ 8. KAUNDĪ

Mādhavī and *Kaundī* both are creepers which blossom in the months of spring and winter respectively. A very beautiful and apt illustration of these two creepers is found in *Vikramorvaśīya:*

(6) निषिञ्चन्माधवीमेतां लतां कौन्दीं च नर्तयन्।
स्नेहदाक्षिण्ययोर्योगात्कामीव प्रतिभाति मे।।[13]

Being greeted as a guest by the southern breeze, king Purūravas expresses his extreme joy thus : Bedewing with honey (impregnating) this *Mādhavī* creeper, and shaking into a dance the *Kaundī* creeper and thus uniting *sneha* (honey and affection) and *dākṣiṇya* (southerliness and courtesy) in itself, it appears to me like a lover. *Mādhavī,* also called *Vāsantī* creeper, blossoms and bears sweet floral juice in spring season. The *Kaundī,* also called *Māghī,* blossoms in the month of *māgha* two months before the spring. Kālidāsa had portrayed this natural phenomenon in a lavish poetic veil. The *Vāyu* is compared to a lover who has two beloveds. One, *Mādhavī,* young still, the other *Kaundī,* grown up and somewhat elderly. He is attached to the former, but tries to please the other by dancing with her. Here many words have double meanings. *Niṣiñcan* denotes: (1) besprinkling, *i.e.,* generating floral nectar; (2) impregnating. *Nartayan* means: (1) shaking; (2) making her dance. *Snehadākṣiṇya* also express double meanings. The breeze shows *sneha* (making the flowers unctuous with honey) to *Mādhavī* and *dākṣiṇya* (southerliness) to *Kaundī*, which simply moves with it. *Sneha* in the other case means love leading to actual enjoyment. *Sneha* in both its senses and *dākṣiṇya* are the principal qualifications of a lover.[14] This verse is a beautiful illustration of *Nisarga-rati* also—love between breeze and two creepers.

Here is found a beautiful blend of plant science and the science of love.

9. PADMA 10. PADMINĪ 11. PUṆḌARĪKA 12. BISA 13. RAKTAKAMALA

Lotus, the king of flowers, is fondly loved by the worshipper of flora—Kālidāsa. He has referred to lotus, lotus-plant, lotus-fibre at more than 175 places in his works. *Padma, Padminī, Puṇḍarīka, Bisa, Raktakamala* all these words, denote lotus. Kālidāsa has used more than 30 words for this magnificent fragrant flower. He knows minutest details of this flower. For details my paper, entitled 'sixty-four Lotus Blossoms in Kālidāsa'[15] can be gone through.

(7) इदं रुणद्धि मां पद्ममन्तःकूजितषट्पदम्।
मया दष्टाधरं तस्याः ससीत्कारमिवाननम्।।[16]

(Purūravas says) This lotus having in it a humming bee obstructs me, appearing, as it does, like the face of my beloved with a hissing sound when I bite her lower lip. The king compares Urvaśī's mouth to a lotus and the humming sound of the bee in the interior of the lotus to the murmuring of hissing sound produced by Urvaśī due to pain caused by his biting her lower lip.

(8) गतं भयं भीरु सुरारिसम्भवं
त्रिलोकरक्षी महिमा हि वज्रिणः।
तदेतदुन्मीलय चक्षुरायतं
महोत्पलं प्रत्युषसीव पद्मिनी।।
(निशावसाने नलिनीव पङ्कजम्।।)[17]

King Purūravas says to Urvaśī thus: O timid one, the fear arising from the foe of gods has vanished, for the power of the wielder of the thunderbolt guards the three worlds. Open then your long eyes, just as the lotus-plant blows open its lotuses in the morning. Here *Padminī* denotes a lotus-plant and *mahotpala* the big blue lotuses. Urvaśī's long eyes are as pretty as the blue lotuses.

(9) मधुकर मदिराक्ष्याः शंस तस्याः प्रवृत्तिं
वरतनुरथ वासौ नैव दृष्टा त्वया मे।
यदि सुरभिमवास्यस्तन्मुखोच्छ्वासगन्धं
तव रतिरभविष्यत्पुण्डरीके किमस्मिन्?।।[18]

Love-lorn Purūravas addresses a bee thus: Or why, you have not at all seen that beautiful damsel, my sweet-heart. If you had enjoyed the sweet odour of her breath, could you have ever fixed your affection on this lotus? Here, the fragrant *Puṇḍarīka* indicates the odorous mouth-breeze of Urvaśī. A beautiful blend of plant science and erotoloty can be relished here.

(10) पश्चात्सरः प्रति गमिष्यसि मानसं त-
त्पाथेयमुत्सृज बिसं ग्रहणाय भूयः।
मां तावदुद्धर शुचो दयिताप्रवृत्या
स्वार्थात्सतां गुरुतरा प्रणयिक्रियैव।।[19]

Love-lorn Purūravas addresses a Rājahaṁsa thus : You may go to the lake Mānasa afterwards. Leave aside lotus-stalks, the provision for your journey, you may take it up again. First relieve me of my grief by providing me with some news regarding my darling, for the performance of the business of a supplicant is more important in the estimation of good than their own interest. Here, *bisa* denotes a lotus-stalk. Lotus-fibres are the choicest eatables of swans. Therefore, they carry with them the lotus-stalks on their journey to lake Mānasa.

(11) स्फुरता विच्छुरितमिदं रागेण मणेर्ललाटनिहितस्य।
श्रियमुद्वहति मुखं ते बालातपरक्तकमलस्य।।[20]

King Purūravas addresses Urvaśī thus: This your face, brightened by the refulgent redness of the jewel placed on your crest, possesses the beauty of the red lotus shone upon by the morning sun. Here Urvaśī's beautiful face with the jewel placed on her crest appears like a red lotus blossomed by the morning sun. 'Urvaśī's face was tinged red by the red lustre of the gem and so wore the splendour of a lotus steeped in the light of the young sun'.[21]

14. RĀJAJAMBŪ

(12) महदपि परदुःखं शीतलं सम्यगाहुः
प्रणयमगणयित्वा यन्ममापद्गतस्य।
अधरमिव मदान्धा पातुमेषा प्रवृत्ता
फलमभिमुखपाकं राजजम्बूद्रुमस्य।।[22]

Love-lorn Purūravas addresses a female cuckoo thus : It is truly observed that the distress of others, howsoever painful, is but cool; since, disregarding the request of me who is plunged in misery, this impassioned bird (female cuckoo) had set about tasting the fruit of the *Rājajambū* (rose-apple)-tree, about to ripen, as if it were the lower lip of her lover. Cuckoos are very fond of sipping the juice of *jambūphala* (rose-apple). The word *Rāja* prefixed indicates 'excellence', a *jambū* tree of the best kind.

15. SALLAKĪ

Elephants are very fond of eating the fresh twigs of the *sallakī* tree.

(13) अयमचिरोद्गतपल्लवमुपनीतं प्रियकरेणुहस्तेन।
अभिलषतु तावदासवसुरभिरसं सल्लकीभङ्गम्।।[23]

Seeing an elephant, Purūravas says thus : Let him first relish this twig of the *sallakī* tree, fetched to him by his sweetheart in her trunk, which has put forth fresh sprouts and which has a juice sweet like liquor. This verse is a beautiful illustration of *paśu-rati*—love between elephant and his spouse. Besides plant science and erotology, Kālidāsa was well-versed in Zoology too. He fully knew the food habits of different animals and birds.

16. KADAMBA

The *kadamba* flowers blossom at the advent of the rainy season. Women use this flower as decoration on their heads, especially in the parting of their hair.

(14) रक्तकदम्बः सोऽयं प्रियया घर्मान्तशंसि यस्यैकम्।
कुसुममसमग्रकेसरविषममपि कृतं शिखाभरणम्।।[24]

(Purūravas says) Here is the red *kadamba*-tree, a blossom of which indicates the end of summer, and rough on account of the incomplete formation of the filaments, was used by my sweetheart as an ornament for her tresses.

At the roar of clouds, the *kadamba*-tree puts forth its blossoms or when sprinkled with the first rain-drops. Therefore, whenever a *kadamba* puts forth buds, it indicates the end of summer season as is described by different poets :

मरुन्नवाम्भःप्रविधूतसिक्ता कदम्बयष्टिः स्फुटकोरकेव।[25]

17. YŪTHIKĀ

Yūthikā is a kind of jasmine. Women use *yūthikā*-flowers to decorate their tresses.

(15) मदकल युवतिशशिकला गजयूथप यूथिकाशबलकेशी।
स्थितयौवना स्थिता ते दूरालोके सुखालोका।।[27]

Love-lorn Purūravas asks an elephant thus : Did you, O lord of the herd of elephants, intoxicated with rut see from a distance that the lady is charming to look on, who is ever in youth, whose tresses are adorned with the *yūthikā* flowers, and who ranks foremost among women? Here, *yūthikā*-flowers are described as decorating the beautiful hair of Urvaśī. Here, Kālidāsa has blent plant-science with the art of female decoration too.

18. HARICANDANA 19. MANDARA 20. KALPATARU

Haricandana, Mandāra and *Kalpataru*—all these are celestial trees often described as found in th divine garden of Lord Indra. In all, there are five celestial trees, the other two being *Santānaka* and *Pārijāta*. Kālidāsa has referred to all these five in his works.

(16) मुञ्चति न तावदस्याः कम्पं कुसुमसमबन्धनं हृदयम्।
पश्य हरिचन्दनेन स्तनमध्योच्छ्वासिना कथितम्।।[28]

Regarding Urvaśī, the king says thus : Her heart frail like the stem of a flower, does not yet give up its tremor which is indicated by the sandal paste throbbing between the breasts. A woman's heart is often represented as frail. *Kusumasamabandhana* expresses the delicate condition of Urvaśī's heart. Women used to smear their breasts with sandal paste. Urvaśī, being a celestial nymph, had used the paste of the celestial sandal tree-*Haricandana*.The heavenly sandal was visible because Urvaśī's upper garment was probably displaced a little in her unconscious state :

(17) मन्दारपुष्पैरधिवासितायां
यस्याः शिखायामयमर्पणीयः।
सैव प्रिया सम्प्रति दुर्लभा मे
किमेनमस्त्रोपहतं करोमि।।[29]

(King Purūravas says) She, in whose tresses fragrant with the flowers of the *Mandāra* tree, this jewel is fit to be placed, that my sweet darling is now unobtainable to me. Why shall I then soil it with my tears? *Mandāra* is a divine tree. Its flowers are favourite with the celestials. Urvaśī used to decorate her tresses with *Mandāra* flowers so did Śacī, the consort of Lord Indra—मन्दारशून्यानलकांश्चकार।[30]

(18) गन्धोन्मादितमधुकरगीतै-
वाद्यमानैः परभृततूर्यैः।
प्रसृतपवनोद्वेल्लितपल्लवनिकरः
सुललितविविधप्रकारैर्नृत्यति कल्पतरुः।।[31]

Kalpataru, the heavenly tree, dances in a number of attractive ways to the accompaniment of the songs of the bees exhilarated with fragrance, and the playing of musical instruments in the form of the notes of the cuckoos, with the clusters of its foliage waving in the blowing gale. King Purūravas, in his love-lorn state, sees a *Kalpataru* dancing and hismelf dances in imitation of it. This is a *carcarī* song wherein is described the beautiful dance of the celestial tree. This verse comprises the trio of *gīta, vādya* and *nṛtya.* Hence, it is a beautiful illustration of *saṅgīta* along with plant-science. Here, bees are singing the songs, the cuckoos are providing accompaniment on musical instruments and the celestial tree is dancing in a number of charming styles. This is a marvellous sight to enjoy.

I conclude this paper with an *anyokti-śloka* showered on the celestial tree-*kalpataru :*

औदार्यं भुवनत्रयेऽपि विदितं सम्भूतिरम्भोनिधे-
र्वासो नन्दनकानने परिमलो गीर्वाणचेतोहरः।
एवं दातृगुणोत्करः सुरतरोः सर्वोऽपि लोकोत्तरः
स्यादर्थिप्रवरार्थितार्पणविधावेको विवेको यदि।।[32]

REFERENCES & NOTES

1. *Flora and Plant Kingdom in Sanskrit Literature* - 'Ten Longing Trees in Kālidāsa' by Prof. Sushma Kulshreshtha
2. *Kumārasambhava* - quoted in Mallinātha's commentary on 3.6
3. *Flora and Plant Kingdom in Sanskrit Literature*- 'Forty Images of Mango blossoms in Kālidāsa' by Prof. Sushma Kulshreshtha
4. *Vikramorvaśīya* (Edited by M.R. Kale) - 2.7
5. *Vikramorvaśīya* - Notes on 2.7, p. 312
6. *Vikramorvaśīya* - 2.23
7. *Vikramorvaśīya* - 3.3-7
8. *Raghuvaṁśa* - 6.67
9. *Vikramorvaśīya* - 4.20
10. *Vikramorvaśīya* - Notes on 4.20, p. 357
11. *Vikramorvaśīya* - 3.16
12. *Abhijñānaśākuntala* - 5.28

13. *Vikramorvaśīya* - 2.4
14. *Vikramorvaśīya* - Notes on 2.4, p. 310
15. *Flora and Plant Kingdom in Sanskrit Literature* - 'Sixty-four Lotus Blossoms in Kālidāsa' by Prof. Sushma Kulshreshtha
16. *Vikramorvaśīya* - 4.21
17. *Vikramorvaśīya* - 1.5
18. *Vikramorvaśīya* - 4.22
19. *Vikramorvaśīya* - 4.15
20. *Vikramorvaśīya* - 4.42
21. *Vikramorvaśīya* - Comment by M.R. Kale, p. 366
22. *Vikramorvaśīya* - 4.13
23. *Vikramorvaśīya* - 4.23
24. *Vikramorvaśīya* - 4.30
25. *Uttararāmacarita* - 3.42
26. *Śiśupālavadha* - 1.25
27. *Vikramorvaśīya* - 4.24
28. *Vikramorvaśīya* - 1.6
29. *Vikramorvaśīya* - 4.35
30. *Raghuvaṁśa* - 6.23
31. *Vikramorvaśīya* - *Pariśiṣṭa* - 4.9
32. *Subhāṣitaratnabhāṇḍāgāra* - *Prakaraṇam 5, Vṛkṣānyoktayaḥ, Kalpadrumaḥ* - 35, p. 248

Section II

FLORA IN COLLECTIVE WORKS OF KĀLIDĀSA

कालिदासकाव्यामृतनिर्झरी

SIXTY-FOUR LOTUS BLOSSOMS IN KĀLIDĀSA

Sushma Kulshreshtha

कमले कमलोत्पत्तिः श्रूयते न च दृश्यते।
बाले! तव मुखाम्भोजे दृष्टमिन्दीवरद्वयम्।।[1]

According to an anecdote, the second line of this *Samasyāpūrti padya* was accomplished by none other than Kālidāsa. Kālidāsa was well versed in plant science and he possessed commendable knowledge of the plant-kingdom of India. He was very fond of plants, trees and flowers of this country. He has mentioned about 120 plants and trees in his works. He has referred to more than forty kinds of flowers in his works. He had a careful eye for colour. He knew all the uses of various flowers. Some flowers were used by women for decoration, while some flowers were offered to deities. Kālidāsa had full knowledge of the habitat of flowers and also the time of their bloom. It is remarkable that he had an intimate knowledge of the form and colour of the flowers. Glancing at his references to different flowers, it appears that the lotus in its various forms and varieties was his most favourite flower. He has made 177 references to this lucky flower that has achieved '*Saubhāgya*' at the hands of Kālidāsa. He has used 30 different words for this lovely flower.

In the present paper, an attempt is made to show Kālidāsa's expertise in plant science with reference to only one flower-*kamala*- Lotus.

Kālidāsa has used the following 30 words denoting *kamala* or lotus. Each word signifies some speciality, variety or colour of the flower. These words with their number of usages (given in bracket) and etymology are :

1. Abja (2) - अप् + जन् + ड = अप्सु जायते इति।
2. Ambhoja (2) - आप् (अम्भ्)+ असुन् = अम्भस्, अम्भसि जायते इति।
3. Ambuja (7) - अम्ब + उण् = अम्बु, अम्बुनि जायते इति।
4. Amburuha (1) - अम्ब + उण् = अम्बु। अम्बुनि रोहति इति।
5. Aravinda (13) - अर+ विन्द् + श = अरान् चक्राङ्गानीव पत्राणि विन्दते। Red or blue lotus.
6. Bisinī (1) - बिस+ इनि + ङीप्।
7. Indīvara (2) - Blue lotus.

8. Kamala and (29) - कम् + अल् + अच्। कं जलमलति भूषयति।
9. Kamalinī (29)
10. Kuśeśaya (2) - कुशे + शी + अच्, अलुक स.।
11. Kuvalaya (4) - कोः पृथिव्याः वलयमिव, उप. स.। Blue lotus.
12. Kokanada (1) - कोक + नद् + अच्। कोकान् चक्रवाकान् नादयति। Red lotus.
13. Nalinī (13) - नल + इनि + ङीप्।
14. Nīlotpala (6) - नीलम् उत्पलम्। Blue lotus.
15. Padma (29) - पद् + मन्।
16. Padminī (4)
17. Paṅkaja (14) - पञ्च् विस्तारे कर्मणि करणे वा घञ्, कुत्वम्। पङ्के जायते इति।
18. Puṇḍarīka (6) - पूंड् + ईकन् नि०। White lotus.
19. Puṣkara (3) - पुष्क + रा+ क। पुष्कं पुष्टिं राति। Blue lotus.
20. Rājīva (1) - राजी दलराजी अस्त्यस्य व। Blue lotus.
21. Sarasija (4) - सृ + असुन् = सरस्। सरसि जायते इति।
22. Saroruha (3) - सृ + असुन् = सरस् सरसि रोहति इति।
23. Saroja (2) - सृ + असुन् = सरस्। सरसि जायते इति।
24. Sthalakamala (1) - स्थल + अच् = स्थलम्। स्थले जायमानं कमलम्।
25. Sthalāravinda (1) - स्थल + अच् =स्थलम्। स्थले जायमानमरविन्दम्।
26. Tāmarasa (5) - तामर + सस् + ड=तामरे जले सस्ति। Red lotus.
27. Utpala (18) - उद् + पल् + अच्। उत्क्रान्तं पलं मांसम्। Blue lotus.
28. Vanaja (1) - वन् + अच् = वनम्। वने जायते इति। Blue lotus.
29. Vārija (1) - वृ + इञ् = वारि। वारिणि जायते इति।
30. Vāriruha (1) - वृ + इञ् = वारि।

Lotuses are of different varieties and colours. Kālidāsa has referred to *Ambuja, Kamala, Kamalinī, Nalinī, Padma* and *Paṅkaja* most frequently. He has made references to white, golden, blue and red lotuses. He has used *Puṇḍarīka* for white lotus. For blue lotus, he has used seven names, *viz., Indīvara, Kuvalaya, Nīlotpala, Puṣkara, Rājīva, Utpala and Vanaja*. For red lotus, he has used three words, viz., *Arvinda, Kokanada* and *Tāmarasa*.

Kālidāsa has referred to this beautiful flower 177 times. Sometimes, he refers to lotus to describe the beauty of his hero or heroine. Sometimes, he uses this flower as standard of comparison. At various places lotus serves the purpose of decoration and ornamentation too. Sometimes, the poet blends his description of this flower with some other *Śāstra* or *Vidyā*. In fact, if I cite all the 177 references to lotus here, it would form a book. Therefore, I present here

64 illustrations of lotus symbolising 64 arts from all the four poetic works of Kālidāsa. This will enable the connoisseur to have a glimpse of the beauty of this magnificent flower and the high expertise of the Kavikulaguru in many sciences particularly the plant science.

ILLUSTRATIONS

I. LOTUS

1. AMBUJA

Kālidāsa has used *ambuja* as an *upamāna* to the face and feet.

(1) सुखाश्रुपूर्णेन मृगाङ्कमौलेः कलत्रमेकेन मुखाम्बुजेन।
तस्यैकनालोद्गतपञ्चपद्मलक्ष्मीं क्रमात्षड्वदनीं चुचुम्ब।।[2]

This is a rare painting of six lotuses at a time. Pārvatī with her one *mukhāmbuja* kissed the six *vadanapadmas* of his son Ṣaḍānana. It appeared as if five lotuses had bloomed in one *nāla* representing the *Ṣaḍvadanī padmalakṣmī* of Kārttikeya.

(2) गात्राणि कालीयकचर्चितानि सपत्रलेखानि मुखाम्बुजानि।
शिरांसि कालागुरुधूपितानि कुर्वन्ति नार्यः सुरतोत्सवाय।।[3]

(3) अन्येऽपि संनह्य महारणोत्सवश्रद्धालवः स्वर्गिगणास्तमन्वयुः।
स्ववाहनानि प्रबलान्यधिष्ठिताः प्रमोदविस्मेरमुखाम्बुजश्रियः।।[4]

In both these illustrations, *ambuja* is used as *upamāna* to the face.

(4) हारैः सचन्दनरसैः स्तनमण्डलानि
श्रोणीतटं सुविपुलं रसनाकलापैः।
पादाम्बुजानि कलनूपुरशेखरैश्च
नार्यः प्रहृष्टमनसोऽद्य विभूषयन्ति।।[5]

(5) काञ्चीगुणैः काञ्चनरत्नचित्रै-
र्नो भूषयन्ति प्रमदा नितम्बान्।
न नूपुरैर्हंसरुतं भजद्भिः
पादाम्बुजान्यम्बुजकान्तिभाञ्जि ।।[6]

In both these illustrations, *ambuja* is used as *upmāna* to the feet.

(6) पयोधरैः पुण्यजनाङ्गनानां
निर्विष्टहेमाम्बुजरेणु यस्याः।
ब्राह्मं सरः कारणमाप्तवाचो
बुद्धेरिवाव्यक्तमुदाहरन्ति।।[7]

This is the river *Sarayū* whose source, persons of reliable testimony declare to be the lake *Brāhma (Mānasasarovara)*. The pollen of its golden lotuses is enjoyed by (has on account of their sporting in it adhered to) the breasts of the wives of the *Puṇyajanas* (the *Yakṣas*). For, the Invisible Principle (*Prakṛti* or productive principle) is the cause of intelligence, the great principle. Here, the pollen of the golden lotuses of *Mānasasarovara* is described as adorning the breasts of the *yakṣāṅganās*.

2. KAMALA 3. KAMALINĪ 4. NALINĪ

Kamala is spoken of as blooming with sunrise and closing with sunset. It is supposed to be the abode of goddess Lakṣmī (*Kālidāsa-Kośa,* p. 6). Māgha has beautifully described the blooming of *kamala* and the closing of *kumuda* at sunrise simultaneously :

कुमुदवनमपश्रि श्रीमदम्भोजषण्डं
त्यजति मुदमुलूकः प्रीतिमांश्चक्रवाकः।
उदयमहिमरश्मिर्याति शीतांशुरस्तं
हतविधिलसितानां ही विचित्रो विपाकः।।[8]

The beauty of lotus at sunrise comes to a close at sunset :

(7) एभिः साधो हृदयनिहितैर्लक्षणैर्लक्षयेथा
द्वारोपान्ते लिखितवपुषौ शङ्खपद्मौ च दृष्ट्वा।
क्षामच्छायं भवनमधुना मद्वियोगेन नूनं
सूर्यापाये न खलु कमलं पुष्यति स्वामभिख्याम्।।[9]

(8) तस्मिन्काले नयनसलिलं योषितां खण्डितानां
शान्तिं नेयं प्रणयिभिरतो वर्त्म भानोस्त्यजाशु।
प्रालेयास्त्रं कमलवदनात्सोऽपि हर्तुं नलिन्याः
प्रत्यावृत्तस्त्वयि कररुधि स्यादनल्पाभ्यसूयः।।[10]

(Yakṣa says to the cloud) The tears of women angry with their lovers have at that time to be wiped off; therefore quit the path of the sun quickly. For he also, having returned to remove the dew-tears from the lotus-face of the lotus-plant, would be not a little incensed against thee obstructing his rays. Here, *kamala* and *Nalinī* both adorn this verse. The word *Nalinī* here is used in the sense of a lotus-plant.[11]

A beautiful woman's face, soft body or eye is compared with a lotus. One's soft and beautiful palm also is compared with it. Pārvatī was so beautiful that when she was observing penance, her face, greatly scorched by the rays of the sun in that manner, bore the beauty of a day-lotus. But gradually, only round the long corners of her eyes, dark colour made its appearance :

(9) तथातितप्तं सवितुर्गभस्तिभिर्मुखं तदीयं कमलश्रियं दधौ।
अपाङ्गयोः केवलमस्य दीर्घयोः शनैः शनैः श्यामिकया कृतं पदम्।।[12]

The breath of a *nāyikā's* mouth is often compared with the odour of a lotus. The breath of

Pārvatī's mouth possessed a fragrance similar to that of a full-blown lotus :

(10) चुम्बनादलकचूर्णदूषितं शङ्करोऽपि नयनं ललाटजम्।
उच्छ्वसत्कमलगन्धये ददौ पार्वतीवदनगन्धवाहिने।।[13]

Śiva, too, when his third eye on the forehead was pained by her hair-powder in the act of kissing, held it to the breath of Pārvatī's mouth, whose fragrance was like that of a full-blown lotus. This verse is a beautiful illustration of *gandhotpannā vaiṣayikī rati, cumbana* and *puruṣāyita* as Mallinātha comments :

अत्र हरचक्षुष्यलकचूर्णकथनाद्देव्या उपरिभावः सूचितः।[14]

Kālidāsa has beautifully blent plant science with erotology in this verse.

(11) स व्यबुध्यत बुधस्तवोचितः शातकुम्भकमलाकरैः समम्।
मूर्च्छनापरिगृहीतकैशिकैः किंनरैरुषसि गीतमङ्गलः।।[15]

Śiva, accustomed to be praised by the wise, woke up at dawn along with the beds of golden lotuses, auspicious songs being sung for him by *kiṁnaras* who took up the *kaiśika* melody in a series of rising notes. Śiva woke up at dawn and the golden lotuses blossomed in the *Mānasa* lake. It is said that golden lotuses abounded in this lake. Kālidāsa has beautifully blent plant science with musicology in this verse. The intricacies of music described in this verse have been critically examined and elaborated by the writer of these lines in a book.[16]

The *rasika nāgarakas,* rich people and kings used to have pleasure-gardens, pleasure-lakes etc. in their mansions and palaces. There they enjoyed swimming, sporting, drinking, dancing, music etc. King Agnivarṇa also had beautiful pleasure-lakes full of lotuses :

(12) यौवनोन्नतविलासिनीस्तनक्षोभलोलकमलाश्च दीर्घिकाः।
गूढमोहनगृहास्तदम्बुभिः स व्यगाहत विगाढमन्मथः।।

(13) घ्राणकान्तमधुगन्धकर्षिणीः पानभूमिरचनाः प्रियासखः।
अभ्यपद्यत स वासितासखः पुष्पिताः कमलिनीरिव द्विपः।।[17]

King Agnivarṇa of impetuous love sported in the artificial pleasure-ponds where the lotuses were unsteady on account of the agitation of the waters caused by the breasts of the wanton women, right-erect by reason of their youthfulness, and where the rooms for amorous pleasure were hidden beneath their waters. He in company of his wanton women drew near the newly constructed little drinking grounds inviting on account of the sweet odour of wine agreeable to the sense of smell, as an elephant, the friend of its mate, resorts to the blooming lotus-beds.

Here, the poet has very beautifully brought out the libido of King Agnivarṇa, the beauty of the pleasure-ponds with blossoming lotuses and the strong liking of elephants for the lotuses. Thus, here, the poet has blent plant science with erotology and *Hastividyā* too.

It has been the practice among the young damsels that they decorate themselves with seasonal flowers and adorn their hands with sportive lotuses (*līlākamala*). Such a description we find in *Meghadūta :*

(14) हस्ते लीलाकमलमलके बालकुन्दानुविद्धं
नीता लोध्रप्रसवरजसा पाण्डुतामानने श्रीः।
चूडापाशे नवकुरबकं चारुकर्णे शिरीषं
सीमन्ते च त्वदुपगमजं यत्र नीपं वधूनाम्।।[18]

In Alakāpurī, the women have lotuses in their hands for sport, the inlaying of young *Kunda* flowers in their hair, beauty made yellowish-white by the pollen of *Lodhra* blossom on their faces, fresh *Kurabaka* flowers in their braids of hair, charming *Śirīṣa* flowers in their ears, and *Kadamba* flowers springing up at thy approach in the partings of their hair.

This verse makes mention of different flowers blossoming in different seasons, *viz.*, the lotus blooms in *Śarad*, the *kunda* in *Hemanta,* the *lodhra* in *Śiśira, kurabaka* in *Vasanta,* the *śirīṣa* in *Grīṣma* and the *kadamba* in *Varṣā.* This brings forth the *Sarvartusamṛddhi* of Alakāpurī. The damsels of Alakā used to decorate themselves with flower-ornaments instead of gold or gem or pearl ornaments. This establishes their *nāgarikatva* as is said in *Sāroddāriṇī* commentary :

अत्र कनकाद्याभरणभारपरिहारेण कुसुमालङ्कारधारणं नारीणां नागरिकत्वं प्रतिपादयति। निसर्गसुकुमारशरीराणां चतुरसुन्दरीणां कनकरत्नमयाद्याभरणपरिहारेण पुष्पालङ्कारधारणमेव प्रायः प्रीतिनिबन्धनमिति।

Vallabhadeva also gives a similar comment :

तदेतेन कनकालङ्कारनिरासेन योषितां नागरत्वमुक्तं सर्वर्तुसमृद्धिश्च।[19]

Līlākamala or the sportive lotus has a long history in our country. A detailed study of *Līlākamala* has been presented in a paper entitled '*Līlākamala* in Sanskrit Literature.'[20]

Kālidāsa has referred to lotus or golden lotus at a number of places in *Ṛtusaṁhāra :*

(15) कमलवनचिताम्बुः पाटलामोदरम्यः
सुखसलिलनिषेकः सेव्यचन्द्रांशुहारः।
व्रजतु तव निदाघः कामिनीभिः समेतो
निशि सुललितगीते हर्म्यपृष्ठे सुखेन।।

(16) सोन्मादहंसमिथुनैरुपशोभितानि
स्वच्छप्रफुल्लकमलोत्पलभूषितानि ।
मन्दप्रभातपवनोद्गतवीचिमाला-
न्युत्कण्ठयन्ति सहसा हृदयं सरांसि।।

(17) कनककमलकान्तैश्चारुताम्राधरोष्ठैः
श्रवणतटनिषक्तैः पाटलोपान्तनेत्रैः।
उषसि वदनबिम्बैरंससंसक्तकेशैः
श्रिय इव गृहमध्ये संस्थिता योषितोऽद्य।।

(18) कनककमलकान्तैराननैः पाण्डुगण्डै-
रुपरिनिहितहारैश्चन्दनार्द्रैः स्तनान्तैः।
मदजनितविलासैर्दृष्टिपातैर्मुनीन्द्रान्
स्तनभरनतनार्यः कामयन्ति प्रशान्तान्।।[21]

5. PADMA 6. PADMINĪ

Kālidāsa has referred to *Padma* and *Padminī* at 33 places in different contexts in his works. Lotus blooms at sunrise but on Mountain Himālaya, its blooming is somewhat peculiar as is described in *Kumārasambhava*.

(19) सप्तर्षिहस्तावचितावशेषाण्यधो विवस्वान्परिवर्तमानः।
पद्मानि यस्याग्रसरोरुहाणि प्रबोधयत्यूर्ध्वमुखैर्मयूखैः।।[22]

Whose lotuses, growing in the lakes on the highest summits, and left after being collected by the hands of the seven sages, the sun, moving on a lower level, blossoms by means of his rays shooting upwards.

The face of a beautiful woman is compared to a lotus. A lotus possesses numerous qualities, *viz.*, beauty, charm, grace, fragrance and delicacy but Pārvatī's face possessed even more as describes our poet :

(20) चन्द्रं गता पद्मगुणान्न भुङ्क्ते पद्माश्रिता चान्द्रमसीमभिख्याम्।
उमामुखं तु प्रतिपद्य लोला द्विसंश्रयां प्रीतिमवाप लक्ष्मीः।।[23]

The unsteady Goddess of beauty could not enjoy (possess) the charms of the lotus when with the moon, and of the lunar graces when with the lotus; but when she betook herself to the face of Umā, she enjoyed the pleasure coming from the charms peculiar to both. 'Pārvatī's face combined in itself the special beauties of both, the lotus and the moon, such as unfading freshness, fragrance, loveliness etc. and thus excelled both; this is poetically and strikingly described in this *śloka*'.[24]

Although a lotus surrounded by black-bees looks beautiful but Pārvatī's face with beautiful dark tresses left no occasion for the lotus even to talk of comparison :

(21) लग्नद्विरेफं परिभूय पद्मं समेघलेखं शशिनश्च बिम्बम्।
तदाननश्रीरलकैः प्रसिद्धैश्चिच्छेद सादृश्यकथाप्रसङ्गम्।।[25]

(22) क्लमं ययौ कन्दुकलीलयापि या तया मुनीनां चरितं व्यगाह्यत।
ध्रुवं वपुः काञ्चनपद्मनिर्मितं मृदु प्रकृत्या चससारमेव च।।[26]

Pārvatī, who was tired even by playing with the ball, entered the course of life of anchorites, verily her body was composed of gold lotuses, as it was delicate by nature and yet tough (full of substance). Here, the word *kāñcanapadma* is very appropriately chosen; it not only bears resemblance to her bodily complexion, but also indicates softness and, at the same time, power to resist any destructive influence.

(23) मुखेन सा पद्मसुगन्धिना निशि प्रवेपमानाधरपत्रशोभिना।
तुषारवृष्टिक्षतपद्मसम्पदां सरोजसन्धानमिवाकरोदपाम्।।[27]

By Pārvatī's face, which was as fragrant as the lotus itself and which shone, with the quivering leaf of the nether lip, she at night restored the beauty of lotuses to the water of the stream, the wealth of lotuses of which was destroyed by the showers of snow in winter season. Pārvatī's face is compared to the fragrant lotus. Her trembling lower lip is compared to the petal of lotus. Here *padma* is used twice and *saroja* once in this verse.

(24) यत्रोन्मत्तभ्रमरमुखराः पादपा नित्यपुष्पा
हंसश्रेणीरचितरशना नित्यपद्मा नलिन्यः।
केकोत्कण्ठा भवनशिखिनो नित्यभास्वत्कलापा
नित्यज्योत्स्नाः प्रतिहततमोवृत्तिरम्याः प्रदोषाः।।[28]

Where in Alakāpurī, the trees are ever-blossoming and noisy with intoxicated bees, the lotus-ponds have ever-blooming lotuses and girdles formed of the rows of swans, the domestic peacocks have their tails ever-shining and their necks uplifted by their cries, and evenings are ever moonlit and pleasant on account of the course of darkness being obstructed. All beauty and prosperity is always present in Alakā as it is a celestial place.

(25) निवातपद्मस्तिमितेन चक्षुषा नृपस्य कान्तं पिबतः सुताननम्।
महोदधेः पूर इवेन्दुदर्शनाद्गुरुः प्रहर्षः प्रबभूव नात्मनि।।[29]

Lotus is a famous standard of comparison for eyes too. Looking intently at (*lit.* drinking up) the lovely face of his son Raghu, with eyes, motionless like a lotus in a breezeless place, King Dilīpa could not control his great joy within himself (his joy overflew all it bounds), as the great ocean its flood at the sight of the moon.

When Princess Indumatī chose Prince Aja as her consort, the people of his side were extremely happy. Kālidāsa has used lotus to depict human emotions and sentiments too thus :

(26) प्रमुदितवरपक्षमेकतस्त-
त्क्षितिपतिमण्डलमन्यतो वितानम्।
उषसि सर इव प्रफुल्लपद्मं
कुमुदवनप्रतिपन्ननिद्रमासीत् ।।[30]

Poet Māgha was so impressed by this verse, that he also used this image in his description of early morning thus :

कुमुदवनमपश्रि श्रीमदम्भोजषण्डं
त्यजति मुदमुलूकः प्रीतिमांश्चक्रवाकः।
उदयमहिमरश्मिर्याति शीतांशुरस्तं
हतविधिलसितानां ही विचित्रो विपाकः।।[31]

(27) श्रियः पद्मनिषण्णायाः क्षौमान्तरितमेखले।
अङ्के निक्षिप्तचरणमास्तीर्णकरपल्लवे।।[32]

Lotus is the abode of Goddess Lakṣmī. The Queens of King Daśaratha saw in dreams that they were waited upon by Lakṣmī with a fan of a lotus in her hand as is seen in this verse :

(28) बिभ्रत्या कौस्तुभं न्यासं स्तनान्तरविलम्बिनम्।
पर्युपास्यन्त लक्ष्म्या च पद्मव्यजनहस्तया।।[33]

By the grace of *Anasūya*, the holy river Gaṅgā flows near sage Atri's hermitage. This river abounds in golden lotuses that are plucked by the seven sages :

(29) अत्राभिषेकाय तपोधनानां सप्तर्षिहस्तोद्धृतहेमपद्माम्।
प्रवर्तयामास किलानुसूया त्रिस्त्रोतसं त्र्यम्बकमौलिमालाम्।।[34]

Elephants are very fond of lotuses, lotus-plants and lotus-stalks specially when they are in the company of their dear mates and in a sportive mood in water. Kālidāsa has painted such scenes in *Raghuvaṁśa :*

(30) स नौविमानादवतीर्य रेमे
विलोलहारः सह ताभिरप्सु।
स्कन्धावलग्नोद्धृतपद्मिनीकः
करेणुभिर्वन्य इव द्विपेन्द्रः।।[35]

(31) चित्रद्विपाः पद्मवनावतीर्णाः
करेणुभिर्दत्तमृणालभङ्गाः ।
नखाङ्कुशाघातविभिन्नकुम्भाः
संरब्धसिंहप्रहृतं वहन्ति।।[36]

(32) तां जानीथाः परिमितकथां जीवितं मे द्वितीयं
दूरीभूते मयि सहचरे चक्रवाकीमिवैकाम्।
गाढोत्कण्ठां गुरुषु दिवसेष्वेषु गच्छत्सु बालां
जातां मन्ये शिशिरमथितां पद्मिनीं वान्यरूपाम्।।[37]

(Yakṣa says to cloud) Thou canst know her who is tacitum and in the absence of me, her companion, solitary like a *cakravākī,* to be my second life (my wife); I imagine that young woman filled with ardent longing, to have become changed in appearance like a lotus-plant blighted by winter, during these heavy days (of separation) that are now passing. Here, the comparison of Yakṣī with *Śiśiramathitā padminī* very aptly paints the true picture of a love-lorn *nāyikā*.

7. PAṄKAJA

Kālidāsa has referred to *paṅkaja* at 14 places in his works using it sometimes as *upamāna,* sometimes to depict a particular situation or mood of a person or sometimes to describe the beauty of a particular limb of a *nāyikā*. Now some illustrations are presented for the enjoyment of the connoisseur :

(33) यथा प्रसिद्धैर्मधुरं शिरोरुहैर्जटाभिरप्येवमभूत्तदाननम्।

न षट्पदश्रेणिभिरेव पङ्कजं सशैवलासङ्गमपि प्रकाशते।।[38]

As Pārvatī's face looked pretty by her decorated tresses, so it did by her matted hair also. A lotus does not look beautiful only by the swarms of bees, but even by its union with moss. Pārvatī was observing a rigorous penance. Still her face looked beautiful just as a lotus looks beautiful with moss also. Pārvatī's face was ever beautiful so is lotus too. A thing of beauty is a joy for ever.

(34) दिनेषु गच्छत्सु नितान्तपीवरं
तदीयमानीलमुखं स्तनद्वयम्।
तिरश्चकार भ्रमराभिलीनयोः
सुजातयोः पङ्कजकोशयोः श्रियम्।।[39]

As days rolled on, *Sudakṣiṇā's* full and plumpy breasts, with dark nipples, put to shame, as it were, the loveliness of two charming lotus-buds surmounted by black bees. Here, *Sudakṣiṇā's* breasts excelled in beauty and left lotus-buds far behind.

(35) इदमुच्छ्वसितालकं मुखं तव विश्रान्तकथं दुनोति माम्।
निशि सुप्तमिवैकपङ्कजं विरताभ्यन्तरषट्पदस्वनम्।।[40]

At the sudden demise of his beloved sweet-heart Indumatī, King Aja laments thus : This face of your's with its dishevelled curly hair and with speech altogether ceased, like a solitary lotus closed at night with the humming of the bees in the inside silenced, torments me, my dear. Indumatī's face is compared to a lotus but definitely in a different state of sentiment.

II. WHITE LOTUS

8. PUṆḌARĪKA

Kālidāsa has referred to *puṇḍarīka* six times in his works. *Puṇḍarīka* is white lotus. It has been used as *upamāna* to the face and to the eyes as is seen in the following verses :

(36) नूनमुन्नमति यज्वनां पतिः शार्वरस्य तमसो निषिद्धये।
पुण्डरीकमुखि पूर्वदिङ्मुखं कैतकैरिव रजोभिरावृतम्।।[41]

(37) प्रबुद्धपुण्डरीकाक्षं बालातपनिभांशुकम्।
दिवसं शारदमिव प्रारम्भसुखदर्शनम्।।[42]

White lotus flowers are described as the umbrella of the autumn season :

(38) पुण्डरीकातपत्रस्तं विकसत्काशचामरः।
ऋतुर्विडम्बयामास न पुनः प्राप तच्छ्रियम्।।[43]

Kālidāsa has composed a very beautiful verse where the word *puṇḍarīka* has been used four times. Goddess Lakṣmī holds a white lotus in her hand. Puṇḍarīkākṣa is Lord Viṣṇu's epithet as his eyes are as beautiful as a white lotus. The name of Agnikoṇa *diggaja* is also Puṇḍarīka and the name of King Nabha's son is also Puṇḍarīka. Now, relish the beauty of *Puṇḍarīka* :

(39) तेन द्विपानामिव पुण्डरीको
राज्ञामजय्योऽजनि पुण्डरीकः।
शान्ते पितर्याहृतपुण्डरीका
यं पुण्डरीकाक्षमिव श्रिता श्रीः॥[44]

A son named Puṇḍarīka was born to King Nabha who was invincible to kings as the elephant Puṇḍarīka is to other elephants. When his father was dead the Royal Fortune taking with her a white lotus went over to him, as she went to the lotus-eyed god Viṣṇu.

III. BLUE LOTUS

The sight of beautiful blue lotuses is a delicious feast to the eyes of the beholder. Kālidāsa has referred to blue lotuses at 35 different occasions in his works. He has used seven different words denoting blue lotus. They are-*utpala, nīlotpala, indīvara, kuvalaya, puṣkara, rājīva* and *vanaja*. A beautiful woman's eyes are compared with it. Blue lotus is used as an ear-ornament also by beautiful damsels. The complexion of a *nāyaka* is also compared with the colour of blue lotus. Sometimes, pleasure-ponds abounding in blue lotuses are described.

9. UTPALA 10. NĪLOTPALA

(40) प्रवातनीलोत्पलनिर्विशेषमधीरविप्रेक्षितमायताक्ष्या।
तया गृहीतं नु मृगाङ्गनाभ्यस्ततो गृहीतं नु मृगाङ्गनाभिः॥[45]

The timid (unsteady) glances, not at all dissimilar to the blue lotus tremulous in a strong wind,-did the female fawns borrow them from Pārvatī, or she, with elongated eyes, from them? Here, Pārvatī's glances are compared to blue lotus.

(41) सा लाजधूमाञ्जलिमिष्टगन्धं गुरूपदेशाद्वदनं निनाय।
कपोलसंसर्पिशिखः स तस्या मुहूर्तकर्णोत्पलतां निनाय॥[46]

Pārvatī, following the instructions of the priest, bent her face towards the smoke of agreeable smell, arising from the (burning) handful of rice, the smoke, touching her cheek with its forepart, attained for a moment the state of the ear-lotus. During the religious wedding rites, the smoke near Pārvatī's cheeks appeared like a blue-lotus-ear-ornament. Beautiful women used to wear blue-lotus as ear-ornaments. A similar idea is also found in *Raghuvaṁśa,* where the wedding rites of Indumatī are being performed :

(42) हविःशमीपल्लवलाजगन्धी पुण्यः कृशानोरुदियाय धूमः।
कपोलसंसर्पिशिखः स तस्या मुहूर्तकर्णोत्पलतां प्रपेदे॥[47]

There rose up from that fire the sacred smoke fragrant with the scent of oblations, *Śamī*-leaves and *Lājas,* which as its spire passed by Indumatī's cheeks looked for a moment like a lotus on her ear.

Rati also used to wear blue-lotus as an ear-ornament. She remembers how once she had beaten Kāmadeva with her blue-lotus-ear-ornament during their love-sports :

(43) स्मरसि स्मर मेखलागुणैरुत गोत्रस्खलितेषु बन्धनम्।
च्युतकेशरदूषितेक्षणान्यवतंसोत्पलताडनानि वा।।[48]

Dost thou remember, O Cupid! my binding thee with the strings of my waist-band whenever I was addressed with a wrong name by thee, or my beatings of thee with lotuses used as ear-ornaments, hurting thy eyes with pollen-dust dropping from them? Strange is the world of lovers where *nāyikās* beat their sweet-hearts with blue lotuses in their pleasure-sports.

(44) तस्याः सुजातोत्पलपत्रकान्ते प्रसाधिकाभिर्नयने निरीक्ष्य।
न चक्षुषोः कान्तिविशेषबुद्ध्या कालाञ्जनं मङ्गलमित्युपात्तम्।।[49]

The beauticians decorating Pārvatī, looking that her eyes were as charming as the petals of a lovely (*lit.* well-grown) blue lotus, took up collyrium (for putting it into them), not because they thought it would add to their beauty, but because it was auspicious to do so. Here, Pārvatī's eyes are compared with blue lotus.

Not only the human beings, the birds and animals also derive pleasure in presenting lotuses or the pollen-dust of lotuses to each other during their love-sports. Śrīrāma describes one such scene to Sītā thus :

(45) अत्रावियुक्तानि रथाङ्गनाम्नामन्योन्यदत्तोत्पलकेसराणि।
द्वन्द्वानि दूरान्तरवर्तिना ते मया प्रिये सस्पृहमीक्षितानि।।[50]

Here, my dear Sītā, couples of unseparated *cakravāka* birds who interchanged lotus fibres among themselves (who gave lotus-stalks to each other) were wistfully gazed at by me, situated as I was at a place far off from thee. Flowers are the source of joy not to human beings alone but to all—birds and animals too. Looking at the tender love-sports of *cakvavāka* couples, Śrīrāma recalls his own love-pleasures. Thus, the description of lotus brings forth human sentiments also with utmost tenderness.

(46) भालेक्षणाग्नौ स्वयमञ्जनं स भङ्क्त्वा दृशोः साधु निवेश्य तस्याः।
नवोत्पलाक्ष्याः पुलकोपगूढे कण्ठे विनीलेऽङ्गुलिमुज्जघर्ष।।[51]

Lord Śaṅkara Himself prepared collyrium and put it Himself in the blue-lotus-like eyes of Pārvatī. A rare fortunate occasion for a bride and a unique sight to glance at for any beholder indeed!

The female wreath-makers also decorate themselves wearing blue-lotuses as ear-ornaments as is described in *Meghadūta :*

(47) विश्रान्तः सन्व्रज वननदीतीरजातानि सिञ्च-
न्नुद्यानानां नवजलकणैर्यूथिकाजालकानि।
गण्डस्वेदापनयनरुजाक्लान्तकर्णोत्पलानां
छायादानात्क्षणपरिचितः पुष्पलावीमुखानाम्।।[52]

Blue lotuses are often used to describe the colour of clouds and of the temple of elephants as is seen in the following verses of *Ṛtusaṁhāra :*

(48) नितान्तनीलोत्पलपत्रकान्तिभिः
क्वचित्प्रभिन्नाञ्जनराशिसंनिभैः ।
क्वचित्सगर्भप्रमदास्तनप्रभैः
समाचितं व्योम घनैः समन्ततः।।[53]

Appearing somewhere like having the lustre of the blue petals of the blue lotuses, in some places looking like the heap of powdered collyrium, in others resembling the breasts of pregnant women, the clouds have covered the sky.

(49) वनद्विपानां नववारिदस्वनै-
र्मदान्वितानां ध्वनतां मुहुर्मुहुः।
कपोलदेशा विमलोत्पलप्रभाः
सभृङ्गयूथैर्मदवारिभिश्चिताः ।।[54]

Lovers are very fond of *Pānagoṣṭhīs*-drinking sessions when they are in the company of their sweethearts. It has been the convention with lovers that they sip wine mixed with blue lotuses or petals of blue lotuses. Thus, the wine becomes odorous and kindles their ardent desire for love-sports. A scene of a *pānagoṣṭhī* can be relished here :

(50) सुगन्धिनिःश्वासविकम्पितोत्पलं
मनोहरं कामरतिप्रबोधकम्।
निशासु हृष्टाः सह कामिभिः स्त्रियः
पिबन्ति मद्यं मदनीयमुत्तमम्।।[55]

In winter-nights, ladies filled with delight, drink in the company of their lovers attractive, excellent, intoxicating wine which inflames their desire for sexual pleasure and the blue lotus flowers in which are shaken by their sweet-odoured breath.

11. INDĪVARA 12. KUVALAYA

(51) इन्दीवरश्यामतनुर्नृपोऽसौ त्वं रोचनागौरशरीरयष्टिः।
अन्योन्यशोभापरिवृद्धये वां योगस्तडित्तोयदयोरिवास्तु।।[56]

Here, the bodily complexion of a prince is compared to a blue lotus.

(52) ज्योतिर्लेखावलयि गलितं यस्य बर्हं भवानी
पुत्रप्रेम्णा कुवलयदलप्रापि कर्णे करोति।
धौतापाङ्गं हरशशिरुचा पावकेस्तं मयूरं
पश्चादद्रिग्रहणगुरुभिर्गर्जितैर्नर्तयेथाः ।।[57]

Pārvatī's fondness for wearing petals of a blue lotus as an ear-ornament is described in this verse.

IV. RED LOTUS

The glimpse of beautiful pink and red lotuses is a fabulous feast to the eyes of the beholder. *Aravinda* is said to be one of the five flower-arrows of the Flower-god Cupid :

अरविन्दमशोकश्च चूतश्च नवमल्लिका।
नीलोत्पलश्च (कुरबकश्च) पञ्चैते पुष्पबाणस्य सायकाः।।

Dīpaśikhā Kālidāsa has referred to red lotuses at 19 different places in his works. He has used three different words denoting a pink and red lotus. They are *Aravinda, Kokanada* and *Tāmarasa*. A beautiful woman's face, a child's face or a happy man's face is compared with a red lotus. A woman's feet are also compared with a red lotus. The odorous breath of a woman is also compared to the fragrance of a red lotus. It was a convention among *nāgarakas* and *nāgarikās* to hold sportive-lotuses (pleasure-lotuses) in their hands. For this sportive lotus, Kālidāsa has used two words-*līlāravinda* and *līlākamala*.[58] Pleasure-ponds are also described as abounding in red lotuses. Now, I present some beautiful pictures of red lotuses for the enjoyment of connoisseurs.

13. ARAVINDA

(53) उन्मीलितं तूलिकयेव चित्रं सूर्यांशुभिर्भिन्नमिवारविन्दम्।
बभूव तस्याश्चतुरस्रशोभि वपुर्विभक्तं नवयौवनेन।।[59]

Pārvatī's body, fully unfolded by fresh youth, appeared charming, in its perfect symmetry, like a painting, gradually grown under the brush of a painter or like a pink lotus blossoming under the rays of the sun. Here, Pārvatī's charming persona is compared with *aravinda*-pink lotus. *Aravinda* is so called because it has petals resembling the spokes of a wheel (अराकाराणि पत्राणि विन्दति इति (अर + विद् + अ(शः) by *Vārttika* on Pāṇini III. 1.138).

(54) सरसीष्वरविन्दानां वीचिविक्षोभशीतलम्।
आमोदमुपजिघ्रन्तौ स्वनिःश्वासानुकारिणम्।।[60]

King Dilīpa and Queen Sudakṣinā smelt the fragrance of the red lotus-flowers in large lakes, cool by contact with ripples and imitating or resembling their own breath. They enjoyed the beauty and the sweet fragrance of the red lotuses blossoming in lakes.

(55) सुगन्धिनिःश्वासविवृद्धतृष्णं बिम्बाधरासन्नचरं द्विरेफम्।
प्रतिक्षणं संभ्रमलोलदृष्टिर्लीलारविन्देन निवारयन्ती।।[61]

Pārvatī, her eyes agitated through confusion, was keeping off, every moment, with a sportive red lotus, a bee hovering round her *bimba*-like lower lip, with its thirst (desire) excited by her fragrant breath. Pārvatī was the beautiful daughter of *Nagādhirāja* Himālaya. She used to hold a sportive red lotus in her hand as was the convention among rich sphisticated princes and princesses.

(56) कश्चित्कराभ्यामुपगूढनालमालोलपत्राभिहतद्विरेफम्।
रजोभिरन्तःपरिवेषबन्धि लीलारविन्दं भ्रमयाञ्चकार।।[62]

In Indumatī's *svayaṁvara,* a certain king began to turn round a red pleasure-lotus, the stem of which he held in his hands, which with its revolving petals warded off the bees and which formed a circle in its interior by means of pollens.

(57) काचिद् विभूषयति दर्पणसक्तहस्ता
बालातपेषु वनिता वदनारविन्दम्।
दन्तच्छदं प्रियतमेन निपीतसारं
दन्ताग्रभिन्नमवकृष्य निरीक्षते च।।[63]

A certain woman with a mirror in her hand is decorating her red lotus-like face in the new beams of the morning sun, and is pulling out and observing her lip whose essence has been sipped by her lover and which has been bitten by the ends of teeth. This verse indicates the red lotus-like beauty of a *nāyikā's* face and her *adharāmṛtapāna* by her lover.

(58) मन्देन खिन्नाङ्गुलिना करेण कम्पेन तस्या वदनारविन्दात्।
परामृशन्घर्मजलं जहार हरः सहेलं व्यजनानिलेन।।[64]

Being seen by Agni during their love-sports, Pārvatī was in wrath. Lord Śaṅkara was appeasing her in various ways. He wiped off with his fingers the drops of sweat on her red lotus-like face and served her with a fan. Strange are the ways of lovers; what to say of Śiva and Pārvatī!

(59) इत्यन्धकारातिसुतस्य दैत्यवधाय युद्धोत्सुकमानसस्य।
सर्वं शुचिस्मेरमुखारविन्दं गीर्वाणवृन्दं वचसा ननन्द।।[65]

When Kārttikeya assured the gods of the killing of demons, they became very happy. When a person is happy, his face glitters and blossoms like the red lotus. Similarly, a smile glittered on the red lotus-like faces of the gods.

(60) सैषा स्थली यत्र विचिन्वता त्वां
भ्रष्टं मया नूपुरमेकमुर्व्याम्।
अदृश्यत त्वच्चरणारविन्द-
विश्लेषदुःखादिव बद्धमौनम्।।[66]

While returning from Laṅkā, Śrīrāma says to Sītā thus : This is the very spot where searching for thee, I saw one anklet which had dropped down upon the ground—an anklet which kept silent through grief of separation, as it were, from thy red lotus-like feet. Here, Sītā's feet are compared with red lotus.

14. KOKANADA

Kokanada is so called as it stimulates the *cakravāka* birds to produce sounds (कोकान् चक्रवाकान् नदति नादयति). They are very fond of red lotuses and their pollen. A number of poets have described *kokanadas :*

(i) नीलनलिनाभमपि तन्वि तव लोचनं धारयति कोकनदरूपम्।[67]

(ii) किञ्चित्कोकनदच्छदस्य सदृशे नेत्रे स्वयं रज्यतः।[68]

(iii) भिन्नेषु रक्तकिरणैः किरणेष्विहेन्दो-
रुच्चावचैरुपगतेषु सहस्रसंख्याम्।
दोषापि नूनमहिमांशुरसौ किलेति
व्याकोशकोकनदतां दधते नलिन्यः।।[69]

(61) इत्थं निशम्य वचनं युधि तारकस्य
कम्प्राधरो विकचकोकनदारुणाक्षः।
क्षोभात्त्रिलोचनसुतो धनुरीक्षमाणः
प्रोवाच वाचमुचितां परिमृश्य शक्तिम्।।[70]

This is the only verse where Kālidāsa has referred to *kokanada*. When a person is in wrath his eyes become red. In the battlefield, Kārttikeya became excessively angry listening to the words of demon, Tāraka. Hence, his eyes turned red like *kokanada*-red lotus.

15. TĀMARASA

(62) शुशुभिरे स्मितचारुतराननाः
स्त्रिय इव श्लथशिञ्जितमेखलाः।
विकचतामरसा गृहदीर्घिका
मदकलोदकलोलविहङ्गमाः ।।[71]

The artificial house-ponds with red lotuses full blown with birds fond of water and uttering indistinct notes through intoxication, looked charming like women having faces more bewitching by their smiles, and zones jingling because they were loosened.

King Daśaratha had pleasure-ponds in his palace which abounded in red lotuses. Here, the poet has compared red lotuses with the beautiful faces of King Daśaratha's damsels.

(63) हेमतामरसताडितप्रिया तत्कराम्बुविनिमीलितेक्षणा।
खे व्यगाहत तरङ्गिणीमुमा मीनपंक्तिपुनरुक्तमेखला।।[72]

Pārvatī struck her lover with a golden red lotus, and had her eyes closed, when struck by the water from Śiva's hands, she sported in the celestial river Ganges in the sky, her girdle being rendered superfluous by the row of fish (in the river) gathering round her waist. Golden red lotuses are described as growing in the Heavenly Ganges. Pārvatī was enjoying water-sports in the celestial river with her lover Śiva and striking him with a golden red lotus which was in abundance there.

(64) दष्टतामरसकेसरत्यजोः क्रन्दतोर्विपरिवृत्तकण्ठयोः।
निघ्नयोः सरसि चक्रवाकयोरल्पमन्तरमनल्पतां गतम्।।[73]

In the lake, the small distance has now become great, between the crying and helpless *cakravāka* birds, who have given up the half-bitten red lotus-filaments, and whose necks are turned round in order to have a glimpse of each other. The lake is full of red lotuses. *Cakravāka* birds are poetically represented as the types where the most perfect conjugal love abides. They are enjoying their love-sports and are eating, out of excessive love, the filament of one red lotus from their two mouths. Suddenly, the night approaches and they have to part from each other, leaving the half bitten red lotus-filament. This is their destiny.

I have presented a beautiful garland, a *vaijayantīmālā* of 64 lotuses of different colours and varieties, plucked up from the lovely lotus-lakes (poetic works) of Kālidāsa. Kavikulaguru has used 30 different words denoting lotus. Here, 15 words expressing lotus have been presented in 64 illustrations. I wish to present the complete *kamalavana* of Kālidāsa in a book in the near future.

Many words denoting lotus have very beautiful feminine forms. These forms have different shades of meanings. Sometimes, the word indicates a group of lotuses, sometimes, it indicates a lotus-plant and sometimes, it indicates a lotus-pond or pond and sometimes, it may indicate some rare meaning too. These feminine forms of the words denoting lotus have been used by Kavikulaguru and other poets too. I wish to present the enumeration of some of these words in their feminine form to arouse interest in connoisseurs and researchers. These words are :

1. Abjinī
2. Ambhojinī
3. Amburohiṇī
4. Aravindinī
5. Bisinī
6. Indīvariṇī
7. Kamalinī
8. Kuvalayinī
9. Nalinī
10. Nīlotpalinī
11. Padminī
12. Paṅkajinī
13. Puṣkariṇī
14. Sarojinī
15. Saroruhiṇī
16. Sthalakamalinī
17. Sthalāravindinī
18. Tāmarasī
19. Utpalinī
20. Vanajā

The eyes of beautiful women are often compared to lotus, hence these words come into existence : *Indīvarākṣī, kamalākṣī, kuvalayākṣī, nalinākṣī, nīlotpalākṣī, padmākṣī, padmapalāśākṣī, paṅkajākṣī, saroruhākṣī, sarojākṣī, utpalākṣī etc.* Sometimes, these words are used for address also. I conclude my paper with a beautiful verse from *Amaruśataka* where a lover appeases his beloved sweetheart in a most novel manner and using a beautiful address too for her :

कोपस्त्वया यदि कृतो मयि पङ्कजाक्षि!
सोऽस्तु प्रियस्तव किमस्ति विधेयमन्यत्।
आश्लेषमर्पय मदर्पितपूर्वमुच्चै-
रुच्चैः समर्पय मदर्पितचुम्बनं च।।[74]

REFERENCES & NOTES

1. *Śṛṅgāratilaka* - 17
2. *Kumārasambhava* - 11.25
3. *Ṛtusaṁhāra* - 4.5
4. *Kumārasambhava* - 14.13
5. *Ṛtusaṁhāra* - 3.20
6. *Ṛtusaṁhāra* - 4.4
7. *Ṛtusaṁhāra* - 13.60
8. *Śiśupālavadha* - 11.64
9. *Meghadūta* - 2.19
10. *Meghadūta* - 1.43
11. *The Meghadūta of Kālidāsa* edited by Gopal Raghunath Nandargika - 1.43, Notes, p. 46
12. *Kumārasambhava* - 5.21
13. *Kumārasambhava* - 8.19
14. *Kumārasambhava* - 8.19, Mallinātha's Commentary
15. *Kumārasambhava* - 8.85
16. *Kālidāsa - Sāhitya evaṁ Saṅgīta-kalā,* pp. 205, 218, 234-38
17. *Raghuvaṁśa* - 19.9,11
18. *Meghadūta* - 2.2
19. *Meghadūta* - 2.2, Notes, p. 80
20. *Erotics in Sanskrit and English Literature - I : Kālidāsa and Shakespeare* (Sushma Kulshreshtha) - pp. 207-218
21. *Ṛtusaṁhāra* - 1.28; 3.11; 5.13; 6.32
22. *Kumārasambhava* - 1.16
23. *Kumārasambhava* - 1.43
24. *Kumārasambhava of Kālidāsa* (Ed. M.R. Kale) - Notes on 1.43, p. 245)
25. *Kumārasambhava* - 7.16
26. *Kumārasambhava* - 5.19
27. *Kumārasambhava* - 5.27
28. *Meghadūta* - 2.3
29. *Raghuvaṁśa* - 3.7
30. *Raghuvaṁśa* - 6.86
31. *Śiśupālavadha* - 11.64
32. *Raghuvaṁśa* - 10.8
33. *Raghuvaṁśa* - 10.62

34. *Raghuvaṁśa* - 13.51
35. *Raghuvaṁśa* - 16.68
36. *Raghuvaṁśa* - 16.16
37. *Meghadūta* - 2.22
38. *Kumārasambhava* - 5.9
39. *Raghuvaṁśa* - 3.8
40. *Raghuvaṁśa* - 8.55
41. *Kumārasambhava* - 8.58
42. *Raghuvaṁśa* - 10.9
43. *Raghuvaṁśa* - 4.17
44. *Raghuvaṁśa* - 18.8
45. *Kumārasambhava* - 1.46
46. *Kumārasambhava* - 7.81
47. *Raghuvaṁśa* - 7.26
48. *Kumārasambhava* - 4.8
49. *Kumārasambhava* - 7.20
50. *Raghuvaṁśa* - 13.31
51. *Kumārasambhava* - 9.26
52. *Meghadūta* - 1.27
53. *Ṛtusaṁhāra* - 2.2
54. *Ṛtusaṁhāra* - 2.15
55. *Ṛtusaṁhāra* - 5.10
56. *Ṛtusaṁhāra* - 6.65
57. *Meghadūta* - 1.48
58. *Erotics in Sanskrit and English Literature - I : Kālidāsa and Shakespeare* (Sushma Kulshreshtha)- Līlākamala in Sanskrit Literature, pp. 207-218
59. *Kumārasambhava* - 1.32
60. *Raghuvaṁśa* - 1.43
61. *Kumārasambhava* - 3.56
62. *Raghuvaṁśa* - 6.13
63. *Ṛtusaṁhāra* - 4.14
64. *Kumārasambhava* - 9.20
65. *Kumārasambhava* - 13.17
66. *Raghuvaṁśa* - 13-23
67. *Gītagovinda* - 10
68. *Uttararāmacarita* - 5.36
69. *Śiśupālavadha* - 4.46
70. *Kumārasambhava* - 17.16
71. *Raghuvaṁśa* - 9.37
72. *Kumārasambhava* - 8.26
73. *Kumārasambhava* - 8.32
74. *Amaruśataka* - 133

FORTY IMAGES OF MANGO BLOSSOMS IN KĀLIDĀSA

Sushma Kulshreshtha

साकूतमधुरकोकिलविलासिनीकण्ठकूजितप्राये।
शिक्षासमयेऽपि मुदे रतलीलाकालिदासोक्ती।।

Dīpaśikhā Kālidāsa, a peerless poet *par excellence,* was acquainted with and affluent in various systems of Philosophy, several schools of religious beliefs, Politics, Economics, Dramaturgy, Erotology, Music and Fine Arts and Plant-science too. Just as the works of Kālidāsa abound in numerous references to Philosophy, Musicology and Erotics etc., in the same way multiple references to more than 120 plants and trees adorn his works. In *Kumārasambhava* and *Raghuvaṁśa* only, there are references to more than 50 and 80 plants and trees respectively.

Kavikulaguru Kālidāsa has referred to all the aforementioned 120 plants and trees at a number of places in his works in the course of his narratives and descriptions as well as in the usage of similes, metaphors and *utprekṣās.* At places, the poet has referred to these plants and trees drawing references to some other *Śāstra* or Science *viz., Āyurveda* (Science of medicine), *Sangitasastra* (Musicology) and *Kāmaśāstra* (Erotics or Erotology) also. The blend of plant-science or *Vṛkṣāyurveda* with that of musicology and erotology and other *śāstras* too has lent additional charm to many of these references.

In the present paper, an attempt is made to bring forth the expertise of Kālidāsa in plant-science or *Vṛkṣāyurveda* discussing at length only one tree *Āmra*-mango, his most favourite one. Here, forty images (out of 45 images) of the mango-blossom or mango-tree found in the works of Kālidāsa are presented for the enjoyment of the connoisseurs.

ĀMRA (CŪTA) (Mangifera Indica Linn)

Āmra or mango is the king of Indian fruits. Not only in India, but also all over the world mango is loved by many. It has hundreds of varieties. Its other names are : *Kāmaśara, Cūta, Rasāla, Kāmavallabha, Vāmāṅga, Sahakāra, Kīreṣṭa* and *Mādhavadruma :*

आम्रः कामशरश्चूतः रसालः कामवल्लभः।
वामाङ्गः सहकारश्च कीरेष्टो माधवद्रुमः।।

Kālidāsa has referred to *Āmra* or *Cūta* at a number of places in the *Kumārasambhava* and almost every time he has blent his description with some other *Śāstra* or *Vidyā* which brings forth his vast erudition. Some examples are presented herewith :

ILLUSTRATIONS :

1. चूताङ्कुरास्वादकषायकण्ठः पुंस्कोकिलो यन्मधुरं चुकूज।
मनस्विनीमानविघातदक्षं तदेव जातं वचनं स्मरस्य।।[1]

Among the birds, the male and the female cuckoo are the luckiest and the most famous ones for singing. The poetic eulogy showered on the sweet notes of music is that of male cuckoo which is a zoologically proved fact and was known to our magnificent poet. For the music of the male cuckoo, he very adeptly uses the term 'पुंस्कोकिलकूजित'. पञ्चम, the fifth note of music is generated from the throat of कोकिल[2]. In spring, the king of seasons, mango trees are full of mango sprouts. The male cuckoo feasts on these and by sipping the fresh juice of these sprouts, he sings sweetly with an impassioned throat. This is his melodious music which becomes Cupid's eloquent mandate empowered to break down the pride of the high-minded damsels.

Here the word कषाय denotes various meanings-(i) a throat tinged with passion; (ii) a throat clear on account of the astringency of the mango-sprout; (iii) a throat which has become reddish brown by the juice of mango-sprouts; (iv) a throat which is सुरभित (fragrant) and hence capable of producing sweet sounds.[3]

Ladies having a proper sense of their honour are called मनस्विनी (High-minded lady). When a lady's lover is attracted to another woman, the wrath generated out of jealousy is called 'मान' :

स्त्रीणामीर्ष्याकृतः कोपो मानोऽन्यासङ्गिनि प्रिये।[4]

As soon as the high-minded ladies listen to the sweet notes uttered by the male cuckoo, they at once give up their मान with regard to their sweet hearts as if they have been directed by the eloquent command of the God of Love :

कोकिलकूजितश्रवणानन्तरं स्मराज्ञप्ता इव मानं जहुरित्यर्थः।[5]

Now in a single verse, we come across the poet's high expertise in the science of love, science of seasons, science of trees, science of birds and science of music.

The picturesque idea of the above verse has been brought out in other works too. Some illustrations are cited here :

(i) त्यजत मानमलं बत विग्रहैर्न पुनरेति गतं चतुरं वयः।
परभृताभिरितीव निवेदिते स्मरमते रमते स्म वधूजनः।।[6]

(ii) प्रियसखीसदृशं प्रतिबोधिताः किमपि काम्यगिरा परपुष्टया।
प्रियतमाय वपुर्गुरुमत्सरच्छिदुरयाऽदुरयाचितमङ्गनाः।।[7]

(iii) दत्तं प्रियाभिर्बहुमानपूर्वमासाद्य चूतासवमन्यपुष्टाः।
आमोदिभिः पञ्चमरागभेदैः प्राबोधयन्पञ्चशरावलेपम्।।[8]

2. हरितारुणचारुबन्धनः कलपुंस्कोकिलशब्दसूचितः।
वद सम्प्रति कस्य बाणतां नवचूतप्रसवो गमिष्यति।।[9]

The voice of the cuckoo becomes clear and sweet when it tastes the mango-sprouts. Hence, the melodious voice of the cuckoo indicates the presence of mango blossoms. When Kāma was reduced to ashes by the fire of Śiva's fury, Rati lamented thus : 'Say, by whom the fresh blossom of the mango tree, the beautiful stem of which is reddish-green and the sprouting of which is proclaimed by the notes of the male cuckoo, will now be employed as his arrow?' Here also Kālidāsa refers to the music of पुंस्कोकिल.

3. पार्वती तदुपयोगसम्भवां
विक्रियामपि सतीं मनोहराम्।
अप्रतर्क्यविधियोगकारिता-
माम्रतेव सहकारतां ययौ।।[10]

During their love-sports, Śiva asks Pārvatī to drink the wine brought for her by the presiding deity of the Gandhamādana. When Pārvatī drank the wine, she underwent a *vikriyā,* a change, which made her even more attractive and enchanting as a common mango-tree is changed by some indefinable power in Nature into a special and fragrant kind of *sahakāra.* The *vikriyā,* the change, is generally for the worse (न हि विक्रिया कुत्रापि मनोहरा भवति-नारायण:) but the change made Pārvatī more beautiful. *Āmra* and *sahakāra* both signify the mango-tree but the latter refers to a particular species whose blossoms are exceedingly fragrant (सहकारोऽतिसौरभ इत्यमर:). This verse poses before us a big question. An ordinary mango-tree cannot be transformed into one of the *sahakāra* species unless it is treated with some magical charms which is expressed by अप्रतर्क्यविधियोग or the inscrutable power of the Creator. अप्रतर्क्यविधियोग may refer to मणिमन्त्रौषधकालादियोग too as is explained by commentator Nārāyaṇa. It means an ordinary mango tree can be transformed into the fragrant species of *sahakāra* by the magical usage of jewels, gems, *mantras* or verses of sacred texts and medicinal herbs during a particular time. Such treatment can definitely bring radical changes in a tree. Pārvatī too underwent just a similar magical change after drinking the wine. Those who are well versed in Plant science and Agricultural science know very well that trees and plants are given varied types of treatment which bring forth amazing improvements resulting in the better quality and variety of flowers and fruits. This very fact was known to Kālidāsa.

Commenting on this verse, Vallabhadeva also expresses surprise that *āmra* can contain *āmratā* only and *sahakāra* can contain *sahakāratā* only. How is it possible that *āmratā* can be changed into *sahakāratā* :

अप्रतर्क्यो दुर्ज्ञेयो यो विधियोगो दैवव्यापारस्तेन विनिर्मितां कृताम्। आम्रता हि केनचिद् दैवभावात् सहकारतां सम्पद्यते वयं न विद्म: (जानीम:)। कस्मिन् देशे कविना आम्रसहकारयो: प्रकृतिविकारभावो दृष्टोऽस्माभिर्हि सामान्यविशेषभावस्तयोरुपलब्ध:। तथा चोक्तम्–

अपुष्पफलवानाम्र: पुष्पितश्चूत उच्यते।
पुष्पै: फलैस्तु संयुक्त: सहकार उदाहृत:।।[11]

Kālidāsa has answers for this query with the appropriate inclusion of अप्रतर्क्यविधियोग. A poet of high calibre alone can make such wonderful remarks. On the one hand, he is describing the amorous sports of Śiva and Pārvatī while on the other, he describes the beauty of Pārvatī which has been enhanced by the magical charm rendered to her by the divine wine provided by the wish-giving trees and brought by the presiding deity of the Gandhamādana forest. Here, we find *Pārvatīgata rūpotpannā* and *gandhotpannā vaiṣayikī rati* very beautifully painted by Dīpaśikhā Kālidāsa.

4. परलोकविधौ च माधव स्मरमुद्दिश्य विलोलपल्लवाः।
निवपेः सहकारमञ्जरीः प्रियचूतप्रसवो हि ते सखा।।[12]

O Mādhava (Vasanta), in the memorial rites for Kāma, offer the spray of fragrant mango blossoms with trembling young leaves as your friend was very fond of mango-flowers. Here, Kālidāsa once again uses *sahakāra* and *cūta* in one verse. He blends here the plant-science with the *nivāpa* ceremony, a rite performed after death.

5. सद्यः प्रवालोद्गमचारुपत्रे नीते समाप्तिं नवचूतबाणे।
निवेशयामास मधुर्द्विरेफान्नामाक्षराणीव मनोभवस्य।।[13]

Madhu, the Spring season, having fitted up the arrow of Kāma in the shape of young mango blossoms with fresh leaves as its beautiful feathers, immediately inscribed on it the letters, as it were, of the name of the Mind-born (Cupid), in the shape of the bees.

The mango blossom is one of the five floral arrows of Cupid :

अरविन्दमशोकश्च चूतश्च नवमल्लिका।
नीलोत्पलञ्च पञ्चैते पुष्पबाणस्य सायकाः।।

It was usual with great warriors to have their names inscribed on their arrows :

बाणाक्षरैरेव परस्परस्य नामोर्जितं चापभृतः शशंसुः।[14]

Here, Kālidāsa has blent plant-science with war-science and erotology.

6. अथ स ललितयोषिद्भ्रूलताचारुशृङ्गं
रतिवलयपदाङ्के चापमासज्य कण्ठे।
सहचरमधुहस्तन्यस्तचूताङ्कुरास्त्रः
शतमखमुपतस्थे प्राञ्जलिः पुष्पधन्वा।।[15]

Then the God of the Flower-Bow, having his bow with its ends curved beautifully as the arching eyebrows of graceful women, slung over his neck bearing the marks of Rati's bracelets and having his arrow of young sprouts of the mango-tree deposited in the hands of his bosom friend Madhu (Spring), approached with folded hands the God of a Hundred Sacrifices (Indra). Here, the imprint of Rati's bracelets over the neck of Kāma indicates their amorous embrace.

7. महीभृतः पुत्रवतोऽपि दृष्टि-
स्तस्मिन्नपत्ये न जगाम तृप्तिम्।
अनन्तपुष्पस्य मधोर्हि चूते
द्विरेफमाला सविशेषसङ्गा।।[16]

The eyes of the Mountain-lord, though blessed with a son, were never satiated by the sight of this child of his (Pārvatī); the circling bees are specially drawn to the mango blossoms, though the spring season blooms with countless flowers. In the midst of an endless shower of beautiful flowers in vernal season, the fresh mango-sprouts excel all.

8. लग्नद्विरेफाञ्जनभक्तिचित्रं
मुखे मधुश्रीस्तिलकं प्रकाश्य।
रागेण बालारुणकोमलेन
चूतप्रवालोष्ठमलञ्चकार ।।[17]

The Vernal Beauty, having displayed on her forehead a *tilaka* (the *tilaka* flower) artistically painted with a black pigment in the shape of the bees that clinged to it, ornamented her lip in the form of the tender mango-shoots with a red tint (red lac) mellow like dawn's first light. Here plant-science is beautifully mingled with seasonology and the art of make-up.

Kālidāsa has referred to *cūta* or *sahakāra* at a number of places in *Raghuvaṁśa* and almost every time he has blent his description with some other *Śāstra* or *Vidyā* or some novel fancy which brings forth his vast erudition. Now some examples are presented herewith from *Raghuvaṁśa:*

9. तं प्राप्य सर्वावयवानवद्यं
व्यावर्ततान्योपगमात्कुमारी ।
न हि प्रफुल्लं सहकारमेत्य
वृक्षान्तरं कांक्षति षट्पदाली।।[18]

At last (during *svayaṁvara),* Princess Indumatī approached Aja who was faultless in all his limbs (handsome) and gave up the idea of going to any other prince; as a row of bees does not long for any other tree when it reaches a full-blossomed mango tree. It is a choice expression. Aja was the most handsome and the worthiest, hence Princess Indumatı dropped the idea of finding any other prince. Mango is the king of fruits, hence the row of bees also does not like to go to any other tree when it reaches the most fragrant mango tree. The choice of the best is longed by all.

10. हस्तेन हस्तं परिगृह्य वध्वाः
स राजसूनुः सुतरां चकासे।
अनन्तराशोकलताप्रवालं
प्राप्येव चूतः प्रतिपल्लवेन।।[19]

That Prince Aja shone still brighter on taking the hand of his bride Indumatī with his own, as does the mango-tree after having received with its foliage the shoots of an *Aśoka*-creeper clung to it. Here, Aja is compared to a mango-tree and Indumatī to *Aśokalatā*, hence a beautiful simile. Mango and *Aśoka* both are longing trees and their longing is fulfilled too.

11. मनोज्ञगन्धं सहकारभङ्गं
पुराणशीधुं नवपाटलञ्च।
संबध्नता कामिजनेषु दोषाः
सर्वे निदाघावधिना प्रमृष्टाः।।[20]

The time of summer that brought together the odoriferous piece of mango blossom, the odoriferous old wine and the odoriferous fresh *Pāṭala,* thereby made amends for all its sins against the tribe of lovers. Lovers, when they are enjoying love-sports with their darling damsels, love old wine with odoriferous fresh mango-sprouts and fresh *Pāṭala*. By providing these longed items to the tribe of lovers, the summer season washes its sins. Mango is one of the foremost arrows of the Cupid and by sipping old wine with fresh mango blossoms, the lovers delve deep in Cupid's world. Here also, a beautiful example of plant-science with the science of love can be seen.

12. मिथुनं परिकल्पितं त्वया
सहकारः फलिनी च नन्विमौ।
अविधाय विवाहसत्क्रिया-
मनयोर्गम्यत इत्यसाम्प्रतम्।।[21]

At the sudden demise of Princess Indumatī, Aja laments thus : The mango tree and the *Priyaṅgu* creeper have been, indeed, designed by you for a marriageable couple. For this reason it is improper for you to depart without having celebrated the auspicious ceremonies of their nuptials.

The matching of a tree with a creeper, and even the celebration of a sham marriage between them is a favourite idea with the poets. Indumatī had also longed to organise the wedding ceremony of the *sahakāra* with *phalinī* which she could not perform. On the *mithunabhāva* of *sahakāra* and *phalinī,* commentator Hemādri quotes thus :

मिथुनं परिकल्पितं त्वया सहकारः फलिनी च, "विवाहकरणं प्रयोगरत्नावल्याम्।" "विवाहमङ्गलाचार-(मङ्गलाचारा Ms.) गीतनेपथ्यसंयुता। वृक्षेणोद्वाहिता श्यामा जायते कुसुमाकुला (कुसुमान्विता Ms.)।।"[22]

The other names of *Phalinī* are *Śyāmā* and *Priyaṅgu*. We can compare the affecting scene when Śakuntalā bids farewell to her favourite creepers and the reply that the sage Kaṇva makes :

सङ्कल्पितं प्रथममेव मया तवार्थे
भर्तारमात्मसदृशं सुकृतैर्गता त्वम्।
चूतेन संश्रितवती नवमालिकेय-
मस्यामहं त्वयि च सम्प्रति वीतचिन्तः।।[23]

13. एषा त्वया पेशलमध्ययापि
घटाम्बुसंवर्धितबालचूता ।
आह्लादयत्युन्मुखकृष्णसारा
दृष्टा चिरात्पञ्चवटी मनो मे।।[24]

Śrīrāma says to Sītā thus : This Pañcavaṭī, where the young mango-trees were reared up with jarfuls of water poured by yourself, though of slender waist, and where the black antelopes are looking towards us with their heads raised, being seen after a long time, gladdens my mind. To rear up the plants and trees with jarfuls of water is one of the favourite pastimes of the *nāyikās*. Sītā, Pārvatī and Śakuntalā all have a high regard for plants and trees and they perform their duty towards them with utmost care and interest.

14. दक्षिणेन पवनेन सम्भृतं
प्रेक्ष्य चूतकुसुमं सपल्लवम्।
अन्वनैषुरवधूतविग्रहा-
स्तं दुरुत्सहवियोगमङ्गनाः।।[25]

The mistresses seeing the mango blossoms with the foliage put forth by the southern breeze gave up the love-quarrels with King Agnivarṇa and won him over to their side, whose separation they thought, would be unbearable to them. In spring season, fresh mango blossoms arouse extreme love in loving couples. Therefore, at the glance of the mango-sprouts, the damsels of Agnivarṇa gave up their love-quarrels. Mango blossoms have immense power of attraction and influence indeed!

15. यत्स भग्नसहकारमासवं
रक्तपाटलसमागमं पपौ।
तेन तस्य मधुनिर्गमात्कृश-
श्चित्तयोनिरभवत्पुनःपुनः।।[26]

King Agnivarṇa drank wine mixed with the small bits of mango-sprouts squeezed together and performed by receiving contact of the red *pāṭala*-flowers. By virtue of such acts his Fancy-Born god Cupid who was emaciated by the departure of the spring again became fresh. It is the usual pastime among lovers that they enjoy drinking wine with their sweet-hearts. It appears that the drinking of wine with mango-sprouts and *pāṭala*-flowers was liked by the *Nāgarakas* in olden times.

Mango blossoms are described as being used in the worship of Cupid, one of whose five arrows are supposed to be made of these blossoms. The mango-leaf is fancied as the lip of the goddess of spring. Mango blossoms are stated to be fragrant. The summit of the mountain *Āmrakūṭa (Amarakaṇṭaka)* is said to have abounded in mango-trees.

16. छन्नोपान्तः परिणतफलद्योतिभिः काननाम्रै-
स्त्वय्यारूढे शिखरमचलः स्निग्धवेणीसवर्णे।
नूनं यास्यत्यमरमिथुनप्रेक्षणीयामवस्थां
मध्ये श्यामः स्तन इव भुवः शेषविस्तारपाण्डुः।।[27]

Spring is the Lord of seasons and mango is the king of trees and fruits. Hence, *Ṛtusaṁhāra* abounds in the description of mango-blossoms, mango-trees and mango-fruits. We get colourful pictures of this most powerful arrow of the god of love, Cupid. Now sip the nectar of this *rasāla :*

17. प्रफुल्लचूताङ्कुरतीक्ष्णसायको
द्विरेफमालाविलसद्धनुर्गुणः ।
मनांसि भेत्तुं सुरतप्रसङ्गिनां
वसन्तयोद्धा समुपागतः प्रिये।।

18. वापीजलानां मणिमेखलानां
शशाङ्कभासां प्रमदाजनानाम्।
चूतद्रुमाणां कुसुमान्वितानां
ददाति सौभाग्यमयं वसन्तः।।[28]

A lover addresses his beloved darling thus : O dear! the warrior spring season has approached with the young mango blossoms for its sharp arrows and with the row of black bees as its radiant bow-string, to pierce the hearts of those addicted to sexual pleasures. This spring season lends additional charm to the waters of the lakes, to jewelled girdle-strings, to moon-light, to women and to mango-trees bent with blossoms. The young mango blossoms are the sharp arrows of Cupid capable of piercing the hearts of loving couples.

The fresh mango-sprouts kindle love not only among human couples but amongst birds too.

19. ताम्रप्रवालस्तबकावनम्रा-
श्चूतद्रुमाः पुष्पितचारुशाखाः।
कुर्वन्ति कामं पवनावधूताः
पर्युत्सुकं मानसमङ्गनानाम्।।

20. पुंस्कोकिलश्चूतरसासवेन
मत्तः प्रियां चुम्बति रागहृष्टः।
कूजन् द्विरेफोऽप्ययमम्बुजस्थः
प्रियः प्रियायाः प्रकरोति चाटु।।[29]

The mango-trees bent with the clusters of reddish sprouts, with their branches adorned with blossoms (*mañjarīs*) and appearing beautiful, being shaken by breezes, kindle passionate desires in damsels' hearts. The male cuckoo, maddened with the liquor of the juice of mangoblossoms, is kissing with ardent love and joy his mate, this sweetly humming black-bee, intent on sipping the honey of the lotus, too, is performing agreeable acts for his beloved and thus enlivening her. This is the magical charm of the mango-blossoms which madden the loving couples whether they are human couples or bird-couples or otherwise.

21. आकम्पयन् कुसुमिताः सहकारशाखा
विस्तारयन् परभृतस्य वचांसि दिक्षु।
वायुर्विवाति हृदयानि हरन्नराणां
नीहारपातविगमात् सुभगे वसन्ते।।

22. नेत्रे निमीलयति रोदिति याति शोकं
घ्राणं करेण विरुणद्धि विरौति चोच्चैः।
कान्तावियोगपरिखेदितचित्तवृत्ति-
र्दृष्ट्वाध्वगः कुसुमितान् सहकारवृक्षान्।।[30]

Shaking the blossoming branches of the mango-tree and spreading in all quarters the sweet notes of the male cuckoo, the spring breeze, pleasant due to the cessation of dew-fall, is blowing, pilfering the hearts of men. Beholding the blossoming mango-trees, the traveller, with his mind stricken with separation from his beloved darling, shuts his eyes, weeps, grieves, covers (closes) his nose with the hand and laments loudly. The sight of mango blossoms arouses deep desire of love amongst loving couples and its glance becomes painful for a love-lorn person who is in separation from his beloved darling.

23. समदमधुकराणां कोकिलानां च नादै-
र्कुसुमितसहकारैः कर्णिकारैश्च रम्यः।
इषुभिरिव सुतीक्ष्णैर्मानसं मानिनीनां
तुदति कुसुममासो मन्मथोद्दीपनाय।।

24. रुचिरकनककान्तिं मुञ्चतः पुष्पराशीन्
मृदुपवनविधूतान् पुष्पितांश्चूतवृक्षान्।
अभिमुखमभिवीक्ष्य क्षामदेहोऽपि मार्गे
मदनशरनिघातैर्मोहमेति प्रवासी।।

25. आकम्पितानि हृदयानि मनस्विनीनां
वातैः प्रफुल्लसहकारकृताधिवासैः।
उत्कूजितैः परभृतस्य मदाकुलस्य
श्रोत्रप्रियैर्मधुकरस्य च गीतनादैः।।[31]

With the sweet notes of cuckoos and intoxicated black bees, with blossomed mango-trees and with charming *karṇikāra* flowers, the Flower-Month (*caitra-masa*) is paining, so to arouse love, the minds of proud damsels, with very sharp arrows as it were. Beholding in front of his way, blossomed mango-trees, shaken by the gentle breeze and dropping heaps of *mañjarīs* (blossoms) radiant as shining gold, the traveller already thin in body, faints being struck by the arrows of Cupid. The hearts of women are made to quiver by breezes fragrant with blossomed mango-trees, by the sweet notes of the intoxicated male cuckoos and by the black-bees' appealing music, pleasant to the ears. In all the above quoted three verses, the magnificence of mango-blossoms is beautifully picturised.

26. रक्ताशोकविकल्पिताधरमधुर्मत्तद्विरेफस्वनः
कुन्दापीडविशुद्धदन्तनिकरः प्रोत्फुल्लपद्माननः।
चूतामोदसुगन्धिमन्दपवनः शृङ्गारदीक्षागुरुः
कल्पान्तं मदनप्रियो दिशतु वः पुष्पागमो मङ्गलम्।।

27. आम्री मञ्जुलमञ्जरी वरशरः सत्किंशुकं यद्धनु-
ज्यां यस्यालिकुलं कलङ्करहितं छत्रं सितांशुः सितम्।
मत्तेभो मलयानिलः परभृता यद्वन्दिनो लोकजित्
सोऽयं वो वितरीतरीतु वितनुर्भद्रं वसन्तान्वितः।।[32]

With the red flowers of *aśoka* made to serve as the lower lip full of nectar, with the humming of intoxicated black-bees, with the garland of *kunda* flowers as the radiant row of teeth and the full-blown lotus as the face, with gentle breezes perfumed with the odour of mango-blossoms and the preceptor in the initiation (training) of love—may spring, the beloved friend of Cupid, grant you all, happiness for ever. May that Bodiless one (Cupid), the conqueror of the worlds, in company with his beloved friend Spring, ever shower on you happiness! He whose excellent arrow is the charming mango blossom, whose bow is the beautiful *kiṁśuka* flower, whose bow-string is the row of black-bees, whose spotless, white umbrella is the moon, whose rutty elephant is the fragrant breeze from the *Malaya* mountain and whose bards are the sweet-singing cuckoos. Thus, *Ṛtusaṁhāra* comes to a close having given the blessings of the Spring and the Cupid to one and all. The mango-shoots have played a dominant role in the life of young lovers in spring the king of all seasons.

28. अनसूया-हला शकुन्तले, इयं स्वयंवरवधूः सहकारस्य त्वया कृतनामधेया वनज्योत्स्नेति नवमालिका। एनां विस्मृतासि।

शकुन्तला-तदात्मानमपि विस्मरिष्यामि। (लतामुपेत्यावलोक्य च।) हला, रमणीये खलु काल एतस्य लतापादपमिथुनस्य व्यतिकरः संवृत्तः। नवकुसुमयौवना वनज्योत्स्ना स्निग्धपल्लवतयोपभोगक्षमः सहकारः। (इति पश्यन्ती तिष्ठति)।[33]

Anasūya-Friend Śakuntalā, here is the *Jasmine* creeper, the self-selecting bride of the mango-tree to which you have given the name *Vanajyotsnā*. You have forgotten it.

Śakuntalā-Then I shall even forget my ownself. (Approaching the creeper and gazing) Friend, at a very charming time, indeed, has taken place the union of this couple-the creeper and the tree. The *vanajyotsnā* with its early blossoms is in its youth; and the mango-tree, on account of its beautiful leaves, appears capable of enjoyment (stands looking at them).

Matching of tree with a creeper is a favourite idea with our poets. Kālidāsa also fondly paints this idea here and there in his works. Joyous union of *vanajyotsnā* and *sahakāra* indicates the happy union of Śakuntalā and Duṣyanta ultimately.

29. प्रियंवदा-सखि, दिष्ट्यानुरूपस्तेऽभिनिवेशः। सागरमुज्झित्वा कुत्र वा महानद्यवतरति। क इदानीं सहकारमन्तरेणातिमुक्तलतां पल्लवितां सहते।[34]

Priyamvadā-Friend, your choice (attachment) is worthy of you. Where to shall a great river bend its course if not to the sea? What tree except the mango can support the *Atimukta* creeper, having an exuberance of foliage?

Here also Kālidāsa points the *mithunabhāva* between *Sahakāra* and *Atimuktalatā*. *Atimuktalatā* or *madhavīlatā*. 'अतिमुक्तः पुण्ड्रकः स्याद्वासन्ती माधवी लता' इत्यमरः। Monier Williams quotes-'The beauty and fragrance of the flower of this creeper give them a title to all the praises which Kālidāsa and Jayadeva bestow on them. It is a gigantic and luxurient climber, but when it meets with nothing to grasp, it assumes the form of a sturdy tree, the highest branches of which display, however, in the air, their natural flexibility and inclination to climb.'[35]

30. शकुन्तला-(उपेत्य लतामालिङ्ग्य) वनज्योत्स्ने चूतसंगतापि मां प्रत्यालिङ्गेतोगताभिः शाखाबाहाभिः।

काश्यपः —

सङ्कल्पितं प्रथममेव मया तवार्थे
भर्तारमात्मसदृशं सुकृतैर्गता त्वम्।
चूतेन संश्रितवती नवमालिकेय-
मस्यामहं त्वयि च सम्प्रति वीतचिन्तः।।[36]

Śakuntalā-(Approaching and embracing the creeper). Vanajyotsnā, although you are united with the mango-tree, do you embrace me, in return, with your arm-like twigs that point in this direction.

Kāśyapa-You have, by your merit, been wedded to a husband worthy of you, and one whom I had at the very outset intended for you. This *Navamālikā* has resorted to the mango-tree; as regards it and you, I am now free from anxiety.

Kālidāsa is fond of matching a tree with a creeper. Here the *mithunabhāvā* between the mango-tree and the *Navamālikā* creeper is established very beautifully.

31. अभिनवमधुलोलुपस्त्वं तथा परिचुम्ब्य चूतमञ्जरीम्।
कमलवसतिमात्रनिर्वृतो मधुकर विस्मृतोऽस्येनां कथम्।।[37]

O Bee, how is it that you, ever longing for fresh honey, having in that manner kissed the mango-blossom, have now forgotten it, being satisfied with a mere residence in the lotus!

This song is being sung by Queen *Haṁsapadikā*. *Cūtamañjarī* is most attractive in summer season. Here *Cūtamañjarī* refers to Śakuntalā and *Madhukara* to Duśyanta.

32. (ततः प्रविशति चूताङ्कुरमवलोकयन्ती चेटी। अपरा च पृष्ठतस्तस्याः।)

प्रथमा-

आताम्रहरितपाण्डुर जीवितसर्वं वसन्तमासस्य।
दृष्टोऽसि चूतकोरक ऋतुमङ्गल त्वां प्रसादयामि।।

द्वितीया-परभृतिके, किमेकाकिनी मन्त्रयसे।

प्रथमा-मधुकरिके, चूतकलिकां दृष्ट्वोन्मत्ता परभृतिका भवति।

× × × ×

33. द्वितीया-सखि, अवलम्बस्व मां यावदग्रपादस्थिता भूत्वा[38]
कामदेवार्चनं करोमि।

× × × ×

द्वितीया-
त्वमसि मया चूताङ्कुर दत्तः कामाय गृहीतधनुषे।
पथिकजनयुवतिलक्ष्यः पञ्चाभ्यधिकः शरो भव।।[39]

Mango blossoms are of a reddish-green and grey colour and all-in-all the life of the spring season. Women propitiate the mango-sprout who is the harbinger of the spring season. The cuckoo is maddened at the sight of a mango blossom and worships the God of love saying thus :

Here do I offer you, O mango blossom, to the God of love, who has taken up his bow. Do you become the most effective arrow of his five flower arrows, having for your mark the young wives of men journeying abroad ?

In olden times, kings used to organise spring festivals in their kingdom. Kāmadeva was worshipped with the offering of fresh mango blossoms which are one of his five flower-arrows.

Once King Duṣyanta prohibited the spring festival in his kingdom. Even the trees blooming in the spring and the birds residing in them obeyed the order of His Majesty :

34. चूतानां चिरनिर्गतापि कलिका बध्नाति न स्वं रजः
सन्नद्धं यदपि स्थितं कुरबकं तत्कोरकावस्थया।
कण्ठेषु स्खलितं गतेऽपि शिशिरे पुंस्कोकिलानां रुतं
शङ्के संहरति स्मरोऽपि चकितस्तूणार्धकृष्टं शरम्।।[40]

The bud of the mango, though long since burst forth, does not form (develop) its pollen; × × × × even the God of Love puts back, in fear, his arrow half-drawn out of the quiver. This verse is a beautiful illustration of *mālāviśeṣokti* :

35. मुनिसुताप्रणयस्मृतिरोधिना मम च मुक्तमिदं तमसा मनः।
मनसिजेन सखे प्रहरिष्यता धनुषि चूतशरश्च निवेशितः।[41]

(King Duṣyanta says to Vidūṣaka). This mind of mine is freed from darkness which obstructed the memory of my love for the hermit's daughter, and at the same time the mango-blossom-shaft has been affixed to his bow by the mind-born God, wishing to strike me. By gazing at fresh mango blossoms, Duṣyanta is stricken by the *cūtabāṇa* of Kāmadeva and is engrossed in the loving memory of his sweet-heart.

36. विसृज सुन्दरि सङ्गमसाध्वसं
तव चिरात्प्रभृति प्रणयोन्मुखे।
परिगृहाण गते सहकारतां
त्वमतिमुक्तलताचरितं मयि।।[42]

(King Agnimitra says to Mālavikā) Give up, Oh sweet one, this fear of union, and now that I, who have for long been devoted to you, have become like the mango-tree, do you assume the part of the *Atimukta*-creeper towards me. King Agnimitra, who is eagerly yearning for Mālavikā's love, asks her to embrace him closely. The *Atimuktalatā* is seen to coil itself or grasp with its tendrils the mango-tree on which it is propped up. This plant is identified with fragrant *kastūrī mogarā.*

37. आमत्तानां श्रवणसुभगैः कूजितैः कोकिलानां
सानुक्रोशं मनसिजरुजः सह्यतां पृच्छतेव।
अङ्गे चूतप्रसवसुरभिर्दक्षिणो मारुतो मे
सान्द्रस्पर्शः करतल इव व्यापृतो माधवेन।।[43]

King Agnimitra says that like a noble person the Spring who feels so much for him in his present suffering, first inquires of him in gentle soft words, as one would do an ailing friend, as to how far his love-torture is bearable and then strokes him gently by way of encouragement. The words of the spring are the sweet notes of cuckoos, while the southern breeze fragrant with mango-blossoms represents the stroking of his hand.

38. अग्रे विकीर्णकुरबकफलजालविभिद्यमानसहकारम्।
परिणामाभिमुखमृतोरुत्सुकयति यौवनं चेतः।।[44]

(King Agnimitra says to Vidūṣaka) Here before us the youth of spring now attaining its ripeness, with the *kurabaka* flowers scattered and the mango-tree bursting with fruit, fills the mind with longing. Here, the mango-tree laden with fruits is beautifully described which fills the king's mind with eagerness. The king knows that as the spring is coming to a close, the days of love-enjoyment will be very soon over. Kālidāsa has described mango-blossoms many times in his works but the reference to mango-fruits is found in this illustration only.

39. इदमसुलभवस्तुप्रार्थनादुर्निवारं
प्रथममपि मनो मे पञ्चबाणः क्षिणोति।
किमुत मलयवातोन्मूलितापाण्डुपत्रै-
रुपवनसहकारैर्दर्शितेष्वङ्कुरेषु ।।[45]

(King Purūravā says to Viduṣaka) In the first place, love smites my mind, which is difficult to turn away from its longing after an unattainable object; what then (how much more will it be tormented), when the mango-trees in the garden, the seared leaves of which have been plucked off by the southern breeze, present to my view their tender sprouts? The sight of mango blossoms arouses love-longing in a lover.

40. अग्रे स्त्रीनखपाटलं कुरबकं श्यामं द्वयोर्भागयो-
र्बालाशोकमुपोढरागसुभगं भेदोन्मुखं तिष्ठति।
ईषद्बद्धरजःकणाग्रकपिशा चूते नवा मञ्जरी
मुग्धत्वस्य च यौवनस्य च सखे मध्ये मधुश्रीः स्थिता।।[46]

Here is the *kurabaka* flower, towards its tip whitish-red like the nail of a lady's finger and at its sides black; the new *Aśoka* blossom stands ready to burst, charming on account of its accumulated redness, and on the mango-tree the new blossom appears greyish towards its tips on account of the pollen being but slightly formed; so my friend, Vernal Beauty stands between infancy and youth. The sight of mango blossoms is the advent of youth of the spring season.

Here, I have presented 40 varied images and pictures of the mango-tree, its blossoms and fruits in the works of Kālidāsa. The sight of a mango-tree laden with *mañjarīs* (mango blossoms) and afterwards laden with a cluster of fruits is a delicious feast to the eyes of the beholder. The sight of *cūta-mañjarīs* arouses excessive love in loving couples. Those who are fond of fruits enjoy the delicious and pleasant taste of the mango-fruit. There are a number of fruits in our country but no other fruit can excel mango in any respect.

I wish to conclude this paper with a panegyric composed by Paṇḍitarāja Jagannātha wherein is described the miserable plight of a number of other fruits thus. Out of jealousy towards mango, the sweet water took shelter inside the coconut, the jackfruit got thorns on its body, the water-melon got divided into two pieces, the banana's face turned downwards, the grape got dried up and shortened and the rose-apple got blackened. Although the water, the coconut, the jack-fruit, the water-melon, the banana, the grape and the rose-apple, all are famous for their sweet and delicious taste but before mango, they lose their existence :

आकर्ण्याम्रफलस्तुतिं जलमभूत्तन्नारिकेलान्तरं
प्रायः कण्टकितस्तथैव पनसः जातं द्विधोर्वारुकम्।
आस्तेऽधोमुखमेव कादलफलं द्राक्षाफलं क्षुद्रतां
श्यामत्वं बत जाम्बवं गतमहो मात्सर्यदोषादिह।।[47]

REFERENCES & NOTES

1. *Kumārasambhava* - (Kale Edition)-3.32
2. *Saṅgītadarpaṇa* .
षड्जं वदति मयूरः पुनः स्वरमृषभं चातको ब्रूते।
गान्धाराख्यं छागो निगदति च मध्यमं क्रौञ्चः।।
गदति पञ्चममञ्चितवाक्, पिको रटति धैवतमुन्मददर्दुरः।
शृणि समाहतमस्तककुञ्जरो गदति नासिकया स्वरमन्तिमम्।। 170-171
3. *Kumārasambhava* - Mallinātha's commentary on 3.32-
चूताङ्कुराणामास्वादेन कषायकण्ठो रक्तकण्ठः। 'सुरभावपथे रक्ते कषायः' इति केशवः।
4. *Kumārasambhava* - 3.32, Notes, p. 62
5. *Kumārasambhava* - Mallinātha's commentary on 3.32
6. *Raghuvaṁśa* - 9.47
7. *Śiśupālavadha* - 6.8
8. *Pārvatīpariṇaya* - 3.3
9. *Kumārasambhava* - 4.14
10. *Kumārasambhava* - 8.78
11. *Kumārasambhava* - Vallabhadeva's commentary on 8. 78
12. *Kumārasambhava* - 4.38

13. *Kumārasambhava* - 3.27
14. *Raghuvaṁśa* - 7. 38
15. *Kumārasambhava* - 2.64
16. *Kumārasambhava* - 1.27
17. *Kumārasambhava* - 3.30
18. *Raghuvaṁśa* - 6.69
19. *Raghuvaṁśa* - 7.21
20. *Raghuvaṁśa* - 16.52
21. *Raghuvaṁśa* - 8.61
22. *Raghuvaṁśa* - Notes on 8.61, p. 761
23. *Abhijñānaśākuntala* (Kale Edition) - 4.13
24. *Raghuvaṁśa* - 13.34
25. *Raghuvaṁśa* - 19.43
26. *Raghuvaṁśa* - 19.46
27. *Meghadūta* - 1.18
28. *Ṛtusaṁhāra* - 6.1, 4
29. *Ṛtusaṁhāra* - 6.17,16
30. *Ṛtusaṁhāra* - 6.24, 28
31. *Ṛtusaṁhāra* - 6.29, 30, 34
32. *Ṛtusaṁhāra* - 6.36, 38
33. *Abhijñānaśākuntala* - 1. p. 28
34. *Abhijñānaśākuntala*- 3. p. 100
35. *Sir Monier Williams' Works* - Vol. V. p. 124
36. *Abhijñānaśākuntala*- 4.13
37. *Abhijñānaśākuntala*- 6.1
38. *Abhijñānaśākuntala*- 6.2, p. 206
39. *Abhijñānaśākuntala*- 6.3
40. *Abhijñānaśākuntala* - 6.4
41. *Abhijñānaśākuntala* - 6.8
42. *Mālavikāgnimitra* - 4.13
43. *Mālavikāgnimitra* - 3.4
44. *Mālavikāgnimitra* - 5.4
45. *Vikramorvaśīya* - 2.6
46. *Vikramorvaśīya* - 2.7
47. *Paṇḍitarājajagannātha-Kāvyagranthāvalī-Prasphuṭitānyoktayaḥ*-252

卐 卐 卐

TEN LONGING TREES IN KĀLIDĀSA

Sushma Kulshreshtha

There are some poetic conventions in our country. One such concerns is with regard to the *dohadavṛkṣas*-longing trees. It was supposed by our poets that some trees had different longings and they had to be satisfied before they put forth their blossoms. 'दोहम्' आकर्षं ददाति (दा + क) इति दोहदः. The ardent irresistible desire of a pregnant woman is called '*dohada*' as-प्रजावती दोहदशंसिनी ते.[1] and

उपेत्य सा दोहददुःखशीलतां यदेव वव्रे तदपश्यदाहृतम्।
न हीष्टमस्य त्रिदिवेऽपि भूपतेरभूदनासाद्यमधिज्यधन्वनः।।[2]

The desire of trees is also called '*dohada*'. On the fulfilment of *dohada,* the trees put forth untimely blossoms as Śrīharṣa says :

इष्टेन पूर्तेन नलस्य वश्यास्स्वर्भोगमत्रापि सृजन्त्यमर्त्याः।
महीरुहो दोहदसेकशक्तेराकालिकं कोरकमुद्गिरन्ति।।[3]

We get references to a number of *dohadavṛkṣas*, longing trees in Sanskrit literature. Popular among them with their botanical names are :

1. Priyaṅgu (Callicarpa Maczophylla)
2. Bakula (Mimusops Elengi Linn)
3. Aśoka (Saraca Indica Linn)
4. Tilaka (Wendlandia Exeratapers)
5. Kurabaka (Rhododendron Arborium)
6. Mandāra (Erythrina Indica Roxb)
7. Campaka (Michelia Champaca)
8. Cūta (Mango) (Mangifera Indica Linn)
9. Nameru (Calophyllum Inophylla)
10. Karṇikāra (Amalatāsa) (Cassia Fistula Linn)

Each tree has got its own longing which is related to a *Śṛṅgāriṇī nāyikā*. The lovely longings of the aforementioned ten trees are as follows :

स्त्रीणां स्पर्शात्प्रियङ्गुर्विकसति बकुलः सीधुगण्डूषसेकात्
पादाघातादशोकस्तिलककुरबकौ वीक्षणालिङ्गनाभ्याम्।
मन्दारो नर्मवाक्यात्पटुमृदुहसनाच्चम्पको वक्त्रवाता-
च्चूतो गीतान्नमेरुर्विकसति च पुरोनर्तनात्कर्णिकारः।।[4]

All these longings are fulfilled by lovely young women by accomplishing different love-acts. In this paper, an attempt is made to show the expertise of Kālidāsa in plant-science, erotology and poetic conventions discussing at length the illustrations pertaining to these ten longing trees.

1. PRIYAṄGU (Callicarpa Maczophylla)

Priyaṅgu (प्रिय + गम् + कु) is a particular creeper said to put forth blossoms at the touch of women. *Mātaṅgalīlā* mentions-प्रियङ्गुश्यामाङ्गप्रकृतिरपि.[5] The other names of *Priyaṅgu* are *Phalinī* and *Śyāmā*. It is said that *phalinī* is the sweetheart of *sahakāra*-the mango tree.

Examples :

1. मिथुनं परिकल्पितं त्वया
सहकारः फलिनी च नन्विमौ।
अविधाय विवाहसत्क्रिया-
मनयोर्गम्यत इत्यसाम्प्रतम्।।[6]

At the sudden demise of Princess Indumatī, Aja laments thus : The mango tree and the *priyaṅgu* creeper have been, indeed, designed by you for a marriageable couple. For this reason it is improper for you to depart without having celebrated the auspicious ceremonies of their nuptials.

The matching of a tree with a creeper, and even the celebration of a sham marriage between them is a favourite idea with the poets. Indumatī had also longed to organise the wedding ceremony of the *sahakāra* with *phalinī* which she could not peform. On the *mithunabhāva* of *sahakāra* and *phalinī,* commentator Hemādri quotes thus :

मिथुनं परिकल्पितं त्वया सहकारः फलिनी च, "विवाहकरणं प्रयोगरत्नापल्याम्।" "विवाहमङ्गलाचार-(मङ्गलाचारा Ms.) गीतनेपथ्यसंयुता। वृक्षेणोद्वाहिता श्यामा जायते कुसुमाकुला (कुसुमान्विता Ms.)।।"[7]

2. श्यामालताः कुसुमभारनतप्रवालाः
स्त्रीणां हरन्ति धृतभूषणबाहुकान्तिम्।
दन्तावभासविशदस्मितचन्द्रकान्तिं
कङ्केलिपुष्परुचिरा नवमालती च।।[8]

The *śyāmā* creepers whose shoots are bent due to their flowery burden surpass the charm of women's arms adorned with ornaments. In fact, the *priyaṅgu* or the *śyama* creepers put forth their blossoms when touched by beautiful women. When their *dohada* is fulfilled, these creepers have huge flowery blossoms. Hence, they excel the charm of women's arms by which they were touched.

3. श्यामास्वङ्गं चकितहरिणीप्रेक्षणे दृष्टिपातं
वक्त्रच्छायां शशिनि शिखिनां बर्हभारेषु केशान्।
उत्पश्यामि प्रतनुषु नदीवीचिषु भ्रूविलासा-
न्हन्तैकस्मिन्क्वचिदपि न ते चण्डि! सादृश्यमस्ति।।[9]

A woman's delicate frame is often compared to this creeper. In his imagination Yakṣa sees his Yakṣī's delicate figure in *priyaṅgu* creepers.

4. प्रियङ्गुकालीयककुङ्कुमाक्तं
स्तनेषु गौरेषु विलासिनीभिः।
आलिप्यते चन्दनमङ्गनाभि-
र्मदालसाभिर्मृगनाभियुक्तम् ॥[10]

Amorous damsels, exhausted with intoxication, are rubbing over their white bosoms sandle-paste mixed with *priyaṅgu, kālīyaka* (black *aguru), kuṅkuma* (saffron) and *mṛganābhi* (musk). The powder of *priyaṅgu*-flowers was mixed in sandal-paste and used by women for different purposes.

5. पाकं व्रजन्ती हिमजालशीतै-
राधूयमाना सततं मरुद्भिः।
प्रिये प्रियङ्गुः प्रियविप्रयुक्ता
विपाण्डुतां याति विलासिनीव॥[11]

Becoming ripe and constantly being shaken by breezes, cooled by snow in Hemanta season, the *priyaṅgu* creeper, O dear, is looking pale like a young lady separated from her lover.

Poet Māgha also remembers *priyaṅgu* creeper while describing winter season :

कुसुमयन्फलिनीरलिनीरवै-
र्मदविकासिभिराहितहुंकृतिः।
उपवनं निरभर्त्सयत प्रिया-
न्वियुवतीर्युवतीः शिशिरानिलः॥[12]

Medicinal Value :

प्रियङ्गुः शीतलो वाति दाहपित्तज्वरास्त्रजित्।
मुखकान्तिप्रजननो गात्रदौर्गन्ध्यनाशनः॥ मदनविनोदः।

2. BAKULA (KESARA) (Mimusops Elengi Linn)

(Illustrations from *Kumārasambhava* only)

Kesara denotes three different plants, *viz.*, Mimusops Elengi Linn, Rottlera Tinctoria and Mesua Ferrea. In *Saṁhitā* and *Nighaṇṭugranthas, Kesara* has been used to denote *Nāgakeśara, Padmakeśara* and *Bakula*. Most of the scholars are of the view that *Kesara* is cultivated and found in Kashmir. Kālidāsa has used *Kesara* to denote *Bakula* flower which is one of the most fragrant white flowers known as *Maulaśrī* or *Maulasirī*. In Sanskrit literature, *Kesara* is used in the sense of *Puṣpaparāga* or filament of a lotus or of any flower or vegetable too. *Kesara* or *Bakula* is a *dohadavṛkṣa* that requires *Śīdhugaṇḍuṣaseka-mukhamadirā* or pouring of wine through the mouth of a beautiful dame.

Examples :

1. स्रस्तां नितम्बादवलम्बमाना पुनः पुनः केसरदामकाञ्चीम्।
न्यासीकृतां स्थानविदा स्मरेण मौर्वीं द्वितीयामिव कार्मुकस्य।।[13]

When Pārvatī was coming to the *āśrama* of Śiva to serve Him, she was again and again drawing up with her hand her girdle-string composed of *Bakula*-flowers, slipping off her hips, which was, as it were, a second string for his bow deposited there by Cupid who knew the proper place for it. The gridle-string made of fragrant *Bakula* flowers was adding to the charm of Pārvatī.

2. आर्द्रकेसरसुगन्धि ते मुखं
मत्तरक्तनयनं स्वभावतः ।
अत्र लब्धवसतिर्गुणान्तरं
किं विलासिनि! मधुः (मदः) करिष्यति।।[14]

The presiding deity of Gandhamādana forest brought wine for Pārvatī to honour her. Śiva said-O sportive lady! Since your mouth possesses the fragrance of fresh *Bakula* flowers and the corners of your eyes are naturally rose-red, then, what other grace can a mouthful of wine impart to you? The intoxication of wine brings two changes; it renders the mouth fragrant and colours the eyes red making them look more attractive. Since, Pārvatī already possessed these two qualities there was nothing more that wine could accomplish in her case. Pārvatī was *a padminī nāyikā* so naturally her mouth was fragrant like fresh *Bakula* flowers and she was *vilāsinī*. Hence, the corners of her eyes were red. This verse is a beautiful illustration of *Pārvatīgata rūpotapannā* and *gandhotpannā vaiṣayikī rati*. Here Kālidāsa has blent plant science with erotology very successfully.

3. तस्य जातु मलयस्थलीरते-
धूतचन्दनलतः प्रियाक्लमम्।
आचचाम सलवङ्गकेसर
श्चाटुकार इव दक्षिणानिलः।।[15]

Once, when Śiva was sporting with his beloved Pārvatī on the grounds of the Malaya mountain, the southern breeze that had been rustling through sandalwood-groves and blowing through clove-orchards came wafting their pollen and like a sweet-spoken lover or adulator removed the tiresomeness of Pārvatī born of sexual sports (pleasure-sports). Here, *kesara* has been used in the sense of the filaments of *Lavaṅga* flower. सलवङ्गकेसरः and धूतचन्दनलतः- these two epithets indicate fragrance and coolness of the breeze. The southern breeze acted as a चाटुकार-an adept adulator or flatterer who drank (dried) up the sex-fatigue of Pārvatī. Here, the usage आचचाम (drank up) is wonderful. In today's world, we come across this word चाटुकार many times. If a person wishes to be a real चाटुकार, he should be able to drink up the fatigue of his lord or beloved. Then only he can succeed in his ventures. This fact was known to Kālidāsa two thousand years ago. Thus in this verse, we find a blend of plant science, erotology and sociology too.

Medicinal Values :

(i) बकुलः शीतलो हृद्यो विषदोषविनाशनः।
मधुरश्च कषायश्च मदाढ्यो हर्षदायकः।। राजनिघण्टौ।

(ii) पुष्पं कषायं शीतं पित्तकफास्रजित्। राजनिघण्टौ।

(iii) बकुलस्य फलं रुक्षं विशदं स्तम्भनं गुरु।
कषायं मधुरं शीतं लेखनं कफपित्तहृत्।
दन्तदाढ्यकरं ग्राहि विबन्धाध्मानवातकृत्।
तद्बीजं दन्तचालघ्नं न स्याच्छीर्षरुजापहम्।। शालिग्रामनिघण्टौ।

3. AŚOKA (Saraca Indica Linn)

(Illustrations from *Kumārasambhava* only)

Jonesia Aśoka Roxb is a tree of moderate size belonging to the leguminous class with magnificent red flowers. Aśoka is a *dohadavṛkṣa,* longing (wishing) tree. The longing of a pregnant woman for particular objects is called *dohada*. There are some *dohadavṛkṣas* which at budding time long to be touched by the foot or the mouth of a lovely woman. It's a poetic convention (*kavisamaya*) that the *Aśoka* requires to be struck by beautiful females with their feet adorned with tinkling anklet bells, so that it is able to bring forth flowers :

सनूपुररवेण स्त्रीचरणेनाभिताडनम्।
दोहदं यदशोकस्य ततः पुष्पोद्गमो भवेत्।।[16]

The jingling anklet bells worn by women produce musical sounds. Music, be it of human beings or birds or animals, encompasses and influences the whole world. Music is three-fold : Vocal, Instrumental and Dance. The splendour of music is to be witnessed in our poetic conventions too that are related to the yearning (longing) trees.

The Aśoka tree becomes laden with blossoming flowers when kicked by the beautiful damsels whose feet are adorned with tinkling anklet bells. The sounds of anklet bells resemble the sounds of idiophones or *ghanavādyas*. The *Nameru* tree blossoms listening to the music and the *Karṇikāra* tree blooms seeing a dance performed before it. Hence, in poetic convention too, music has its significant place where the vocal, instrumental and dance recitals performed by beautiful ladies enable the *Nameru, Aśoka* and *Karṇikāra* trees to blossom :

नूपुरान्वितपादेन तरुण्या ताडितो भृशम्।
अशोकः केसरो वक्त्रसीधुसिक्तश्च फुल्लति।। प्रयोगरत्नावल्याम्।

स्त्रीणां स्पर्शात्प्रियङ्गुर्विकसति बकुलः सीधुगण्डूषसेकात्
पादाघातादशोकस्तिलककुरबकौ वीक्षणालिङ्गनाभ्याम्।
मन्दारो नर्मवाक्यात्पटुमृदुहसनाच्चम्पको वक्त्रवांता-
च्चूतो गीतान्नमेरुर्विकसति च पुरोनर्तनात्कर्णिकारः।।[17]

Examples :

1. असूत सद्यः कुसुमान्यशोकः
स्कन्धात्प्रभृत्येव सपल्लवानि।
पादेन नापैक्षत सुन्दरीणां
सम्पर्कमासिञ्जितनूपुरेण ।।[18]

Madhu (the vernal season), Kāma's bosom friend unfolded in that forest assuming his true form, where Śiva was practising *Samādhi*. At once, the *Aśoka* tree showered sprays of flowers and fresh leaves blooming straight from the trunk without waiting for the delicate touch of a pretty woman's foot adorned with jingling anklet bells for blossoming. This is the only verse where Aśoka tree blooms without its longing fulfilled by the touch of beautiful dames. This verse proves that Kālidāsa was aware of the poetic conventions, different types of *dohadas* of different trees and various fine arts, *viz.*, music and dance. The word *āsiñjitanūpureṇa* denotes instrumental music and dance.

2. अशोकनिर्भर्त्सितपद्मराग-
माकृष्टहेमद्युतिकर्णिकारम्।
मुक्ताकलापीकृतसिन्धुवारं
वसन्तपुष्पाभरणं वहन्ती।।[19]

In Spring season, Pārvatī wore a decoration of spring flowers. The *Aśoka* blossoms put the rubies into shame, the *Karṇikāra* sprays stole the lustre from gold and the *Sindhuvāra* buds shone like a necklace of pearls. Hence, the red *Aśoka* flowers, the yellow *Karṇikāra* flowers and the white *Sindhuvāra* flowers worn by Pārvatī enhanced her natural charm. Here, Kālidāsa has fully utilized the flower-kingdom to decorate his heroine. *Karṇikāra* is also a *dohada*-tree which requires dancing by a damsel for its blooming.

Medicinal Values :

अशोकः शीतलस्तिक्तो ग्राही वर्ण्यकषायकः।
दोषापची तृषादाहकृमिशोषविशास्त्रजित्।।
अशोकस्य त्वचा रक्तप्रदरस्य विनाशिनी।। शालिग्रामनिघण्टौ।

4. TILAKA (Wendlandia Exeratapers)

At being gazed by beautiful women, the *Tilaka* tree puts forth its lovely blossoms. Its other name is *Śrīmān*-तिलकः श्रीमान्नाम वृक्षः। 'तिलकः क्षुरकः श्रीमान्' इत्यमरः।[20]

Examples :

1. उपचितावयवा शुचिभिः कणैरलिकदम्बकयोगमुपेयुषी।
सदृशकान्तिरलक्ष्यत मञ्जरी तिलकजाऽलकजालकमौक्तिकैः।।[21]

A cluster of blossoms of *Tilaka*-tree, fully devoloped in its parts by white pollens and coming in contact with swarms of bees, appeared equal in beauty with the net-like ornament of pearls worn in the hair. There are *mañjarīs* in *Tilaka*-tree as they are in mango tree. The beauty of *yamaka* is also enjoyable in this verse.

2. अलिभिरञ्जनबिन्दुमनोहरैः कुसुमपंक्तिनिपातिभिरङ्कितः।
न खलु शोभयति स्म वनस्थलीं न तिलकस्तिलकः प्रमदामिव।।[22]

Verity it is not that the *Tilaka* tree did not decorate the sylvan site-the tree marked as it was with bees alighting on rows of flowers and hence looking beautiful like spots of collyrium, as decorates a young woman the mark of musk painting. Here, the beauty of the *tilaka* flowers along with the beauty of *yamaka* is to be enjoyed.

3. लग्नद्विरेफाञ्जनभक्तिचित्रं मुखे मधुश्रीस्तिलकं प्रकाश्य।
रागेण बालारुणकोमलेन चूतप्रवालोष्ठमलञ्चकार।।[23]

The Vernal Beauty, having displayed on her forehead the *tilaka*-flower artistically painted with black pigment in the shape of the bees that swarmed over it, ornamented her lip in the form of the young mango-leaf with a red tint (red lac) mellow like the light of the morning sun. Here, *tilaka*-flower is serving as the *tilaka* on the forehead of *vasantalakṣmī*.

4. दूरलग्नपरिमेयरश्मिना वारुणी दिगरुणेन भानुना।
भाति केसरवतेव मण्डिता बन्धुजीवतिलकेन कन्यका।।[24]

With the reddish sun whose rays are shooting widely apart and lessening (in number), the western quarter appears like a damsel adorned with the *tilaka* mark of a *bandhujīva* flower having filaments. Although there is no direct mention of *tilaka*-flower in this verse, it can be presumed that the western quarter appeared like a maiden adorned with a *tilaka* mark in the form of *bandhujīva* and *tilaka*-flower. Shri Sures Chandra Banerji has referred to this verse in his *Kālidāsa-Kośa* mentioning *tilaka*-flower.[25]

Medicinal Value :

तिलकः कटुकः पाके रसे चोष्णो रसायनः।
कफकुष्ठकृमीन् हन्ति मुखदन्तगदान्हरेत् ।। भावप्रकाशनिघण्टौ।

5. KURABAKA (Rhododendron Arbarium)

Being embraced by beautiful women, *Kurabaka* puts forth red blossoms. *Kurabaka* (ईषत् रवो यत्र इति कुरव + कन्) (Apte's Sanskrit-Hindi Dictionary, p. 286) appears to have been used by women to decorate the top-knot of their hair. It is described as blossoming in spring.

Examples :

1. विरचिता मधुनोपवनश्रियामभिनवा इव पत्रविशेषकाः।
मधुलिहां मधुदानविशारदाः कुरबका रवकारणतां ययुः।।[26]

The *Kurabakas,* which appeared like ornamental leaves painted in amatory sports on the person of the Vernal Beauty by her lover the spring, and which were liberal in giving nectar to the bees became the cause of their humming. Here we find personification of *madhu* and *upavanaśrī*. A similar idea on the ornamental leaves being painted on a young woman's person can be relished in the following verse of *Mālavikāgnimitra* :

2. रक्ताशोकरुचा विशेषितगुणो बिम्बाधरालक्तकः
प्रत्याख्यातविशेषकं कुरबकं श्यामावदातारुणम्।
आक्रान्ता तिलकक्रियापि तिलकैर्लीनद्विरेफाञ्जनैः
सावज्ञेव मुखप्रसाधनविधौ श्रीर्माधवी योषिताम्।।[27]

3. हस्ते लीलाकमलमलके बालकुन्दानुविद्धं
नीता लोध्रप्रसवरजसा पाण्डुतामानने श्रीः।
चूडापाशे नवकुरबकं चारु कर्णे शिरीषं
सीमन्ते च त्वदुपगमजं यत्र नीपं वधूनाम्।।[28]

Yakṣa says to the cloud-messenger : In Alakāpurī, the women have lotuses in their hands for sport, the inlaying of young *kunda* flowers in their hair, beauty made yellowish-white by the pollen of *lodhra* blossom on their faces, fresh *kurabaka* flowers in their braids of hair, charming *śirīṣa* flowers in their ears, and *kadamba* flowers springing up at thy approach in the partings of their hair. The damsels of Alakāpurī decorate their braids of hair with fresh *kurabaka* flowers.

4. रक्ताशोकश्चलकिसलयः केसरश्चात्र कान्तः
प्रत्यासन्नौ कुरबकवृतेर्माधवीमण्डपस्य।
एकः सख्यास्तव सह मया वामपादाभिलाषी
काङ्क्षत्यन्यो वदनमदिरां दोहदच्छद्मनास्याः।।[29]

(Yakṣa gives to the cloud-messenger a description of the vicinity of his house). Hereon are the red *Aśoka* with its waving sprouts, and the beautiful *Bakula*-tree, in the vicinity of the bower of the *Mādhavī*-creepers hedged in by *Kurabaka*-plants; the former longs with me for thy friend's (my wife's) beautiful foot and the latter desires with me the wine from her mouth, under the pretext that it is an operation essential in causing their blossoming. According to this description, it appears that *kurabaka*-plants were used for hedging of the garden also. It is remarkable that three longing trees, *viz., Aśoka, Bakula* and *Kurabaka* and the longing of two trees (of *Aśoka* and *Bakula*) are mentioned in this verse.

5. कान्तामुखद्युतिजुषामचिरोद्‌गतानां
शोभां परां कुरबकद्रुममञ्जरीणाम्।
दृष्ट्वा प्रिये सहृदयस्य भवेन्न कस्य
कन्दर्पबाणपतनव्यथितं हि चेतः।।

6. मधुसुरभि मुखाब्जं लोचने लोध्रताम्रे
नवकुरबकपूर्णः केशपाशो मनोज्ञः।
गुरुतरकुचयुग्मं श्रोणिबिम्बं तथैव
न भवति किमिदानीं योषितां मन्मथाय।।[30]

Having witnessed the great charm of the blossoms of the *kurabaka*-tree, newly appearing and possessing the radiant loveliness of the faces of damsels, the heart of what sensitive man, O dear, would not be pained with the fall of the arrows of Cupid? × × × Their lotus-like faces sweet-smelling with wine, their eyes red like *lodhra* flowers, their charming, abundant tresses adorned with new *kurabaka*-blossoms, their very heavy breasts and also their round hips;—what, of damsels, does not arouse passion? The radiant *kurabaka*-blossoms arouse excessive passion in loving couples. Beautiful damsels decorate their tresses with *kurabaka*-flowers.

6. MANDĀRA (Erythrina Indica Roxb)

At being greeted with soft and pleasing words uttered by pretty damsels, the *Mandāra* tree puts forth its blossoms. *Mandāra* (मन्द् + आरक्) is a coral tree or *Vidruma*-tree. Its other names are : *Pravālavṛkṣa, ratnavṛkṣa, mandaṭa, raktakandala, hemakandala, ratnakandala, latāmaṇi* etc. It is one of the five celestial trees adorning the divine garden of Lord Indra. The five celestial trees are : *Mandāra, Pārijāta, Santānaka, Kalpavṛkṣa* and *Haricandana.*

Examples :

In olden times (these days also), distinguished guests were greeted with the offering of flower-garlands.[31] Presentation of these garlands was a token of high honour and love extended to a distinguished person. The *mandāramālā* offered to King Duṣyanta by Lord Indra indicates his high applause :

1. अन्तर्गतप्रार्थनमन्तिकस्थं जयन्तमुद्वीक्ष्य कृतस्मितेन।
आमृष्टवक्षोहरिचन्दनाङ्का मन्दारमाला हरिणा पिनद्धा।।[32]

Indra fastened a garland of *mandāra*-flowers bearing marks of the heavenly sandal rubbed off (by it) from his bosom, smiling and looking up at Jayanta, who was standing by with an inward longing for the same. In this verse, two celestial trees *mandāra* and *haricandana* are referred to.

मति मानहेतुर्भवति।[33]

According to this *nirukti, mālā* is a token of high esteem. 'मां शोभां लाति'- according to this *nirukti, mālā* brings beauty and good fortune. Now are presented some beautiful illustrations of *mandāra* flowers from the works of Kālidāsa :

2. तत्रागारं धनपतिगृहानुत्तरेणास्मदीयं
दूराल्लक्ष्यं सुरपतिधनुश्चारुणा तोरणेन।
यस्योपान्ते कृतकतनयः कान्तया वर्धितो मे
हस्तप्राप्यस्तबकनमितो बालमन्दारवृक्षः।।[34]

Yakṣa says to the cloud-messenger : There to the north of Kubera's building stands my house visible from afar, by the arched-doorway as beautiful as the rainbow. Close to this is a young *mandāra* tree bent down by the cluster of flowers, within reach of hand and reared by my wife as an adopted son. People used to rear plants and trees like their own offsprings and extend extreme love to them.

3. असम्पदस्तस्य वृषेण गच्छतः
प्रभिन्नदिग्वारणवाहनो वृषा।
करोति पादावुपगम्य मौलिना
विनिद्रमन्दाररजोऽरुणाङ्गुली।।[35]

Indra, having for his vehicle the rutting elephant of the Eastern quarter, touches, with his crest, the feet of that Wealthless God Śiva who goes about on a bull, and makes their toes red with the pollen-dust of the full-blown *mandāra*-flowers. Who can describe the greatness of Śiva before whom even Indra bows his head. Indra is fond of *mandāra*-flowers. Hence, his crest is adorned with full-blown *mandāra*-blossoms with red pollen-dust.

4. क्रियाप्रबन्धादयमध्वराणा-
मजस्रमाहूतसहस्रनेत्रः।
शच्याश्चिरं पाण्डुकपोललम्बा-
न्मन्दारशून्यानलकांश्चकार।।[36]

(Sunandā describes a king to princess Indumatī). This king, in his unremitted course of sacrificial ceremonies, perpetually invited the thousand-eyed god Indra, and thus made the tresses of Śacī, which were pendent on her pale cheeks, long destitute of *mandāra*-flowers. Śacī, the consort of Indra, is very fond of *mandāra*-flowers with which she decorates her tresses. But when she is *proṣitabhartṛkā,* she does not adron her hair–प्रोषितभर्तृका हि केशरसंकारं न कुर्वन्ति.'[37]

5. मन्दारपुष्पैरधिवासितायां
यस्याः शिखायामयमर्पणीयः।
सैव प्रिया सम्प्रति दुर्लभा मे
किमेनमस्त्रोपहतं करोति।।[38]

(Purūravā says) she, in whose hair scented with the flowers of the *mandāra*-tree this jewel is fit to be placed, that my sweet-heart (Urvaśī) is now unobtainable to me; why shall I then soil it with my tears? *Mandāra* appears to be a favourite flower with the celestials. Urvaśī used to perfume her tresses with *mandāra*-flowers.

There are beautiful *mañjarīs* in *Mandāra* tree. The sixth day of the bright fortnight of the month of *Māgha* is called *Mandārasaṣṭhī*. *Mandāra* denotes *Arka*-tree and *Dhattūra*-tree also.

Medicinal Values :

पारिभद्रः कटूष्णः स्यात्कफवातनिकृन्तनः।
अरोचकहरः पथ्यो दीपनश्चापि कीर्तितः।। धन्वन्तरिनिघण्टौ।

7. CAMPAKA (Michelia Champaca)

At being greeted with gracious and sweet smiles passed by charming damsels, the *campaka* tree puts forth its lovely blossoms. *Campaka* (चम्प + ण्वुल्) is a big tree and its flowers are yellowish white or golden yellow in colour and very fragrant. Women are stated to decorate their heads with these flowers. The writer of this paper is writing these lines sitting in front of a big *campaka* tree laden with thousands of *campaka* flowers and herself having decorated her tresses with *campaka-gajarās* on 31st May, 2002 at 9.30 p.m. at Rajawala, Dehradun. Today is dark night and the *campaka* flowers are glittering at the top of the tree. There is a beautiful reference to this flower :

अद्यापि तां कनकचम्पकदामगौरीम्।[39]

Although *campaka* is a very fragrant and beautiful flower, Kālidāsa has mentioned this only once and that too in *Ṛtusaṁhāra* thus :

1. ईषत्तुषारैः कृतशीतहर्म्यैः
सुवासितं चारु शिरश्च चम्पकैः।
कुर्वन्ति नार्योऽपि वसन्तकाले
स्तनं सहारं कुसुमैर्मनोहरैः।।[40]

In mansions rendered slightly cool with snow, ladies, also in the spring season, perfume their beautiful tresses with *campaka* blossoms and wear on their breasts, garlands made of lovely flowers.

Many poets have composed beautiful *anyokti-ślokas* on *campaka*. Some are cited here for the enjoyment of the connoisseurs :

(i) साधारणतरुबुद्ध्या न मया बद्धस्तवालवालोऽपि।
लज्जयसि मामिदानीं चम्पक भुवनाधिवासिभिः कुसुमैः।।

(ii) यद्यपि खदिरारण्ये गुप्तौ वस्ते हि चम्पको वृक्षः।
तदपि च परिमलमतुलं दिशि दिशि कथयेत्समीरणस्तस्य।।

(iii) केनात्र चम्पकतरो बत रोपितोऽसि
कुग्रामपामरजनान्तिकवाटिकायाम् ।
यत्र प्रवृद्धवनशाकविवृद्धिलोभा-
द्धो भग्नवाटघटनोचितपल्लवोऽसि।। विज्जकायाः।

(iv) कोपं चम्पक मुञ्च याचकजनैरायासितस्त्वं सखे!
मा म्लासीः परितो विलोकय तरुः कस्तेऽधिरूढस्तुलाम्।
कोपश्चेन्नियतस्तवास्ति हृदये धात्रे तथा कुप्यतां
येन त्वं हि सुवर्णवर्णकुसुमामोदोऽद्वितीयः कृतः।।

(v) सन्त्येकेऽपि महीरुहाः प्रतिदिनं संसक्तमत्तालय-
स्तत्तादृग्गुणिनो लवङ्गलवलीमाकन्दकुन्दादयः।
आशास्यं जनुरस्य चम्पकतरोर्यत्कोरकान्तर्दलं
स्वैरङ्गैरुपमीय राजरमणी सासूयमालोकते।।[41]

These verses tell the story of the *campaka*-tree and its flowers fully. Why Kālidāsa has not mentioned this flower more abundantly is yet to be found out.

Medicinal Values :

चम्पकं कुसुमं शीतं चक्षुष्यं विशदं शुभम्।
चम्पकं कटुकं तिक्तं कषायं मधुरं हिमम्।। क्षेमकुतूहले।
निहन्ति कफपित्तास्त्रं मूत्रकृच्छ्रचिषं कृमीन्।। कैय्यदेवनिघण्टौ।

8. CŪTA (ĀMRA) (Mangifera Indica Linn)
(Illustrations from *Kumārasambhava* only)

At being greeted with the perfumed mouth-breeze of beautiful damsels, the mango-tree puts forth its fragrant blossoms called *cūta-mañjarīs* or *āmra-mañjarīs*.

Āmra or mango is the king of Indian fruits. Not only in India, mango is loved by many all over the world. It has hundreds of varieties. Its other names are : *Kāmaśara, Cūta, Rasāla, Kāmavallabha, Vāmāṅga, Sahakāra, Kīreṣṭa* and *Mādhavadruma :*

आम्रः कामशरश्चूतः रसालः कामवल्लभः।
वामाङ्गः सहकारश्च कीरेष्टो माधवद्रुमः।।

Kālidāsa has referred to *Āmra* or *Cūta* at a number of places in the *Kumārasambhava* and almost every time he has blent his description with some other *Śāstra* or *Vidyā* which brings forth his vast erudition. Some examples are presented herewith :

Examples :

1. चूताङ्कुरास्वादकषायकण्ठः पुंस्कोकिलो यन्मधुरं चुकूज।
मनस्विनीमानविघातदक्षं तदेव जातं वचनं स्मरस्य।।[42]

Among the birds, the male and the female cuckoo are the luckiest and the most famous ones for singing. The poetic eulogy showered on the sweet notes of music is that of male cuckoo which is a zoologically proved fact and was known to our magnificent poet. For the music of the male cuckoo, he very adeptly uses the term 'पुंस्कोकिलकूजित'. पञ्चम, the fifth note of music is generated from the throat of कोकिल[43]. In spring, the king of seasons, mango trees are full of mango sprouts. The male cuckoo feasts on these and by sipping the fresh juice of these sprouts, he sings sweetly with an impassioned throat. This is his melodious music which becomes Cupid's eloquent mandate empowered to break down the pride of the high-minded damsels.

Here the word कषाय denotes various meanings-(i) a throat tinged with passion; (ii) a throat clear on account of the astringency of the mango-sprout; (iii) a throat which has become reddish brown by the juice of mango-sprouts; (iv) a throat which is सुरभित (fragrant) and hence capable of producing sweet sounds.[44]

Ladies with a proper sense of their honour are called मनस्विनी (High-minded lady). When a lady's lover is attracted to another woman, the wrath generated out of jealousy is called 'मान' :

स्त्रीणामीर्ष्याकृतः कोपो मानोऽन्यासङ्गिनि प्रिये।[45]

As soon as the high-minded ladies listen to the sweet notes of the male cuckoo, they at once give up their मान for their sweet hearts as if they have been directed by the eloquent command of the God of Love :

कोकिलकूजितश्रवणानन्तरं स्मराज्ञप्ता इव मानं जहुरित्यर्थः।[46]

Now in a single verse, we come across the poet's high expertise in the science of love, science of seasons, science of trees, science of birds and science of music.

The picturesque idea of the above verse has been brought out in other works too. Some illustrations are cited here :

(i) त्यजत मानमलं बत विग्रहैर्न पुनरेति गतं चतुरं वयः।
परभृताभिरितीव निवेदिते स्मरमते रमते स्म वधूजनः।।[47]

(ii) प्रियसखीसदृशं प्रतिबोधिताः किमपि काम्यगिरा परपुष्टया।
प्रियतमाय वपुर्गुरुमत्सरच्छिदुरयाऽदुरयाचितमङ्गनाः।।[48]

(iii) दत्तं प्रियाभिर्बहुमानपूर्वमासाद्य चूतासवमन्यपुष्टाः।
आमोदिभिः पञ्चमरागभेदैः प्राबोधयन्पञ्चशरावलेपम्।।[49]

2. हरितारुणचारुबन्धनः कलपुंस्कोकिलशब्दसूचितः।
वद सम्प्रति कस्य बाणतां नवचूतप्रसवो गमिष्यति।।[50]

The voice of the cuckoo becomes clear and sweet when it tastes the mango-sprouts. Hence, the melodious voice of the cuckoo indicates the presence of mango-blossoms. When Kāma was reduced to ashes by the fire of Śiva's fury, Rati lamented thus : 'Say, by whom the fresh blossom of the mango-tree, the beautiful stem of which is reddish-green and the sprouting of which is proclaimed by the notes of the male cuckoo, will now be employed as his arrow?' Here also Kālidāsa refers to the music of पुंस्कोकिल.

3. पार्वती तदुपयोगसम्भवां
विक्रियामपि सतीं मनोहराम्।
अप्रतर्क्यविधियोगकारिता-
माम्रतेव सहकारतां ययौ।।[51]

During their love-sports, Śiva asks Pārvatī to drink the wine brought for her by the presiding deity of the Gandhamādana. When Pārvatī drank the wine, she underwent a *vikriyā,* a change, which made her even more attractive and enchanting as a common mango-tree is changed by some indefinable power in Nature into a special and fragrant kind of *sahakāra*. The *vikriyā,* the change, is generally for the worse (न हि विक्रिया कुत्रापि मनोहरा भवति-नारायणः) but the change made Pārvatī more beautiful. *Āmra* and *sahakāra* both signify the mango-tree but the latter refers to a particular species whose blossoms are exceedingly fragrant (सहकारोऽतिसौरभ इत्यमरः). This verse poses before us a big question. An ordinary mango-tree cannot be transformed into one of the *sahakāra* species unless it is treated with some magical charms which is expressed by अप्रतर्क्यविधियोग or the inscrutable power of the Creator. अप्रतर्क्यविधियोग may refer to मणिमन्त्रौषधकालादियोग too as is explained by commentator Nārāyaṇa. It means an ordinary mango tree can be transformed into the fragrant species of *sahakāra* by the magical usage of jewels, gems, *mantras* or verses of sacred texts and medicinal herbs during a particular time. Such treatment can definitely bring radical changes in a tree. Pārvatī too underwent just a similar magical change after drinking the wine. Those who are well versed in Plant science and Agricultural science know very well that trees and plants are given varied types of treatment which bring forth amazing improvements resulting in the better quality and variety of flowers and fruits. This very fact was known to Kālidāsa.

Commenting on this verse, Vallabhadeva also expresses surprise that *āmra* can contain *āmratā* only and *sahakāra* can contain *sahakāratā* only. How is it possible that *āmratā* can be changed into *sahakāratā* :

अप्रतर्क्यो दुर्ज्ञेयो यो विधियोगो दैवव्यापारस्तेन विनिर्मितां कृताम्। आम्रता हि केनचिद् दैवभावात् सहकारतां सम्पद्यते वयं न विद्मः (जानीमः)। कस्मिन् देशे कविना आम्रसहकारयोः प्रकृतिविकारभावो दृष्टोऽस्माभिर्हि सामान्यविशेषभावस्तयोरुपलब्धः। तथा चोक्तम्—

अपुष्पफलवानाम्रः पुष्पितश्चूत उच्यते।
पुष्पैः फलैस्तु संयुक्तः सहकार उदाहृतः।।[52]

Kālidāsa has answers for this query with the appropriate inclusion of अप्रतर्क्यविधियोग. A poet of high calibre alone can make such wonderful remarks. On the one hand, he is describing the amorous sports of Śiva and Pārvatī while on the other, he describes the beauty of Pārvatī which has been enhanced by the magical charm rendered to her by the divine wine provided by the wish-giving trees and brought by the presiding deity of the Gandhamādana forest. Here, we find *Pārvatīgata rūpotpannā* and *gandhotpannā vaiṣayikī rati* very beautifully painted by Dīpaśikhā Kālidāsa.

4. परलोकविधौ च माधव स्मरमुद्दिश्य विलोलपल्लवाः।
निवपेः सहकारमञ्जरीः प्रियचूतप्रसवो हि ते सखा।।[53]

O Mādhava (Vasanta), in the memorial rites for Kāma, offer the spray of fragrant mango blossoms with trembling young leaves as your friend was very fond of mango-flowers. Here, Kālidāsa once again uses *sahakāra* and *cūta* in one verse. He blends here the plant-science with the *nivāpa* ceremony, a rite performed after death.

5. सद्यः प्रवालोद्गमचारुपत्रे नीते समाप्तिं नवचूतबाणे।
निवेशयामास मधुर्द्विरेफान्नामाक्षराणीव मनोभवस्य।।[54]

Madhu, the Spring season, having fitted up the arrow of Kāma in the shape of young mango-blossoms with fresh leaves as its beautiful feathers, immediately inscribed on it the letters, as it were, of the name of the Mind-born (Cupid), in the shape of the bees.

The mango blossom is one of the five floral arrows of Cupid :

अरविन्दमशोकश्च चूतश्च नवमल्लिका।
नीलोत्पलश्च पञ्चैते पुष्पबाणस्य सायकाः।।

It was usual with great warriors to have their names inscribed on their arrows :

बाणाक्षरैरेव परस्परस्य नामोर्जितं चापभृतः शशंसुः।[55]

Here, Kālidāsa has blent plant-science with war-science and erotology.

6. अथ स ललितयोषिद्भ्रूलताचारुशृङ्गं
रतिवलयपदाङ्के चापमासज्य कण्ठे।
सहचरमधुहस्तन्यस्तचूताङ्कुरास्त्रः
शतमखमुपतस्थे प्राञ्जलिः पुष्पधन्वा।।[56]

Then the God of the Flower-Bow, having his bow with its ends curved beautifully as the arching eyebrows of graceful women, slung over his neck bearing the marks of Rati's bracelets and having his arrow of young sprouts of the mango-tree deposited in the hands of his bosom friend Madhu (Spring), approached with folded hands the God of a Hundred Sacrifices (Indra). Here, the imprint of Rati's bracelets over the neck of Kāma indicates their amorous embrace.

7. महीभृतः पुत्रवतोऽपि दृष्टि–
स्तस्मिन्नपत्ये न जगाम तृप्तिम्।
अनन्तपुष्पस्य मधोर्हि चूते
द्विरेफमाला सविशेषसङ्गा।।[57]

The eyes of the Mountain-lord, though blessed with a son, were never satiated by the sight of this child of his (Pārvatī); the circling bees are specially drawn to the mango blossoms, though the spring season blooms with countless flowers. In the midst of an endless shower of beautiful flowers in vernal season, the fresh mango-sprouts excel all.

8. लग्नद्विरेफाञ्जनभक्तिचित्रं
मुखे मधुश्रीस्तिलकं प्रकाश्य।
रागेण बालारुणकोमलेन
चूतप्रवालोष्ठमलञ्चकार ।।[58]

The Vernal Beauty, having displayed on her forehead a *tilaka* (the *tilaka* flower) artistically painted with a black pigment in the shape of the bees that clinged to it, ornamented her lip in the form of the tender mango-shoots with a red tint (red lac) mellow like dawn's first light. Here plant-science is beautifully mingled with seasonology and the art of make-up.

Medicinal Values :

पक्वं तु मधुरं वृष्यं स्निग्धं बलसुखप्रदम्।
गुरुवातहरं हृद्यं वर्ण्यं शीतमपित्तलम्।।
कषायानुरसं वह्निश्लेष्मशुक्रविवर्धनम्।। भावप्रकाशनिघण्टौ।

9. NAMERU (Calophyllum Inophylla)

At being greeted with melodious singing by beautiful women, the *Nameru* (नम् + एरु) tree puts forth its lovely blossoms. 'Mallinātha gives *Sura-punnāga* as its synonym. Its flowers appear to have been used as decoration especially of the head. *Nameru* trees are described as affording a pleasant shade.'[59]

Examples :

1. गणा नमेरुप्रसवावतंसा भूर्जत्वचः स्पर्शवतीर्दधानाः।
मनःशिलाविच्छुरिता निषेदुः शैलेयनद्धेषु शिलातलेषु।।[60]

Śiva's attendant troops (demigods called pramathas), with the flowers of *nameru* trees for their ear-ornaments, clad in birch-barks soft to the touch, and annointed with mineral (red arsenic) dyes, sat on the rocks coated with fragrant resin. It is remarkable that the attendants of Śiva are decorating their ears with *nameru*-flowers. Mostly women adorn their ears with flowers but here *Śivagaṇas* are decorating their ears with *nameru*-flowers. It is but natural for them as per their description found in *Kālikāpurāṇa :*

विचित्ररूपाभरणा जटाचन्द्रार्धमण्डिताः।
आकाशमार्गे गच्छन्तमनुगच्छन्ति नित्यशः।।
ध्यानस्थं परिचर्यन्ति सलिलादिभिरीश्वरम्।
नानाशस्त्रधराः शम्भोर्गणास्तु प्रमथाः स्मृताः।।
अपरे गायनास्तालमृदङ्गपणवादिभिः।
नृत्यन्ति वाद्यं कुर्वन्तो गायन्ति मधुरस्वरम्।।
षट्त्रिंशत्कोटयश्चैते हरस्य सकला गणाः।।[61]

2. विशश्रमुर्नमेरूणां छायास्वध्यास्य सैनिकाः।
दृषदो वासितोत्सङ्गा निषण्णमृगनाभिभिः।।[62]

King Raghu's soldiers reposed (rested) in the shade of *Nameru*-trees, seated on stone slabs, the surface whereof was perfumed with the naval musk of the recumbent deer. Here, tired soldiers are enjoying the pleasant shade of *Nameru*-trees.

3. दृष्टिप्रपातं परिहृत्य तस्य कामः पुरःशुक्रमिव प्रयाणे।
प्रान्तेषु संसक्तनमेरुशाखं ध्यानास्पदं भूतपतेर्विवेश।।[63]

Having avoided Śiva's glance, as one does the quarter wherein shines Venus, when starting on a journey, Kāma entered Śiva's place of contemplation screened all round with the thickly interwoven branches of *Nameru*-tree. *Nameru*-trees had formed an arbour there, their branches forming a canopy. This proves that *Nameru*-trees have very thickly interwoven and shady branches and also that it was a good place for Kāma to hide himself from Śiva.

4. खर्जूरीस्कन्धनद्धानां मदोद्गारसुगन्धिषु।
कटेषु करिणां पेतुः पुन्नागेभ्यः शिलीमुखाः।।[64]

The sting mouthed black bees fell from the *punnāga* flowers on the temples which were fragrant on account of the emission of ichor of elephants that were tied to the trunks of *Kharjūra*-

trees. Some people are of the view that *Nameru* and *Punnāga* are the same flowers. Mallinātha gives *Nāga-keśara* as the synonym of *Punnāga*. But, the botanical name of *Nāga-keśara* is Mesua ferrea (see Hooker, I. 277).

Medicinal Value :

पुन्नागो मधुरः शीतः सुगन्धिः पित्तनाशकृत्।।
भूतविद्रावणं चैव देवतानां प्रसाधनः।। धन्वन्तरिनिघण्टौ।

10. KARṆIKĀRA (AMALATĀSA) (Cassia Fistula Linn)

(Illustrations from *Kumārasambhava* only)

At being greeted with a lovely dance performance in front of it by the beautiful damsels, the *Karṇikāra*-tree puts forth its blossoms. *Karṇikāra* blossoms in spring season. In Sanskrit literature, *Karṇikāra* is used in the sense of golden *Campā, Kaṭhacampā, Mandāra* or *Amalatāsa*. It seems, Kālidāsa has used *Karṇikāra* in the sense of golden *Campā* and at places in the sense of *Amalatāsa* too.

Examples :

1. उमापि नीलालकमध्यशोभि विस्त्रंसयन्ती नवकर्णिकारम्।
चकार कर्णच्युतपल्लवेन मूर्ध्ना प्रणामं वृषभध्वजाय।।
अथोपनिन्ये गिरिशाय गौरी तपस्विने ताम्ररुचा करेण।
विशोषितां भानुमतो मयूखैर्मन्दाकिनीपुष्करबीजमालाम्।[65]

Umā bowed so low to the Bull-emblemed God that the tender young leaf shoot at her ear slipped and fell and the fresh *Karṇikāra* flowers shining in the midst of her blue-black tresses got loosened. Then, Pārvatī offered to Śiva, given to asceticism, a rosary of the seeds of lotuses grown in the Mandākinī and dried up by the rays of the Sun, with her hand which had a rosy complexion. Here, plant-science is mingled with erotology as Pārvatī's *Nāyikālaṅkāra Bhāva* is found in these verses.

2. अशोकनिर्भर्त्सितपद्मरागमाकृष्टहेमद्युतिकर्णिकारम् ।
मुक्ताकलापीकृतसिन्धुवारं वसन्तपुष्पाभरणं वहन्ती।।[66]

For critical comments on this verse, please see the heading '*Aśoka*'.

3. वर्णप्रकर्षे सति कर्णिकारं दुनोति निर्गन्धतया स्म चेतः।
प्रायेण सामग्र्यविधौ गुणानां पराङ्मुखी विश्वसृजः प्रवृत्ति।।[67]

The *Karṇikāra* flower, though of gorgeous colour, pained the mind by its odourlessness. Generally, the mind of the Creator is averse to bestowing the entirety of excellence on any one thing. It appears that *Karṇikāra* here denotes *Amalatāsa*.

Medicinal Values :

कर्णिकारो दीर्घफलः स्वर्णाङ्गः स्वर्णभूषणः।
आरग्वधो गुरुः स्वादुः शीतलस्त्रंसनोत्तमः।।
तत्फलस्त्रंसनं रुच्यं कुष्ठपित्तकफापहम्।
ज्वरे तु सततं पथ्यं कोष्ठशुद्धिकरं परम्।। भावप्रकाशनिघण्टौ।

Thus, Kālidāsa has presented a beautiful garden comprising all the ten longing trees with their eye-catching splendour of lovely blossoms. The longing of each tree differs from that of the other. In fact, all the longings of these trees are love-acts desired by these trees and fulfilled by amorous *nāyikās*. In fact, touching with hand and foot, gazing, embracing, uttering soft words, smiling and laughing, pouring fragrant mouth-breeze or pouring wine through mouth, singing and dancing, all these acts are love-acts which will be liked and enjoyed by any human being or animal or plant or tree. Similarly, trees and creepers also desire and long for loving acts and being satisfied they, in turn, put forth lovely and fragrant blossoms. These trees bring forth a pleasant message that we should extend good and courteous behaviour towards one and all to lead a happy and prosperous life on earth.

I conclude this paper with three verses from *Vālmīki Rāmāyaṇa* wherein is described the natural beauty of the forests and gardens near the Kailāsa mountain. These forests and gardens abound in trees laden with blossoming flowers. Here, seven longing trees find special mention :

कर्णिकारवनैर्दीप्तैः कदम्बबकुलैस्तथा।
पद्मिनीभिश्च फुल्लाभिर्मन्दाकिन्या जलैरपि।।
चम्पकाशोकपुंनागमन्दारतरुभिस्तथा।
चूतपाटललोध्रैश्च प्रियङ्ग्वर्जुनकेतकैः।।
तगरैर्नारिकेलैश्च प्रियालपनसैस्तथा।
एतैरन्यैश्च तरुभिरुद्भासितवनान्तरे।।[68]

REFERENCES & NOTES

1. *Raghuvaṁśa* (Edited by G.R. Nandargikar) - 14.45
2. *Raghuvaṁśa* - 3.7
3. *Naiṣadhīyacarita* - 3.21
4. *Kumārasambhava* (Ed. by M.R. Kale) - Quoted in Notes on 3.26
5. *Mātaṅgalīlā* - 3.9, Quoted in Apte's Sanskrit-Hindi Kośa, p. 694
6. *Raghuvaṁśa* - 8.61
7. *Raghuvaṁśa* - Notes on 8.61, p. 761
8. *Ṛtusaṁhāra* - 3.18
9. *Meghadūta* - 2.43
10. *Ṛtusaṁhāra* - 6.14
11. *Ṛtusaṁhāra* - 4.11

12. *Śiśupālavadha* - 6.62
13. *Kumārasambhava* - 3.55
14. *Kumārasambhava* - 8.76
15. *Kumārasambhava* - 8.25
16. *Kumārasambhava* - Quoted in Mallinātha's commentary on 3.26
17. *Kumārasambhava* - Quoted in Notes on 3.26
18. *Kumārasambhava* -3.26
19. *Kumārasambhava* - 3.53
20. *Raghuvaṁśa* - Mallinātha's commentary on 9.41; Apte's Sanskrit-Hindi Kośa, p. 1037.
21. *Raghuvaṁśa* - 9.44
22. *Raghuvaṁśa* - 9.41
23. *Kumārasambhava* - 3.30
24. *Kumārasambhava* - 8.40
25. *Kālidāsa Kośa* (Sures Chandra Banerji) - p. 13
26. *Raghuvaṁśa* - 9.32
27. *Mālavikāgnimitra* - 3.5
28. *Meghadūta* - 2.2
29. *Meghadūta* - 2.17
30. *Ṛtusaṁhāra* - 6.20, 33
31. *Kāmasūtra* - 4.1.36
32. *Abhijñānaśākuntala* - 7.2
33. *Śabdakalpadruma* - *mālā śabdaḥ*
34. *Meghadūta* - 2.14
35. *Kumārasambhava* - 5.80
36. *Raghuvaṁśa* - 6.23
37. *Raghuvaṁśa* - 6.23 quoted in Mallinātha-ṭīkā
38. *Vikramorvaśīya* - 4.35
39. *Caurapañcāśikā* - 1
40. *Ṛtusaṁhāra* - 3.6
41. *Subhāṣitaratnabhāṇḍāgāra*-Vṛkṣānyoktayaḥ-campakaḥ - 64, 65, 67, 70, 71, pp. 249-250.
42. *Kumārasambhava* - (Kale Edition), 3.32
43. *Śaṅgītadarpaṇa* -

    षड्जं वदति मयूरः पुनः स्वरमृषभं चातको ब्रूते।
    गान्धाराख्यं छागो निगदति च मध्यमं क्रौञ्चः।।
    गदति पञ्चममञ्चितवाक् पिको रटति धैवतमुन्मददर्दुरः।
    शृणि समाहतमस्तककुञ्जरो गदति नासिकया स्वरमन्तिमम्।। 170-171

44. *Kumārasambhava* - Mallinātha's commentary on 3.32 -
    चूताङ्कुराणामास्वादेन कषायकण्ठो रक्तकण्ठः। 'सुरभावपथे रक्ते कषायः' इति केशवः।
45. *Kumārasambhava* - 3.32, Notes, p. 62
46. *Kumārasambhava* - Mallinātha's commentary on 3.32

47. *Raghuvaṁśa* - 9.47
48. *Śiśupālavadha* - 6.8
49. *Pārvatīpariṇaya* -3.3
50. *Kumārasambhava* - 4.14
51. *Kumārasambhava* - 8.78
53. *Kumārasambhava* - Vallabhadeva's commentary on 8.78.
54. *Kumārasambhava* - 4.38
55. *Kumārasambhava* - 3.27
56. *Raghuvaṁśa* - 7.38
57. *Kumārasambhava* - 2.64
58. *Kumārasambhava* - 1.27
59. *Kālidāsa Kośa* - (Sures Chandra Banerji) - p. 9
60. *Kumārasambhava* - 1.55
61. *Kālikāpurāṇa* - Quoted in *Kumārasambhava* - 1.55, Notes, p. 250
62. *Raghuvaṁśa* - 4.74
63. *Kumārasambhava* - 3.43
64. *Raghuvaṁśa* - 4.57
65. *Kumārasambhava* - 3.62, 65
66. *Kumārasambhava* - 3.53
67. *Kumārasambhava* - 3.28
68. *Vālmīki Rāmāyaṇa* - 7.26.4-6

卐 卐 卐

MANGO BLOSSOM & MALE CUCKOO IN KĀLIDĀSA

(Abstract)

Sushma Kulshreshtha • Abha Kulshreshtha

Purā kavīnām gaṇanāprasaṅge kaniṣṭhikādhiṣṭhitakālidāsa.
Adyāpi tattulyakaverabhāvādanāmikā sārthavatī babhūva.

Kavikułaguru Kālidāsa, the global poet, excels all other Sanskrit poets in the description of flora and fauna. He is well versed in many sciences, *viz.*, Botany or Plant Science or the *Vṛkṣāyurveda,* Zoology or *Prāṇivijñāna,* Musicology or *Saṅgītaśāstra,* Erotics or *Kāmaśāstra* etc., etc. His erudition in many *vidyās* and *śāstras* knows no bounds. Kālidāsa has referred to more than 120 plants and trees in his seven world-famous works. In the same manner, he has made references to a number of animals and birds with their music and dance too.

The mango blossom blooms magnificently in almost all the works of Kālidāsa. Mango is *phalarāja* that blossoms in *Ṛturāja Vasanta,* the spring season. The male cuckoo, the *Puṁskokila,* and its sweet music is also found referred to in almost all the works of Kālidāsa.

In the present paper an attempt is made to show the expertise of Kālidāsa in flora and fauna with special reference to mango and male cuckoo and its music.

Mango, the king of Indian fruits, is *āmra, kāmaśara, cūta, rasāla, kāmavallabha, vāmaṅga, sahakāra, kīreṣṭa, mādhavadruma* and *mākanda*. All these synonyms of mango bear different shades of meaning that are brought to light by our poet in various references. All these references to mango blossom have been carefully dealt with at length in this paper. The medicinal (Āyurvedic) qualities and values of mango blossom and mango fruit have also been given. Similarly, the male cuckoo, a lovable bird, is *puṁskokila, parabhṛta, kokila* and *anyapuṣṭa* that is referred to at a number of places in different contexts. Male cuckoo is very famous for its sweet notes which are described by Kālidāsa with utmost beauty and grandeur. In this paper, all the references pertaining to the music of the male cuckoo have been discussed at length.

Among the numerous references to the mango and the male cuckoo, many bear testimony to the erudition of Kālidāsa in musicology and erotology too, besides the knowledge of plant science and zoology. Kālidāsa has very efficiently blent four *śāstras, viz.*, flora, fauna, musicology and erotology in the following verse of *Kumārasambhava :*

Cūtāṅkurāsvādakaṣāyakaṇṭhaḥ
puṁskokilo yanmadhuraṁ cukūja.
Manasvinīmānavighātadakṣaṁ
tadeva jātaṁ vacanaṁ smarasya.

The strain of sweet music that was warbled out by the male cuckoo, whose voice had become impassioned by his feasting on the mango-sprouts, became the mandate of Cupid competent to break down the pride of high-minded damsels.

Besides Kālidāsa, Paṇḍitarāja Jagannātha is another great poet who has referred to the mango blossom and the sweet notes of the male cuckoo at a number of places in his works. A comparative study of Kālidāsa and Paṇḍitarāja Jagannātha with reference to *Āmra* and *Puṁskokila* will bring to light many facets of flora and fauna. A beautiful *anyokti* of Paṇḍitarāja Jagannātha which refers to mango tree and the sweet *pañcama* note of the male cuckoo is presented herewith :

Rasāla! tava mādhurīprathitasatphalaṁ pakṣiṇaḥ
caranti nahi te yasaḥ prakaṭayanti kāṣṭhāṣu te.
Pikastu navapallavagrasanameva kurvan svaraiḥ
prakāśayati dīkṣu te mṛdulapañcamākhyairyaśaḥ.

Thus, after a careful study of all the references of the mango blossom and the male cuckoo, it can be said with affirmity that Dīpaśikhā Kālidāsa is a poet *par excellence* in flora and fauna too.

卐 卐 卐

Section III

FLORA IN SANSKRIT LITERATURE

संस्कृतसाहित्यामृतनिर्झरी

LĪLĀKAMALA IN SANSKRIT LITERATURE*

Sushma Kulshreshtha • Ila Ghosh

Kavikulaguru Kālidāsa has enriched Sanskrit literature with numerous novel motifs. One such motif is *Līlākamala* or the sportive lotus. He has used *Līlākamala* on four different occasions in his works. We get its first reference in *Meghadūta* where the young damsels of Alakāpurī decorating themselves with seasonal flowers, are having sportive lotuses in their hands :

हस्ते लीलाकमलमलके बालकुन्दानुविद्धं
नीता लोध्रप्रसवरजसा पाण्डुतामानने श्रीः।
चूडापाशे नवकुरबकं चारुकर्णे शिरीषं
सीमन्ते च त्वदुपगमजं यत्र नीपं वधूनाम्।।[1]

The second reference is found in *Raghuvaṁśa* in the description of *Indumatīsvayaṁvara*. Kings, aspirants of the maiden-princess Indumatī, were showing love-gestures of various kinds. A certain king began to turn round a pleasure lotus. He held its stem in his hands, which, with its revoling petals, warded off the bees and which formed a circle in its interior by means of pollens :

कश्चित्कराभ्यामुपगूढनालमालोलपत्राभिहतद्विरेफम्।
रजोभिरन्तः परिवेषबन्धिः लीलारविन्दं भ्रमयाञ्चकार।।[2]

The remaining two references adorn *Kumārasaṁbhava*. In the third canto, when Cupid, while looking at Śaṅkara in a *Samādhi* posture, his hand drooping through fear does not notice the bow and arrow dropping down from his hand, enters Pārvatī, reviving as it were, by the grace of her person, his prowess, almost deadened. She was keeping off, with a pleasure lotus, a bee hovering round her *bimba*-like lower lip, with its thirst excited by her fragrant breath :

सुगन्धिनिःश्वासविवृद्धतृष्णं बिम्बाधरासन्नचरं द्विरेफम्।
प्रतिक्षणं संभ्रमलोलदृष्टिर्लीलारविन्देन निवारयन्ती।।[3]

Again, in the sixth canto, the poet uses this motif. Pārvatī, who was by her father's side listening to her own marriage proposal, counts the petals of her sportive lotus with a downcast glance :

एवं वादिनि देवर्षौ पार्श्वे पितुरधोमुखी।
लीलाकमलपत्राणि गणयामास पार्वती।।[4]

We do not get the reference of *Līlākamala* in *Rāmāyaṇa, Mahābhārata* or the works of Bhāsa. In the context of *āhāryābhinaya,* although Bharatamuni refers to innumerable *alaṅkāras* worn by males and females, he makes no reference to *Līlākamala.* In later literary compositions of Bhāravi, Māgha and Subandhu too, it has not been referred to. In the *Kādambarī* of Bāṇabhaṭṭa, this motif has been used twice but in a less important context. In the first context, the reddishness of the palms of damsels is praiseworthier than that of the pleasure-lotus :

यत्र च कन्यकाजनस्य करतलान्येव लीलाकमलानि।[5]

In another context of joy-sports, Kādambarī strikes the forehead of Cāmaragrāhiṇī with *Līlākamala :*

कृतदुष्टस्मितां चामरग्राहिणीं विहस्य लीलाकमलेन शिरसि विघट्टयन्तीम्।।[6]

Śrīharṣa has used this motif, thrice in his *Naiṣadhīyacarita* but there too, that speciality or the subtlety of suggestiveness is not relished which is there in Kālidāsa.[7] In all these places, the prime intention of the poet is to establish the supremacy of the face or the palm of the heroine and not that of *Līlākamala.*

This grand motif of Kālidāsa has been elaborately used in Indian sculpture and painting too. Prof. B.S. Upadhyaya considers this to be the tendency of the Gupta Period. Damsels are shown holding a sportive lotus in their hands in the sculptures and paintings of the Gupta period.[8]

In the Gūjarīmahala museum of Gwalior, there is one *toraṇadvāra-paṭṭa* brought from Pavaya where are encarved two beautiful damsels, one of whom standing in front is holding in her hand a *sanālakamala.*

In Cave No. 1 at Ajanta, there is found a painting of a beautiful lady holding *sanālakamala* in her hand. The lotus flower is protruding low a little, in the same manner, her face too, that reminds us of Pārvatī, having downcast glances. This cave belongs to the 5th century.

This peculiar motif of literature, art and day-to-day life of people reached other neighbouring countries also. In the Sigaria caves of Sri Lanka (5th cent.), a painting of a nymph deserves mention. She is holding in her left hand, a half-blossomed lotus and two lotus-buds.

Now the question arises as to what is this *līlākamala.* We quote here the views of some scholars. According to Sir Monier Williams, *līlākamala* is a woman's toy-lotus.[9] In the opinion of Dr. Hira Lal Shukla, *līlākamala* is *vilāsanalina* or *krīḍāpadma* (sportive lotus). To imitate the behaviour of the lover, a lotus held in hand by a damsel is known as *līlākamala.*[10] Dr. B.S. Upadhyaya opines that *līlāravinda* denotes decoration of the contemporary Gupta period . . . Ladies having completed their decoration and about to leave their abodes, used to hold *līlāravinda.*[11] Acharya Hajariprasad Dwivedi also enumerates this under *alaṅkāras* or *maṇḍanas* of damsels.[12] But this motif, in the hands of Kālidāsa is not that limited. In order to know different shades of meaning of this motif and to reach the root of this *līlākamala,* we need a thorough study of the meanings of the *samastapada līlākamala* and also the meanings of the *vyastapadas līlā* and *kamala* both.

The conventional meaning of the *samastapada līlākamalam* is लीलार्थं लीलायै वा आधृतं कमलं लीलाकमलम्। The dictionary-meaning of *Līlā,* is *Keli, Vilāsa,*[13] *Krīḍā, Manorañjana,*[14] *Saundarya, Lāvaṇya, Lālitya, Strī-ceṣṭā* or *hāva* originated due to an erotic feeling.[15]

Līlā is a special technical term of *Nāṭyaśāstra, Kāmaśāstra* and *Kāvyaśāstra.* The definitions like इष्टजनस्यानुकृतिर्लीला ज्ञेया प्रयोगज्ञैः। and

प्रेम्णा जनस्य या चेष्टा याऽनुरागाधिक्येन वा।
क्रियतेऽनुकृतिः सेह लीलोक्ता मुनिसत्तमैः।।[16]

etc., reveal the following facts :

(i) Like *Vilāsa, Vicchitti, Vibhrama, Līlā* is one of the natural graces of women.[17]

(ii) *Līlā* is a love-gesture born of excessive and acute love.

(iii) Imitation of the loved one is *līlā.*

(iv) The purpose of *līlā* is *cittavinodana* (entertainment of mind).[18]

Barring the references of *līlākamala,* Kālidāsa has used that word *līlā* denoting the meaning of *hāva, bhāva, ceṣṭā, krīḍā, chavi, śobhā, cārutā* and in the occurrence of an act without any deliberate effort or knowledge; *e.g.,* लीलाचतुराम् (कुमार. I.47); लीलाखेलम् (रघु. IV.22); लीलास्मितम् (रघु. V.70); लीलागतिः (रघु. VII.7); लीलाञ्चित (कुमार. I.34); लीलागार (रघु. VIII.95); सलीलम् (रघु. VI.18); कन्दुकलीलया (कुमार. V.9) etc.

The etymology of *Līlā* is 'लियं लाति इति'. There are two roots in this word ली and ला. The meaning of 'ली' is *laya, śleṣaṇa, saṁśleṣaṇa,* embracing and absorption etc. The meaning of 'ला' is *ādāna* or *grahaṇa.* Thus, the formation of *Līlā* is लियं + ला + क + टाप्. Any such action, effort, stage, element, means, beauty, decoration, embellishment, adornment, emotion or gesture which leads one to attraction, mutual meeting, absorption, joy, merriment, bliss or *rasa,* is called *līlā.* For example, in *Kṛṣṇalīlā* and *Rāmalīlā,* the actions of Kṛṣṇa and Rāma are *Līlā* because they attract the mind and heart of people towards themselves, entertain them, recreate them and also delight them. In the presence of Rāma and Kṛṣṇa, the performance of their actions by their devotees or actors is also *līlā* because it includes an element of imitation.

The etymological meaning of *kamala,* 'कं जलमलंति भूषयति' (कम् + जल + अच्) denotes *kamala* as a beautifying element of water. *Kamala, padma* or lotus is one of the most beautiful flowers of our nation which is famous for its form, qualities, colours, fragrance, beauty and attraction. *Padma,* the peerless symbol of Indian wisdom, thought, philosophy, literature, arts, life, watery creation, *jīva* and *mukta puruṣa,* being associated in Hindu mythology with numerous gods and goddesses due to its purity and detachment from objects, has become their synonym too, *e.g.,* पद्मेशयः, पद्मनाभः (विष्णुः), पद्मासनः (ब्रह्मा), कमला, कमलालया, पद्मा (लक्ष्मी), कमलाकान्तः etc.

Haṭhayoga propounds the existence of eight *kamalas* in our body from *mūlādhāra* to *lalāṭa.* In literature, *kamala* and its associates like *patra, mṛṇāla, dala, bisasūtra* have become standards of comparison of the heroes and heroines or the symbol of their emotions; sometimes their embellishments and *kavisamaya* too. In painting and sculpture too, *padma* has been assigned its due place in varied forms in *kamalavallarī, kamalāsana, kamalākāra alaṅkṛta prabhāmaṇḍala* (Kālidāsa too refers to it 'छायामण्डललक्ष्येण पद्मा पद्मातपत्रेण)[19] etc. *Padmabandha* is a peculiar variety of poem-composition, *padmarāga* is a gem, *padma* is the *nidhi* of Kubera, *padma* is a number, *padminī* is a special type of *nāyikā, padmakośa* is a peculiar hand-gesture, *padmāsana* is a type of *yogāsana* and above these all is the magnificent motif *Līlākamala*.

While discussing the afore-quoted references, we come to know the following facts pertaining to *Līlākamala :*

(i) In Kālidāsa literature, two words for this motif have been used : *Līlākamala* and *Līlāravinda. Līlākamala* was red, whitish red or pink lotus. *Aravinda,* a synonym of *kamala,* also denoted red colour. The word लीलातामरस[20] used by poet Amaruka also indicates its reddishness. 'करतलान्येव लीलाकमलानि' mentioned by Bāṇabhaṭṭa also confirms its red colour. This red colour of lotus was suggestive of the love of *nāyaka-nāyikā* too.

(ii) *Līlākamala* was *sanālakamala* which was held in hand with *nāla.*[21]

(iii) These *kamalas* through their fragrance, attracted bees.[22]

(iv) *Līlāravinda* and *Līlākamala,* though appearing identical, denoted two different shades of meanings. *Aravinda* was a symbol of youth, amorous feelings and gestures, desire, longing and *vilāsa.* That is why Kālidāsa compares the body of Pārvatī, fully unfolded by fresh youth, with a lotus blooming under the rays of the sun :

उन्मीलितं तूलिकयेव चित्रं सूर्यांशुभिर्भिन्नमिवारविन्दम्।
बभूव तस्याश्चतुरस्रशोभि वपुर्विभक्तं नवयौवनेन।।[23]

Holding its stem in the hand and turning round the pleasure-lotus was a peculiar love-gesture of a king mentioned in *Indumatī-svayaṁvara.*[24] *Aravinda* arouses sensuality. According to Indian *Devaśātra, aravinda*[25] is the first arrow of *Pañcaśara Kāmadeva.* That is why *Līlāravinda* firstly adorns the hands of Pārvatī who is bubbling with fresh youth, beauty and charm.

Kamala symbolized *rūpa, varṇa, prabhā, rāga, ābhijātya, lāvaṇya, mādhurya, śrī, sampatti* and *saubhāgya.* The sign of *padma* in the hands of a female is considered auspicious according to *Sāmudrika Śāstra.*[26] Kālidāsa himself considers a hand auspicious which is like a lotus saying 'कुशेशयताम्रतलकरतल'[27] and जालग्रथिताङ्गुलिं · · · भिन्नमिवैकपङ्कजम्[28]. The *Śakunaśastra* (science of omens) declares the blossoming of lotuses, beholding lotus in dream and a pond adorned with lotus plants or blooming lotuses as extremely auspicious.

The eight *maṅgalas* encarved on the *toraṇa*-gate of Sanchi comprise lotus too. That is why the hand of Pārvatī, who succeeded in her resolve of practising severe penance to win Śiva, is adorned with a pleasure-lotus. Counting of petals of her sportive lotus by Pārvatī having a downcast look reveals her bashfulness befitting a damsel, grandeur of feminity and her supreme fortune and beauty to win over the love of her beloved Lord. Utilizing this motif of a pleasure-lotus in two different shades of *Llīlāravinda* and *līlākamala,* the great poet Kālidāsa with utmost efficiency has very effortlessly revealed the long sojourn of self-development of the *rūpagarvitā*

Pārvatī, her severest penance and austerities after knowing *satya* (truth), to achieve Śiva through *sundaratva* (beauty) and the transformation of a natural lotus into a glittering golden lotus. The charming maidens of Alakāpurī too hold *līlākamala* which is indicative of their beauty and fortune and not the *līlāravinda*.

(v) According to Kālidāsa, *līlāravinda* was used by males and females belonging to special class, while *līlākamala* was used by ladies only. Among his heroines, the poet has adorned Pārvatī alone with *līlākamala*. *Līlākamalas* are seen in the hands of the damsels of Alakā too. Pārvatī and the pretty maidens of Alakā, both are celestial beings. Defining various types of women on the basis of their nature, Kālidāsa describes *devaśīlā* damsels as 'गन्धपुष्परता हृद्या'.[29] *Kamala* is matchless among the fragrant flowers. Hence, the propriety of *līlākamala* in the hands of celestial damsel Pārvatī.

(vi) *Līlākamala* denoted union, good fortune and beauty, not the separation or misfortune. That is why, love-lorn Yakṣī is not holding *līlākamala*. Śrīharṣa also depicts Damayantī, giving up the pleasure-lotus, when she is in a state of separation.[30]

(vii) By joining *līlā* with *kamala,* Kālidāsa created a novel motif as *līlākamala* and contributed a significant arena to the convention of holding of a pleasure-lotus which was prevalent in the life of common people and also in painting and sculpture.

Now, we should try to find out the seed of our poet's novel creation. *Līlākamala* was his magnificent creation, no doubt, but *kamala* alone had been established as a symbol or peculiar motif in Indian philosophy, religion, thought and art long before Kālidāsa. According to Indian philosophy, this creation originates from water :

आपोमयाः सर्वरसाः सर्वमापोमयं जगत्।[31]

Therefore, this Earth is fancied in the form of a lotus in water.[32] In Bhāgavata religion, all the forms of Lord Viṣṇu, be it Vāsudeva, Pradyumna, Aniruddha, Saṅkarṣaṇa or Kṛṣṇa are shown with *padma* or *kamala* in their hands. This Creation is the *Līlā* of Viṣṇu or the fruit of his desire of creating. Therefore, the *padma* worn by Viṣṇu is *Līlāpadma* only. According to *Pādmasaṁhitā,* Vāsudeva holds *sarasija* for Creation, *cakra* for existence, *śaṅkha* for salvation and *gadā* for destrtuction :

स्थित्यै चक्रं सरसिजं दधानं सृष्टये पुनः।
मुक्तये पाञ्चजन्यं च गदां संहतये तथा।।[33]

This *padma* has been categorically referred to in famous works on architecture like *Aparājitapṛcchā* and *Rūpamaṇḍana* and in the *Purāṇas* too while describing *Viṣṇu-Pratimā-Lakṣaṇa*. According to *Viṣṇudharmottarapurāṇa,* Viṣṇu is holding that eternal *kamalanāla* in his fourth hand on which is seated Lord Brahmā on a blossomed lotus. The idol of Lord Viṣṇu in a Śeṣaśāyī form, found in Devagarh, also comprises a similar lotus. Kālidāsa himself has mentioned the shapes of Viṣṇu furnished with lotus.[34]

The second deity is Sūrya who is described and carved as being adorned with lotus flowers in his hands. It has been well indicated in *Bṛhatsaṁhitā*[35] and *Matsyapurāṇa* that in idols of Sūrya. He should be shown as seated on a chariot with a lotus in his hands :

रथस्थं कारयेद्देवं पद्महस्तं सुलोचनम्।[36]

A full-bloomed lotus is shown in the hand of Sūrya-idols found in Bodhagaya, Khandagiri and Mathura. The lotus is blossomed by the rays of the Sun. Sūrya, the abode of lustre is the symbol of Saccidānanda Brahma and lotus is the symbol of Jīva-hṛdaya. Hence, Sūrya and *kamala* are having long-existing relationship.

Under the influence of Mahāyāna school, a novel image of Bodhisattvas like Padmapāṇi Avalokiteśvara, Mañjuśrī and Vajrapāṇi was formed. In Cave No. 2 in Bāghakalā, Buddha is encarved with Bodhisattvas on both of his sides. On one side is shown Bodhisattva Padmapāṇi holding a lotus in his hand with its stalk. On his head, there is a diadem where too are encarved bloomed lotuses. On the other side is shown Bodhisattva Maitreya who is holding bunches of lotus flowers in his hands. In Caves Nos. 1 and 17, Bodhisattva Avalokiteśvara is shown holding in a very charming gesture a lotus-flower with its stalk in his right hand. In the sculpture of the Gupta period, the nectar-pitchers shown in the hands of Bodhisattvas do have the shapes of lotus-buds.

Among the goddesses, the relation of Lakṣmī with lotus is long-existing. In seals found from Harappa and Mohanjodaro in Indus civilization, a *devī* is shown in a standing posture, in between two lotus-stalks with buds originated from a round-shaped pond.[37] In the *Śrīsūkta* of *Ṛgveda,* Śrī and Lakṣmī appear as one and the same goddess adorned with a garland of lotus flowers round her neck.

On the *Vedikāstambha* of Bharahuta (2nd cent. B.C.) is encarved deity Sirima with his head surrounded with lotus-shaped lustrous halo. There was a lotus in his hand which is now in a shattered form.[38] Lakṣmī holding a lotus with its stalk is encarved in the ancient seals[39] found in Ujjayinī in the 2nd cent. B.C., on coins of the Śaka ruler Ages[40] and also on coins of Samudragupta, Kumaragupta and Skandagupta.[41]

Goddess Lakṣmī encarved on Lakṣmī-idols of the Śuṅga period and on clay-idols and engraved on stone-slabs of Bodhagaya and Khandagiri is also shown as *Kamalahastā*. There is a remarkable similarity in the description of beauty of goddess Lakṣmī in *Brahmavaivartapurāṇa* and of Pārvatī in *Kumārasambhava*. After the completion of full decoration, goddess Lakṣmī holds a lotus encircled by humming bees :

करेण पद्मं भ्रमरोपगीतं वैदूर्यनालं च शुभं गृहीत्वा।
स्वरूपमूढेषु सुरासुरेषु दृष्टिं ददौ चारु मनोऽभिरामा।।[42]

The idols of Umā and Gaurī are also adorned with a lotus in their hands.[43] *Aparājitapṛcchā* refers to five different epithets of Gaurī : Lalīyā, Līlā, Līlāṅgī, Lalitā and Līlāvatī. Amongst these, Līlā holds *padma* in her hand :

मृणालयुग्मं ललीया लीला पद्मं च पुस्तकम्।[44]

Although the work *Aparājitapṛcchā* belongs to the 13th century, yet the material collected here does prove the existence of some very ancient established tradition. Goddess Sāvitrī and Goddess Sarasvatī are also enjoined with *padma,* but the lotus worn by them is white-coloured. Dīpaśikhā Kālidāsa did adopt this special motif of lotus that was excessively prevalent in various branches of Indian philosophy and religion, not in the same form but in a novel and elegant form of pleasure-lotus or sportive lotus. He described it as '*Līlākamala*' and not as '*Līlāpadma*'. Although *padma* and *kamala* became synonyms in later period, there might have been some remarkable difference between the two initially.

In complete Vedic literature, the word *padma* is more abundantly used than *kamala.* The word *kamala* is used only once in *Atharvaveda* in a *Sūkta* entitled *Garbhadoṣanivāraṇa* seen by Ṛṣī Mātṛnāma. Probably, *kamala* used here denotes *garbhadvāra* or *garbhāśaya :*

यः कृणोति मृतवत्सामवतोकामिमां स्त्रियम्।
तमोषधे त्वं नाशयास्याः कमलमञ्जिवम्।।[45]

Padma being expressive of purity, piety and dissociation from worldly attachment is plentifully associated with Brahmā, Viṣṇu and Buddha.

Kamala expresses the feelings of this world as well as those of the other world too. The *Līlākamala* of Kālidāsa is a *sanālakamala* full of fragrant pollen. *Sanālakamala* is the symbol of that instant born infant that has come out of his mother's womb, yet is joined with the *garbha* with a *nāla*. Indirectly, this *sanālakamala* symbolizes that Brāhmī creation which is originated from *Padmanābha* Viṣṇu. Lakṣmī is His Līlāsahacarī, his beloved consort. Therefore, She too holds a lotus in her hand. Umā or Pārvatī is the half form of Ardhanārīśvara Śiva. Hence, Her hands are also embellished with *kamala* which is a symbol of *sṛṣṭi-līlā*.

In Indian tradition, a king is considered to be an *aṁśa* of deities like Viṣṇu and of Lokapālas like Indra.[46] A female, particularly a bride, is considered as Likṣmī.[47]

Thus, the *Līlāravinda* or *Līlākamala* of poet Kālidāsa is the *laukika* form of *kamala* associated with different gods and goddesses.

Through his brilliant imagery, poet Kālidāsa pre-adding *līlā* to *kamala,* did attach that meaning of the word *līlā* that had been established as a love-gesture by that time, that was expressive of excessive love of the hero and the heroine and which included the element of imitation too. The *ādāna* of *liya* or the etymological meaning of *līlā* was also included in it. Hence, this *Līlākamala* or sportive lotus plays a grand role in the mutual attraction, union, oneness and absorption of Śiva and Pārvatī.

This *Līlākamala,* fancied and perceived by Kālidāsa was not merely a lotus worn for pleasure, but it was a symbol or imitation of Viṣṇu-*kamala* or Śrī-*kamala* too. This *Līlākamala* was not merely a decoration enhancing the beauty of female palms or a part of the *Ṣoḍaśa Śṛṅgāra,*[48] but was a live symbol and a special motif suggestive and expressive of that long-existing attraction of males and females prevalent right from the moment of creation of this world, their longing, their amorous sports, their beauty, their brilliance, their well-being and their piety of *antaḥkaraṇa*. In later times, this grand motif of Kālidāsa was forgotten and remained merely a toy or an ornament.

REFERENCES & NOTES

* This paper was originally written in Hindi by Dr. Ila Ghosh and has been translated and elaborated in English by Prof. Sushma Kulshreshtha.

1. *Meghadūta* (Kale Ed.) - *Uttaramegha*. 2
2. *Raghuvaṁśa* (Nandargikar Ed.) - VI. 13
3. *Kumārasambhava* (Kale Ed.) - III. 56
4. *Kumārasambhava* - VI. 84
5. *Kādambarī* - *Kanyāntaḥpuravarṇanā*, p. 528
6. *Kādambarī* - *Kādambarīvarṇanā*, p. 543
7. *Naiṣadhīyacarita*—

   (i) विलेखितुं भीमभुवो लिपीषु सख्याऽतिविख्यातिभृतापि यत्र।
   अशाकि लीलाकमलं न पाणिरपारि कर्णोत्पलमक्षि नैव।। VI.64

   (ii) अपास्तपाथोरुहि शायितुं करे करोषि लीलाकमलं किमाननम्।
   तनोषि हारं कियदस्तुणः स्ववैरदोषनिर्वासितभूषणे हृदि।। IX. 105

   (iii) करस्थताम्बूलजिघत्सुरेकिका विलोकनैकाग्रविलोचनोत्पला।
   मुखे निचिक्षेप मुखद्विराजतारुषेव लीलाकमलं विलासिनी।। XV.77
8. *Kālidāsa ke Subhāṣita* - p. 163
9. *A Sanskrit-English Dictionary* - p. 903
10. *Kālidāsakoṣa* - p. 325
11. *Kālidāsa ke Subhāṣita* - p. 163
12. *Kālidāsa kī Lālityayojanā* - p. 143
13. *Śabdakalpadruma* - Part IV., p. 228
14. *Amarakoṣa* - *Ist Kāṇḍa, Nāṭyādivarga*, 32
    द्रवकेलिपरिहासः क्रीडा लीला च नर्म च।
15. *Amarakoṣa* - 31- हेलालीलेत्यमी भावाः क्रियाः शृङ्गारभावजाः।
16. *Nāṭyaśāstra* - XXIV.14; *Kāmaśāstra*
17. *Nāṭyaśāstra* - XXIV.12
18. *Ujjvalanīlamaṇi* -
    अप्राप्तवल्लभसमागमनागिकाग़ः
    सख्याः पुरोऽत्र निजचित्तविनोदबुद्ध्या।
    आलापवेशगतिहास्यविलोकनाद्यैः
    प्राणेश्वरानुकृतिमाकथयन्ति लीलाम्।।
19. *Raghuvaṁśa* - IV.5
20. *Amaruśataka* - 60
    लाक्षालक्ष्मललाटपट्टमभितः केयूरमुद्रा गले
    वक्त्रे कज्जलकालिमा नयनयोस्ताम्बूलरागोऽपरः।
    दृष्ट्वा कोपविधायि मण्डनमिदं प्रातश्चिरं प्रेयसो
    लीलातामरसोदरे मृगदृशः श्वासाः समाप्तिं गताः।।
21. *Raghuvaṁśa* -
    कश्चित्कराभ्यामुपगूढनालम्। VI.13
22. *Raghuvaṁśa* - VI.13
23. *Kumārasambhava* - I. 32

24. *Raghuvaṁśa* -
    तां प्रत्यभिव्यक्तमनोरथानां महीपतीनां प्रणयाग्रदूत्यः।
    प्रवालचेष्टा इव पादपानां शृङ्गारचेष्टा विविधा बभूवुः।। VI.12
25. अरविन्दमशोकं च चूतञ्च नवमल्लिका।
    नीलोत्पलञ्च पञ्चैते पञ्चबाणस्य सायकाः।।
26. *Bṛhatsaṁhitā* - LXX.10
    मत्स्यस्वस्तिकवेदिकाव्यञ्जनकैः शङ्खातपत्राम्बुजैः।
    पादे पाणितलेऽथवा युवतयो गच्छन्ति राज्ञीपदम्।।
27. *Raghuvaṁśa* - VI.18
28. *Abhijñānaśākuntala* - VII.16
29. *Nāṭyaśāstra* - XXIV.102
30. *Naiṣadhīyacarita* - IX. 105
31. *Mahābhārata* - I.179.18
32. *Śatapatha Brāhmaṇa* - VII.4.1.8
33. *Pādmasaṁhitā* - II.14
34. *Raghuvaṁśa* - X.60
35. *Bṛhatsaṁhitā* - LVIII.47
    बिभ्राणः स्वकररुहे पाणिभ्यां पङ्कजे मुकुटधारी।
    कुण्डलभूषितवदनः प्रलम्बहारो विहङ्गवृतः।।
36. *Matsyapurāṇa* - 260
37. Manke, *Further Excavation* - Plate 94, No. 430.
38. C. Sivaram Murti, *A Guide to the Archaeological Galaries of the Indian Museum* - Plate D.
39. Winsent Smith, *Catalogue of the Coins in the Indian Museum* - Part I, p. 153, Plate 19.
40. R.B. White Head, *Catalogue of Coins in the Punjab Museum,* Lahore.
41. Rakhaldas Bannerjee, *Prācīna Mudrā,* p. 158. *Alen Catalogue* - Plate 2, No. 3
42. *Brahmavaivartapurāṇa* - I. 41
43. *Aparājitapṛcchā* - 22.8, 10
44. *Aparājitapṛcchā* - 222.24
45. *Atharvaveda* - VIII. 6.9
46. *Manusmṛti* - VII 4-5; *Raghuvaṁśa* - III.11
47. *Śatapathabrāhmaṇa* - XIII.2.6.7; *Mālavikāgnimitra* - V.6; *Saundarananda* - VI.26
48. Bhagavat Sharan Upadhyaya; *Kālidāsa ke Subhāṣita* - Quoted on p. 175 :This became a part of the sixteen *śṛṅgāras* in poets of *Rītikāla :*
    अंग शुचि मंजन वसन माँग महावर केश
    तिलक भाल तिल चिबुक में भूषण मेंहदी वेश।
    मिस्सी काजल अगरजा बीरी और सुगन्ध
    पुष्पकली युत होय कर तब नवसप्त निबन्ध।।

卐 卐 卐

EROTICISM AND FLOWER BLOSSOMS IN GĀTHĀSAPTAŚATĪ

Sushma Kulshreshtha • Abha Kulshreshtha

Gāthāsaptaśatī (or *Gāhāsattasaī*) is a marvellous anthological treatise composed and compiled in Mahārāṣṭrī Prakrit by King Hāla Sātavāhana who reigned sometime during the first half of the first century A.D. This is a *Koṣakāvya* comprising 700 *Gāthās* divided into seven *Śatakas*. King Hāla has himself stated that he has composed, rather compiled only seven hundred *gāthās* adorned with figures of speech out of ten millions of such verses[1]. *Gāthā* is a verse which is composed in Prakrit and in a metre which resembles Sanskrit *Āryā*.

There are four human goals, *viz., dharma* (religion or religious duties), *artha* (wealth and property), *Kāma* (enjoyment and pleasure) and *mokṣa* (emancipation or liberation from worldly attachments) prescribed by our *ṛṣis* for the proper regulation of life. The *gāthās* are based on all these four but are mainly centred upon erotic sentiment. It may be observed that the village women, young or adult, form, as it were, the *nāyikās* in this type of natural erotic sentiment and the village men, young or grown up, the *nāyakas*. In the Indian villages flourishing in agriculture, the most pleasurable and joyous life of the rustic people and their wives, the farmers and their wives, sons and daughters of the village headman, other ordinary householders and their spouses and their sons and daughters are elegantly depicted in these Prakrit *gāthās*.

It can be said with affirmity that the human character and the proclivities of human mind remain the same in every clime and in all times. It may be observed that the *vibhāva* (ensuant feeling), *anubhāva* (manifestation of feeling), *vyabhicāribhāva* (accessory feeling), *sambhoga* (love in association or union), *vipralambha* (love in separation), *cauryarata* and *asatīrata* (illicit and unbridled type of love)—all these belonging to the *sthāyibhāva rati* (and also to other *sthāyibhāvas)* agitate, everywhere and always, the human mind in the same manner. *Śāstras* and *vidyās* are created very often to instruct people to control such agitations and excitements of mind. It appears that King Hāla has compiled this *Gāthāsaptaśatī*-a collection of erotic verses with the prime purpose of imparting instruction to all types of people to behave appropriately in all situations.

Gāthāsaptaśatī provides a good picture of the society as existing in ancient India specially in the Deccan. In the *gāthās* of this treatise are painted word-pictures which bring forth different moods and situations of the erotic sentiment. Herein, the connoisseur will find a beautiful description of a love-lorn lady in iresome love, a love-struck lady, a wife keeping her husband under control, a wife separated due to quarrel, a wife whose husband is living abroad, a lady in separation from her beloved, a lady approaching a rendezvous, an unchaste lady, a beloved darling, a lascivious lady, a daughter and a daughter-in-law etc. etc. Similarly, we find *gāthās* that describe the mental state of different types of males who are lustful, libidinous, attached to their wives, attracted towards other women, are of hollow or weak love, are of deceitful nature, are guilty of adultery etc.

Rural life and the erotic life of ancient Indian people is depicted in the *Gāthāsaptaśatī* picturesquely. The composers of these *gāthās* have referred to many plants, trees, flowers, birds and animals in different contexts. At least twentytwo varieties of flowers are described in the *Gāthāsaptaśatī*. They with their botanical names are as follows :

1. Utpala (Nymphaea Stellata Willd) Lotus
2. Kadamba (Anthocephalus Indicus A. Rich)
3. Kandoṭa-Blue Lotus
4. Kamala (Nelumbo Nucifera Garten) Lotus
5. Kusumbha (Corthamus Tinctorius Linn) Safflower
6. Kāśa (Saccharum Sponatum Linn)
7. Kunda (Jasminum Pubecenes Willd)
8. Kuruvaka (Rhododendron Arborium)
9. Kuvalaya (Nymphaea) Water Lily
10. Tāmarasa-Red Lotus
11. Nalinī-A Variety of Lotus
12. Nīlotpala-Blue Lotus
13. Palāśa [Buttea Monosparma (Linn) Kuntz]
14. Pāṭala or Pāṭalā (Stereospermus Suoveolens)
15. Puṇḍarīka-White Lotus
16. Bakula (Mimusops Elengi Linn)
17. Madhūka (Madhuea Indica J.F.)
18. Maruvaka
19. Mālatī (Jasminum Gradiflorum Linn)
20. Śirīṣa (Albizia Lebbeck Benth)
21. Śephālikā (Vitex Trifolia Linn)
22. Saptalā (Navamālikā) (Jasminum Arborescens Roxb)

These flowers are mentioned in the *Gāthāsaptaśatī* on different occasions and with different purposes too. Sometimes they are used to form simile or metaphor. Sometimes they are mentioned to bring forth a particular state of mind of a particular person. Sometimes they are described in the form of imparting some instruction to a person through *anyāpadeśa*. In the present paper, an attempt has been made to show the expertise of the poets of *Gāthāsaptaśatī* who are well-versed in different *Śāstras,* including plant science and eroticism too. In almost all the *gāthās* where a flower, a plant or a tree is described, there is some delightful and enjoyable erotic state also to be found. A brief study of the twelve flowers is presented herewith, citing relevant *gāthās* with critical comments.

1. KADAMBA (Anthocephalus Indicus A. Rich)

Examples :

(1) अच्छीइँ ता थइस्सं दोहिँ वि हत्थेहिँ वि तस्सिं दिट्ठे।
अङ्गं कलम्बकुसुमं व पुलइअं कहँ णु ढक्किस्सं।। णरसीहस्स।
(अक्षिणी तावत्स्थगयिष्यामि द्वाभ्यामपि हस्ताभ्यां तस्मिन्दृष्टे।
अङ्गं कदम्बकुसुममिव पुलकितं कथं नु च्छादयिष्यामि।। नरसिंहस्य।)[2]

Context : *Nāyikā* speaks to her female friend who is admonishing her to observe *māna* towards *Nāyaka*.

He, the beloved, having been glanced at by me, I may possibly cover up my eyes with my hands. But, how shall I cover up my whole body which is horripilated, like a *kadamba* flower. This is a beautiful *gāthā* which describes the excessive love of a *nāyikā* towards her beloved. She cannot conceal her love as it is revealed through the horripilation on her body at the lovely sight of her *nāyaka*. Kavikulaguru Kālidāsa also describes *Kadambaromāñca* thus : *aṅgaib sphuradḥ-ālakadambakalpaiḥ.*[3]

(2) गन्धं अग्घाअन्तअ पक्ककलम्बाणँ वाहभरिअच्छ।
आससु पहिअजुआणअ घरिणिमुहं मा ण पेच्छिहिसि।।
(गन्धमाजिघ्रन्पक्वकदम्बानां बाष्पभृताक्ष।
आश्वसिहि पथिकयुवन् गृहिणीमुखं मा न प्रेक्षिष्यसे।।)[4]

Context : Some experienced person is consoling a young traveller whose eyes are filled with tears as he presumes that his wife might have died due to the unbearable pangs of separation in the rainy season.

O travelling young chap with your eyes filled with tears due to smelling the odour of full-blown (ripe) *Kadamba* flowers! cheer up, it cannot be that you will not ever have the chance of seeing the face of your beloved wife. The fragrance of the ripe *Kadamba* indicates the long existence of the rainy season. Hence, the worry of the young traveller.

(3) पप्फुल्लघणकलम्बा णिद्धोअसिलाअला मुइअमोरा।
पसरन्तोज्झरमुहला ओसाहन्ते गिरिग्गामा।।
(प्रोत्फुल्लघनकदम्बा निर्धौतशिलातला मुदितमयूराः।
प्रसरन्निर्झरमुखरा उत्साहयन्ति गिरिग्रामाः।।)[5]

Context : Inspiration for love-pleasures in the rainy season.

The mountain villages encourage people for love-sports as they are adorned with dense clusters of *Kadamba* trees glittering with blossoming flowers, have stone-slabs washed by waters, have peacocks in a pleasant mood and have resounding fountains. This *gāthā,* very beautifully describes the *uddīpana,* the *śilāśayana,* the merrimaking in viewing the peacock-dances and also the *maṇita* which is reflected in the resounding fountains.

2. KANDOṬA (NĪLOTPALA) BLUE LOTUS

(4) सरए सरम्मि पहिआ जलाइँ कन्दोट्टसुरहिगन्धाइं।
धवलच्छाइँ सअण्हा पिअन्ति दइआणँ व मुहाइं।
(शरदि सरसि पथिका जलानि कन्दोट (नीलोत्पल) सुरभिगन्धीनि।
धवलाच्छानि सतृष्णाः पिबन्ति दयितानामिव मुखानि।।)[6]

Context : Information of change in the rendezvous to a *nāyikā* by a female friend.

In autumn thirsty travellers drink the white and clear waters of the lake, sweet perfuming due to the presence of the blue lotuses as if they kiss the faces of their beloved darlings.

In autumn, travellers start touring. As soon as they behold the blue lotuses, they at once are engrossed in the memory of the beautiful faces of their darlings. Hence, they drink the sweet-scented waters of the lake presuming as if they are caressing and kissing the mouth of their beloveds. This verse indicates that now rendezvous cannot be fixed near the lake as there is a heavy movement of travellers. This *gāthā* refers to the art of kissing also.

3. KAMALA (Nelumbo Nucifera Garten) LOTUS

(5) कमलं मुअन्त महुअर पिक्ककइत्थाणँ गन्धलोहेण।
आलेक्खलड्डुअं पामरो व्व छिविऊण जाणिहिसि।।
(कमलं मुञ्चन्मधुकर! पक्वकपित्थानां गन्धलोभेन।
आलेख्यलड्डुकं पामर इव स्पृष्ट्वा ज्ञास्यसि।।)[7]

Context : Someone admonishes through *anyāpadeśa* a *nāyaka* who has abandoned a *nāyikā* adorned with virtues and is infatuated towards another who is devoid of good qualities.

O bee who leaves the lotus flower on account of your attraction for the smell of a ripe wood apple (*kapittha* fruit)! you will know by your touch how hard they are just as a blockhead deceives himself by touching *laḍḍū* (sweet-meat) painted in a picture.

The idea is that an idiot does not know the difference between a delicate flower *kamala* and a hard fruit *kapittha*. Similarly, a lack-brain *nāyaka* described above is unable to differentiate between a *nāyikā* who is embellished with virtuous graces and the other *nāyikā* who lacks them.

4. KUSUMBHA (Carthamus Tinctorius Linn) Safflower

(6) सहिआहिँ भण्णमाणा थणए लग्गं कुसुम्भपुप्फं त्ति।
मुद्धबहुआ हसिज्जइ पप्फोडन्ती णहवआइं।। व (वा) लाइच्चस्स।
(सखीभिर्भण्यमाना स्तने लग्नं कुसुम्भपुष्पमिति।
मुग्धवधूर्हस्यते प्रस्फोटयन्ती नखपदानि।। बालादित्यस्य)।।[8]

Context : Description of an innocent *mugdhā nāyikā*.

Having been asked by her female friends as to whether any saffron-flower had stuck to her breast, the ignorant newly-wed lady was laughed at by them when she endeavoured in vain to wipe away the nail-marks of her lover. This *gāthā* refers to the art of nail-marks.

5. TĀMARASA-RED LOTUS

(7) जई सो ण वल्लहो व्विअ गोत्तग्गहणेण तस्स सहि कीस।
होइ मुहं ते रविअरफंसव्विसदं व तामरसम्।। सुसीलस्स।
(यदि स न वल्लभ एव गोत्रग्रहणेण तस्य सखि किमिति।
भवति मुखं तव रविकरस्पर्शविशद (विकसित) मिव तामरसम्।।
सुशीलस्य।)[9]

Context : A female friend speaks to a *nāyikā* who is concealing her love towards a *nāyaka*.

O friend! if he is not dear to you, how is it that your face assumes similarity to a lotus opened by the touch of the sun's rays as soon as his name is referred to by anybody.

The beautiful and cheerful face of a damsel is often compared to a lotus flower.

6. NALINĪ-A VARIETY OF LOTUS

(8) *Gāthāsaptaśatī* - 7.19

Please see its elaboration under title SAPTALĀ.

7. PALĀŚA (Buttea Monosparma (Linn) Kuntz)

(9) कीरमुहसच्छहेहिं रेहइ वसुहा पलासकुसुमेहिं।
बुद्धस्स चलणवन्दणपडिएहिँ व भिक्सुसंघेहिं।।
(कीरमुखसदृक्षै राजते वसुधा पलाशकुसुमैः।
बुद्धस्य चरणवन्दनपतितैरिव भिक्षुसंघैः।।)[10]

Context : *Nāyikā's* words to her beloved who is ready to proceed on a long tour and she wants to stop him.

The earth appears magnificent with the red flowers of the *Palāśa* trees that resemble the beats of the parrots as if they were the congregated monks fallen, for worship, at the feet of the Buddha.

By describing the beautiful red *Palāśa* flowers which are adorning the earth, the *nāyikā* draws a picture of the vernal season and hence, wishes to stop the journey of her beloved. Secondly, by comparing the *Palāśa* flowers with the congregation of Buddhist monks, she indicates inauspicious omen also. The appearance of a *Sanyāsin* at the time of the commencement of journey is considered inauspicious. 'By comparing the fresh *Palāśa* blossoms with Buddhist monks, the poet has opened a novel arena in the history of simile'—is the view of Dr. Jagannatha Pathak.[11]

8. PĀṬALA OR PĀṬALĀ (Stereospermus Suoveolens)

(10) रन्धणकम्मणिउणिए मा जूरसु रत्तपाडलसुअन्धं।
मुहमारुअं पिअन्तो धूमाइ सिही ण पज्जलइ।। भीमसामिणो।
(रन्धनकर्मनिपुणिके मा क्रुध्यस्व रक्तपाटलसुगन्धम्।
मुखमारुतं पिबन्धूमायते शिखी न प्रज्वलति।। भीमस्वामिनः।)[12]

Context : A lascivious person expresses his libido towards his sweetheart by citing the example of fire.

O (lady) expert in the art of cooking! do not feel depressed, the fire in your oven smokes only, but does not blaze and it does so in order to inhale the breath of your mouth that is so odorous as the red *Pāṭala* flowers. This *gāthā* describes the fragrance of the mouth-breath of a *nāyikā* which is like that of sweet-smelling *Pāṭala*-blossoms. This *gāthā* has been quoted by Bhojarāja in his *Sarasvatīkanṭ hābharaṇa* as an illustration of *gandhotpannā vaiṣayikī rati*.[13]

(11) *Gāthāsaptaśatī*—7.19

Please see its elaboration under title SAPTALĀ.

9. MADHŪKA (Madhuea Indica J.F.)

(12) अग्घाइ छिवइ चुम्बइ ठेवइ हिअअम्मि जणिअरोमञ्चो।
जाआकवोलसरिसं पेच्छह पहिओ महुअपुप्फं।।
(आजिघ्रति स्पृशति चुम्बति स्थापयति हृदये जनितरोमाञ्चः।
जायाकपोलसदृशं पश्यत पथिको मधूकपुष्पम्।।)[14]

Context : This verse brings forth the fact that a person loves anything which resembles any limb of his or her beloved.

Look here! the traveller, with his hair standing on end, smells, caresses, kisses and puts on his chest the *Madhūka* flower which resembles the cheek of his darling wife. The *gāthā* refers to the art of kissing too.

10. MĀLATĪ (Jasminum Grandiflorum Linn)

(13) *Gāthāsaptaśatī*—7.19

Please see its elaboration under title SAPTALĀ.

11. ŚEPHĀLIKĀ (Vitex Trifolia Linn)

(14) सुप्पउ तइओ वि गओ जामोत्ति सहीओ कीस मं भणह।
सेहालिआणँ गन्धो ण देइ सोत्तुं सुअह तुम्हे।। सिरिसत्तिस्स।
(सुप्यतां तृतीयोऽपि गतो याम इति सख्यः किमिति मां भणथ।
शेफालिकानां गन्धो न ददाति स्वप्तुं स्वपित यूयम्।। श्रीशक्तेः।)[15]

Context : Some *Virahotkanṭhitā nāyikā's* reply to her female friends on the non-arrival of her beloved.

O friends! why do you direct me thus—"Go to sleep, even the third watch of the night is already over." The odour of the *Śephālikā* flowers, disturbs my sleep. Therefore, please you all go to sleep.

Endearingly waiting for her beloved, a *nāyikā* was awake till the third watch of the night was already past. She was unable to sleep as the sweet smelling *Śephālikā* flowers began blossoming after midnight. The fragrance of the *Śephālikā* blossoms was so madenning that she longed only for the early arrival of her beloved. A similar verse is found in *Sāhityadarpaṇa* which is composed by Viśvanātha himself :

शेफालिकां विदलितामवलोक्य तन्वी
प्राणान् कथञ्चिदपि धारयितुं प्रभूता।
आकर्ण्य सम्प्रति रुतं चरणायुधानां
किं वा भविष्यति न वेद्मि तपस्विनी सा।।[16]

In this verse is described the *Maraṇāsanna* state of a *nāyikā*.

12. SAPTALĀ (NAVAMĀLIKĀ) (Jasminum Arborescens Roxb)

(15) णलिणीसु भमसि परिमलसि सत्तलं मालइं पि णो मुअसि।
तरलत्तणं तुइ अहो महुअर जइ पाडला हरइ।।
(नलिनीषु भ्रमसि परिमृद्नासि सप्तलां मालतीमपि नो मुञ्चसि।
तरलत्वं तवाहो मधुकर यदि पाटला हरति।।)[17]

Context : A female messenger showers words of *Upālambha* through *anyāpadeśa* on a wavering *nāyaka*.

O bee! you hover near the lotus flowers, press the *Saptalā* or *Navamālikā* flowers and do not let the *Mālatī* flowers alone. I do not know if the *Pāṭalā* flower will remove your wavering in love. A bee hovers round the lotuses, presses the *Navamālikā* and sips the *Mālatī* till it finally reaches the *Pātalā* or the *Alipriyā* flower. Similarly, the female messenger addresses a shaky lover thus-you hover round a *nāyikā,* you press some other one and you do not let alone even another one. Your unsteadiness in love will meet an end when you would come into contact of my friend. A wavering lover is often compared to a bee or a *Madhukara.*

Thus, we find that the composers of *Gāthāsaptaśatī* were adept in many *śāstras* and *vidyās,* including plant science and erotology. They were well-acquainted with minutest details of different flowers and well-versed in minutest intricacies of the erotic sentiment.

REFERENCES & NOTES

1. *Gāthāsaptaśatī* - (Ed. Dr. Jagannath Pathak), 1.3
2. *Gāthāsaptaśatī* - 4.14
3. *Kumārasambhava* - 3.68
4. *Gāthāsaptaśatī* - 6.65
5. *Gāthāsaptaśatī* - 7.36
6. *Gāthāsaptaśatī* - 7.22
7. *Gāthāsaptaśatī* - 7.41
8. *Gāthāsaptaśatī* - 2.45
9. *Gāthāsaptaśatī* - 4.43
10. *Gāthāsaptaśatī* - 4.8
11. *Gāthāsaptaśatī* - p. 179
12. *Gāthāsaptaśatī* - 1.14
13. *Sarasvatīkaṇṭhābharaṇa*-5.89
14. *Gāthāsaptaśatī* - 7.39
15. *Gāthāsaptaśatī* - 5.12
16. *Sāhityadarpaṇa* (Ed. Dr. Satyavrat Singh) - p. 236.
17. *Gāthāsaptaśatī* - 7.19

卐 卐 卐

CONTRIBUTION OF PT. JAGANNĀTHA MIŚRA TO RĀGA-ICONIFICATION IN RASAKALPADRUMA

(WITH SPECIAL REFERENCE TO FLORA)

Sushma Kulshreshtha • Jagdish Sahai Kulshreshtha

Pt. Jagannātha Miśra flourished in Orissa in the 18th century (1725-1775 A.D.). His encyclopaedic work *Rasakalpadruma,* a voluminous compilation on 'Rasa' deals primarily with everything pertaining to *Rasa* as interpreted in works on rhetorics and erotrics and secondarily with many topics related to other *Śāstras viz.*, 64 arts, musicology etc. A number of great musicologists have adorned Orissa with their remarkable treatises on musicology. Some of them are Gajapati Nārāyaṇa Deva (or Puruṣottama Miśra, according to some) who wrote *Saṅgītanārāyaṇa,* Harichandana, who composed *Saṅgītamuktāvalī* and Kṛṣṇadāsa who authored *Gītaprakāśa*. Pt. Jagannātha Miśra has quoted many times from these works and from other treatises too on musicology *viz., Saṅgītasāra* of Harināyaka, *Saṅgītaratnamāla* of Mammaṭācārya and others.

Pt. Jagannātha Miśra deals with musicology in the 6th Pallava and 5th Dala of *Rasakalpadruma.*[1] He defines the three-fold music thus :

गीतं वाद्यं च नृत्यं च त्रयं सङ्गीतमुच्यते।
गीतवाद्ये उभे एव सङ्गीतमिति केचन;
तत्तिर्यङ्नरदेवादिमनोहारि प्रकीर्तितम्।।[2]

Music is eternal bliss. It delights everyone alike, be a human being, a divine being, a bird or an animal. The musical rāgas fill with utmost pleasure the hearts of all the creatures residing in the three worlds :

यैस्तु चेतांसि रज्यन्ते जगत्त्रितयवासिनाम्।
ते रागा इति कथ्यन्ते मुनिभिर्भरतादिभिः।।[3]

According to Jagannātha Miśra, the number of rāgas is sixteen thousand because sixteen thousand gopīs presented their compositions in these rāgas before their beloved Lord Kṛṣṇa. Among these, thirtysix *rāgas* and *rāgaṇīs* are popular :

गोपीभिर्गीतमारब्धमेकैकं कृष्णसन्निधौ।
तेन जातानि रागाणां सहस्राणि तु षोडश।।
एषु रागेषु षट्त्रिंशद्रागा जगति विश्रुताः।
सन्ति मेरोश्चतुर्दिक्षु सर्वे तेऽपीति केचन।।[4]

There are different ways of classifying *rāgas* in Indian Music. There developed a novel way of classifying *rāgas,* namely the gender-classification. *Rāgamālā* (1576 A.D.) and *Nartananirṇaya*

(16th cent.) of Puṇḍarīka Viṭṭhal of Karnataka present the first gender-classification of *rāgas* (one from the mouth of Girijā and one from each of the five faces of Śiva), each of which has consorts and sons.[5] Jagannātha Miśra also presents gender-classification of *rāgas* enumerating six *rāgas* and their thirty *rāgiṇīs*. He presents three different sets of views regarding six *rāgas* and their thirty *rāgiṇīs* alongwith their names.[6] His first gender-classification of *rāgas* is as follows :

रागाः षडेव तु प्रोक्ता रागिण्यस्त्रिंशदेव हि।
भैरवोऽथ वसन्तश्च रागो मालवकौशिकः।।
श्रीरागो मेघरागश्च नटनारायणस्तथा।
एते पुमांसः षड्रागाः क्रमात्तद्रागिणीं वदेत्।।
भैरवी कैशिकी चैव भाषा वेलावली तथा।
वङ्गाली चेति रागिण्यो भैरवस्यैव वल्लभाः।।
गौरी गुण्डकिरी चैव वराडी च क्षमावती।
कार्णाटी चेति रागिण्यः प्रिया मालवकौशिकी।।
गान्धारी देवगान्धारी मालवश्रीश्च शावरी।
रामकिर्यपि रागिण्यः श्रीरागस्य प्रिया इमाः।।
लुलिता मालशी गौरी नाटी देवकिरी तथा।
मेघरागस्य रागिण्यो भवन्तीमाः सुदुर्लभाः।
तारामणिस्तथाभीरी कामोदी गुज्जरी तथा।
ककुभा चेति रागिण्यो नटनारायणप्रियाः।।[7]

Pt. Jagannātha Miśra describes the *phala* of this gender classification :

रागं चेदालपेत्पूर्वं तत्पत्नीं तदनन्तरम्।
अन्यपत्नी न गातव्या नृपाज्ञायां न दूषणम्।।[8]

We find an iconographic description of *rāgas* or, in other words, beautiful word pictures of *rāgas* and their *rāgiṇīs* in the works on music. In his *Rāgavibodha,* Somanātha (1609 A.D.) explicitly states that a *rāga* possesses a dual form; (i) *nādatma,* full of *dhvani* (sound carrying implied meaning) and constituted of musical notes, *Ṣaḍja* etc. and (ii) *devamaya,* having a deific form :

सुस्वरवर्णविशेषं रूपं रागस्य बोधकं द्वेधा।
नादात्मं च देवमयं तत्क्रमतोऽनेकमेकं तु।।[9]

Puṇḍarīka Viṭṭhala, Śrīkaṇṭha, Catura Dāmodara, Somanātha and Basava Bhūpala in their works *Rāgamālā, Rasakaumudī, Saṅgītadarpaṇa, Rāgavibodha* and *Śivatattvaratnākara* respectively, have given beautiful word pictures, iconographic descriptions and *dhyāna-ślokas* of *rāgas* and *rāgiṇīs*. Besides these treatises, we get such descriptions in other works too, e.g., *Rasakalpadruma, Rāgasāgara, Catvāriṁśacchatarāganirūpaṇa* etc. Pt. Jagannātha Miśra has given an iconographic description (*Rāgamūrttayaḥ)* of the following sixty-two *rāgas* and *rāgiṇīs* :

(A) SAMPŪRṆARĀGĀḤ

1. Śrīrāga	2. Naṭṭarāga
3. KarṇṇāṭaṆ	4. Revagupta
5. Vasanta	6. Bhairava
7. Baṅgāla	8. Somarāga
9. Amarapañcama	10. Kāmoda
11. Megharāga	12. Draviḍagauḍa
13. Varādī	14. Gurjjarī
15. Toḍī	16. Mālavaśrī
17. Saindhavī	18. Devakirī
19. Rāmakirī	20. Prathamamañjarī
21. Naṭṭa	22. Velāvalī
23. Gauḍī	24. Naṭa
25. Ghaṇṭārava	26. Naṭanārāyaṇa
27. Bhūpati	28. Śaṅkarabharaṇa

(B) ṢĀḌAVARĀGĀḤ

29. Gauḍa	30. Karṇṇāṭagauḍa
31. Deśīrāga	32. Dhannāsikā
33. Kolāhala	34. Vallālī
35. Deśākhya	36. Śāvarī
37. Khambhāvatī	38. Harṣapurī
39. Mallārī	40. Huñchikā
41. Śrīkaṇṭhikā	42. Bhaulī
43. Tātā	44. Sālaṅkagauḍa
45. Ābhīrī	46. Madhukarī
47. Chāyā	48. Nīlotpalā

(C) AUḌAVARĀGĀḤ

49. Madhyamādi	50. Mallāra
51. Deśapāla (Kedāra)	52. Mālava
53. Hindola	54. Bhairava
55. Nāgadhavani	56. Goṇḍakirī
57. Lalita	58. Pratāpavelāvalī
59. Turuṣkagauḍa	60. Gandhāra
61. Pulindī	62. Megharañjī

Now, I herewith present a study of these iconographic descriptions of eleven *rāgas* and *rāgiṇīs* as presented by Pt. Jagannātha Miśra comparing them with their word-pictures found in other treatises.

1. RĀGA VASANTA OR VASANTIKĀ

(i) शिखण्डिबर्होच्चयबद्धचूडः
पुष्णन् पिकं चूतलताङ्कुरेण।
भ्रमन्मुदाराममनङ्गमूर्तिः
मतो मतङ्गस्य वसन्तरागः।। (रसकल्पद्रुमः - VI. 5. 906)

With a high crown (diadem) spread wide like the plumage of a peacock, encouraging cuckoo (to sing) with the mango-*mañjarī,* the cupid-figured one, roaming in the garden with pleasure, is Rāga Vasanta according to Mataṅga.

(ii) चूताङ्कुरेणैव कृतावतंसो
विघूर्णमानारुणनेत्रपद्मः ।
पीताम्बरः काञ्चनचारुदेहो
वसन्तरागो युवतिप्रियश्च।। (रसकल्पद्रुमः - VI. 5.907)

With ear-ornaments of mango-*mañjarīs* and red eyes of a red lotus, having a charming golden figure, clad in yellow robes, is Rāga Vasanta, the darling of the young damsels.

(iii) शिखण्डिबर्होच्चयबद्धचूडा(डः)
कर्णावतंसी कृतशोभनाम्रा(म्रः)।
इन्दीवरश्यामतनुः सुचित्रा[1]
वसन्तिका[2] स्यादलि[3]मञ्जुलश्रीः।।

1. तनुर्विलासी; 2. वसन्तकः; 3. स्यात्फल

(रागकल्पद्रुमः - p. 20; सङ्गीतदर्पणः - II. 71; शिवतत्त्वरत्नाकरः - VI. 8. 105, p. 552)

With ear-ornaments of mango-*mañjarīs* and a high crown (diadem) spread wide like the plumage of a peacock, her body dark like the blue lotus and the black bee, charming and voluptuous is Vasanta, the beloved of spring.

(iv) शृङ्गारवनसमीपे नर्तन्तां युवतिजनकदम्बैश्च।
शुकपिकशारियुक्तं ध्यायेन्मे मनसि सन्ततं वासन्तम्।।

(रागसागरः - III.17)

Parrots, cuckoos and Śāri birds encircle Vasanta, the Lord of spring, who dances in the garden of voluptuosity (Love) surrounded by young charming damsels. May I remember him always!

All these iconographic word pictures present Rāga Vasanta before the eyes of the readers. The description at No. (ii) presents a beautiful combination of green, yellow, red and golden colours, thereby showing the scenic beauty of a garden in spring season.

2. MEGHARĀGA

(i) पर्यङ्के प्रियया सार्द्धमासीनमुपवीजयन्।
पीताम्बरः सुभूषाद्यो मेघरागो घनद्युतिः।।

(रसकल्पद्रुमः - VI. 5.914)

Dressed in yellow, adorned with beautiful ornaments, his body lustrous like blue clouds, playing the lute and sitting on the bed with his beloved is Rāga Megha.

(ii) नीलोत्पलाभवपुरिन्दुसमानवक्त्रः[1]
पीताम्बरस्तृषितचातकयाच्यमानः।
पीयूषमन्दहसितो घन[2]मध्यवर्ती
वीरेषु राजति युवा किल मेघरागः।।

1. नीलः; 2. द्रुम

(सङ्गीतदर्पणः - II.76 ; शिवतत्त्वरत्नाकरः - VI. 8. 116. p. 554)

The young Megha Rāga, his body lustrous like a blue lotus, the divine smile of his moon-like face is sweeter than *pīyūṣa* (*amṛta*), dressed in yellow amidst heavy clouds, he glitters among the heroes. The thirsty *cātaka* birds, that drink only raindrops, beholding him, cry out for water.

There is total resemblance in Rāga Megha and the clouds.

3. RĀMAKIRī RĀMAKALĪ RĀMAKRĪ OR RĀMAKRIYĀ

(i) स्वर्णप्रभाभासुरभूषणाढ्या
नीलं निचोलं वपुषा वहन्ती।
कान्ते पदोपान्तमधिश्रितेऽपि
मानोन्नता रामकिरी प्रदिष्टा।।

(रसकल्पद्रुमः - VI. 5. 925)

(ii) हेमप्रभाभासुरभूषणा च[1]
नीलं निचोलं वपुषा वहन्ती।
कान्ते समीपे कमनीयकण्ठा[2]
मानोन्नता रामकली मतेयम्।।

1. नि; 2. पदमाश्रितेऽपि।

(सङ्गीतदर्पणः - II. 60; शिवतत्त्वरत्नाकरः - VI. 8.83. p. 548)

Radiant like gold, her attire deep blue, Rāmakirī or Rāmakalī is adorned with glittering ornaments. Haughty and pretending anger, her voice becomes sweeter when the lover is near her.

(iii) यक्षिणी पद्मवदना यक्षकिन्नरदुर्लभा।
वीणाहस्ता पर्वतस्था रामक्रीरुच्यते बुधैः।।

(चत्वारिंशच्छतरागनिरूपणम् - p. 10)

A Yakṣī (nymph) with the lotus-like face, for Yakṣas (fauns) and Kinnaras (centaurs) hard to possess. *Viṇā* (lute) in hand and standing on a mountain, she is called Rāmakirī by the wise.

(iv) वीरासने निवासान्तां (? समासीनां) शरकोदण्डधारिणीम्।
जम्बूफलनिभां देवीं ध्याये रामक्रियां सदा।।

(रागसागरः - III. 18)

I worship (see) Devī Rāmakriyā who is sitting in the posture of heroes. holding a bow and an arrow and is dark like the *jambū* fruit.

4. HINDOLA HINDOLIKĀ OR HINDOLĀ

(i) नितम्बिनीमन्दतरङ्गितासु
दोलासु खेलासुखमादधानः।
खर्वः कपोतद्युतिकर्वुरश्री-
र्हिन्दोलरागः कथितो मुनीन्द्रैः।।

(रसकल्पद्रुमः - VI. 5. 970)

(ii) नितम्बिनीम[1]न्दतरङ्गितासु
दो[2]लासु खेलासुखमादधानः।
खर्व्वः[3]कपोत[4]द्युतिकामयुक्तो
हिन्दोलरागः कथितो मुनीन्द्रैः।।

1. वृ; 2. डो; 3. तासां; 4. कपोल

(रागकल्पद्रुमः - p. 20; सङ्गीतदर्पणः - II. 58; चत्वारिंशच्छतरागनिरूपणम् - p. 20;
शिवतत्त्वरत्नाकरः - VI 8.79, p. 548)

Dwarf, with the lustre of a dove, on a swing pleasantly placed for play, Hindola is gently rocked, the sages say, by ladies with broad hips.

(iii) नितम्बिनी सुन्दरगौरगात्रा
वीणां दधाना सुरपुष्पगन्धी।
स्वर्णप्रभाश्रीः कमलायताक्षी
हिन्दोलिकेयं कथिता मुनीन्द्रैः।।

(रागकल्पद्रुमः - p. 20)

Her beautiful, pale golden body is fragrant like the celestial flowers. Well-figured, long-lotus-eyed. Hindolikā holds a lute, say the sages.

(iv) न्यग्रोधाग्रजटाग्रबद्धकनकप्रद्योतडोलासने
श्रीकृष्णं कमलैश्च पूजितसदाभक्तिप्रयुक्तात्मकाम्।
गौराङ्गीं मणिभूषणीं मुरलिकानादप्रियां मे मनो
हिन्दोलां वरचित्रवस्त्रलसितां तुङ्गस्तनीं ध्यायति।।

(रागसागरः - III. 61)

My heart dreams of Hindolā, whose breasts are firm and who is dressed in beautiful and colourful garments. With the lotus flowers, she worships Lord Śrī Kṛṣṇa, who sits on a golden swing tied to the hanging roots of a banyan tree. She loves to listen to the sweet notes of the flute, her heart full of adoration and her fair limbs adorned with jewels.

5. LALITA OR LALITĀ

(i) प्रफुल्लसप्तच्छदमाल्यधारी
युवाऽतिगौरोऽलसलोचनश्रीः।
विनिःसृतो वासगृहात्प्रभाते
विलासिवेशो ललितः प्रदिष्टः।।

(रसकल्पद्रुमः - VI. 5. 974)

The young, fair-complexioned, beautiful-eyed Lalita is adorned with a garland of sweet-fragranced seven-fold flowers. Dressed in amorous attire and coming out of his dwelling apartment, he is called Lalita.

(ii) प्रफुल्लसप्तच्छदमाल्यधारी[1]
युवा[2] च गौरोब्जदलायताक्षः।[3]
विनिःश्वसन्[4] दैव[5] वशात्[6] प्रभाते
विलासवेषा ललिता प्रदिष्टा।।
(यस्याः पतिः सा ललिता प्रदिष्टाः)

1. युक्ता or नीलकण्ठा; 2. रुचा or गौरी; 3. गौरोत्पललोच श्रीः or कृराङ्गी तरुणी चलाक्षी or सुगौरकान्तिर्युवती सुदृष्टिः; 4. विनिर्गता; 5. श्वास; 6. विनिःश्वसन्ती सहसा। (चत्वारिंशच्छतरागनिरूपणम्, p. 20; सङ्गीतदर्पणः - II. 63; शिवतत्त्वरत्नाकरः - VI. 8.89. p. 549)

The young and fair Lord of Lalita is adorned with a garland of sweet-fragranced seven-fold flowers. His lovely laughing eyes look long like the petal of the white lotus. It is dawn. Lalitā, overwhelmed by fate deeply sighs, dressed to meet her lover.

Or in another reading; Lalitā is young and fair and wearing a garland of seven-fold flowers. Her long eyes resemble the petal of the lotus. Overwhelmed by fate, at dawn, she is sighing to meet her lover.

(iii) अतिस्निग्धोऽतिगौरश्च दिव्यगन्धानुलेपनः।
मृगपाणिर्जटाधारी योगी ललितसंज्ञकः।।

(चत्वारिंशच्छतरागनिरूपणम् - p. 14)

This very fair and amiable yogī, smeared with divine perfumed unguents, with tangled locks and a deer in his hand is known as Lalitā.

(iv) चामीकराभा ललिता सुमुग्धा
वीणाधरा कोकिलपाणिपद्मा।
कल्पद्रुमाधःस्थलसंस्थितापि
पयोधरामण्डितकोटिकामा।।

(चत्वारिंशच्छतरागनिरूपणम् - p. 13)

Lalitā, attractive due to her innocence, is glittering like gold. While she holds a lute, a cuckoo perches on her lotus-like hand. Although she is seated beneath the wishing tree, her breasts all unadorned, she is having thousands of desires.

(v) वीणापुस्तकपाणिं मञ्जुलकेलिं सुखेन जल्पन्तीम्।
अरुणारविन्दनयनां ललितां सङ्गीतमातृकां ध्याये।।

(रागसागरः - III.7)

A lute and a book in her hands, Lalitā appears to be the Goddess of Music. Pleasingly playful, she speaks lightly, her eyes are like the red lotuses. I worship her.

6. MEGHARAÑJĪ

(i) श्रुतौ दधाना नवकर्णिकार-
मारामगा केशरपुञ्जकाञ्ची।
अध्यापयन्ती स्वकरस्थशारीं
श्रीरामरामेति च मेघरञ्जी।।

(रसकल्पद्रुमः - VI. 5. 979)

Present in the pleasure-garden, adorned with fresh *Karṇikāra* flowers in her ears, wearing girdlestring of *Keśara,* teaching her beloved female Śari bird, who is in her hand, to uttar Śrīrāma, Rāma, she is Megharañjī.

(ii) विद्युल्लताङ्गीं विबुधेन्द्रपूजा-
सन्धानहस्तार्पितपुष्पमालाम्।
नीलाम्बराडम्बरसन्नितम्बिनीं
भजामि नित्यं घनमेघरञ्जीम्।।

(रागसागरः - III. 3)

Daily do I adore Megharañjī who brings in her hands flower-garlands for the worship of Indra, the God of rains. Her body looks like lightning, a blue veily attire adorns her beautiful hips.

7. TOḌĪ

(i) उन्निद्रपङ्केरुहचारुनेत्री कुरङ्गशावं कलमाङ्कुरेण।
सम्भावयन्ती विपिनोपकण्ठे तोडीयमिन्दीवरदामरम्या।।

(रसकल्पद्रुम - VI. 5.920)

Having long and beautiful eyes like a lotus, pleasing her pet young deer with sprouts of *kalama* near a forest, wearing a girdle-string of blue lotuses and looking charming, she is Toḍī.

(ii) मृणालकुन्देन्दुसमानगात्री विलिप्तदेहा हरिचन्दनेन।
विनोदयन्ती विपिने कुरङ्गं तोडी विपञ्चीं दधती कराभ्याम्।।

(रसकौमुदीः - II. 134)

(iii) तुषारकुन्दोज्ज्वलदेहयष्टिः काश्मीरकर्पूरविलिप्तदेहा।
विनोदयन्ती हरिणं वनान्ते वीणाधरा राजति टोडिकेयम।।

(सङ्गीतदर्पणः - II. 212)

(iv) कलितविपञ्ची विपिने लालितहरिणाऽरुणाम्बराहरिणी।
धवलाङ्गरागरचना मृदुवचना भूषिता तोडी।।

(रागविबोधः - V. 180)

White-complexioned like a lotus, a *kunda* flower and the moon, her body smeared with *Haricandana,* or Kāśmīra-karpūra or white unguent, pleasing her pet dear in the forest, holding a *vipañcī* lute in her hands, soft-spoken, charming and adorned is Toḍī.

8. KĀMODA OR KĀMODĪ

(i) अक्षमालां करे कृत्वा वसानस्तारवीं त्वचम्।
जपन् जह्नुसुतातीरे कामोदः परिकीर्तितः।।

(रसकल्पद्रुमः - VI. 5. 912)

At the banks of the holy river Ganges, holding *Akṣamālā* in his hands, wearing tree barks and worshipping Lord Śiva, is Kāmoda.

(ii) भर्त्रा समं पाथसि हेमवर्णा
पयोविहारेण सरोरुहाणि।
विचिन्वती सौरभमोदमाना
कामोदनाम्ना कथिता मुनीन्द्रैः।।

(रसकल्पद्रुमः - VI. 5. 913)

Golden-comlexioned, enjoying *Jalavihāra* with her beloved consort, delighting by the fragrance of flower and collecting lotuses, is she known by the name of Kāmoda or Kāmodī by the sages.

(iii) पीताम्बरा काकलिनादिनीयं सुकेशपाशा विपिने रुदन्ती।
विलोकयन्ती भयमुद्वहन्ती कामोदिका नाथमनुस्मरन्ती।।

(रसकौमुदीः - II. 148)

(iv) पीतं वसाना वसनं सुकेशी वने रुदन्ती पिकनाददूना।
विलोकयन्ती विदिशोऽतिभीता कामोदिका कान्तमनुस्मरन्ती।।

(सङ्गीतदर्पणः - II. 244)

(v) पीतांशुका सुकेशी शितिः स्मरन्ती पतिं भयाकुलदृक्।
पिकनादेन विदूना कामोदी कानने रुदती।।

(रागविबोधः - V. 187)

Beautiful-haired, yellow-attired, singing in *Kākali* note, distressed at listening to the sound of cuckoo, frightened and crying in the forest, beholding in the quarters with timid eyes and remembering her beloved consort, is she Kāmodikā.

9. BHAIRAVA

(i) सचन्द्रहासं फलकं दधानो
निबद्धकक्षो दृढबद्धकक्षः।
गतीर्विचिन्वन्बहुधा पदातिः
प्रचण्डरूपः किल भैरवोऽयम्।।

(रसकल्पद्रुमः - VI. 5. 908)

Having tied locks, holding the *Phalaka* with Candrahāsa, fully equipped (to attack), finding out his way many times, as a *padāti* and looking fierce is Bhairava.

(ii) गङ्गाधरश्चन्द्रकलोत्तमाङ्गो भुजङ्गमव्यूहविभूषिताङ्गः।
शुभ्राम्बरः शूलविभूतिधारी स भैरवाख्यो जयति प्रकामम्।।

(रसकौमुदी - II. 104)

(iii) गङ्गाधरः शशिकलातिलकस्त्रिनेत्रः
सर्पैर्विभूषिततनुर्गजकृत्तिवासाः ।
भास्वत्त्रिशूलकर एष नृमुण्डधारी
शुभ्राम्बरो जयति भैरव आदिरागः।।

(सङ्गीतदर्पणः - II. 198)

(iv) डमरुत्रिशूलधारी पन्नगहारी सितो लसद्भसितः।
धृतशशिगङ्गोऽतजरोऽजिनविकटो भैरवोऽसमदृक्।।

(रागविबोधः - V. 178)

Dressed in white attire, holding Gaṅgā on his head and Candrakalā on his foreheadā as *tilaka,* smeared with ashes, wearing elephant skin and human skulls, adorned by serpent-ornaments, holding a glittering trident and a *ḍamaruka* in his hands, victorious is the three-eyed Bhairava, the first (chief) rāga.

10. DHANĀŚRĪḤ OR DHANNĀSIKĀ OR DHANĀSĪ

(i) दूर्वादलश्यामतनुर्मनोज्ञा
कान्तं लिखन्ती फलके विदग्धा।
बाला गलल्लोचनवारिबिन्दु-
निस्यन्दसिक्ता कथिता धनासी।।

(रसकल्पद्रुमः - VI. 5. 943)

Very skilled, charming and young, dark like the *dūruā* grass, wet with the stream of tears coming out of her eyes due to her love-lorn state and painting her beloved consort on the canvas, is

Dhanāsī or Dhanāśrī

(ii) नीलोत्पलश्यामलमूर्तिरेषा प्रियं लिखन्ती विरहेण युक्ता।
श्रीखण्डचर्चाविलसत्कुचास्था धन्नासिका भाति मनोज्ञवेषा।।

(रसकौमुदी - II. 118)

(iii) दूर्वादलश्यामतनुर्मनोज्ञा कान्तं लिखन्ती विरहेण दूना।
श्वेते कपोले नयनारविन्दनिष्यन्दनिर्धू(धौं)तकुचा धनाश्रीः।।

(सङ्गीतदर्पणः - II. 287

(iv) दूर्वाभनिभा विरहासहा लिखन्ती पटे पतिं रुदन्ती।
स्नपितकुचा सितगल्ला स्थिरधम्मिला धनाश्रीः।।

(रागविबोधः - IV. 177)

Dark-complexioned like the blue lotuses or the green *dūrvā* grass, her face and bosom smeared with *Śrīkhaṇḍa,* painting her beloved consort on the canvas with tears coming out of her lotus-like eyes and sprinkiling her breasts due to her unbearable love-lorn state, dressed in attractive attire and elegant is Dhannāsikā or Dhanāśrīḥ.

11. KEDĀRA OR DEŚAPĀLA

अयमेव केदार इति केषाञ्चिन्मते। यथा . . .

(i) चिरप्रवासी जलदावलोका-
द्विचिन्तयन्नीलसरोरुहाक्षीम्।
कामी युवा गीतकलाभिलाषी
केदाररागस्तरुणोऽरुणाभः ।।

(रसकल्पद्रुमः - VI. 5.968)

Dwelling abroad for long, gazing at the clouds and remembering zealously his beloved blue-lotus-eyed darling, red-complexioned, young, juvenile and libidinous, and an ardent lover of the art of music, is the rāga Kedāra.

(ii) गङ्गाधरः सुन्दरचन्द्रमौलिर्भुजङ्गमोद्भासुरयज्ञसूत्रः।
ध्याने निविष्टो धृतयोगपीठः केदाररागो जटिलो विभाति।।

(रसकौमुदी - II. 146)

(iii) जटां दधानः सितचन्द्रमौलिर्नागोत्तरीयो धृतयोगपीठः।
गङ्गाधरो ध्याननिमग्नचित्तः केदाररागः कथितस्तपस्वी।।

(सङ्गीतदर्पणः - II. 237)

(iv) जटिलोऽहियोगपट्टः सविधुशकलमौलिरुल्लसद्भसितः।
गङ्गाधरस्तपस्वी ध्यानरतोऽतीव केदारः।।

(रागविबोधः - V. 208)

Holding Gaṅgā on his head and beautiful Candrakalā on his forehead, adorned by glittering serpent-*yajña-sūtra* (or wearing serpent-uttarīya) and observing *dhyāna* on the *Yogapīṭha,* does shine the matted-locked ascetic, the Kedāra rāga.

Going minutely through the iconographic descriptions of the afore-said eleven *rāgas* and *rāgiṇīs*, we come to the following conclusion :

1. These descriptions present before our eyes the complete *nādatma* or the deific form of the concerned *rāga* or *rāgiṇī*.
2. There is more verbal similarity in the verses of Rasakaumudī. *Saṅgītadarpaṇa, Rāgakalpadruma* and *Śivatattvaratnākara.*[10]
3. In the verses of *Rāgavibodha,* there is more ideological similarity, and scanty verbal similarity due to employment of different metre.[11]
4. All the verses of iconographic description are masterpieces of literary art. A critical as well as comparative appraisal of these works is the need of the day.
5. While writing all these word-pictures, Śrīkaṇṭha is indebted to his Guru Puṇḍarīka Viṭṭ hala, Dāmodara to Śrīkaṇṭha; and Somanātha to Śrīkaṇṭha and Dāmodara. Basava Bhūpala is indebted to all his predecessors.
6. Our Pt. Jagannātha Miśra has gone elaborately through and fully utilized all the works present before him. Taking content material and marry times similar vocabulary too, he has presented his verses which have resemblance with one or the other works of his predecessors. Thus, he has followed all his predecessors and is indebted to all of them, although he has his own contribution too. It would be praiseworthy if researches are carried out on the contribution of Pt. Jagannātha Miśra to different *Śāstras*, particularly musicology. A detailed comparative study of the iconographic description of the sixty-two *rāgas* and *rāgiṇīs* presented by Pt. Jagannātha Miśra will definitely open new vistas for the future researchers.

REFERENCES & NOTES

1. *Rasakalpadruma* - VI. 5. 874-1037
2. *Rasakalpadruma* - VI. 5. 874
3. *Rasakalpadruma* - VI. 5. 875
4. *Rasakalpadruma* - VI, 5. 876-77
5. *Sumati-Saṅgītābharaṇam, Gems of Indian Music and Musicology* (Ed. Sushma Kulshreshtha); Rāga-Iconification in Indian Music (R. Sathyanarayana), p. 73
6. *Rasakalpadruma* - VI. 5.878-884; 885-892; 893-898.
7. *Rasakalpadruma* - VI. 5.878-884
8. *Rasakalpadruma* - VI, 5.899
9. *Rāgavibodha* - V. 11

10&11. *Gems of Indian Music and Musicology,* Rāgadhyāna-Ślokas - A Comparative Study (Dr. A. N. Jani), p. 100

SELECT BIBLIOGRAPHY

1. *Catvāriṁśacchatarāganirūpaṇam* (See *Kālidāsa-Saṅgīta-Mañjarī-2, Ṛtusaṁhāra-Saṅgīta-Surabhi;* Sushma Kulshreshtha and J.S. Kulshreshtha, Eastern Book Linkers, Delhi, 1992).
2. *Nartananirṇaya* (Puṇḍarīka Viṭṭhala) (See *Sumati-Saṅgītābharaṇam,* Ed. Sushma Kulshreshtha, Pratibha Prakashan, Delhi 1994; p. 73 & 90).
3. *Rāgakalpadruma* (See *Kālidāsa-Saṅgīta-Mañjarī-2).*
4. *Rāgamālā* (Puṇḍarīka Viṭṭhala) (See *Sumati-Saṅgītābharaṇam)*; p. 73, 90).
5. *Rāgavibodha* (Somanātha), Adyar, 1945.
6. *Rāgasāgara* (See *Kālidāsa-Saṅgīta-Mañjarī-2).*
7. *Rasakalpadruma* (Pt. Jagannātha Miśra), Orissa Sahitya Akademi, Bhubaneshwar, 1965.
8. *Rasakaumudī* (Śrīkaṇṭha), Ed. A. N. Jani; G.O.S. No. 143, Baroda, 1963.
9. *Śivatattvaratnākara* (Keladi Basava Bhūpāla), Vol. 1, Oriental Research Institute, University of Mysore, Mysore, 1965.
10. *Saṅgītadarpaṇa* (Catura Dāmodara), Ed. K.V. Sastri, S.M.S. No. 34, Tanjore, 1952.
11. *Sumati-Saṅgītābharaṇam,* Ed. Sushma Kulshreshtha, Jagdish Sahai and Abha Kulshreshtha, Pratibha Prakashan, Delhi, 1994.

Section IV

FLORA : VEDIC & SCIENTIFIC PERSPECTIVE

वनस्पतिविज्ञानरसझरी

VEDIC FLORA : A STUDY

Bidyut Lata Ray

PROLEGOMENON

The *Ṛgveda* or the *Veda* of verses is the mot ancient and the most important text of Vedism. It is available in the form of a collection of 1028 hymns (*Sūktas*), divided into ten 'circles' (*maṇḍala*). The main feature of the *Ṛgveda* is to depict the glory of thc gods and goddeses. The deities worshipped by the Vedic people are mainly *Agni* (the fire), *Indra, Varuṇa, Viṣṇu, Rudra, Sabitā, Marūt, Sūrya* (the sun), *Vāyu* (the air), *Soma, Dyāvāpṛthivī* (the world), *Mitra, Pūṣā, Uṣā* (morning), *Parjanya, Aśvin* and *Yama* etc. Evidently, most of these deities relate to the natural environment in which we live. Since the *Vedas* are the sacred texts of the Āryan culture, it is quite obvious that the Āryans were worshipping the components of natural creations as gods and goddesses. It is true that the physical world outlined in the Vedic hymns and *sūtras* plays an important role in shaping the habits, customs, manners and culture of the Vedic people.

The *Vedas* depict the cosmology, cosmogong, astronomy, astrology, philosophy, science, society, history, geography, tradition, culture, language and literature etc. According to the *Vedas*, the Universe is divided into three parts, each sometimes duplicated and even tripled. They are the earth, the *antarīkṣa* and the sky.[1] Space is conceived, in fact, like an ocean, divided into two, three or four seas. For the sun, the common Vedic notion is that it has a bright and a dark face. The *nakṣatra* or lunar mansions appear perhaps in the most recent parts of the *Ṛgveda*. It is seen that the astronomical phenomena are latent in the Vedic hymns in mythical forms. Further, the four *Vedas,* viz. *Ṛg, Yaju, Sāma* and *Atharva,* deal with some cities, towns, countries, states, rivers, mountains, lakes, forests, trees, birds, animals, the earth, the air, the water, the fire, the climate, the herbs, the plants, the flowers, the fruits, the vegetables and the weeds etc. Moreover, some place names are available from the Vedic hymns. All the above items together focus on the Vedic culture and civilization prevailing at that time. This also shows the vast knowledge of the Vedic seers about their surrounding nature and natural resources. The world of plants, herbs, flowers and fruits exhibits the social life, custom and tradition of the Vedic people. The other living organisms like animals, birds and insects add to the above knowledge more concretely. In the present study, an attempt has been made to survey the Vedic flora and plant world in order to uncover various aspects of Vedic civilization and culture. The *Ṛgveda* mentions a large number of trees, plants, grains, flowers and grasses in connection with the performance of sacrifices.

PLANTS

The Ṛgveda includes a plant named *Arṭu*[2], from the wood of which the axle of a chariot was sometimes made. The botanical name of this species is colosanthes indica. Other varieties are *Ajaśṛṅgi*[3], *Adhyāṇ ḍā*[4], *Apāmārga* (Achyranthes aspera)[5], *Amatā* (Emblica officinalis)[6], *Amūlā* (Kmethoica superba)[7], *Arāṭaki*[8], *Arundhatī*[9], *Arka* (Calotropis gigantca)[10], *Alāpu* (Lagenaria Vulgaris)[11], *Avakā* (Blyxa octandra[12], *Aśvavāra* or *Aśvavāla* (Saccharum Spontancum)[13], *Ādāra*[14], *Ābayu* (mustard plant)[15], *Uśanā* (a plant)[16], *Eraṇḍa* (Ricinus Communis)[17], *Aukṣagandhi*[18], *Kavīra* (Copparis aphylla)[19], *Kumuda* (Namphaca esculenta)[20], *Kuṣṭha* (Costus speciosus or Arabicus)[21], *Jaṅgiḍa* (Tarminalia arjuneya)[22], *Jāmbila* (Citron)[23], *Tājadbhaṅga*[24], *Tilvaka* (Symplocos racemosa)[25], *Taudi*[26], *Trāyamāṇa*[27], *Narācī*[28], *Nalada* or *Naladi* (nard)[29], *Nyastikā* (Andropagon aciculatus)[30], *Pāṭā* (Clypea hemandifolia)[31], *Pilā*[32], *Pūtika* (Guilandina Bonduc or Basella cordifalia)[33], *Pṛśricparṇi* (Hermionitis Cordifolia)[34], *Praprotha*[35], *Pramaganda,*[36], *Pramandani*[37], *Prasū* (young shoot)[38], *Baja* (mustard plant)[39], *Bimba* (Momordica monadelpha)[40], *Bāṅga* (hemp)[41], *Mañjiṣùhā* (madder)[42], *Madāvalī* (intoxicating)[43], *Madugha* (honey plant)[44], *Viṣāṇkā*[45], *Vihalha*[46], *Virudh* (plant)[47], *Śana* (hemb)[48], *Saphaka*[49], *Śipāla* (Blyxa octandra)[50] *Sarṣapa* (mustard)[51], *Saha*[52], *Sahadeva*[53], *Sahadevī*[54], *Sahamāna*[55], *Silāci*[56] and *Silāñjāla*[57] etc. Beside the above, the names of some water plants and weeds are also mentioned in the Vedic literature.

WATER PLANTS & WEEDS

Some plants like lotus, lily etc. grow in water. Similarly, different kinds of weeds germinate in the water medium. Some weeds are found floating in water and some grow on the soil inside water. Among the water plants, *Āṇḍika* (lotus)[58], *Kiyāmba*[59], *Kumuda* (lily)[60], *Puṇḍarīka* (lotus blossom)[61] and *Puṣkara* (lotus flower)[62] are the prominent names traced in Vedic literature. The name *Āla*[63] denotes weed. *Bisa*[64] is identified with lotus fibre and *Śalūka*[65] with lotus shoot.

HERBS & GRASSES

The word *Tṛṇa*[65A] is found in Vedic literature. It is identified with grass. It was used as straw to roof in a house or hut.[66] The other varieties of grasses referred to in Vedic texts are *Durvā* (Panicum dactylon)[67], *Iṣīkā* (reed grass)[68], *Ulapa*[69], *Kāśa* (Saccharum spontancum)[70], *Kuśa* (Poa cynosuroides)[71], *Drabha*[72], *Balbaja*[73], *Viraṇa*[74], *Śāda*[75], *Sugandhitijana*[76], *Sairya*[77] and *Satmba*[78], etc. Moreover, some grass-related words are spotted. These are *Naḍa* (reed)[79], *Naḍvatā* (reed bed), *Piñjula* (bundle of grass)[80], *Śara* (redd)[81], *Saṣpa* (young grass)[82] and *Sumbala* (straw)[83]. *Sara*[84] is a kind of herb mentioned in the *Ṛgveda*. The word is also applied to the soma plant[85] and the sacrificial straw.[86] Prasū in the *Ṛgveda*[87] denotes the young shoots of grass or herbs used at the sacrifices.

GRAINS & CREEPERS

The Vedic texts mention a number of grains and grain-creepers which add to the knowledge of our evironment. Some of the grains are used as food grains by Vedic people. Nowadays, such species are also available in nature and some are also cultivated by the people. The word *Aṇu*[88] symbolises the grain in general. The list of grains mentioned in Vedic literature includes *Kulmāsa* (beans)[89], *Garmut* (wild bean)[90], *Godhūma* (wheat)[91], *Taṇḍala* (rice grains)[92], *Tila* (Sesmum)[93], *Dhāna* (grains of corn)[94], *Dhānya* (grain)[95], *Pūlpa* or *pūlya* (shrivelled grain)[96], *Pryaṅyu* (Pranicum italicum)[97], *Masūra* (Ervum hirsulum)[98], *Yava* (barley)[99], *Vrīhi* (rice)[100], *Śāli* (rice)[101], *Śasya* (corn)[102] and *Plāśuka* (fast growing rice)[103], etc. After harvesting the paddy plants, we get *Palāla* (straw)[104], and the paddy grains. By way of processing rice and husk (*Tuṣa*)[105] are separated. *Taila* (Oil)[106] obtained from the seeds of sesamum is also referred to in the Vedic hymns.

Among the creepers, the prominent names are *Alasālā*[107], *Nīlāgalasālā* or *Nīlākalasālā*[108] and *Vratati*[109], etc. Besides, many names of fruits, flowers and seeds are also found in Vedic literature.

FLOWERS FRUITS & SEEDS

The word *Puṣpa*[110], meaning flower is mentioned in the Vedic literature. Among flowers, lotus *(puṣkara)*[111], lily *(kumuda)*[112], *Aśmagandhā* (Physalis flexuous), etc. are common names. *Āmalaka*[114] denotes a fruit. Another fruit mentioned is the *Urvārū* or *Urvāvuka*[115], which means cucumber. the flowers and of *Palāśa*[116] and *Śalmali*[117] are traced in the Vedic texts. In general *Bīja* (seed)[118] is mentioned in this literature. The opertion of sowing seed (*vap*) is being several times referred to in the *Ṛgveda*[119] and later[120]. In a metaphorical sense the term is used in the *Upaniṣads* of the classes of beings according to origin, of which the *Chāndogya Upaniṣad*[121] enumerates three, the *Aitareya*[122] four. The former list includes *aṇḍa-ja* (egg-born), *jīva-ja* (born alive) and *udbhiji-ja* (produced from sprouts), while the atter adds *sveda-ja* (sweat-corn), *i.e.* generated by hot moisture.

TREES

The names of many big and small trees are found in the four *Vedas, Brāhmaṇas, Āraṇyakas* and *Upaniṣads*. Vedic *Sūtras* also mention some of their varieties. The word *Vṛkṣa*[123] in the *Vedas* generally stands for the tree. *Druma*[124] is also another word used for the tree. Two words *Vayā*[125] and *Śākhā*[126] have been employed to mean the branch of a tree. *Valka*[127] stands for the bark and *Valśa*[128] for the twig of the tree. The words *Dāru*[129], *Kṛmuka*[130] and *Krumuka*[131] stand for the wood. *Vakala*[132] is used for the bast. The big trees are *Aśvattha* (Ficus religiosa)[133], *Nyagrodha* (Ficus indica)[134], *Bilva* (Aigle marmelos)[135], *Udambara* (Ficus glomerata)[136], *Karkandhu* (Zizyphus jujuba)[137], *Kākambira*[138], *Kārṣmarya* (Gmelina arborca)[139], *Kiṁśuka* (Butea frondosa)[140], *Khadira* (Acacia catechu)[141], *Kharjura* (Phanix silestris)[142], *Talāśa* (Flacourtia cataphracta)[143], *Palāśa* (Butca frondosa)[144], *Pippala* (berry)[145], *Badava* (jujube)[146], *Rohitaka* (Andersonia Rohitaka)[147], *Pūtudru* (Deodar)[148], *Prakṣa* (Ficus infectoria)[149], *Plakṣa* (Ficus infectoria)[150], *Śamī*[151], *Śālmali* (Salmalia malabarica)[152], *Śiṁśapā (Dalbergia Śiśu)*[153], *Haridsu* (Pinces deodoxa)[154] and *Sphūrjaka* (Diosphyros embryopteris)[155], etc. Out of the above trees, some are grown wildly and some are planted by the people for their use in the treatment of diseases. Vedic people also knew the medicinal value of all these trees, plants, herbs, creepers, grains, flowcrs, fruits, shoots and seeds. As they lived in the forests. depending on the nautral resources, they gradually practised cultivating those varieties of plants which were helpful for their living. Thus, *Kṛṣi*[156] was the main occupation of the Vedic people. In the *Atharvaeda Pṛthī Vainya* is credited with the origination of ploughing[157], and even in the *Ṛgveda* the Aśvins are spoken of as concerned with the sowing of grain by means of the plough.[158]

Thus, the nature and the natural resources like the earth, air, water, fire, mountains, forests, lakes, rivers, seas, oceans, etc. have been described in the *Vedas* and Vedic texts as gods and goddesses. Vedic hostile groups worshipped them with the notion that the deities have been manifested in nature in different forms to help them live. The entire plant world noted above goes a long way in solving their problems of living and earning bread and butter. Vedic people were using medicinal plants and herbs in the cure of diseases. Nowadays, such a cure is known as Āyurvedic treatment, which was actually developed during the Vedic period.

REFERENCES & NOTES

1. Ray, B.L., *Studies in Sanskrit Indology and Culture* - Classical Publishing Company, New Delhi, 1998, p. 11.
2. *Ṛgveda* - VIII. 46, 27 also, *Atharvaveda* - XX. 131, 17
3. *Atharvaveda* - IV.37. This plant is equated with *Viṣāṇin* (The Odina pinnata). Its othername is *Avāṭakī* (*AV.* - IV. 37.6)
4. *Śatapatha Brāhmaṇa* - XIII.8, 1, 16
5. *Atharvaveda* - IV.17, 6; 18, 7; 19, 4; VII. 65,2. This plant is described in the *Atharvaveda* - (IV.17, 2) as 'revertive' (punaḥ-sara), because it has reverted leaves.
6. *Jaiminīya Upaniṣad Brāhmaṇa* - I. 38, 6
7. *Atharvaveda* - V.31, 4. This plant has no root. Its botanical name is Methonica superba, which was used for poisoning arrows.
8. *Atharvaveda* - IV. 37, 6
9. *Atharvaveda* - IV. 12.1; V. 5, 5.9; VI. 59, 1.2; VIII. 7, 6; XIX. 38, 1. This plant possesses healing properties in case of wounds, as a fabrifuge, and as inducing cows to give milk. Being a climber, it attaches itself to trees like the *Plakṣa, Aśvattha, Nyagrodha* and *Parṇa* (*AV.* V. 5,5)
10. *Atharvaveda* - VI. 72, 1
11. *Atharvaveda* - VIII. 10, 29.30
12. *Atharvaveda* - VIII. 7, 9; 37. 8-10. The Gandharvas are said to eat this plant (*AV.* - IV. 37, 8). Its later name is *Śaivāla*, and it is identical with the *Śīpāla*.
13. *Maitrāyaṇī Saṁhitā* - III. 7, 9; This is a species of reed.
14. *Śatapatha Brāhmaṇa* - IV. 5.10, 4. This plant was prescribed as a substitute for *Soma*. It is identified with *Pūtīka*.
15. *Atharvaveda* - VI. 16, 1
16. *Śatapatha Brāhmaṇa* - III. 4, 3, 13; IV. 2, 5, 15. *Soma* was prepared from this plant.
17. *Śāṅkhāyana Āraṇyaka* - XII. 8
18. *Atharvaveda* - IV. 37, 3. The name of this plant denotes some sort of fragrant plant.
19. *Taittirīya Saṁhitā* - II. 4, 9, 2
20. *Atharvaveda* - IV. 34. 5. It is identified with the white water-lily.
21. *Atharvaveda* - I. 65. It grew especially on the mountains, alongwith *Soma,* on the high peaks of the Himālayas, where the eagles nest. Like *Soma*, it is said to have grown in the third heaven under the famous *Aśvattha* tree.
22. *Atharvaveda* - II. 4; XIX. 34, 35. It is a healing plant. It was used as an amulet against the diseases like fevers and rheumatic pains.
23. *Maitrāyaṇī Saṁhitā* - III. 15.3
24. *Atharvaveda* - VIII. 8. 3. It has been identified with the castor-oil plant in the *Kauśika Sūtra*.
25. *Śatapatha Brāhmaṇa* - XIII. 8, 1, 16. A tree near which it is inauspicious to construct a grave.
26. *Atharvaveda* - X. 4, 14
27. *Atharvaveda* - VIII. 2, 6
28. *Atharvaveda* - V. 31, 4. It is a poisonous plant.
29. *Atharvaveda* - VI. 102, 3. This plant is mentioned as used for a garland.
30. *Atharvaveda* - VI., 139, 1

31. *Atharvaveda* - II. 27, 4. It is a medicinal plant.
32. *Atharvaveda* - IV. 37, 3. This is the name of some fragarant plant.
33. *Kāṭhaka Saṁhitā* - XXXIV. 3. This plant is usually identified with the *Guilandina Bonduc*. It is used as a substitute for the *Soma* plant.
34. *Atharvaveda* - II. 25, 1. This plant has been used as a protection against evil beings procuring abortion.
35. *Pañcaviṁśa Brāhmaṇa* - VIII. 4, 1. This plant is used as a substitute for *Soma*.
36. *Ṛgveda* - III. 53, 14
37. *Kauśika Sūtra* - VIII. 17. This word denotes a sweet-scented plant.
38. *Ṛgveda* - I. 95, 10
39. *Atharvaveda* - VIII. 6, 3.6.7.24. This plant was used against a demon of disease.
40. *Jaiminīya Upaniṣad Brāhmaṇa* - III. 5, 6
41. *Atharvaveda* - XI. 6, 15
42. *Aitareya* - III.2, 4. (*Āraṇyaka*); *Śāṅkhāyana* - VIII. 7 (*Āraṇyaka)*
43. *Atharvaveda* - VI. 16, 2
44. *Atharvaveda* - I. 34, 4. *Ṛgveda* - VI. 70, 1.5
45. *Atharaveda* - VI. 44, 3.
46. *Atharvaveda* - VI. 16, 2
47. *Ṛgveda* - I. 67. 9. This plant has practically the same sense as *Oṣadhi*.
48. *Atharvaveda* - II. 4, 5. This plant grows in the forest.
49. *Atharvaveda* - IV. 34, 5. It is so called because its leaves are shaped like hoofs (*śapha*).
50. *Ṛgveda* - X. 68. 5
51. *Chāndogya Upaniṣad* - III. 14, 3
52. *Atharvaveda* - XI. 6, 15
53. *Ṛgveda* - I. 100, 17
54. *Atharvaveda* - VI. 59, 2
55. *Atharvaveda* - II. 25, 2; IV. 17, 2; VIII. 2, 6; 7, 5
56. *Atharvaveda* - V. 5, 1.8
57. *Atharvaveda* - VI. 16, 4. This plant is perhaps a 'grain creeper'.
58. *Atharvaveda* - IV. 34, 5; V. 17, 16. This is one edible plant, apparently with fruit or leaves of egg-shape akin to the lotus.
59. *Ṛgveda* - X. 16, 13; *Atharvaveda* - XVIII. 3, 6. According to the funeral hymn in the *Ṛgveda* (as mentioned above), these plants grow on the place where the body of the dead was burnt.
60. *Atharvaveda* - IV. 34.5. This plant identified with lily that grows in water.
61. *Ṛgveda* - X. 142, 8. This plant denotes the blossom of the lotus.
62. *Ṛgveda* - VI. 16, 13; VII. 33, 11. This word denotes the blue lotus flower.
63. *Atharvaveda* - VI. 16, 3
64. *Atharvaveda* - IV. 34, 5
65. *Atharvaveda* - IV. 34, 5

65A. *Ṛgveda* - I. 161., 1; 162, 8; X. 102, 10; *Atharvaveda* - II. 30, 1; VI. 54, 1

66. *Aitareya Brāhmaṇa* - III. 22, VIII. 24
67. *Ṛgveda* - X. 16, 13; 134, 5; 142, 8
68. *Atharvaveda* - VII. 56, 4; XII. 2, 54
69. *Ṛgveda* - X. 142, 3
70. *Ṛgveda* - X. 100, 10

71. *Śatapatha Brāhmaṇa* - II. 5, 2, 15; III. 1, 2, 16; V. 3, 2, 7
72. *Ṛgveda* - I. 191, 3
73. *Atharvaveda* - XIV. 2, 22, 23 *Taittirīya Saṁhitā* - II. 2, 82; *Kāṭhaka Saṁhitā* - X.10; *Maitrāyaṇi Saṁhitā* - II. 25
74. *Śatapatha Brāhmaṇa* - XII 8, 1, 15
75. *Ṛgveda* - IX 15,6; *Vājasaneyī Saṁhitā* XXXV.1
76. *Taittiviya Saṁhitā* - VI 2,8,4, *Kaṭhaka Saṁhitā* - XXXV. 6; *Aitareya Brāhmaṇa* - I.28,28; *Śatapatha Brāhmaṇa* - III.5,2, 27. *Pañcaviṁśa Brāhmaṇa* - XXXIV. 13,5
77. *Ṛgveda* - I. 191, 3
78. *Atharvaveda* - VIII. 6, 14
79. *Ṛgveda* - VIII 1. 33
80. *Vājasaneyī Saṁhitā* - XXX. 16.*Taittiriya Braāhmaṇa* - III,4,12,1
81. *Ṛgveda* - I. 191,3; *Atharvaveda* - IV. 7.4
82. *Vājasaneyī Saṁhitā* - XIX 13, 81; XXI 29; *Aitareya Brāhmaṇa* - VII, 5, 3, 8, 4; *Statapatha Brāhmaṇa* - XII 7, 2, 8 ; 9, 1 , 2. The word denotes young or sprouting grass.
83. *Śatapatha Brāhmaṇa* - XII. 5, 2, 3. The word has been identified with straw and dried cotton fibre.
84. *Ṛgveda* - I. 51, 3; X. 79, 3
85. *Ṛgveda* - III. 5, 6; IV. 5, 7
86. *Ṛgveda* - V. 21, 4
87. *Ṛgveda* - I. 95, 10; III. 5, 8; VII. 9, 3; 35, 7; VIII. 6, 20. The word denotes young shoots of grass or herbs used at the sacrifice.
88. *Vājasaneyī Saṁhitā*, XVIII. 12
89. *Chāndogya Upaniṣad* - I. 10, 2, 7
90. *Taittirīya Saṁhitā* - II. 4, 4, 1, 2
91. Maitrāyaṇī *Saṁhitā* - I. 2, 8; *Vājasaneyi Saṁhitā* - XVIII. 12; XIX. 22, 89; XXI. 29
92. *Atharvaveda* - X. 9, 26; XI. 1, 18; XII. 3, 18, 29, 30
93. *Atharvaveda* - IV. 7, 3; II. 8,3; VI. 140, 2; XVIII. 3, 69
94. *Ṛgveda* - I. 16, 2; III. 35, 3; 52, 5
95. *Ṛgveda* - VI. 13, 4
96. *Atharvaveda* - XIV. 2, 63
97. *Taittirīya Saṁhitā* - II. 2, 11, 4; *Taittirīya Brāhmaṇa* - III. 8, 14, 6
98. *Vājasaneyī Saṁhitā* - XVIII. 12
99. *Ṛgveda* - I. 23, 15; 66, 3; 117, 21; 135, 8; 176, 2; II. 2, 6; 14, 11; V. 85, 3; VII. 3, 4; VIII. 2, 3; 22, 6; 63, 9; 78, 10
100. *Ṛgveda* - V. 53, 13. The word is identified with *dhānya bīja* (rice seeds)
101. Macdonell, A.A. and Keith, A.B., *Vedic Index of Names and Subjects,* Volume II, MLBD, Delhi, Reprint 1995, p. 376.
102. *Atharvaveda* - VII. 11, 1; VIII. 10, 24.
103. *Śatapatha Brāhmaṇa* - V. 3, 3, 2.
104. *Atharvaveda* - VIII. 6, 2. The meaning of the word is 'straw' in which sense it occurs in the *Kauśka Sūtra* (lxxx. 27)
105. *Atharvaveda* - IX. 6, 16; XI. 1, 12, 29; 3, 5; XII. 3, 19. It is the husk of grain and very often used for a fire.
106. *Atharvaveda* - I. 7, 2
107. *Atharvaveda* - VI. 16, 4
108. *Atharvaveda* - VI. 16, 4
109. *Ṛgveda* - VIII. 40.6; *Nirukta,* I. 14; VI. 28.
110. *Atharvaveda* - VIII. 7.12
111. *Ṛgveda,* VI. 16, 13; VII. 33, 11
112. *Atharvaveda* - IV. 34, 5
113. *Śatapatha Brāhmaṇa* - XIII. 8, 1, 16
114. *Chāndogya Upaniṣad* - VII. 3, 1

115. *Ṛgveda* - VII. 59; *Atharvaveda* - XIV. 1, 17
116. *Kauṣītaki Brāhmaṇa* - X. 2; *Śatapatha Brāhmaṇa* - I. 5, 4, 5; V. 2, 1, 17
117. *Ṛgveda* - VII. 50, 3
118. *Ṛgveda* - X. 94, 13; 101, 3
119. *Ṛgveda* - X. 94, 13; 101, 3
120. *Atharvaveda* - X. 6, 33
121. *Chāndogya Upaniṣad* - VI. 3, 1
122. *Aitareya Upaniṣad* - III. 3
123. *Ṛgveda* - I. 164, 20, 22; II. 14, 2; 39, 1; IV. 20, 5; V. 78, 6
124. *Ṣaḍviṁśa Brāhmaṇa* - V. 11; *Nirukta,* IV. 19; V. 26; IX. 23.
125. *Ṛgveda* - II. 5, 4; V. 1, 1; VI. 7, 6; 13, 1; VIII. 13, 6, 17
126. *Ṛgveda* - I. 8, 8; VII. 43, 1; X. 94, 3
127. *Taittirīya Saṁhitā* - II. 5, 3, 5; III. 7, 4, 2; *Taittirīya Brāhmaṇa* -I. 4, 7, 6
128. *Taittirīya Saṁhitā* - VII. 3, 9, 1; *Ṛgveda* - II. 8, 11; *Atharvaveda* - VI. 30, 2
129. *Ṛgveda* - VI. 3, 4; X. 145, 4; *Atharvaveda* - X. 4, 3.
130. *Kāṭhaka Saṁhitā* - I. 180; *Śatapatha Brāhmaṇa,* VI. 6, 2,11
131. *Taittirīya Saṁhitā* - V. 1, 9, 3
132. *Taittirīya Brāhmaṇa* - III. 7, 4, 2
133. *Ṛgveda* - I. 135, 8; X. 97, 5; *Atharvaveda* - III. 6, 1; IV. 37, 4
134. *Ṛgveda* - I, 24, 7; *Atharvaveda* - IV. 37, 4; V. 5, 5
135. *Atharvaveda* - XX. 136, 13
136. *Atharvaveda* - XIX. 31, 1. The wood of this tree is like that of other kinds of fig tree—*Aśvattha, Nyagrodha* and *plakṣa*-was considered suitable for use in the sacrifice (*Taittirīya Saṁhitā* - III. 4, 8, 4)
137. *Kāṭhaka Saṁhitā* - XII. 10; *Maitrāyaṇī Saṁhitā* - III. 11, 2; *Vājasaneyī Saṁhitā* - XIX. 23, 91
138. *Ṛgveda* - VI. 48, 17
139. *Taittirīya Saṁhitā* - V. 2, 7, 3.4; VI. 2, 1, 5
140. *Ṛgveda* - X. 85, 20
141. *Ṛgveda* III. 53. 19; *Atharvaveda* - III. 6, 1; V. 5, 5; VIII. 8, 3
142. *Taittirīya Saṁhitā* - II. 4, 9, 2. of *Yajurveda.*
143. *Atharvaveda* VI. 15, 3
144. *Kauṣītakī Brāhmaṇa* X. 2; *Śatapatha Brāhmaṇa* - I. 5, 4, 5
145. *Ṛgveda* -I. 164, 20
146. *Kāṭhaka Saṁhitā of Yajurveda* - XII. 10
147. *Maitrāyaṇī Saṁhitā* - III. 9, 3
148. *Atharvaveda* - VIII. 2, 28
149. *Taittirīya Saṁhitā* - VI. 3, 10, 2
150. *Atharvaveda* - V. 5, 5
151. *Atharvaveda* - VI. 11, 1; 30, 2, 3
152. *Ṛgveda* - VII. 50, 3
153. *Ṛgveda* - III. 53, 19
154. *Śatapatha Brāhmaṇa* - XIII. 8, 1, 16
155. *Śatapatha Brāhmaṇa* - XIII. 8, 1, 16
156. *Ṛgveda* - I. 23, 15; X. 34, 13
157. *Atharvaveda* - VIII. 10. 24
158. *Ṛgveda* - I. 117. 21

卐 卐 卐

THE CONCEPT OF PLANT SCIENCE IN ANCIENT INDIAN LITERATURE

Mukta Biswas

Ancient India is known all over the world for her rich cultural heritage. Indian civilization was highly developed and influenced the development of other civilizations of the world. From the studies of ancient literature it is evident that Indians in ancient times made tremendous progress in art, religion, literature, philosophy etc. There is a general impression that in the field of science ancient Indians made little contribution or not at all. Contrary to the general belief, India made significant contributions to many branches of science like Astronomy, Mathematics, Chemistry and Botany which were both original and fundamental. Sanskrit is the treasure house of the wisdom of ancient Indians in science.

The present write-up is an attempt to discuss ancient India's contribution to the field of Plant Science. The study of plant life can be traced back to very ancient times. The knowledge on the rich plant kingdom is reflected in the ancient works like *Ṛgveda, Atharvaveda, Upaniṣads, Mamusaṁhitā* etc. Dependence on plants for food and shelter necessitated pre-Vedic Indians to study the plants and plant life in a scientific way. There are references that agriculture, horticulture, sylviculture were greatly developed in India during the Vedic period. The science of botany, on which all these applied sciences were based, was known in ancient time as Vṛkṣāyurveda, i.e., the knowledge of tree life. This science was also called Bheṣajavidyā as a major portion of the medicinal substances used were plant-products. The Vṛkṣāyurveda, a work on plants, by sage Parāśara who belonged to 100 B.C. is one of the most significant ancient works on Botany. The work Vṛkṣāyurveda of Surapāla of the llth C.A.D. and the Vṛkṣāyurveda section of the *Agnipurāṇa* dealt with plants and their treatment. These works reveal a profound and in-depth knowledge of plant science. No systematic work on Vṛkṣ āyurveda belonging to the early period is available now. There are, however, references to this subject scattered in different ancient texts from which it is possible to procure an account of this science. The information gathered from ancient works could be arranged according to modern botanical terminology as: (i) Classification and Morphology, (ii) Physiology, (iii) Ecology and (iv) Taxonomy.

CLASSIFICATION AND MORPHOLOGY

The Ṛgveda[1] categorised the plants into various categories based on their morphological characters and other properties. Plants were classified into three broad classes viz. Vṛksa (tree), Oṣadhi (herb useful to man), and Vīrudh (minor herb). According to another classification based on their form of growth, plants were divided into *Vṛkṣa* and *Druma* (tree), *Viśākha* (shrub with spreading branches), *Sasa* (herb), *Aṁsumalin* (Spreading or deliquescent plant), *Stambinī* (bushy plant), Vratatī (climber), Pratanvatī (creeper) and Alasāla (creeper spreading on the ground).

The *Atharvaveda*[2] further classified 'Sasa' into Prastṛṇatī (expanding), Ekaśuṅga (one sheothed or spathed), Aṁśumatī (having many stalks or branches) and Kāṇḍinī (jointed). Different parts of a plant body are found to be mentioned in the *Ṛgveda*. The *Atharvaveda*[3] gave an almost complete enumeration of parts of a plant described in a hymn as : "Rich in sweets the roots, rich in sweets the tips of them, rich in sweets the middle of the plants (stem); rich in sweets the leaves, rich in sweets the flowers of them".

The *Mahābhārata*[4] also contained an analogy which mentioned various parts of a tree, including the trunk, branches, nodes, leaves, flowers, fruits and seeds. The *Viṣṇu Purāṇa*[5] classified the principal parts of a plant into mūla or pāda (the subterranean part) and Tūla or Vistāra (subaerial part). In ancient times leaves of a tree were classified as Ekapatra, Dvīpatra, Tripatra or Saptaparṇa and so on according to the number of their leaflets. Such classification of plants was in existence around 5000 years ago, whereas Theophrastus, the Greek scholar, who was considered to be the founder of modern botany in the West, made classification of the plants around 300 B.C. Parāśara in 100 B.C. classified the flowering plants into various families such as Samīganiya, Pupīlikāgaṇiya, Svastikagaṇīya and Kurcāgaṇītya. In modern times (1700 AD) the flowering plants are classified into Leguminoesae, Rutaceae, Cruciferae, Composite etc.

It may be highlighted that the classification of flowering plants made by Parāśara is an agreement with that of modern-day classification. It is worth mentioning that both external and internal morphology of plants was known to the ancient Indians. Mention of the words like Bījakoṣa (seed vessel), Śasya (endosperm) and Bījapatra (cotyledon) in early works revealed the acquaintance of ancient Indians about the different parts of the seed.

Parāśara in his work gave a detailed description of Rasakoṣa, i.e. plant-cell. He stated that plant cells contain Kalaveṣṭana (outer wall), Sūkṣma Patraka (inner wall), Rañjakayukta Rasāśraya (sap with colouring matter) and Anvasva (not visible to the naked eye).

In modern era Robert Hook (1665 AD) revealed that plants contain compartments (cells) which are honeycomb types in structure.[6] Significantly, descriptions of plant cells given by Parāśara bear similarity with that of Robert Hook made in modern age with the help of a microscope.

PHYSIOLOGY

Plants have been regarded as living beings since Vedic times. Ancient works like *Ṛgveda, Manusaṁhitā* and *Mahābhārata*[8] reveal possession of knowledge regarding the consciousness of trees and plants. An important aspect of plant physiology is photosynthesis. The process of photosynthesis was known to the ancient Indians. They knew that plants absorb food from soil in a state of solution.

The phenomena of absorption, transport and preparation of food in the leaves of plants in the presence of solar energy and air were known to them. The Sanskrit name "Pādapa" (the one who drinks water by foot) for plant substantiates this notion. The process of photosynthesis is found to be described in the *Mahābhārata*[9] where it is said that just as water is sucked through the lotus petiole, so also plants with roots drink (absorb and draw up through the stem) water, i.e. watery solution with air.

American scientists Dixon and Jolly as recently as 1894 proposed the theory of suction force to explain the process of absorption of water by plants.[10] *Suśrutasaṁhitā* mentioned that ṛtu (proper season), i.e. suitable temparature, conditions for germination of seeds. Guṇaratna's commentary on

Saddarsansamuccaya further mentiond that the seeds of banyan, *aśvattha* and *nimba* sprout during the rainy season under the influence of weather and air. The suitability of particular seasons for planting of different saplings was found out. Thus, it is clear that post-Vedic Indians had the knowledge that air, warmth and water are necessary for germination of seeds and growth of plants.

ECOLOGY

Ancient Indians classified plants in accordance with the nature of the soil in which they grew, *e.g. Jāṅgala* (arid), *Ānūpa* (marshy), and *Sādhāraṇa* as they knew that the growth and development of plants depend to a great extent on climate and soil. Jaṅgala was described as a region of open spaces where a steady dry wind blows. In such areas there were few rivers and rivulets and consisted of dry and rough sand. The plants found in such a region were known as *Khadira* (Acacia catechu), *Asana* (Terminalia tomentosa), and *Badarī* (Zizyphus jujuda), among others.

The Anūpa region was stated to be a marshy tract bordered by seas. Some of the plants grown in this region were Vañjula (cane or reed), Hintāla (a kind of palm) and Nārikela (coconut). The Sādhāraṇa region had some of the features common to the other two regions. Mandāra, Pārijātaka (coral tree) and Santāna (kalpa tree) were some of the plants found in this region. Ancient people could correlate climatic variations like excessive rainfall, drought etc. with the types of plants grown in a certain locality.

TAXONOMY

A scientific and rational procedure was adopted in the nomenclature of plants in ancient times as well. For example, plants were named in accordance with their special association, medicinal and other properties, environmental association and other noticeable peculiarities. Medicinal properties were utilized in naming plants such as Dadrughna (curer of eczema) and Arśoghosa (curer of piles). Examples of naming plants on the basis of some dynastic utility are Dantadhāvana tree (cleaning of teeth), of which the twig is used as a tooth brush. Morphological features were embodied in Tripatra (three leafed), Śatamūlī (hundred rooted). The *Matsyapurāṇa*[11] mentions *Jalaja, i.e.,* water plants which emphasised the environmental association.

Ancient Indian botanists made notable contributions to the field of agriculture. Knowledge of rotation of crops by fallowing the land and by cultivating different crops alternately in the same field is found to be described in the ancient work like *Taittirīyasaṁhitā*.[12] Roxburgh believes that for the practice of crop rotation the western world is indebted to India.

The references to cuttings and graftings of plants are found in the treatise like *Bṛhatsaṁhitā, Arthāśāstra, Manusaṁhitā* etc. Ancient people were aware that for successful agriculture, crops and plants must be protected from diseases. Hence, they acquired the knowledge of plant pathology for understanding the causes, symptoms and cures of plant diseases.

The *Atharvaveda*[14] refers to the destruction of corn by pestiferous insects. Sāyaṇa's commentary on *Atharvaveda* gives a long list of such pests. Among the remedies suggested were the removal of affected parts of the plants and taking of preventive measures against fresh infections through the wound.

Agnipuraṇā says that if the fruit of a tree continues to be spoilt, it should at first be cut with a weapon, then it should be smeared with a mixture of Vidaṅga, ghee and mud, and then cold water should be sprinkled over it.[15] Flowers and fruits were produced abundantly if a mixture of Kulatha,

Māsa, Mudga, Yava, Tila and ghee in cold water was sprinkled over a tree. Barrenness of plants was also considered as a disease for which certain remedies were prescribed.

According to *Agnipurāṇa,* Phalanāśa (loss of fruits) could be averted by spraying the leaves and branches of the tree concerned with the mixture of Vidaṅga, ghee, powdered mudge etc., and cold water should be sprinkled with a paste of horsegram, blackgram, greengram, barley and sesamum. For the proper growth and nourishment of a mango tree, cold water in which fish has been washed, should be sprinkled.

Application of crushed fish meat mixed with Vidaṅga and rice would make the trees bear fruits. It was prescribed as a panacea for curing the diseases of various trees.[16] Sprinkling with the admixture of excreta of sheep and goat, pulverised barley and seasamum that were allowed to be soaked in meat and water for seven nights would also increase the bearing of fruits and flowers in all kinds of trees.[17]

In conclusion it could be said that knowledge of plant science played a vital role in the development of agriculture and medicinal science in ancient days. Moreover, it helped in trade and commerce in various ways. Most of the commodities involved in the trade were plant products and even the transport vessels were made of wood.

Acquirement of the knowledge of this branch of science also had its impact on the cultural life of ancient people by way of making dresses, furniture, vehicles etc. from plants and trees. It is revealed that India cultivated plant science, in howsoever rudimentary a form, at a time when most of the seats of ancient civilization knew little or nothing about it.

REFERENCES & NOTES

1. *Oṣadhi prati modadvaṁ puṣpavatī prasūbarīḥ asvaiba sujitvarīvīrudhaḥ pārayiṣnabaḥ, RV.* X. 97.3
2. *Prastṛṇatī stambinīrekaṣuṅgāḥ pratanvatīroṣubhīra aṁśumatīḥ kāṇḍinīryā viśakhā hvayāmi te vīrudha.....* *AV,* VIII, 7.4
3. *Madhumanmūlaṁ madhumadagramāsāṁ madhumanmadhvaṁ vīrudha babhuva,*
   mamdhumatparnaṁ madhumat puṣpamāsāṁ modhoḥ.
   saṁbhakta amrtasya bhaksoh, AV, VIII, 7,12
4. *MBh,* I, 65-66
5. *VP* - II, 7.37-39
6. *Cf. SHI,* p. 79
7. *Antaḥ saṁjñā bhaventyete sukhaduḥkha samanvitā - MS.* I. 49
8. *Uṣmato mlāyate parnaṁ tvak phalaṁ puṣpamedaca*
   mlāyate ṣīryate cāpi sprśastenātra bidyate, MBh - XII. 184,II
9. *Vaktreṇotpalanālena yathordhvaṁ jalamādadet*
   tatha pavanasaṁyuktaḥ padaiḥ pibati pādapaḥ - MBh, XII,184, 16
10. *Cf. SHI.* p. 83
11. *Mat.,* p. 118. 39-41
12. *Tat. S.,* V. I. 7.3
13. *Upavanavinoda,* p.115
14. *AV,* VI, 50

15. *Biphalā syurghanā vṛkṣā śastrenādau hi śodhanaṁ Vidaṅga ghṛtapaṅkāktān secayacchītavāriṇā, AP,* 282, 9-10.
16. *Vidaṅga tandulapetaṁ matsyaṁ māṁsaṁ hi dohadaṁ sarvesāṁ viseṣeṇa vṛkṣānāṁ rogamardānaṁ, AP.* 282. 13
17. *Gomāṁsamudakañcaiba saptarātraṁ nidhāpayet utsekaḥ sarvavṛkṣaṇāṁ phalapuspādivṛdhidaḥ. AP.,* 282 .12

ABBREVIATIONS

AP	-	*Agnipurāṇa*
AV	-	*Atharvavedasaṁhitā*
MBh	-	*Mahābhārata*
MS	-	*Manusmṛti*
Mat. P	-	*Matsyapurāṇa*
RV	-	*Ṛgvedasaṁhitā*
Tat. S	-	*Taittirīyasaṁhitā*
Vp	-	*Viṣnupurāṇa*
SHI	-	*Scientific Heritage of India*

BIBLIOGRAPHY

Agnipurāṇaṁ - ed. by Pt. Panchanan Tarkaratna, published by Natabar Chakraborty in Бangabasi Electro Machine Press, Calcutta

Atharvavedasaṁhitā - Hindi translation with text by K. Trivedi, 1912-21

Mahābhārata - With Nīlakaṇṭha's commentary, Poona, 1929-36

Manusmṛtī - ed.by V.L. Pansikar, NSP, 1933

Matsyapurāṇaṁ - ed by P. Tarkaratna, Calcutta, 1316 B.S.

Ṛgvedasaṁhitā - ed. by R.C. Dutta, Calcutta, 1963

Taittirīyasaṁhitā - by A.M. Sastri and K. Pangacharya, Mysore, 1900-02.

Upavanavinoda - ed. by G.P. Majumdar, Calcutta, 1935

Viṣṇupurāṇaṁ - by P.Tarkaratna, Bangabasi Press, 1331 BS.

Banarji, S.C., *A Companion to Sanskrit Literature*, Motilal Banarasidass, Delhi.

Nagaraj,V. *Scientific Heritage of India, Viśvasaṁskṛtam*, Bangalore, 1997

The Cultural Heritage of India Vol. VI, The Ramkrishna Mission Institute of Culture, Calcutta

Scientific Heritage of India, The Mythic Society, Bangalore

Seal, B.N., *Positive Sciences of the Ancient Hindus*, Delhi, 1958

卐 卐 卐

CLASSIFICATION OF PLANTS & PLANT SUBSTANCES IN SANSKRIT LITERATURE

Nirmal Trikha

Classification of Plants and Plant Substances is a subject which comes under plant Taxonomy. Plant Taxonomy is a Systematic Botany which deals with the nomenclature, description, identification and classification of plants into various natural groups based on resemblances and differences in their morphological characteristics. A study of ancient Sanskrit literature reveals the systematization of Plant Science by Indians and their scientific approach for the nomenclature and classification of plants and plant substances.

The *Ṛgveda* and the *Atharvaveda* name some plants based on morphological characteristics and other peculiarities. 'Apāmārga' is described as 'Pratyāvṛta' because it has perverted leaves.[1] 'Arundhatī' is called, 'Hiraṇyavarṇā'[2] (golden coloured) and 'Lomavakṣā'[3] (with hairy stem). 'Aśvavāra' or 'Aśvavāla' is the name of the tree which has hair resembling the tail of a horse. The 'Āṇḍīka' has fruits of the shape of 'Aṇḍa' (egg).[4] Arātaki (Odina pinnata) is a plant which is described as goat-horned (Ajaśṛṅga)[5]. 'Aśvattha' (Ficus religiosa) is called Vaibādha (the destroyer) because it plants its roots in the 'Khadira' and other[6] trees and destroys them.[7] The epithet 'nāna-vīrya'[8] (of manifold powers) is applied to medicinal plants as they possess medicinal properties. The A.V. mentions all the medicinal plants and herbs by describing their forms and characteristics, e.g. pra-stṛṇatiḥ (expanding), stambinih (bushy),[9] eka-śuṅgah (single-spathed), pra-tanvatiḥ (expanding), aṁśumatī (having many shoots), kāṇḍinih (jointed), vi-śākhāh (having spreading branches), Jīvala (growing up again), naghāriṣ ā (harmless) and madhumatī (sweet).

Nomenclature of plants on the basis of the peculiarity of their leaves (parṇa), flowers (puṣpa), fruits (phala) and root (mūla) has been referred to in the *Aṣṭādhyāyī* of Pāṇini.[10] For instance, Śaṅkhapuṣpī (Andropogon aciculatus) is a herb which has flowers white like conch-shell (śaṅkha). Some plants derive their names from the season in which they bloom.[11] The *Kāśikā* mentions *'Vāsantī Kundalatā'* (Jasminum multiflorm) flowering in the spring season as an example.

Parāśara is a pioneer in the field of Botany as far as nomenclature is concerned. Shri N.N. Sircar[12] has righty pointed out the importance of *Vṛkṣāyurveda* of Parāśara for the identification of plants :

"Without, therefore, a knowledge of the *Vṛkṣāyurveda*, botanical synonyms of plants used in the *Vaidyaka* treatises cannot be properly interpreted and identified in many cases, and that is why it is not possible for one, these days to become conversant with the identities of the vegetable drugs of Indian Pharmacopoeias."

Caraka, Suśruta and other authors of the medical treatises have adopted three types of synonyms for medicinal plants. The Botanical,[13] Theraputic[14] and habitats or special events are the three factors which form the basis of their system of nomenclature.

The plant world is divided into three categories in the Vedic literature, *e.g.*, trees, herbs and creepers (vṛkṣa, oṣadha and vīrudh) *Vṛkṣa* denotes any tree. *Oṣadha* is a plant possessing a healing quality. *Vīrudh* is a term for minor vegetable growths.

The *Ṛgveda* classifies plants into four groups, *e.g.*, flowering, non-flowering, fructiferous and non-fructiferous.[16] The four-fold classification based on morphological and some other special characteristics is found in the Atharvaveda. These four-fold divisons are: which have flowers, which have no flowers, those which have fruits and those which are fruitless.[17]

The *Atharvaveda*[18] classifies medical herbs on the basis of colour, *e.g.*, twany, bright, real, spotted, swarthy, black.

Manusmṛti classifies plants[19] into Oṣadhi, Vanaspati, Vṛkṣa, Guccha, Gulma, Tṛṇa, Pratāna and Vallī. Oṣadhi is a plant which withers away after fructificaion and bears lots of flowers and fruits.[20] Vanaspati is a tree that bears fruits without evident flowers. Vṛkṣa bears fruits and flowers.[21] Gulma (succulent shrubs), Guccha (bushes), Tṛṇa (grass), Pratāna (creeper with stems spreading on the ground) and Vallī (climbers) are grown from seed (Bīja) and Stem (kāṇḍa).[22]

The *Aṣṭādhyāyī* divides the plant kingdom conveniently into two divisions, *e.g.*, *Oṣadhi* and *Vanaspati*.

The *Carakasaṁhitā* classifies plants on the basis of external and floral characters, dietic or medicinal values. The plants are classified according to the following three distinct principles, e.g.

1. Botanical (udbhijjādi)
2. Dietic (annapānādi)
3. Medicinal (virecanādi)

According to botanical principle, Caraka has divided plants into four categories :[24]

(i) Vanaspatis (Trees having fruits without evident flowers)
(ii) Vṛkṣa or Vānaspatya (Trees bearing both fruits and flowers)
(iii) Vīrudha (Creepers without expanding stems).
(iv) Auṣadhi (plants which wither away when their fruits become ripe).[25]

The important groups of dietic (*annapānādi*) classification of plants are mentioned below :

(i) Śūkadhānya.[26] (Monocotledons)
(ii) Śamīdhānya.[27] (Di-cotyledons)
(iii) Śākavargah.[28] (Group of vegetables)
(iv) Phalavarga.[29] (Group of fruits)
(v) Haritavarga.[30] (Class of Greens)

In the medicinal (*Virecanādi*) classification, Caraka has classified plants according to the plant products used in medicine. The root, bark, sāra (aqueous extract), secretions, fibre, juice, tender leaves, latex, fruits, flowers, ashes, oils, thorns, matured leaves, sprouts, etc. are used in medicine.[31] The plants having the therapeutically used roots are sixteen.[32] The plants having the therapeutically most useful fruits are nineteen.[33] There are three plants whose latex is useful[34] and another three plants which have useful bark.[35]

Caraka has classified plants in accordance with their medicinal power to cure deranged *Vāyu (Vāta)*, Phlegm (*Pitta*) and Bile (*Kapha)*.

According to the simplest, easiest and the most systematic classification in the C.S., the plant substances have been classified into fifty groups, each containing ten plant substances : [36]

(i) Jīvanīya[37] (Life-promoters)

(ii) Brihaṇīya[38] (Roborants)

(iii) Lekhanīya[39] (Weight reducing)

Musta (Cyperus rotundus Linn.)
Kuṣṭha (Sanssurea lappa C.S. Clarke)
Laridrā (Curcuma longa Linn.)
Dāruharidrā (Berberis aristata B.C.)
Vacā (Acorus calamum. Linn.)
Ativiṣā (Aconitum heterophyllum wall)
Kaṭurohinī (Picrorhiza kurroa Royle ex Benth)
Citraka (Plumbago zeylanica Linn)
Cirabilva (Pongamia pinnata Merr.)
Laimavatī (Iris versicolor)

(iv) Bhedanīya[40] (Purgative)

(v) Sandhānīya[41] (Wound healing)

(vi) Dīpanīya[42] (Digestive stimulants)

(vii) Balya[43] (Strength giving)

(viii) Varṇya[44] (Complexion promotors)

(ix) Kaṇṭhya[45] (Good for voice)

(x) Hṛdhya[46] (Cardic tonics)

Āmra (Mangifera indica Linn.)
Āmrātaka (Spondias pinnata Kurz)
Likuca (Artocarpus lakooca Roxb.)
Karamada (Carissa carandes Linn)
Vṛkṣāmala (Tamarindus indica Linn)
Amalavetasa (Rheum emodi wall)
Kuvala (Zizypus sativa Gaert)
Badara (Zizyphuz jujuba Lam)
Dādima (Punica granatum Linn)
Mātuluṅga (Citrus decumana Linn)

(xi) Triptighna[47] (Appetisers)

(xii) Arshioghnana[48] (Anti-Hemorrhoidals)

(xiii) Kuṣṭhaghna[49] (Cure for Dermatosis)

(xiv) Kaṇḍughna[50] (Anti-Itching)
(xv) Kṛmighna[51] (Anti-Infection)
(xvi) Viṣaghna[52] (Poison killer)
(xvii) Stanyajanan[53] (Galactogogues)
(xviii) Stanyashodhaka[54] (Galacto-purificators)
(xix) Shukrajanana[55] (Spermmatopoietics)
(xx) Shukrashodhaka[56] (Semeno-purifiers)
(xxi) Svedopaga[57] (Persperation inducing)
(xxii) Vamanopaga[58] (Adjuvants of emesis)
(xxiii) Virecanopaga[59] (Puragatives)
(xxiv) Āsthāpanopaga[60] (Adjuvants of non-oily type of enema)
(xxvi) Anuvāsanopaga[61] (Adjuvants of oily type of enema)
(xxvii) Shirovirecanopaga[62] (Adjuvants in Errhines)
(xxviii) Chardi Nigrahaṇa[63] (Anti-Emetics)
(xxix) Tṛṣṇānigrahana[64] (Anti-thirst)
(xxx) Hikkā-nigrahaṇa[65] (Anti-Hicough)
(xxxi) Purīṣasaṅgrahanīya[66] (Bowel-binding)
(xxxii) Purīṣavirajahīya[67] (Corrective of fecal Pigments)
(xxxiii) Mūtrasaṅgrahaṇīya[68] (Urinary Astrigents)
(xxxiv) Mūtravirajanīya[69] (Corrective of Urinary pigments)
(xxxv) Mūtravirecanīya[70] (Diuretics)
(xxxvi) Kāśahara[71] (Anti-cough)
(xxxvii) Śvāsahara[72] (Anti-Bronchitus)
(xxxviii) Śothahara[73] (Anti-Dropsy)
(xxxix) Jvarahara[74] (Cure for fever)
(xl) Śramahara[75] (Anti-Fatigue)
(xli) Dāhapraśamana[76] (Anti burning sensation)
(xlii) Śītapraśamana[77] (Anti-cold)
(xliii) Udardapraśamana[78] (Anti-Urticarials)
(xliv) Aṅgamardapraśamana[79] (Cure for malaise)
(xlv) Śūlapraśamana[80] (cure for pain)
(xlvi) Śoṇitasthāpana[81] (Haemostatics)
(xlvii) Vedanāsthāpana[82] (Sedatives)
(xlviii) Sajñāsthāpana[83] (Restoratives of consciousness)
(xlix) Prajāsthāpana[84] (Procreatants)
(l) Vayahsthāpana[85] (Longevity promoters)

The above mentioned fifty groups of plant substances are further classified by Caraka into ten groups in the following way :

Group	Decades of Plant substance
I	1-6
II	7-10
III	11-16
IV	17-20
V	21-27
VI	28-30
VII	31-35
VIII	36-40
IX	41-45
X	46-50

Numerically speaking, the plant substances are not five hundred in the above classification. Sometimes, one and the same plant substance is repeated in the groups due to its various functions. A few non-plant substances too have crept in the group. But, the attempt of Caraka in the sphere of classification of plants and plant substances, based on their medicinal value, cannot be underestimated.

Another classification of plant substances into six categories has been done by Caraka having only taste in view :[86]

(i) Sweet group of plant substances[87]
(ii) Sour group of plant substances[88]
(iii) Strong group of plant substances[89]
(iv) The pungent group of plant substances[90]
(v) The bitter group of plant substances[91]
(vi) The Astringant group of plant substances[92]

Besides taste, the plant substances have also been classifical by Caraka according to their potencies *vipāka* and specific action.[93]

Suśruta, classification of plants into Vanaspati, Vṛkṣa or Vānaspatya Virudha and Oṣadhi is identical with that of Caraka.[94] He clasifies medicinal plants into thirty-five groups. Classification of plants on the basis of dietic value, also finds place in the Suśruta saṁhitā. Characteristic flora is the basis of the classification of soil in the Suśruta saṃhitā.[95]

The *Arthaśāstra* of Kauṭilya classifies crops according to the time of sowing. It classifies forest products into timber trees, group of bamboos, rope making material, plants that yield leaves for writing material, group of medicines, poisons, fire wood and fodder, plants used for preparing liquor, etc. The Arthaśāstra has classified plants according to the land suitable for their growth also.[97]

Varāhamihira, in his *Bṛhatsaṁhitā,* has given the botanical classification[98] of plants into: (i) Taru, Vṛkṣa, Druma, Pādapa, (ii) Gulma and (iii) Latā, Vallī. Another system of classification of plants appears to be on the basis of the genders of their names[99]. The trees are also classified into Kaṇṭakin[100] (thorny), Phalin[101] (phaladruma, phalataru), Puṣpadruma and Kṣīrin[102] (trees with milky sap). The classification of plants according to the soil on which they grow, is also found in the Bṛhatsaṁhitā. The botanical classification of plants into Śūkadhānya[103] and Kośa-dhānya[104] or ŚamīJāti[105] corresponds to the modern botanical classes of mono-cotyledons and di-cotyledons respectively.

The Vana-auṣadhivarga and Vaiśyavarga of Amarakoṣa deal with the botanical classification of plants into Vānaspatya, Vanaspati, Auṣadha, Kṣupa, Stamba, Gulma, Vallī, Latā, Tṛṇa and water plants.[106]

Śukranītisāra has classified trees into fruit-bearing trees[107] and thorny trees.[108] According to the Vaiśeṣikas like Praśastapāda, the seven categories of plants are Vṛkṣa tṛṇa, oṣadhi, gulma, latā, avatāna, and vanaspati.

The *Vṛkṣāyurveda* of Parāśara classifies plants on the basis of comparative morphology. A few examples of Gaṇa Vibhāga (classification of plants into familites) based on floral characters,[109] their resemblances and differences are noted below :

(i) Samīgaṇīyam[110] (belonging to the family of Leguminosea)

(ii) Puplikagaṇīyam[111] (belonging to the family of Rutaceae)

(iii) Tripuṣpagaṇīyam[112] (family of Cucurbitacea)

(iv) Mallikāgaṇīyam[113] (family of Apocynaceae)

(v) Svastikāgaṇīyam[114] (family of Cruciferae)

(vi) Kurchapuṣpagaṇīyam.[115]

The Upavanavinoda contains a chapter on the classification of plants.

Thus, the survey of Plant Taxonomy in ancient Sanskrit literature clearly proves that an exhaustive attempt was made both with respect to nomenclature as well as the classification of plants. Systematization of any branch of knowledge through proper nomenclature and classification appears to be a speciality of ancient Indians. The classification of plants was based on external or floral characteristics as well as medical or dietic use. Caraka, followed by Suśruta, has somewhat accepted the broad Vedic classification. They have recognized as subclasses some of the classes of plants enumerated by Manu. Positive attempts in the field of classification of plants have been made in the *Arthaśāstra, Bṛhatsaṁhitā, Amarakośa, Śukranītisāra,* works on *Vaiśeṣika, e.g., Prashastapādabhāṣya*, *Kandalī* of Śrīdhara and Kiraṇāvalī of Udayana. The elaborate classification of plants in the *Vṛkṣāyurveda* is based on morphological characteristics. Though the classification of plants into families and genus is generally not found in the ancient Sanskrit literature, some advancement in this direction is clearly discernible in the *Vṛkṣāyurveda.*

REFERENCES & NOTES

1. *A.V.* 17,2 *Cf.* Roth-St. Peterburg Dictionary, Whitney Translation of the *A.V.* 180
2. *A.V.* V . 5.7 हिरण्यवर्णे सुभगे शुष्मे।
3. *Maittrayaṇī Saṁhitā*-लोमवक्षणे।
4. *A.V.* IV 34,5-आण्डीकम्
5. *A.V.* IV 37. 4.6.
6. *A.V.* III,6, Such plants are called Parasite plants.

7. *A.V.* XII. 1.2.
8. *A.V.* VIII, 7;,4,8,13,27;
9. प्रस्तृणाती स्तम्बिनीरेकशुङ्गा प्रतन्वतीरोषधीरावदामि अंशुमती: काण्डिनीर्या विशाखा ह्वयामि ते।।
   वीरुधो वैश्वदेवीरुग्रा: पुरुषजीवनी:।।
   जीवला नघारिषा जीवन्तीमोषधीमहम्।
   अरुन्धतीमुन्नयन्तीं पुष्पां मधुमतीमिह . . . ।।
10. *A.V.* IV 1.64.
11. *A.V.* IV. 3.43
12. An Introduction to the *Vṛkṣāyurveda* of Parāśara, *Journal of the Royal Asiatic Society of Bengal*, vol. XVI. No. 1. p. 124.
13. परिचयज्ञापिका संज्ञा
14. गुणप्रकाशिका संज्ञा
15. *Taittirīya Saṁhitā*, ii, 5,3,2.
16. य: फलिनिर्य अफल अपुष्प यश्च पुष्पिणि:। X. 97.15
17. पुष्पवती: प्रसूमती: फलिनीरफला उत। VII. 7. 27
18. *A.V.* VIII.7.1.
19. All the plants grown from seed (Bīja) and stalk (Kāṇḍa) are called 'Udbhija' according to *Manusmṛti*, I. 46
   उद्भिज्जा: स्थावरा: सर्वे बीजकाण्ड प्ररोहिण:। *Manusmṛurti*, I. 46
20. ओषध्य: फल पाकान्ता बहुपष्पफलोपगा:।। *Manusmṛurti*, I. 46 II
21. अपुष्पा: फलवन्तो ये तो वनस्पतय: समृता:। *Manusmṛurti*, I.47
   पुष्पिण: फलिनश्चैव वृक्षास्तूभयत: स्मृता:।।
22. गुल्मगुच्छं तु विविधं तथैव तृणजातय:।
   बीजकाण्डरुहाण्येव प्रताना वल्ल्य एव च।।
23. Agrawala, V.S., *India as known to Pāṇini*, p. 210-11
24. औद्भिदं तु चतुर्विधम्। वनस्पतिर्वीरुधश्च वानंस्पत्यस्तथौषधि: ।। *C.S.* I .72.
25. फलैर्वनस्पति: पुष्पैर्वानस्पत्य: फलैरपि।
   ओषध्य: फलपाकान्ता: प्रातनैर्वीरुध: स्मृता:।। *C.S.* I.73
26. अथ शूकधान्यवर्ग: —
   रक्तशालिर्महाशालि: कलम: शकुनहृत:।
   तूर्णको दीर्घशूकश्च गौर: पाण्डुकलाङ्गुलौ।।
   सुगन्धको लोहवाल: सारिवाख्य: प्रमोदक:।
   पङ्गस्तपनीयश्च ये चान्ये शालय: शुभा:।। *C.S. Sūtrasthāna* XXVII, 8-9
27. Śamīdhanya comprises different varieties of pulses (*C.S.* XXVII, 24-34)
28. It includes leaves, roots, fruits, flowers, etc. *C.S.*XXCII. 124.I
   शाकवर्गीऽयं पत्रकन्दफलाश्रय:।।
29. This group contains fruits which are commonly used- *C.S.* XX VII.165 II
   Group of fruits- *C.S* XXVII. 125-165
   फलवर्गोऽयगुल्म: प्रयोपयोगिक:।।
30 *C.S.* XXVII, 166-176 These are the vegetables used uncooked in the salad term.
31. मूलत्थकसार निर्यासनालस्वरसपल्लथा:।
   क्षारा: क्षीरं फलं पुष्पं भस्म तैलानि कण्टका:।। *CS.* I- 75
32. *C.S.* I. 78-79
33. *C.S.* I. 82-84
34. *C.S.* I. 115
35. *C.S.* I. 117

36. *C.S.* Sūtra Sthāna - IV. 8
37. *C.S.* Sūtra Sthāna - IV.9- (i)
38. *C.S.* Sūtra Sthāna - IV. 9- (ii)
39. मुस्तकुष्ठहरिद्रादारुहरिद्रावचातिविषाकटुरोहिणी चित्रकचिरबिल्वहैमवत्य इति दशेमानि लेखनीयानि। *C.S.* 9- (iii)
40. *C.S.* IV. 9- (iv)
41. *C.S.* IV. 9 -(v)
42. *C.S.* IV. 9-(vi)
43. *C.S.* IV. 10-(i)
44. *C.S.* IV. 10-(ii)
.45. *C.S.* IV. 10-(iii)
46. आम्राम्रातकलिकुचकरमर्दवृक्षाम्लाम्लवेतसकुवलबदरदाडिममातुलुङ्गानीति दशेमानि हृद्यानि भवन्ति। *C.S.* IV. 10- (iv)
47. *C.S.* IV. 11- (ii)
48. *C.S.* IV11- (iii)
49. *C.S.* IV11- (iv)
50. *C.S.* IV 11-(v)
51. *C.S.* ICV11-vi)
52. *C.S.* IV12 - (i)
53. *C.S.* IV12 - (ii)
54. *C.S.* IV - (iii)
55. *C.S.* IV -12 - (iv)
56. *C.S.* IV- 12 - (v)
57. *C.S.* IV - 13 - (i)
58. *C.S.* IV- 13 - (ii)
59. *C. S.* IV - 13 - (iv)
60. *C.S.* IV. 13 - (v)
61. *C.S.* IV 13 - (vi)
62. *C.S.* IV 13 - (vii)
63. *C.S.* IV 14 - (i)
64. *C.S.* IV. 14 - (ii)
65. *C.S.* IV. 14 - (iii)
66. *C.S.* IV 15 - . (i)
67. *C.S.* IV 15 - (ii)
68. *C.S.* IV 15 - (iii)
69. *C.S.* IV 15 - (iv)
70. *C.S.* IV 15 - (v)
71. *C.S.* IV 15 - (i)
72. *C.S.* IV 16 - (ii)
73. *C.S.* IV16 - (iii)
74. *C.S.* IV 16 - (iv)
75. C.S IV 16 - (v)
76. *C.S.* IV 17 - (i)
77. *C.S.* IV 17 - (ii)
78. *C.S.* IV 17 - (iii)
79. *C.S.* IV 17 - (iv)
80. *C.S.* IV 17 - (v)
81. *C.S.* IV. 18 - (i)
82. *C.S.*IV 18 - (ii)
83. *C.S.* IV 18 - (iii
84. *C.S.* IV 18 - (iv)
85. *C.S.* IV 18 - (v)
86. सरभेदत: - *C. S.* Vimānasthānam VIII. 145

87. *C.S.* Vimānasthānam VIII. 139 - (i)
88. *C.S.* Vimānasthānam VIII. 140 - (i)
89. *C.S.* Vimānasthānam VIII. 141- (i)
90. *C.S.* Vimānasthānam VIII. 142 - (i)
91. *C.S.* Vimānasthānam VIII. 143 - (i)
92. C.S. Uimanasthanam VIII. 144 - (i)
93. रसवीर्यविपाकैश्च प्रभावैश्च प्रचक्ष्महे। *C.S.* XXXVII. (i)
94. तासां स्थावरश्चतुर्विधाः । वनस्पतयो वृक्षा वीररुध् ओषधय इति। तासु अपुष्पाः फलवन्तो वनस्पतयः पुष्पफलवन्तो वृक्षाः। प्रतानवत्यः स्तम्बिन्यश्च वीरुधः। फलपाकनिष्ठा ओषधय इति। *S. S. Sutrasthāna.* I. 23
95. *S. S. Sutrasthāna* - XXXV. 34-42
जाङ्गल, अनुप, साधारण।
96. *A.S.* II. 25.42
97. *A.S.* XXXIV, 116-17
98. वृक्षगुल्मलताश्च *Br. Sam.* XXXIX. 14
99. स्त्रीसंज्ञास्तरवः *Br. Sam.* XLII. 14
100. *Br. Sam.* XLVII. 4. LII. 84
101. *Br. Sam.* LII. 84-5
102. *Br. Sam.* XXXV. 17
103. *Br. Sam.* L.30
104. *Br. Sam.* VII. 8
105. *Br. Sam.* VIII. 10
106. वानस्पत्यः फलैः पुष्पात्, तैरपुष्पाद् वनस्पतिः।
ओषध्यः फल-पाकान्ताः स्युरवन्ध्यः फलेग्रहिः।। *Amarakoṣa*, II. 4.6
ह्रस्व-शाखा-शिफः क्षुपः। *Amarakoṣa* II. 4.8
अप्रकाण्डे स्तम्ब-गुल्मौः। *Amarakoṣa* II. 4.9
वल्ली तु व्रततिर्लता। *Amarakoṣa* II. 4.9
मूलात् चाऽग्रं गता लता। *Amarakoṣa* II. 4.11
107. IV. 4 48-51
108. IV.4. 57-61
109. अंगैश्चैतैश्च वृक्षवल्लीगुल्मानां साधर्म्यं वैधर्म्यं तुल्यातुल्प्रकृतिमयिसमौक्ष्य गणविभागम्।
110. बीजकाण्ड पुष्पांगसूचीयाध्यायः
111. बीजकाण्ड पुष्पांगसूचीयाध्यायः
112. बीजकाण्ड पुष्पांगसूचीयाध्यायः
113. बीजकाण्ड पुष्पांगसूचीयाध्यायः
114. बीजकाण्ड पुष्पांगसूचीयाध्यायः
115. बीजकाण्ड पुष्पांगसूचीयाध्यायः
116. *A Concise History of Science in India*, National Science Academy, p 386.

卐 卐 卐

FLORA : A SCIENTIFIC STUDY

S.K. Singhal

Plants are an integral part of our life. Life is not possible without them. There is a relationship between plants and animals (human beings). It is not a new relationship but very old since human beings came to the earth. Early men lived in forests and were nomadic in nature. In the beginning they did not know the value of the plants. But when they settled down, they started taking keen interest in nature and its products. They discovered many useful plants. They provide us with a lot of items, which we use everyday. Animals are also equally important. Their importance cannot be neglected. Plants and animals are divided into two groups on the basis of characters. There are 3,50,000 species of plants and 11 million species of animals.

The early man of the Stone Age depended totally on plants for his survival and developed means for utilizing natural resources. As the human civilization progressed its multifarious needs also increased. This led to a better understanding and appreciation of the plant kingdom and its economic importance. Man discovered that the plants could be used as food, for making clothes, medicines, decoration etc. Plants do the process of photosynthesis and synthesize the food for themselves and animals. The three basic needs of man like food, clothing and shelter are being provided for, by plants or their derivatives. All the animals, whether carnivorous, omnivorous or herbivorous, depend on plants.

1. Plants provide us with food, which is the basic need of each and every one. The main source of food is cereals (*wheat, rice,* and *maize*), vegetables, pulses, fruits etc. These are good sources of proteins, vitamins, minerals, carbohydrates etc. They provide use with energy as well as help in repairing the damaged parts of the body.

2. Man requires clothes for covering the body. Plants are a good source of the fibres. These fibres are *cotton* (Gossypium herbaceum), *Sun hemp* (*paṭsana*) (Crotolaria Juncea), *Pineapple* (Ananas comosus). We use all these fibres in making clothes, bags, ropes.

3. Plants give us rubber and latex. Many plants, specially xerophytes and succulents, exude a whitish viscous liquid known as latex. These organic compounds become hard on exposure to air. Christopher Columbus, during his adventure in the New World, noticed that natives of Haiti played with a ball that could bounce and was also waterproof. There are two types of rubber. Natural rubber and synthetic rubber. Natural rubber is obtained from plants. It has isoprene. Nowadays artificial rubber is also prepared, which is more durable. Thiokol and Neoprene are the Synthetic rubber. Thiokol is used in rocket as a fuel.

4. *Sugar* is derived from the Sanskrit word *śarkarā* that means sweet. It is universally present in all actively metabolising cells in the form of simple sugar like glucose. This form of sugar liberates the energy as it is oxidised. All the animals use this energy. Sugar is present in

ripe fruits, sugarcane plant (stem), and sugar beet. From the remains of the sugar a black colour product Molasses is obtained. This is used in making alcohol (Ethyl alcohol). It is used in drinking, antifreezer and in making varnish, drugs. Dry residue left at various stages is known as press mud. It is used as fertilizer, as an animal feed and for the extraction of wax and also in making carbon paper and polish.

5. A large number of wild plants are important sources of medicines. The medicinal plants possess various alkaloids, glycosides and tennins etc. which produce a specific physiological action in the human body. Plants also form an integral part of the Indian system of medicine. Homoeopathy, Ayurveda and Unani systems of medicine use the medicinal properties of these plants. All parts of the plants can be used for preparing medicines. In fact, Homoeopathy owes its origin to the plant kingdom. Dr. Samuel Hanhemann, "Father of Homoeopathy", while translating a "materia medica" from English to German, found that the "Peruvian Bark" (i.e. Cinchona) produced the same symptoms in a healthy individual which it was supposed to cure. Homoeopathy stands on this basic principle of "Similia Similibus Curantur". Both Homoeopathy and classical system of medicine use the bark of *Cinchona* to treat malaria. Homoeopathic medicine is "China" and Allopathic is "*Quinin*".

"Allium Cepa", derived from *onions* is used to treat cold and influenza. "Allium Sativa" (*Garlic*) is useful in the treatment of Colitis and "Zingiber officianale" (Ginger) is used for the treatment of Diarrhoea caused by eating *water-melons* and drinking impure water.

Aconite (Sweet poison) is used for the treatment of fever, pain, cough and diarrhoea. Apart from this, their sphere of action has also not left the third generation diseases untouched. Hypertension, Diabetes and Cancer have found great cures in the medicines derived from plants. "Rauwolfia Serpentina" is used to treat high blood pressure. The seed of "Syzgium Jabolicum" (*Jāmuna*) is used to treat sugar or diabetes. "Cinnamon" is known for its effects on cancer.

"Azadirachta Indica" (*Nīma*) has an excellent action on skin. "Gossypium" (cotton plant) acts as an emmenagogue. "Granatum" (pomegranate) aids in the expulsion of tapeworms, acting as a vermifuge. Medicines prepared from "Janosia Aśoka" (Ashoka Tree) are used in the treatment of uterine disorders in females. *"Ficus Religiosa" (Pīpala)* has a very effective treatment for bleeding disorders like piles, epistaxis and dysentry. *"Anacardium Orientale"*, (*Badāma*) prepared from almonds, is said to improve concentration in students and intellectuals and treat "Brain Fags" in them.

"Mint" (*Pudīnā*) is another medicinal plant. Its leaves are used for treatment of nausea, sickness and vomiting. *"Clove"* (*Lauṅga*) has warming qualities and is used as a stimulant, anti-septic and antispasmodic drug. It is a common constituent of many tooth pastes and mouth wash.

6. Plants are useful in increasing the fertility of soil. They also conserve the soil. The roots of leguminous plants like Pea, Gram etc. have the rhizobium bacteria, which fix the nitrogen into nitrate and save a large quantity of fertilizers. It also saves money. This makes the farmer economically strong and prosperous. Plants tightly bind the soil and prevent its erosion through water, air. Waste of plants like leaves, roots, stem mixed in the soil and decomposed by the microbes increase the fertility of soil.

7. Spices and condiments do not possess any nutritive value. Hence, they cannot be considered food. However, these are added only for increasing the taste and flavour of food. So, they are called food adjuncts. Spices are obtained from any part of the plant like Rhizome, bark, flower, leaves, fruits, seeds etc. The common spices are coriander, turmeric etc.

8. **Forest :** the word forest is derived from the Latin word foris. It means outside. It is generally used to include all vegetation occurring outside the premises of human dwellings and cultivation. Forests are of immense value to the life and prosperity of human beings. They greatly influence the social and economical status of a nation. Many of these are obtained from the forest. Timber is an important one and is used in ship-building, furniture making, plywood etc. But the products like oil, drugs, spices, gum, resins are also obtained. The common tree like Kadamba (*Kadamba*), Mango, Mulberry, Red Sandalwood, Indian Rosewood (*kālī Śiśama*), White Sandalwood, Bamboo etc. are used in making various things.

卐 卐 卐

DEFENCE MECHANISM IN PLANTS

Vandana Gupta

INTRODUCTION

Darwin had very rightly propounded the theory of 'The Survival of the Fittest', which says that only the fittest (strongest) of the living beings can survive in this world. The weaker are bound to become the prey of the stronger ones. God has provided various defence mechanisms to animals to protect them from others like a chameleon can change its colour to protect itself, a tortoise carries its shell on its back just in case of emergency and so on

The animal kingdom as a whole is directly or indirectly parasitic upon the plant kingdom. This being so, plants must either fall a victim to various classes of animals, particularly the herbivorous ones, which live exclusively on a vegetable diet. In order to survive they have been provided with special organs or devices to repulse or avoid the attack of their enemies. Being fixed to the ground they cannot, of course, manocuvre when attacked by animals.

VARIOUS DEVICES OF DEFENCE PRESENT ON THE SURFACE OF PLANT BODY

(i) Thorns, Spines, Prickles and Bristles

They are all sharp, pointed, hard structures specially developed to ward off herbivorous animals. Small spinous plants, commonly called thirtles, are beset with numerous spines and prickles all over their body so that no animal dare attack them.

(a) Thorns are modifications of branches and originate from deeply-seated tissues of the plant body. They are straight and hard and can pierce the body of thick-skinned animals. Plants like lemon (citrus), pomegranate (punica), duranta etc. are well provided with thorns for self-defence.

(b) Spines are modifications of leaves or parts of leaves and serve the purpose of defence. These are seen in pineapple, date-palm, dragger plant or Adam's needle (Yucca) etc. In dragger plant (Yucca) each leaf ends in a very sharp pointed spine and is directed obliquely outwards. It acts as a sort of dagger or pointed spike, protecting the plant against grazing animals.

(c) Prickles are also hard and pointed like thorns, but are usually curved and have a superficial origin; they are further irregularly distributed on the stem, branch or leaf. They are found in rose, coral tree, silk cotton tree etc. Cane and Pisonia, which are large climbing shrubs, are elaborately armed with numerous sharp prickles and spines for self-defence (as well as for climbing).

(d) Bristles are short, stiff and needle-like hair, usually growing in cluster and not infrequently barbed. Their walls are often thickened with deposition of silica or calcium carbonate. Bristles can be located in prickly pear (opuntia) and in many other cacti.

(ii) Stinging Hair

Nettles (Bichuti) develop stinging hair on their leaves or fruits or all over their body. Each hair has a sharp siliceous apex which breaks off even when touched lightly. The sharp point penetrates the body and inflicts a wound. The acid poison of the hair contained in its bulbous base is instantly injected into the skin of the victim's body. This evidently causes a sharp burning pain which is often followed by inflammation.

(iii) Glandular Hair

Many plants produce glandular hair on their leaves, branches and fruits. These glandular hair secrete a sticky substance which is a kind of a gum. If any animal feeds upon such a plant the glands stick to its mouth, and the animal finds it difficult to brush them off. Plants bearing glandular hair are thus never attacked by grazing animals. Tobacco (Nicotiana) is one such plant having glandular hair.

(iv) Hair

A dense coating of hair or presence of stiff hair on the body of the plant is always repulsive to animals as these hair stick on to their throat and cause a choking sensation. *e.g.* cut-weed (Gnaphalium) and many gourd plants (Cucurbila).

OTHER DEVICES OF DEFENCE

(v) Poisons

Many plants secrete poisonous and irritating substances. Such plants are carefully avoided by animals which can by intuition distinguish between poisonous and non-poisonous ones.

(a) Latex is the milky juice secreted by certain plants. It always contains some waste products, and often irritating and poisonous substances so that it causes inflammation and even blisters when it comes in contact with the skin. *e.g.* banyan, fig, peepul, garden poppy etc. contain latex.

(b) Alkaloids are in many cases exteremly poisonous and a very minute quantity is sufficient to kill a strong animal. There are various kinds of them found in plants e.g. morphine in opium poppy (Papaver), nicotine in tobacco (Nicotiana), daturine in Datura, quinine in Cinchona etc.

(c) *Irritating Substance.* Plants like many aroids possess needle-like or otherwise sharp and pointed crystals of calcium oxalate, i.e. raphides. These crystals, when such plants are fed upon, prick the tongue and the throat and cause irritation. Therefore, such plants never fall victims of grazing animals.

(vi) Bitter Taste and Repulsive Smell

These are also effective mechanisms to ward off animals. Paederia foetida emits a bad smell so that no animal likes to go near it. Plants like sacred basil (ocimum), mint etc. also emit a strong disagreeable odour.

(vii) Waste Products

Apart from latex, alkaloids etc., the presence of many other waste products such as tannin, resin, essential oils and silica also keep plants free from the attack of animals.

(viii) Mimicry

Certain plants also protect themselves against grazing animals by imitating the general appearance, colour, shape or particular feature of another plant or animal which has developed a special weapon of defence. For instance, there are certain aroids which resemble multi-coloured and variously spotted snakes. Leaves are also spotted and striped in many species of Bowstring Hemp (Sansevieria) and other allied plants. Herbivorous animals, possibly mistaking them for snakes or some other deadly creatures, carefully avoid them. Another aroid, called snake or cobra plant (Arisaema) common in Shillong and Darjeeling during the rains, expands like the hood of a cobra. This act of imitating the appearance, colour or any particular feature of another plant or animal is called mimicry.

Plants have also to protect themselves against the attack of many parasitic fungi and growing insects, and also against the scorching rays of the sun. This they do by developing a thick cuticle, cork and bark.

卐 卐 卐

MANGO MIAN!!

Jagan Nath

[Every season is mango season. This is one fruit that has its takers always. The mango legend is as rich as diverse. Mangoes are closely associated with the history of Indian horticulture. This fruit was spread to the continental and sub-continental world by the Muslim missionaries. It is a tree that is revered by both the Hindus and the Buddhists. Little wonder, it is described in the Hindu texts as 'kalpavṛṣksha', or the wish-yielding tree.]

Please dont touch. This was the watchword that greeted visitors to the International Mango Festival just concluded in New Delhi.

And to ensure that the "order" was strictly obeyed, a guard was posted at each table where the fruit was on display. This left no scope for any mischief.

The people present there were sorely disappointed, for they had gone to the show in the fond hope of tasting the luscious varieties of the fruit. Instead, they were handed over saltish snacks.

But there was a consolation prize, too. The newsmen, when they left, were given a mango pack as a parting gift. It was found to contain unripe bottle-green mangoes which took three to four days to ripen.

Indeed, the Talkatora Indoor Stadium, the venue of the festival, wore a festive look. A distinct mango flavour pervaded there.

(As many as 500 varieties of the mango were placed on tastefully decorated tables).

In all about 1,000 varieties are being grown in India, but only half of them were available for exhibition.

The mangoes came not only from India, but also from Costa Rica, Jamaica, Kenya, Gambia, Venezuela, Puerto Rico and Pakistan.

Some of the prominent mango-growing States of India are Punjab, Uttar Pradesh, Bihar, Andhra Pradesh, Orissa, Assam, Maharashtra, and Tamil Nadu.

India is producing 10 million tons of mangoes per annum. Andhra Pradesh is the largest producer, with 28,000 tons, followed by Uttar Pradesh 18,000 tons and Maharashtra 14,000 tons.

Mangoes at the New Delhi Festival were in all shapes, sizes and colours. The smallest, named Moti Dana, weighed just 2 grams, akin to a green pea.

Among the heaviest varieties was an exhibit from Rataul (Meerut). It was named Jam-e-Jam and weighed an astonishing 2 kilograms. Then there were the long ones. Potvakot, grown all over Western Uttar Pradesh, was 8 inches long, while Karela was a mind-boggling 9 inches long.

The popular mango varieties include Alphanso, Khas-ul-Khas, Rataul, Rumani, Safaida, Rajwala (one mango weighs more than one kg.) Raspunia, Langra and Dussehri.

India is the largest mango producer in the world, accounting for 60 per cent of the global production. Mangoes are grown in an area of 2,500,000 hectares of land in the country.

A spokesman of the Agricultural and Processed Food Product Export Development Authority (APEDA) told me that India was exporting fresh mangoes to about 40 countries, including the U.K., Canada, Russia, Saudi Arbia and Kuwait.

There is a heavy demand for Indian mangoes in Russia and Bangladesh. The Langra variety sells like hot cakes in Russia.

Mango is a cash crop, a good foreign exchange earner.

According to the spokesman, mango exports have been steadily rising since 1990-91. In 1993-94, the exports touched the Rs. 500 million mark.

The organisation of the International Mango Festival is trying to attract more foreign buyers and ultimately encourage them to travel to India. This is intended to help the promotion of business with this country.

Besides, it also helps in creating awareness among local citizens and domestic travellers of the fruit, which has immense potential for export.

The Festival was one of the many events organised by Delhi Tourism to attract both domestic and foreign tourists to the Capital.

Incidentally, India is the original home of this delicious fruit. This is evidenced by the fact that its botanical name is Mangifera Indica.

Young and old, rich and poor, high and low all enjoy eating mangoes. So was it in the centuries gone by.

The story of mangoes dates back to 4,000 years. The fruit, some say, is an incarnation of Prajāpati, the lord of creatures.

Mangoes earned praise from Alexander the Great, who became an ardent mango fan after he invaded India in 326 B.C. Poet Amir Khusro immortalised the fruit.

The mango tree has been described in the ancient Hindu books as Kalpavṛikṣa, or the "wish-granting tree." And the epic Rāmāyaṇa mentions the virtues of the mango.

It is depicted on the stūpas and other sculptures. It is also found in many paintings. Mango-shaped silver pendants and caskets in wood or papier mache are seen in craft bazars of India.

Ambi is an old, very old, mango motif. It is used in weaving needle work and textile printing. Other motifs may come and go but Ambi goes on for ever.

As in art, so in poetry. Sanskrit and later poets always praised the mango. The tree figures in many folk and tribal songs of love and longing. Mango poems and songs are written to this day. There are mango riddles and sayings too.

Mango is closely associated with the history of Indian horticulture.

It was introduced to several countries of the continental and sub-continental world by Muslim missionaries, Spanish voyagers and Portuguese explorers in the 15th and 16th centuries.

Kāma (Cupid, the god of love) tips his arrows with five spring flowers. One of these is the mango flower.

Strings of mango leaves are hung around for luck or auspiciousness at weddings and other ceremonies. Dry mango twings are cast into the holy fire.

The mango is, thus, a sacred tree. Both Hindus and Buddhists revere it. The tree finds mention in the Jātaka stories of the previous births of the Buddha. Many other tales also centre around the mango.

The mango is the richest source of Beta Carotens (the precursor mother or Vitamin A), a good source of Vitamin C, easily digestible sugars, a fair source of Vitamin B Complex and Niacin and minerals.

Mango parties have been common during the mango season since time immemorial. Mirza Ghalib, the renowned Urdu poet, once threw such a party. His poet friends came and enjoyed the Mirza's hospitality. They ate the luscious part and threw the seed out of the window.

One of the invitees saw that an ass came to the pile of mango seeds, sniffed it and went away. He drew the attention of Ghalib and remarked: "Look, Mirza Sahib, even asses do not eat mangoes." Showing great presence of mind, Ghalib retorted: "Only those who are asses ignore this food from heaven."

At one time kings and nobles had their own mango gardens. They had many choice varieties and encouraged their gardeners to produce new varieties, Shah-pasand (King's liking) and Begum-pasand (Queen's liking) are tell-tale names.

Mughal Emperor Akbar (16th century) had a personal orchard of over 100,000 mango-trees. Many of them are still bearing fruit in Darbhanga, Bihar State.

However, it is not because of this that the mango is called the 'King of Fruits'. The title comes from its abundance and popularity. It is a ruler of the hearts, it will remain so for ever.

卐 卐 卐

YAJÑA YOGA AND FRUITS IN WASTELAND AND ENVIRONMENT

Darshananand

One of the most important gifts of Nature is 'Earth'. Every human being is born on earth, lives on earth and dies on earth. Similar is the case with all flora and fauna of the whole world. We all are wholly and solely dependent on earth. What we eat, comes out of earth. What we drink comes out of earth, food and other crops, fruits and vegetables all grow on earth.

To have a healthy environment 'earth' alongwith other natural resources must be protected, specially in these days of pollution. Pollution has been classified into several heads like air-pollution, water-pollution, noise-pollution and soil-pollution.

Of these, air-pollution is most hazardous. This is caused by exhaust fumes and gases from rising industries, running vehicles, population, insanitation and others. These polluting fumes and gases are very harmful and poisonous as well.

On the other hand, ruthless cuttings of trees, forests and orchards and burning of jungles are going on in full swing. This is resulting in lack of oxygen and excess of deadly pollutants in air, which we are forced to inhale, causing thereby deterioration of many diseases which sometimes prove fatal.

These pollutants include carbon-dioxide, carbon monoxide, sulphurdioxide, nitrous oxide, methane, lead, tobacco smoke (nicotine, tar or charcoal : benzopyrine, nitrosemine; acetal dehyde, acrolene, hydrogen cyanide and formaldehyde), chloro-florocarbons (CFCs) and others.

Besides, vacant and unutilized plots of land turn into eroded land, savines etc. and disturb the environment. As such, earth must be best utilized. Protection and conservation of 'earth' is possible by several means and one of these is by covering the wasteland with vegetation like trees, specially fruit trees.

However, all this may be possible only when there is love for earth, land, soil, trees, fruits and 'Nature' as a whole. Yoga is one of the best and pious means for reaching near Nature. During Yajña, the burning materials in 'havana' emit scented fumes in air, which make the whole atomosphere pleasantly odorous, healthy and free from pollution.

While performing Yajña, the aspirants with their concentrated and peaceful minds develop will-power and a spiritual awakening in themselves, which result into exposure of their inner hidden potentialities.

Yajña and yoga, sādhana, meditation, prāṇāyāma, chanting of Veda mantras and other spiritual performances, with peaceful mind, pure heart and earnest ideas, awaken people's consciousness to feel that they are reaching nearer and nearer to Nature and God. These performances also create love for Nature. Swami Sivananda of Rishikesh has explained that teachings of sages and seers are that one should dwell in solitude, cleanse his heart and thoughts, meditate, harm none and love all.

A large area of land, to the tune of 1295.74 lac hectares, is estimated to be lying waste in our country (HTC, 8). Out of this, non-forest-degraded area is 936.85 lac hectares and forest-degraded area is 358.89 lac hectares (HTC, 8). Such wastelands are in various forms like banjar, usar, ravines, river-banks, low-lying areas and others. India has a total of about 70.0 lac hectares of wasteland under usar, out of which an area of 12.90 lac hectares is only in Uttar Pradesh (Pathak, 20), which is followed by the state of Gujarat, having an area of 12.15 lac hectares under usar.

Further, only 30 percent of cultivated land in our country is under irrigation and the remaining 70% of cultivation is done without irrigation (Jakhar, 10). These areas are either drought-prone or have no irrigation facilities and depend only on rain. The only means of watering crops of these areas is rain water, which is collected in ponds and 'diara' lands for utilizing in future. The cultivated area depending on rain has been estimated to be 14 crore hectares (Anon., 1).

Again, it is estimated that 40,000 hectares of cultivable land is becoming saline every year and the problem of plant growth under salt affected soil is more of concern in arid and semi-arid regions of the Indian sub-continent (Iyengar *et. al.*, 9). It has also been estimated that the country has extensive strips of coastal dune sand along 5600 km. of coastline occurring in different climatic ranges from-semi-arid to sub-humid regions (Iyengar *et. al.*, 9).

However, under the conditions mentioned above, the question of even thinking of any arrangements for irrigation facility in wastelands, therefore, does not arise at all. These dry wastelands are left only to the mercy of God. Off and on stray cattle are, of course, found roaming in search of vegetation. There, they get almost nothing to graze but they do erode the soil. Further, regular grazing, over-grazing, cattle ranching and torrential rains in forest areas too cause long-term damage to land. Ultimately, such forest areas are also turned into eroded wasteland (Dubey, 6). In a reference to the alarmingly bad state of environment in the world, it has been estimated that 25,000 Mt. of material is removed from top soil every year (UNEP, 35).

For control of such soil damages, it has been opined that all Nations have to translate into action various measures to prevent further degradation of earth in relation to their development process and conserve the total eco-systems alongwith the entire bio-diversity (Parmeshwarappa, 19). Thus, with a view to conserving soils and making improvement in day-to-day (i) polluting environment and (ii) deteriorating ecological balance, by covering wasteland with suitable useful trees, a new 'Ministry of Environment and Forests' was created in our country in January, 1985 (HTC, 7). These programmes were planned to be implemented through the National Wasteland Development Board under this Ministry.

Surprisingly enough, much attention was paid in switching over, with a great zeal, to plantation of only few species of plants like Eucalyptus, Acacias, Prosopis, Parkinsonia etc. and inclusion of fruit trees in the programme was entirely ignored. Maximum importance was given to Eucalyptus plants. Farmers, orchardists and general public were made to understand its economics and industrial value in such a refined manner that this resulted into mass coverage of land with Eucalyptus plants.

Such plantations may easily be seen all round during a rail or road journey in rural or urban areas. Even cultivable fertile land, fit for growing food and various horticultural crops, was not spared.

National highways and various other road-sides were also covered with shadeless, dense and thorny jungles of Eucalyptus and Acacias. This coverage has developed into dangerous pockets of day-to-day crimes and various misdeeds. These have become sources of accidents also. Most of the space on both sides of railway lines and canals and river banks has also been covered in the same fashion.

Similar observations were made by others also. According to a report, social forestry projects were turned out to be the conversion of fertile food-growing land into pulp wood plantations for industry (Shiva, 25).

In another report some good teak forests were converted into commercial plantations of Eucalyptus, Acacias etc. (HTC, 7). Such unsystematic plantations have also been discouraged from time to time (HTC, 7; Kurian, 11; Sharma; 24). Seeing all these, peasants of Korate-gere taluka in Tumkur district and Shimoga district in Karnataka state (India), uprooted Eucalyptus plants from Government nurseries and replanced with other species (Shiva, 25).

Government have, therefore, now realized to give priority to integrated wasteland development by putting wasteland to sustainable use for generating greater employment opportunities through various connected schemes. To give it a positive push, the National Wasteland Development Board has been reconstituted (Anon., 4). The wasteland development work has now been withdrawn from the Ministry of Environment and Forests and assigned to the Ministry of Rural Development (Anon., 4).

The Union Government have now instructed various states to identify such wasteland, prepare projects for annual and five-year plans and get implemented in co-ordination with various Government/ non-Government departments/organizations and individuals as well (Anon., 4; HTC, 8). The reconstituted National Wasteland Development Board is supposed to ensure these implementations, monitor and watch the progress.

This has also been found agreeable to the Government now that horticultural crops have a greater potential for generating employment in rural areas and, therefore, emphasis is being given for growing fruit orchards in degraded and other waste and fallow lands for increased production of fruits (Anon., 3; PTI, 22).

Again, to develop post harvest technologies and export potential of fruits, recently a scheme of Rs. 662 crore was finalised by the Union Ministry of Agriculture (Anon., 3). This will also increase the country's capacity to earn more foreign exchange. The Forestry Research Wing of Uttar Pradesh under a scheme of 'Association of Elite Mother Trees' (AEMT) has, besides various forest trees, also included fruits of aonla and jamun for revegetating wasteland like usar, ravines, sandy and brackish water areas in plains and denuded slopes of the Himalayan and Vindhya ranges of this state (PTI, 23).

The fact that fruits are very healthful, rich sources of vitamins and minerals, of great medicinal value and that fruits must find a suitable place in our daily diet, need no justificaiton now. Swami

Sivananda Maharaj of Rishikesh says in his book Sādhana that one should take fruits and milk, live on the banks of the Ganges, do japa and meditation to attain self-realisation and become Brahman. He has also communicated in his meassage to give always like the Ganges, the fruit trees and sandal trees.

Besides increasing production of fruits in our country, fruit trees will also save the soil from being eroded and converted into ravines, clean the polluted environment, supply oxygen to live, help in good rainfall, check floods, provide shade, flowers, fodder, fuel, timber etc. There are a number of fruits which can very well be grown in wasteland. These fruit trees thrive easily in areas of low rainfall, having unfertile dry soils. These are hardy enough to tolerate various hard weather conditions like frost, hot wind and others. These do not require much cultural care as well. Some fruits respond quite well even in usar soils, which may be alkaline-usar (pH above 8.5, E.C. less than 4 milimhose/cm., Exchangeable Sodium more than 15 per cent) or saline-usar (pH upto 8.5, E.C. more than 4 milimhose/cm., Exchangeable Sodium less than 15 per cent). Generally, most of the usars are alkaline-usars. Selection of a particular fruit for growing in usar, depends upon the degree of its tolerance to salts present in it. Some fruit trees are less tolerant (pH near about 7.0), some medium tolerant (pH 9.8) and some highly tolerant (pH 10.5).

Before planting any fruit plant in usar pits, which are dug in summer, should be left open as such. After the onset of rains, rain water should be allowed to fill in the pit, after which water should be thrown out of it. This practice should be repeated twice or thrice, after which pits are filled in with soil, 2-4 baskets of farm yard manure and 5-10 kg. of pyrite or gypsum (according to the presence of salt in the soil). The whole mixture is then allowed to rot for a month before actual planting (Pathak, 20).

Aonla (*Emblica officinalis* Gaertn.)—the richest source of vitamin-C, among all the commonly grown fruits, thrives well in usar, in which its tree is medium to highly tolerant. It can also grow in ravines and other wastelands. Seedling Desi aonlas grow wild upto a height of even above 1300 metres from sea level. Earlier, aonla was classified under minor fruits, but after knowing about its excellent qualities and usefulness, it has become a very important fruit now. This resulted into an increase in area with such a repid speed that the areas under aonla reached above 400 hectares only in Pratapgarh district of Uttar Pradesh (Nand, 18), against an area of only about 18 hectares (45 acres) in the year, 1956-58 (Nand, 14).

Problems of unfruitfulness in aonla orchards, specially in Banarasi variety, have been observed for the last several years. This appeared mainly due to pollination problem, self-sterility in flowers and use of scions, which were having more of male flowers and only few or no female flowers at the time of propagation (Bajpai, 5; Pathak, 20).

However, by accommodating few trees of self-fertile varieties in an aonla grove, fruitfulness may be assured through cross-pollination, provided the trees of the orchard were propagated from scions of female flowers. Planting of orchards of only self-fertile varieties like Chakaiya, Francis, Krishna and Kanchan may also lead to fruitfulness (Pathak, 20).

The variety (Narendra ,7) (Nadiya-ke-paar) is also self-fertile. Top-working one branch each of all the unfruitful trees with Desi variety of aonla may also result in fruitfulness. The latest technique adopted for propagation of aonla plants is by budding (Nand, 13; Pathak *et. al.*, 21; Singh, 27; Srivastava, 33; Teotia and Asthana, 34). Aonla orchards of choice varieties can best be established by budding in situ. Seedling and inferior aonla trees growing wild can, therefore, also be easily converted into imporved varieties by top-working.

Guava (*Psidium quajava,* L.), is another sumptuous fruit, next to aonla in respect of its Vitamin-C content and quite fit for growing in soils of drought-prone areas. It is less to medium tolerant in usar. The plant is very hardy. Even water-logged, low-lying and flood-hit areas are also well suited for guava cultivation. Guava has been found the only and best fruit crop for gowing successfully along the banks of rivers Gaṅgā and Jamunā (Nand, 15; 17). Propagation is done by patch budding and stooling, besides inarching. For root stocks of these, guava seedling plants suit well.

Ber (*Ziziphus mauritiana* Lamk.) is suitable for dry land horticulture in unfertile banjar lands, ravines and alkaline soils. The tree is highly tolerant to usar salts. To some extent, it can withstand water-logging also. Propagation is done by ring or shield budding. To avoid mortality in lifting, good orchards may be developed by budding in situ. Seedlings growing wild may also be top-worked.

Bael (*Aegle marmelos* L.), Jamun (*Syzigium cumini* Skeels.) and Kaitha (*Feronia limonia* Swingle : Rutaceae) also thrive in ravines, unfertile and dry banjar land. Bael thrives also in marshy lands and soils of 5-10 pH value (Singh and Roy, 29). Jamun also thrive to some extent, under water-logged conditions and is medium to highly tolerant in usar. Promising varieties of bael and jamun can now easily be multiplied by budding and their trees of inferior qualities may be top-worked with choice varieties. Bael and jamun fruits act as medicine for various diseases. Jamun trees are shady and fit well also for planting along road sides and railway lines. Kaitha (wood-apple) trees are highly tolerant to salts of usar soils. Its fruits make very good jelly, pickles and chutney. It has curative effect in dysentery and stomach diseases.

Custard-apple (*Annona squamosa* L.) , Lasorā (*Cordia myxa:* Ehretiacea), Star-goose-berry (*Phyllanthus disticus* : Euphorbiaceae), Fig (*Ficus carica* L.), Promegranate (*Punica granatum* L.), Shahtoot (*Morus alba* L. and *M. nigra* L.), Pear (*Pyrus communis* L.), Phālsā (*Grewia asiatica* L.) and Karaundā (*Carissa carandas* L.) may also be added to the list of plants for growing in wastelands.

Lasorā and Karaundā plants show tendencies of high tolerance towards salts of usar, while those of custard-apple, pomegranate and phālsā show medium tolerance. The tree of fig is less-medium tolerant and those of star-goose-berry shahtoot and pear are less tolerant. Lasorā is specially useful for pickles. Star-goose-berry (Harfareori) fruits are sour in taste and make good pickles. Fig fruit is medicinal. Its propagation is done by cuttings. Pomegranate fruits are nutritious and very refreshing and are good also for patients. Propagation is done by cuttings. Pomegranate plants flourish also in saline wastelands.

Monkey jack (*Artocarpus lakoocha* Roxb: Moraceae), Tamarind (*Tamarindus indica* L.), Khirni (*Mimusops hexandra* Roxb.: Sapotaceae), Mahuwa (*Bassia latifolia* Roxb.), Goolar (*Ficus glomerata* Roxb. : Moraceae), carambola (*Averrhoa Carambols,* L.) and Panida (*Flacourtia cataphracta* Roxb. : Flacourtiaceae), may further be listed for such plantations. Trees of these fruits are huge in size and are very shady and suit also for plantation along National highways and other road-sides.

Tamarind and mahuwa trees are highly tolerant to usar, while rest of these trees are less tolerant.

Monkey jack thrives also in marshy lands. Trees also stand water logging. Wood is not affected by white ants. Unripe fruits are used for preparing curries and pickles. Tamarind pulp is used for preparing chutney. Khirni bears small beautiful golden yellow-coloured sweet fruits, available durintg May-June. Mahuwa is an important industrial tree. Its flowers are utilized as food and friuts taken fresh or as vegetables. Mahuwa is also medicinal. Green unripe goolar fruits are useful for preparing curries and are good for eye sight. Goolar leaves are utilied as fodder, Carambola fruirs are available during December-January, when these are turned into chutney, pickles, preserves and squash. Paniala fruits are sourish sweet and are eaten fresh. Trees grow in humid regions and fruits ripen in July-August.

Hog-plum (*Spondias pinnata,* Kurz. : Anacardiaceae), Drumstick (*Moringa oleifera* Lamk.), Date-palm (*Phoenix dictylifera* L. : Palmae) and Tenti (*Capparis decidua* Edgew : Capparidaceae) are other horticultural crops for growing in wasteland. Date-palm and tenti are highly tolerant to usar salts, while hog-plum and drumstick are less tolerant. Hog-plum fruits are best utilized for preparing tasteful pickles. Its plants may be propagated by seeds or cuttings.

Drumstick (Sahjan) trees also do not require much care and flourish well at neglected places like road-sides and others. Its pods are utilized in making curries and pickles. It is also of a great medicinal value. Datepalm is tasteful and rich in calorific value. Tenti shrubs, though are seen growing wild without any care in dry wastelands, may further be encouraged by planting in a planned way. This will courage tenti-pickle industry for better employment.

Observations made regarding growing many of the above mentined fruit trees in wastelands are also in conformity to observations made by other authors (Nand, 15, 16, 17; Pathak, 20; Singh, 26; Singh, 28; Singh, 30). Scopes of plantations of ber, phalsā, fig, gauva and pomegranate in respect of their tolerance/semi-tolerance to various degrees of salinity of soil/irrigation water, have also been reported (Manchanda and Agarwal, 12).

Emphasis has been given to work out the production technology of some wild-growing drought-hardy indigenous fruits of Rajasthan under dryland, saline irrigation and run off farming conditions (Singh, 31). These fruits are Kair, Khejri, Kumthi, Pilu (*Salvadora oleoides* Decne., Salvadoraceae;) and Jharbery (*Ziziphus nummularia* Wight and Arn. Syn. *Z. rotundifolia* Lam.) *Rhamnus nummularia* Burm., f.(Rhamnaceae), Lasorā and Karaundā (Singh, 31).

Again, plantation in coastal areas is also a problem. During question hours in the Rajya Sabha, as televised on 28th November, 1992, "Sea water often runs in coastal areas, which again flows back to sea. This further increase salinity in coastal soils and as such a scheme has been planned out for decreasing salinity of coastal areas in four districts of Gujarat, including Surat and Bhroach."

In an investigation conducted at the Central Salt and Marine Chemicals Research Institute, Bhavanagar, crops of sugar-beat, white onion, Pusa Ruby tomato and many cereals were found tolerant/semi-tolernant in seashore soils, when irrigated with sea water of various degrees of salinity (Iyengar *et. al.*, 9).

Further, in a note on Salvadora, it has been reported that *Salvadora persica* (Chota pilu, Jhal or Kharjal; Salvadoraceae) is mainly suited to arid and semi-arid conditions and that it grows on highly saline and non-saline wasteland and on the sea coast as well (Anon., 2). Fruits of both the species of Salvadora mentioned above, are edible (Singh *et. al.*, 30).

REFERENCES & NOTES

1. Anon, (1991), Krishi Somachar, Delhi DD, 1st January, 1991.
2. Anon, (1991), Discipline of phytosalinity, CSMCRI, Bhavnagar. Personal communication from E.R.R., Iyengar, 7th Jan. 1991. (Note on Salvadora) : 1-2.
3. Anon, (1992), National programme, Delhi DD and AIR, 28th Nov., 1992
4. Anon, (1992), 'Banjar bhoomi ke vikas par kendra ka zore'. Rashtriya Sahara, Delhi, 13th Oct., 1992
5. Bapai, P.N., (1957), Blossom biology and fruit set in *Phyllanthus emblica,* Indian J. Hort., 14(2) : 99-102
6. Dubey, O.P., (1992), Eat greens for good health, N.I.P. (Alld.) mag 8th Nov., 1992 : III
7. HTC, (1986), Ansari warns against commercial plantations. HT, 29th Aug., 1986
8. HTC, (1992), Wastelands.
9. Iyengar, E.R.R., J.B. Pandya and J.S. Patolia (1991), Seashore Farming—a new approach of biosaline research. Pers. Communication from E.R.R. Iyengar, 7th Jan. 1991, (Reprint) : 105-111
10. Jakhar, Balram, (1992), Talk given in Krishi Darshan, Delhi DD, 17th Nov., 1992
11. Kurian, K.K., (1984), Ecologists' war on Eucalyptus. H.T. 11th Feb., 1984.
12. Manchanda, H.R. and M.C. Agarwal, (1991), Use of brackish water for agriculture, Journ. IEI (H) Dec., 1991 : 46-48
13. Nand, Darshana, (1962), Budding in Aonla (*Phyllanthus emblica*), Sci. and Cult., 28 (10); 486
14. Nand, Darshana, (1969), Some outstanding varieties of aonla (*Phyllanthus emblica,* L.) Bhadari Abhinandan Granth. (Spl. number 'Gardening') : 11-15
15. Nand, Darshana, (1986), Best use of Ganga bank. Paper read and presented in symposium "Ganga as a source", organised by National Academy of Sciences, India, Allahabad, 30th-31st March, 1986
16. Nand, Darshana, (1987), Scope of growing Horticultural crops in Wastelands. Paper read and presented at a symposium on "Inputs of Science and Technology in the development of Wastelands", organised by the National Academy of Sciences, India, Allahabad, 4th April, 1987
17. Nand, Darshana, (1991), Gangā ki talhatī men Amrood kā bāgh lagāyen. Vigyan, April, 1987
18. Nand, Darshana, (1992), Aonla aur uskī bāghwani, (under publication)
19. Parmeshwarappa, S., (1992), Only one Earth. IEI News, 42 N (4); 4
20. Pathak, R.K., (1990), Phalon ki khetī, Gram Vikas Prakashan, Allahabad
21. Pathak, R.K., C.M. Ojha, R. Dwivedi, Hari Om, (1991), Studies on the effect on methods and duration of budding in aonla. Ind. J. Hort. 48(3); 207-12.
22. PTI (1992), Horticulture main thrust in eighth plan. NIP (Allahabad), 8th Nov., 1992
23. PTI (1993), Plan to protect 'Elite Trees'. NIP (Allahabad), 23rd Jan., 1993 : 5

24. Sharma, Shardendu, (1993), Sikurtā paryāvaran jhulastā desh, Dainik Jagran (Saptahik parishishtha). 3rd Jan., 1993 : 1-2.

25. Shiva, Vandana, (1991), Real, pseudo-environmentalists battle it out. Pioncr, 4th Dec., 1991.

26. Singh, K.P., (1990), Krishi Darshan, Delhi DD, 10th Feb., 1990.

27. Singh, L.B., (1952), A new technique for propagating aonla. (*Phyllanthus emblica*)., Sci., and Cult., 17 : 345-46.

28. Singh, R.N., (1974), Hardy aonla ideal for dry regions, Ind. Hort., Oct.-Dec., 1974.

29. Singh, R.N. and S.K. Roy, (1984), The Bael. ICAR Technical Bulletin.

30. Singh, Umrao, A.M. Wadhwani, B.M. Johri, (1983), Dictionary of Economic Plants in India, ICAR, New Delhi.

31. Singh, R.N., (1991), A general talk for utilization of Wasteland for fruit production, Indian J. Hort. 48(2) : ii-iii.

32. Sivananda, Swami (1958), Sādhanā. Veda Vedanta Forest University, Sivananda Nagar, Rishikesh : 501.

33. Srivastava, R.P., (1964), Aonla Propagation, Indian Hort., 8 : 15-16.

34. Teaotia, S.S., and M.P., Asthana, (1960), Propagating aonla by Budding, Gardening, 2 (8) : 19-20.

35. UNEP, (1992), Only One Earth, IEI, News, 42N(4) : 4.

卐 卐 卐

CASCADE II

(HINDI)

FLORA & FLORAL ARTS

ILĀ-KALĀŚRĪḤ

वनस्पतिकलारसझरी

इला-कलाश्रीः

भास्वद्वंशवतंसकीर्तिरमणीरङ्गप्रसङ्गस्वन-
द्वादित्रप्रथमध्वनिर्विजयते वल्मीकजन्मा मुनिः।
पीत्वा यद्वदनेन्दुमण्डलगलत्काव्यामृताब्धेः किम-
प्याकल्पं कविनूतनाम्बुदमयी कादम्बिनी वर्षति।।

तया स्रजा मङ्गलपुष्पमय्या विशालवक्षःस्थललम्बया सः।
अमंस्त कण्ठार्पितबाहुपाशां विदर्भराजावरजां वरेण्यः।।

धूपोष्मणा त्याजितमार्द्रभावं केशान्तमन्तःकुसुमं तदीयम्।
पर्याक्षिपत्काचिदुदारबन्धं दूर्वावता पाण्डुमधूकदाम्ना।।

अन्तर्गतप्रार्थनमन्तिकस्थं जयन्तमुद्वीक्ष्य कृतस्मितेन।
आमृष्टवक्षो हरिचन्दनाङ्का मन्दारमाला हरिणा पिनद्धा।।

CASCADE II

(HINDI)

FLORA & FLORAL ARTS

ILĀ-KALĀŚRĪḤ

वनस्पतिकलारसझरी

इला–कलाश्रीः

कुलगुरुरबलानां केलिदीक्षाप्रदाने
परमसुहृदनङ्गो रोहिणीवल्लभस्य।
अपि कुसुमपृषत्कैर्देवदेवस्य जेता
जयति सुरतलीलानाटिकासूत्रधारः।।

साहित्ये सुकुमारवस्तुनि दृढन्यायग्रहग्रन्थिले
तर्के वा मयि संविधातरि समं लीलायते भारती।
शय्या वास्तु मृदूत्तरच्छदवती दर्भाङ्कुरैरास्तृता
भूमिर्वा हृदयङ्गमो यदि पतिस्तुल्या रतिर्योषिताम्।।

आकर्ण्याम्रस्तुतिं जलमभूत्तन्नारिकेलान्तरं
प्रायः कण्टकितस्तथैव पनसः जातं द्विधोर्वारुकम्।
आस्तेऽधोमुखमेव कादलफलं द्राक्षाफलं क्षुद्रतां
श्यामत्वं बत जाम्बवं गतगहो मात्सर्यदोषादिह।।

Section IX-Flora in Bṛhattrayī & Individual Poets

Section X-Plant Science & Erotology

Section XI-Flora in Astrology & Smṛti Literature

Section V

INTRODUCTION & FLORAL ARTS
विषयप्रवर्तन-पुष्पकलाश्रीः

संस्कृतवाङ्मय एवं वनस्पतिजगत्

(विषय-प्रवर्तन)

श्रीधर वासिष्ठ

सभ्यता एवं संस्कृति के वास्तविक रूप को जानने एवं पहचानने के लिए सर्वोत्तम माध्यम होता है सम्बद्ध जाति का वाङ्मय। यह वाङ्मय दो रूपों में उपलब्ध हो सकता है लिखित एवं भाषित। भाषित वाङ्मय में नये-नये तथ्य तथा उत्तरकालीन घटनायें अपना प्रभाव डालती रहती हैं और वह कथाओं, परम्पराओं तथा लोकगीतों आदि के माध्यम से लोकानुरंजन तथा प्रबोधन करता रहता है। लिखित वाङ्मय में सभ्यता एवं संस्कृति का निश्चित स्वरूप अपरिवर्तित रूप में सदियों सहस्राब्दियों में उपलब्ध होता रहता है परन्तु इसमें कठिनाई यह होती है कि समय के साथ-साथ भाषा के स्वरूप में भी परिवर्तन होता रहता है। अतः प्राचीन भाषा में निबद्ध वाङ्मय को समझना तथा उसमें लिखित तथ्यों को जानना दुस्साध्य कार्य हो जाता है। परन्तु भारतीयों का यह सौभाग्य है कि इनकी संस्कृति की संवाहिका संस्कृत भाषा सहस्राब्दियाँ बीत जाने के पश्चात् भी अपने वास्तविक रूप को यथावत् सुरक्षित रखे हुए है। संस्कृत भाषा आज भी उसी रूप में बोली, समझी तथा लिखी जा सकती है जिस रूप में सहस्राब्दियों पूर्व वाल्मीकि, व्यास, अश्वघोष आदि ने बोली, समझी तथा लिखी थी। इसलिए संस्कृत भाषा में लिखित हमारी सभ्यता तथा संस्कृति को जानने तथा समझने के लिए हमें किसी प्रकार की कठिनाई नहीं होती। आज हमारा यह प्रयास है कि भविष्य में भी संस्कृत का यह स्वरूप निरन्तर बना रहे ताकि आगे आने वाली पीढ़ियों को संस्कृत भाषा में निबद्ध ज्ञान प्राप्त करने में कठिनाई न हो।

भारतीय जन सदा प्रकृति के निकट रहे हैं या यूँ कहें कि प्रकृतिस्थ रहे हैं। प्रकृति का सर्वोत्तम रूप जैव प्रकृति है और वनस्पति-जगत् उसका प्राणवान् स्वरूप है। सामान्यतया वनस्पति से अभिप्राय भूमि में उत्पन्न होने वाले सभी उद्भिजों से लिया जाता है जिसमें छोटे-से-छोटे पौधे से लेकर बड़े-से-बड़े वृक्षों की गणना हो सकती है परन्तु पारिभाषिक रूप से वनस्पति का अर्थ बड़ा पेड़ ही होता है। वनस्पतिः अर्थात् वन का पति। वन का पति तो बड़ा वृक्ष ही हो सकता है। संस्कृत वाङ्मय में इस अर्थ में इसका अधिकतर प्रयोग हुआ है। श्रीराम के वनवास के समय का वर्णन करते हुए कालिदास ने वनस्पति का इसी अर्थ में प्रयोग किया है। चित्रकूट में भरत द्वारा श्रीरामचन्द्र की खड़ाऊँ लेकर चले जाने के बाद श्रीरामचन्द्र एक बड़े वृक्ष के नीचे सीता की गोद में लेटकर विश्राम करने लगे।

प्रभावस्तम्भितच्छायमाश्रितः स वनस्पतिम्।
कदाचिदङ्के सीतायाः शिश्ये किञ्चिदिव श्रमात्।।[1]

इसी प्रकार कुमारसम्भव में कामदेव को अपने वश में करने के प्रयास को विफल करते हुए भगवान् शिव ने अपने तीसरे नेत्र की अग्नि से भस्म कर दिया। कालिदास ने उसका वर्णन करते हुए लिखा कि जैसे आकाशीय बिजली किसी बड़े पेड़ को तोड़कर रख देती है, उसी प्रकार भगवान् शिव ने कामदेव को समाप्त कर दिया—

वनस्पतिं वज्र इवावभज्य।[2]

ये बड़े पेड़ योद्धाओं के शस्त्र के रूप में भी काम आते थे। भासकृत अभिषेक नाटक का यह पद्य दर्शनीय है जहाँ अशोक वाटिका के रक्षक जाकर रावण को हनुमान् के विषय में बताते हैं—

अस्मदीयैर्महावृक्षैरस्मदीया महाबलाः।
क्षिप्रमेव हतास्तेन किङ्करा द्रुमयोधिना।।[3]

शब्दों की दो प्रकार की प्रवृत्ति होती है—व्युत्पत्तिलभ्य और प्रवृत्तिलभ्य। यहाँ वनस्पति प्रवृत्तिलभ्य अर्थ में ही प्रयुक्त होने लगा जिससे व्युत्पत्तिलभ्य अर्थ का प्रयोग अपने आप में मन्द पड़ गया। वनस्पतियाँ भारतीय संस्कृति में सदा ही महत्त्वपूर्ण रही हैं। उनका हरा रंग मानव के लिए सदा ही महत्त्वपूर्ण माना गया है। इसीलिए वैदिक ऋषि ने अथर्ववेद में लिखा—

भूमिष्ट्वा पातु हरितेन विश्वभृत्।[4]

अर्थात् विश्व का भरण-पोषण करने वाली यह भूमि अपनी हरी वनस्पतियों से आप सब की रक्षा करे। हिमालय को इसलिये शैलाधिराज कहा जाता है क्योंकि उसमें वे वनस्पतियाँ उत्पन्न होती हैं जिनका यज्ञ के अङ्ग के रूप में प्रयोग होता है—

यज्ञाङ्गयोनित्वमवेक्ष्य यस्य सारं धरित्रीधरणक्षमं च।
प्रजापतिः कल्पितयज्ञभागं शैलाधिपत्यं स्वयमन्वतिष्ठत्।।[5]

वेदों में अनेक ऐसी औषधियों का वर्णन है जो मनुष्य को नीरोग करती हैं—

शंनो देवी पृश्निपर्ण्यशं निर्ऋत्या अकः।[6]

अर्थात् पृश्निपर्णी (जलकुम्भी) नाम की औषधि हमारे लिए कल्याणकारी हो। इसने रोगों के लिए दुःख पैदा कर दिए हैं अर्थात् रोग समाप्त कर दिए हैं।

उद्गातां भगवती निवृतौ नाम तारके।
विक्षेत्रियस्य मुञ्चतामधमं पाशमुत्तमम्।।[7]

अर्थात् भगवती (वैष्णवी/लघुशतावरी/तुलसी/अपराजिता/विष्णुक्रान्ता) नामक औषधि तथा तारका (देवताड़वृक्ष/इन्द्रवारुणी) औषधि हमारे क्षेत्रिय (आनुवंशिक) रोग के पाश को काटे। ये दोनों औषधियाँ निर्ऋत्य (तेज) बढ़ाने वाली हैं।

आजकल हम दशमूलारिष्ट आदि औषधियों का नाम प्रायः सुनते हैं। दशमूल वृक्षों की विशेषता अथर्ववेद में ही उल्लिखित कर दी गई थी—

दशवृक्ष मुञ्चेमं रक्षसो ग्राह्या अधियैनं जग्राह पर्वसु।
अथो एवं वनस्पते जीवानां लोकमुन्नय।।[8]

जोड़ों का दर्द या संधिवात रोग बड़ी आयु के लोगों को सदा से पीड़ित करता रहा है। इसे वेद में रक्षोग्राही रोग के नाम से जाना गया है अर्थात् जैसे राक्षस किसी को पकड़कर बाँध लेता है वैसे ही संधिवात रोग (Arthraitis)

शरीर के जोड़ों को पकड़कर मनुष्य को कष्ट देता है। इसलिए वैदिक ऋषि ने दशवृक्ष योग से तैयार की गई औषधि द्वारा मनुष्यों के जीवन को उन्नत करने के लिए मार्ग सुझाया है।

शरीर की वृद्धि के लिए अस्थि, मांस, मज्जा, त्वचा, रोम आदि सभी की वृद्धि अपेक्षित होती है। हड्डी आदि के टूटने पर उसे जोड़ने की आवश्यकता होती है। इसके लिए सर्वोत्तम औषधि है—रोहणी। अथर्ववेद का ऋषि उसी औषधि से प्रार्थना करता है कि हे कष्ट को दूर करने वाली रोहणी! तू इस मनुष्य को स्वस्थ कर दे—

रोहण्यसि रोहण्यस्थनश्छिनस्य रोहणी।
रोहयेदमरुन्धती।[9]

ऋग्वेद में सोमरस की बड़ी महिमा गायी गई है। यह सोमलता से तैयार किया जाता है। ऋग्वेद का पूरा नवम मण्डल सोम की महिमा से मण्डित है।

असृग्रन् देववीतयेऽत्यासः कृत्व्या ह वा।
क्षरन्त पर्वतावृधः।[10]

अर्थात् पर्वतों पर उत्पन्न होने वाला सोमरस बहता हुआ पानपात्र में गिरता है। यह देवताओं को अर्पण करने के लिए होता है। यह तेज गति से दौड़ने वाले घोड़ों की-सी शक्ति देता है।

ऋग्वेद के अरण्यानि सूक्त में वनस्पतियों को देवता के रूप में आह्वान करते हुए ऋग्वैदिक ऋषि उससे कहता है कि तू जंगल में ही क्यों छिपी रहती है? नगर को भी क्यों हराभरा नहीं करती? जंगल में गौएं चरती हैं। लताकुंज घरों जैसे दिखाई देते हैं और लोग जंगल से हरीभरी वस्तुओं-फल, कन्दमूल तथा पशुओं का चारा गाड़ियों में डालकर अपने गाँवों को ले आते हैं।

उत गाव इवादन्त्युत वेश्मेव दृश्यते।
उतो अरण्यानि सायं शकटीरिव सर्जति।[11]

वनस्पति का नाम सुनते ही हमारे मस्तिष्क में औषधियों की भावना जाग उठती है। राम-रावण युद्ध में जब लक्ष्मण रावण से युद्ध करते हुए मूर्छित हो गए और उन्हें मृत हुआ मानकर श्रीरामचन्द्र जीवन त्याग करने की बात कहने लगे तब सुषेण नामक वानर वैद्य ने श्रीरामचन्द्र जी को आश्वासन दिया कि लक्ष्मण मृत नहीं, वह केवल मूर्छित हुए हैं। उन्होंने हनुमान् को गन्धमादन पर्वत से चार महत्त्वपूर्ण औषधियाँ लाने के लिए कहा—

पूर्वं तु कथितो योऽसौ वीर जाम्बवता तव।
दक्षिणे शिखरे जातां महौषधिमिहानय।।
विशल्यकरणीं नाम्ना सावर्ण्यकरणीं तथा।
संजीवकरणीं वीर संधानीं च महौषधिम्।।[12]

ये चारों औषधियाँ तत्काल लाभ देने वाली हैं और इनके प्रयोग से सुषेण वैद्य ने लक्ष्मण तथा मूर्छित एवं मृत वानरों को तत्काल ठीक कर दिया। आश्चर्य की बात यह है कि सुषेण को उन औषधियों के उत्पन्न होने का स्थान भी ज्ञात था।

उत्तरकालीन साहित्य में पदे-पदे वनस्पति-जगत् की सुगन्धि उपलिप्त है। यहाँ पर कालिदास-साहित्य से कुछ उदाहरण प्रस्तुत करने की चेष्टा की जा रही है। कुमारसम्भव में अनेक स्थलों पर वनस्पति-जगत् का मनुष्य-प्रकृति के

साथ मणिकाञ्चन संयोग बैठाया गया है। वसन्त ऋतु में पलाश के अर्ध विकसित रक्ताभ पुष्प ऐसे लगते हैं जैसे वनस्थली-नायिकाओं के शरीर पर वसन्त के नखक्षत हों–

बालेन्दुवक्राण्यविकासभावाद् बभुः पलाशान्यतिलोहितानि।
सद्यो वसन्तेन समागतेन नखक्षतानीव वनस्थलीनाम्।।[13]

ऐसा माना जाता है कि कर्णिकार पुष्प सुगन्धि-रहित होता है। इस सुन्दर दिखने वाले पुष्प में सुगन्धि का अभाव कवि कालिदास के मन को कष्ट देता है। वह समझते हैं कि विधाता किसी भी जीव अथवा वस्तु को सभी गुणों से पूर्ण नहीं करना चाहते।

संस्कृत साहित्य में कुछ कविसमय हैं, अर्थात् कवियों की मान्यतायें हैं जिनमें निम्नलिखित उल्लेखनीय हैं:

स्त्रीणां स्पर्शात्प्रियङ्गुर्विकसति बकुलः सीधुगण्डूषसेकात्
पादाघातादशोकस्तिलककुरबकौ वीक्षणालिङ्गनाभ्याम्।
मन्दारो नर्मवाक्यात्पटुमृदुहसनाच्चम्पको वक्त्रवाता-
च्चूतो गीतान्नमेरुर्विकसति च पुरोनर्तनात्कर्णिकारः।।

इसका अर्थ है कि अशोक वृक्ष स्त्रियों के पादाघात से, तिलक वीक्षण से (देखने मात्र से) कुरबक (सदाबहार) आलिङ्गन से, प्रियङ्गु (अंगूर लता) स्पर्श से, बकुल (मौलसिरी) मदिरा के कुल्ले की बौछार से, मन्दार प्रेम वाक्य बोलने से, चम्पक मुधर हँसी से, आम्र (आम का पेड़) धीरे से फूँक मारने से, नमेरु (रुद्राक्ष) गीत गाने से तथा कर्णिकार सामने नाचने से फलते-फूलते हैं। यह वनस्पतिजगत् का मनुष्यजगत् से सामञ्जस्य का उदाहरण है परन्तु वसन्त के आगमन पर हिमालय पर्वत पर विद्यमान अशोक वृक्ष सुन्दरियों के नूपुरों से सुशोभित पादप्रहार की अपेक्षा किए बिना ही अपने स्कन्ध से पल्लवित, पुष्पित होने लगा।

असूत सद्यः कुसुमान्यशोकः स्कन्धात्प्रभृत्येव सपल्लवानि।
पादेन नापैक्षत सुन्दरीणां सम्पर्कमासिञ्चितनूपुरेण।।[14]

कोयल (पुंस्कोकिल) का कूजना मनस्विनियों के मान को तोड़ने वाला कामदेव का वचन बन जाता है क्योंकि पुंस्कोकिल ने आम के अंकुरों के स्वाद से अपने कण्ठस्वर को तीखा कर लिया था।

आम्राङ्कुरास्वादकषायकण्ठः पुंस्कोकिलो यन्मधुरं चुकूज।
मनस्विनीमानविघातदक्षं तदेव जातं वचनं स्मरस्य।।[15]

पुष्पगुच्छ रूपी स्तनभृत तथा रक्तपुष्प रूपी लाल होठों वाली लता नायिकाओं ने अपनी शाखा रूपी भुजाओं से वृक्षनायकों का आलिंगन कर लिया।

पर्याप्तपुष्पस्तबकस्तनाभ्यः स्फुरत्प्रवालोष्ठमनोहराभ्यः।
लतावधूभ्यस्तरवोप्यवापुर्विनम्रशाखाभुजबन्धनानि ।।[16]

रघु के दिग्विजय-प्रसङ्ग में कालिदास ने भारत देश में चारों दिशाओं में उपलब्ध अखरोट, रुद्राक्ष, नारियल, खजूर, ताड़ आदि अनेक वृक्षों तथा वनस्पतियों का उल्लेख किया है। वसन्त ऋतु ने भले ही कमलों का छाता बना लिया हो और खिलते हुए काश पुष्पों की चामर डुलवाई हो परन्तु वह दिग्विजय के लिए निकले हुए रघु की शोभा को प्राप्त नहीं कर सका।

पुण्डरीकातपत्रस्तं विकसत्काशचामरः।
ऋतुर्विडम्बयामास न पुनः प्राप तच्छ्रियम्।।[17]

धान की रखवाली करने वाली महिलाएँ गन्ने के खेत में बैठकर रघु की यशोगाथा गाती थीं।

इक्षुच्छायनिषादिन्यस्तस्य गोप्तुर्गुणोदयम्।
आकुमारकथोद्घातं शालिगोप्यो जगुर्यशः।।[18]

दिल्ली में लोग सप्तपर्ण पुष्पों की सुगन्धि से सुपरिचित हैं। असम प्रदेश में हाथी के मद की सुगन्धि वाले सप्तपर्ण वनस्पति के फूलों का वर्णन करते हुए कालिदास ने हाथियों द्वारा प्रतियोगिता में अधिक सुगन्धि उत्पन्न करने के लिए सात बार मदस्राव करने का उल्लेख किया है।

प्रसवैः सप्तपर्णानां मदगन्धिभिराहताः।
असूययेव तन्नागाः सप्तधैव प्रसुस्रुवुः।।[19]

रघु ने बंदी राजाओं को उखाड़कर वैसे ही जमा दिया जैसे धान की रुपाई होती है। इस प्रकार लगाई गई धान अधिक फल देने वाली होती है। इसी प्रकार बंदी राजाओं ने रघु को अत्यधिक धन सम्पत्ति देकर बढ़ाया।

आपादपद्मप्रणताः कलमा इव ते रघुम्।
फलैः संवर्धयामासुरुत्खातप्रतिरोपिताः।।[20]

थके हुए रघु को विश्राम देने के लिए गंगा के जलकणों से युक्त वायु भूर्जपत्रों में मरमर ध्वनि करती हुई तथा कीचक वंशों में संगीत उत्पन्न करती हुई बहने लगी।[21] कालिदास ने मेघदूत में अलकापुरी की पहचान करवाते हुए वनस्पतिजगत् और वहाँ की सुन्दरियों के ताल-मेल का वर्णन किया है। अलकापुरी की वधुएँ हाथ में नीलकमल लिए रहती हैं। बालों में कुन्दपुष्प लगाती हैं। लोध्रपुष्प की रज से मुख को सुशोभित करती हैं। जूड़े में कनकाम्बरम् पुष्प लगाती हैं। कानों में सुन्दर शिरीष के फूल तथा बालों में कदम्ब के पुष्प सजाती हैं।[22] शकुन्तला की विदाई के समय वनस्पतियों ने अपनी-अपनी ओर से उपहार भेजे जिनमें पीला वस्त्र, लाक्षा रस तथा अनेक आभूषण सम्मिलित थे।[23] शकुन्तला के रूप-सौन्दर्य को देखकर मोहित हुए राजा को विदूषक माढव्य कहता है कि जल्दी उसे सम्भाल, नहीं तो इंगुदी फल मिश्रित तेल से चिकने बालों वाले किसी तपस्वी के हाथ पड़ जायेगी।

तेन हि लघु परित्रायतामेनां भवान्। मा कस्यापि तपस्विन इङ्गुदीतैलचिक्कणशीर्षस्य हस्ते पतिष्यति।[24]

संस्कृत वाङ्मय में वनस्पतियों का चित्रण मानव प्रकृति के संयोग से ही किया गया है। इसका सर्वोत्तम उदाहरण शकुन्तला का वनस्पति प्रेम है।

पातुं न प्रथमं व्यवस्यति जलं युष्मास्वपीतेषु या
नादत्ते प्रियमण्डनापि भवतां स्नेहेन या पल्लवम्।
आद्ये वः कुसुमप्रसूतिसमये यस्या भवत्युत्सवः
सेयं याति शकुन्तला पतिगृहं सर्वैरनुज्ञायताम्।।[25]

वस्तुतः वनस्पतिजगत् का वर्णन संस्कृत वाङ्मय में इतना विशाल है कि उसके लिए कई महाग्रन्थों को रचने की आवश्यकता है।

सन्दर्भ–सङ्केत

1. रघुवंशम् – 12. 21
2. कुमारसम्भवम् – 3. 74
3. अभिषेकनाटकम् – 3. 5
4. अथर्ववेद: – 5. 28. 5
5. कुमारसम्भवम् – 1. 17
6. अथर्ववेद: – 2. 25. 1
7. अथर्ववेद: – 2. 8. 1
8. अथर्ववेद: – 2. 9. 1
9. अथर्ववेद: – 4. 12. 1
10. ऋग्वेद: – 9. 46. 1
11. ऋग्वेद: – 10. 146. 3
12. रामायणम्–युद्धकाण्डम् – 101. 31
13. कुमारसम्भवम् – 3. 29
14. कुमारसम्भवम् – 3. 26
15. कुमारसम्भवम् – 3. 32
16. कुमारसम्भवम् – 3. 39
17. रघुवंशम् – 4. 17
18. रघुवंशम् – 4. 20
19. रघुवंशम् – 4. 23
20. रघुवंशम् – 4. 37
21. रघुवंशम् – 4. 74
22. मेघदूतम् – 2. 2
23. अभिज्ञानशाकुन्तलम – 4. 15
24. अभिज्ञानशाकुन्तलम् – 2 अङ्क
25. अभिज्ञानशाकुन्तलम् – 4. 9

卐 卐 卐

वटबीजश्री

संस्कृतवाङ्मय एवं वनस्पतिवैभव

(विषय-प्रवर्तन-विस्तरण)

कौशल्या गुप्ता

वट-बीज को उँगली के हल्के से स्पर्श-मात्र से उठा लिया तो भूत-वर्तमान-भविष्य उठा लिया— त्रिकाल-सृष्टि के रहस्य का, निसर्ग का, कवि-मन का, मानव की जिज्ञासा के औचित्य-अनौचित्य का, वृक्षायुर्वेद का, स्रष्टा के सामर्थ्य का, विश्व-दर्शन-विज्ञान का, विश्व ब्रह्माण्ड के एकांश का, अन्तःसलिल से तृप्त अधोमूल ऊर्ध्वशाख-स्कन्धों से छूटती जटाओं से धरा में प्रवेश-द्वार खोजती खोलती वट-वृक्ष की छवि का।

कितना भी कहो, कितना ही खोजो, कितना ही लिखो, पर वट-बीज का मौन में मुखर 'नेति', 'नेति' स्वर निकलता ही रहेगा। प्रत्येक देश, नगर, वनस्थल, जलस्थल, गिरिशिखर के प्रत्येक तृण, वृक्ष, लता, स्कन्ध, पुष्प, बीज, फल की यही गाथा है, यही महाकाव्य है। पशु-पक्षी, कृमि-कीट, सरीसृप, मधु-लोभी भ्रमर, उड़ते फूलों सी तितली में, मनु-सन्तान मानव के प्राण-सञ्चार में, प्राण-स्पन्दन में इसी का स्पन्दन है।

जङ्गम-सृष्टि के अवतरण से पूर्व स्थावर-सृष्टि आविर्भूत हुई। उसके बिना जङ्गम का अस्तित्व नहीं था। उसका जीपन-प्राणाधार तो स्थापर है।

इन सीमाओं में 'विश्व-साहित्य में वनस्पति जगत्', 'संस्कृत-वाङ्मय में वनस्पति जगत्' और 'World-Flora' विषयों पर संगोष्ठी और चर्चा सुसाहसिक प्रयास है। जैसे वट-बीज ब्रह्माण्ड का कुछ तो समेटे है अपने में। इस प्रयास में भी अनेक श्रम-प्रयत्न सिमटे हैं, श्रम है अध्ययन के निष्कर्म का। अतः परिणति तो सफल होगी ही। विषय-प्रवर्तन का प्रयत्न संगोष्ठी के निषय को दी हुई संज्ञाओं से ही करूँगी।

'Flora of the World' से आज जो सामान्यतः गृहीत होता है, वह है सब वृक्ष, लता, गुल्म, फूल, फल और बीज इस संसार के। किन्तु वस्तुतः Flora से अभिप्रेत है—किसी स्थूल निशेष के भू-तत्त्वों के परिणामस्वरूप निशेष निसर्ग-प्रकृति में उत्पन्न उद्‌भिज् अर्थात् मनुष्य के प्रयत्न हस्तक्षेप के बिना प्रकृति-जात उद्‌भिज किसी प्रान्त विशेष में—वह गिरि-स्थल हो, जल स्थल हो, मरु-स्थल हो या धरा-स्थल। संगोष्ठी के विषय में 'Flora' शब्द का सीमित अर्थ विस्तृत हो जाता है और आज के सामान्य प्रयोग में उसी प्रकार पारिभाषिक दृष्टि से ''वनस्पति'' शब्द का सीमित अर्थ विस्तार लेता है 'वनस्पति जगत्' शब्द में।

चिकित्सा योग्य को सुश्रुत ने द्रव्य कहा है और औषधि का पर्याय भी माना है। चरक ने कहा है औषधि द्रव्य स्थावर और जंगम है। प्रकारान्तर से मनुस्मृति, चरक, सुश्रुत आदि सभी के स्थावर-वृष्टि के प्रकारों में से एक है 'वनस्पति' और स्थावर सृष्टि का पर्याय है उद्‌भिद् या उद्‌भिज्ज। ये चतुर्विध हैं —

वनस्पति, वृक्ष या वानस्पत्य, वीरुध और औषधि। मनु गुच्छ, गुल्म, प्रतान, और उपभेद करते हैं। इनका अन्तर निम्नलिखित से स्पष्ट हो जाता है—

1. अपुष्पाः फलवन्तः वनस्पतयः— जैसे वट, गूलर (उदुम्बर), प्लक्ष (पिलखन), अश्वत्थ (पीपल) ये गुह्यपुष्प हैं अर्थात् फूल सामान्य रूप से बाहर नहीं होता, फल के अन्दर ही छिपा होता है।

2. पुष्पफलवन्तः वृक्षाः (चरक-कथित वानस्पत्य) जैसे आम्र, शाल, पलाश, कोविदार, मन्दार आदि।

3. प्रतानवन्त्यः स्तम्बिन्यः वीरुधः अर्थात् लता, वल्ली जैसे माधवी, प्रियङ्गु, गुडूची।

4. फलपाकनिष्ठाः औषधयः (फल के पकने के बाद रहने वाली, जैसे शालि, गोधूम आदि। और अब 'औषधि' केवल रोग-निवारक 'दवाई' द्योतक है।

निष्कर्ष में शैवाल (काई) से लेकर गिरि-शिखर-स्पर्धी देवदारु तक सब और वनस्पति-जगत् के अन्तर्गत हैं अब।

राजशेखर ने काव्यमीमांसा में पुष्पों के विषय में कहा है—

शोभान्धोगन्धरसैर्फलार्चनाभ्यां च पुष्पयोनि।
षोढादर्शितमेतत् स्यात् सप्तममनुपयोगि।।

फूलों के सात उपयोग हैं या कहें फूलों के सात लाभ हैं— शोभा, अन्न, सुगन्ध, रस, फल और पूजा-विधि दायी होने के कारण। अभिप्राय यह है कि कविजन के लिए इन छः प्रकार से फूलों का वर्णन उपयोगी और उपादेय है, अन्य नहीं, कहा नहीं, पर अभिप्राय सम्भवतः यह रहा होगा कि चिकित्साशास्त्र-विहित औषधि के रूप में नहीं। मरण, उच्चाटन आदि के प्रयोग में तो निषिद्ध ही है।

राजशेखर ने अपनी उसी कृति काव्यमीमांसा में फल भी छः प्रकार के कहे हैं— रस-भोग की दृष्टि से। (रस-भोग में बाधक तत्त्व को व्याज कहा है) अन्तर्व्याज (विकुच-बड़हल), बहिर्व्याज (केला), उभयव्याज (आम), सर्वव्याज (अर्जुन, ककुभ) बहुव्याज (पनस-कटहल), निर्व्याज (कपित्थ, द्राक्षा)। छिलका, गुठली, और बीज फल के रस-भोग में बाधक (व्याज) हैं।

पहले कहा जा चुका है कि जङ्गम-सृष्टि का उद्भव उद्भिज् अर्थात् वनस्पति के कारण हुआ। आदियुग में इसका उपयोग शोभादायी, गन्धदायी और पूजार्चना के योग्य होना वैकल्पिक रहा होगा। प्राणधारण के लिए भोजन का प्राप्ति-उत्स वनस्पति का सर्वप्रथम और प्रमुख प्रयोजन था। भ्रूण से लेकर महायात्रा के अन्तराल तक प्राणायु इसी पर आश्रित है, शेष अवशेष ये हैं, उपादेयता है—

वनस्पति के आकार-प्रकार के वर्णन और तत्सम्बद्ध प्रकृति-चित्रण में, ऋतु-वर्णन में, उत्सव-अनुष्ठान में, लौकिक-अलौकिक मिथकों में, उपमा-उपमेय आदि अलङ्कारों में, कवि-सुकुमार प्रयोग और कवि-समय में, तद्भूत सङ्गीत में, वास्तुकला, स्थापत्य कला, चित्रकला में, अङ्ग-सज्जा सामग्री में, वसन-वस्त्र-वेषभूषा में और अन्य-अन्य उपयोग-प्रयोग हैं 'वनस्पति-जगत्-प्राप्य' उपादानों के।

आकार-प्रकार के अन्तर्गत वृक्ष, वल्ली, लता, गुल्म का विभाजन आता है और अनेक बार नामकरण का कारण भी जैसे 'चलदल' पीपल के लिए, स्वर्णमाल कर्णिकार के लिए।

प्राय सब ही चिकित्सा शास्त्रों में और काव्यों में वनस्पति जगत् का वर्णन ऋतुओं के अनुसार होता है। कालिदास के काव्यों में स्पष्ट होता है कि ग्रीष्म ऋतु में प्रसङ्ग हैं शिरीष, पाटल, चन्दन, उशीर आदि का। चन्दन + उशीर ग्रीष्म-दाह को सह्य बनाने के उपकरण हैं। वर्षा-ऋतु का चित्र कदम्ब, अर्जुन, केतकी आदि की छवि से उभरता है।

शरत्-ऋतु वर्णन में काश, सप्तच्छद, कुमुद, बन्धूक, कोविदार, शेफालिका अनिवार्य है। हेमन्त में नवप्रवाल-सस्य (गेहूँ आदि), यदशालि, कार्पास है। वसन्त-श्री की तो आम्र-मञ्जरी, कर्णिकार, पलाश, शाल्मलि, शाल, मन्दार के फूलों से शृङ्गार-सज्जा होती है।

चिकित्सा-शास्त्रियों ने ऋतुओं के अनुसार फूल, फल, कन्द, मूल, पत्ते, शस्य आदि के भोग-प्रयोग का विधान किया है। शल्य-चिकित्सा और औषध-चिकित्सा में हजारों उद्भिज् का प्रयोग-विधान है। चिकित्सा-शास्त्रों में वर्णित और काव्यों की विविध भंगिमाओं में 'दोहद' सामान्य है। सुश्रुत के अनुसार गर्भ के चौथे मास में गर्भस्थ शिशु की हृदय-गति सुनाई देने लगती है (गर्भप्रव्यक्तिभावात् चेतना धातुरभिव्यक्तिर्भवति।) तब गर्भिणी 'दौहृदिनी' और उसकी उस समय की उत्कट इच्छा 'दौहृद' है। चरक और सुश्रुत के मत से 'अलब्ध' दौहृद हानिकर है। कवि-जगत् में वह 'दौहृद' वृक्ष-दोहद रूप ले अवतरित हुआ। प्रसङ्ग से कह दूँ कि गर्भिणी का दोहद वृक्ष (पुल्लिङ्ग) का दोहद बन गया। यह कवि-समय है और एक सुकुमार मान्यता है।

स्त्रीणां स्पर्शात्प्रियङ्गुर्विकसति बकुलः सीधुगण्डूषसेकात्
पादाघातादशोकस्तिलककुरबकौ वीक्षणालिङ्गनाभ्याम्।
मन्दारो नर्मवाक्यात्पटुमृदुहसनाच्चम्पको वक्त्रवाता-
च्चूतो गीतान्नमेरुर्विकसति च पुरोनर्तनात्कर्णिकारः।।

नायिका के अङ्ग-स्पर्श, अङ्ग-स्पृष्ट पदार्थ या अङ्ग-क्रिया-भंगिमा से अनेक वृक्ष कुसुमोन्मुखी होते हैं। पुष्पविकास में मन्थर अशोक के दोहद को कालिदस ने 'मालविकाग्निमित्र' के गति-चक्र का केन्द्र-बिन्दु बनाया। गर्भिणी सीता के गङ्गादर्शन-दोहद के व्याज से भवभूति के राम ने सीता का परित्याग किया उत्तर राम चरित में।

वाल्मीकि, भास, कालिदास, भारवि आदि के काव्यों में प्रकृति-चित्रण, अलङ्कार प्रयोगों से यह तो निश्चित है कि उन्होंने प्रकृति और वनस्पति जगत् को एकाङ्गीभाव से समोया था। रामायण में वाल्मीकि ने वन-काण्ड में पीत-वर्णी कर्णिकार पुष्पों से सीता की केश-सज्जा की थी। रावण द्वारा सीता-हरण होने पर विरही राम ने कर्णिकार से सीता के विषय में पूछा था— और भी लता, पादप, पशु-पक्षी से पूछा था।

शरद् ऋतु में खिलने वाली शेफालिका के फूलों को नवविवाहिता पद्मावती उदयन को दिखाने के लिए आकुल-आतुर हो गई थी— दिन में मुक्ता प्रवाल के गुच्छों सी दिखती शेफालिका की कलियाँ और विहान में वृन्त-च्युत धरा पर बिखरे शेफालिका फूलों की सुन्दर छवि है।

मृग यदि दुष्यन्त को कण्वाश्रम तक ले आया, तो केसर वृक्ष ने उसको छिपने का अवकाश दिया। नवमल्लिका 'वन-ज्योत्स्ना' के जल-सिंचन से मधु-पान में बाधित उड़े भ्रमर ने दुष्यन्त को शकुन्तला के पास पहुँचने का अवसर दिया। इसी सुघटना के स्मृति-रूप में सखीद्वय ने केसर के फूलों की माला को नारियल के खोल में शकुन्तला के पतिगृह जाने के क्षण के लिए रखा था। शिरीष केसर का अवतंस स्वेद-म्लान हो गया शकुन्तला के कपोलों पर, जैसे जल-सेचन से कान्त शकुन्तला। इसी छवि को विरही दुष्यन्त चित्र में उँकेरना चाहता था।

शिरीष— केसर-सक्त कपोलों वाली शकुन्तला, केसर वृक्ष के पीछे खड़ा दुष्यन्त, और इन दोनों का पुत्र, सर्वदमन, सिंह-शावक के केसर मर्दन करता था। 'केसर' शब्द का विभिन्न छवियों में और अर्थों में प्रयोग कवि का शब्द-क्रीडा-कौशल है।

कुछ ऐसी छवि भी सामने आती है जो केवल कवि दृष्ट और अनुभूत थी। यूँ तो कवि निज अनुभूति को सर्वानुभूत पदार्थ के उपमान के माध्यम से सहृदय रसिक मन पर आरोपित करता है— किन्तु 'अर्कस्योपरि च्युता

नवमल्लिका' कालिदास ने ही देखी होगी। कहाँ आख का क्षुप और कहाँ नवमल्लिका? पर कालिदास ने दोनों को एक साथ देखा होगा— नवमल्लिकी लता और उसी के नीचे उगे आख पर उसके टपकते फूल को जैसे कण्व के आश्रम में कण्व-पोषित शकुन्तला।

उसी भाँति भारवि के किरातार्जुनीय में —

मुखरसौ विद्रुमभङ्गलोहितैः शिखाः पिशङ्गीः कलमस्य बिभ्रती।
शुकावलिर्व्यक्तशिरीषकोमला धनुश्रियं गोत्रभिदोऽनुगच्छति।।

कृष्ण-वर्णी बीज-युक्त पीत-वर्णी सूर्यमुखी के फूल को उड़ते-उड़ते दस्यु तोते को हरण करते तो मैंने भी देखा है। नीलाकाश में हरी तूलिका से काली-पीली रेखा खिंचती चली जाती थी पेड़ की शिखा तक।

शकुन्तला नखों से शुकोदर सुकुमार नलिनी-पत्र पर दुष्यन्त के लिए मदन-लेख लिखती थी। विरह-अवधि का एक-एक दिन गिनती थी 'देहली दत्त पुष्पा'। यक्षिणी। एक दिन बीतने पर देहली पर एक फूल धर देती थी। विरहिणी सीता समय व्यतीत करने को कुन्द-माला गूँथ-गूँथ कर नदी में प्रवाहित कर देती थी, वह माला राम को मिली, राम पहचान लेते हैं कि इसमें गुम्फन-कला सीता की है, और दिङ्नाग ने नाटक का नामकरण 'कुन्दमाला' कर दिया।

इसी प्रकार संस्कृत-साहित्य की अनेक काव्य-कृतियों वृक्ष-लताओं के प्रसङ्ग-प्रयोगों से कथानक की गति में या वर्णन-चित्रों में सौन्दर्य और छवि-माधुर्य का समावेश हुआ है।

उपर्युक्त के अतिरिक्त कितने ही क्षेत्र और विषय हैं जिनका आधार उद्भिज्-प्राप्त पदार्थ हैं। उनके बारे में केवल संकेत-मात्र दे रही हूँ —

1. उद्‌भिज्-सृजन और मानव-सृजन से सम्बद्ध कितनी ही संज्ञा दें सामान्य हैं। पुष्प, ऋतु, क्षेत्र, क्षेत्री, फल, सेचन, ऋतुमती, रजस्, ऋतुकाल, वन्ध्य इत्यादि।

2. निरामिष भोजन, सब फूल, फल, कन्द, पत्र, काण्ड, धान्य, तेल आदि सब वनस्पति जन्य हैं। मधुर, तिक्त, कटु, कषाय, अम्ल, लवण— षट्-रस रसना-जिह्वा के स्वाद हैं। इनका अनुभव स्वादु-ग्रन्थि कुछ खाकर ही पाती हैं। काव्य-अनुरञ्जन का स्रोत रस है। काव्य-रस-निष्पत्ति और उससे होने वाले रसोद्रेक के विषय में काव्यमीमांसाकार राजशेखर कहते हैं—

वक्ता, शब्द, अर्थ और रस— इन सबके होने पर भी जिसके बिना वाङ्मधु स्रवित नहीं होता, वह पाक है और वह काव्य-पाक नौ प्रकार का है, उनके नाम फलों के ऊपर हैं—पिचुमन्द-पाक, बदर-पाक, मृद्वीका-पाक, वार्ताक-पाक, तिन्तिणी-पाक, सहकार-पाक, क्रमुक-पाक, त्रपुस-पाक और नारिकेल-पाक। (भारवि के काव्य को नारिकेल-पाक कहते हैं—इसी से उक्ति प्रसिद्ध हुई—'नारिकेलफलसमं वचो भारवेः')। सहृदय जन पाक-आस्वादन से काव्य-रस की निष्पत्ति पाते हैं।

3. उत्सव, अनुष्ठान, संस्कार, सामाजिक-गोष्ठी, पान-गोठी सब ही में उद्भिज्-जगत् की छवि जुड़ी है। वसन्तोत्सव, शरद्-उत्सव, सीमन्तोन्नयन संस्कार आदि।

4. 'देवता और वृक्षों से सम्बद्ध' मिथकों में पुष्प, वृक्ष, लताओं का महत्त्व अलग से ही विस्तृत और व्यापक अध्ययन का विषय है। वैष्णवों द्वारा तुलसी वन्द्य है, तो शैवों का रुद्राक्ष। देवी को जपा चढ़ाते हैं। यह भी कह दूँ कि शिव को धतूरा, आक, भाँग आदि चढ़ाये जाते हैं— वे विषपायी जो हैं।

'अश्वत्थ सनातन' तो सनातन है-उसकी कथा सनातन, उसका वैशिष्ट्य सनातन, उसका दर्शन सनातन। उसी के नीचे सिद्धार्थ 'बोधि' पाकर बुद्ध बन गए और उनका दर्शन दिग्-दिगन्तर में व्याप्त हो गया। इसके अतिरिक्त निम्नलिखित विषयों पर शोध अपेक्षित है —

वनस्पति-जगत् से प्राप्त (1) भोज्य ओर पेय (2) वसन एवं वेश-सामग्री, (3) गन्ध-प्रसाधन के पदार्थ, (4)

लेखन-उपादान, (5) अस्त्रों-शस्त्रों की योजना-आयोजना, (6) चित्र-कला के साधन, (7) पर्णकुटी से लेकर आवास-प्रासाद और देवमन्दिर के निर्माण-सहायक, (8) औषध-चिकित्सा-द्रव्य-विवरण-सारिणी दीर्घकाय है।

वनस्पति-जगत् के सदस्यों पर आधारित स्थलों के नाम (पाटलिपुत्र, आदि) और व्यक्तिगत संज्ञायें (कणाद, चाणक्य, पिप्पलाद, याज्ञवल्क्य, इक्ष्वाकु, वंशीधर, आदि)-ये भी गवेषणा योग्य हैं।

वनस्पति-जगत् के अन्य विविध आयाम विस्तृत रूप में वराहमिहिर की बृहत्संहिता के गन्ध-युक्ति, कान्दर्पिकम्, वास्तु-विद्या, कुसुमलतावृक्षायुर्वेद, काण्डारोप्या उदकार्गला अध्यायों में वर्णित हैं।

कौटिल्य के अर्थशास्त्र के अन्त में परघात प्रयोग प्रकरण (शत्रु-मारण-औषध-प्रयोग), प्रलम्भनप्रकरण (औषधियों से भूख-प्यास नष्ट करने या आकृति-परिवर्तन के द्वारा शत्रु-प्रवञ्चन), भैषज्यमन्त्रप्रयोग (जादू-टोना) और स्वावलेपघातप्रतीकार (शत्रु-आघात के प्रतीकार) में वृक्ष-लताओं की विशद भूमिका है।

अब कह दूँ कि मृणाल से अलग किया कमल कुम्हला जाता है, किन्तु जननी-संयुक्त नाल से अलग किया सद्योजात शिशु जड़-चेतन, स्थावर-जंगम सबका स्पर्श-अनुभव सकल-इन्द्रियों से पाने को नयनोन्मीलन करता है। आयु-अवधि समाप्त होने पर वंश का वंशज वंश-वाहन अन्तिम-यात्रा करता है।

उस 'पर' ने 'एकोऽहं बहुधा स्याम्' की उद्घोषणा की जिसकी गूँज, अनुगूँज, ध्वनि-प्रतिध्वनि, नाद, सङ्गीत, कण-कण में है, अणु-अणु में है, मेरे वट-बीज में है। नतभाव से कहूँ—वट-बीज की छुअन अन्तर्मन में बाकी है।

卐 卐 卐

माल्यग्रथनकला

(पुष्पमालाग्रथन एवं पुष्पाभूषणविरचन)

इला घोष

विभिन्न प्रकार के पुष्पों से अलंकरण बनाने की कला प्राचीन भारत की एक मनोरम कला थी। ललितविस्तर की शिल्पसूची में 'माल्यग्रथनम्' के रूप में तथा शुक्रनीतिसार में 'पुष्पादिग्रथनम्' के रूप में इस कला का उल्लेख हुआ है।

संस्कृत साहित्य में माल्य शब्द का प्रयोग दो अर्थों में हुआ है—

प्रथम-पुष्प के अर्थ में, यथा रामायण में —

'विटपी माल्यधारिणः' 'तानि माल्यानि जातानि मुनीनां तपसा तदा' जैसे सन्दर्भ[1]।

द्वितीय-पुष्पों से रचित माला के अर्थ में, यथा कुमारसम्भव का निम्नलिखित सन्दर्भ —

माल्येन तां निर्वचनं जघान।[2]

अतः माल्यग्रथनविकल्पाः से अभिप्राय पुष्पों को सुन्दर कलात्मक ढंग से गूँथकर या बाँधकर माला, करधनी, कर्णाभूषण, शिरोभूषण आदि बनाने की कला है। मानवीय सभ्यता के उस प्रथम चरण में जब मनुष्य ने स्वर्णादि धातुओं का प्रयोग नहीं सीखा था तब माल्य ही मा नव के प्रथम प्रसाधन बने। पुष्पों के उज्ज्वल वर्ण, मादक गंध, कोमल स्पर्श एवं सर्वसुलभता ने ही इन्हें अलंकरण के रूप में सर्वप्रिय बनाया।

प्राचीन भारत में माल्य देवता और मनुष्य दोनों के ही नेपथ्य विधान (वेशभूषा धारण) का अनिवार्य अंग था।[3] नागरक प्रातःकाल प्रसाधनविधि के अंतर्गत माल्य धारण करने के पश्चात् ही अपने दैनिक कर्तव्यों को प्रारम्भ करता था। रात्रि में सम्मर्दन आदि से शीघ्र म्लान न होने वाली कुरण्ट पुष्प की माला अधिक प्रयोग में लाई जाती थी।।[4] स्त्री पति के पास अभिगम करते समय अंगराग आदि के साथ पुष्पमाला भी धारण करती थी।[5]

दैनन्दिन जीवन में पुष्प अलंकरणों का उपयोग इतना अधिक था कि 'माल्यग्रन्थन' एक स्वतन्त्र शिल्प या कला के रूप में विकसित हुआ।

माला

माल्य अर्थात् पुष्पनिर्मित आभूषणों में प्रमुख है— माला। कलाकार की कोमल कल्पना के साथ क्रमशः एक के बाद एक सूत्र में पिरोए गए पुष्पों से रचित होने के कारण ही इसकी संज्ञा माला है; जो परवर्ती युग में पंक्ति या परम्परा का वाचक बन गया। दृष्टि को या मन को हर लेने के कारण यह ''हार''; शिल्पी की मनोरम कल्पना और सौन्दर्य चेतना का सर्जन होने के कारण 'स्रज्' तथा बाँधने के लिए फीते या रस्सी का कार्य करने के कारण 'दाम' कहा गया है।

वैदिककाल से लेकर वर्तमान युग तक रचित सम्पूर्ण संस्कृत साहित्य में शायद ही कोई ऐसी कृति हो जिसमें किसी न किसी प्रसंग में माल्य का उल्लेख न हुआ हो।

ऋग्वेद में अश्विनी कुमारों को कमल-पुष्प की माला (पुष्करस्रज/10/84/3) धारण करने वाला कहा गया है। रामायण में अयोध्या की समृद्धि का वर्णन करते हुए आदिकवि लिखते हैं कि अयोध्या में ऐसा कोई भी नागरिक नहीं था जो गन्धमाला का उपभोग न करता हो—

नाकुण्डली नामुकुटी नास्त्रग्वी नाल्पभोगवान्।[6]

कमलों की माला धारण करती हुई वनवासिनी सीता की उपमा पद्मिनी से दी गई है—

कमलानां च शुभां मालां पद्मिनीव च बिभ्रती। (अरण्यकाण्ड - 46.16)

संस्कृत साहित्य में वर्णित कतिपय विशिष्ट मालाओं के सन्दर्भ इस प्रकार हैं—

(1) सिर पर धारण की जाने वाली मालाएँ

अमरकोश के अनुसार ऐसी मालाओं की सामान्य संज्ञा— माल्य, माला और स्रज् है। केशमध्य में धारण की गई माला की विशिष्ट संज्ञा **गर्भक**, शिखा से लटकती हुई माला की **प्रभ्रष्टक** और सामने की ओर रखी गई माला की **ललामक** है।[7]

ये मालाएँ एक ही जाति के पुष्पों से या भिन्न वर्ण और गन्ध वाले पुष्पों की मिश्रित संयोजना से बनाई जाती थी। कालिदास के अनुसार वर्षा ऋतु में स्त्रियाँ कदम्ब, केसर और केतकी की सुन्दर आयोजना से रचित मालाओं को सिर पर धारण करती थीं—

मालाः कदम्बनवकेसरकेतकीभिरायोजिताः शिरसि बिभ्रति योषितोऽद्य।[8]

कुछ हरापन लिए हुए बकुल के साथ खिले हुए श्वेत मालती पुष्पों और किञ्चित रक्तिम जूही की कलियों का संयोजन निश्चय ही मनोज्ञ होता था—

शिरसि बकुलमालां मालतीभिः समेतां
विकसितनवपुष्पैर्यूथिकाकुड्मलैश्च।।[9]

सिर पर धारण किए जाने वाले माल्य-आभरण 'शेखरक' और 'आपीड' कहे जाते थे इनकी सुरुचिपूर्ण योजना एक स्वतन्त्र कला मानी गई थी।

स्त्रियाँ अपनी लम्बी वेणी को भी पुष्प माल्य से अलंकृत करती थीं। ऐसी मालाओं या गजरों को 'वेणीस्रक्'[10] कहा जाता था।

आखेट आदि के प्रसंग में केशों को वनमाला से बाँध लिया जाता था—

ग्रथित मौलिरसौ वनमालया।[11]

विवाह के अवसर पर वधू के केशों को दूर्वायुक्त मधूक दाम से बाँधा जाता था—

पर्याक्षिपत्काचिदुदारबन्धं दूर्ववता पाण्डुमधूकदाम्ना।[12]

(2) कँधे से लटकती हुई लम्बी मालाएँ

ऐसी मालाएँ कालिदास को अत्यन्त प्रिय हैं, वे प्रायः पुरुषों के प्रसंग में इन मालाओं का वर्णन करते हैं यथा—

अंसार्पितलम्बहार को धारण किए हुए पाण्ड्य देश के राजा (रघुवंश - 6.60); **अंसलम्बिकुटजार्जुनस्रज** से शोभित अग्निवर्ण (रघुवंश - 19.37) आदि।

(3) कण्ठ में धारण की जाने वाली मालाएँ

ये मालाएँ अनेक प्रकार की होती थीं—

(क) वक्ष:स्थल को सुशोभित करने वाले पुष्पहार

ग्रीष्म ऋतु में स्त्रियों के चन्दन चर्चित वक्ष:स्थल पर लटकते हुए तुषार— गौर पुष्पहार कालिदास को अत्यन्त प्रिय हैं—

पयोधराश्चन्दनपङ्कचर्चितास्तुषारगौरार्पितहारशेखरा:।[13]

अंगनाओं के वक्ष:स्थल पर अर्पित हारयष्टि सोये हुए मन्मथ को जगा देती है।[14]

अमरकोश के अनुसार कण्ठ से वक्षस्थल तक सीधी लटकती हुई मालाओं की संज्ञा प्रालम्ब है।[15]

महाकवि कालिदास ने रघुवंश में अज के वक्ष:स्थल पर लम्बमान स्वयम्वर माला का सुन्दर वर्णन किया है जो इन्दुमती के बाहुपाश के समान शोभित हो रही थी—

तया स्त्रजा मङ्गलपुष्पमय्या विशालवक्ष: स्थललम्बया स:।
अमंस्त कण्ठार्पितबाहुपाशां विदर्भराजावरजां वरेण्य:।।[16]

(ख) घुटनों तक लटकती मालिकाएँ

अपेक्षाकृत पतली और जानु तक लटकने वाली मालाओं को बाणभट्ट ने 'मालिका' कहा है। पारिजात पुष्पों और बीच-बीच में पल्लवों को गूँथकर बनाई गई ऐसी मालिकाओं को धारण करने वाली वन देवी का सुन्दर वर्णन कादम्बरी में हुआ है—

पारिजातकुसुमपल्लवग्रथिताभिराजानुलम्बिनीभि: कण्ठमालिकाभिराच्छादितविग्रहया।[17]

मालाओं की भी माला अर्थात् एक साथ कई लड़ियों को धारण करने के कारण भी संभवत: इन्हें मालिका कहा जाता था। ये मालिकाएँ क्रमश: कण्ठ से स्कन्ध प्रदेश तक के भाग को सुशोभित करते हुए शरीर को आच्छादित कर देती थीं।

(ग) घुटनों तक लटकती हुई 'वैकक्षक' मालाएँ

महाकवि बाणभट्ट श्वेत कुसुमों से गूँथी गई; घुटनों तक लटकती हुई उन लम्बी मालाओं का वर्णन करते हैं, जिनकी विशेष संज्ञा वैकक्षक थी। यौवराज्याभिषेक के अवसर पर चंद्रापीड़ ऐसी ही वैकक्षक मालाएँ पहने हुए थे—

सितकुसुमग्रथिताभिराजानुलम्बिनीभिरिन्दुकरकलापकोमलाभि:
वैकक्षकस्त्रग्भि: निरन्तरनिचितशरीरतया . . .।[18]

विवाह के अवसर पर वर को भी इन मालाओं से सज्जित कया जाता था। वर वेश में ग्रहवर्मा वैकक्षक मालाओं को धारण किए हुए थे। बाणभट्ट ने इस माला की उपमा कामदेव के धनुष से दी है—

कार्मुकेणेव कौसुमेन दाम्ना विरचितवैकक्षकविलास:।

(हर्षचरित - उ. 4, पृ. 249)

अमरकोश के अनुसार कण्ठ से उर:स्थल तक यज्ञोपवीत के समान तिरछी लटकने वाली माला को वैकक्षक कहा जाता था।[19]

वासुदेव शरण अग्रवाल के मत में— वे लम्बी मालाएँ जो बाँये कंधे से दाहिनी ओर एवं दाहिने कंधे से बाईं ओर जाती हुई बीच में स्वस्तिकाकार दिखाई देती थीं, वैकक्षक कही जाती थीं।[20]

(घ) पैरों का स्पर्श करती हुई 'आप्रपदीन' माला

चरणों तक लटकती हुई या धरणितल का स्पर्श करने वाली अत्यन्त लम्बी मालाएँ बाणभट्ट को विशेष प्रिय हैं। ऐसी मालाओं से अधिष्ठित देवी लक्ष्मी का एक चित्र–

धरणितलचुम्बिनीभिः कण्ठकुसुममालाभिः अधिष्ठिताम्।[21]

हर्ष की माता यशोमती ने भी सती होते समय ऐसी ही लम्बी माला धारण की थी–

आप्रपदीनां कण्ठे गुणकुसुममालां यमदोलामिवारूढाम्।[22]

इनके अतिरिक्त विशेष अवसरों के लिए कुछ विशिष्ट मालाएँ इस प्रकार थी–

(अ) कौतुकमालिका

महाकवि भास ने विवाह के अवसर पर वधू द्वारा धारण की जाने वाली माला को **कौतुक मालिका** कहा है इसमें पुष्पों के साथ **अविधवाकरण सपत्नीमर्दन** नामक औषधियाँ भी गूँथ दी जाती थीं। इसे गूँथने का कार्य इस कार्य में कुशल कुलीन स्त्रियाँ ही करती थीं।[23]

(ब) मधूकमाला

विवाहादि अवसरों पर मांगलिक पुष्पों से ही मालाएँ बनाई जाती थीं। इन्दुमती ने अज को जो स्वयंवरमाला पहनायी थी उसमें दूर्वा के साथ मधूकपुष्प गूँथे हुए थे–

किञ्चिद्विस्रंसिदूर्वाङ्कमधूकमाला।[24]

तया स्रजा मङ्गलपुष्पमय्या।।[25]

(स) बकुलमाला

अपनी मादक गंध के कारण बकुल या केसर पुष्प की मालाएँ विलासी स्त्री-पुरुषों को विशेष प्रिय थी। बकुल मालाएँ लम्बे समय तक ताजी और सुगंधित बनी रहती थीं। अनुसूया ने शकुन्तला की विदाई के लिए बहुत पहले से ही ऐसी माला गूँथ कर सुरक्षित रख दी थी–

एतन्निमित्तमेव कालान्तरक्षमा निक्षिप्ता मया केसरमालिका।[26]

हर्ष के जन्मोत्सव पर कन्नौज के युवकों ने केसर मालाएँ ही धारण की थीं–

स्कन्धावलम्बमान केसरमाला . . . युवानः।[27]

आचार्य कवि राजशेखर के अनुसार म्लान हो जाने पर भी बकुल मालाएँ त्यागी नहीं जाती थीं–

म्लानापि मोच्या न केसरस्रग्।[26]

'मालतीमाधवम्' में माधव द्वारा गूँथी गई और मालती द्वारा धारण की गई बकुलमाला दीर्घकाल के बाद भी माधव के लिए; मालती के अभिज्ञान का चिह्न बन जाती है।[29]

(ङ) करवीरमाला

मृच्छकटिक में रक्तवर्णी करवीर पुष्पों से ग्रथित करवीरमाला का उल्लेख हुआ है। जो वध से पूर्व चारुदत्त को पहनाई गई थी।[30] शव साधना में शव को लाल पुष्पों की माला से अलंकृत किया जाता था।[31]

(च) वन्दनमाला

गृह-प्रवेश, विजयोत्सव, वरयात्रा आदि के प्रसंग में स्वागत और अभिनन्दन के लिए तोरणों की आधी ऊँचाई पर बाँधी गई मांगलिक मालाओं को वन्दनमाला कहा जाता था-

तोरणार्द्धे च माङ्गल्यं दाम वन्दनमालिका।

इसमें पुष्पों के साथ आम्रपल्लव गूँथे जाते थे अथवा यह पूर्ण रूप से हरित आम्रपल्लवों से ही रचित होती थी।

कादम्बरी में कुमार चन्द्रपीड के लिए निर्मित भवन के गृहप्रवेश के अवसर पर इस वन्दनमाला का उल्लेख हुआ है—

आबद्धहरितवन्दनमालम् . . . उपपादिताशेषगृहप्रवेशमङ्गलं भवनं जगाम। (पृ. 297)

मेखला

मालाओं की भाँति ही पुष्पों को गूँथकर छोटी-छोटी मालिकाओं की लड़ियों से मेखला या करधनी भी बनाई जाती थीं। लड़ियों की संख्या के अनुसार इनकी विशिष्ट संज्ञाएं थीं। एक लड़ वाली करधनी को 'काञ्ची', आठ लड़ वाली को 'मेखला', सोलह लड़ वाली को 'रसना', पच्चीस लड़ वाली को 'कलापक' कहा जाता था।[32]

मेखला के लिए मादक गन्ध वाले बकुल पुष्प ही अधिक रुचिकर थे। समाधिलीन शिव को मुग्ध करने के लिए पार्वती ने जब शिव के आश्रम में प्रवेश किया तब वे केसर काञ्ची पहने हुए थीं-

स्रस्तां नितम्बादवलम्बमाना पुनः पुनः केसरदामकाञ्चीम्।[33]

कई लड़ों वाली मेखला को गूँथना निश्चय ही एक समय सापेक्ष कला थी। प्रायः प्रेमी स्त्री-पुरुष मिल-जुलकर ऐसी विलासमेखलाओं को गूँथते थे-

असमाप्य विलासमेखलाम्।[34]

कालिदास के ही समान बाणभट्ट ने भी बकुल मालिकाओं से रचित मेखला को धारण करने वाली नन्दन वन की देवी का सुन्दर चित्र प्रस्तुत किया है।[35]

इन सूत्र ग्रथित माल्यों के साथ ही सूत्र में अग्रथित कई सुन्दर अलङ्करणों की रचना भी इस कला के अंतर्गत होती थी। राजप्रसादों के कन्यान्तःपुर में कला निपुण स्त्रियाँ पुष्पाभरणों की रचना करती थीं।[36] कुसुमप्रसाधन प्रायः ऋतुपुष्पों से बनाए जाते थे।

रचितं रतिपण्डित त्वया स्वयमङ्गेषु ममेदमार्तवम्।
ध्रियते कुसुमप्रसाधनम् . .।[37]

ऐसे अलङ्करणों का सर्वाधिक वर्णन कालिदास साहित्य में हुआ है। उनकी नायिकाओं के ऋतुओं के अनुसार प्रिय पुष्प अलङ्करण है।

शरद् ऋतु में हाथ में लीलाकमल, हेमन्त में केशपाश में ताजे कुन्द के पुष्प, वसन्त में चूड़ापाश में नव कुरबक, ग्रीष्म में कानों में कोमल शिरीष के पुष्प तथा वर्षा में सीमन्त को सुशोभित करता हुआ कदम्ब का पुष्प।[38]

वसन्तु ऋतु में पार्वती द्वारा धारण किए जाने वाले पुष्पाभरण, पद्मरागमणि, स्वर्ण और मुक्ताकलाप की शोभा को भी हर लेते हैं—

अशोकनिर्भर्त्सितपद्मरागमाकृष्टहेमद्युति कर्णिकारम्।
मुक्ताकलापीकृतसिन्दुवारं वसन्तपुष्पाभरणं वहन्ती।।[39]

कतिपय प्रसिद्ध पुष्प अलङ्करण इस प्रकार हैं—

अवतंस

सामान्य रूप से अलङ्कार अर्थ का वाचक होते हुए भी अवतंस शब्द विशेष रूप से कर्णाभूषण के अर्थ में ही प्रयुक्त हुआ है। संस्कृत साहित्य में कानों को अलंकृत करने वाले पुष्पावतंसों के अनेक उदाहरण प्राप्त होते हैं।

अत्यन्त सुकुमार शिरीष पुष्प का अवतंस कालिदास को विशेष प्रिय है—

अवतंसयन्ति दयमानाः प्रमदाः शिरीषकुसुमानि।[40]

ग्रीष्म ऋतु में यह अलका की वधुओं का भी कर्णभूषण बनता है।[41]

सम्भवतः इन्हें सूत्र में गूँथकर या बाँधकर कानों में बाँध लिया जाता था यथा शकुन्तला द्वारा धारण किया जाने वाला **आगण्डविलम्बिकेसर कर्णार्पितबन्धन शिरीष पुष्प का आभरण।**[42]

स्तबक (गुच्छे) या मंजरियों में खिलने वाले पुष्पों से रचित अवतंस कानों से बाँधकर पहने जाते थे अतः इनकी संज्ञा 'निबन्धनीय' थी। सूत्र में बाँधकर लटका लिए जाने के कारण ये बाह्य गति के साथ हिल उठते थे—

स्ववाहनक्षोमचलावतंसाः।[43]

ककुभ-मञ्जरियों से भी इच्छानुकूल अवतंस बनाए जा सकते थे।[44]

नमेरु पुष्प[45] एवं **तमाल-प्रवाल**[46] के अवतंसों का वर्णन भी कालिदास ने किया है तथापि सुगन्धित पुष्पों के अवतंस ही अङ्गनाओं को अधिक प्रिय थे।[47]

कर्णपूर

कानों को पूरी तरह से आच्छादित कर देने या सौन्दर्य से पूर्ण कर देने के कारण ही इनकी संज्ञा कर्णपूर थी। कर्णपूर की रचना पुष्पस्तबक और पुष्प दोनों से ही की जाती थी। बाणभट्ट ने हर्ष के जन्मोत्सव पर नृत्य करती हुई स्त्रियों द्वारा कानों में धारण किए गए शिरीषस्तबक के कर्णपूरों से सुनहली धूप के भी हरित हो जाने का वर्णन किया है।[48]

समुल्लसद्भिः शिरीषकुसुमस्तबककर्णपूरैः शुकपिच्छमय इव हरिच्छायोऽभूदातपः।

वर्षा ऋतु में नवीन कदम्ब के पुष्प नववधुओं के कर्णपूर बनते थे—

विकचनवकदम्बैः कर्णपूरं वधूनां रचयति जलदौघः कान्तवत्काल एषः।[49]

तो वसन्त में कर्णिकार के स्वर्णिम पुष्प।[50]

कर्णपूर पुरुषों के कानों को भी अलंकृत करते थे। हर्षचरित में बाणभट्ट द्वारा धारण किए गए; दूब की नाल में गूँथकर बनाए गए गिरिकर्णिका पुष्प के कर्णपूर का वर्णन हुआ है।

कानों को छेदकर पहने जाने वाले ये आभरण 'आवेध्य' वर्ग के अन्तर्गत आते थे। कुछ पुष्प अलङ्करणों को कानों के ऊपर या स्वर्णाभूषणों के ऊपर खोंस लिया जाता था ऐसे अलङ्करणों की संज्ञा 'निवेश्य' थी; यथा—

कर्णेषु च प्रवरकाञ्चनकुण्डलेषु
नीलोत्पलानि विविधानि निवेशयन्ति।[51]

कर्णाभूषण के रूप में उत्पल[52] और कुवलय[53] का वर्णन कालिदास ने विशेष अभिरुचि के साथ किया है।

अग्रथित आभूषणों में वे पुष्प अलङ्करण भी आते हैं जो केशों को अलंकृत करते थे। इन्हें निवेश्य वर्ग में रखा जा सकता है क्योंकि इन्हें वेणी या जूड़े में खोंस लिया जाता था—

निवेशितान्तःकुसुमैः शिरोरुहैः।[54]

घननील कुञ्चित केशों में नवमालती की शोभा अपूर्व होती थी—

केशान्नितान्तघननीलविकुञ्चिताग्रा-
नापूरयन्ति वनिता नवमालतीभिः।[55]

खिले हुए मल्लिका-पुष्प भी वेणी में गूँथ लिए जाते थे जो कन्दुक क्रीड़ा आदि के समय वेणी के तीव्र गति से हिलने के कारण गिरने लगते थे।[56]

वसन्त ऋतु में चञ्चल नील अलकों को कभी अशोक के लाल पुष्प[57] अलंकृत करते थे तो कभी चम्पक के सुगन्धित पुष्प।[58] मानव शरीर, देवप्रतिमा आदि के अलङ्करण के साथ ही पुष्प माल्यभवनों[59], तोरणद्वारों[60], वेदिकाओं, सभामण्डपों, शयनगृहों, शैय्याओं, वाद्ययंत्रों[61] और मंगलकलशों[62] को भी अलंकृत करते थे।

रामायण में श्वेत मालाओं से अलंकृत राजभवनों का एक चित्र देखा जा सकता है—

सितमेघनिभं चापि राजवेश्म सुतोरणम्।
शुक्लमाल्यकृताकारं दिव्यगन्धसमुक्षितम्।।[63]

पुष्पमाल्य भारतीय पूजा-अर्चना का भी अभिन्न अंग था। पुत्र-प्राप्ति के लिए नन्दिनी गाय की सेवा करने वाले राजा दिलीप की पत्नी सुदक्षिणा प्रतिदिन गन्धमाल्य से नन्दिनी की अर्चना करती थीं।[64]

प्राचीन भारत में नागरक के गृह में अतिथि-मित्रों का सत्कार पुष्पमालाओं से होता था।[65] माल्योपहार आंतरिक सौहार्द और प्रेम को तो अभिव्यक्त करता ही था, साथ ही यह विशिष्ट सत्कार और सम्मान का भी प्रतीक था। देवराज इन्द्र द्वारा राजा दुष्यन्त को पहनाई गई मन्दार माला इसका उदाहरण है—

राजा—**स खलु मनोरथानामप्यभूमिर्विसर्जनावसरसत्कारः।**
मन्दारमाला हरिणा पिनद्धा।[66]

वस्तुतः माला **'माति मानहेतुर्भवति'** इस निरुक्ति[67] के अनुसार मान का ही प्रतीक थी। माला श्री और सौभाग्य की वृद्धि करने वाली समझी जाती थी अतः *'मां शोभां लाति'* इस व्युत्पत्ति के अनुसार यह एक अन्वर्थ संज्ञा थी। चरक के अनुसार गन्धमाल्य का सेवन सौभाग्य, आयुष्य, पुष्टि और बल को प्रदान करने वाला, चित्त को प्रसन्न करने वाला तथा काम्य होता है—

वृष्यं सौभाग्यमायुष्यं काम्यं पुष्टिबलप्रदम्।
सौमनस्यमलक्ष्मीघ्नं गन्धमाल्यनिषेवणम्।।[68]

अतः स्नान के पश्चात् स्त्री-पुरुष प्रतिदिन अंगराग आदि के साथ ही पुष्पमाल्य भी धारण करते थे—

अपि स्नातो जामातेति। सुमनोवर्णकमानयामि।[69]

नागरक के बहिः प्रकोष्ठ में एक वेदिका पर अनुलेप, सौगन्धिकपुटिका आदि के साथ माल्य भी सर्वदा सुलभ होते थे।[70]

यद्यपि प्रसंग और अभिरुचि के अनुसार सभी प्रकार के ऋतु पुष्पों की मालाएँ उपयोग में लाई जाती थीं तथापि ग्रीष्म में कमल और उत्पल (नीलकमल) की मालाएँ विशेष शीतल मानी जाती थीं—

स्रजः सकमलोत्पलाः। (अष्टांगहृदय-सूत्रस्थान - 4.35)

श्वेत पुष्पों का भी विशेष महत्व था। इनसे आभिजात्य सात्त्विकता तथा पवित्रता का भाव अभिव्यक्त होता था। गोष्ठी-विहार आदि के समय स्त्रियाँ परिमित आभूषणों के साथ केशों में प्रायः श्वेत पुष्प गूँथती थीं।[71]

राज्याभिषेक के अवसर पर अभिषिच्यमान राजा श्वेत पुष्प मालाएँ ही धारण करता था।[72] सत्कार के लिए श्वेत पुष्प उपहार में दिए जाते थे—

सितकुसुम . . . सत्कृतैः सूत्रधारैः।[73]

इस प्रकार दैनन्दिन जीवन में माल्य के बहुविध उपयोग ने 'माल्यग्रथन' को एक शिल्पकला के रूप में विकसित किया। यद्यपि स्त्री और पुरुष दोनों ही इस कला में नैपुण्य प्राप्त करते थे तथापि प्रायः नायक अपनी प्रिया को प्रसन्न करने के लिए सुन्दर मालाओं को रचकर उनका प्रसाधन करते थे—

शिरसि बकुलमालां मालतीभिः समेतां
विकसितनवपुष्पैर्यूथिकाकुड्मलैश्च ।
विकचनवकदम्बैः कर्णपूरं वधूनां
रचयति जलदौघः कान्तवत् काल एषः।।[74]

महाकवि भवभूति के 'मालतीमाधव' में इस कला के सम्बन्ध में कई महत्वपूर्ण सन्दर्भ प्राप्त होते हैं—

यह एक सुन्दर हस्तशिल्प था जिसमें अन्य कलाओं की भाँति ही विदग्धता की अपेक्षा रहती थी—

माधवश्रीहस्तनिर्माणमनोहरा बकुलमाला।[75]

विदग्धरचनामनोहरां स्रजमभिनिर्मातुमारब्धवान्।।[76]

सुन्दर रचना के लिए चित्त की एकाग्रता आवश्यक थी इसके अभाव में वह विरचना हो जाती थी—

मालतीमुखावलोकनविहस्ततया विषगरचितैकभागाम्।
एकपार्श्वविषमप्रतिबद्धेयं विरचना।।[77]

इस मनोरम कला सृष्टि की सार्थकता प्रिया की प्रसन्नता में ही समझी जाती थी—

तद्भवतु कृतार्थता वैदग्ध्यस्य। फलतु निर्माणरमणीयता।
समासादयतु एष भर्तृदारिकायाः कण्ठावलम्बनमहार्घताम्।[78]

माल्यग्रथन की अनेक व्यक्तिगत शैलियाँ थीं। विशिष्ट प्रकार का गुम्फन कलाकार की पहचान का कारण होता था। 'कुन्दमाला' नाटक इसका एक सुन्दर उदाहरण है। गोमती नदी के जल में बहकर आई हुई, विशिष्ट रचनाविन्यास वाली कुन्द पुष्पों की माला को देखकर श्रीराम निर्वासिता सीता का स्मरण कर रोमांचित हो उठते हैं—

रामः -(निर्वर्ण्य रोमाञ्चमभिनीय)

वत्स! दृष्टपूर्वमिदं कुसुमरचनाविन्यासकौशलम्। . . . क्व वान्यत्रेदृशस्यावस्थानम्![79]

महाकवि राजशेखर पुष्पमाल्य के सम्बन्ध में कई महत्वपूर्ण रहस्यों को उद्घाटित करते हैं। यथा— मालतीमाला विमर्दन के योग्य नहीं है। म्लान होने पर भी केसर माला का परित्याग नहीं किया जाता।[80]

कोरण्ड पुष्प की माला जैसे-जैसे सूखती है अधिक लाल होती जाती है आदि।[81]

संस्कृत साहित्य में पुष्प माल्य महाकवियों की कोमल कल्पना से जुड़कर अनेक मनोरम भावों का अभिव्यञ्जक हुआ है। श्रीहर्ष के अनुसार दमयन्ती के अंगों की रचना कमल, कुवलय, चम्पक आदि पुष्पों से करते हुए, विधाता ने मानों कामदेव के अर्चन के लिए कुसुमस्त्रज की ही रचना की है।[82]

क्योंकि पुष्प कामदेव के बाण बनकर दमयन्ती के हृदय को बेंधते हैं अतः उसकी सखियाँ माला गूँथते हुए सुई की नोक से पुष्पों को व्यथित करती हैं।[83]

काव्य और नाट्य के साथ ही शास्त्रों में भी माल्य संबंधी उल्लेख प्राप्त होते हैं। भरत मुनि आहार्य अभिनय के अंतर्गत आभरण और वस्त्र के साथ माल्य का भी परिगणन करते हैं।[81] उनके अनुसार संरचना की दृष्टि से माल्य पाँच प्रकार के होते हैं[82]—

(1) वेष्टिम – बीच-बीच में दूर्वा आदि लगाकर या लपेट कर बनाए गए माल्य अथवा ऐसे माल्य जो शरीर के अंग विशेष को घेर लें।

(2) वितत – फैला कर धारण की गई एक जैसी अनेक मालाएँ जिनसे शरीर का वह भाग पूरी तरह आच्छादित हो जाए। बाणभट्ट को ऐसी मालाएँ विशेष प्रिय हैं।

(3) संघात्य – जो अनेक पुष्पों के समूह से खचित हों या कई लड़ों को बीच-बीच में मिलाकर एक लड़ बना दी गई हो।

(4) ग्रन्थिमत् – जो सुई से धागे में पिरोकर नहीं अपितु पुष्प नाल में गाँठ लगाकर रचे गए हों।

(5) प्रलम्बित – जो दूर तक लटकने वाले हों।

राजानक रुय्यक ने इनके अतिरिक्त—

(6) मुक्तक – जो केवल एक पुष्प से बना हो;

(7) मञ्जरी – अनेक छोटे-छोटे पुष्पों से युक्त शाखा तथा

(8) स्तबक – पुष्पगुच्छ का भी उल्लेख किया है।

माल्य भारतीय चित्रकला और मूर्तिशिल्प का भी विषय बना है। रामायण के एक महत्वपूर्ण सन्दर्भ के अनुसार लङ्का के राजप्रासाद की भित्तियों पर गजलक्ष्मी के ऐसे सुन्दर चित्र रचे गए थे जिनमें देवी लक्ष्मी के दोनों ओर चित्रित गज अपनी सूँड में नीलकमलों की माला लिए हुए थे—

नियुध्यमानाश्च गजाः सुहस्ताः
तथैव पद्मोत्पलदामहस्ताः।
लक्ष्मीस्तथा पद्मवितानहस्ता
गृहान्तरे राजति तस्य संस्था।। (सुन्दरकाण्ड - 5.18)

प्राचीन भारतीय मन्दिरों और प्रासादों में माल्य आकृतियों को स्तम्भों और तोरणद्वारों पर उकेरा गया है। देव, गन्धर्व और यक्ष प्रतिमाएँ माल्यों से अलंकृत हैं। देवगढ़ के दशावतार मन्दिर तथा खजुराहो के मन्दिरों में अधिकांश स्त्री प्रतिमाएँ पुष्प माल्यों से शोभित हैं। बिड़ला संग्रहालय भोपाल में विद्यमान सिंह वाहिनी दुर्गा प्रतिमा के केशों को कदम्ब एवं कुमुदिनी पुष्पों

से सजाया गया है। (आकृति—210)

संस्कृत साहित्य में 'माल्य' शब्द का प्रयोग पुष्प निर्मित माला और पुष्प अलंकरण दोनों के लिए ही हुआ है। पुष्पमाल्य अपने रूप, वर्ण, सुरभि और मार्दव से चक्षु, घ्राण और त्वक् तीनों इन्द्रियों को एक साथ तृप्त करता हुआ जीवन की ताजगी, स्फूर्ति, आनन्द, उल्लास और उत्सव का सूचक था अतः विषाद के अवसरों पर इसका उपयोग नहीं होता था यथा—

श्रीराम के वनगमन पर अयोध्या के नागरिकों ने बहुवर्णी पुष्प मालाओं का परित्याग कर अपना शोक व्यक्त किया था।[86] महाराजा दशरथ की मृत्यु पर सम्पूर्ण नगर ही पुष्पसज्जा से रहित[87] और माल्य-आपण माल्यरहित हो गए थे—

माल्यापणेषु राजन्ते नाद्य पण्यानि वै तथा।[88]

सीता के विरह में श्रीराम को पुष्प ही निष्प्रयोजन प्रतीत होने लगे थे—

पश्य लक्ष्मण पुष्पाणि निष्फलानि भवन्ति मे।[89]

वस्तुतः 'माल्यग्रथन विकल्पः' जीवन के शृङ्गार की कला थी। यह प्रेम की ऐसी मूक भाषा थी जिसे मानव ने कोमल पुष्पों के बहुवर्णी वैविध्य के माध्यम से मुखर किया था।

सन्दर्भ-सङ्केत

1. रामायण-अरण्यकाण्ड - 73.20, 25
2. कुमारसम्भव - 7.19
3. माल्यानां मुण्डमालादीनां देवतापूजनार्थं ग्रथनं विकल्पाः।
   कामसूत्र - 3.15 पर यशोधर की टीका, पृ. 88
4. कामसूत्र - 1.4.4
5. कामसूत्र - 4.1.24
6. रामायण, बालकाण्ड - 1.60.10
7. माल्यं माला स्रजौ मूर्ध्नि केशमध्ये तु गर्भकः।
   प्रभ्रष्टकं शिखालम्बि पुरोन्यस्तं ललामकम्।। अमरकोश-काण्ड, 2, मनुष्यवर्ग, 6.135
8. ऋतुसंहार - 2.21
9. ऋतुसंहार - 2.25
10. विद्धशालभञ्जिका - 2.13
11. रघुवंश - 9.51
12. कुमारसम्भव - 7.14
13. ऋतुसंहार - 1.6
14. ऋतुसंहार - 1.7
15. प्रालम्बमृजुलम्बि स्यात्। अमरकोश - 2.6.136
16. रघुवंश - 6.84
17. कादम्बरी - पृ. 435
18. कादम्बरी - पृ. 339
19. वैकक्षकं तु तत् यत्तिर्यक् क्षिप्तमुरसि। अमरकोश - 2.6.136
20. कादम्बरी एक सांस्कृतिक अध्ययन - पृ. 124

21. हर्षचरित – उच्छ्वास 4, पृ. 224
22. हर्षचरित – उच्छ्वास 5, पृ. 195
23. स्वप्नवासवदत्ता – अंक, 3
24. रघुवंश – 6.25
25. रघुवंश – 6.84
26. अभिज्ञानशाकुन्तल – अंक 3
27. हर्षचरित – उच्छ्वास 4, पृ. 223
28. विद्धशालभञ्जिका – 3.5
29. मालतीमाधव – अंक 9, पृ. 429
30. मृच्छकटिक – 10.21
31. रक्तस्रगाभरणस्य. . . शवस्य, हर्षचरित – उ. 3
32. एकयष्टिर्भवेत् काञ्ची मेखला त्वष्टयष्टिका।
    रसना स्यात् षोडशभिः कलापः पञ्चविंशकः।। अमरकोश, काण्ड – 2.6.108 पर रत्नप्रभा टीका।
33. कुमारसम्भव – 3.55
34. रघुवंश – 8.64
35. कादम्बरी – पृ. 435
36. मधुकरिके! विरचय कुसुमाभरणकानि। कादम्बरी – पृ. 533
37. कुमारसम्भव – 4.18
38. मेघदूत – 2.2
39. कुमारसम्भव – 3.53
40. अभिज्ञान शाकुन्तल – 1.4
41. मेघदूत – 2.2
42. अभिज्ञानशाकुन्तल – 6.18
43. कुमारसम्भव – 7.38
44. ऋतुसंहार – 2.21
45. कुमारसम्भव – 1.55
46. रघुवंश – 13.49
47. कृतावतंसैः कुसुमैः सुगन्धिभिः। ऋतुसंहार – 2.18
48. हर्षचरित – उ. 4, पृ. 227
49. ऋतुसंहार – 2.25
50. ऋतुसंहार – 6.6
51. ऋतुसंहार – 3.19
52. मेघदूत – 1.28
53. मेघदूत – 1.48
54. ऋतुसंहार – 5.8
55. ऋतुसंहार – 3.19
56. अविरलवेणिवेल्लिदभल्लवलनधुदविअसिदमल्लिअं। विद्धशालभञ्जिका – 2.7
57. चलेषु नीलेष्वलकेष्वशोकम्। ऋतुसंहार – 6.6
58. सुवासितं चारु शिरश्च चम्पकैः। ऋतुसंहार – 6.3
59. माल्यदामभिराकीर्णम्। रामायण–सुन्दरकाण्ड – 4.53
60. ऋज्वायतां हि मुखतोरणलोलमालाम्। स्वप्नवासवदत्ता – 5.3

61. रघुवंश - 8.34
62. पल्लवललामहेमकलशे बद्धवनमालादाम्नि . . .। हर्षचरित - उ. 7, पृ. 361
63. रामायण-सुन्दरकाण्ड - 4.53
64. रघुवंश - 2.1
65. कामसूत्र - 4.1.36
66. अभिज्ञानशाकुन्तल - 7.2
67. शब्दकल्पद्रुम - मालाशब्द
68. चरकसंहिता - सूत्रस्थान - 5.93
69. स्वप्नवासवदत्त - अंक 4
70. कामसूत्र - 1.4.4
71. कामसूत्र - 4.1.25
72. रामायण, अयोध्या - 3.9
73. हर्षचरित - उ. 4, पृ. 242
74. ऋतुसंहार - 2.25
75. मालतीमाधव - 6, पृ. 281
76. मालतीमाधव - अंक 1, पृ. 45
77. मालतीमाधव - अंक 1, पृ. 66; अंक 2, पृ. 88
78. मालतीमाधव - अंक 1, पृ 64-65
79. कुन्दमाला - अंक, 3, पृ. 67
80. विद्धशालभञ्जिका - 3.5
81. कोरण्डकुसुममाला ग्लायन्ती सुष्ठु रक्तत्वं दर्शयति। विद्धशालभञ्जिका - अंक 3, पृ. 81
82. नैषधीयचरित - 2.96
83. नैषधीयचरित - 6.67
84. नाट्यशास्त्र 23.10
85. नाट्यशास्त्र - 23.11
86. रामायण-अयोध्याकाण्ड - 114.23
87. रामायण-अयोध्याकाण्ड - 72.28
88. रामायण-अयोध्याकाण्ड - 72.41
89. रामायण-किष्किंधाकाण्ड - 1.44

卐 卐 卐

शेखरकापीडयोजनकला

(शिर:पुष्पमालायोजना)

इला घोष

वात्स्यायन ने शेखरक और आपीड योजना को चतुष्षष्टि कलाओं के अन्तर्गत एक स्वतन्त्र कला माना है। शेखरक और आपीड शिर पर धारण किए जाने वाले दो पुष्प रचित अलङ्कार हैं अत: यह कला 'माल्यग्रथन' का ही अंग है तथापि स्वतन्त्र कला के रूप में इसके परिगणन का अभिप्राय टीकाकार यशोधर के अनुसार इस प्रकार है—

ग्रथनविकल्प एवायं किन्तु योजनं कलान्तरम्।[1]

सुन्दर ढंग से इसकी योजना में भी एक प्रकार की कलात्मकता है; अत: यह एक स्वतन्त्र कला मानी गई है।

कोश ग्रन्थों में 'शेखर' और 'आपीड' दोनों शब्द ही शिखा स्थित माल्य के अर्थ में प्रयुक्त हैं—

शब्दरत्नावली के अनुसार—

शिखाविन्यस्तमालायामापीड: शेखरोऽपि च।

अमरकोश के अनुसार दोनों एक दूसरे के पर्याय हैं—

आपीड: शिखास्थितमाल्यं तत्पर्याय: शेखर:।[2]

यशोधर के अनुसार दोनों में सूक्ष्म भेद है—शेखर शिखास्थान में अवलम्बन्यास से (लटकाकर) पहना जाता है। (सम्भवत: इसकी रचना शिखराकार होती है।) आपीड मण्डलाकार गूँथा जाता है। इसे समग्र सिर को घेरते हुए काष्ठिका (काँटे) आदि की सहायता से पहना जाता है।[3]

ये दोनों ही नागरक के नेपथ्यविधान (वेशभूषाधारण) के प्रमुख अंग थे।

महाकवि कालिदास ने कुसुम-शेखर और कुसुम-आपीड का शब्दश: उल्लेख न करते हुए भी शिर पर धारण की जाने वाली मौलिमालाओं का अनेकश: वर्णन किया है।[4] उर्वशी को शिखाभरण के रूप में रक्त कदम्ब का पुष्प प्रिय है[5] तो महाराज दशरथ की अन्त:पुरिकाओं को रंगबिरंगे पुष्पों की मालाएँ।[6]

समग्र संस्कृत साहित्य में कुसुम-शेखर का सर्वाधिक वर्णन बाणभट्ट की रचनाओं में हुआ है। महाराज शूद्रक के मस्तक को आमोदित-मालती-कुसुम-शेखर अलंकृत करते हैं;[7] तो राजकुमार चन्द्रापीड की पहचान ही चन्द्रमा की किरणों के समान उज्ज्वल मालती-कुसुम-शेखर से होती है—

शशिकरकलापो मालतीकुसुमशेखरोऽभिलक्ष्यते।[8]

महाकवि बाणभट्ट सम्राट हर्ष द्वारा धारण की गई मुण्डमाला का भी वर्णन करते हैं जो मुखचंद्र को परिवेशमण्डल की भाँति अलंकृत करती थी—

उत्फुल्लमालतीमयेन मुखशशिपरिवेषमण्डलेन मुण्डमालागुणेन परिकल्पितकेशान्तम्।[9]

मुण्डमाला ऐश्वर्य और राजशक्ति का प्रतीक मानी जाती थी—

परमेश्वरचिह्नभूतां शशिकलामिव कल्पयित्वा सितकुसुममुण्डमलिकां शिरसि।[10] मुण्डमाला और शेखर दोनों का एक साथ संयोजन भी होता था। विवाह के अवसर पर ग्रहवर्मा ने मुण्डमाला के मध्य कुसुम-शेखर धारण किया था।—

उत्फुल्लमुण्डमालामध्याध्यासितकुसुमशेखरेण शिरसा। हर्षचरित - उ. 4, पृ. 249

कुसुमशेखर का अतिशययुक्त काव्यात्मक वर्णन भी कादम्बरी में हुआ है—

जिस समय राजा शूद्रक की सभा भंग होती है तब एक साथ उठे हुए राजाओं के मालती कुसुम-शेखरों के हिलने से भौंरों के झुण्ड उड़ने लगते हैं।[11]

चन्द्रापीड की दिग्विजय यात्रा के समय सैन्य प्रस्थान से उठी हुई धूल; राजाओं के शेखरों से गिरी हुई कुसुम-रज से मानों और अधिक बढ़ जाती है—

प्रोत्साह्यमान इव नरपतिकुसुमशेखरसहस्रपरिच्युतैः कुसुमशेखररजोभिः।[12]

अधीनस्थ राजाओं और सामन्तों के शेखररज से कथानायक सम्राट् के चरणों का रञ्जित होना भी संस्कृत कवियों का प्रिय विषय रहा है। यथा— रघुवंश में महाराज रघु के चरणों का वर्णन—

प्रस्थानप्रणतिभिरङ्गुलीषु चक्रुर्मौलिस्रक्च्युतमकरन्दरेणुगौरम्।[13]

इस प्रकार संस्कृत साहित्य में प्राप्त सन्दर्भों से इस कला के सम्बन्ध में निम्न तथ्यों का ज्ञान होता है

शेखरक और आपीड की योजना प्राचीन भारत की एक कमनीय कला थी। इसकी रचना और कल्पना कलात्मक और अभिरुचि की परिचायक थी। राजा, महाराजा, सामन्तों और सम्भ्रान्त नागरिकों की दैनन्दिन साज-सज्जा का यह अभिन्न अंग थी। कालिदास के युग में मौलि-माला या मौलिस्रक का ही अधिक प्रयोग होता था। बाणभट्ट के युग में इसने शेखर या मुकुट का रूप ले लिया। शेखर की रचना पुष्प-मालाओं से की जाती थी। प्रतिदिन स्नान के पश्चात् राजा गण अपने मस्तक पर सुगन्धित पुष्पों से रचित शेखर धारण करते थे। यथा महाराज शूद्रक के वर्णन प्रसंग में—

विरचितामोदिमालतीकुसुमशेखरः।[14]

विशिष्ट अतिथि के प्रति सम्मान और आत्मीयता की अभिव्यक्ति सिर पर शेखरक की रचना द्वारा की जाती थी। कादम्बरी की सखी मदलेखा ने स्वयं चन्द्रापीड के मस्तक पर मालती-मालाओं से शेखर की रचना की थी—

मालतीकुसुमदामभिरारचितशेखरं कृत्वा।[15]

विवाह के अवसर पर वर-वधू को भी शेखर और आपीड से सज्जित किया जाता था। राजशेखर स्वयंवर के प्रसंग में द्रौपदी द्वारा धारण किए गए शेखर[16] का और महाकवि भवभूति मालती के विवाह नेपथ्य में कुसुम-आपीड[17] का वर्णन करते हैं।

शेखर और आपीड की रचना के लिए श्वेत, खिले हुए मालती पुष्प ही अधिक प्रयुक्त होते थे। इनसे केशों की शोभा वैसे ही निखर उठती थी जैसे नक्षत्र खचित आकाश की। अभिसारिकाएँ रात्रि में अभिसार के अनुकूल नीलवेश के साथ ही नील कमलों के शेखर धारण करती थीं।[18] नर्तकियाँ कभी-कभी रक्त कुरण्ट पुष्प के शेखर भी धारण करती थीं जो उनकी लम्बी वेणी के साथ नितम्ब देश तक लटकते रहते थे—

नितम्बबिम्बलम्बिविकचकुरण्टकशेखरा: प्रदीप्ता इव रागाग्निना।[19]

ग्रीष्म ऋतु में खिले हुए चम्पे की मालाएँ सिर पर धारण की जाती थीं—

स्त्रजश्च मौलौ सितचम्पकानां ग्रीष्मेऽपि सोऽयं शिशिरावतार:।[20]

वर्षा ऋतु में स्त्रियाँ कदम्ब, केसर मालाएँ सिर पर धारण करती थीं; तथापि शेखर और मुण्डमाला (आपीड) की रचना मालती पुष्पों की माला से ही होती थी।

आपीड के सम्बन्ध में वाल्मीकि ने एक महत्वपूर्ण तथ्य का निर्देश किया है तदनुसार यह दाक्षिणात्यों का विशिष्ट शिरोभूषण था—

कुर्वन्ति कुसुमापीडाञ्शिर:सु सुरभीनमी · · दाक्षिणात्या नरा यथा।।[21]

वर्तमान समय में शेखरक और आपीड विवाह के अवसर पर वर द्वारा धारण किए गए सेहरे के रूप में दिखाई देता है।

सन्दर्भ-सङ्केत

1. कामसूत्र - 1.3.15 पर यशोधर की टीका, पृ. 88
2. शब्दकल्पद्रुम - शेखर शब्द के प्रसंग में उद्धृत।
3. शेखरकस्य शिखास्थानेऽवलम्बन्यासेन परिधापनात्। आपीडस्य च मण्डलाकारेण ग्रथितस्य काष्ठिकायोगेन परिधापनात्। कामसूत्र - 1.3.15 पर यशोधर की टीका।
4. रघुवंश - 17.23; ऋतुसंहार - 2.21, 25
5. विक्रमोर्वशीय - 4.61
6. रघुवंश - 9.67
7. कादम्बरी - पृ. 27
8. कादम्बरी - पृ. 260
9. हर्षचरित - उ. 2, पृ. 126-27
10. हर्षचरित - पृ. 360
11. कादम्बरी - पृ. 41
12. कादम्बरी - पृ. 353
13. रघुवंश - 4.88

14. कादम्बरी - पृ. 49
15. कादम्बरी - पृ. 579
16. बालभारत - 1.27
17. एष सितकुसुमापीड इति। मालतीमाधव - अंक 6, पृ. 267
18. नीलाब्जैः शेखरश्रीः। विद्धशालभञ्जिका - 3.7
19. हर्षचरित - उ. 4, पृ. 224
20. काव्यमीमांसा - अ. 18, पृ. 255
21. रामायण-अयोध्याकाण्ड - 93.13

卐 卐 卐

गन्धयुक्तिकला

(सुगन्धयोजना)

इला घोष

वात्स्यायन-वर्णित चौंसठ कलाओं में एक महत्त्वपूर्ण कला है—'गन्धयुक्ति' अर्थात् सुगन्ध की योजना। ललितविस्तर की शिल्प सूची में भी इसकी गणना हुई है। विभिन्न प्रकार के सुगन्धित द्रव्यों का निर्माण एवं उनका प्रसङ्गानुकूल सुरुचिपूर्ण उपयोग प्राचीन भारत की एक कमनीय कला थी।

गन्ध धातु से अच् प्रत्यय लगकर निष्पन्न 'गन्ध' शब्द का सामान्य अर्थ है— आमोद। सुरभि-असुरभि भेद से स्थूल रूप से यह दो प्रकार का होता है। महाभारत में गन्ध दस प्रकार के कहे गए हैं— इष्ट, अनिष्ट, मधुर, अम्ल, कटु, निर्हारी, संहत, स्निग्ध, रुक्ष एवं विशद।[1] इष्ट गन्ध को सुगन्ध, नासिका को तृप्त करने वाली गन्ध को सुरभि, आकर्षक गन्ध को निर्हारी, अति आकर्षक को आमोद और जगन्मनोहर गन्ध को परिमल कहते हैं। (अमरकोश - 1.5.10-11)

गन्ध पृथ्वी का गुण है। औषधियाँ एवं जल इसी गन्ध को धारण करते हैं। प्रत्येक पार्थिव तत्त्व में यही गन्ध बसी हुई है। वैदिक ऋषि की वाणी में—

(i) **यस्ते गन्धः पृथिवि संबभूव**
यं बिभ्रत्योषधयो यमापः।

(ii) **यस्ते गन्धः पुरुषेषु स्त्रीषु पुंसु भगो रुचिः।**
यो अश्वेषु वीरेषु यो मृगेषूत हस्तिषु।
कन्यायां वर्चो यद् भूमे ······ ।

अथर्ववेद-काण्ड - 12.1.23; 25

प्रकृति ने मानव को उपहार के रूप में पुष्प, चंदन, केसर, कुंकुम जैसे अनेक सुगन्धित द्रव्य प्रदान किए हैं। निसर्ग का ऋतुचक्र वर्ष भर नानाविध सुमनों की सुगन्ध बिखेरता रहता है तो ऋतुराज वसंत 'सुरभिमधुनिषेक' से समग्र चराचर को ही गन्धमय कर देता है। निसर्ग के ही इन उपादानों का बहुविध संयोजन कर मानव ने गन्धयुक्ति की कला विकसित की है।

जिस प्रकार सुन्दर रूप मनुष्य की चक्षु इन्द्रिय को तृप्ति देता है; उसी प्रकार सुन्दर गन्ध भी नासिका को तृप्त करते हुए आनन्द देती है; जैसा कि रामायण में स्वयं आदिकवि ने कहा है—

गुहासमीरणो गन्धान्नानापुष्पभवान् वहन्।
घ्राणतर्पणमभ्येत्य कं नरं न प्रहर्षयेत्।। अयोध्याकाण्ड - 94.14

सुगन्ध में एक अद्‌भुत आकर्षण होता है। गन्ध के साथ यौन आवेग भी सम्बद्ध होते हैं। अतः चिरन्तन काल से ही स्त्री-पुरुष यौन आकर्षण हेतु अपने शरीर की गन्ध को बढ़ाने के लिए भी सुगन्धित द्रव्यों का प्रयोग करते आए हैं। कलाप्रेमी भारत के नागरक-नागरिकाओं को सम्भवतः सर्वाधिक प्रेम सुगन्धित द्रव्यों से ही रहा है। वाल्मीकि का साक्ष्य इसका प्रमाण है। अयोध्या के नागरिकों में ऐसा कोई भी व्यक्ति नहीं है, जो सुगन्ध का उपयोग न करता हो।

कौटिल्य के अर्थशास्त्र में चन्दन, अगुरु, तैलपर्णिक, भंद्रश्रीय (कपूर), कालेयक आदि सुगन्धित द्रव्यों के उत्पत्ति स्थान, प्रकार एवं गुणों का विस्तृत वर्णन हुआ है।[2] चन्दन नौ रङ्गों का तथा छह प्रकार की गन्ध वाला होता है। देवसभ नामक स्थान में उत्पन्न चन्दन रक्त वर्ण और पद्मगन्धि होता है। उत्तम चन्दन लघु, स्निग्ध, हृद्य गन्ध वाला, वर्ण विकार से रहित, शीतल और संतापहारी होता है।

अगुरु असम के जोङ्गक और दोङ्गक नामक स्थानों में अधिक उत्पन्न होता है। समुद्र के पास सिंहलादि देशोत्पन्न अगर खश अथवा नवमालिका की गन्ध वाला होता है। उत्तम अगर के निम्न गुण हैं—

गुरुस्निग्धं पेशलगन्धिनिर्हार्यग्निसहमसंप्लुतधूमं विमर्दसहमित्यगुरुगुणाः।

इन सुगन्धित द्रव्यों की विशेषता यह है कि पीसने, पकाने, आग में जलाने या अन्य द्रवों के साथ मिलाने पर भी इनकी गन्ध बनी रहती है।[3]

वराहमिहिर की बृहत्संहिता में 'गन्धयुक्ति' अध्याय 77 के अन्तर्गत निम्नलिखित सुगन्धित यौगिकों की निर्माण-विधि एवं उपयोग का वर्णन हुआ है— गन्धोदक, गन्धद्रव्य, गन्धधूप, गन्धतेल, शिरःस्नान, स्नानचूर्ण, पटवास एवं मुखवास। गन्धार्णव एवं सर्वतोभद्र जैसे विशिष्ट गन्ध द्रव्यों का भी वर्णन प्राप्त है। वराहमिहिर के अनुसार गणित के प्रकार एवं प्रस्तार भेद से गन्धों की संख्या एक लाख चौहत्तर हजार सात सौ बीस तक हो सकती है। नकुल, चम्पक, अतिमुक्तक, उत्पल आदि के समान कृत्रिम गन्ध भी बनाई जा सकती है।[4]

संस्कृत साहित्य में इस कला से निर्मित द्रव्यों के दैनन्दिन उपयोग के असंख्य सन्दर्भ प्राप्त होते हैं जिन्हें निम्न शीर्षकों में विवेचित किया जा सकता है—

(1) गन्धोदक

यह जल में सुगन्धित द्रव्यों को मिलाकर तैयार किया जाता था। प्राचीन भारत में नागरक की दिनचर्या ही सुगन्ध के उपयोग से प्रारम्भ होती थी। दन्तधावन के लिए वह जिस दातून का प्रयोग करता था, वह गन्धोदक से सुवासित होती थी। दन्तधावन का उल्लेख रामायण काल से ही प्राप्त होने लगता है।[5] लगभग एक सप्ताह पूर्व से ही सुगन्धकारी भृत्यों द्वारा उसे सुवासित करने की प्रक्रिया प्रारम्भ हो जाती थी। हर्रे के चूर्ण से मिश्रित गोमूत्र में सात दिन तक डूबे हुए दन्तकाष्ठ को, समभाग में इलायची, दालचीनी, तेजपत्र, अञ्जन, मधु, नागकेसर और कूठ के मिश्रण से बने हुए गन्धोदक में भिगो कर सुवासित किया जाता था। तत्पश्चात् चार भाग जायफल, दो भाग तेजपत्र, एक भाग इलायची और एक भाग कर्पूर के मिश्रण से बने बारीक, गन्धचूर्ण दन्तकाष्ठ पर मसलकर इन्हें धूप में सुखाकर रखा जाता था।[6] वराहमिहिर के अनुसार इस विधि से निर्मित दन्तकाष्ठों के सेवन से स्वास्थ्य, सौन्दर्य और माङ्गल्य की वृद्धि होती है।[7]

राजा-महाराजाओं एवं सम्भ्रान्त नागरिकों के स्नानार्थ बनाए गए सुगन्धित जल के रूप में भी गन्धोदक का उपयोग होता था। रामायण के अनुसार महाराज दशरथ के लिए प्रतिदिन स्नानविधि के ज्ञाता भृत्यों द्वारा, काञ्चन घटों में, हरिचन्दन से सम्पृक्त जल प्रस्तुत किया जाता था—

हरिचन्दनसम्पृक्तमुदकं काञ्चनैर्घटैः।
आनिन्युः स्नानशिक्षज्ञा यथाकालं यथाविधि।।[8]

यह गन्धोदक प्रातः काल प्रस्तुत किए जाने वाले मांगलिक अभिहारिक का अभिन्न अङ्ग था।

महाकवि भास भी गणिका वसन्तसेना के शरीर से निकलती हुई सुरभिस्नान की दूर तक फैलने वाली सुगन्ध का उल्लेख करते हैं।[9]

बाणभट्ट ने कादम्बरी में; महाराज शूद्रक को गन्धोदक से स्नान कराए जाने का एक सुन्दर चित्र प्रस्तुत किया है।

स्नानभूमि के मध्य एक कनक द्रोणी में गन्धोदक भरा जाता था; जिसमें स्नान से पूर्व शूद्रक कुछ समय तक अवगाहन करते थे। एक ओर कलशों में अति सुगन्धित जल भरा हुआ होता था जिसकी परिमल से आकृष्ट भ्रमर-समूह से कलशों का मुख भाग अन्धकार पूर्ण हो रहा था। यह गन्धोदक चन्दन-रस एवं केसर के पृथक्-पृथक् मिश्रण से तैयार किया गया था।[10]

कादम्बरी के कन्यान्तःपुर में उन कनक दीर्घिकाओं का वर्णन है जो गन्धोदक से भरी जाती थीं।[11]

क्रीडा वापियों को मकरमुख प्रणाली से बहकर आए हुए गन्धोदक से पूर्ण किया जाता था। हर्षचरित 4 - पृ. 243

राजप्रासादों एवं सम्पन्न नागरिकों के हर्म्यतलों को ग्रीष्म ऋतु में शीतल, सुवासित करने के लिए भी गन्धोदक का उपयोग होता था। रामायण[12], ऋतुसंहार[13] एवं परवर्ती संस्कृत साहित्य[14] में इसके सन्दर्भ प्राप्त होते हैं।

बाणभट्ट चन्दनरस में कस्तूरी के मिश्रण से बनाए गए सुगन्धित जल से आस्थान मण्डप की मणि भूमि एवं स्वर्ण स्तम्भों को धोए जाने का उल्लेख करते हैं।[15]

हिमगृहों को भी शीतल-सुगन्धित करने के लिए गन्धोदक कूपों से जल निकाल कर हिमगृह की जल द्रोणिकाओं में भरा जाता था।[16]

आचार्य कवि राजशेखर श्वेत चन्दन रस से प्रक्षालित सौध तलों पर समय बिताना अति सुखद मानते हैं।[17]

विरहदशा में ताप शान्ति के लिए भी यह लाभकारी था। कादम्बरी में हिमगृह के मध्य कादम्बरी की कुसुमशय्या के चारों ओर पतली नालियों से कर्पूर रस प्रवाहित किए जाने का उल्लेख हुआ है।[18]

दशकुमारचरित में शीतोपचार के लिए हरिचन्दन, उशीर और कर्पूर जैसे शीतल द्रव्यों के मिश्रण से स्नान जल तैय्यार किए जाने का वर्णन हुआ है।[19]

(2) सुगन्धित कल्क कषाय-चूर्ण एवं शिरःस्नान

स्नान से पूर्व विभिन्न प्रकार के सुगन्धित कल्क एवं कषाय चूर्णों का प्रयोग किया जाता था। सम्भवतः आँवला आदि कुछ कषैले पदार्थों से बनने के कारण इसे कषाय कहा जाता था। रामायण में इनका नामतः उल्लेख है।[20] कालिदास ने शरीर के तैलीय अंश को दूर करने के लिए स्नान पूर्व लोध्रकषाय[21] लोध्रकल्क एवं कालेयक मिश्रित अंगराग[22] के प्रयोग का वर्णन किया है।

स्नान से पहले सिर पर कषाय चूर्ण का लेप किया जाता था तत्पश्चात् सुगन्धित जल से केश धोए जाते थे अतः इसकी संज्ञा शिरःस्नान थी। बृहत्संहिता के अनुसार नृपतियोग्य शिरःस्नान-दालचीनी, कूठ, रेणुका, नालिका, स्पृक्का, बोल, तगर, नेत्रवाला, नागकेसर एवं गन्धपत्र को समभाग में पीस कर बनाए जाते थे।

स्त्रियाँ ग्रीष्म ऋतु में निदाघ का शमन करने के लिए अपने केशों को स्नान कषाय से वासित करती थीं।[23]

कादम्बरी में शिरःस्नान के रूप में सुगन्धित आमलक के प्रयोग का उल्लेख है।[24]

(3) अङ्गराग अनुलेप एवं सुगन्धित चूर्ण

स्नान पूर्व एवं पश्चात् शरीर को रंगने के लिए प्रयुक्त अङ्गराग में भी सुगन्धित द्रव्यों का प्रयोग होता था। रघुवंश के अनुसार अत्रि ऋषि की पत्नी अनुसूया ने सीता को उपहार में जो अङ्गराग दिया था; उसकी सुगन्ध से वन के भ्रमर भी आकर्षित हो जाते थे—

अनसूयातिसृष्टेन पुण्यगन्धेन काननम्।
सा चक्रुरङ्गरागेण पुष्पोच्चलितषट्पदम्।। 12.17

स्नान के पश्चात् सम्पूर्ण शरीर अथवा वक्षःस्थल एवं मस्तक पर सुगन्धित लेप का प्रयोग प्राचीन प्रसाधन विधि का

अनिवार्य अङ्ग था। स्नान पश्चात् यह कार्य होने के कारण ही सम्भवतः इसे अनुलेप कहा जाता था।

शरीर की त्वचा को स्निग्ध, उज्ज्वल, कांतियुक्त एव सुवासित करने के लिए अगुरु, केसर, चन्दन आदि के मिश्रण से सुगन्धित लेप तैयार किए जाते थे। ग्रीष्म एवं वसन्त में शीतल, स्निग्ध एवं हल्का होने के कारण चन्दन का लेप ही अधिक रुचिकर होता था। इसे और अधिक सुगंधित करने के लिए कभी-कभी कस्तूरी मिला दी जाती थी—

प्रियङ्गुकालीयक कुङ्कुमाक्तं स्तनेषु गौरेषु विलासिनीभिः।
आलिप्यते चन्दनमङ्गनाभिर्मदालसाभिर्मृगनाभियुक्तम्।।

ऋतुसंहार - 6.14

हर्षचरित में बलाशना नामक औषधि को घी में पकाकर कुंकुम कल्क के मिश्रण से अंगराग और मुखलेप तैयार किए जाने का वर्णन हुआ है। उ. 4, पृ. 244

नैषधीयचरित में 'यक्षकर्दम' नामक सुगन्धित द्रव्य का उल्लेख है जिसका प्रयोग स्नान से पूर्व किया जाता था। यह कर्पूर, अगुरु, कस्तूरी, चन्दन और कक्कोल इन पाँच सुगन्धित द्रव्यों के योग से बनाया जाता था। (नैषधचरित - 21.7. मल्लिनाथ की टीका)

राजभवनों में एक विशेष कक्ष अनुलेप के लिए होता था जिसे 'विलेपनभूमि' कहा जाता था। कादम्बरी में ऐसी विलेपन भूमि का मनोरम वर्णन हुआ है, जहाँ मृगमद, कर्पूर तथा कुङ्कुम से वासित चन्दन का अनुलेप प्रस्तुत रहता था, जो परिमलाकर्षित अलिकुलों से निरन्तर झङ्कृत होता रहता था।[25] तापशान्ति के लिए उशीरानुलेप की भी चर्चा हुई है।[26]

पुष्प, पुष्प-रेणु एवं कर्पूर आदि से बने हुए सुगन्धित चूर्ण से मुख वर्ण को उज्ज्वल किया जाता था। कालिदास ने अलकापुरी की वधुओं द्वारा इस प्रसाधन द्रव्य के प्रयोग का सुन्दर वर्णन किया है।[27]

(4) गन्ध तेल

गन्धतेल का उपयोग मुख्यतः शिर की मालिश और केशों को सुवासित करने के लिए होता था। हर्षचरित में सहकार तेल का उल्लेख है।[28] सहकार एक प्रकार का सुगन्धित आम था जिससे तेलादि सुगन्धित द्रव्य बनते थे।[29]

कृष्णागुरु का तेल मोटी बाँस की नलियों में भरकर पत्तों में लपेटकर सुरक्षित रूप से सुदूर प्रान्तों में भेजा जाता था।[30] राजभवनों में दीपक भी सुगन्धित तेल से जलाए जाते थे। रामायण और कादम्बरी में गन्ध तैल से वासित 'सुरभिगन्धोद्गारिणी दीपिकाओं' का वर्णन हुआ है[31] और अधिक सुगन्ध के लिए दीपों की बत्तियाँ 'कामशर' नामक धूप से बनाई जाती थीं—

क्वापि कामशरवृत्तवर्तयो यं महासुरभितैलदीपिकाः। नैषधचरित - 18.6

(5) गन्धद्रव्य पटवास मुखवास आदि

सुगन्धित पत्र-पुष्प, कर्पूर आदि के रस से बनाए गए गन्धद्रव्य का उपयोग शैय्या, वस्त्र, अलङ्कार, पात्रादि को अधिवासित करने के लिए होता था। वस्त्रों को वासित करने के लिए प्रयुक्त गन्धद्रव की विशेष संज्ञा पटवास थी। बृहत्संहिता के अनुसार दालचीनी, खश तथा गन्धपत्र के तीन भाग एवं छोटी इलायची के आधे भाग का चूर्ण बनाकर कस्तूरी और कर्पूर का बोध देने से उत्तम पटवास तैयार होता है।[31a]

उत्तरीय वस्त्रों को बहुमूल्य गन्ध से वासित करने के उल्लेख भास के 'चारुदत्त'[32] एवं शूद्रक के 'मृच्छकटिक'[33] में प्राप्त होते हैं।

आभूषणों को भी सुरभित किया जाता था जैसे कि कादम्बरी द्वारा कानों में पहनी गई कर्पूर से वासित केतकी की कली[34], हर्ष के जन्मोत्सव पर उपहार में लाई गईं स्नानीय चूर्ण से अवकीर्ण पुष्पमालाएँ[35] वसन्तसेना द्वारा धारण की गई सौरभ्यानुविद्ध माला[36] आदि। सुगन्ध प्रेम की चरम सीमा तो यह थी कि सुगन्धि रखने के पात्रों को भी पहले अधिवासित कर

लिया जाता था।[37] हर्षचरित में कुङ्कुम से अधिवासित मणिमय पात्रों का उल्लेख है।[38] वायु को सुगन्धित करने के लिए गवाक्षों की जालियों में चन्दन और कर्पूर चूर्ण रख दिया जाता था।[39]

मुख को सुगन्धित करने वाला गन्धद्रव्य मुखवास कहा जाता था। इसका प्रयोग प्राय: ताम्बूल के साथ होता था। बृहत्संहिता के अनुसार— कक्कोल, पूग (सुपारी), लवली फल और पारिजात से आमोदित ताम्बूल मद और मोद के साथ ही निम्न गुणों को उत्पन्न करता है—

कामं प्रदीपयति रूपमभिव्यनक्ति
सौभाग्यमावहति वक्त्रसुगन्धितां च।
ऊर्जं करोति कफजांश्च निहन्ति रोगां-
स्ताम्बूलमेवमपरांश्च गुणान् करोति।। 77.33

वात्स्यायन के अनुसार प्राचीन भारत का नागरक प्रात:काल प्रसाधन विधि को सम्पन्न कर; मुखवास युक्त ताम्बूल खाकर ही अपने दैनिक कार्यों को प्रारम्भ करता था। कामसूत्र के टीकाकार यशोधर के अनुसार गन्धयुक्ति की प्रक्रिया से प्रस्तुत मुखवास गुटिका का भी प्रयोग होता था।[40]

हर्षचरित में 'पारिजातपरिमल' नामक गन्धद्रव का अनेकश: उल्लेख हुआ है—

गुञ्जन्मधुकरकुलपीयमानपारिजातपरिमलानि। उ. 4, पृ. 221

यह पाँच सुगन्धित द्रव्यों से बना सुगन्धित मसाला या मुखशोधक था—

अतिसुरभिसहकारकर्पूरकक्कोललवङ्गपारिजातकपरिमलमुचा मुखेन · · ·। उ. 1, पृ. 39

इसमें इलायची और चम्पक का मिश्रण भी होता था।[41]

(6) धूप

धूप वह सुगन्धित द्रव्य है जो जलने पर निस्ताप धूम के साथ सुगन्ध बिखेरता है। बृहत्संहिता में अनेक प्रकार के मनोहारी धूपों; यथा— पिण्डधूप, नरेन्द्रधूप आदि की निर्माण विधि वर्णित है।[42]

भारत में धूप-धूम के बहुविध प्रयोग प्रचलित थे। रामायण में श्रीराम के राज्याभिषेक के अवसर पर पुरवासियों द्वारा राजमार्ग को धूपगन्ध से अधिवासित किए जाने का वर्णन है।[43] विशिष्ट अवसरों पर अन्त:पुर तथा नगरद्वारों पर धूप जला दिए जाते थे[44]; जो बहुत दूर से ही आगन्तुक को उत्सव की सूचना देते थे। धूप तैयार करने वाले शिल्पियों की विशेष संज्ञा 'धूपक' थी।[45]

धूप-धूम का उपयोग शिर:स्नान से आर्द्र केशों को सुखाने के लिए भी होता था।[46] हेमन्त और शिशिर में स्त्रियाँ सुरतोत्सव के लिए अपने केशों को कालागुरु धूप से धूपित करती थीं। कालिदास के अनुसार उज्जयिनी में सौध गवाक्षों से निकलती हुई केशसंस्कार की धूम इतनी अधिक होती थी कि आषाढ़ के प्रथम मेघ उससे पोषण प्राप्त करते थे।[47] कादम्बरी में यही धूप-धूम सघन अन्धकार की सृष्टि करती थी।[48]

कालिदास ने धूप-धूम से वस्त्रों को अधिवासित करने का भी उल्लेख किया है।[49]

इस प्रकार सुगन्ध प्राचीन भारत के सम्भ्रान्त जीवन का एक अभिन्न अंग थी। गन्ध उत्सवों को आमोदित करते हुए मानवीय आनन्द को अभिव्यक्ति देते थे तो दु:ख और शोक की व्यञ्जना सुगन्ध के परित्याग से होती थी; रामायण में महाराज दशरथ के निधन का प्रसङ्ग—

चन्दनागुरुसम्पृक्तो धूपसम्मूर्च्छितोऽमल:।
प्रवाति पवन: श्रीमान् किं नु नाथ यथा पुरा।। अयोध्याकाण्ड - 72.28

राजभवनों में सुगन्धित द्रव्य इतनी अधिक मात्रा में संचित होते थे कि वे 'गन्धिक भवन' के समान प्रतीत होते थे।[50]

वाल्मीकि के अनुसार मनोज्ञ गन्ध को निःसृत करते हुए ये राजभवन चन्दनगिरि के समान प्रतीत होते थे।

अयोध्याकाण्ड - 15.34

कौटिल्य के अनुसार चन्दनादि सुगन्धित द्रव्यों की विशेष संज्ञा सार थी। राजकोशों में इनका संग्रह किया जाता था।[51] गणिकाओं के भवन भी गन्धयुक्ति के केन्द्र होते थे—

सुक्खविअन्ति ओलविदकुङ्कुमपत्थरा सालिअदि कत्थूरिआ,
विसेसेण घिस्सदि चन्दणरसो, संजोईअन्ति गन्धजुत्तीयो।

मृच्छकटिक - अं. 4, पृ. 239

श्रीहर्ष के एक महत्त्वपूर्ण उल्लेख के अनुसार सुगन्धित द्रव्यों के क्रय-विक्रय हेतु पृथक् बाजार थे; जिनकी संज्ञा 'विलेपन आपण' थी। सन्ध्या काल यहाँ बड़ी चहल-पहल दिखाई देती थी। भीड़-भाड़ और कोलाहल के कारण कस्तूरी के साथ तुल जाते हुए भौरों को भी ग्राहक नहीं जान पाते थे।[52] केसर की पण्यवीथियों (गलियों) में मार्ग केसर से लाल होकर ऐसे प्रतीत होते थे मानों सूर्य की भूमि पर गिरी हुई किरणें हों।[53]

अन्तःपुर की परिचारिकाएँ सर्वदा सुगन्धित द्रव्यों को साथ लेकर चलती थीं; यथा—महाश्वेता के साथ ताम्बूल करङ्कवाहिनी तरलिका[54], चन्द्रापीड के साथ पत्रलेखा आदि।

गन्ध भारतीय पूजा-अर्चना का भी अभिन्न अंग थी।[55] भिन्न-भिन्न प्रकार की गन्ध भिन्न-भिन्न देवताओं को प्रिय मानी जाती थीं।[56]

गन्ध भाव सम्प्रेषण का भी माध्यम थी। सुगन्धित वस्तुएँ प्रियजनों को उपहार में दी जाती थीं। वाल्मीकि के अनुसार अनसूया ने सीता देवी को दिव्य माला अङ्गराग और अनुलेप प्रीतिदान के रूप में दिए थे।[57]

वात्स्यायन प्रेम सम्बन्धों को बढ़ाने के लिए ऐसे उपहारों के आदान-प्रदान को विशेष महत्त्व देते हैं—

तत्र महार्हगन्धमुत्तरीयं . . . स्पृहणीयं . . . दद्यात्।
वाससि च कुङ्कुमाङ्कम् . . . । कामसूत्र - 5.2.22; 5.4.38

कादम्बरी ने चन्द्रापीड को अभिज्ञान के रूप में जो वस्तुएँ भेजी थीं उनमें—

हरचन्द्रखण्डस्थूलशकलञ्जकर्पूरम्, अतिबहलमृगमदामोदमनोहरञ्चमलयजविलेपनम् (कर्पूर और चन्दन का लेप) भी था।

कादम्बरी - पृ. 601

प्राग्ज्योतिष्पुर के कुमार ने हर्षवर्धन को उपहार में निम्न सुगन्धित द्रव्य प्रेषित किए थे

सहकार लता का रस, कृष्णागुरु का तेल, काले अगुरु के ढेर, गोशीर्ष नामक चन्दन की राशियाँ, कर्पूर, कस्तूरी, कक्कोल फल, लवंगपुष्प की मञ्जरियाँ एवं जायफल के गुच्छे।[58]

राजभवनों में पुत्रजन्मादि शुभ अवसरों पर ऐसे उपहारों के ढेर लग जाते थे। हर्ष के जन्म पर सामन्त स्त्रियों द्वारा लाए गए उपहारों की सूची इस प्रकार है—

स्नानीय चूर्णों से अवकीर्ण पुष्पमालाएँ, स्फटिक मणि के टुकड़ों के समान कर्पूर के खण्ड, कुंकुम से वासित मणिमय पात्र, सहकार तैल से सिक्त खदिर, पारिजात परिमल से भरी हुई थैलियाँ, सिन्दूर पात्र, पटवास चूर्ण से भरे पात्र एवं ताम्बूल के छोटे पौधे।[59]

अभ्यागत बन्धुओं एवं आत्मीय जनों की सुगन्धित पदार्थों से सपर्या भारतीय संस्कृति की पहचान ही बन गई थी।[60]

न केवल जन समाज अपितु उसका चित्रण करने वाला कवि भी पवित्र सुगन्धित वेश से युक्त होता था। राजशेखर की दृष्टि में सुगन्ध शुचिता का ही अङ्ग थी। यह पवित्रता वस्तुतः सरस्वती का ही सम्मान था—

नित्यं शुचिः स्यात्। . . . सविलेपनमात्रं वपुः; . . . सकुसुमं शिर इति।
शुचिशीलनं हि सरस्वत्याः संवननमामनन्ति। (काव्यमीमांसा - अ. 10, पृ. 121)

संस्कृत कवियों को गन्ध द्रव्यों से इतना अधिक प्रेम था कि वे अपनी नायिकाओं की सृष्टि भी गन्धद्रव्यों से ही कर लेते थे यथा दण्डी की नायिका अवन्तिसुन्दरी की रचना—

समस्तमकरन्दकस्तूरिकासम्मितेन मलयजरसेन प्रक्षाल्य कर्पूररागेण सम्मृज्य निर्मितेव रराज।

(दशकुमारचरित - पू.पी., उ. 5, पृ. 109)

यह मनोज्ञ कला चित्रकार की तूलिका का भी विषय बनी है। अजन्ता में कुमार गौतम के स्नान का एक मनोहर दृश्य अंकित है। कुमार एक स्फटिक की चौकी पर बैठे हैं। समीप ही एक परिचारिका थाली में सुगन्धित द्रव्य लिए खड़ी है। पार्श्वभाग से एक परिचारक सुगन्धित जल से भरा कलश लेकर आ रहा है। एक परिचारिका प्रसाधन सामग्री लेकर स्नान-भूमि की ओर आ रही है। यह अजन्ता के विश्व प्रसिद्ध चित्रों में से एक है।

भारतीय मूर्तिशिल्प भी इस गन्ध से अछूता नहीं है। खजुराहो के मन्दिरों में दर्पण हाथ में लेकर कपोलों पर सुगंधित चूर्ण लगाती हुई नारी मूर्तियों का मनोरम अङ्कन हुआ है।[61]

इस प्रकार गन्धयुक्ति प्राचीन भारत की एक समुन्नत कला थी। गन्ध द्रव्यों का निर्माण अधिकांशतः नैसर्गिक उपादानों से ही होता था। तत्काल गन्ध पाने के लिए पत्रपुष्प को हाथ से मसलकर रस निकाल लिया जाता था[62] या सीधे पुष्पों के प्रयोग से शय्या आदि को वासित किया जाता था।[63] गन्धद्रव्य बनाने के लिए यन्त्र से दबाकर रस निकाला जाता था।[64] किसी वस्तु की नैसर्गिक गन्ध को बदलने या बढ़ाने के लिए उसमें अन्य द्रव्य मिला दिए जाते थे।[65]

हजारों प्रकार के गन्धों के निर्माण में कला का कौशल तो था ही इसके साथ ही सुरुचिपूर्ण पद्धति से अवसर के अनुकूल गन्ध का उपयोग भी कलात्मक अभिरुचि, आभिजात्य एवं सौन्दर्यबोध का परिचायक था। वात्स्यायन के अनुसार अनुलेप का प्रयोग उचित मात्रा में ही होना चाहिए। लेप की प्रभूत मात्रा अनागरकता का परिचय देती है। स्त्री-पुरुषों को विहार के लिए जाते समय भी हल्के अनुलेप एवं मृदु सुगन्ध का ही प्रयोग करना चाहिए।[66]

स्वच्छता, ताजगी, स्फूर्ति, स्वास्थ्य और श्रीवृद्धि के साथ ही इनके अन्य प्रयोजन भी थे। इस मनोवैज्ञानिक तथ्य से सभी भली-भाँति परिचित थे कि दुर्गन्ध विराग का कारण होती है तो सुगन्ध कामोद्दीपन का। अतः शय्या गृहों को बहुल सुगन्ध से आमोदित किया जाता था।[67]

देववाणी संस्कृत में निबद्ध साहित्य, कला की अधिष्ठात्री देवी सरस्वती का वह मणिदर्पण है, जिसमें प्राचीन भारतीय कलाएँ अपने उज्ज्वलतम् रूप में प्रतिबिम्बित हुई हैं। गन्धयुक्ति के सन्दर्भ वैदिक साहित्य से ही प्राप्त होने लगते हैं। रामायण के कवि भी यथाप्रसङ्ग इनका वर्णन करते हैं। महाकवि कालिदास को पुष्पों की नैसर्गिक गन्ध अधिक प्रिय है। 'पुष्पावतंस-सुरभीकृतकेशपाशाः', 'सुवासितं चारु शिरश्च चम्पकैः' से मुग्ध होते हुए भी कवि गन्धयुक्ति की महिमा को भी जानते हैं। इन सन्दर्भ में कवि का वैशिष्ट्य यह है कि वे गन्धद्रव्यों के वर्णन के साथ ही उनके निर्माण की प्रक्रिया, प्रयोजन एवं वैशिष्ट्य को भी रेखाङ्कित करते चलते हैं; यथा— लोध्र कषाय के प्रयोग से तैलीय त्वचा रुक्ष हो जाती है, धूप-धूम की ऊष्मा केशों के आर्द्रभाव को दूर करती है; अगरबत्ती अगरु-सार से बनती है; धूप की गन्ध धूम के साथ ऊपर की ओर उठती हुई अधिक देर तक और अधिकर दूर तक फैलती है—

संचारिते चागुरुसारयोनौ धूपे समुत्सर्पति। रघुवंश - 6.8

बाणभट्ट की रचनाओं में सुगन्ध का संभार अधिक है, जो तत्कालीन सामन्ती विलास और सम्भ्रान्त वर्ग के कृत्रिम गन्धद्रव्यों के प्रति क्रमशः बढ़ते हुए प्रेम को सूचित करता है।

इस प्रकार गन्धयुक्ति जीवन के उमङ्ग, आनन्द और उल्लास की सूचक थी। यह यौवन के अनुदासीनत्व का प्रतीक थी[68]; जीवन को सुन्दर कलात्मक ढंग से जीने एवं आनन्द के सम्पूर्ण उपभोग की कला थी। प्राचीन भारत के स्त्री-पुरुष बड़े ही मनोयोग के साथ; अन्य कलाओं के साथ इसे भी अधिगत करते थे। जीवन के मधुर रतिफल का आस्वाद लेते हुए अन्त में 'सर्वगन्धः सर्वरसः' उस परम पुरुष को प्राप्त करने का प्रयत्न करते थे।[69]

सूर्या के विवाह में जिस पुष्कर गन्ध का देवताओं ने उपयोग किया था; पृथ्वी की उसी मधुगन्ध से; अनुराग और प्रेम से; सौमनस्य और सद्भाव से जीवन और जगत् को आमोदित, वासित करने की कला है—'गन्धयुक्ति'—

यस्ते गन्धः पुष्करमाविवेश
यं संजभ्रुः सूर्याया विवाहे।
अमर्त्याः पृथिवी गन्धमग्रे तेन मा
सुरभिं कृणु मा नो द्विक्षत कश्चन।। अथर्ववेद - 12.1.24

सन्दर्भ-सङ्केत

1. महाभारत -14.50.40-42
2. अर्थशास्त्र - 2.11.44-76
3. अर्थशास्त्र - 2.11.75
4. तुल्यैः पत्रतुरुष्कबालतगरैर्गन्धः स्मरोद्दीपनः।
   सव्यामो बकुलोऽयमेव कटुकाहिंगुप्रधूपान्वितः।।
   नुष्णेगोत्पलगन्धिकः समलयः पूर्वो भवेच्चम्पको।
   जातीत्वक्सहितोऽतिमुक्तक इति ज्ञेयः सकुस्तुसम्बुरुः।। बृहत्संहिता - 77.7
5. शुक्लानंशुमतश्चापि दन्तधावनसंचयान्। रामायण - अयोध्या - 91.75
6. बृहत्संहिता - 77.31-33
7. बृहत्संहिता - 77.34
8. रामायण-अयोध्या - 65.10
9. विटः-सुरभिस्नानधूपानुविद्ध इव गन्धः। चारुदत्त - अं. 1
10. कादम्बरी कथामुख - पृ. 45-47
11. कादम्बरी - पृ. 532
12. पुष्पसंचयचित्रेषु चन्दनागुरुगन्धिषु।
    प्रासादवरवर्येषु शीतलासु सुगन्धिषु ।। रामायण-अयोध्याकाण्ड - 88.7
13. ऋतुसंहार - 1.3
    क्षालिताश्च हिमवालुकाम्बुभिः। रेजुः · · · · मणिकुट्टिमा भुवः।।
14. नैषधीयचरित - 18.7
15. कादम्बरी-कथामुख - पृ. 50
16. कादम्बरी-कथामुख - पृ. 613
17. श्रीखण्डद्रवधौतसौधतलको रम्यः क्षणः वर्तते। विद्धशालभञ्जिका - 2.23

18. कादम्बरी - पृ. 617
19. दशकुमारचरित - पूर्वपी., उ. 5, पृ. 121
20. कल्कांश्चूर्णकषायांश्च स्नानानि विविधानि च। रामायण-अयोध्याकाण्ड - 91/74
21. कुमारसम्भव - 7.17
22. कुमारसम्भव - 7.9
23. ऋतुसंहार - 1.4
24. कादम्बरी-कथामुख - पृ. 45
25. कादम्बरी-कथामुख - पृ. 49
26. अभिज्ञानशाकुन्तल - अं. 3
27. नीता लोध्रप्रसवरजसा पाण्डुतामानने श्रीः। मेघदूत - 2.2
28. हर्षचरित - उ. 2, पृ. 221
29. सहकार-सुगंधद्रव्यभेदः सहकारफलेनैव क्रियते। हर्षचरित - शंकरकृत संकेतटीका, पृ. 38
30. हर्षचरित - उ. 7, पृ. 387
31. अध्यात्मरामायण - सुन्दरकाण्ड - 4.53
    कादम्बरी - उत्तर भाग, पृ. 10

31a. बृहत्संहिता - 77/12
32. चारुदत्त - अं. 1
33. मृच्छकटिक - अ. 1
34. कादम्बरी - पृ. 619
35. हर्षचरित - उ. 4, पृ. 221
36. मृच्छकटिक - अं. 1
37. कर्पूरपल्लवरसेनाधिवासय गन्धपात्राणि। कादम्बरी - पृ. 532
38. हर्षचरित - उ. 4, पृ. 221
39. जालजालधृतचन्द्रचन्दनक्षोदमेदुरसमीरशीतलम्। नैषधीयचरित - 18.5
40. कामसूत्र - अधि. 1.4.5 पर जयमङ्गला टीका
41. चूतचम्पकलवलीलवङ्गककक्कोलवन्तेलालता-
    मिश्रितानि ससहकाराणि कर्पूरपूरितानि पारिजातकवनानि। हर्षचरित - उ. 2, पृ. 112-113
42. हरीतकीशंखघनद्रवाम्बुभिर्गुडोत्पलैः शैलकमुस्तकान्वितैः।
    नवान्तपादादिविवर्धिताः क्रमाद्भवन्ति धूपा बहवो मनोहराः।। बृहत्संहिता - 77.10
43. रामायण-अयोध्याकाण्ड - 7.17
44. रामायण-अयोध्याकाण्ड - 3.13
45. रामायण-अयोध्याकाण्ड - 83.14
46. धूपोष्मणा त्याजितमार्द्रभावं
    केशान्तमन्तःकुसुमं तदीयम्। कुमारसम्भव - 7.14
47. ऋतुसंहार - 4.5;5.12
48. मेघदूत - 1.36
49. ऋतुसंहार - 6.15
50. कादम्बरी - राजकुलवर्णन, पृ. 279
51. कोशाध्यक्षः कोशप्रवेश्यं रत्नं सारं कुप्यं वा . . . प्रतिगृह्णीयात्। अर्थशास्त्र - 2.11.1
52. नैषधीयचरित - 2.92

53. रुचयोऽस्तमितस्य भास्वतः स्खलिता यत्र निरालयाः खलु।
अनुसायमभुर्विलेपनापणकश्मीरजपण्यवीथयः ।। नैषधीयचरित - 2.90

54. गृहीतविविधकुसुमताम्बूलाङ्गरागपटवासचूर्णया। कादम्बरी - पृ. 474
कुसुमपटवासताम्बूलतालवृन्ताङ्गरागभृङ्गारधारिणा उपास्यमानाम् . . . । कादम्बरी - पृ. 289

55. अपरिमितकुसुमधूपविलेपन . . . अम्बादेवीसपर्य्यामाततान। कादम्बरी - 201

56. गन्धो मलयजो यस्तु दैवे पैत्र्ये च सम्मतः।
तत्पङ्को वा रसो वापि चूर्णो वा विष्णुतुष्टिदः।।
कृष्णागुरुसकर्पूरः सहितो मलयोद्भवैः।
वैष्णवीप्रीतिदो गन्धः कामाख्याश्च भैरव।। कालिकापुराण - अ. 68

57. रामायण-अयोध्याकाण्ड - 118.18-21

58. हर्षचरित - उ. 7, पृ. 386

59. हर्षचरित - उ. 4, पृ. 221

60. नायकमित्राणां च स्रगनुलेपनताम्बूलदानैः पूजनं न्यायतः। कामसूत्र - 4.1.36
गन्धकुसुमाक्षतघनसारताम्बूलादिनानाजातिवस्तुनिचयेन पूजां तस्मै कारयामास। दशकुमारचरित - पूर्वपीठिका - पृ. 114

61. कंदरिया महादेव मंदिर, वाम वहिरंग, वामनमंदिर, वामवहिरंग

62. कादम्बरी - पृ. 614

63. कादम्बरी - कथामुख - पृ. 51

64. विद्धशालभञ्जिका - 3.14

65. केतकीकुसुमवासिनस्य खदिरस्थान्योगन्धोद्गारः। विद्धशालभञ्जिका - 3, पृ. 70

66. गृहीतमात्रयानुलेपः। कामसूत्र - 1.4.5
प्रभूतानुलेपनादिग्रहणादनागरकः स्यात्। कामसूत्र -जयमंगला टीका
परिमिताभरणं सुगन्धिता नात्युल्बणमनुलेपनम्। . . . इति वैहारिको वेशः। कामसूत्र - 4.1.25

67. उत्तरकादम्बरी - पृ. 111

68. अनुदासीनं यौवनमस्य पटवासगन्धः सूचयति। चारुदत्त - अं. 1
यः पण्यस्त्रीरतिपरिमलोद्गारिभिर्नागराणाम्
उद्दामानि प्रथयति शिलावेश्मभिर्यौवनानि।। मेघदूत - 1.27

69. गन्धेन लभते कामं गन्धो धर्म्मप्रदः सदा।
अर्थानां साधको गन्धो गन्धे मोक्षः प्रतिष्ठितः।। कालिकापुराण।

卐 卐 卐

वृक्षायुर्वेदकला

(उपवनरचना)

इला घोष

मानव ने प्रकृति की जिस हरी-भरी गोद में जन्म लिया है, पुष्पों की जिस मधु गन्ध से वह उच्छ्वसित हुआ है, वनस्पति जगत् के जिस अवदान से वह पुष्ट हुआ है, निसर्ग की जिस पावन सुन्दरता ने मन को उदात्तता दी है, जिन हरे भरे कुञ्जों की सघन छाया ने उसे विश्रान्ति दी है, उसी निसर्ग को अपने समीप बसा लेने की, आत्मीय बना लेने की कला है— **वृक्षायुर्वेदयोगाः।**

आयुर्वेद का अर्थ है— आयु को देने वाला वेद या शास्त्र। वृक्षायुर्वेद वृक्षों को दीर्घायुष्य एवं स्वास्थ्य प्रदान करने वाला शास्त्र है। इस शास्त्र का जीवन में उपयोग अर्थात् वृक्षों के रोपण, पोषण, चिकित्सा, दोहद आदि के द्वारा मनचाहे फल और फूलों की समृद्धि को प्राप्त करने की कला है— वृक्षायुर्वेदयोगाः।[1]

इस कला का प्रयोजन या उद्देश्य है— मनोरम उद्यान या बगीचे की रचना। संस्कृत भाषा में बगीचे के लिए उपवन, आराम और उद्यान शब्दों का प्रयोग हुआ है। उप-वन वह है जो गुणों में वन के समीप हो या छोटा सा वन ही है। आ-राम शब्द 'रम्' धातु से बना है जिसका अर्थ है 'रमना'। आराम वे हैं जहाँ मानव-मन रम जाए, विश्रान्ति और आनन्द प्राप्त करे। उद्यान वे हैं जो मनुष्य को वृक्षों के समान उत्-ऊपर, यान-उठने की-बढ़ने की प्रेरणा दें, फल के समान माधुर्य और पुष्पों के समान रूप, रस और गन्ध की शोभा बिखेरने के लिए प्रेरित करें।

प्राचीन भारत में उद्यान, नगर निवेश एवं भवन-वास्तु के अनिवार्य अंग माने गए थे। वराहमिहिर के अनुसार उद्यानों से युक्त नगरों में देवता सर्वदा निवास करते हैं—

रमन्ते देवता नित्यं पुरेषूद्यानवत्सु च। बृहत्संहिता - 56.8

संस्कृत साहित्य में शायद ही कोई ऐसी कृति हो जिसमें नगर एवं प्रासाद वर्णन के प्रसंग में उपवन का वर्णन न हुआ हो। देवलोक का नन्दनवन; लंकापुरी की अशोकवनिका (रामा., सुन्दर); अयोध्या के उद्यान और आम्रवन (रामायण - बाल., 5.12); नागरकों के विहार के लिए नगर के समीपवर्ती वन (पुरोपकण्ठवनानि, रघु., 14.30); राजभवनों के प्रमदवन (अभिज्ञान., अंक 6, विक्रम., अं. 2), कन्यान्तःपुरों के क्रीडोद्यान (कादम्बरी); अनेक प्रकार के लतामण्डप (विक्रम., अं. 2, पृ. 164 स्वप्न., अं. 2) तथा गन्धपुष्पों की वीथियाँ इसी कला की देन हैं।

एक विद्या या ज्ञान की शाखा के रूप में प्राचीन भारत में वृक्षायुर्वेद का अपना शास्त्र था जिसका संक्षिप्त विवेचन बृहत्संहिता के 55वें अध्याय में हुआ है। इस विवेचन तथा साहित्य में प्राप्त सन्दर्भों के आधार पर इस कला के सम्बन्ध में निम्नलिखित तथ्यों का ज्ञान होता है—

(1) वृक्ष एवं उपवन लगाने के योग्य स्थान

सरोवर, नदी आदि जल स्त्रोतों के तटवर्ती स्थानों को वृक्षारोपण के लिए उत्तम माना गया था। तालाबों के जल से जहाँ वृक्षों को जीवन मिलता था वहीं जलाशय की शोभा भी छायादार वृक्षों से मानी जाती थी—

प्रान्तच्छायाविनिर्मुक्ता न मनोज्ञा जलाशयाः।
यस्मादतो जलप्रान्तेष्वारामान् विनिवेशयेत्।। बृहत्संहिता - 55.1

अतः उपवन प्रायः जलस्त्रोतों के समीप या तटप्रदेश पर ही लगाए जाते थे। उज्जयिनी में शिप्रा की ठंडी वायु से कम्पित उद्यानों की कतारें[2] दिखाई देती हैं तो हिमालय की वादियों में मालिनी नदी के तट पर लतावलय से युक्त कुञ्ज।[3]

राजभवनों तथा नागरकों के गृहों में जहाँ ये प्राकृतिक जलस्त्रोत नहीं होते थे वहाँ कुँआ, वापी (चौकोर या गोल आकार का तालाब या बावड़ी) तथा दीर्घिका (आयाताकार लम्बे तालाब) बनावाए जाते थे।[4]

यक्ष के उद्यान में मरकत मणि से जड़ी हुई सीढ़ियों वाली एक मनोरम वापी[5] थी तो अग्निमित्र के प्रमदवन में कमलों से युक्त सुन्दर दीर्घिका।[6]

(2) वृक्षारोपण के लिए भूमि तैयार करना

कोमल मिट्टी वाली भूमि सभी वृक्षों के लिए हितकारी मानी जाती थी। भूगि को अधिक उर्वर और मृदु बनाने के लिए पहले तिल बोया जाता था। जब पौधे फूलने लगते थे तब उन्हें मसलकर मिट्टी के साथ मिला दिया जाता था। यह बगीचा लगाने के लिए भूमि का प्रथम प्रतिकर्म या संस्कार था।

(3) मांगलिक वृक्षों का प्रथम रोपण

मिट्टी तैयार हो जाने पर नगरोद्यानों या गृहोद्यानों में सर्वप्रथम मंगल वृक्ष लगाए जाते थे। अरिष्ट (नीम), अशोक, पुन्नाग, शिरीष और प्रियंगु मंगल वृक्ष माने गए थे।[7]

मेघदूत में यक्षप्रिया द्वारा लगाए गए उद्यान में हम माधवीलता के मण्डप के समीप तरंगित पल्लवों वाले रक्त अशोक को पाते हैं।[8] एक कोने में है-लाल-लाल गुच्छों वाला मन्दार का छोटा सा वृक्ष जिसकी शाखाओं को हाथ से ही झुकाया जा सकता था— **हस्तप्राप्यस्तबकनमितो बालमन्दारवृक्षः।** मेघदूत - 2.15

(4) उपवन की बाड़ लगाना

उपवन की सुरक्षा के लिए नाना प्रकार के पुष्प युक्त पादपों की बाड़ लगायी जाती थी। यक्ष के उद्यान में माधवीमण्डप के चारों ओर कुरबक[9] वृक्षों की बाड़ लगाई गई थी। दशार्ण देश के उपवनों में केतकी[10] की बाड़ें लगायी गई थीं जो वर्षा ऋतु में खिले हुए पुष्पों से सफेद दिखाई देती थीं। कुरबक की पत्तियों को पशु नहीं खाते तथा यह गुलाबी फूलों के गुच्छों से बड़ा मनोरम दिखाई देता है, केतकी के फूल काँटेदार होते हैं तथा इनकी सुगन्ध बड़ी तीव्र होती है। अतः बाड़ के लिए इनका प्रयोग किया जाता था। नगरों को घेरने के लिए शाल जैसे विशाल वृक्ष लगाए जाते थे जो ऋतु आने पर मनोहारी फूलों से लद जाते थे। रामायण की अयोध्या शाल वृक्षों[11] से घिरी हुई थी। शाल वृक्षों के पुष्पों को तोड़ने के खेल से भारतीय मूर्ति शिल्प में 'शालभञ्जिका' मुद्रा का जन्म हुआ है।

शाल्मली (सेमल), शमी, बड़, गूलर आदि वृक्ष ग्रामों या नगरों की सीमा निर्धारण के लिए भी लगाए जाते थे।[12] अतः हरे भरे स्निग्ध वृक्षों को देखकर नगर की समीपता का अनुमान कर लिया जाता था—

सोपस्नेहतया वृक्षाणामभितः खल्वयोध्या भवितव्यम्।

(5) पादपसंरोपण

वृक्षारोपण की कई विधियाँ थीं–छोटे पौधों का रोपण, वृक्ष की शाखा का रोपण या कलम लगाना तथा शाखा युक्त वृक्ष का रोपण।

छोटे पौधों को लगाने के लिए पौध तैयार कर ली जाती थी। इन्हें शिशिर ऋतु में लगाना उत्तम माना जाता था। शाखा युक्त पौधे को अधिक ठंडे मौसम में अर्थात् हेमन्त ऋतु में तथा शाखा–प्रशाखा से युक्त बड़े पौधे को वर्षा ऋतु में रोपा जाता था। वृक्षारोपण के लिए एक स्थान से पौधे को उखाड़कर दूसरे स्थान पर लगाने की क्रिया– पौध प्रतिरोपण कही जाती थी। वराहमिहिर इस सन्दर्भ में एक महत्त्वपूर्ण तथ्य का निर्देश करते हैं कि प्रतिरोपण करते समय वृक्ष को पूर्व–वत् दिशा में लगाना वृक्ष की समृद्धि और विकास के लिए उत्तम होता है।[13]

पौध प्रतिरोपण से पहले पेड़ को उखाड़ने की क्रिया की जाती थी इसे विरोपण कहा गया है। विरोपण से पूर्व वृक्ष के मूल से लेकर शाखा तक एक विशिष्ट लेप किया जाता था जो घी, खस, तिल, शहद, वायविडंग, दूध और गोबर के मिश्रण से तैयार किया जाता था।

कटहल, अशोक, केला, जामुन, लिकुच, दाडिम (अनार), द्राक्षा (दाख), बिजौरा और अतिमुक्तक वृक्षों की शाखाएँ या कलम लगाई जाती हैं अतः इन वृक्षों की शाखा काटकर गोबर से लेपकर लगाई जाती थी या जड़ के पास से सावधानी से काटकर इसे लगाया जाता था।[14] बहुत पास–पास उत्पन्न हुए एक दूसरे का स्पर्श करने वाले तथा मिली हुई जड़ों वाले वृक्ष पीड़ित होने के कारण ठीक से फल नहीं पाते अतः वृक्षारोपण के समय समुचित दूरी का ध्यान रखना भी आवश्यक था। दो वृक्षों के मध्य बीस हाथ की दूरी उत्तम, सोलह हाथ की दूरी मध्यम और बारह हाथ की दूरी अधम मानी गई थी।

वृक्षारोपण में नक्षत्रों के प्रभाव का आकलन भी प्राचीन वृक्षायुर्वेद के ज्ञाता विद्वानों ने किया था। तदनुसार उत्तरा, रोहिणी, मृगशिरा, रेवती, चित्रा, अनुराधा, मूल, विशाखा, पुष्यश्रवण, अश्विनी और हस्त नक्षत्र वृक्षारोपण के लिए उत्तम माने गए थे।[15]

(6) पौधों का सिञ्चन

वृक्षायुर्वेद के अनुसार ग्रीष्म ऋतु में प्रातःकाल और सायं काल दिन में दो बार, शीतकाल में एक दिन छोड़कर दूसरे दिन तथा वर्षाकाल में भूमि के सूखने पर वृक्षों को सींचना चाहिए।

वृक्षवाटिका के पौधों को सींचने का वर्णन साहित्य में अनेकशः हुआ है। छोटे–छोटे घड़ों से बाल पादपों को सींचने का कार्य प्रायः किशोरी कन्याएँ ही किया करती थीं। संस्कृत साहित्य की नायिकाओं सीता[16], पार्वती[17], शकुन्तला[18] आदि को वृक्षों की यह परिचर्या विशेष प्रिय है।

शकुन्तला और उसकी सखियों का प्रथम दर्शन ही वृक्षवाटिका के पौधों को सींचते हुए होता है–

अये एतास्तपस्विकन्यकाः स्वप्रमाणानुरूपैः सेचनघटैः बालपादपेभ्यः पयो दातुम् इत एवाभिवर्तन्ते।

अंक–1

प्रत्येक पादप को पर्याप्त जल मिल सके इसके लिए मूल भाग में आलवाल (क्यारियों) बनी होती थीं जिन्हें घड़े के जल से भर दिया जाता था।[19]

बाल पादपों (छोटे पौधों) तथा वृक्षकों (कुछ बड़े पौधों या छोटे वृक्षों) को घड़े के जल से सींचा जाता था। शाखी (शाखा युक्त बड़े वृक्षों) को सींचने के लिए नहरें बना दी जाती थीं—

कुल्याम्भोभिः पवनचपलैः शाखिनो धौतमूलाः। अभिज्ञानशाकुन्तल - 1.15

जामुन, वेतस, वानीर, कदम्ब, अदुम्बर, अर्जुन, वञ्जुल, नक्तमाल, तिलक और कटहल आदि वृक्षों को बहुत अधिक जल की आवश्यकता होती है अतः ये वृक्ष अनूप (बहुत जल वाले) देश में ही लगाए जाते हैं।

(7) वृक्षचिकित्सा

वृक्षायुर्वेद का एक महत्त्वपूर्ण अंग रोगी वृक्षों की चिकित्सा है। आवश्यकता से अधिक शीत, वात तथा धूप वृक्षों के रोग के कारण हैं। इनसे वृक्षों के पत्ते पीले हो जाते हैं, शाखाएँ सूखने लगती हैं, वृद्धि रुक जाती है तथा शाखाओं से रस टपकने लगता है। इनकी चिकित्सा निम्नविधि से करनी चाहिए—

(i) **शस्त्र-शोधन**-वृक्ष के सूखे और सड़े अंगों को शस्त्र से काट दें।

(ii) **लेपन**-वृक्ष की डालियों पर वायविडंग, घी और गीली मिट्टी का लेप करें।

(iii) **सिञ्चन**-तत्पश्चात् दूध मिले जल से पौधे को सींचें।

फल-पुष्प से रहित बन्ध्य वृक्ष संतानहीनता के समान दुःख देते हैं।[20] उनकी चिकित्सा के लिए नाना प्रकार के उर्वरकों का छिड़काव किया जाता था। बृहत्संहिता में उर्वरक या छिड़काव हेतु घोल तैयार करने की विधि इस प्रकार बताई गई है—

(i) कुलथ, उड़द, मूँग, तिल और जौ दूध में डालकर उबालें। ठण्डा हो जाने पर उस दूध से वृक्ष को सींचें।

(ii) भेड़ और बकरी के मेंगन का चूर्ण दो आढक, तिल एक आढक, सत्तू एक प्रस्थ, जल एक द्रोण और गोमांस एक तुला; इन सबको एक पात्र में डालकर सात दिन तक रखें फिर इस घोल से वृक्ष, लता और गुल्म को सींचें। (55.16-18)

(8) बीजोपचार

बीजों को सुरक्षित रखने, अधिक फल और पुष्प प्राप्त करने तथा उन्नत किस्म के बीजों को बनाने की कला को बीजोपचार कहा जाता है। कौटिल्य के अर्थशास्त्र में बीजों की सुरक्षा के लिए महत्त्वपूर्ण जानकारी प्राप्त होती है। तदनुसार-ईख आदि काण्ड बीजों को शहद, घी और सूअर की चर्बी में डुबोकर गोबर में लपेटकर रखना चाहिए। कन्द (नौल्व) को शहद और घी से लेपकर तथा गुठली के भीतर से निकलने वाले बीजों को गोबर में मिलाकर रखना चाहिए (2.24.33)। बृहत्संहिता में बीज से पुष्प और फल सहित पौधा उत्पन्न करने तथा वृक्ष के बीजों से वल्ली (लता) बनाने की विधि बताई गई है।

(i) बीज से पुष्पसहित पौधा उगाना

दस दिन तक दूध में डूबे हुए बीज को घी के हाथ से चुपड़ें फिर गोबर से उसे बार-बार रूखा, करें, सूकर और हरिण के मांस को जलाकर उसकी धूप दें फिर मछली और सूअर की चर्बी के साथ परिकर्म (तिल को बोने एवं मिलाने से मृदुल) युक्त भूमि में बोएँ तथा दूध युक्त जल से सींचें तो उस स्थान से जो वृक्ष उत्पन्न होगा वह फूल के साथ होगा (55.19-20)।

(ii) एक ही दिन में वृक्ष बनकर फल लग जाना

अंकोल फल के कल्क या तेल से अथवा लसोड़े के कल्क अथवा तेल से बीज को सौ भावना देकर (सौ बार गीला कर) ओले से भीगी हुई मिट्टी में बोने पर वह बीज तुरन्त अङ्कुरित होकर फलभार से झुकी हुई शाखा बन जाता है—

वापितं करकोन्मिश्रं मृदि तत्क्षणजन्मकम्।
फलभारान्विता शाखा भवतीति किमद्भुतम्।। बृहत्संहिता - 55.28

(iii) वृक्ष के बीज से लता बनाना

वृक्षायुर्वेद की कला में इस प्रकार के मनोरम प्रयोग भी मिलते हैं।

इमली की लता बनाने के लिए इमली के बीज को-धान, उड़द तथा तिल का चूर्ण, सत्तू एवं सड़े माँस के मिश्रण से गीला करें फिर हल्दी की धूप दें। इस विधि से उपचारित बीज को बोने पर इमली की लता बनती है (बृहत्संहिता - 55.21)।

बीज से तत्काल लता बनाने के लिए अन्य प्रयोग थे। सुन्दर पत्तों वाली, मण्डप को ढक लेने वाली कपित्थ (कैंथ) की लता को तत्काल उगाने की विधि बृहत्संहिता (55.22-26) में प्राप्त होती है—

उप्तं च बीजं चतुरंगुलाधो मत्स्याम्भसा मांसजलैश्च सिक्तम्।
वल्ली भवत्याशु शुभप्रवाला विस्मापनी मण्डपमावृणोति।।

साहित्य में भी इस प्रकार की लताओं का उल्लेख हुआ है अशोक, शमी और आम के वृक्ष ही होते हैं पर कालिदास अशोकलता[20] और शमीलता[21] का तथा बाणभट्ट सहकारलता[20] का वर्णन करते हैं। सम्भवतः उस प्राचीन युग में वृक्षायुर्वेद की कला से ऐसी लताएँ उगाई जाती थीं, ये काल्पनिक[33] लताएँ नहीं थीं।

(9) वृक्षदोहद

फल-पुष्पों की अत्यधिक समृद्धि और अकाल पुष्पोद्गम (बिना मौसम के फूल खिलाने) के लिए वृक्षदोहद का वर्णन संस्कृत साहित्य में बहुलता से हुआ है।

'दोहद' शब्द का सामान्य अर्थ है इच्छा अथवा लालसा किन्तु गर्भ चिह्न[24] और गर्भिणी स्त्री की लालसा[25] के अर्थ में यह रूढ़ हो गया है। वृक्षों के सन्दर्भ में यह विशेष रूप से पुष्पोद्गम और कहीं-कहीं फलोद्गम के अर्थ में भी प्रयुक्त हुआ है। शब्दार्णव के अनुसार—

कुशल व्यक्ति द्वारा तरु, गुल्म और लता में जिन द्रव्यों और क्रियाओं से अकाल पुष्पोद्गम कराया जाता है उसे दोहद कहते हैं।[26]

कौटिल्य दोहद के स्थान पर मूल शब्द 'दौहृद' का प्रयोग करते हैं और समय पर वृक्षों की दौहृद क्रिया को आवश्यक मानते हैं— काले दौहृदं च (अर्थशास्त्र - 2.24.33)। इस प्रसंग में वे पौधों के कुछ बड़े (प्ररूढ) हो जाने पर उनके लिए छोटी मछलियों की गीली खाद और स्नुही (सैंड़े) के दूध से सिंचाई आवश्यक मानते हैं।[27]

स्पष्ट है कि वर्तमान रासायनिक या प्राकृतिक उर्वरकों या खाद के अर्थ में दोहद शब्द का प्रयोग हुआ है। मोनियर विलियम्स के अनुसार दोहद एक प्रकार का सुगन्धित द्रव्य है जिसका प्रयोग खाद की भाँति किया जाता है।[28]

कर्पूरमञ्जरी में हम चम्पकलता के आलवाल को कस्तूरी-कर्पूर आदि से पूर्ण किए जाने का उदाहरण भी पाते हैं।[29]

दोहदधूप

नैषध महाकाव्य में फलसमृद्धि के लिए दाडिम (अनार) वृक्ष को दोहद धूप दिए जाने का उल्लेख हुआ है—

फलानि धूमस्य धयानधोमुखान् स दाडिमे दोहदधूपिनि द्रुमे। 1.82

इसी सन्दर्भ में मल्लिनाथ की टीका में दाडिम की फलवृद्धि के लिए कई प्रयोग बताए गए हैं—

(i) भेड़ के माँस से युक्त जल से सींचना तथा उसके बालों और माँस का धूप (धुआँ) देना।

(ii) मत्स्यमाँस, घी और त्रिफला का लेप।

(iii) बकरी अथवा भेड़ के माँस से लेप और धूप का प्रयोग।

इस प्रकार फल समृद्धि के लिए उर्वरक के साथ धूप का भी प्रयोग किया जाता था। धूप से पौधे कीड़ों और रोगों से मुक्त होते थे।

संस्कृत साहित्य में स्त्रियों की विभिन्न क्रियाओं से अशोक, बकुल, चम्पक आदि में पुष्पोद्गम का वर्णन हुआ है तथा इसे कवि समय या कवि प्रसिद्धि कहा गया है। कवि प्रसिद्धि के अनुसार— सुन्दर स्त्रियों के स्पर्श से प्रियंगु, मुखमदिरा के सिंचन से बकुल, पदाघात से अशोक, वीक्षण अथवा अवलोकन से तिलक, आलिंगन से कुरबक, नर्म वचन से मन्दार, मृदु हास्य से चम्पक, मुखवायु से आम्र, गान से नमेरु और नृत्य से कर्णिकार पुष्पित होता है।[30]

कालिदास यक्षप्रिया के पादाघात से अशोक एवं मुखमदिरा के सिंचन से बकुल वृक्ष के पुष्पित होने का वर्णन करते हैं—

रक्ताशोकश्चलकिसलयः केसरश्चात्रकान्तः
प्रत्यासन्नौ कुरबककवृतेर्माधवीमण्डपस्य।
एकः सख्यास्तव सह मया वामपादाभिलाषी
काङ्क्षत्यन्यो वदनमदिरां दोहदच्छद्मनास्याः ।। मेघदूत - 2.18

मालविकाग्निमित्र नाटक की सुखद परिणति में अशोक-दोहद की महती भूमिका है। मालविका के पादाघात से अशोक पुष्पित होता है और महारानी धारिणी प्रसन्न होकर अग्निमित्र से उसका विवाह करवा देती है।

साहित्य में दोहद का इस रूप में वर्णन होने पर भी वृक्षायुर्वेद में इस दोहद का उल्लेख नहीं है।

साहित्य में अकाल पुष्पोद्गम के अन्य सन्दर्भ भी हैं। रत्नावली नाटिका में नायक उदयन द्वारा दोहद क्रिया से नवमल्लिका को पुष्पसमृद्धि से युक्त किए जाने का वर्णन है—

अद्य किल भर्त्ता श्रीपर्वतादागतस्य श्रीखण्डदासनामधेयस्य धार्मिकस्य सकाशादकालकुसुमसंजननदोहदं शिक्षयित्वा नवमालिकां कुसुमसमृद्धिशोभितां करिष्यति इति। अं. 2, पृ. 55

प्रस्तुत कला के सन्दर्भ में अत्यन्त महत्त्वपूर्ण यह है कि वृक्ष दोहद की कला विशेष रूप से सीखी जाती थी। स्वयं राजा भी इसे सीखते थे। श्रीपर्वत से आए हुए धार्मिक से यह कला सीखी गई थी। पाँचवी-छठवीं शताब्दी में श्रीपर्वत तन्त्र मन्त्र और अनेक चमत्कारों का केन्द्र माना जाता था। सम्भवतः वृक्ष-दोहद के मूल में भी चमत्कार की कल्पना पनपने लगी थी।

इस प्रकार 'वृक्षायुर्वेदयोगाः' वृक्षों की समृद्धि के लिए अनेक प्रकार के प्रयोग की कला थी। प्राचीन भारत में गृहोद्यानों की देखभाल प्रायः स्त्रियाँ, कुमारी कन्याएँ ही करती थीं। वे इस कला को सीखती थीं। वात्स्यायन ने इसे भार्या (विवाहिता पत्नी) का विशेष कर्त्तव्य बताया है। उनके अनुसार गृहिणी साफ-सुथरी जगह में नित्य प्रयोग में आने वाली सब्जियाँ, ईख, जीरा, सौंफ, सरसों आदि मसालों की क्यारियाँ तथा तमाल के गुल्म लगवाए। बेला, चमेली, मालती, तगर, कदम्ब, जपा आदि पुष्पों के पौधे लगाए तथा बैठने के लिए चबूतरे बनवाए।[31]

राजभवनों में भी प्रमदवनों की देख-भाल प्रायः स्त्रियाँ ही करती थीं इन्हें उद्यानपालिका[32] या उद्यानपाली[33] कहा जाता था। ये प्रमदवन नाना प्रकार के सुगन्धित पुष्पों, फलदार वृक्षों, सदाबहार पौधों, लताकुञ्जों और कदलीगृहों से शोभित होते थे। इस कला के माध्यम से इन उपवनों को सभी ऋतुओं की पुष्प-शोभा से सम्पन्न कर लिया जाता था।[34]

प्रिय के साथ लता-पादपों की पुष्प समृद्धि को देखना परम आनन्द और सौभाग्य का क्षण होता था—

धारिणी-इच्छाम्यार्यपुत्रेण सहाशोकवृक्षस्य प्रसूनलक्ष्मीं प्रत्यक्षीकर्तुम्।

मालविकाग्निमित्र - अं. 5

अपने प्रिय को पुष्पों की शोभा दिखाना सम्मान और गौरव का विषय माना जाता था—

पद्मावती-आर्यपुत्र इहागत्येमां कुसुमसमृद्धिं दृष्ट्वा संमानिता भवेयम्।

स्वप्नवासवदत्त - अं. 4

वृक्षायुर्वेद की कला से ऐसे समय भी पादप को पुष्पसमृद्धि से युक्त किया जा सकता था जब अन्य पौधों के फूल समाप्ति की ओर होते थे—

राजा-अयम्. . .इदानीमनन्यसाधारणीं शोभामुद्वहति।
सर्वाशोकतरूणां प्रथमं सूचितवसन्तविभवानाम्।
निवृत्तदोहदेऽस्मिन्संक्रान्तानीव कुसुमानि।। मालविकाग्निमित्र - 5.5

कृषि विभाग के अध्यक्ष (सीताध्यक्ष) एवं उसके सहयोगियों के लिए भी कृषितन्त्र के साथ ही वृक्षायुर्वेद का ज्ञान आवश्यक माना गया था।[35]

यह केवल उपवन लगाने की ही कला नहीं थी अपितु वनस्पति जगत् के साथ हृदय से जुड़ने की आत्मीय सम्बन्धों को बनाने की कला थी तभी तो अपने हाथ से लगाए गए लता पादपों में प्रथम पुष्प का उद्गम जीवन का उत्सव[36] बन जाता है तो ये लता पादप परम सुहृद[37] और आत्मीय। पार्वती पादपों को अपत्य (संतान) स्नेह[38] से सींचती हैं तो शकुन्तला सोदर स्नेह[39] से। ऋषि कण्व को जितनी चिन्ता शकुन्तला के विवाह की है उतनी ही नवमल्लिका के विवाह की भी।[40]

यह आत्मीयता और स्नेह एकतरफा नहीं है। वृक्ष भी मनुष्य के सुख-दुःख, हास-अश्रु के अभिन्न सङ्गी[41], नायक नायिका के प्रणय व्यापारों के साक्षी[42], विषण्ण हृदय के विश्रान्ति स्थल[42] हैं।

यह केवल कोमलहृदय कवि की मञ्जुल कल्पना नहीं है शास्त्रों का भी यही अनुभव है। तभी तो वृक्षायुर्वेद कहता है—

प्रत्यारोपण के लिए वृक्ष को उखाड़ने से पूर्व स्वयं स्नान और चन्दनादि अनुलेप से पवित्र होकर वृक्ष की पूजा करें। ऐसे पौधे उन्हीं पत्तों के साथ लग जाते हैं अर्थात् सूखते नहीं है।[44]

मनुष्य और वनस्पतिजगत् की इस आत्मीयता को बढ़ाने की कला है—वृक्षायुर्वेदयोगाः। यह विज्ञान और कला, चमत्कार और प्रयोग का रोचक समन्वय है।

सन्दर्भ-सङ्केत

1. रोपणपुष्टिचिकित्सावैचित्र्यकृतो गृहोद्यानार्थाः। कामसूत्र - 1.3.15 पर यशोधर की टीका
2. सिप्रातरङ्गानिलकम्पितासु विहर्तुमुद्यानपरंपरासु। रघुवंश - 6.35
3. इमामुग्रातपवेलां प्रायेण लतावलयवत्सु मालिनीतीरेषु ससखीजना शकुन्तला गमयति।
   अभिज्ञानशाकुन्तल - अं. 1
4. मध्ये कूपं वापीं दीर्घिकां च खानयेत्। कामसूत्र - 4.1.8
5. वापी चास्मिन् मरकतशिलाबद्धसोपानमार्गा। मेघदूत - 2.16
6. पत्रच्छायासु हंसा मुकुलितनयना दीर्घिकापद्मिनीनाम्। मालविकाग्निमित्र - 2.12
7. अरिष्टाशोकपुन्नागशिरीषाः सप्रियङ्गवः।
   मङ्गल्याः पूर्वमारामे रोपणीया गृहेषु वा। बृहत्संहिता - 55.3
8. रक्ताशोकश्चलकिसलयः। मेघदूत - 2.18
9. प्रत्यासन्नौ कुरबकवृतेर्माधवीमण्डपस्य। मेघदूत - 2.18
10. पाण्डुच्छायोपवनवृतयः केतकैः सूचिभिन्नैः। मेघदूत - 1.25
11. महतीं सालमेखलाम्। रामायण-बालकाण्ड - 5.12
12. शाल्मलीशमीक्षीरवृक्षानन्तेषु सीम्नां स्थापयेत्। अर्थशास्त्र - 2.1.3
13. अजातशाखांश्छिशिरे जातशाखान् हिमागमे।
    वर्षागमे च सुस्कन्धान्यथादिक् प्रतिरोपयेत्।। बृहत्संहिता - 55.6
14. बृहत्संहिता - 55.5
15. बृहत्संहिता - 55.31
16. इमानि खलु प्रत्यग्राभिषिक्तानि वृक्षमूलानि अदूरगतां मैथिलीं सूचयन्ति।
    योऽस्याः करः श्राम्यति दर्पणेऽपि स नैति खेदं कलशं वहन्त्याः। प्रतिमानाटक - 5.3
17. अतन्द्रिता सा स्वयमेव वृक्षकान्घटस्तनप्रस्रवणैर्व्यवर्धयत्। कुमारसम्भव - 5.14
18. स्रस्तांसावतिमात्रलोहिततलौ बाहू घटोत्क्षेपणात्। अभिज्ञानशाकुन्तल - 1.28
19. सेकान्ते मुनिकन्याभिस्तत्क्षणोज्झितवृक्षकम्।
    विश्वासाय विहङ्गानामालवालाम्बुपायिनाम्।। रघुवंश - 1.51

    कथं पश्यन्न दूयसे।
    सिक्तं स्वयमिव स्नेहाद्वन्ध्यमाश्रमवृक्षकम्।। रघुवंश - 1.70
20. अशोकलताप्रवालम्। रघुवंश - 7.21
21. शमीलतां छेत्तुमृषिर्व्यवस्यति। अभिज्ञानशाकुन्तल - 1.18
22. सहकारलता रसानां च . . .। हर्षचरित - उ. 7, पृ. 387

23. श्री भगवतशरण उपाध्याय अशोक और शमीलता को काल्पनिक लता मानते हैं। कालिदास का भारत - भाग 1, पृ. 62

24. सुदक्षिणा दोहदलक्षणं दधौ। रघुवंश - 3.1

25. प्रजावती दोहदशंसिनी ते। रघुवंश - 14.45

26. तरुगुल्मलतादीनामकाले कुशलैः कृताम्।
पुष्पाद्युत्पादकं द्रव्यं दोहदं स्यात्तु तत्क्रिया।।

27. प्ररूढांश्चाशुष्ककटुमत्स्यांश्च स्नुहिक्षीरेण वापयेत्। अर्थशास्त्र - 2.24.34

28. मोनियर. कोश. - पृ. 499

29. कर्पूरमञ्जरी - जव., 1, पृ. 52

30. मेघदूत - 2.18 पर मल्लिनाथ की टीका

31. कामसूत्र - 4.1.6-7

32. अनयोरेव उद्यानपालिकयोः · · ·। अभिज्ञानशाकुन्तल - अं. 6

33. प्रथमकुसुमनिर्गमनिवेदनागताम् उद्यानपालीम् अशेषाभरणदानेन सम्मानयन्तीम्। कादम्बरी - पृ. 545

34. ऋद्धसर्वर्तुवृक्षवाटिका। नैषधीचरित - 18.10

35. सीताध्यक्षः कृषितन्त्रशुल्ववृक्षायुर्वेदज्ञस्तज्ज्ञसखो वा। अर्थशास्त्र - 2. 24.1

36. आद्ये वः कुसुमप्रसूतिसमये यस्या भवत्युत्सवः। अभिज्ञानशाकुन्तल - 4.9

37. अनुमतगमना शकुन्तला तरुभिरियं वनवासबन्धुभिः। अभिज्ञानशाकुन्तल - 4.9

38. देवदारुं पुत्रीकृतोऽसौ वृषभध्वजेन।
यो . . . स्कन्दस्य मातुः पयसां रसज्ञः।। रघुवंश - 2.36

39. अस्ति मे सोदरस्नेहोऽप्येतेषु। अभिज्ञानशाकुन्तल - अं., 1

40. भर्तारमात्मसदृशं सुकृतैर्गता त्वम्।
चूतेन संश्रितवती नवमालिकेय-
मस्यामहं त्वयि च सम्प्रति वीतचिन्तः।। अभिज्ञानशाकुन्तल - 4.13

41. विलपन्निति कोशलाधिपः करुणार्थग्रथितं प्रियां प्रति।
अकरोत्पृथिवीरुहानपि स्नुतशाखारसबाष्पदूषितान्।। रघुवंश - 8.70

42. लतावलय! संतापहारक आमन्त्रये त्वां भूयोऽपि परिभोगाय। अभिज्ञानशाकुन्तल - अं. 3

43. इहागतोऽस्मि प्रमदवनम्। यावदिदानीं भागधेयनिर्वृत्तं दुःखं विनोदयामि। स्वप्नवासवदत्त - अं. 3

44. बृहत्संहिता - 55.8

卐 卐 卐

प्राचीन भारतीय प्रसाधन

शैलेश कुमार मिश्र

सौन्दर्य की समग्रता अलंकरण से होती है। अलंकरण की प्रवृत्ति केवल मनुष्य में ही नहीं वरन् प्रकृति भी स्वयं को विभिन्न रूपों में सजाती रहती है। प्रकृति की इसी अवर्ण्य सजावट पर मुग्ध कविहृदय कदाचित् कह उठता है 'पयसा कमलं कमलेन पयः पयसा कमलेन विभाति सरः।'

अलंकरण या प्रसाधन मानव की प्रवृत्ति है। प्रसाधन का भिन्न-भिन्न स्वरूप भिन्न-भिन्न कालों में दृष्टिगत होता रहा है। वनवासी राम ने भी सीता को वन्य पुष्पों और मनःशिला से अलंकृत किया तथा श्रीकृष्ण भी वन में गोचारण करते हुए ग्वालबालों के साथ वनमाला, गुञ्जा के हार, अङ्गराग, मोरपंख आदि से प्रसाधन किया करते थे।

आदर्शवादियों की यह भ्रान्त धारणा है कि प्रसाधन निरर्थक और आदर्श से च्युत करने की वस्तु है। यह विचारणीय है कि जो बाह्य प्रसाधन में तत्पर होगा, उसी का अन्तःकरण भी सुसज्जित होगा। प्रसाधन की अपनी-अपनी कोटियाँ हैं। बुद्ध, गाँधी जैसे महात्माओं में भी प्रसाधन था किन्तु उसकी अपनी कोटि थी। उनका प्रसाधन एक नैसर्गिक अलंकरण था, उसमें कृत्रिमता न थी। जीवन प्राचीन काल से ही प्रसाधन से ओत-प्रोत रहा है अतएव साज-सज्जा अवांछनीय नहीं है। प्रसाधन की पद्धति वांछनीय या त्याज्य हो सकती है। वर्तमान युग में प्रसाधन समस्त विश्व में अपनी विस्तृत और विकसित सत्ता स्थापित कर चुका है, जीवन का अभिन्न अंग बन गया है। ऐसे समय में जब विदेशी प्रसाधन पद्धति का अन्धानुकरण भारतीय समाज कर रहा है तब प्राचीन भारतीय प्रसाधन की विशिष्टताओं का उल्लेख अनिवार्य हो जाता है। विदेशी पद्धति के अनुकरण से बहुत-सी हानियाँ हो रही हैं अतः ऐसे में हमें प्रसाधन की उस पद्धति का अवलोकन करना चाहिए जो मानवमात्र के सौन्दर्यवर्धन के साथ-साथ स्वास्थ्यवृद्धि भी करती थी।

प्रसाधन एक कला है। प्राचीन काल में प्रसाधन-कला में निपुण पुरुष या स्त्रियों की चर्चा प्राचीन ग्रन्थों में मिलती है। प्रसाधन कला में निपुण स्त्री के लिए महाभारत में 'सैरन्ध्री' शब्द प्रयुक्त है। विराट् के राज्य में अज्ञातवास कर रही द्रौपदी भी 'सैरन्ध्री' नाम से जानी जाती थी—

साहं ब्रुवाणा सैरन्ध्री कुशला केशकर्मणि। महाभारत-विराट्पर्व-3.18

कुमारसम्भव में पार्वती की आँखों में प्रसाधिकाओं द्वारा मंगलजनक काजल लगाए जाने का उल्लेख है—

तस्याः सुजातोत्पलपत्रकान्ते प्रसाधिकाभिर्नयने निरीक्ष्य।
न चक्षुषोः कान्तिविशेषबुद्ध्या कालाञ्जनं मङ्गलमित्युपात्तम्।। कुमारसम्भव - 7. 20

नायिका या स्वामिनी के प्रसाधन का ध्यान रखने वाली प्रसाधिका को कादम्बरी में 'ताम्बूलकरङ्कवाहिनी' नाम दिया गया है—

ताम्बूलकरङ्कवाहिनी इति कृत्वा मया प्रेषिता। कादम्बरी - पत्रलेखावर्णन

कालिदास ने रघुवंश में पुरुष प्रसाधक का उल्लेख किया है—

तं धूपाश्यानकेशान्तं तोयनिर्णिक्तपाणयः।
आकल्पसाधनैस्तैस्तैः उपसेदुः प्रसाधकाः।। रघुवंश - 17. 22

शरीर के विभिन्न हिस्सों के प्रसाधन की चर्चा संस्कृत साहित्य में मिलती है। इसे अधोविन्यस्त रूप में देखा जा सकता है—

1. केशप्रसाधन

घुंघराले काले और कोमल केशपाश की प्रशंसा प्राचीन काल से होती आ रही है। संस्कृतकवियों ने मेघों की तरह काले काले नायिकाओं के केशपाश की खूब चर्चा की है।

सुन्दर केश की विशिष्टताओं का उल्लेख चरकसंहिता में इस प्रकार मिलता है—

एकैकजा मृदवोऽल्पाः स्निग्धाः शुद्धमूलाः कृष्णाः केशाः प्रशस्यन्ते।

अर्थात् बाल अलग-अलग हों तथा एक मूल से एक ही केश निकलना चाहिए। बाल काले और मृदु होने चाहिए।

इस तथ्य का समर्थन बुद्धचरित में भी मिलता है—

पृथक् पृथक् मूलरुहा समुद्गताः। बुद्धचरित-8.52

सिर पर तेल लगाने की प्रथा का उल्लेख चरकसंहिता में प्राप्त होता है। आचार्य चरक कहते हैं कि तेल से आर्द सिर में कभी दर्द नहीं होता तथा केश झड़ना, केश पकना आदि रोग दूर होते हैं—

नित्यं स्नेहार्द्रशिरसः शिरःशूलं न जायते।
न खालित्यं न पालित्यं न केशाः प्रपतन्ति च।।
बलं शिरःकपालानां विशेषेण विवर्धते।
दृढमूलाश्च दीर्घाश्च कृष्णाः केशा भवन्ति च।।

चरकसंहिता - सूत्रस्थान-5. 79-80

केशों में अगर (अगुरु) के धुएँ देने की प्रथा प्राचीन काल में थी। अगुरु सुगन्धित होता है तथा इसका धूम दुर्गन्धनाशक, मैलजूँनाशक तथा रोगोत्पादक जीवाणुओं को नष्ट करने वाला होता है। केशसंस्कार की इस विधि की चर्चा कालिदास ने अपने कई ग्रन्थों में की है। पूर्वमेघ में उज्जयिनी वर्णन का यह प्रसंग—

जालोद्गीर्णैरुपचितवपुः केशसंस्कारधूपैः। पूर्वमेघ -32

ऋतुसंहार में भी अगुरुधूम से धूपित केशवाली स्त्रियों का उल्लेख है—

कालागुरुप्रचुरचन्दनचर्चिताङ्ग्यः पुष्पावतंससुरभीकृतकेशपाशाः।
श्रुत्वा ध्वनिं जलमुचां त्वरितं प्रदोषे शय्यागृहं गुरुगृहात्प्रविशन्ति नार्यः।।

ऋतुसंहार - 2.22

गात्राणि कालीयकचर्चितानि सपत्रलेखानि मुखाम्बुजानि।
शिरांसि कालागुरुधूपितानि कुर्वन्ति नार्यः सुरतोत्सवाय।। ऋतुसंहार - 4.5

अगुरु के स्थान पर कालागुरु का प्रयोग किया गया है। कालिदास ने कालागुरु के उद्गम स्थान के रूप में प्राग्ज्योतिष अर्थात् आसाम को इंगित किया है—

चकम्पे तीर्णलौहित्ये तस्मिन्प्राग्ज्योतिषेश्वरः।
तद्गजालनतां प्राप्तः सह कालागुरुद्रुमैः।। रघुवंश - 4.81

धूम देने के लिए बाल गीले रखे जाते थे—

धूपोष्मणा त्याजितमार्द्रभावं केशान्तमन्तःकुसुमं तदीयम्। कुमारसम्भव - 7.14

सूखे बालों में धूप देने से वे टूट जाते थे। बालों में धूप इस मात्रा में दी जाती थी कि बाल सूख जाएँ। अधिक मात्रा में धूप देने से उनके रुखड़े हो जाने तथा टूट जाने का भय रहता था—

कुण्ठत्वमायान्ति गुणाः कवीनां साहित्यविद्याश्रमवर्जितेषु।
कुर्यादनार्द्रेषु किमङ्गनानां केशेषु कृष्णागुरुधूपवासः।।

विक्रमाङ्कदेवचरित - 1.4

अगुरु के साथ अन्य औषधीय द्रव्यों के प्रयोग का उल्लेख भी संस्कृत के प्राचीन ग्रन्थों में मिलता है। कादम्बरी में आँवले के प्रयोग की भी चर्चा है—

वारविलासिनीकरमृदितसुगन्धामलकालिप्तशिरसो . . .। कादम्बरी-शूद्रकवर्णन

केशविन्यास के सौन्दर्यवर्धन के लिए पुष्पों से केशशृङ्गार का उल्लेख संस्कृत साहित्य में मिलता है। देश और काल के अनुसार खिलने वाले फूलों से नायिकाएँ केशशृङ्गार करती थीं। उत्तरमेघ में विभिन्न फूलों से केशसज्जा का उल्लेख है—

अलके बालकुन्दानुविद्धं
चूडापाशे नवकुरबकं चारुकर्णे शिरीषं
सीमन्ते च त्वदुपगमजं यत्र नीपं वधूनाम्।। उत्तरगेघ - 2

अलका की अभिसारिकाओं की अलकों से मन्दारपुष्पों के मार्ग में गिरे होने का उल्लेख कालिदास इन शब्दों में करते हैं—

गत्युत्कम्पादलकपतितैर्यत्र मन्दारपुष्पैः। उत्तरमेघ - 9

कालिदास ने सुन्दरियों द्वारा कदम्ब, मौलसिरी, केतकी की मालाओं से तथा मालती के फूलों के साथ जूही की कलियों की मालाओं से केशपाश को अलंकृत करने की चर्चा बड़े सरस शब्दों में की है—

मालाः कदम्बकेसरकेतकीभिरायोजिताः शिरसि बिभ्रति योषितोऽद्य। ऋतुसंहार - 2. 9
शिरसि बकुलमालां मालतीभिः समेतां विकसितनवपुष्पैर्यूथिकाकुड्मलैश्च।
विकचनवकदम्बैः कर्णपूरं वधूनां रचयति जलदौघः कान्तवत्काल एषः।।

ऋतुसंहार - 2. 25

इसी प्रकार अशोक के फूलों से सुसज्जित केशों, कर्णिकार से युक्त कानों की प्रशंसा कालिदास ने की है—

कर्णेषु योग्यं नवकर्णिकारं चलेषु नीलेष्वलकेष्वशोकम्।
पुष्पं च फुल्लं नवमल्लिकायाः प्रयान्ति कान्तिं प्रमदाजनानाम्।। ऋतुसंहार - 6.6

दूर्वाङ्कुर से केशसज्जा की चर्चा विक्रमोर्वशीय में मिलती है—

पवित्रदूर्वाङ्कुरलाञ्छितालका। विक्रमोर्वशीय - 3.12

बँधे हुए केशपाश को धम्मिल्ल कहते थे। इस धम्मिल्ल में रत्न भी गूँथे जाते थे—

मुक्ताजालग्रथितमलकम्। पूर्वमेघ - 63

केशविन्यास के भिन्न-भिन्न प्रकार थे। भिन्न-भिन्न प्रदेशों में अलग-अलग प्रकार की केशरचना का उल्लेख भरत अपने नाट्यशास्त्र में करते हैं। अवन्ति देश की स्त्रियाँ घुंघराले बालों वाली होती हैं। गौड़ देश की स्त्रियों के केश शिखा की तरह लम्बी वेणी वाले होते हैं। आभीर देश की युवतियाँ दो वेणियाँ (चोटियाँ) बनाती हैं—

अवन्तीयुवतीनां तु शिरः सालककुन्तलम्।
गौडीनामलकप्रायं स शिखापाशवेणिकम्।।
आभीरयुवतीनां तु द्विवेणीधरमेव च।
शिरः परिगतं कार्यं नीलप्रायमथाम्बरम्।। नाट्यशास्त्र - 21. 64-65

2. तिलकप्रसाधन

प्रांगलिक कार्यार्थ या सौन्दर्यवृद्धि के लिए मस्तक पर तिलक लगाने का वर्णन संस्कृत साहित्य में प्राप्त होता है। तिलक करने के लिए गोरोचन, हरिताल, मनःशिला (मैनसिल) आदि द्रव्यों का प्रयोग किया जाता था। कादम्बरी में चाण्डालकन्या के वर्णन के प्रसंग में गोरोचन से तिलक करने का उल्लेख है—

आकपिलगोरोचनारचिततिलकतृतीयलोचनाम्। कादम्बरी-चाण्डालकन्यावर्णन

राजा हर्ष द्वारा तीर्थमृत्तिका और गोरोचन का तिलक लगाने का वर्णन हर्षचरित में मिलता है—

तीर्थमृदा गोरोचनया च रचिततिलकाः। हर्षचरित

मनःशिला और हरिताल प्राचीन भारतीय चिकित्साशास्त्र में प्रयुक्त होने वाले रसायन हैं जिनका प्रयोग तिलक करने के लिए भी होता था। कुमारसम्भव में यह वर्णन मिलता है कि मेना ने गीली हरताल और मैनसिल में अंगुलियाँ डुबो कर पार्वती के माथे पर तिलक कर दिया—

अथाङ्गुलिभ्यां हरितालमार्द्रं माङ्गल्यमादाय मनःशिलां च।
तमेव मेना दुहितुः कथंचिद् विवाहदीक्षातिलकं चकार।। कुमारसम्भव - 7. 23

दमयन्ती के लाल तिलक की प्रशंसा करते हुए श्रीहर्ष कहते हैं कि दमयन्ती के ललाट की सीमा पर आए घुंघराले काले बाल मैनसिल रूपी दीपक से उत्पन्न काजल के धुएँ की घुंघराली पंक्ति के समान सुशोभित हुए—

ललाटिकासीमनि चूर्णकुन्तला बभुः स्फुटं भीमनरेन्द्रजन्मनः।
मनःशिलाचित्रकदीपसम्भवा भ्रमीभृतः कज्जलधूमवल्लयः।। नैषधीयचरित - 15. 33

तिलक पर अभ्रक के चमकीले चूर्ण चिपकाने का वर्णन भी नैषधीयचरित में मिलता है जिसकी तुलना चमकदार बिन्दियों से की जा सकती है—

चन्द्राभमाभ्रं तिलकं दधाना तद्वन्निजास्येन्दुकृतानुबिम्बम्।
सखीमुखे चन्द्रमसे ससर्ज चन्द्रानवस्थामिव कापि यत्र।। नैषधीयचरित - 6. 62

शीतलता के लिए चन्दन का तिलक किया जाता था।—

पर्य्युषितधूसरचन्दनरसतिलकालंकृतललाटपट्टया। कादम्बरी-पत्रलेखावर्णन

3. नेत्रप्रसाधन

आँखों की सुरक्षा और सुन्दरता के लिए अंजन का प्रयोग प्राचीन ग्रन्थों में मिलता है। चरकसंहिता में प्रतिदिन अंजन लगाने का उपदेश किया गया है—

सौवीरमञ्जनं नित्यं हितमक्ष्णोः प्रयोजयेत्।
पञ्चरात्रेऽष्टरात्रे वा स्रावणार्थे रसाञ्जनम्।। चरकसंहिता-सूत्रस्थान -5.15

अंजन और सुरमा के प्रयोग के साक्ष्य सिन्धु सभ्यता में भी मिले हैं। सिन्धु सभ्यता के अवशेषों में सुरमादानी और शलाकाएँ मिली हैं। अंजन या सुरमा लगाने के लिए सोने, चाँदी, तांबा या लोहे की शलाकाएँ बनती थीं। अंगुली से भी शलाका का काम लिया जाता था। आयुर्वेदीय ग्रन्थों में पाँच प्रकार की चर्चा है— नीलांजन, रसांजन, पुष्पांजन, स्रोतांजन और सौवीरांजन।

अंजन लगाने का उल्लेख कुमारसम्भव में है—

विलोचनं दक्षिणमञ्जनेन सम्भाव्य तद्वञ्चितवामनेत्रा।
तथैव वातायनसन्निकर्षं ययौ शलाकामपरा वहन्ती।। कुमारसम्भव - 7.59

भगवान् शङ्कर ने अपने ललाट मे स्थित नेत्र की अग्नि में काजल बनाकर नवोत्पलसदृश आँखों वाली पार्वती की आँखों में काजल लगा दिया तथा अंगुली में लगे अंजन को पोंछने के लिए अंगुली को अपने नीले कण्ठ में रगड़ लिया—

भालेक्षणाग्नौ स्वयमञ्जनं स भङ्क्त्वा दृशोः साधु निवेश्य तस्याः।
नवोत्पलाक्ष्याः पुलकोपगूढे कण्ठे विनीलेऽङ्गुलिमुज्जघर्ष।। कुमारसम्भव - 9.26

अंजन के स्थान पर काजल लगाने की प्रथा भी है—

वाससितं स्वेदजलं कज्जलमलिनाश्रुवारिणा मिश्रम्।
कुचतटपतितं तस्याः प्रयागसम्भेदसलिलमनुकुरुते।। कुट्टिनीमत - 298

अर्थात् नायिका के गौरवर्ण शरीर से टपका श्वेत स्वेदजल आँखों में लगे काजल से मिलकर जब स्तनों के किनारे पर आकर मिलता है तब प्रयाग के गंगायमुना के संगम की सी शोभा प्रकट होती है। प्रसाधिकाओं द्वारा पार्वती की आँखों में काजल लगाए जाने का उल्लेख कुमारसम्भव में प्राप्त होता है—

तस्याः सुजातोत्पलपत्रकान्ते प्रसाधिकाभिर्नयने निरीक्ष्य।
न चक्षुषोः कान्तिविशेषबुद्ध्या कालाञ्जनं मङ्गलमित्युपात्तम्।। कुमारसम्भव - 7.20

दमयन्ती के अञ्जनाञ्चित नेत्रों की शोभा श्रीहर्ष ने इस शब्दों में व्यक्त की है—

नलिनं मलिनं विवृण्वती पृषतीमस्पृशति तदीक्षणे।
अपि खञ्जनमञ्जनाञ्चिते विदधाते रुचिगर्वदुर्विधम्।। नैषधीयचरित - 2.3

4. कपोलप्रसाधन

नायिका के कपोलों के सौन्दर्य की चर्चा करते संस्कृत कवि थकते नहीं। सौन्दर्य-निरूपण में महत्त्वपूर्ण भूमिका अदा करने वाले कपोल नायिका की विभिन्न भावभंगिमाओं के वाहक होते हैं।

कपोलों पर चित्रकर्म, पत्रभंग, लोध्ररज आदि का प्रयोग होता था। कपोलों पर चित्रकर्म के लिए तमालपत्र का प्रयोग होता था। अनुलेपन के लिए चंदन, कस्तूरी आदि का भी उपयोग होता था। कपोलों पर उसी प्रकार चित्रकर्म होता था। जिस प्रकार आजकल मेंहदी से हथेली पर चित्ररचना की जाती है। इस प्रकार की चित्र-विचित्र आकृतियों के चित्रण को मकरिका, नवमञ्जरी, वैशिषिका, तमालपत्र आदि नाम दिए गए थे। सौन्दरनन्द का यह श्लोक प्रासंगिक होगा—

पत्युस्ततो दर्पणसक्तपाणेर्मुहुर्मुहुर्वक्त्रमवेक्षमाणा।
तमालपत्रार्द्रतले कपोले समापयामास विशेषकं तत्।। सौन्दरनन्द - 4.20

लोध्र के फूलों के पराग कपोलों पर लगाए जाते थे। कुमारसम्भव में पार्वती के कपोलों पर लोध्रकाषाय लगाए जाने का उल्लेख है—

कर्णार्पितो लोध्रकषायरूक्षे गोरोचनाक्षेपनितान्तगौरे।
तस्याः कपोले परभागलाभाद् बबन्ध चक्षूंषि यवप्ररोहः।। कुमारसम्भव - 7.17

यह लोध्रपराग पांडुर वर्ण का होता है तथा पसीने को सुखाता है अतः इसका प्रयोग पाउडर की तरह होता था। लोध्र का एक नाम भिल्ल भी है। आचार्य सुश्रुत ने बतलाया है कि लोध्र के पानी से चेहरे को धोने से फोड़े, फुंसी रक्तपित्तजन्यरोग सद्यः विनष्ट होते हैं—

भिल्लोदककषायेण तथैवामलकस्य वा।
प्रक्षालयेन्मुखं नेत्रे स्वस्थः शीतोदकेन वा।।
नीलिकां मुखशोषं च पिडिकां व्यंगमेव च।
रक्तपित्तकृतान् रोगान् सद्य एव विनाशयेत्।।

सुश्रुतसंहिता-चिकित्सास्थान - 24.15-16

लोध्रपराग से नायिका के कपोलों को सजाना कवियों को अत्यन्त प्रिय था। माघकवि के काव्य की नायिका का यह सौन्दर्यवर्णन द्रष्टव्य है—

अधरेष्वलक्तकरसः सुदृशां विशदं कपोलभुवि लोध्ररजः।
नवमञ्जनं नयनपङ्कजयोः विभिदे न शङ्खनिहितात्पयसः।। शिशुपालवध - 8.46

मेघदूत में वर्णित अलकापुरी की स्त्रियाँ भी इससे अछूती न थीं—

नीता लोध्रप्रसवरजसा पाण्डुतामानने श्रीः। उत्तरमेघ - 2

5. ओष्ठप्रसाधन

शरीर के अंग प्रत्यंग के सौन्दर्य की चर्चा हो और ओठों की विवेचना न हो तो चर्चा अधूरी रह जाती है। नायिका के लाल होठों की तुलना पके हुए बिम्बफल से की जाती रही है। किसी चपल-चटुल नायक के शब्दों में नायिका के होठों की तरह लाल बिम्बफल को कुतरने का सौभाग्य भी शुकशावक को वर्षों की तपस्या से मिलता है।

शिखरिणि क्व नु नाम कियच्चिरं किमभिधानमसावकरोत्तपः।
सुमुखि येन तवाधरपाटलं दशति बिम्बफलं शुकशावकः।।

ध्वन्यालोक-प्रथम उद्योत

ओठों को लाल बनाने के लिए आलक्तक का प्रयोग होता था। ओठों पर मोम का प्रयोग होता था जिससे आलक्तक ठीक जमता था तथा ओठ चिकने होते थे—

वर्णविशेषापेक्षा प्रसाधने नो रतिप्रसङ्गेषु।
ओष्ठे मदनासङ्गो नो पुरुषविशेषसंभोगे।। कुट्टिनीमत - 310

यहाँ मोम के लिए श्लेषात्मक मदन शब्द का प्रयोग है। कुमारसम्भव में पार्वती के ओठों पर मोम लगाए जाने की चर्चा है।

रेखाविभक्तिः सुविभक्तगात्र्याः किञ्चिन्मधुच्छिष्टविमृष्टरागः।
कामप्यभिख्यां स्फुरितैरपुष्यदासन्नलावण्यफलोधरोष्ठः।। कुमारसम्भव - 7.18

दमयन्ती के ओठों की लाली को चमकाने के लिए भी मोम लगाया गया था—

निवेशितं यावकरागदीप्तये लगत्तदीयाधरसीम्नि सिक्थकम्।
रराज तत्तैन नितस्तुमुत्सुकं मधूनि निर्धूंग सुधाराधर्गिणि।। नैषधीयचरित 15.43

ओठों पर महावर लगाकर लोध्र का चूर्ण छिड़कने की चर्चा भी यत्र तत्र मिलती है। ओष्ठप्रसाधन की ये विधियाँ होठों के सौन्दर्य और स्वास्थ्य को ध्यान में रखकर बनाई गई है।

6. श्रोत्रप्रसाधन

कानों के मण्डनार्थ उसमें शिरीष के फूल, अशोक के पल्लव आदि लगाए जाते थे। नवकदम्ब के कर्णपूर बनाए जाने का उल्लेख भी मिलता है। यथा अभिज्ञानशाकुन्तल में—

कृतं न कर्णार्पितबन्धनं सखे शिरीषमागण्डविलम्बिकेसरम्। अभिज्ञानशाकुन्तल - 6.18

शैवालमञ्जरी से कानों को सजाने की चर्चा कादम्बरी में है—

अपहृताशेषशिरीषसौभाग्याभिः शैवालमञ्जरीभिः कृतकर्णपूरम्।

कादम्बरी-चन्द्रापीडवर्णन

अशोक के पल्लवों के कर्णपूर की चर्चा भी कादम्बरी में है—

लोहितायमानं कर्णपूराशोकपल्लवैः। कादम्बरी-कादम्बरीवर्णन

कालिदास ने नवकदम्ब, कर्णिकार तथा शिरीष आदि फूलों को कर्णाभरण के रूप में प्रयोग किया है—

विकचनवकदम्बैः कर्णपूरं वधूनां रचयति जलदौघः कान्तवत्काल एषः।

ऋतुसंहार - 2.25

कर्णेषु योग्यं नवकर्णिकारं चलेषु नीलेष्वलकेष्वशोकम्। ऋतुसंहार - 66

अलका की सुन्दरियों के कानों में सुशोभित शिरीष की यह चर्चा भी प्रासंगिक है—

चूडापाशे नवकुरबकं चारुकर्णे शिरीषम्। उत्तरमेघ - 2

कानों को सुसज्जित करने वाले ये विभिन्न फूल आज सोने चाँदी के फूलों का रूप ले चुके हैं।

7. स्तनप्रसाधन

स्तनों पर विभिन्न प्रकार के चित्रकर्म, पत्रभंग आदि बनाए जाते थे। केसर, कस्तूरी, चंदन आदि सुगंधित द्रव्यों का लेप स्तनों पर किया जाता था। कालिदास को स्तनों की सज्जा के लिए चन्दन और हार बहुत प्रिय है—

हारैः सचन्दनरसैः स्तनमण्डलानि . . . । ऋतुसंहार - 3. 20

सचन्दनाम्बुव्यजनोद्भवानिलैः सहारयष्टिस्तनमण्डलार्पणैः। ऋतुसंहार - 1. 2

चन्दन का लेप स्तनसज्जा का प्रमुख अंग था—

निश्शेषश्च्युतचन्दनस्तनतटं निर्मृष्टरागोधरः। काव्यप्रकाश-प्रथमोल्लास

कपोलों की तरह स्तनों पर भी पत्तों को काटकर लगाया जाता था। विभिन्न प्रकार के लेप ऋतुओं के अनुसार लगाए जाते थे। वसन्तकाल में प्रियंगु, कालीयक, कुंकुम के पत्रलेखों के साथ कस्तूरमिश्रित चन्दन से आर्द्र हार विलासिनियों के गौर स्तनों की शोभा बनाते हैं—

प्रियंगुकालीयककुंकुमाक्तं स्तनेषु गौरेषु विलासिनीभिः।
आलिप्यते चन्दनमङ्गनाभिर्मदालसाभिर्मृगनाभियुक्तम्।। ऋतुसंहार - 6.14

स्तनेषु हाराः सितचन्दनार्द्रा भुजेषु सङ्गं वलयाङ्गदानि। ऋतुसंहार - 6.7

स्तनों पर पत्रभंग रचना का उल्लेख कादम्बरी में मिलता है—

कामिनीकुचपत्रभंगेषु वक्रता। कादम्बरी-तारापीडवर्णन

हरिण इव हरिणलाञ्छने न लिखितो गुरुपत्रभंगः पयोधरभारि।

कादम्बरी-विलासवतीवर्णन

निपुणिके! लिख मणिशालभञ्जिकास्तनेषु कुंकुमरसपत्रभंगान्। कादम्बरी

कपोलों की तरह स्तनों पर किए गए चित्रकर्म को मकरिका कहते थे। नैषधीयचरित में ऐसे चित्रकर्म का वर्णन

मिलता है—

आलिख्य सख्याः कुचपत्रभङ्गीमध्ये सुमध्या मकरीं करेण।
यत्रालपत्तामियमालि! यानं मन्ये त्वदेकावलिनाकनद्याः।। नैषधीयचरित - 6.69

8. पादप्रसाधन

मेघदूत की **लाक्षारागं चरणकमलन्यासयोग्यां** पंक्ति से मालूम होता है कि पैरों के मण्डन के लिए आलक्तक या महावर का प्रयोग किया जाता था। पैरों को रंगने की यह प्रथा अति प्राचीन है। कुमारसम्भव का प्रसंग है कि एक स्त्री अपने पैरों में महावर लगवा रही थी। शिवजी की बारात देखने की उत्सुकता से वह उसे बीच में ही छोड़कर महावर लगे गीले पैरों से छाप बनाती हुई दौड़ पड़ी—

प्रसाधिकालम्बितमग्रपादमाक्षिप्य काचिद् द्रवरागमेव।
उत्सृष्टलीलागतिरागवाक्षादलक्तकाङ्कां पदवीं ततान।। कुमारसम्भव - 7.58

भारवि ने भी नर्तकियों के मन के अनुराग की तुलना आलक्तक के लाल रंग से की है—

अविरलमलसेषु नर्तकीनां द्रुतपरिषिक्तमलक्तकं पदेषु।
स वपुषमिव चित्तरागमूहर्नमितशिखानि कदम्बकेसराणि।। किरातार्जुनीय - 10.43

महावर से चाण्डालकन्या के चरण ऐसे लाल हो गए थे मानों महिषासुर के ताजे रक्त की लालिमा हो और चाण्डलकन्या दुर्गा की तरह लग रही थी—

अतिबहलपिण्डालक्तकरसरागपल्लवितपादपङ्कजाम् अचिरमृदितमहिषासुर-
रुधिररसचरणामिव कात्यायनीम्। कादम्बरी-चाण्डालकन्यावर्णन

कालिदास ने ऋतुसंहार में अलक्तकयुक्त चरणकमलों की शोभा का वर्णन इस प्रकार किया है—

नितान्तलाक्षारसरागरञ्जितैः नितम्बिनीनां चरणैः सनूपुरैः।
पदे पदे हंसरुतानुकारिभिः जनस्य चित्तं क्रियते समन्मथम्।। ऋतुसंहार - 1. 5

शकुन्तला की विदाई के अवसर पर आश्रम के पेड़ पौधों ने जो उपहार दिए उनमें चरणोपभोगसुलभ लाक्षारस भी एक था—

निष्ठ्यूतश्चरणोपभोगसुलभो लाक्षारसः केनचित्। अभिज्ञानशाकुन्तल - 4.5

पैरों के प्रसाधनार्थ आलक्तक या महावर को महत्त्व दिया जाता था क्योंकि इससे रंगे पैरों के लाल तलुवे ही प्रशंसा के योग्य माने जाते हैं। आज भी जिस प्रकार पश्चिम भारत में मेंहदी का अधिकाधिक प्रचलन है उसी प्रकार पूर्व में महावर का प्रचलन है।

9. अङ्गराग

अङ्गराग स्नान के पश्चात् शरीर पर सुगंधित द्रव्यों का लेप है। स्नान के अनन्तर सुगन्धित क्रीम, पाउडर आदि

लगाने को इस अंगराग का आधुनिक स्वरूप मान सकते हैं। अंगराग के लिए कस्तूरी, चंदन, कुंकुम, गोरोचन आदि का प्रयोग होता था। कालिदास ग्रीष्म ऋतु में चन्दन के प्रयोग की खूब चर्चा करते हैं।

निशाः शशाङ्कक्षतनीलराजयः क्वचिद्विचित्रं जलयन्त्रमन्दिरम्।
मणिप्रकाराः सरसं सचन्दनं शुचौ प्रिये यान्ति जनस्य सेव्यताम्।।

ऋतुसंहार - 1.2

पयोधरों पर चन्दन-लेप का उल्लेख कई स्थानों पर मिलता है। कालिदास को भी 'पयोधराश्चन्दनपङ्कचर्चिता:' अतिप्रिय हैं।

चन्दन के साथ कपूर के मिश्रण के लेप की चर्चा नैषधीयचरित में मिलती है—

मृषाविषादाभिनयादयं क्वचिज्जुगोप निःश्वासततिं वियोगजाम्।
विलेपनस्याधिकचन्द्रभागताविभावनाच्चापललाप पाण्डुताम्।।

नैषधीयचरित - 1.51

जैसे-जैसे वातावरण में शैत्य बढ़ता है और गर्मी कम होती जाती है वैसे-वैसे कालागुरु और कस्तूरी का प्रयोग बढ़ता जाता है—

गात्राणि कालीयकचर्चितानि सपत्रलेखानि मुखाम्बुजानि।
शिरांसि कालागुरुधूपितानि कुर्वन्ति नार्यः सुरतोत्सवाय।। ऋतुसंहार - 4.5

जब वसन्तकाल में सर्दी और गर्मी का मिश्रित मौसम आ जाता है तो प्रियंगु, कालीयक, कुंकुम के साथ मृगनाभि अर्थात् कस्तूरी और चन्दन का प्रयोग स्तनों पर किया जाता है—

प्रियंगुकालीयककुंकुमाक्तं स्तनेषु गौरेषु विलासिनीभिः।
आलिप्यते चन्दनमङ्गनाभिर्मदालसाभिर्मृगनाभियुक्तम्।। ऋतुसंहार - 6.14

अंगराग या सुगन्धित द्रव्यों का लेप भारतीय परम्परा में स्वस्थ जीवन की पहचान है। आचार्य चरक ने गंधमाल्य के प्रयोग को पुष्टिप्रद, बलवर्द्धक, आयु बढ़ाने वाला तथा चित्त प्रसन्न करने वाला बतलाया है—

वृष्यं सौगन्ध्यमायुष्यं काम्यं पुष्टिबलप्रदम्।
सौमनस्यमलक्ष्मीघ्नं गन्धमाल्यनिषेवणम्।। चरकसंहिता-सूत्रस्थान - 5.93

इन शारीरिक प्रसाधनों के अतिरिक्त कई अन्य प्रसाधन भी किए जाते थे जिनमें स्नानविषयक प्रसाधन, अभ्यंग, वर्णप्रसाधन, भ्रुवों का प्रसाधन आदि अनेक प्रकार मुख्य रूप से उल्लेख्य हैं।

प्राचीन भारतीय साहित्य में वर्णित प्रसाधन या अलंकरण का उद्देश्य मात्र विलासिता या आकर्षण नहीं था। ये प्रसाधन मांगल्य के सूचक, सौन्दर्यवर्धक, स्वास्थ्यप्रद तथा भारत की पारम्परिक कला के वाहक थे। आधुनिक काल में प्रसाधन की सामग्री, प्रसाधन की विधियों का जितना विकास हुआ है उतनी ही विकृति भी इसमें आ गई है। पाश्चात्य

प्रसाधनों के अन्धानुकरण से स्वास्थ्य पर प्रतिकूल प्रभाव पड़ने लगा है। भारतीय चिन्तकों ने प्रसाधनों के प्रयोग में कई बातों पर बल दिया है यथा-देश तथा काल के अनुरूप प्रसाधन का प्रयोग। शरीर के सौन्दर्यवर्धन के लिए किए जाने वाले ये प्रसाधन भारतीय औषधीय परम्परा से संबंध रखते हैं अतः सर्वथा निर्दुष्ट और स्वास्थ्यप्रद हैं। इन प्राचीन भारतीय प्रसाधनों की एक और विशेषता यह है कि इनमें कृत्रिमता नहीं है। इनका प्रकृतिप्रदत्त होना एक विशिष्ट गुण है जो स्वास्थ्य की दृष्टि से सर्वथा उपयुक्त है। उस समय प्रसाधन की वस्तुएँ सर्वजनसुलभ थीं। आधुनिक प्रसाधन तो धनवानों की चहारदीवारी तक सीमित है। आधुनिक प्रसाधनिक द्रव्यों की कई खामियाँ उसकी विकृति का कारण है। इनमें रासायनिकता का पुट अधिक होता है अतः कभी-कभी उनके दीर्घकालीन प्रयोग से त्वचा की विवर्णता तथा अन्य विकृतियाँ आ जाती हैं।

आधुनिक प्रसाधन के द्रव्यों से होने वाली हानियों को देखते हुए अब प्रसाधन के प्रयोग आयुर्वेदीय तथा प्राचीन भारतीय शास्त्रीय योगों की ओर मुड़ रहे हैं। विभिन्न औषधीय पादपों द्रव्यों के महत्त्वपूर्ण गुणधर्म से परिचित होने के बाद पाश्चात्य देश इन पर कब्जा जमाने के लिए पेटेंट कानून का रास्ता अख्तियार कर रहे हैं पर सत्य तो यह है कि ये महत्त्वपूर्ण प्राकृतिक प्रसाधनिक द्रव्य सदियों से हमारी संस्कृति में रचे-बसे हैं तथा उसका अभिन्न अंग हैं।

卐 卐 卐

Section VI

FLORA IN VEDIC EPIC & PURĀṆIC LITERATURE

वेदपुराणामृतनिर्झरी

पुष्करश्री

पुष् · पुष्प · पुष्कर
(वैदिकवाङ्मय के सन्दर्भ में)

प्रवेश सक्सेना

पुष्,[1] पुष्प और पुष्कर तीनों में 'पुष्' है (अंग्रेजी का पुश (Push) नहीं।) पुष् धातु है जिसका अर्थ होता है पोषण करना, पालना, पोसना। इससे पुष्ट, पुष्टि, पुष्टिककर्म पुष्टिवर्धन जैसे वैदिक शब्द सिद्ध होते हैं। पुष् से ही बनता है 'पुष्कर'।[2] पर पुष्प बनता है पुष्प् धातु (अच् के साथ) से जिसका अर्थ होता है विकसना, खिलना। वनस्पतियों की बात जब की जाती है तो उनका सर्वाधिक आकर्षक व सुन्दर अङ्ग 'पुष्प' ही होता है। 'पुष्प' एक ओर वृक्ष या लता की जीवन्तता का प्रतीक होता है तो दूसरी ओर 'फल' की आशा का रूप होता है। हर स्थान, हर देश की वनस्पतियाँ, वृक्ष, लताएं, पुष्प अलग-अलग प्रकार के होते हैं क्योंकि उनका जीवन स्थान-विशेष या देश-विशेष की जलवायु पर निर्भर करता है इसलिए हर स्थान, हर देश के वाङ्मय में स्थानीय वृक्षों, लताओं, फूलों व फलों का वर्णन प्रायः मिल जाता है। जब वैदिक वाङ्मय की वनस्पतियों (Flora) की बात आती है तो ओषधियों, वृक्षों, लताओं की प्रचुरता तो दिखाई पड़ती है पर पुष्प 'नामों' का उल्लेख नहीं के बराबर है। यहाँ तक कि स्वयं 'पुष्प'[3] शब्द भी कुछ गिनती के स्थानों में ही प्रयुक्त हुआ है। अथर्ववेद (19.44.5) में 'पुष्प' का एक सुन्दर प्रयोग मिलता है दिव्य अञ्जन रूपी भैषज को सम्बोधित करते हुए कहा गया है—

सिन्धोगर्भोऽसि विद्युतां पुष्पम्।

तू सिन्धु का गर्भ है और बिजलियों का फूल है।[4] अर्थात् नदियों की स्यन्दनशक्ति तथा विद्युत् का तेज तुझमें है। पुष्प के अतिरिक्त उसके अन्य पर्याय जैसे कुसुम, प्रसून सुम, सून, सुमन आदि भी वैदिक वाङ्मय में अनुपस्थित हैं। लौकिक साहित्य में प्रकृतिवर्णनों में जो पुष्पों की समृद्धि तथा विविधवर्णी फूलों का सुकुमार कोमल संसार दृष्टिगोचर होता है उसका नामो-निशान यहाँ नहीं है। यद्यपि फूलों से परिचित तो वैदिक ऋषि हैं क्योंकि ऋग्वेद (X. 97.15) में फूल रहित और फूलों वाली वनस्पतियों का उल्लेख हुआ है।

अपुष्पा याश्च पुष्पिणीः।[5]
ताः बृहस्पति प्रसूताः
ने! मुञ्चत्वंहसः।।

इसी प्रकार अथर्ववेद में घर के आगे पीछे दूर्वा के उद्यान तथा फूलों की बात आई है—

आयने ते परायणे दूर्वा रोहन्तु पुष्पिणीः।।[6]

यहाँ 'फूलों वाली दूब' अर्थ लिया है ग्रिफिथ ने— Dūrva grass-'Panjcum Da Clylon' a creaping grass with flower bearing branches erect. By far the most common and useful grass in India. It grows everywhere abundantly and flowers all the year.[7]

पुष्पों की यह अनुपस्थिति कुछ आश्चर्यजनक लगती है क्योंकि वैदिक ऋषि अन्यथा प्रकृति के सभी तत्त्वों, उपादानों से परिचित ही नहीं उनके प्रति 'देवताभाव' भी रखता है। सूर्य, पवन, धरती, आकाश, नदियाँ सभी तो उसकी सौन्दर्यानुभूति का अङ्ग बने हैं तथा सूक्तों में उनकी प्रशंसाएं अभिव्यक्त हुई हैं। इस अभाव के कारण अनुमानित ही किए जा सकते हैं—

1. वैदिक ऋषि सम्भवतः सौन्दर्यबोध से अधिक महत्त्व उपयोगिता को देते हैं तभी वनस्पतियों और औषधियों का प्रचुरता से वर्णन करते हैं। फूलों वाली और फूलों से रहित, फलवाली और फलरहित औषधियाँ वर्णित हुई हैं परन्तु उनकी दृष्टि फूलों के सौन्दर्यमात्र पर अटकी नहीं रह सकी है। वनस्पतियों के औषधिपरक गुणों पर ही उनका ध्यान अधिक रहा है।
2. लौकिक संस्कृत साहित्य में जो पुष्प-समृद्धि, पुष्पों की विविधता मिलती है उस काल में हो सकता है वे 'फूल' उगाए ही न जाते हों।

   वैदिक संस्कृति मूलरूप से अरण्य संस्कृति है जहाँ स्वयं उग जाने वाली वनस्पतियों और औषधियों की प्रचुरता है। 'उपवन-विकास' की सम्भावनाएँ वहाँ नहीं थीं।
3. वैदिक आर्य जिस प्रदेश के वासी रहे हों वहाँ वैसे फूलों के पाए जाने की सम्भावना न रही हो जैसे बाद के साहित्य में वर्णित है। उस स्थान व समय की जलवायु भी उसके अनुकूल नहीं रही हो। पर जो भी हो वैदिक वाङ्मय में जिस पुष्प का वर्णन हुआ है वह पुष्पराज 'कमल' है जो लताओं पर नहीं आता, जल में उगता, विकसता है। 'कमल' के पर्याय 'पुण्डरीक' और 'पुष्कर' ही एकाधिक बार वर्णित हुए हैं। 'कमल' के अतिरिक्त एक स्थान पर 'पलाश किंशुक' का वर्णन हुआ है जहाँ पतिगृह जाते समय सूर्य की बैलगाड़ी को पलाश के लाल फूलों से सजाया गया वर्णित किया है—

सकिंशुकं शाल्मलिं विश्वरूपं हिरण्यवर्णं सुवृतं सुचक्रम्।
आ रोह सूर्ये अमृतस्थलोकं स्योनं पत्ये वहतुं कृणुष्वा।।[8]

अर्थात् किंशुकों (फूलों) से युक्त शाल्मलि की लकड़ी से बने रथ पर वधू चढ़े।

इस वर्णन के अतिरिक्त बस 'पुष्कर' है जो सर्वाधिक बार वर्णित हुआ है। 'कमल' नाम केवल एक स्थान पर आया है जहाँ गर्भ-द्वार रूपी कमल का उल्लेख हुआ है—'तमोषधे त्वं नाशयस्याः कमलमञ्जिवम्'[9] तैत्तिरीयसंहिता (7.3.18) में 'कमलाय' उल्लिखित हुआ है। इन उद्धरणों के अतिरिक्त 'कमल' के 'पुष्कर' और 'पुण्डरीक' पर्याय प्रयुक्त हुए हैं। पुण्डरीक 'श्वेत कमल' का प्रसिद्ध नाम है। यह सम्भवतया पुंड्र (श्वेत) से बना है अथवा अन्य पुष्पों का गर्व चूर्ण करने वाला होने से कमल का पर्याय बना है। श्वेत कमलों अर्थात् पुण्डरीकों से परिपूर्ण सरसियों या तालाबों का वर्णन ऋग्वेद में एक स्थान पर हुआ है जो वैदिक ऋषि के सौन्दर्य-बोध को उद्घाटित करता है—

आयने ते परायणे दूर्वा रोहन्तु पुष्पिणीः।[10]
ह्रदाश्च पुण्डरीकाणि समुद्रस्य गृहा इमे।।

अर्थात् हे अग्ने (परमात्मन्)! तेरे आगमन पर व जाने पर हमारी इस निवासभूमि में पुष्पवाली लताएं और दूबें उगें। उसमें नाना जलाशय हों जिनमें कमल हों। समुद्र के इस प्रदेश में हमारे निवास स्थान हों (जिससे हम दाह को न प्राप्त हों)। अथर्ववेद (6.106.1) में घर की काम्यशोभा का वर्णन करते हुए कहा गया है—

आयने ते परायणे दूर्वा रोहन्तु पुष्पिणीः।
उत्सो वा तत्र जायतां ह्रदो वा पुण्डरीकवान्।।

अर्थात् घर के आगे-पीछे दूर्वा का उद्यान हो। उसमें बहुत प्रकार के फूल उत्पन्न हों, वहाँ पानी का हौद हो, कमलों वाला तालाब हो। ग्रिफिथ ने 'ह्रदो वा पुण्डरीकवान्', का अनुवाद किया है 'lake with blooming lotuses'। इन दोनों उदाहरणों से प्रतीत होता है कि वैदिक युग में उपवनों में पुष्पवाले वृक्ष लगाने की परम्परा भले ही न रही हो परन्तु तालाबों में कमल उगाने की परम्परा जरूर रही होगी। 'वास्तु' को, 'घर' को सौन्दर्यशाली बनाने के लिए दूब तो लगाई ही जाती थी, कमल भी जल में रोपित किए जाते थे। पुण्डरीकों अर्थात् श्वेतकमलों का उल्लेख ब्राह्मणग्रन्थों में भी हुआ है।[11] ऐतरेय आरण्यक[12] में भी एक बार 'पुण्डरीक' उल्लिखित हुआ है। उपनिषदों में भी 'पुण्डरीक' का प्रयोग दार्शनिक भावनाओं को अभिव्यक्त करने के लिए हुआ है—'**यथा पुण्डरीकम्**'[13] जिसे शांकरभष्य में वर्णित किया गया है

यथा पुण्डरीकं शुक्लं तद्वदपि च वासनारूपं कस्यचिद्भवति।[14]

अर्थात् और जिस तरह पुण्डरीक (श्वेतकमल) सफेद रंग का होता है, उस प्रकार भी किसी की वासनाओं का रूप होता है। 'यही नहीं एक और स्थान पर सूर्य को दिशाओं का पुण्डरीक ('श्वेतकमल') कहकर नमस्कार किया गया है तथा स्वयं मनुष्यों में 'पुण्डरीक' बनने की बात कही गई है—

प्रातरादित्यमुपतिष्ठते दिशामेकपुण्डरीकमस्यहं
मनुष्याणामेकपुण्डरीकं भूयासमिति।[15]

छान्दोग्योपनिषद् (1.6.7) में पुरुष के नेत्रों को 'पुण्डरीक' से उपमित किया गया है पर उन्हें कवि के बैठने के स्थान (कप्यास अर्थात् गुदा) की तरह लाल बताया गया है। इस प्रकार यहाँ 'पुण्डरीक' अपने मूलार्थ श्वेतकमल से भिन्न 'लाल कमल' को अभिव्यक्त करता है। पञ्चविंशब्राह्मण (18.9.6) में 'पुण्डरीक' को नक्षत्रों के प्रकाश से उत्पन्न बताया गया है जो इस पुष्प के दिव्यमूल की ओर सङ्केत करता है। अथर्ववेद में एक स्थान पर मानवहृदय की तुलना 'पुण्डरीक' से की गई है—

पुण्डरीकं नवद्वारं त्रिभिर्गुणैरभिरावृतम्।
तस्मिन्यद्यक्षमात्मन्वत्तद्वै ब्रह्मविदो विदुः।। अथर्ववेद - 10.8.43

नवद्वार वाला कमल तीन गुणों से घिरा हुआ है। उसमें जो आत्मा वाला पूज्य देव है उसे ब्रह्मज्ञानी जानते हैं। मैक्डानल एवं कीथ ने 'वैदिक इण्डेक्स ऑफ नेम्स एण्ड सब्जेक्ट्स' (पृ० 536) में 'पुण्डरीक' को मानव-हृदय से उपमित माना है जिसमें 'आत्मा' निवास करती है। अन्य विद्वान् नवद्वार वाला शरीर मानते हैं। एक स्थान पर कमल पत्र की माला का भी उल्लेख हुआ है।[16]

इस प्रकार से 'पुण्डरीक' श्वेतकमल वैदिक वाङ्मय में एक ओर तालाबों में विकसित होकर घर की शोभा बढ़ाता था तो दूसरी ओर सूर्य का, हृदय का उपमान भी था। पुण्डरीक अर्थात् कमलवत् जीवन जीने का प्रतीक भी था (उपनिषद् में)।

'पुष्कर' जैसा कि प्रारम्भ में कहा जा चुका है पुष्टि अर्थ वाली धातु से बना शब्द है जो 'कमल' का पर्याय तो है ही अन्य अर्थों में भी प्रयुक्त हुआ है। वैदिक वाङ्मय में 'पुष्कर' से बने शब्द पुष्करिणी, पुष्करसृज्, पुष्करसाद आदि भी प्रयुक्त हुए हैं। सर्वप्रथम ऋग्वेद में 'पुष्कर' शब्द आया है जो 'नील कमल' का नाम है—

त्वामग्ने पुष्करादध्यथर्वा निरमन्थत
मूर्ध्नो विश्वस्य वाधतः।। ऋग्वेद - 6.16.13

अर्थात् हे अग्ने! तुझे आधार देने वाले सब विश्व के मुख्य स्थान रूप 'पुष्करपत्र' के ऊपर अथर्वा ने मन्थन करके उत्पन्न किया था।' यहाँ सातवलेकर के अनुसार सिर में स्थित सहस्रार कमल की ओर सङ्केत है जो सब शरीर का आधार है परन्तु ग्रिफिथ ने इस मन्त्र का अर्थ यों किया है—

'Agni, Atharvan brought thee forth, by rubbing, from the flower lotus. The head of viśva of the priest.' उनके अनुसार यहाँ 'पुष्कर' अर्थात् द्यौ का आलङ्कारिक रूप में वर्णन है। वैसे भी निरुक्त में 'पुष्कर' जल के नामों में से एक है। अतः 'पुष्कर' अर्थात् अन्तरिक्ष स्थित जलों में से विद्युत्-अग्नि की उत्पत्ति को भी दर्शा सकता है। ऋग्वेद के ही एक अन्य मन्त्र में 'पुष्कर' का प्रयोग हुआ है—

ब्रह्मणा दैव्येन विश्वे देवाः
पुष्करे त्वाददन्त।। ऋग्वेद - 7.33.11

अर्थात् हे वसिष्ठ, तुझे दिव्य मन्त्रों के साथ विश्वेदेवों ने तुझे 'पुष्कर' में धारण किया। ग्रिफिथ ने इस मन्त्रांश का अनुवाद इस प्रकार किया है—

'All the gods laid thee on a lotus blossom.'

यह मन्त्र बाद की उन पौराणिक गाथाओं का आधार माना जा सकता है जिनमें कमल से देवोत्पत्ति बताई गई है जैसे ब्रह्मा को नाभिकमल से उद्भूत बताया जाता है तथा 'पद्मनाभ' कहा गया है। 'पुष्कर' का उपर्युक्त मन्त्र में एक अर्थ 'जलकुम्भ' या 'यज्ञ-कलश' भी किया गया है जिसका प्रयोग यज्ञ में किया जाता था। विल्सन व सायण ने 'पुष्कर' का अर्थ 'तालाब' लिया है। पाश्चात्य विद्वान् उस यज्ञपात्र को 'पुष्कर' मानते हैं जिसमें यज्ञ का स्रुवा पड़ा रहता है। अथर्ववेद में ओदन का महत्त्व बताते हुए कहा गया है—'पुष्करमस्य गन्धः'।

अर्थात्—'पुष्कर इसका गन्ध है'। कहने का भाव यही जान पड़ता है कि 'अन्न' की गन्ध 'पुष्कर' या नील-कमल की गन्ध की तरह होती है। सुगन्धित अन्न पुष्टिकारक होता है। स्वाद-रस के साथ-साथ अन्न की 'गन्ध' भी मनुष्य को आकर्षित करती है। अथर्ववेद के एक अन्य मन्त्र में पृथिवी की गन्ध को कमल में आविष्ट हुआ बताया है—

यस्ते गन्धः पुष्करमाविवेश यं संजभ्रुः सूर्याया विवाहे।
अमर्त्याः पृथिवि गन्धमग्रे तेन मा सुरभिं कृणुमानो द्विक्षत कश्चन।[17]

अर्थात् हे पृथिवी! जो तुम्हारी गन्ध कमल में प्रविष्ट हुई है पहले जिस गन्ध को वायु आदि देवता उषा के विवाह के समय (सूर्योदयकाल में) धारण करते हैं, उस सुगन्धि से हमें सुगन्धित करो। कोई भी हम लोगों से द्वेष न करे। पृथिवी की विशेषता है गन्ध। यही गन्ध वनस्पतियों में, औषधियों तथा फूलों में पाई जाती है। यहाँ कमल में स्थित गन्ध को पृथिवी की गन्ध बताया गया है। लौकिक साहित्य में सूर्य द्वारा कमल के विकसित होने की बात का उल्लेख बहुधा होता है। यहाँ भी उषाकाल में कमल के विकसने तथा वायु द्वारा उस गन्ध को धारण करने का तथ्य बताया गया है। पुष्प में आबद्ध गन्ध को गन्धवाही पवन ही दूर-दूर तक पहुँचाता है। सुगन्ध की विशेषता होती है वह मन को प्रसन्न करती है तभी 'गन्ध' का प्रयोग शृङ्गार के रूप में, औषध के रूप में सदा से होता आया है। आज भी अरोमा थेरेपी द्वारा चिकित्सा की जाती है। यहाँ भी द्वेष व द्रोह-राहित्य के लिए 'पुष्करगन्ध' की बात कही गई है।

यजुर्वेद में भी 'पुष्कर' का प्रयोग एक बार हुआ है—

अपां पृष्ठमसि योनिरग्नेः समुद्रमभितः पिन्वमानम्।
वर्धमानो महा ँ आ च पुष्करे दिवो मात्रया वरिम्णा प्रथस्व।।[18]

अर्थात् तुम जलों के ऊपर रहने वाले हो और अग्नि के उत्पन्नकर्ता हो। तुम समुद्र को बढ़ाते हो, सब ओर वृद्धि को प्राप्त होते हुए बड़े जल में (महान् पुष्करे) सब प्रकार स्थित हो और द्युलोक की तेज शक्ति से और पृथ्वी की विशालता से चारों ओर विस्तृत हो। यहाँ निरुक्त (5.14) के आधार पर 'पुष्कर' का अर्थ जल ही गृहीत हुआ है। 'पुष्कर' पुष्प का अर्थ यहाँ संगत भी नहीं जान पड़ता।

जो भी हो 'पुष्कर' अर्थात् कमल के प्रति रुचि इस बात से अभिव्यक्त होती है कि यहाँ ऐसे तालाबों का वर्णन है जहाँ 'पुष्कर' पैदा होते थे। ऐसे तालाबों को 'पुष्करिणी' कहा जाता था। स्वभावतः पुष्करिणियों के आस-पास का वातावरण मनमोहक व आकर्षक होता था। कई बार ऐसे वर्णन मिलते हैं—

यथा वातः पुष्करिणी समीङ्गयति सर्वतः (ऋग्वेद - 10.78.7)

अर्थात् जैसे वायु पुष्करयुक्त तालाबों को चारों ओर से हिलाता है। ऋग्वेद के ही एक और मन्त्र में दाता के घर को पुष्करिणी की तरह सुसज्जित बताया गया है—

भोजस्य इदं वेश्म पुष्करिणी इव परिष्कृतम्। ऋग्वेद - 10.107.10

अथर्ववेद के 4.34 सूक्त के 5-6-7 मन्त्रों की टेक ही है—

उप त्वा तिष्ठन्तु पुष्करिणीः समन्ताः।

अर्थात् तुम्हारे चारों तरफ 'पुष्करिणियाँ' विद्यमान रहें। स्वर्ग का वर्णन करते हुए ये कामनाएँ की गई हैं। ग्रिफिथ ने इस पंक्ति का अनुवाद इस प्रकार किया हैं— Whole lakes with lotus-blossom shall approach thee'.

अथर्ववेद के इन मन्त्रों में 4.34.5 मन्त्र महत्त्वपूर्ण है क्योंकि इसमें 'कुमुद' नामक फूल का वर्णन है तथा उसके बिस या तन्तु तथा कन्द का भी वर्णन है—

आण्डीकं कुमुदं सं तनोति बिसं शालूकं शफको मुलाली।

अण्डे के समान बढ़ने वाले आनन्ददायक कमलकन्द के समान बढ़ने वाले को ठीक तरह फैलाता है। ग्रिफिथ ने इसका अनुवाद यों किया हैं— The oval-fruited lotus spreads his fibre, there bloom the nenuphar and water-lilies.

ग्रिफिथ के अनुसार आण्डीकम् अण्डे के आकार के फल या वल्ब वाला कोई दूसरा जल का पौधा भी हो सकता है। कुमुद या तो श्वेतकमल है अथवा लाल कमल जिसका फल खाने योग्य होता है। शालूकं, शफक और मुलाली कुछ अपरिचित, जल में होने वाले पौधे हो सकते हैं अथवा कमल के ही अन्य भेद। लौकिक संस्कृत में 'कुमुद' को सूर्योदय के समय नहीं 'चन्द्रोदय' के काल में विकसित होने वाला माना गया है।

अथर्ववेद में ही एक और स्थान पर 'पुष्कर' के विषय में कहा गया है कि जिस देश में जाने या अनजाने ब्राह्मणी का अपहरण होता है, वहाँ कमल वाले तालाब नहीं होते और कमलों के बीज तथा बीज वाले बिस या मृणाल नहीं होते—

नास्य क्षेत्र पुष्करिणी नाण्डीकं जायते बिसम्।[19]
यस्मिन्राष्ट्रे निरुध्यते ब्रह्मजायाचित्त्या।। अथर्ववेद - 5.17.16

इस मन्त्र से एक ओर ब्राह्मणस्त्री या विदुषीस्त्री का महत्त्व स्थापित होता है क्योंकि उसके अपमान के फलस्वरूप कमलयुक्त तालाब विकसित नहीं होते, दूसरी 'कमल' एक पवित्र पुष्प के रूप में स्थापित होता है क्योंकि जहाँ पुण्यकार्य होते हैं वहीं पुष्कर खिलते हैं।

पुण्यता, पवित्रता एवं सुन्दरता तथा मधुरगन्ध के कारण ही व्यक्तित्व की साजसज्जा के रूप में 'पुष्करों' का प्रयोग होता था। 'पुण्डरीक माला' का उल्लेख पूर्व में किया जा चुका है। ऋग्वेद में अश्विनौ को 'पुष्करस्त्रज'– कमल माला से सुसज्जित विशेषण मिला है–

गर्भं ते अश्विनौ देवा वा धत्तां पुष्करस्त्रजा।[20]

अर्थात् कमल माला धारण करने वाले अश्विदेव, तेरे गर्भ का धारण करे। अथर्ववेद[21] में अश्विनौ के सम्बन्ध में कहा गया है–

तावन्मे अश्विना वर्च आ धत्तं पुष्करस्त्रजौ

अर्थात् कमलमाला धारण करने वाले अश्वि देव उतना तेज मेरे लिए धारण करो। अश्वि देवों का प्रातःकाल से घनिष्ठ सम्बन्ध वेदों में अभिव्यक्त हुआ है। तभी प्रातःकाल विकसित होने वाले कमल पुष्पों की माला से उन्हें सुसज्जित कहा गया है। दूसरी ओर अश्विदेव मधुविद्या या मधुतत्त्व[22] के संरक्षक देव भी हैं और कमल भी एक मधुरता से परिपूर्ण पुष्प है। यही कारण है पुष्कर या कमल भारतीय जनमानस में एक महत्त्वपूर्ण प्रतीक के रूप में अंकित है। यह पूरा ब्रह्माण्ड ही खिला कमल है। वह उत्पत्ति, निर्माण, विकास और जीवन का प्रतीक है। इसीलिए पौराणिक वर्णनों में हर देवी-देवता किसी न किसी रूप में कमल से जुड़ा है। संसार में रहते हुए उससे वैसे ही अलिप्त रहें जैसे जल में रहते हुए भी कमल अलिप्त रहता है– यह सन्देश भी हमें इस पुष्प से मिलता है।

व्यावहारिक रूप में कमल के पत्ते का पात्र के रूप में प्रयोग भी वर्णित हुआ है–

पुष्करपर्णम् पात्रम्। (अथर्ववेद - 8.10.6)[22]

'पुष्कर' उस पात्र को भी कहा जाता था जिसमें 'स्त्रुवा' पड़ा रहता है। सम्भवतः दोनों (कमल तथा पात्र) के आकार के सादृश्य के आधार पर यह प्रयोग शुरु हुआ होगा। ऋग्वेद (8.72.11)[23] ऐतरेयब्राह्मण (7.5) में तो यही अर्थ सुनिश्चित है परन्तु ऋग्वेद (7. 72.11) में 'पुष्कर' का अर्थ तालाब भी किया गया है–

'कुओं के भी सूख जाने पर अग्नि से प्रेरित मेघ पृथ्वी के पास आकर 'तालाबों' को मीठे पानी से भर देते हैं।' 'पुष्कर' निरुक्त[24] (5.14) में उदक का नाम भी है तभी सम्भवतः 'तालाब' को भी 'पुष्कर' नाम मिला होगा। निरुक्त में तो 'पुष्कर' के अन्य अर्थ भी दिए गए हैं–

पुष्करमन्तरिक्षम्। पोषति भूतानि। उदकं पुष्पकरम्। पूजाकरम्।

पूजयितव्यम्। इदमपीतरत् पुष्करमेतस्मादेव। पुष्करं वपुष्करं वा।[25]

अर्थात् पुष्करम् का अर्थ है अन्तरिक्ष– यह उत्पन्न प्राणियों को पुष्ट करता है। (पोषति) जल 'पुष्करम्' कहलाता है क्योंकि यह पूजा का साधन (पूजाकरम्) है या पूजा जाने के लिए है (पूज्)। पुष्करम् (कमल) का यह अर्थ भी उसी धातु से निकला है– यह शरीर को अलंकृत करने का साधन (वपुष्करम्) है। निरुक्त में कथित 'अर्थ' इस बात को सङ्केतिक करते हैं कि 'पुष्कर' या 'कमल' व्यक्तित्वसज्जा के काम आता था। अन्य संहिता (तैत्तिरीय संहिता 5.5.14.1, मैत्रायणी संहिता 3.14.12) में 'अश्वमेघ' में पुष्करसाद शब्द का प्रयोग हुआ है।[26] पाश्चात्य विद्वान् यहाँ इसका

अर्थ सर्प' लेते हैं। रॉथ ने एक 'पक्षी' अर्थ कहा है परन्तु तैत्तिरीय-संहिता के भाष्यकार ने इसका अर्थ 'मक्खी' लिया है। 'पुष्करसादः' कमल पर बैठने वाला भँवरा भी हो सकता है क्योंकि लौकिक साहित्य में 'कमल-भँवरा' के सन्दर्भ में कई कवि-समय के प्रयोग मिलते हैं। आधुनिक भाष्यकारों ने यहाँ भी 'पुष्कर' का अर्थ 'तालाब'[27] ही लिया है। देवी चन्द ने अपने अंग्रेजी अनुवाद में 'पुष्करसाद' का अर्थ लिया है— 'bird residing in the tank.' जो भी हो 'पुष्करसाद' शब्द से प्रेरणा लेकर ही बाद के साहित्य में बहुत से देवता 'कमलासन' पर स्थित दिखाए गए प्रतीत होते हैं।[28]

निष्कर्ष रूप में कहा जा सकता है कि वेदों में पुष्पों का वर्णन बहुत कम हुआ है। एक 'कमल' ही है जो जलपुष्प के रूप में वर्णित हुआ है। इस 'पुष्प' के प्राकृतिक सौन्दर्य का वर्णन तो हुआ ही है, दार्शनिक विशेषताएँ भी उभर कर आई हैं, जैसे शतपथ ब्राह्मण में कहा गया है—जल कमल है और पृथ्वी क ल-पत्र है। जैसे जल पर कमलपत्र रखा रहता है उसी प्रकार जल पर पृथ्वी ठहरी हुई है। यह कमल-पत्र रूपी पृथ्वी अग्नि की योनि है—

आपो वै पुष्करं तासामियं पर्णं यथा ह वा इदं पुष्करं
पर्णमप्स्वध्याहितुमेवमियमप्स्वध्याहिता सेयं योनिरग्नेरियम् . . . ।

शतपथब्राह्मण - 7.4.1.8

कितनी सुन्दर उपमा है पृथ्वी की जो जल पर कमल-पत्र सी ठहरी है। बाद के साहित्य में तो 'कमल' शरीर के लगभग हर अङ्ग का उपमान बना है। हर देवता से कमल जुड़ा है कहीं न कहीं।

छान्दोग्योपनिषद् (4.14) में आचार्य उपकोसल से कहते हैं—

'मैं तुझे उस (ब्रह्म) का उपदेश करूँगा—'**यथा पुष्कर पलाश आपो न शिलष्यन्त एवमेव विदि पापं कर्म न शिलष्यन्त इति।**' अर्थात् जैसे कमल के पत्तों पर जल नहीं लिपटता वैसे ही (ब्रह्म को) जानने वाले पापकर्म में नहीं लिपटते।' इसी प्रकार मैत्रायणी उपनिषद् (3.1) में कहा गया है—'शुभाशुभ कर्मों से दबा वह भूतात्मा कहलाता है। इन भूतों का समुदाय ही शरीर है। अतः शरीर भूतात्मा कहलाता है। इसमें स्थित आत्मा कमल-पत्र में स्थित जलबिन्दु की तरह है। प्राकृतिक गुणों से अभिभूत होकर यह मूर्खता से अपने प्रेरणा को नहीं देख पाता।'

इस प्रकार 'कमल' एक चिर प्राचीन प्रतीक है जो वेद में ही नहीं विश्व की सभी संस्कृतियों में उपलब्ध है। मुस्लिम व ईसाई धर्म में भी इस सुन्दर फूल को स्थान मिला है। स्थापत्य-कला में सर्वत्र 'कमल' उकेरा गया है। बहाई-धर्म का मंदिर तो 'कमल मंदिर' (Lotus Temple) ही है। आयुर्वेद में तथा तन्त्र में सर्वत्र व्यापी है 'कमल'। लोक-जीवन काव्य, कला, शिल्प सर्वत्र 'कमल' प्रतिष्ठित रहा है।

सन्दर्भ-सङ्केत

1. परस्मैपदी भ्वादिगण की धातु का रूप बनता है 'पोषति' आदि तो दिवादिगण में 'पुष्यति' आदि और क्रयादिगण में पुष्णाति आदि। अर्थ सर्वत्र समान है।
2. पुष्कं पुष्टिं यति 'पुष्करम्'।
3. (i) मधुमत् पुष्पम्। अथर्ववेद 8.7.12
   (ii) अपां त्वा पुष्पं पृच्छामि। वही 10.8.134
   (iii) पुष्पेभ्यः स्वाहा। यजुर्वेद 22.28
   (iv) तैत्तिरीयसंहिता 5.4.4.2
   (v) पञ्चविंशब्राह्मण 8. 4.1
   (vi) छान्दोग्योपनिषद् 3.1.2
   (vii) बृहदारण्यकोपनिषद् 6.4.1

4. जयशंकर प्रसाद ने कामायनी में जो निम्न पंक्तियों में 'बिजली का फूल' का प्रयोग किया है सम्भवतः उसकी प्रेरणा यहीं से मिली होगी।

   नील परिधान बीच सुकुमार
   मृदुल अधखुला अंग
   खिला हो ज्यों बिजली का फूल।

5. पुष्पवती। अथर्ववेद 8.7.27
6. अथर्ववेद 6.106.1
7. Griffith's footnote No. 1 on AV VI. 106.1
8. ऋग्वेद 10.85.20
9. अथर्ववेद 8.6.9
10. अथर्ववेद 10.142.8
11. तैत्तिरीयब्राह्मण 1.8.2.1; शतपथब्राह्मण 5.5.5.6
12. ऐतरेयारण्यक 3.2.4
13. बृहदारण्यक 2.3.6
14. शाङ्करभाष्य बृहदारण्यक 2.3.6
15. बृहदारण्यक 6.3.6
16. तैत्तिरीयब्राह्मण 1.8.2.1
17. अथर्ववेद 12.1.24
18. यजुर्वेद 11.29
19. No lily grows with oval bulbs, no lotuspool is in his field in whose dominion is detained through senseless love, a Brahmaṇa's dam. Griffith's translation of A.V. 5.17.16
20. ऋग्वेद 10.184.2
21. अथर्ववेद 3.22.4
22. अथर्ववेद 8.4.8, 9.1.9
23. अभ्यारमिदद्रयो निषिक्तं पुष्करे मधु। अवतस्य विसर्जने।। ऋग्वेद 8.72.11
24. शतपथब्राह्मण 6.4.2.2
25. निरुक्त 5.14
26. पुष्करसादः। यजुर्वेद 24.31
27. सातवलेकरभाष्य
28. ऋग्वेद के 'श्री सूक्त' में लक्ष्मी 'पद्मस्थिता' बताई गई हैं।

卐 卐 卐

अथर्ववेद में भैषज्यमयी वनस्पतियाँ

पुष्पा गुप्ता

स्वास्थ्य जीवन की अमूल्य निधि है यह निर्विवाद सिद्ध है। वेदों में प्राप्त होने वाले विभिन्न वनस्पतियों के नाम तथा उनके द्वारा दूर किए जाने वाले रोगों की विस्तृत विवेचना से स्पष्ट है कि वैदिक ऋषि इस विषय में सतत जागरूक थे और इस दिशा में शोधकार्य करने के लिए भरसक प्रयत्नशील भी थे। रोग निवारण में सर्वाधिक प्रयोग वनस्पतियों का ही किया जाता था। 'आयुर्वेद तो पूर्ण रूप से वनस्पतियों का ही वेद है' इस विषय में किसी की भी विप्रतिपत्ति नहीं है। वस्तुतः यह कहना अत्युक्ति नहीं होगी कि आज भी प्रचलित चिकित्सा विज्ञान की सभी विद्याओं का आधार प्रायः वनस्पतियाँ ही हैं।

अथर्ववेद और चिकित्साशास्त्र की अन्य प्रणालियों में एक मौलिक अन्तर यह है कि अथर्ववेद में इन वनस्पतियों को इनके स्वाभाविक रूप में ही धारण करने से अथवा प्रयोग करने से रोग शान्त हो जाता था जबकि अन्य प्रणालियों में वनस्पतियों की जड़, पत्ते, शाख, तन्तु, रस इत्यादि का कुछ प्रक्रियाओं द्वारा रूप परिवर्तन कर दवा बनाकर प्रयोग किया जाता है। इसका कारण सम्भवतः यह रहा होगा कि अथर्ववेद में मंत्रों की शक्ति से शुद्ध और समृद्ध वनस्पतियाँ मूल रूप में ही रोगों को दूर करने में समर्थ थीं। परन्तु बाद में मन्त्रों की शक्ति का उचित प्रयोग न होने से उन वनस्पतियों को प्रयोगात्मक समीक्षण द्वारा प्रभावशाली बनाने का प्रयत्न किया गया। अथर्ववेद में केवल एक दो स्थलों पर वनस्पतियों को दवा रूप में परिवर्तित करने का उल्लेख है।[1]

अथर्ववेद में इन वनस्पतियों का प्रयोग केवल रोग निवारण के लिए ही नहीं किया जाता था अपितु शत्रुओं द्वारा किए गए हिंसक अथवा घातक प्रयोगों के प्रत्यावर्तन के लिए भी किया जाता था।[2] इसकी विस्तृत व्याख्या यथास्थान इसी लेख के अन्तर्गत की जाएगी।

अथर्ववेद में एक स्थान पर वनस्पतियों के रस को ठोस करके जङ्गिड तथा पर्णमणि बनाए जाने का निर्देश भी है[3] जिन्हें धारण करने से अनेक लाभ होते हैं। यह भी इसी लेख में अन्यत्र पल्लवित किया गया है।

इसी प्रकार एक स्थल पर दो पृथक्-पृथक् वृक्षों के मेल से एक तीसरा नया पौधा उत्पन्न होने का उल्लेख है जो उन दोनों वृक्षों के संयुक्त गुणों से युक्त है।[4]

चिकित्सा शास्त्र की दृष्टि से अथर्ववेद सर्वाधिक महत्त्वपूर्ण है। इसमें विभिन्न रोगों के कारण, उनके लक्षण तथा निदान करने वाली विभिन्न वनस्पतियों का उल्लेख है।

वेद में शरीर की समता 'आरोग्य' है और विषमता 'रोग'। अरोग्य की स्थापना के लिए शं शांति आदि पदों का प्रयोग है तो विषमता दूर करने के लिए वाचक पद 'योः' है। इस प्रकार शं योः इन दोनों पदों का संयुक्त अर्थ है ''समता की स्थापना कर विषमता को दूर करना''। वस्तुतः कफ, पित्त वायु का संतुलन ही शरीर में समता स्थापित करता है। और इनका असुन्तलन ही शरीर में रोग रूपी प्रकोप उत्पन्न करता है। रोगों का निदान करने वाली वनस्पतियाँ भी इसी तथ्य की पुष्टि करती हैं।

यह ध्यातव्य है कि वेदों में ओषधि, औषधि और वनस्पति ये तीनों पद 'वृक्ष, पौधा, जड़ी बूटी इत्यादि के द्योतक है। संस्कृत शब्दकोष में भी इसी अर्थ में इन पदों का प्रयोग हुआ है।[5]

अथर्ववेद में वर्णित कुछ महत्त्वपूर्ण वनस्पतियाँ जो भैषज्यमयी होने के कारण चिकित्साविज्ञान की दृष्टि से अत्यन्त महत्वपूर्ण हैं, निम्नलिखित हैं—

मुञ्ज

मुञ्ज घास अपने रस इत्यादि से अनेक रोगों और स्रावों को दूर करता है। यह घावों को भी भरने वाला है।[6] वस्तुतः मुञ्ज स्वयं शुद्ध और पवित्र है। उसके समान ही स्वयं को पवित्र और निर्मल बनाकर रोगमुक्त रखा जा सकता है।

शर

शर भी मुञ्ज का वाचक है। यह मूत्र दोष को दूर करता है। शरीर का समस्त विष मूत्र के माध्यम से बाहर निकल जाता है। जिससे मनुष्य नीरोगी रहता है।[7]

रामा कृष्णा असिक्नि

ये तीनों वनस्पतियाँ रात में उत्पन्न होती हैं और श्वेत कुष्ठ को दूर करती हैं।[8] कुष्ठ दो प्रकार का है (1) पलित अर्थात् श्वेत- जिसमें त्वचा पर सफेद-सफेद धब्बे हो जाते हैं और (2) किलास— जिसमें त्वचा विरूप सी हो जाती है।

उपर्युक्त तीनों वनस्पतियाँ श्वेत कुष्ठ को दूर करती हैं। असिक्नि स्वयं कृष्णवर्ण है अतः उससे त्वचा के सभी धब्बे दूर करने की प्रार्थना की गई है।[9] इनका रस लगाने से केवल वाह्य त्वचा का ही रंग नहीं बदलता अपितु यह इस त्वचा के अन्दर तक प्रवेश कर इसे समरूप कर देता है।[10]

श्यामा आसुरी वनस्पति

दो वृक्षों की कलम के संयोग से उत्पन्न तीसरी श्यामा आसुरी नामक वनस्पति विशेष गुणों से युक्त होती है तथा साधारण कुष्ठ को दूर करती है।[11] यह स्वयं श्यामा है और त्वचा का निश्चित रूप से सरूपीकरण करती है।[12] शरीर के वास्तविक रंग के समान कुष्ठ रोग की त्वचा का रंग बनाना ही सरूपीकरण है।

शण और जङ्गिड

शण और जङ्गिड शोषक रोग को दूर करते हैं। इनमें से शण वनस्पति है और वन से प्राप्त होता है जबकि जङ्गिड एक मणि है जो खेतों में उत्पन्न वनस्पतियों के रस को ठोस करके बनाया जाता है।[13]

राजवल्लभ नामक वैद्यक ग्रन्थ में लिखा है कि शण का फूल रक्तपित्त में लाभकारी है, मलरोधक है और उसका बीज रक्त शुद्धि करता है।[14] यह खट्टा और कषाय है। मल, गर्भ और रक्त का स्राव करवाने वाला है, वमन करवाने वाला तथा वात और कफ को भी दूर करने वाला है।[15]

जङ्गिड मणि वनस्पतियों का ही प्रारूप है जो रोगों को दूर करता है और आयु बढ़ाता है।[16] सबका रक्षक है (रक्षितासि जङ्गिडः, 19.34.1) हिंसक कार्य करने वालों के तेज को दूर करता है (सर्वान्विनक्तु तेजसोऽरसां जङ्गिडस्करत् 19.34.2) बुद्धिहीनता को दूर करता है (अपेतो जङ्गिडामतिम् 19.34.4), हिंसक कृत्यों का नाशक व शत्रुओं का विनाशक है (कृत्यादूषण एवायमको अरातिदूषणः 19.34.4) यह पुरानी और नवीन सभी वनस्पतियों से बढ़कर है।[17] इन्द्र ने इसे बहुत शक्तिशाली बनाया अतः यह सब रोगों और राक्षसों को नष्ट करने वाला है।[18] विशेष रूप से शरीर को अत्यधिक कष्ट पहुँचाने वाली खाँसी, पीठ की बीमारी तथा शरदर्तु में होने वाले ज्वर के लिए बहुत प्रभावशाली है।[19]

सभी औषधियों के गुणों से सम्पन्न (विश्वभेषज:) यह भूतों से भी रक्षा करने में समर्थ है (परि मा भूतात् 19. 35.4)। हजारों सामर्थ्यों से युक्त यह मणि देवों द्वारा किए गए व अन्य सभी हिंसक कृत्यों से धारक की सब तरफ से रक्षा करता है।[20]

वैष्णवी और तारका

दो प्रकार की वैष्णवी और दो प्रकार की तारका, ये चारों वनस्पतियाँ भूमि पर उत्पन्न होती हैं।[21] वैष्णवी को भगवती के नाम से भी जाना जाता है।[22] भूरे और श्वेत रंग वाले यव के अंशों के साथ तथा तिल की मञ्जरियों से प्राप्त ताजा तिल के साथ सेवन करने से ये वनस्पतियाँ असाध्य आनुवंशिक रोगों को समूल नष्ट कर देती हैं।[23]

दशवृक्ष

दशवृक्ष वनस्पति गठिया तथा सन्धिवात को दूर करती है।[24] आजकल यह दशमूल के नाम से प्रसिद्ध है। इसका तैल, घृत, आसव, कषाय, अरिष्ठ आदि आज भी आयुर्वेद में प्रचलित हैं और इनका प्रयोग वातरोग को दूर करने के लिए किया जाता है।

पृश्निपर्णी

यह शरीर की शोभा को नष्ट करने वाले, रक्तह्रास करने वाले, पुष्टि को रोकने वाले तथा गर्भ सुखाने वाले रोगों का नाश करती है।[25] यह मनुष्यों के लिए सुख और व्याधियों के लिए दुःख उत्पन्न करती है। प्रचण्ड रोगबीजों को नष्ट कर रोगों को दूर भगाती है।[26]

इसे चित्रपर्णी, पीठवन, पीतवन और पठौनी भी कहते हैं। वैद्यक ग्रन्थों में इसके विषय में कहा गया है।

त्रिदोषघ्नी वृष्योष्णा मधुरा सरा।
हन्ति दाहज्वरश्वासरक्तातिसारतृड्वमीः।।[27]

पाटा

पाटा नाम की वनस्पति वाद विवाद तथा युद्ध दोनों में ही विजय प्राप्त करवाती है। वाद विवाद के समय इसे मुख में रखने से अथवा कण्ठ पर बाँधने से वक्तृत्व के दोष नहीं होते जिससे वादी की विजय होती है।[28]

भाव प्रकाश में भी इसे श्रेयकारिणी, मुख में वाणी के दोष को दूर करने वाली तथा कण्ठ की पीड़ा को हरने वाली कहा गया है।[29]

टूटे हुए अवयव जोड़ने के कारण तथा घाव जल्दी भरने के कारण इसका प्रयोग युद्ध में विजय प्राप्ति करवाता था। अथर्ववेद में स्पष्ट रूप से कहा गया है कि इन्द्र ने भी पाटा को हाथ पर बाँधा[30] और मुख में धारण किया।[31]

वैद्यक ग्रन्थों में पाटा को तिक्त, गुरु, उष्ण, वात-पित्त ज्वर नाशक तथा टूटे हुए अवयवों को जोड़ने वाली कहा गया है। यह पित्त, दाह और अतिसार को दूर करती है।[31]

वचा

वच नामक वनस्पति उन सभी कृमियों का नाश करती है जो दृश्य हैं अथवा अदृश्य[33], शरीर के अन्दर हैं अथवा बाहर।[34] इतना ही नहीं वचा नामक औषधि से आँतों, सिर और पसलियों में रहने वाले तथा रेंगने वाले सभी कृमियों का नाश हो जाता है।[35] संक्षेप में हर प्रकार के कृमि वचा से नष्ट किए जा सकते हैं।

आजकल वचा को वच नाम से जाना जाता है। इसका चूर्ण शरीर पर लगाने से कृमि बाधा नहीं होती। जल में घोलकर इसका प्रयोग करने से शरीर के अन्दर के कृमि नष्ट हो जाते हैं।

औषधि के विष से यदि मूर्च्छा आती हो तो उसके लिए भी वचा का प्रयोग विहित है।[36]

पर्णमणि

जैसा कि इसके नाम से ही स्पष्ट है, यह औषधियों के रस से बनता है। यह बल बढ़ाने वाला, शत्रुओं को नष्ट करने वाला तथा दीर्घायु और पुष्टि प्रदान करने वाला है।[37] इस प्रकार पर्णमणि अत्यन्त प्रभावशाली है।

ऋषभक

ऋषभक वनस्पतियाँ इन्द्रियों की सामर्थ्य बढ़ाने वाली हैं जिन्हें खोद कर प्राप्त किया जाता है।[38] यह पुरुषों के लिए विशेष रूप से लाभकारी है। पुरुषों की जननेन्द्रिय शक्ति की स्थिरता के लिए ऋषभक वनस्पति का रस लाभप्रद है।[39]

ऋषभक ओषधियों के बीज गर्भाशय को दोषमुक्त कर वन्ध्यत्व को दूर करते हैं। वीर्य को बढ़ाकर उत्तम संतान देते हैं।[40]

वारणा

वारणा नामक वनस्पति का रस विष को दूर करने वाला कहा गया है।[41] विष से उत्पन्न होने वाली मूर्च्छा को दूर करने के लिए तिलौदन दही के साथ खाने का निर्देश है।[42]

अञ्जन

अथर्ववेद में पर्वत पर उत्पन्न होने वाली वनस्पतियों से बने हुए अञ्जन का उल्लेख है जो प्राणियों को अपमृत्यु से बचाने वाला है व आँखों के लिए हितकारी है।[43] यह पाण्डुरोग को भी दूर करता है।[44] इस अञ्जन को धारण करने वालों को दुष्ट भाषण, शाप, हिंसाकर्म, शोक और पीड़ाएँ कष्ट नहीं पहुँचातीं।[45] ज्वर, क्षय, कफविकार, उदावर्तन नामक पेट का रोग और सर्पविष भी इससे दूर हो जाते हैं।[46] यह त्रैककुद और यामुन के नाम से भी जाना जाता है।[47] वैद्यक ग्रन्थों में भी इसके यही गुण बतलाए गए हैं—शीतलं कटुं तिक्तं कषायं चक्षुष्यं रसायनं कफवातविषघ्न च।[48]

रोहिणी

यथा नाम तथा गुण के अनुसार रोहिणी नामक वनस्पति बढ़ाने वाली है। टूटी हुई हड्डी को जोड़ने वाली है।[49] आहत, दग्ध अथवा किसी भी कारण से पिसा हुआ अवयव इस वनस्पति से पूर्ववत् हो जाता है।[50] यह मज्जा, चर्म, रुधिर, हड्डी और माँस को भी बढ़ाती है।[51] तीव्र अस्त्र शस्त्र अथवा पत्थर का घाव भी इससे ठीक हो जाता है।[52] महाभारत में भी वर्णन आता है कि जब योद्धाओं के शरीर बाणों से घातयुक्त हो जाते थे तो वे रात में कोई औषधि लगा कर सो जाते थे। सम्भवतः वे रोहिणी का ही प्रयोग करते हों।

वैद्यक ग्रन्थों में इसे वीरवती, माँसरोहिणी विकषा, प्रहारवल्ली इत्यादि नामों से अभिहित किया गया है।

अपामार्ग

अपामार्ग ओषधियों मे विशेष सामर्थ्य वाली है। सहस्र वीर्यों वाली यह सब रोगों का निवारण करने में समर्थ है।[53] यह आक्रोश दूर कर सहनशक्ति बढ़ाती है।[54] दुःस्वप्न, उदासीनता, निर्बलता, निस्तेजता, बवासीर आदि रोगों को दूर करती है।[55] अत्यधिक भूख, प्यास, इन्द्रिय तथा वाणी दोष, नपुंसकता इत्यादि रोगों का निदान भी अपामार्ग ओषधि से ही होता है।[56] इसके फल विपरीत दिशा में बढ़ते हैं अत: यह विपरीत आचरण के सब दोष दूर करती है।[57] यह वनस्पति जादू टोने

के प्रभाव को भी दूर करती है। किसी को मारने के लिए यदि कोई उसके खेत, पशुओं अथवा घर में कुछ रख देता है तो अपामार्ग वनस्पति से प्रार्थना की गई है कि इस घातक प्रयोग को इसे करने वाले के पास ही भेज दे।[58] इसी तथ्य को स्पष्ट करते हुए पुनः कहा गया है कि जो स्वयं पापकर्म करके दूसरों को नष्ट करना चाहता है, अपामार्ग वनस्पति से उसी का नाश हो जाता है जैसे तपा हुआ पत्थर स्वयं फट जाता है।[59]

अपामार्ग वनस्पति आनुवंशिक रोगों को, चिड़चिड़ेपन को और अन्य सभी यातनाओं को भी दूर करती है।[60] यह वनस्पति तेजस्वी सेना के समान रोगरूप शत्रु पर हमला करती है।[61] वनस्पतियों में यह मुख्य है।[62]

हिन्दी भाषा में इसे लटजीरा और चिरचिरा भी कहते हैं।

मातृनामा

मातृनामा वनस्पति दृष्टिदोष का निवारण करती है। इससे नेत्र ज्योति बढ़ती है और मनुष्य सब कुछ देख पाता है।[63] इसे आखुकर्णी, महाश्रावणिका और घृतकुमारी भी कहते हैं।

अजश्रृंगी

अजश्रृगी अपनी सुगन्ध से जल में रहने वाले रोग कृमियों का नाश करती है।[64] सम्भवतः गुग्गुलू, पीला, नलदी, औक्षगन्धिः और प्रमन्दनी ये पाँचों वनस्पतियाँ मिलकर अजश्रृंगी कहलाती हैं।

कुष्ठ

कुष्ठ वनस्पति हिमालय की ऊँची चोटी पर उत्पन्न होती है[65] तथा सब औषधियों में सबसे अधिक बल प्रदान करने वाली है।[66] क्षय रोग, सिर के रोग, आँखों की कमजोरी तथा शरीर के सभी दोषों को यह दूर करती है।[67] सर्वरोग विनाशक होने के कारण यह अमृततुल्य प्रतीत होती है।[68] हिन्दी में इसे 'कुठ' कहते हैं तथा वैद्यक ग्रन्थों में भी इसकी यही विशेषताएँ बतलाई गई हैं।

लाक्षा

लाक्षा वनस्पति के रस का पान मुनष्यों का भरण-पोषण करता है और उन्हें नीरोगी बनाता है।[69] पीपल, खैर, पलाश आदि अनेक वृक्षों पर यह उत्पन्न होती है।[70] इसका नाम स्परणी भी है।[71] डण्डे, बाण और रगड़ से उत्पन्न होने वाले घावों को यह भरती है।[72] वैद्यक ग्रन्थों में इसका वर्णन बहुत आया है। हिन्दी में इसे 'लाख' कहते हैं।

मधुला

अपने नाम के अनुरूप ही मधुला मधुरता उत्पन्न करने वाली है। यह सत्यपालक है और सत्य से उत्पन्न हुई है।[73]

रेवती

रेवती वनस्पतियों में श्रेष्ठ है[74] और बालों को मजबूत करने वाली और बढ़ाने वाली है।[75]

अरुन्धती

यह वनस्पति गायों को बहुत अधिक दूध देने वाला बनाती है और सब प्राणियों को नीरोगी बनाती है।[76]

सोम

कहीं-कहीं असंख्य ओषधियों में से सोम को मुख्य मानते हुए उन्हें पापरूपी अनेक रोगों से सुरक्षित करने वाला

कहा गया है।[77] यहाँ तक कि आँख, मन, वाणी आदि इन्द्रियों द्वारा जाग्रतावस्था में अथवा स्वप्नावस्था में जो पाप हम करते हैं, उन पापों से उत्पन्न रोग भी सोमादि ओषधियों से दूर हो जाते हैं।[78] ये मृत्यु से भी मनुष्य की रक्षा करती है।[79]

पिप्पली

पिप्पली वनस्पति उन्माद, वात और महाव्याधि का नाश करती है। यह अकेली ही जीवन की आरोग्यता के लिए पर्याप्त है। इस ओषधि की यह प्रतिज्ञा है कि इसका सेवन करने वाला पुरुष मुत्यु को प्राप्त नहीं होता।[80]

चीपुद्रु

चीपुद्रु नामक वनस्पति खाँसी, फोड़े-फुन्सी, रक्तस्राव और चर्मरोग दूर करती है।[81]

नितत्नी

नितत्नी वनस्पति बालों को मजबूत करती है, उन्हें लम्बा करती है और गंजेपन को दूर करती है।[82] यह लता है जिसका रस केश सम्बन्धी सभी दोषों को दूर करता है।[83] यह बालों को काला भी करती है और नरकट घास (जल के स्थान में बढ़ने वाली घास) के समान उन्हें बढ़ाती भी है।[84]

सहस्रपर्णी

सैकड़ों शाखाओं व 33 उपशाखाओं वाली सहस्रपर्णी वनस्पति सौभाग्य की वृद्धि करती है।[85] इससे पति-पत्नी एक दूसरे का वियोग नहीं सह पाते।[86] यह विछुड़े हुए प्रमियों को भी मिलाती है।[87]

आसुरी

यह वनस्पति पति की आसक्ति पत्नी की तरफ ही बनाए रखती है। पति चाहे कहीं भी गया हो, इस वनस्पति के प्रभाव से वह बँध कर अपनी पत्नी के पास ही आता है।[88] यह पति-पत्नी के प्रेम को प्रगाढ़ करती है।

मधु

यह वनस्पति साँप के विष को दूर करती है।[89] तथा मच्छरों को भी नष्ट करती है।[90] भयंकर विष से जो रोगी टेढा-मेढा, कुरूप या ढीले संधि वाला हो गया है अथवा जो अपने मुख को कुटिल करता है, वह भी इस वनस्पति से ठीक हो जाता है।[91] बिच्छू का विष भी इससे दूर हो जाता है।[92]

मुनि

लाल रंग वाली गण्डमाला दूर करने के लिए मुनि नामक वनस्पति की जड़ बहुत उपयोगी है।[93]

दर्भ

दर्भ को उग्र ओषधि माना गया है जो आयु बढ़ाने वाला है। परन्तु न कटे पत्तों वाला दर्भ ही सुख देता है।[94] दुष्ट हृदय की जिह्वा तथा वचनों को चीरने का वर्णन भी है।[95] दर्भमणि का वर्णन भी है जो शत्रुओं को नष्ट करने वाला (सपत्नहा), शक्तिशाली (सहस्वान्) ओषधियों में प्रथम (ओषधीनां प्रथमः) तथा चारों तरफ से रक्षा करने वाला है (विश्वतः न परिपातु)

अन्य वनस्पतियाँ

अथर्ववेद में कुछ ऐसी वनस्पतियों का वर्णन है जिनका नाम नहीं दिया गया। यथा 2.7 में ऐसी वनस्पति का वर्णन है जो पापवृत्ति को हटाने वाली, दिव्य भावों को बढ़ाने वाली तथा क्रोधावेश मे शाप देने की प्रवृत्ति को दूर करने वाली है।

5-14 में घातक प्रयोग को लौटाने वाली वनस्पतियों का उल्लेख है।[96]

शमी पर चढ़े हुए पीपल वृक्ष की औषध बनाकर स्त्री द्वारा सेवन किए जाने पर पुत्रोत्पत्ति होती है।[97] वस्तुतः अश्व शक्ति का प्रतीक है और इस प्रकार अश्वत्थ का प्रतीकात्मक अर्थ ''शक्ति से युक्त पुरुष'' हुआ। शमी स्त्री का प्रतीक है जो शान्त मनोवृत्ति वाली है। ऐसे स्त्री पुरुष के सम्बन्ध से पुरुष संतान उत्पन्न होती है।

6.138 में ऐसी ओषधि का वर्णन भी है जिसके द्वारा बैल, घोड़ों इत्यादि को क्लीब बनाया जाता था।[98] वीर्य की नाड़ियाँ तोड़ दी जाती थीं व अण्डकोषों को नष्ट कर दिया जाता था।[99] पशुओं को बधिया करने की प्रथा आज भी प्रचलित है।

8.7 'ओषधयः' नामक सूक्त में अनेक प्रकार की वनस्पतियों का वर्णन है। कई वनस्पतियाँ पोषण करने वाली, कई घाव भरने वाली, कई वीर्य बढ़ाने वाली हैं। वनस्पतियाँ छोटे पौधों के रूप में, विशाल वृक्षों के रूप में और पृथ्वी के नीचे भी होती हैं। परन्तु सभी विविध शक्तियों से युक्त हैं।[100]

वनस्पतियों को उत्पन्न करने से पहले भूमि पर हल आदि चलाकर भली भाँति तैयार किया जाता था। तत्पश्चात् ईश्वर से प्रार्थना की जाती थी कि वह उत्तम प्रकार से जल बरसाए। वर्षा का जल वनस्पतियों को तेजस्वी बनाता है। भूमि को वनस्पतियों की माता कहा गया है तो पर्जन्य, मित्र, वरुण, चन्द्र और सूर्य को पिता कहा गया है क्योंकि इन पाँचों की शक्ति से ही भूमि वनस्पतियों को उत्पन्न कर पाती है।

वनस्पतियों का संरक्षण, संवर्धन और संपोषण सप्रयत्न किया जाता था।[102]

चूहे, पतङ्गे और शलभ इत्यादि पौधों को नष्ट करने वाले हैं।[103] प्रचण्ड वायु भी वृक्षों के लिए हानिकारक है।[104]

इस प्रकार अथर्ववेद में नानाशक्तियों से युक्त असंख्य चमत्कारिक वनस्पतियों का उल्लेख है। यह कदापि नहीं कहा जा सकता कि ये ऋषियों की कल्पना का परिणाम है क्योंकि साहित्य समाज का दर्पण होता है। जो कुछ समाज में प्रचलित होता है और प्रयोग में लाया जाता है, उसी का वर्णन सहित्य में किया जाता है। यदि अथर्ववेद में ऐसी दिव्य वनस्पतियों का वर्णन है तो वे उस समय अवश्य रही होंगी। इनमें से कुछ वनस्पतियाँ तो आज भी आयुर्वेद में प्रचलित हैं। परन्तु कुछ ऐसी भी हैं जिनके विषय में किसी को ज्ञान नहीं है। इसके दो कारण हो सकते हैं। प्रथम तो वे जो आज उपलब्ध ही नहीं हैं और दूसरे वे जो उपलब्ध तो हैं परन्तु उनके विषय में ज्ञान नहीं है। यदि इस दिशा में शोध कार्य किया जाए तो हो सकता है कि ऐसी ही कुछ और अमूल्य निधि हमारे हाथ लग जाए।

सन्दर्भ-सङ्केत

1. औषधिरथो कृणोमि भेषजम्। अथर्ववेद 8.7.5
2. अरसाः सन्तु कृत्वरीः। वही, 4.18.1
3. वही, 2.4..3
4. वही, 1.24.3
5. ओषधिः-ओष + $\sqrt{}$ धा + कि + ङीष् (1) जड़ी बूटी वनस्पति (2) औषधि का पौधा, फसली पौधा या जड़ी बूटी जो पककर सूख जाती है। संस्कृत हिन्दी कोष, वामन शिवराम आप्टे, प्रकाशक-मोतीलाल बनारसीदास, दिल्ली, 1992, पृ. 231
   औषधि : जड़ी बूटी, वनस्पति, रोगनाशक जड़ी बूटी, वही, पृ. 234
6. अथर्ववेद, 1.2.4

7. यदान्त्रेषु गवीन्योर्यद्वस्तावधि संश्रुतम्।
एवा ते मूत्रं मुच्यतां बहिर्बालिति सर्वकम्।। वही, 1.3.6

8. नक्तं जातस्योषधे रामे कृष्णे असिक्नि च।
इदं रजनि रजय किलासं पलितं च यत्।। अथर्ववेद, 1.23.1

9. वही, 1.23.3

10. आ त्वा स्वो विशतां वर्णः। वही, 1.23.2

11. वही, 1.24.3

12. श्यामा सरूपंकरणी पृथिव्या अध्युद्धृता।
इदमू षु प्र साधय पुना रूपाणि कल्पय।। वही, 1.24.4

13. शणश्च मा जङ्गिडश्च विष्कन्धादभि रक्षताम्।
अरण्यादन्य आभृतः कृष्या अन्यो रसेभ्यः।। अथर्ववेद, 2.4.5

14. तत्पुष्पं रक्तपित्ते हितं मलरोधकं च। बीजं शोणित शुद्धिकरम्।। अथर्ववेद का सुबोध भाष्य, प्रथम भाग भाष्यकार पद्मभूषण डॉ० श्रीपाद दामोदर सातवलेकर स्वाध्याय मण्डल, पारडी, 1985, पृ. 30

15. अम्लः कषायो मलगर्भास्त्रपातनः वान्तिकृत्।
वातकफघ्नश्च।। वही, पृ. 30

16. अथर्ववेद, 2.4.6

17. न त्वा पूर्वा ओषधयो न त्वा तरन्ति या नवाः। अथर्ववेद, 19.34.7

18. अमीवाः सर्वाश्चातयं जहि रक्षांस्योषधे। वही, 19.34.9

19. आशरीकं विशरीकं बलासं पृष्टयामयं।
तक्मानं विश्वशारदमरसां जङ्गिडस्करत्।। वही, 19.34.10

20. मणिः सहस्रवीर्यः परि णः पातु विश्वतः। वही, 2.4.2

21. अमू ये दिवि सुभगे विचृतौ नाम तारके। वही, 3.7.4

22. वही, 2.8.1

23. बभ्रोरर्जुनकाण्डस्य यवस्य ते पलाल्या तिलस्य तिलषिञ्ज्या
वीरुत्क्षेत्रियनाशन्यप क्षेत्रियमुच्छतु।। वही, 2.8.3

24. दशवृक्ष मुञ्चेमं रक्षसो ग्राह्या अभि यैनं जग्राह पर्वसु।
अथो एनं वनस्पते जीवानां लोकमुन्नय।। अथर्ववेद, 2.9.1

25. अरायमसृक्पावानं यश्च स्फातिं जिहीर्षति।
गर्भादं कण्वं नाशय पृश्निपर्णि सहस्व च।। वही, 2.25.3

26. शं नो देवी पृश्निपर्ण्यशं निर्ऋत्या अकः।
उग्रा हि कण्वजम्भनी तामभक्षि सहस्वताम्।। वही, 2.25.1

27. अथर्ववेद का सुबोध भाष्य, भाग 1, पृ. 95

28. नेच्छत्रुः प्राशं जयाति सहमानाभिभूरसि।
प्राशं प्रतिप्राशो जह्यरसान्कृण्वोषधे।। अथर्ववेद, 2.27.1

29. श्रेयसी मुखवाचिका। कफकण्ठरुजावहा। अर्थर्ववेद भाष्य, पृ. 103

30. इन्द्रो ह चक्रे त्वा बाहावसुरेभ्यस्तरीतवे। अथर्ववेद, 2.27.4

31. पाटाभिन्द्रो व्याश्नादसुरेभ्यस्तरीतवे। वही, 2.27.4

32. तिक्ता गुरूरुष्णा वातपित्तज्वरघ्नी।
भग्नसंधानकरी पित्तदाहातिसारशूलघ्नी च।। अथर्ववेद भाष्य, पृ. 103

33. दृष्टमदृष्टमतृहम्। अथर्ववेद, 2.31.2

34. येऽस्माकं तन्वमाविविशुः सर्वं तद् हन्मि जनिम क्रिमीणाम्। वही, 2.31.5

35. अन्वान्त्र्यं शीर्षण्यमथो पार्ष्टेयं क्रिमीन्।
अवस्कवं व्यध्वरं क्रिमीन्वचसा जम्भयामसि।। अथर्ववेद, 2.31.4

36. वि ते मदं मदावति शरमिव पातयामसि।
प्र त्वा चरुमिव येषन्तं वचसा स्थापयामसि।। वही 4.7.4

37. तमस्मभ्यं सहायुषा देवा ददतु भर्तवे। वही, 3.5.3

38. तां त्वा वयं खनामस्योषधिं शेपहर्षणीम्। वही, 2.4.1

39. उच्छुष्मौषधीनां सार ऋषभाणाम्।
सं पुंसामिन्द्र वृष्ण्यमस्मिन्धेहि तनूवशिन्।। वही, 4.4.4

40. यानि मद्राणि बीजान्यृषभा जनयन्ति च।
तैस्त्वं पुत्रं विन्दस्व सा प्रसूर्धेनुका भव।। अथर्ववेद, 3.23.4

41. वारिदं वारयातै वरणावत्यामधि। वही, 4.7.1

42. वही, 4.7.3

43. एहि जीवं त्रायमाणं पर्वतस्यास्यक्ष्यम्।
विश्वेभिर्देवैर्दत्तं परिधिर्जीवनाय कम्।। वही, 4.9-1

44. अथो हरितभेषजम्। वही, 4.9.3

45. नैनं प्राप्नोति शपथो न कृत्या नाभिशोचनम्।
नैनं विष्कन्धमश्नुते यस्त्वा विभर्त्याञ्जन।। वही, 4.9.5

46. त्रयो दासा आञ्जनस्य तक्मा बलास आदहिः। वही, 4.9.8

47. यदि वासि त्रैककुदं यदि यामुनमुच्यसे।
उभे ते भद्रे नाम्नी ताभ्यां नः पाह्याञ्जन।। अथर्ववेद, 4.9.10

48. अथर्ववेद का सुबोध भाष्य, भाग 2, पृ. 31

49. रोहिण्यसि रोहिण्यस्थ्नश्छिन्नस्य रोहिणी। अथर्ववेद, 4.12.1

50. यत्ते रिष्टं यत्ते युतमस्ति पेष्ट्रं त आत्मनि।
धाता तद् भद्रया पुनः संदधत्परुषा परुः।। वही 4.12.2

51. मज्जा मज्ज्ञा सं धीयतां चर्मणा चर्म रोहतु।
असृक्ते अस्थि रोहतु मांसं मांसेन रोहतु।। वही, 4.12.4

52. वही, 4.12.7

53. ईशानां त्वा भेषजानाम् . . .। चक्रे सहस्रवीर्यं सर्वस्मा ओषधे त्वा। वही, 4.17.1

54. वही, 4.17.2

55. दौष्वप्न्यं दौर्जीवित्यं रक्षो अभ्वमराय्यः।
दुर्णाम्नीः सर्वा दुर्वाचस्ता अस्मन्नाशयामसि।। वही, 4.17.5

56. क्षुधामारं तृष्णामारमगोतागनपत्यताग्।
अपामार्ग त्वया वयं सर्वं तदपमृज्महे।। वही, 4.17.7

57. प्रतीचीन फलो हि त्वमपामार्ग रुरोहिथ।
सर्वान्मच्छपथां अधिवरीयो यावया इत:।। वही, 7.65.1

58. वही, 10.1.4

59. वही, 4.18.3

60. वही, 4.18.7

61. सेनेवैषि त्विषीमती। वही, 4.19.2

62. अग्रमेष्योषधीनाम्। वही, 4.19.3

63. त्वयाहं सर्वा भूतानि पश्यानि देव्योषधे। वही, 4.20.2

64. त्वया वयमप्सरसो गन्धर्वांश्चातयामहे।
अजशृङ्ग्ज रक्षः सर्वान्गन्धेन नाशय।। वही, 4.37.2

65. सुपर्वसुवने गिरौ जातं हिमवतस्परि। वही, 5.4.2

66. वीरुधां बलवत्तम:। वही, 5.4.1

67. यक्ष्मं च सर्वं नाशय। अथर्ववेद, 5.4.9
तथा

शीर्षामयमुपहत्यामक्ष्योस्तन्वोरप:।
कुष्ठस्तत्सर्वं निष्करदैवं समह वृष्ण्यम्।। वही, 5.4.10

68. तत्रामृतस्य चक्षणं देवा: कुष्ठमवन्वत्। वही, 5.4.3

69. यस्त्वा पिबति जीवति त्रायसे पुरुषं त्वम्।
भर्त्री हि शश्वतामसि जनानां च न्यञ्चनी।। वही, 5.5.2

70. वृक्षं वृक्षमारोहसि। वही, 5.5.3

71. स्परणी नाम वा असि। वही, 5.5.3

72. यद्दण्डेन यदिष्वा यद्वारुर्हरसा कृतम्।
तस्य त्वमसि निष्कृति:।। वही, 5.5.4

73. ऋतजात ऋतावरि मधु मे मधुला कर:। वही, 5.15.1

74. वसिष्ठं वीरुधानाम्। वही, 6.21.2

75. उत स्थ केशदृंहणीरथो ह केशवर्धनी:। वही, 6.21.3

76. करत् पशस्वन्त गोष्ठमयक्ष्माँ उत पूरुषान्। वही, 6.59.2

77. वही, 6.96.1

78. यच्चक्षुषा मनसा यच्च वाचोपारिम जाग्रतो।
यत् स्वपन्त: सोमस्तानि स्वधया न: पुनातु।। वही 6.96.3

79. उत त्वा मृत्योरोषधय: सोमराज्ञीरपीपरन्। वही, 8.1.17

80. पिप्पल्य: समवदन्तायतीर्जननादधि।
यं जीवमश्नवामहै न स रिष्याति पूरुष:।। वही, 6.109.2

81. विद्रधस्य बलासस्य लोहितस्य वनस्पते।
विसल्पकस्योषधे मोच्छिष: पिशितं चन।। वही, 6.127.1

82. दृंहप्रत्नान् जनयाजातान् जातानु वर्षीयसंस्कृधि। वही, 6.136.2
83. इदं तं विश्वभेषज्यभिषिञ्चामि वीरुधा। वही, 6.136.3
84. केशा नडा इव वर्धन्तां शीर्ष्णस्ते असिताः परि। वही, 6.137.3
85. न्यस्तिका रुरोहिथ सुभगंकरणी मम . . . तया सहस्रपर्ण्या। वही, 6.139.1
86. वही, 6.139.1
87. कामस्य विच्छिन्नं संधेहि वीर्यावति। वही, 6.139.5
88. यदि वासि तिरोजनं यदि वा नद्यस्तिरः।
 इयं ह मह्यं त्वामोषधिर्बद्ध न्यानयत्।। वही, 7.38.5
89. परिसंभृतम् . . . विषमियं वीरूदनीनशत्। वही, 7.56.1
90. भेषज्यथो मशकजम्भनी। वही, 7.56.2
91. अयं यो वक्रो विपरुर्व्यङ्गो मुखानि वक्रा वृजिना कृणोषि।
 तानि त्वं ब्रह्मणस्पत इषीकामिव सं नमः।। वही, 7.56.4
92. शर्कोटस्य विषं . . . आदिषि। वही, 7.56.5
93. अपचितां लोहिनीनां . . .मुनेर्देवस्य मूलेन सर्वा विध्यामि। वही, 7.74.1
94. यस्मा अच्छिन्नपर्णेन दर्भेण शर्म यच्छति। वही, 19.32.2
95. वही, 19.32.4
96. कृत्याः सन्तु कृत्याकृते। वही, 5.14.5
97. शमीमश्वत्थ आरूढस्तत्र पुंसवनं कृतम्।
 तद् वै पुत्रस्य वेदनं वत्र स्त्रीष्वा भरामसि।। वही, 6.11.1
98. त्वं वीरुधां श्रेष्ठतमाभिश्रुतास्योषधे।
 इमं मे अद्य पूरुषं क्लीबमोपशिनं कृधि।। वही, 6.138.1
99. वही, 6.138.4
100. नानावीर्या ओषधिर्या बिभर्ति। वही, 12.1.2
101. वर्षस्य सर्गा महन्तु भूमिम्। वही, 4.15.2
102. पयस्वतीरोषधयः पयस्वन्मामकं वचः।
 अथो पयस्वतीनामाभरेऽहं सहस्रशः।। वही, 3.24.1
103. वही, 6.50.1–2
104. यथा वातो वनस्पतीन् वृक्षान् भनक्त्योजसा। वही, 10.3.13

卐 卐 卐

वाल्मीकि रामायण में वर्णित अलौकिक वनोपवन

अनीता शर्मा

रामायण एक कालजयी एवं बहुआयामी रचना है। साहित्य, संस्कृति, दर्शन, वनस्पतिशास्त्र एवं समाजशास्त्र आदि सभी इस महान् अयन में समाहित हैं। वनस्पतिशास्त्र की दृष्टि से देखा जाए तो इसका धरातल इतना अधिक विस्तृत है कि भारत की तत्कालीन अनेकानेक वृक्ष वल्लरियाँ, इस महाकाव्य में वर्णित वनोपवनों में परिलक्षित हुई हैं। इसका कारण यह है कि रामायण की संकल्पना, जन्म, वर्द्धन एवं परिपोषण प्रकृति की स्नेहिल गोद में ही हुआ था। तमसा के तोय रूपी दुग्ध का पान कर, आश्रम के प्राकृतिक वातावरण में आकार धारण करने वाली इस कृति में दो प्रकार के वनोपवनों का वर्णन हुआ है—एक तो आश्रमों और पर्वतों के प्राकृतिक वातावरण से सम्बद्ध वन और दूसरे अपने चमत्कारिक स्वरूप से चमत्कृत कर देने वाले अलौकिक वनोपवन।

मानव जीवन के रमणीय रूप को रूपायित करने वाली इस रचना में अनेक संस्कृतियों का वर्णन हुआ है यथा मुनि संस्कृति, मानव संस्कृति, असुर संस्कृति, तथा वानर संस्कृति आदि। अलौकिक वन-वाटिकाएँ इन सभी संस्कृतियों का अविभाज्य अङ्ग थे।

देवपुरोहित तेजस्वी मुनि भरद्वाज का आश्रम रमणीय वृक्षावलियों से सुशोभित था। चित्रकूट पर रह रहे भ्राता श्रीराम से मिलने जा रहे भरत ने मुनिश्रेष्ठ भरद्वाज के इसी आश्रम में एक रात्रि सेनासहित निवास किया—

ततस्तथेत्येवमुदारदर्शनः प्रतीतरूपो भरतोऽब्रवीद् वचः।
चकार बुद्धिं च तदाश्रमे तदा निशानिवासाय नराधिपात्मजः॥[1]

पाद्य, अर्घ्य और फलमूल आदि से अतिथि सत्कार कर चुके भरद्वाज मुनि ने सेनासहित भरत का जो दिव्य सत्कार किया, वह अद्वितीय था। विश्वकर्मा दिक्पालों, नदियों, देव, गन्धर्वों एवं अप्सराओं आदि के साथ उन्होंने अलौकिक चैत्ररथ वन का भी आह्वान किया। कुबेर के इस वन में दिव्य वस्त्र और आभूषण ही वृक्षों के पत्ते हैं और दिव्य अङ्गनाएँ ही फल—

वनं कुरुषु यद् दिव्यं वासोभूषणपत्रवत्।
दिव्यनारीफलं शश्वत् तत्कौबेरमिहैव तु॥[2]

आह्वान किए जाने पर ऐसा चैत्ररथ भरद्वाज मुनि के आश्रम में उपस्थित हो गया।

उत्तरेभ्यः कुरुभ्यश्च वनं दिव्योपभोगवत्।
आजगाम नदी सौम्या तीरजैर्बहुभिर्वृता॥[3]

यद्यपि आश्रम में स्थान-स्थान पर बेल, कैथ, कटहल, आंवला, बिजौरा तथा आम के फलों से युक्त वृक्ष सुशोभित हो रहे थे तथापि जो पुष्प देवताओं के उद्यानों में तथा चैत्ररथ वन में हुआ करते थे, वे भी महर्षि के प्रताप

से प्रयागवन में दिखाई देने लगे। वहाँ के पार्थिव वृक्ष भी मुनि के तेज से अलौकिक हो गए। बेल के वृक्ष मृदङ्ग बजाते, बहेड़े के वृक्ष शम्या नामक ताल देते तो पीपल के वृक्ष नृत्य करते थे।

बिल्वा मार्दङ्गिका आसन् शम्याग्राहा बिभीतिकाः।
अश्वत्था नर्तकाश्चासन् भरद्वाजस्य तेजसा।।[4]

देवदारु, ताल, तिलक और तमाल कुबड़े और बौने बनकर हर्षपूर्वक भरत की सेवा हेतु उपस्थित हो गए। शिंशिपा, आमलकी और जम्बू आदि स्त्रीलिंग वृक्ष एवं मालती, मल्लिका एवं जाति आदि वन की लताएँ नारी का रूप धारण करके भरद्वाज मुनि के आश्रम में आ बसीं—

ततः सरलतालाश्च तिलकः सतमालकाः।
प्रहृष्टास्तत्र सम्पेतुः कुब्जा भूत्वाथ वामनाः।।
शिंशिपाऽऽमलकी जम्बूर्याश्चान्याः कानने लताः।
मालती मल्लिका जातिर्याश्चान्याः कानने लताः।
प्रमदाविग्रहं कृत्वा भरद्वाजाश्रमेऽवसन्।।[5]

इन वल्लरियों ने स्त्रियाँ बनकर सेनासहित भरत को आदरपूर्वक भोजन कराया।

ऐसे अद्भुत वन के स्त्रष्टा मुनि भरद्वाज यहाँ इस अलौकिक वन के माध्यम से उस मुनि संस्कृति के प्रतिनिधि दिखाई पड़ते हैं जो स्वान्तःसुखाय परार्थ करती थी। भरद्वाज मुनि अपनी प्रसन्नता के लिए भरत को भोजन करवाना चाहते थे।[6] उनके तपोबल से पार्थिव वृक्ष एवं लताएँ अलौकिक रूप धारण कर अतिथि-सेवा रूपी नृयज्ञ के अनुष्ठान में सहयोगी बने।

मुनिगण जहाँ अपने तेज से इस प्रकार के अलौकिक वनोपवनों की सृष्टि कर सकते थे, वहीं मानव कौशल से ऐसे वनों का निर्माण करने में समर्थ थे। मानव संस्कृति के प्राणभूत एवं इस महान् अयन के महान नायक श्रीराम की अयोध्या में भी अन्तःपुर में विहार योग्य एक अलौकिक अशोकवनिका विद्यमान थी। इस वाटिका में सदा फूल-फल देने वाले रमणीय, मनोरम, दिव्य रस एवं गन्ध वाले वृक्ष थे जो कि मालियों द्वारा तैयार किए गए थे—

सर्वदा कुसुमैः रम्यैः फलवद्भिर्मनोरमैः।
दिव्यगन्धरसोपेतैस्तरुणाङ्कुरपल्लवैः ।।
तथैव तरुभिर्दिव्यैः शिल्पिभिः परिकल्पितैः।
चारुपल्लवपुष्पाढ्यैर्मत्तभ्रमरसङ्कुलैः ।।[7]

इस वन में चन्दन, अगरु, आम, नारियल, रक्तचन्दन, देवदारू, चम्पा, अशोक, पुंनाग, महुआ, कटहल, असन, पारिजात, कदम्ब, अर्जुन, नागकेसर, छितवन, अतिमुक्तक, मन्दार, कदली, प्रियंगु, धूलिकदम्ब, बकुल, जामुन और कोविदार[8] जैसे अनेक पार्थिव वृक्षों के साथ-साथ सुवर्ण के समान पीले, अग्निशिखा के समान उज्ज्वल और नीले अञ्जन के समान श्याम वृक्ष भी थे।[9] यह इन्द्र के नन्दन एवं ब्रह्मा द्वारा निर्मित चैत्ररथ के ही समान रमणीय वाटिका थी।

नन्दनं हि यथेन्द्रस्य ब्राह्मं चैत्ररथं यथा।
तथाभूतं हि रामस्य काननं संनिवेशनम्।।[10]

अयोध्या की अलौकिक वृक्षों से युक्त यह अशोकवाटिका मानव कौशल का अनुपम उद्घोष कही जा सकती है।

रामायण में एक ऐसे सुवर्णमय अलौकिक वन का भी वर्णन हुआ है जिसका निर्माण 'मय' नामक असुर ने किया था।[11] दक्षिण दिशा में विन्ध्यगिरि की गुफाओं और गहन वनों में सीता को खोजते तृषार्त, क्लान्त हनुमान् आदि वानरवीर जल की आशा से ऋक्षबिल नामक गुफा में प्रविष्ट हुए। अन्धकाराच्छन्न इस गुफा में वानरों द्वारा सुवर्णमय, अन्धकाररहित मय-निर्मित वन देखा गया। उस वन के वृक्षों से अग्नि के समान प्रभा निकल रही थी। यह वन साल, ताल, तमाल, पुंनाग, अशोक, धव, चम्पा, नागवृक्ष और कनेर-इन सभी पुष्पित एवं बालसूर्य के समान कान्तिमान् सुवर्णमय वृक्षों से व्याप्त था। विचित्र हिरण्यमय गुच्छे और रक्तिम पत्र मानों वृक्षों के मुकुट थे। फल रूपी सुवर्णमय आभूषणों से विभूषित ये वृक्ष अपने दीप्तिमान् स्वरूप से प्रकाशित हो रहे थे। निर्मल जल में कमल भी सोने के ही थे।[12]

मयासुर के इस अद्भुत् काञ्चन वन एवं किष्किन्धा के दिव्य वृक्षों से परिचित कपिश्रेष्ठ हनुमान् अमरावती तुल्य लङ्का पुरी की अशोक वाटिका को देखकर चमत्कृत रह गए। विश्वकर्मा द्वारा निर्मित इस वाटिका में हनुमान् प्रविष्ट हुए। सुवर्णमय वृक्ष समूह जब वायु के झोंकों से हिले तो उनसे जो सैकड़ों घुंघरुओं के बजने जैसी ध्वनि हुई, तब कपिवर विस्मय से भर उठे।[13] स्वर्गिक कल्पवृक्ष की लताओं एवं वृक्षों से वह भूमि सुशोभित थी। ये वृक्ष एवं लताएँ अलौकिक सौरभ, स्वाद, सौन्दर्य एवं वर्ण से युक्त थे—

संतानकलताभिश्च पादपैरुपशोभिताम्।
दिव्यगन्धरसोपेतां सर्वतः समलङ्कृताम्।।[14]

कनेर, पुंनाग, सप्तपर्ण, चम्पा, उद्दालक आदि पार्थिव वृक्ष एवं सब ऋतुओं में फलने-फूलने के कारण अलौकिक हो गए थे।[15] जैसा कि अभिधान से ही स्पष्ट है कि इस वाटिका में अशोक वृक्ष संख्या में सर्वाधिक थे। सैकड़ों प्रकार के अशोकों में से कुछ सुनहरे वर्ण के थे, कुछ अग्निशिखा के समान रक्त वर्ण के थे, तो कुछ काजल के समान कृष्ण वर्ण के थे—

शातकुम्भनिभाः केचित् केचिदग्निशिखप्रभाः।
नीलाञ्जननिभाः केचित् तत्राशोकाः सहस्रशः।।[16]

वस्तुतः अशोकवाटिका कल्पनातीत प्राकृतिक सौन्दर्य से परिपूर्ण थी। वृक्षों और पुष्पों की विविधता के कारण यह देवोद्यान नन्दन और चैत्ररथ से भी बढ़कर था।[17]

असुर संस्कृति भोगविलासों में लिप्त कामासक्तों की संस्कृति थी। इसी काम-प्रधान स्वभाववश मय-असुर, इन्द्र द्वारा काञ्चन वन से मार भगाया गया तो असुराधिपति रावण श्रीराम से न तो अशोकवाटिका रूपी मुकुटमणि से सुशोभित अपनी लङ्का को बचा पाया और न ही अपने प्राणों को।

पर्वतराज हिमालय अलौकिक वृक्षों, औषधियों एवं फल-मूलों का आकर है। इस पर्वतश्रेष्ठ पर एक अलौकिक विशाल वृक्ष, उत्तर दिशा में सीता की खोज में गए वानरवीरों द्वारा देखा गया। यह वृक्ष भगवान् शङ्कर की यज्ञशाला में स्थित था।[18] पूर्वकाल में पवित्र पर्वतराज पर भगवान् शङ्कर के द्वारा यज्ञ किया गया तो जो होम द्रव्य का स्राव हुआ, उससे अमृत तुल्य स्वादिष्ट फल-मूल उत्पन्न हुए।[19] इन अलौकिक फल-मूलों को एक बार खाने वाला एक मास तक तृप्त बना रहता था—

तदन्नसम्भवं दिव्यं फलमूलं मनोहरम्।
यः कश्चित् सकृदश्नाति मांसं भवति तर्पितः।।[20]

फलाहारी बुद्धिमान् वानर शिखामणियों ने वहाँ जो भी दिव्य औषधियाँ देखीं उन्हें भी दिव्य फल-मूलों के साथ ले लिया और वानरराज सुग्रीव को समर्पित किया।[21]

इन्द्रजित् द्वारा प्रयुक्त ब्रह्मास्त्र का सम्मान रखने हेतु समराङ्गण में श्रीराम एवं सुमित्रानन्दन वानरवीरों सहित घायल हो गए तो सैंकड़ों बाणों से विद्ध वृद्ध ऋक्षराज जाम्बवान् द्वारा पवनकुमार हनुमान् को हिमालय पर्वत पर उत्पन्न होने वाली, दिव्य औषधियाँ लाकर राम लक्ष्मण सहित सम्पूर्ण घायल वानरों को स्वस्थ कराने को कहा।[22] ऋषभ एवं कैलास पर्वत के मध्य स्थित औषधियों के पर्वत से दसों दिशाओं को प्रकाशित करने वाली चार महौषधियाँ शीघ्रातिशीघ्र कपिश्रेष्ठ हनुमान् को लानीं थीं। उनके नाम मृतसञ्जीवनी, विशल्यकरणी, सुवर्णकरणी तथा संधानी थे।[23] इन महौषधियों में अदृश्य होने की अद्भुत् शक्ति थी। ये महौषधियाँ ये जानकर अदृश्य हो गईं कि कोई हमें लेने आ रहा है—

महौषध्यस्ततः सर्वास्तस्मिन् पर्वतसत्तमे।
विज्ञायार्थिनमायान्तं ततो जग्मुरदर्शनम्।।[24]

इसी कारण हनुमान् को वह पर्वतशिखर ही लङ्का में लाना पड़ा। इन महौषधियों की सुगन्ध मात्र से ही राम लक्ष्मण सहित सभी वानरवीर स्वस्थ हुए। उनके शरीर से बाण निकल गए और उनकी सारी पीड़ा जाती रही।[25]

राजा इल की कथा में भगवान् शिव से सम्बद्ध एक अलौकिक वन प्रदेश भी वर्णित है। इस वन में भगवान् शिव अपने सेवकों सहित गिरिराजकुमारी का मनोरञ्जन करते थे। यहाँ सभी पुल्लिग नामधारी वृक्ष स्त्रीलिङ्ग में परिणत हो स्थित थे—

यत्र यत्र वनोद्देशे सत्त्वाः पुरुषवादिनः।
वृक्षाः पुरुषनामानस्ते सर्वे स्त्रीजना भवन्।।[26]

किष्किन्धा सुदृढ़ एवं वैभवपूर्ण वानर साम्राज्य का तुमुल नाद थी। रत्नमयी यह पुरी उन अलौकिक वृक्षों से परिपूर्ण थी जिन्हें स्वयं देवराज इन्द्र द्वारा प्रदान किया गया था—

महेन्द्रदत्तैः श्रीमद्भिर्नीलजीमूतसंनिभैः।
दिव्यपुष्पफलैर्वृक्षैः शीतच्छायैर्मनोरमैः।।[27]

किष्किन्धापुरी के पुष्पित वृक्ष सम्पूर्ण कामनाओं को पूर्ण करने वाले फलों से युक्त थे।[28]

उत्तर भारत में शैलोदा नदी के तट पर स्थित अद्वितीय उत्तर कुरुदेश के अलौकिक वृक्ष सब ऋतुओं में फलने-फूलने वाले, दिव्य गन्ध, दिव्य रस एवं दिव्य स्पर्श प्रदान करने वाले एवं कामनाओं को पूर्ण करने वाले थे।[29] वहाँ अनेक चमत्कारिक वृक्ष थे। कुछ श्रेष्ठ वृक्ष तो फलों के रूप में नाना प्रकार के वस्त्र, मोती, वैदूर्यमणि जटित आभूषण देते थे तो कुछ सुन्दर वृक्ष मणियों के समान विचित्र फल उत्पन्न करते थे।[30] कितने ही वृक्ष विचित्र बिछौनों से युक्त शय्याओं को ही फल के रूप में प्रकट करते थे। ये वृक्ष सुन्दर मालाएँ, बहुमूल्य पेय पदार्थ और विविध भोजन के साथ-साथ रूप और यौवन से प्रकाशित सद्गुणवती कन्याओं को भी जन्म देते थे—

शयनानि प्रसूयन्ते चित्रास्तरणवन्ति च।
मनः कान्तानि माल्यानि फलन्त्यत्रापरे द्रुमाः।।
पानानि च महार्हाणि भक्ष्याणि विविधानि च।
स्त्रियश्च गुणसम्पन्ना रूपयौवनलक्षिता।।[31]

उपर्युक्त वर्णन के आधार पर कहा जा सकता है कि रामायण काल में अलौकिक वनोपवन विद्यमान थे, भले ही इनके वर्णनों में किञ्चित् अतिशयोक्ति रही हो। इनकी सत्ता को नितान्त काल्पनिक मानकर नकारा नहीं जा सकता क्योंकि साहित्य रूपी दर्पण में वही प्रतिबिम्बित होता है जो समाज में विद्यमान हो। रामायणकालीन ये अलौकिक वनोपवन मानवनिर्मित भी थे और असुर निर्मित भी। ये मुनियों के तेज का भी परिणाम थे और देवताओं द्वारा प्रदत्त उपहार भी। ये वन वाटिकाएँ ऐसे वृक्षों से परिपूर्ण थीं जो सब ऋतुओं में फलते-फूलते थे और कामनाओं को पूर्ण करने जैसे चमत्कारिक गुणों से युक्त होते थे। प्रायः इनके वृक्ष पार्थिव ही हैं परन्तु पार्थिव वृक्षों से भिन्न अलौकिक रूप, रस, गन्ध, स्पर्श एवं गुणों को धारण करने वाले हैं। इन्हें हम असुरों के वैभव का, मुनियों के तपोबल का एवं मानवों के कौशल का प्रतीक मान सकते हैं। इन वनोपवनों के विषय में विस्मयकारक तथ्य तो यह है कि मुनि, असुर, मानव आदि विविध संस्कृतियाँ परस्पर वैभिन्न्य रखते हुए भी अलौकिक वनोपवनों के प्रति समभाव से प्रेम रखती हैं। वर्तमान में जिस प्रकार से वनों का दोहन और ध्वंस हो रहा है, उसके चलते भविष्य में पार्थिव वन भी कहीं अलौकिक वनों की भाँति ग्रन्थों के पृष्ठों में ही सिमटकर न रह जाएँ?

सन्दर्भ-सङ्केत

1. श्रीमद्वाल्मीकीय रामायण (गीताप्रेस, गोरखपुर)-काण्ड-2, सर्ग-20, पद्य 24
2. वही - 2.91. 2
3. वही - 2.91. 31
4. वही - 2.91.49
5. वही - 2.91.50-51
6. वही - 2.91.4
7. वही - 7. 42.6-7
8. वही - 7. 42.2-5
9. वही - 7. 42.9
10. वही - 7. 42.15½
11. वही - 4.51.10-13
12. वही - 4.50.24, 26-29
13. वही - 5.14. 40
14. वही - 5.15. 2

15. वही - 5.15. 8, 9, 13
16. वही - 5.15.10½
17. वही - 5.15.11½
18. वही - 4.37. 27
19. वही - 4.37. 29
20. वही - 4.37. 30
21. वही - 4.37.31-32, 35
22. वही - 6.74.28-29
23. वही - 6.74.30-34
24. वही - 6.74. 64
25. वही - 6.74.73-74
26. वही - 7.87.13
27. वही - 4.33.16
28. वही - 4.33.5, 15
29, वही - 4.43. 44
30. वही - 4.43.45-46
31. वही - 4.43.47-48

卐 卐 卐

मतङ्गवन एवं पम्पा पुष्करिणी में वनस्पति

(वाल्मीकि रामायण के अरण्य तथा किष्किन्धाकाण्ड पर आधारित)

अञ्जु बाला

आदिकाव्य रामायण 'चतुर्विंशति साहस्त्री संहिता' के नाम से प्रसिद्ध है क्योंकि इसमें 24 हज़ार श्लोक हैं। गायत्री में भी 24 अक्षर होते हैं। विद्वानों का मत है कि रामायण के प्रत्येक हज़ार श्लोक का प्रथम अक्षर गायत्री मन्त्र के ही अक्षर से प्रारम्भ होता है। भारतीय परम्परानुसार कवि वाल्मीकि ने त्रेतायुग के आरम्भ में रामजन्म के पूर्व ही रामायण की रचना की थी। काव्यात्मक, प्रौढशैली में उपनिबद्ध रामायण में प्रकृति के अनेकविध मनोरम दृश्य उपस्थित हैं। बाल, अयोध्या, अरण्य, किष्किन्धा, सुन्दर, युद्ध, और उत्तरकाण्ड— इन सात काण्डों में विभक्त रामायण भारतीय संस्कृति एवं सभ्यता का अद्वितीय कोश है।[1]

अरण्य तथा किष्किन्धाकाण्ड में मतङ्ग मुनि के आश्रम और पुष्करिणी पम्पा की शोभा दर्शनीय है। वहाँ सर्वत्र प्रसृत वनस्पति-सौन्दर्य श्रीराम के दृष्टिपथ में आता है किन्तु सीता के वियोग से सन्तप्त श्रीराम के लिए वनशोभा तथा उस पर वसन्तर्तु का प्रहार असह्य हो रहा है—

शक्यो धारयितुं कामो भवेदभ्यागतो मया।
यदि भूयो वसन्तो मां न हन्यात् पुष्पितद्रुमः।।[2]

वसन्तर्तु में वन का नवीनपुष्पपल्लवों से सजना, मलयानिल का पुष्पों से सुरक्षित होना,[3] कोकिल का कूजना, कमल का खिलना, पक्षियों का चहचहाना, मयूरों का नृत्य करना आदि (वसन्तर्तु के) स्वाभाविक गुण हैं, जो श्रीराम को उद्दीप्त कर रहे हैं।

मन्मथायाससम्भूतो वसन्तगुणवर्धितः।।
अयं मां धक्ष्यति क्षिप्रं शोकाग्निर्नचिरादिव।
मम त्वं विना वासः पुष्पमासे सुदुःसहः।।[4]

आदि कवि वाल्मीकि वसन्तर्तुकालीन वृक्ष तथा पुष्पों की चर्चा करते हैं। मार्ग में आने वाले अनेकविध वृक्षों का उल्लेख करते हुए कहते हैं—

जम्बूप्रियालपनसा न्यग्रोधप्लक्षतिन्दुकाः।
अश्वत्थाः कर्णिकाराश्च चूताश्चान्ये च पादपाः।।
धन्वना नागवृक्षाश्च तिलका नक्तमालकाः।
नीलाशोकाः कदम्बाश्च करवीराश्च पुष्पिताः।।
अग्निमुख्या अशोकाश्च सुरक्ताः पारिभद्रकाः।[5]

पम्पा सरोवर के तटस्थ वृक्ष उसी के जल से विकसित और पुष्प-गन्ध से सुवासित हैं।

पम्पातीररुहाश्चेमे संसिक्ता मधुगन्धिनः।
मालतीमल्लिकापद्मकरवीराश्च पुष्पिताः।।
केतक्यः सिन्दुवाराश्च वासन्त्यश्च सुपुष्पिताः।
माधव्यो गन्धपूर्णाश्च कुन्दगुल्माश्च सर्वशः।।
चिरिबिल्वा मधूकाश्च वञ्जुला बकुलास्तथा।
चम्पकास्तिलकाश्चैव नागवृक्षाश्च पुष्पिताः।।[6]

मतङ्गवन में पर्वतशिखरों पर अङ्कोल, कुरंट, चूर्णक (सेमल), पाटलि, कोविदार, मुचुकुन्द (नारङ्ग), अर्जुन, केतक, उद्दालक, शिरीष, शीशम, धव, पलाश, चन्दन और नागकेसर आदि पुष्पित पल्लवित वृक्ष शोभायमान हैं।[7] वसन्तर्तु में पुष्पवैभव दर्शनीय है। चैत्रमास में ये वृक्ष परस्पर होड़ लगाकर पुष्पित हैं।[8]

राम लक्ष्मण को पम्पा (पुष्करिणी) के मनोहर वृक्षों को देखने का आग्रह करते हैं जो पुष्पिताग्र लता वल्लरियों से परिवेष्टित हैं।[9]

अमी पवनविक्षिप्ता विनदन्तीव पादपाः।
पुष्पसंछन्नशिखरा मारुतोत्क्षेपचञ्चलाः।।[10]

वायु और वृक्ष के सम्पर्क पर कवि की विविध उत्प्रेक्षाएँ अवलोकनीय हैं यथा वायु द्वारा विक्षिप्त शाखाओं के अग्रभागों का परस्पर ग्रथित हो जाना।[11] काननद्रुमों द्वारा पुष्पवर्षा (मेघ के समान) करके वहाँ भूमि को आच्छादित करना।[12] अन्यत्र कवि ने पुष्प तथा वायु के मध्य किए जा रहे खेल (क्रीड़ा) की सुन्दर उत्प्रेक्षा प्रस्तुत की है मानों वे पुष्प तथा वायु एक दूसरे के पीछे दौड़ रहे हों—

पतितैः पतमानैश्च पादपस्थैश्च मारुतः।
कुसुमैः पश्य सौमित्रे क्रीडतीव समन्ततः।।[13]

वायु से ही नहीं प्रत्युत स्वयं झड़कर गिरे हुए वृक्षपुष्पों से भूमि सुखदायिनी हो गई है। मानों चित्रविचित्र कोमलशय्या (मुलायम बिछौना) तैयार कर दी गई हो।[14] ये वृक्ष शाखाओं पर फूल रूपी मुकुट से शोभित हो रहे हैं।[15] वायु बहुत बलशालिनी है— यह गायन, वादन और नृत्य-कलाओं में निपुण है अतः ऐसी प्रतीत होती है मानो झूमते हुए वृक्षों को नृत्य शिक्षा दे रही हो—

मत्तकोकिलसंनादैर्नर्तयन्निव पादपान्।
शैलकंदरनिष्क्रान्तः प्रगीत इव चानिलः।।[16]

वृक्ष नर्तन ही नहीं कर रहे हैं अपितु गुञ्जायमान भ्रमरों के व्याज से गान भी कर रहे हैं।

अमी मधुकरोत्तंसाः प्रगीता इव पादपाः।।[17]

इस पम्पा का मनोरम रूप मन्दाकिनी के समान प्रतीत हो रहा है।[18] इसका जल शीतल सुगन्धित तथा असंख्य कमलों से युक्त है।[19] इसमें विभिन्न जलीय जीव यथा-कारण्डव, चकवा, हंस और जलकुक्कुट विचरण करते हैं।

एषा प्रसन्नसलिला पद्मनीलोत्पलायुता।
हंसकारण्डवाकीर्णा पम्पा सौगन्धिकायुता।।[20]

पम्पा में विकसित, प्रफुल्लित कमल के लिए कवि विभिन्न पदों का प्रयोग करते हैं यथा-पद्म, नीलोत्पल, अरविन्द, उत्पल, कुमुद तथा नलिनी और पङ्कज आदि।[21] एक स्थल पर शीतलवारिनिधि पम्पा में त्रिविध कमलों की अद्‌भुत छटा निरूपित है जिससे यह पम्पा चित्रविचित्र वर्णों वाले कालीन की शोभा को प्राप्त करती है–

पद्मसौगन्धिकैस्ताम्रां शुक्लां कुमुदमण्डलैः।
नीलां कुवलयोद्‌घाटैर्बहुवर्णां कुथामिव।।[22]

अनेकत्र कवि ने नेत्र के उपमानरूप कमल का उल्लेख किया है। किष्किन्धाकाण्ड में श्रीराम लक्ष्मण से कहते हैं कि वह सीता के नेत्रों के समान कमलकोशदल को ही देखना चाहते हैं।[23] इसके अतिरिक्त सीता के लिए 'पद्मनिभेक्षणा' तथा 'पद्मपत्रविशालाक्षी' पदों का प्रयोग करते हैं।[24]

अरण्यकाण्ड में पम्पा के निर्मल जल को कमलपत्र में लाने का उल्लेख मिलता है।[25] यहाँ उल्लेखनीय है कि पम्पासरोवर की पुष्पवृक्षादि (वनस्पति) सम्पत्ति कभी मलिन नहीं होती और न ही विनष्ट होती। कवि के अनुसार मतङ्गऋषि शिष्य के स्वेदबिन्दु ही वन से फलमूल लाते समय भूमि पर गिरकर (मुनिप्रभाव से) पुष्परूप में परिणत हो गए।[26]

संक्षेपतः यह दिव्य पुष्पराशि अवलोकनीय, आस्वादनीय और वन्द्य हैं।

सन्दर्भ-सङ्केत

1. संस्कृतसाहित्यकोश (राजवंश सहाय हीरा), पृ. 470
2. रामायण (वाल्मीकि) - 4.1.69
3. रामायण (वाल्मीकि) - 4.1.53
4. रामायण (वाल्मीकि) - 4.1.32-33, 41
5. रामायण (वाल्मीकि) - 3.73.3-5
6. रामायण (वाल्मीकि) - 4.1.76-78
7. रामायण (वाल्मीकि) - 4.1.80-82
8. रामायण (वाल्मीकि) - 4.1.91
9. रामायण (वाल्मीकि) - 4.1.9, 83-84
10. रामायण (वाल्मीकि) - 4.1.18 (पूर्वार्द्ध), 20 (पूर्वार्द्ध)
11. रामायण (वाल्मीकि) - 4.1.16
12. रामायण (वाल्मीकि) - 4.1.10, 12
13. रामायण (वाल्मीकि) - 4.1.13
14. रामायण (वाल्मीकि) - 4.1.89-90
15. रामायण (वाल्मीकि) - 4.1.92 (उत्तरार्द्ध)

16. रामायण (वाल्मीकि) - 4.1.15

17. रामायण (वाल्मीकि) - 4.1.18, 20

18. रामायण (वाल्मीकि) - 4.1.94

19. रामायण (वाल्मीकि) - 4.1.98

20. रामायण (वाल्मीकि) - 4.1.63

21. रामायण (वाल्मीकि) - 3.75.21; 4.1.62, 64, 66

22. रामायण (वाल्मीकि) - 3.75.20

23. रामायण (वाल्मीकि) - 4.1.71

24. रामायण (वाल्मीकि) - 4.1.50 (पूर्वार्द्ध), 67 (पूर्वार्द्ध)

25. रामायण (वाल्मीकि) - 3.73.17

26. रामायण (वाल्मीकि) - 3.73.23-25

卐 卐 卐

महाभारत में वनस्पति

आशा लता पाण्डे

वनस्पति-विज्ञान को प्रायः आधुनिक विज्ञान की देन माना जाता है, लेकिन इसके बीज तो हमें संस्कृत-भाषा के प्राचीनतम ग्रन्थ 'ऋग्वेद'[1] में ही प्राप्त हो जाते हैं। वैदिक कर्मकाण्ड में वनस्पतियों का प्रयोग किया जाना,[2] वेद-युगीन-जन के दैनिक जीवन में वनस्पतियों का उपयोग किया जाना तथा प्रकृति के प्रति आर्यों की संवेदनशीलता— ये सभी बातें भारत के प्राचीनतम साहित्य और समाज में वनस्पति के अस्तित्व, ज्ञान व महत्त्व को सिद्ध करती हैं।

भारत के प्राचीन महत्त्वपूर्ण ग्रन्थों की शृङ्खला में ही "महाभारत" भी है। महाभारत के लिए यह कहा गया है कि "जो यहाँ नहीं है, वह कहीं नहीं है"[3]— तो इस दृष्टि से यहाँ वनस्पतियों की उपस्थिति का वर्णन बहुतायत से होना स्वाभाविक ही है। वैसे भी जहाँ वनों,[4] वनश्रेणियों[5] के वर्णन हों, वनपर्व नाम से एक पूरा अध्याय ही हो, वहाँ वनस्पतियाँ तो होंगी ही। वनों में भी महान् वन,[6] कण्टकित-वन, निष्कण्टक वन[7], कदली-वन,[8] कमल-वन[9], शालवन, निर्जन-वन[10] आदि का उल्लेख है। अनुमान लगाया जा सकता है कि महान् वन अत्यन्त विशाल, कण्टकित— काँटों से भरा, कदलीवन- केले के पेड़ों से युक्त, कमलवन- कमल पुष्पों तथा शालवन- शाल वृक्षों की बहुलता से युक्त रहा होगा। इसके अतिरिक्त काम्यक,[11] द्वैत,[12] नन्दन,[13] खाण्डव[14] आदि वनों का भी उल्लेख है। वन के लिए विपिन,[15] अरण्य शब्दों का भी प्रयोग किया गया है। पेड़ों के लिए वृक्ष,[16] तरु,[17] द्रुम,[18] वनस्पति,[19] नग,[20] पादप,[21] जगतीरुह[22] आदि शब्दों का प्रयोग किया गया है। वृक्षों में न्यग्रोध,[23] वट,[24] शमी,[25] पलाश,[26] अश्वत्थ[27] अशोक,[28] शाल[29], शरस्तम्ब (सरकण्डा)[30] ताल (ताड़)[31], ढाक (किंशुक),[32] नल (नरकुल)[33] आदि नामों का उल्लेख है। शाल के वृक्ष का अन्य वृक्षों की अपेक्षा अधिक वर्णन इसकी तत्कालीन बहुलता को सिद्ध करता है। इनके अतिरिक्त तृण,[34] दर्भ (कुशा),[35] धान की क्यारी (केदारखण्ड)[36] भी उल्लिखित हैं। पके हुए धान के विशाल खेत हुआ करते थे।[37] कन्द-मूल-फलों की बहुतायत तो थी ही। वानरसेना के आगे बढ़ने के प्रसङ्ग में कहा गया है कि वे उन सुन्दर पर्वतीय शिखरों पर डेरा डालते हुए आगे बढ़ रहे थे जहाँ फल-मूल की बहुतायत होती तथा मधु और कन्द-मूल प्रचुर मात्रा में उपलब्ध होते।[38] लङ्का के वन में अन्न-जल का बहुत सुभीता था तथा फल और मूल भी प्रचुर मात्रा में उपलब्ध थे।[39]

दैनिक-जीवन में वनस्पतियाँ ईंधन, भोजन,[40] आभूषण, सजावट,[41] स्वागत,[42] खेलकूद[43] तथा पूजा[44] के उपयोग में लाई जाती थीं। रक्त (लाल) तथा श्वेत दोनों ही प्रकार के चन्दनों का उपयोग किया जाता था।[45] फूलों के रस व मधूक पुष्प से पेय पदार्थ बनाए जाते थे।[47] गृह-निर्माण के कर्म में सुशिक्षित एवं विश्वसनीय कारीगरों द्वारा घर बनाते समय सन, राल, मूँज, बल्वज (मोटे तिनकों वाली घास) और बाँस आदि द्रव्यों को घी से सींचकर बड़ी खूबी के साथ भवनरचना का उल्लेख है।[48] तृणों में वीरणस्तम्ब (खस) का वर्णन है।[49] विराट् पर्व में एक वृक्ष का वर्णन तो है लेकिन उसका नाम नहीं दिया गया है। यह वृक्ष ताड़ के बराबर था, जिसकी शाखाएँ बहुत बड़ी थीं और जो ऊपर से सूख गया था। इसकी ऊँचाई दस व्याम थी और इसके आसपास बरगद, पीपल और ढाक के वृक्ष थे।[50] तूल(रुई) का भी उल्लेख प्राप्त है।[51]

वातावरण को शुद्ध रखने के स्थान को सुन्दर बनाने के लिए उपवनों और उद्यानों के निर्माण का प्रचलन था।[52]

सुरम्य तपोवन तो होते ही थे।[53] फूलों से लदे हुए, सुन्दर वृक्षों से युक्त विचित्र वन हुआ करते थे।[54] महाभारत में फूलों से लदे वनस्पति और गुल्म का उल्लेख कई प्रसङ्गों में प्राप्त होता है।[55] राजा कल्माषपाद शापवश जिस वन में गए वह अनेक प्रकार की लताओं, गुल्मों से आच्छादित व विविध प्रकार के वृक्षों से आवृत गहन वन था जो भयङ्कर शब्दों से गूँजता रहता था।[56] गुप्तचर अज्ञातवास में छिपे पाण्डवों को खोजने जिस वन में गए वह निर्जन वन अनेकानेक वृक्षों और लताओं से व्याप्त, विविध लताओं की बहुलता और विस्तार से विलसित तथा नाना गुल्मों से समावृत था।[57]

ऐसे वनप्रदेशों का भी यहाँ वर्णन है, जहाँ फल-फूल और जल की कमी थी।[58] साथ में ऐसा स्थल भी है जहाँ सदा बर्फ़ जमी रहने के कारण कोई वृक्ष नहीं होता।[59] जल के लिए व्याकुल भाइयों के लिए पानी लाने के लिए युधिष्ठिर ने जब नकुल को भेजा तो उनसे कहा कि किसी वृक्ष पर चढ़कर सब दिशाओं में दृष्टिपात करो और जल के किनारे होने वाले वृक्षों को देखो।[60] इनमें जलकमल की बेल, सिन्दुबार (सिन्धुवार), बेंत (वेतस), केवड़ा (केतक), करवीर तथा पीपल के वृक्षों का उल्लेख है।[61] कुछ वृक्ष ऋतु आने पर ही फलते-फूलते थे।[62] वसन्त ऋतु में अशोक, चम्पा, आम, अतिमुक्तक (माधवीलता), पुन्नाग (नागकेसर), कनेर,[63] मौलसिरी, दिव्य पाटल, पाटल, नारियल, चन्दन तथा अर्जुन—ये स्वादिष्ट फलों से युक्त, रमणीय तथा पवित्र महावृक्ष उस वन की शोभा बढ़ा रहे थे।[64]

युधिष्ठिर ने महान् वन में तमाल, ताल, आम, महुआ, नीप, कदम्ब, साल, अर्जुन और कनेर के वृक्ष देखे जो ग्रीष्म ऋतु बीतने पर फूल धारण करते हैं।[65] स्थान-स्थान पर घास-फूस, वृक्ष व लतावल्लरियों के वर्णन तो प्राप्त होते ही हैं।[66] एक स्थल पर ओष्ठ की तुलना बिम्बफल से की गई है।[67] वनस्पतियों का प्रयोग हानिकारक भी होता था। अर्कपत्र (आक के पत्ते) खारे, तीखे, कड़वे और रूखे होते हैं। उनका परिणाम तीक्ष्ण होता है। पाचनकाल में वे पेट के अन्दर आग की ज्वाला-सी उठा देते हैं, अतः उनको खाने से उपमन्यु की आँखों की ज्योति नष्ट हो गई थी।[68]

महाभारत में देववृक्ष, चैत्य [69] व दिव्य सुगन्धित फूलों[70] का वर्णन है। शालिहोत्र मुनि के आश्रम का पवित्र वृक्ष सर्दी, गर्मी और वर्षा को अच्छी तरह सहने वाला है जिसका निर्माण मुनि ने अपनी तपस्या द्वारा किया है।[71] समुद्र-मन्थन के प्रसङ्ग में असंख्य वृक्ष, दिव्य ओषधियों, लताओं के समुदाय से आच्छादित मन्दराचल[72] व सम्पूर्ण कामनाओं का फल देने वाले पारिजात वृक्ष का वर्णन है।[73] ओषधि के रूप में वनस्पतियों का प्रयोग किया जाता था। महाराज संवरण के पृथ्वी पर गिर जाने पर उनके मन्त्री ने राजा के मस्तक को कमल की सुगन्धि से युक्त ठण्डे जल से सींचा,[74] जिससे उनकी मूर्छा दूर हो गई। भीम ने नागों की दी हुई खीर विषनाशक सुगन्धित ओषधियों के साथ खाई थी।[75] कर्ण-अर्जुन युद्ध में पक्ष-विपक्ष ग्रहण करने के समय वृक्ष व ओषधियाँ अर्जुन के पक्ष में आ गई थीं।[76]

वनस्पति-विज्ञान की मुख्यतः दो शाखाएँ होती हैं—

(i) जिसमें प्रकृति से सम्बद्ध पौधों का अध्ययन किया जाए (Pure Botany)।
(ii) जिसमें मानव-जीवन के लिए उपयोगी पौधों का वर्णन किया जाए (Applied Botany)।

महाभारत में दोनों ही प्रकार के उदाहरण प्राप्त हो रहे हैं। पेड़-पौधों के विभिन्न अँगों के स्वरूप, जैसे—बीज, जड़, तना, शाखाएँ, पत्तियाँ, फूल व फल[77] के उद्धरण भी यहाँ हैं। टहनी के लिए शाखा के अतिरिक्त वर्तिका[78] शब्द का भी प्रयोग किया गया है। नागराज तक्षक द्वारा विष से जलाए हुए वटवृक्ष को जब द्विजश्रेष्ठ काश्यप ने अपनी विद्या के बल से जीवित किया तो सबसे पहले उसमें से अङ्कुर निकला, फिर उसमें दो पत्ते हुए। इसी प्रकार क्रमशः पल्लव, शाखा और प्रशाखाओं से युक्त उस महान् वृक्ष को उन्होंने पूर्ववत् खड़ा कर दिया।[79] इस प्रसङ्ग में आदिपर्व में महाभारत रूपी वृक्ष के अङ्गों का सुन्दर और विस्तृत वर्णन द्रष्टव्य है—'महाभारत वृक्ष का बीज है संग्रहाध्याय और जड़ है पौलोम एवं आस्तीक-पर्व। सम्भवपर्व इसके स्कन्ध का विस्तार है और सभा तथा अरण्यपर्व पक्षियों के रहने योग्य कोटर हैं। अरणीपर्व इस वृक्ष का ग्रन्थिस्थल है। विराट और उद्योगपर्व इसका सारभाग है। भीष्मपर्व इसकी बड़ी शाखा और द्रोणपर्व

इसके पत्ते हैं। कर्णपर्व इसके श्वेत पुष्प हैं और शल्यपर्व सुगन्ध। स्त्रीपर्व और ऐषीकपर्व इसकी छाया है तथा शान्तिपर्व इसका महान् फल है। अश्वमेधपर्व इसका अमृतमय रस है और आश्रमवासिकपर्व आश्रय लेकर बैठने का स्थान। मौसलपर्व श्रुतिरूपा ऊँची-ऊँची शाखाओं का अन्तिम भाग है तथा सदाचार एवं विद्या से सम्पन्न द्विजाति इसका सेवन करते हैं।[80] यह अक्षय भारत-वृक्ष है।[81] इसके स्वादु, पवित्र, सरस और अविनाशी पुष्प तथा फल हैं– धर्म और मोक्ष।[82] अन्य स्थलों पर भी महाभारत के चरित्रों की तुलना वृक्ष के अङ्गों से की गई है। दुर्योधन क्रोधमय विशाल वृक्ष के समान है। कर्ण स्कन्ध, शकुनि शाखा और दुःशासन समृद्ध फल-पुष्प हैं। अज्ञानी राजा धृतराष्ट्र ही इसके मूल हैं।[83] इसी प्रकार युधिष्ठिर धर्ममय विशाल वृक्ष हैं। अर्जुन स्कन्ध, भीमसेन शाखा और माद्रीनन्दन इसके समृद्ध फल-पुष्प हैं। श्रीकृष्ण वेद और ब्राह्मण ही इस वृक्ष के मूल (जड़) हैं।[84] ऐसा ही वर्णन नीतिज्ञ राजा का भी किया गया है।[85]

वनस्पतियों से सम्बन्धित कुछ नाम महाभारत में अनेक स्थलों पर मिलते हैं, कुछ अपेक्षाकृत कम स्थलों पर तो कुछ केवल एक ही बार। वनपर्व में राम द्वारा राक्षस की एक बाँह को तिल के पौधे की तरह काट गिराने की उपमा दी गई है।[86] फूलों में कमल का प्रयोग बहुतायत से किया गया है। उपमा में मानव अङ्गों जैसे मुख[87], उंगलियाँ[88], नेत्र, स्तन[89] आदि की सुन्दरता के वर्णन में कमल के विशेषण प्रयुक्त हैं। कोमलता व कान्ति- वर्णन में भी इसका प्रयोग है।[90] सौगन्धिक कमल[91] और सनातन कमल[93], नाभिपद्म[93] और वैजयन्ती माला (जिसके कमल कुम्हलाते नहीं)[94] का वर्णन प्राप्त है। उपमाओं में सर्वाधिक उपमा नेत्रों के लिए प्राप्त है जैसे– पुण्डरीकाक्ष,[95] कमलपत्राक्ष,[96] कमलनयन[97] व लोच्चन राजीवलोचना,[98] पद्मपलाशाक्षी,[99] पद्मगर्भारुणेक्षण,[100] कमललोचन,[101] जलरुहेक्षण,[102] वनजपत्राक्षी,[103] पद्मायतविशालाक्ष,[104] आदि। कमलिनी के लिए तामरसी,[105] शब्द का प्रयोग हुआ है। पम्पावर्णन में भी नीले लाल कमलों का वर्णन है।[106] शारदीय कमल का वर्णन है।[107] कमल के लिए पुण्डरीक[108], पद्म,[109] उत्पल[110] आदि शब्दों का प्रयोग हुआ है। कमल-कुमुदिनी सरोवरों की उपमा प्राप्त है।[111] महाभारत में एक स्थल पर वनस्पतियों की उत्पत्ति का अत्यन्त वैज्ञानिक उल्लेख है, जहाँ जरितारि अग्निदेव से कहते हैं कि वे वनस्पतियों के शरीर हैं। तृण-लता आदि की योनि पृथ्वी और जल अग्नि के वीर्य हैं।[112]

अन्ततः यह कहा जा सकता है कि महाभारत में वृक्षों और लताओं से सुशोभित दुर्गम वन, कमल और उत्पल आदि से अलङ्कृत रमणीय सरोवर, विकसित वृक्षों और लता-वल्लरियों से विभूषित विचित्र कानन, पर्वतों के कुञ्ज, यहाँ तक कि गुफाओं में खिले हुए कमलसमूह, बड़े-बड़े शालवृक्षों के जंगल, फलों से सम्पन्न तपस्वी मुनियों के सुरम्य आश्रम व देववन[113]– यहाँ वनस्पतियों के अस्तित्व व महत्त्व को स्वतः सिद्ध कर रहे हैं। महाभारत में कहा गया है कि जिस हरे-भरे वृक्ष की शीतल छाया का आश्रय लेकर रहा जाए, उसके किसी एक पत्ते से भी द्रोह नहीं करना चाहिए।[114]

सन्दर्भ-सङ्केत

1. ऋग्वेद 1. 32. 5
2. अथर्ववेद 10.7.38
   तैत्तिरीय संहिता VII, 3.19-20
   ओषधिभ्यः स्वाहा मूलेभ्यः स्वाहा तूलेभ्यः स्वाहा काण्डेभ्यः स्वाहा वल्शेभ्याः स्वाहा पुष्पेभ्यः स्वाहा फलेभ्यः स्वाहा। वनस्पतिभ्यः स्वाहा मूलेभ्यः स्वाहा तूलेभ्यः स्वाहा स्कन्धेभ्यः स्वाहा शाखेभ्यः स्वाहा पर्णेभ्यः स्वाहा पुष्पेभ्यः स्वाहा।
3. यदिहास्ति तदन्यत्र यन्नेहास्ति न तत् क्वचित्। (महाभारत)
4. आदिपर्व 139.12, 28 (वनोद्देशे); 148.12; 150.1, 144; 151.1; 152.31, 35; 155.1 (वनेन वनं गत्वा); 162.5;170.43; 175.29 (वनोद्देशे); 184.4; विराट्पर्व 26.7; 38.6; 39.12; 60.7
5. वनपर्व 83. 21; 264. 2

6. आदिपर्व 172.2; 176.46; 2.295; वनपर्व 264.3; 279.27 (वने महति-विशाल वन में); 296.2; विराट् पर्व 25.9; 54.14
7. आदिपर्व 152.27; वनपर्व 264.14; वनपर्व 11.72
8. आदिपर्व 2.178; 63.71 (रम्भोरुं-जांघें कदली-सी शोभा पा रही थीं); 291.14
9. आदिपर्व 136.9 (· · · पद्मवनात् · · ·); वनपर्व 25.1
10. आदिपर्व 182.7; वनपर्व 24.2; 264.8
11. आदिपर्व 2.157, 189; वनपर्व 258.13, 17; 268.22, 311.2
12. आदिपर्व 2.195; 24.13; 25.1; 26.1, 2; वनपर्व 246.27; 256.8; 258.2, 5; 311.3, 5
13. वनपर्व 280.41
14. आदिपर्व 22वां अध्याय; कर्णपर्व 87.69; विराट्पर्व 36.18
15. आदिपर्व 139.27
16. आदिपर्व 50.34, 41; 131.75; 132.5; 133.9; 150.2, 33; 37, 151.4; 152.44; 154.16; 230.16; वनपर्व 277.51; 311.7 आदि। विराट्पर्व 5.33; 9.26; 23.27; 33.16 (महावृक्षो); 41.1; 50.18; 54.16; द्रोणपर्व 46.24 आदि।
17. वनपर्व 288.18
18. आदिपर्व 132.4; 150.4, 32, 35 (काननजा-वनों में उत्पन्न), वनपर्व 286.4, 13; कर्णपर्व 82.19; विराट्पर्व 16.12; द्रोणपर्व 76.31
19. आदिपर्व 50.22, 33, 40, 42; 131.76; 154.16; वनपर्व 311.12; विराट्पर्व 16.17; 33.17, 18
20. आदिपर्व 50.23, 41; 132.9; विराट्पर्व 54.13
21. आदिपर्व 19.26; 152.45; वनपर्व 287.19; 288.14; विराट्पर्व 38.6; 23.26, 27
22. वही 287.3
23. आदिपर्व 2.296; 30.23; विराट्पर्व 23.23
24. वही 30.23 (शाखा की विशालता का उल्लेख) 76.36
25. वही 2.206; विराट्पर्व 5.28, 31; 40.1, 3; 67.12, 22
26. वही 31.8; वनपर्व 297.110; विराट्पर्व 58.55; शल्यपर्व 9.24
27. विराट्पर्व 23.23; आदिपर्व 150.1; 152.44, 45
28. आदिपर्व 82.6; वनपर्व 280.42 (अशोकवनिका-अशोकवाटिका)
29. वही 114.8; 151.1; 154.28; 211.6; वनपर्व 270.10 (शाल के वृक्ष की भाँति ऊँचे) 276.12; 287.8,9, 10; 288. 18; 295.4; 279.29 (शालस्कन्ध-साखू की शाखा के समान उसके कन्धे और बड़ी भुजाएँ); वनपर्व 313.123 (बृहच्छाल इवोत्थितः-शालवृक्ष के समान ऊँचा) कर्णपर्व 85.37
30. वही 129.13
31. वनपर्व 276.12; 280.51; द्रोणपर्व 170.23 (पक्वं तालफलं यथा— आँधी के द्वारा गिराए हुए पके हुए तालफल के समान पृथ्वी पर गिर पड़ा) विराट्पर्व 14.51
32. विराट्पर्व 23.23
33. कर्णपर्व 18.8 (· · · स्थूलं नलं यथा तथा— जैसे मोटे नरकुलों के कुचले जाते समय चर-चर की आवाज होती है)
34. आदिपर्व 139.13
35. वही 43.24; विराट्पर्व 6.1, वनपर्व 83.23
36. वही 3.23
37. वनपर्व 283.18

38. वही 283.20
39. वही 284.1
40. विराट्पर्व 16.19; आदिपर्व 117.25; 119.47; 125.23; वनपर्व 25.3; 280.43; विराट्पर्व 9.13; 28.20
41. आदिपर्व 63.21 (चन्दन फूलों के हार); 126.8; 134.9; (··· शुक्लमाल्यानुलेपनः— श्वेत पुष्पों की माला व श्वेत चन्दन से सुशोभित); वनपर्व 279.66; 67; विराट्पर्व 9.18 (द्रौपदी मल्लिका, उत्पल, कमल और चम्पा के फूलों के सुन्दर व विचित्र हार गूँथ सकती थी); 28.20; 211.4; शल्यपर्व 3.38 (··· कोविदाखरध्वजम् ··· ध्वजा में कचनार वृक्ष का चिह्न); 7. 44
42. आदिपर्व 43.24, 25
43. वही 127.21, 22
44. वही 134.24; वनपर्व 39.65; 279.34 (कुश, लाजा, शमीपत्र का अभिषेक में प्रयोग); 296.26
45. वही 134.19, 24; वनपर्व 279.66-68; शल्यपर्व 9.21
46. वनपर्व 278.40
47. कर्णपर्व 83.30
48. आदिपर्व 146.15
49. वही 13.17
50. विराट्पर्व 23.20-23
51. वनपर्व 20.41
52. आदिपर्व 127.29 (पुरोद्यान); 139.64; 211.5; वनपर्व 283.51, 54
53. वनपर्व 293.39, 40; 294.9, 10; 295.9; 296.12
54. वही 296.30, 31
55. आदिपर्व 150.1, 10; द्रोणपर्व 174.23
56. वही 182.8
57. विराट्पर्व 25.10
58. आदिपर्व 150.8
59. वही, 119.12
60. वनपर्व 312.5, 6, 8
61. वही 312.45

    उपेतं नलिनीजालैः सिन्धुवारैः सवेतसैः।
    केतकैः करवीरैः पिप्पलैश्चैव संवृतम्।।

62. आदिपर्व 64.25; 126.7; विराट्पर्व 56.14
63. वही 211.10; शल्यपर्व 19.51; (लाल कनेर— कर्णिकाराः)
64. वही 63.43, 44; द्रोणपर्व 56.27 (वसन्त ऋतु में खिले किंशुक-पलाश)

    अशोकैश्चम्पकैश्चूतैरनेकैरतिमुक्तकैः ।
    पुन्नागैः कर्णिकारैश्च बकुलैर्दिव्यपाटलैः।।
    पाटलैर्नारिकेलैश्च चन्दनैश्चार्जुनैस्तथा।
    एतै रम्यैर्महावृक्षैः पुण्यैः स्वादुफलैर्युतम्।।

65. वनपर्व 24.17

तमालतालाम्रमधूकनीप
कदम्बसर्जार्जुनकर्णिकारैः।
तपात्यये पुष्पधरैरुपेतं
महावनं राष्ट्रपतिर्ददर्श।।

66. शल्यपर्व 24.63-64; कर्णपर्व 89.4; 90.39; वनपर्व 24.26
67. विराट्पर्व 9.13
68. आदिपर्व 3.50-51, 55
69. वही 150.33; 218.3 (कल्पवृक्ष); वनपर्व 181.5
70. कर्णपर्व 87.87; 88.18
71. वही 154.16
72. वही 17.5-7; 18.18, 22, 26, 27, 28
73. वही 17.37
74. वही 172.9
75. वही 128.25
76. वही 87.40; 89.4
77. आदिपर्व 43.10
78. वही 31.8
79. वही 43.10

अङ्कुरं कृतवांस्तत्र ततः पर्णद्वयान्वितम्।
पलाशिनं शाखिनं च तथा विटपिनं पुनः।।

80. वही, 1.88-92

संग्रहाध्यायबीजो वै पौलोभास्तीकमूलवान्।
सम्भवस्कन्धविस्तारः सभारण्यविटङ्कवान्।।
अरणीपर्वरूपाढ्यो विराटोद्योगसारवान्।
भीष्मपर्वमहाशाखो द्रोणपर्वपलाशवान्।।
कर्णपर्वसितैः पुष्पैः शल्यपर्वसुगन्धिभिः।
स्त्रीपर्वैषीकविश्रामः शान्तिपर्वमहाफलः।।
अश्वमेधामृतरसस्त्वाश्रमस्थानसंश्रयः ।
मौसलः श्रुतिसंक्षेपः शिष्टद्विजनिषेवितः।।

81. वही 1.92
82. वही 1.93
83. वही 1.110
84. वही 1.111
85. आदिपर्व 139.68
86. वनपर्व 279.37 (··· निकृत्तस्तिलकाण्डवत् ···)
87. आदिपर्व 171.11; 135.34
88. वही 120.6, 7

89. विराट्पर्व 14.21
90. आदिपर्व 8.23; 170.9; वनपर्व 263.13
91. वही 2.177, 178
92. वनपर्व 270.43
93. वही 270.44
94. आदिपर्व 67.15
95. वनपर्व 270.61; 280.50; द्रोणपर्व 33.22 (कमलाक्ष नाम है)
96. वही 154.16; 291.3; (कमलपत्राक्षी-आदिपर्व 171.12); शल्यपर्व 6.81 (पद्मपत्राक्ष)
97. कर्णपर्व 91.68
98. आदिपर्व 50.45; 82.87; वनपर्व 293.23
99. वनपर्व 293.27
100. वही 263.13
101. वही 263.22
102. आदिपर्व 139.27
103. वही 170.43
104. वनपर्व 308.19
105. विराट्पर्व 7.7
106. वनपर्व 280.1
107. विराट्पर्व 9.13
108. शल्यपर्व 9.20 (पुण्डरीक-लाल कमल)
109. कर्णपर्व 89.6
110. वही
111. द्रोणपर्व 19.50-51; 56.30
112. आदिपर्व 231.7

    आत्मासि वायोर्ज्वलन शरीरमसि वीरुधाम्।
    गोनिरापश्च ते शुक्रं गोनिस्त्वमसि चाम्भसः।।

113. आदिपर्व 154.24-29
114. विराट्पर्व 16.19

    यस्य चार्द्रस्य वृक्षस्य शीतच्छायां समाश्रयेत्।
    न तस्य पर्णं द्रुह्येत् पूर्ववृत्तमनुस्मरन्।।

卐 卐 卐

श्रीमद्भागवतपुराण में वनस्पतिजगत्

शशिप्रभा गोयल

संस्कृत साहित्य के विशाल महासागर में श्रीमद्भागवतपुराण एक रत्न के समान चमकता है। इसीलिए कहा जाता है 'विद्या भागवतावधिः।' यह ग्रन्थ समस्त विद्याओं का भण्डार है इसीलिए इसे 'परमहंससंहिता' भी कहा जाता है। सभी पुराणों में सृष्टिक्रम का वर्णन है परन्तु भागवत का सृष्टि-वर्णन अद्‌भुत है। स्वयं ब्रह्मा की उत्पत्ति भी कमलकोष से हुई। यह कमल कोष एक अव्यक्त पुरुष की नाभि से उत्पन्न हुआ।

परावरेषां भूतानामात्मा यः पुरुषः नरः।
स एवासीदिदं विश्वं कल्पान्तेऽन्यन्न किञ्चन।।
तस्य नाभेः समभवत् पद्मकोषो हिरण्मयः।
तस्मिञ्जज्ञे महाराजस्वयम्भूश्चतुराननः।। (11.1.8-9)

(सर्वप्रथम अव्यक्त पुरुष हुए। उसकी नाभि से कमलकोष प्रकट हुआ। उसी से ब्रह्मा उत्पन्न हुए। वहीं से सृष्टि का प्रारम्भ हुआ।)

वास्तव में वृक्षादि वनस्पति-जगत् की सृष्टि मानवी सृष्टि से प्राचीन है। यह सातवीं सृष्टि मानी जाती है। प्रथम छः सृष्टियाँ प्राकृत सृष्टि कहलाती हैं। महत् तत्त्व, अहङ्कार, पाँच भूत, इन्द्रियाँ, मन, अविद्या ये प्राकृत सृष्टि मानी जाती हैं। सातवीं सृष्टि वैकृत सृष्टि स्थावर वृक्षादियों की है जो पृथ्वी के रोम हैं। वृक्षादयः रोमसदृशाः एव (2.10.23), रोमाणि वृक्षौषधयः, तनुरुहेष्वोषधिजातयश्च। (8.20.28)

यह वनस्पति जगत् वहाँ छः प्रकार का बताया गया है—

वनस्पत्योषधिलतात्वक्सारा वीरुधो द्रुमाः।
उत्स्रोतसस्तमःप्रायाः अन्तःस्पर्शा विशेषिणः।। (3.10.19)

वनस्पति वे कहलाती हैं जो बिना पुष्प के फलोत्पत्ति करती हैं जैसे पिप्पल इत्यादि। ओषधिः वे हैं जो फल के पक जाने पर विनष्ट हो जाती हैं जैसे गेहूँ, चना इत्यादि। लताएँ वे हैं जो आश्रय से ऊपर चढ़ती हैं जैसे ब्राह्मी, गिलोय आदि। त्वक्साराः— जिनका त्वक् अर्थात् वल्कल बहुत कठोर होता है जैसे बाँस; वीरुधः— वे लताएँ जो ऊपर नहीं चढतीं अपितु धरती पर ही फैलती हैं जैसे खरबूजा इत्यादि की बेलें, द्रुम-वे वृक्ष हैं जिनमें पहले फूल आता है बाद में फल। ऐसा ही वर्णन मनुस्मृति में भी मिलता है।

उद्भिज्जाः स्थावराः सर्वे बीजकाण्डप्ररोहिणः।
अपुष्पाः फलवन्तो ये ते वनस्पतयः स्मृताः।।
ओषधयः फलपाकान्ताः बहुपुष्पफलोपगाः।
पुष्पिणः फलिनश्चैव वृक्षास्तूभयतः स्मृताः।।

गुच्छगुल्मं तु विविधं तथैव तृणजातयः।
बीजकाण्डरुहाण्येव प्रताना वल्ल्य एव च।।
तमसा बहुरूपेण वेष्टिताः कर्महेतुना।
अन्तःसंज्ञा भवन्त्येते सुखदुःखसमन्विताः।। (मनुस्मृति - 1.46-49)

यहाँ अन्तिम पंक्ति बहुत ही महत्त्वपर्ण है जो यह बताती है कि इनमें अन्तःचेतना होती है और ये भी सुख और दुःख का अनुभव कर सकती हैं। इनका प्राणसञ्चार मूल से ऊपर की ओर होता है।

यह सृष्टि पाषाण आदि की सृष्टि से श्रेष्ठ है। ये जीव माने गए हैं। भागवत् पुराण में कहा गया है—

जीवा श्रेष्ठा ह्यजीवानां ततः प्राणभृतः शुभे!
ततः सचित्ताः प्रवरास्ततश्चेन्द्रियवृत्तयः।। (3.29.28)

इस पुराण में समस्त संसार को ही एक वृक्ष के रूप में निरूपित किया गया है—

एकायनोऽसौ द्विफलस्त्रिमूल-
श्चतूरसः पञ्चविधः षडात्मा।
सप्तत्वगष्टविटपो नवाक्षो
दशच्छदी द्विखगो ह्यादिवृक्षः।। (10. 2. 27)

एक पृथ्वी इसका आश्रय है, सुख-दुःख रूपी दो फल हैं, सत्त्व, रजस, तमस ये तीन जड़ें हैं, धर्म-अर्थ-काम-मोक्ष आदि ये चार रस हैं, श्रोत्र, त्वक्, नेत्र, रसना नासिका आदि पाँच इन्द्रियाँ ज्ञानप्राप्ति के साधन हैं, छः स्वभाव हैं— उत्पत्ति, स्थिति, वृद्धि, परिवर्तन, क्षय और विनाश, रस, रुधिर, माँस, मेदा, अस्थि, मज्जा, शुक्र आदि सात प्रकार का वल्कल है, आठ शाखाएँ हैं— भूमि, जल, अग्नि, वायु, आकाश, मन, बुद्धि, अहङ्कार इत्यादि। नव द्वार इसके नौ खोखल हैं, प्राण, अपान, उदान, व्यान, समान, नाग, कूर्म, कृकल, देवदत्त, धनञ्जय इसके दस पत्ते हैं। जीव और ईश्वर इसके ऊपर स्थित दो पक्षी हैं, सत्य ही इस वृक्ष का पुण्य फल है।

इन वृक्षों की महिमा इसी पुराण में श्रीकृष्ण ने इस प्रकार गाई है—

पश्यैतान् महाभागान् परार्थैकान्तजीवितान्।
वातवर्षातपहिमान् सहन्तो वारयन्ति नः।। (10. 23.32)

अहो एषां वरं जन्म सर्वप्राण्युपजीविनम्।
सुजनस्येव येषां वै विमुखा यान्ति नार्थिनः।। (10. 23.33)

पत्रपुष्पफलच्छायामूलवल्कलदारुभिः ।
गन्धनिर्यासभस्मास्थितोक्मैः कामान् वितन्वते।। (10. 23.34)

ये वृक्ष धन्य हैं जो वात, वर्षा, धूप, गर्मी सर्दी सब सहते हुए हमारी रक्षा करते हैं। सभी प्राणियों के सहारे, ये वृक्ष उन सज्जनों के समान हैं जिनके पास से याचक बिना लिए नहीं जाते हैं। ये वृक्ष पत्र, पुष्प, फल, छाया, मूल, वल्कल, काष्ठ, गन्ध, भस्म, अस्थि, इत्यादि से सभी मनुष्यों की कामनाओं को पूर्ण करते हैं।

यह हमारा समस्त भूमण्डल सात द्वीपों में बंटा हुआ है। प्रथम द्वीप है जम्बू द्वीप जिस पर हम सभी वास करते हैं। यह द्वीप नील कमल के कोशस्थानीय जो सात द्वीप हैं उनमें सबसे भीतर का कोश है। इसका विस्तार एक लाख योजन

है और यह कमल के पत्ते के समान गोलाकार है। इसमें नौ–नौ हजार योजन वाले नौ वर्ष हैं जो इनकी सीमाओं का विभाजन करने वाले आठ पर्वतों से बंटे हुए हैं। इनके बीचोंबीच इलावृत्त नामक आभ्यन्तर वर्ष है जिसके बीचोंबीच ऊपर से नीचे तक सुवर्णमय एक लाख योजन ऊँचा मेरुपर्वत है जो कमल की कर्णिका के समान सुशोभित है। इलावृत्त के दक्षिण की ओर एक के बाद एक निषध, हेमकूट और हिमालय नाम के तीन पर्वत हैं। इनसे क्रमशः हरिवर्ष, किम्पुरुष, और भारत वर्ष की सीमाओं का विभाग होता है। इलावृत्त के पूर्व और पश्चिम की ओर उत्तर में नील पर्वत और दक्षिण में निषध पर्वत तक फैले हुए गन्धमादन और माल्यवान् नामक दो पर्वत हैं। ये भद्राश्व और केतुमाल नामक दो वर्षों की सीमा निश्चित करते हैं। इनके सिवा मन्दर, मेरुमन्दर, सुपार्श्व और कुमुद ये चार ऊँचे–ऊँचे पर्वत मेरु के साथ जुड़े हुए हैं जिनके ऊपर क्रमशः आम, जामुन, कदम्ब और बड़ के पेड़ हैं। मन्दराचल की गोद में जो ग्यारह सौ योजन ऊँचा देवताओं का आम्रवृक्ष है उससे बड़े–बड़े, अमृत के समान स्वादिष्ट फल गिरते हैं और उनके फटने से उनका लाला–लाल रस अरुणोदा नामक नदी में परिणत हो जाता है। जामुन के वृक्ष के फलों से जम्बू नामक नदी प्रकट होती है जो मेरुमन्दर पर्वत के दस हजार योजन ऊँचे शिखर से गिरती हुई इलावृत्त के दक्षिण भाग को सींचती है। कदम्ब वृक्ष के पाँच खोखलों से पाँच नदियाँ इलावृत्त के पश्चिमी भाग को सींचती हैं। इसी प्रकार कुमुद के शतवल्श नामक वटवृक्ष की जटाओं से नीचे की ओर बहने वाले अनेक नद निकलते हैं जो इलावृत्त के उत्तरी भाग को सींचते हैं।

यह जम्बूद्वीप खारे पानी के समुद्र से घिरा हुआ है। इससे आगे है प्लक्षद्वीप जहाँ बृहदाकार प्लक्ष (अंज़ीर) का वृक्ष है। यहाँ के लोग सूर्य की उपासना करते हैं। इससे परे शाल्मलीद्वीप है जहाँ पर सेमल का पेड़ है। चौथा द्वीप कुशद्वीप है जहाँ कुश के गुच्छों से निकलता हुआ प्रकाश समस्त दिशाओं को प्रकाशित करता है। पाँचवें क्रौञ्च द्वीप से आगे छठा शाकद्वीप है जहाँ शाक नामक वृक्ष की सुगन्धि चारों ओर फैली हुई है। सातवाँ द्वीप पुष्कर द्वीप है जहाँ पर स्थित कमल ब्रह्मा का आसन है, यहीं पर मानसोत्तर नामक पवित्र पर्वत है।

कैलास पर्वत पर अनेक वृक्षों और फल–फूलों का अद्‌भुत वर्णन मिलता है, जिनमें प्रमुख हैं मन्दार, पारिजात, सरल तमाल, शाल, कोविदार, असन, अर्जुन, आम, कदम्ब नीप इत्यादि लम्बी सूची दी गई है। कैलास पर्वत पर ही अलका पुरी है जिसमें सौगन्धिक वन है जिसमें बहुत से कल्पवृक्ष हैं। यहाँ पर एक वट वृक्ष भी है जो सौ योजन ऊँचा है, और 75 योजन तक उसकी शाखाएँ फैली हुई हैं। इससे वहाँ गर्मी का नाम निशान भी नहीं है। इसी वृक्ष के नीचे शिवजी ने तपस्या की थी। भगवान् विष्णु के वैकुण्ठ में नैःश्रेयस नामक एक और वन है जो कल्पद्रुमों से परिपूर्ण है। विष्णु तुलसी दल से अपने आप को सजाते हैं। क्षीर सागर में त्रिकूट नामक पर्वत पर ऋतुमान् नामक उद्यान है और इस उद्यान में सहस्त्रों वृक्षों का वर्णन है जो इस पुराण के आठवें स्कन्द में देखा जा सकता है। इसी प्रकार मनु की पुत्री देवहूति का विवाह कर्दम ऋषि से हुआ जिनका आश्रम विविध वृक्षों से समलङ्कृत था। (तृतीय स्कन्ध) इसी प्रकार इस पुराण में वैश्रम्भक, सुरसन, नन्दन, पुष्पभद्रक, मानस, चैत्ररथ्य इत्यादि अनेकों वनों का वर्णन किया गया है। उत्तानपाद के पुत्र ध्रुव ने भी मधुवन में तप किया और केवल कपित्थ और बदरीफल खाकर जीवन–यापन किया। राजा पृथु के यज्ञ के उत्सव पर वृक्षों ने क्षीरादि भेंट किए। प्रचेतादि दश पुत्र जब भ्रमण कर रहे थे तो उन्होंने जो एक विशाल जलाशय देखा उसमें अनेक रंग वाले कमलों का वर्णन है। एक बार इन्हीं प्रचेतादि ऋषि पुत्रों ने वृक्षों को जलाने के लिए जब मुख से वायु छोड़ी तो सोमदेव ने उन्हें मना करते हुए कहा—

मा द्रुमेभ्यो महाभागा दीनेभ्यो द्रग्धुमर्हथ।
विवर्धयिषवो यूयं प्रजानां पतयः स्मृताः।। (7.2.15)

अरे ये वृक्ष तो तुम्हारी भलाई के लिए निरन्तर कार्य करते हैं, इन वृक्षों को मत जलाओ। इसी प्रकार जब एक बार दैत्य परशु से वृक्षों का संहार करने लगे तो दैत्यराज हिरण्यकशिपु ने उनको कहा कि वृक्षों का उच्छेद उचित नहीं है।

इस पुराण में तुलसी और कमल की महिमा सर्वत्र ही गाई गई है। वृन्दावन ही तुलसी वन है। इस में अनेक वृक्ष हैं जिनकी शाखाएँ श्री कृष्ण के स्पर्श से अमर हो चुकी हैं। श्री कृष्ण पर्यावरण के प्रथम संरक्षक हैं। उन्होंने तालालिसंकुल वन को धेनुक नाम दैत्य के भय से मुक्त कराया। मुञ्जाटवी में दावनल को नष्ट किया। वृन्दावन के कन्दमूल फल खाकर ही श्री कृष्ण बड़े हुए। वे सदैव पाँच प्रकार के फूलों से बनी वैजयन्ती माला को धारण करते थे। गोपियाँ यमुना के तट पर अशोक वन में कृष्ण को ढूँढती हुई अनेक वृक्षों और लताओं से इनका पता पूछती हैं। उद्धव तो वृन्दावन के ही गुल्म लता ओषध के रूप में जन्म लेना चाहते हैं। प्रायः लोग अपने घरों के द्वारों को रम्भा, पूग आदि वृक्षों से अलङ्कृत करते थे। लोग एक दूसरे को चन्दन, अगुरु, कुङ्कुम, कुश, कमल आदि से पूजते थे।

वस्तुतः मनुष्य और वृक्ष परस्पर एक दूसरे पर आश्रित हैं। इनमें दोनों में ही प्राण शक्ति है। प्राणो हि जीवमुपधावति तत्र तत्र (11.3.39)। शापवश मनुष्य भी वृक्ष योनि को प्राप्त करते हैं। कुबेर के पुत्र नल कूबर और मणिग्रीव मदिरा पीकर उन्मत्त हो गए तो नारद ने उनको शाप देकर वृक्ष बना दिया।

उद्धव जब श्रीकृष्ण से पूछते हैं—आपकी भक्ति किस प्रकार करनी चाहिए तो श्रीकृष्ण कहते हैं—**उद्यानादीनां निर्माणे उद्यमः करणीयः।**

ममार्चास्थापने श्रद्धा स्वतः संहत्य चोद्यमः।
उद्यानोपवनाक्रीडपुरमन्दिरकर्मणि ।। (11.12.38)

योगाभ्यास में भी हृदय को कमल के समान वर्णित किया गया है। शरीर में स्थित चक्र सभी कमल के समान हैं। अन्त में मनुष्य अन्न में ही समा जाता है। प्रलय काल में भी मनु ने वनस्पतियों और ओषधियाँ की रक्षा की। क्या इससे अधिक पर्यावरण संरक्षण कहीं अन्यत्र देखने को मिल सकता है? यहाँ मनुष्य और प्रकृति का परस्पर आन्तरिक सम्बन्ध है और वनस्पतिजगत् पर ही प्राणिमात्र का सम्पूर्ण अस्तित्व टिका हुआ है।

卐 卐 卐

Section VII

FLORA IN POETIC WORKS OF KĀLIDĀSA

कालिदासकाव्यामृतनिर्झरी

कालिदास-साहित्य एवं पादपपुष्पफलसमृद्धि

प्रभुदयालु अग्निहोत्री

1. इङ्गुदी

यह तापस वृक्ष है। तपोवनों में इसकी स्थिति प्रसिद्ध थी। इसके फलों से तेल निकाला जाता था जिसे तपस्विजन अपने मुण्डित सिर पर मलते थे। शाकुन्तल में विदूषक राजा से कहता है कि इस अनाघ्रात पुष्प (शकुन्तला) को बचाइए। कहीं ऐसा न हो कि यह किसी इङ्गुदी तेल लगाए हुए चिकने सिर वाले तापस के हाथ लग जाए—**तेन हि लघु परित्रायतां भवान्। मा कस्यापि तपस्विनः इङ्गुदीतेलमिश्रचिक्कणशीर्षस्य हस्ते पतिष्यति।।** (शाकु. 2.11 के नीचे)। इङ्गुदी के बीजों से निकाला हुआ तेल दीपों में भी जलाया जाता था। निर्वासित सीता को रात्रि-वास के लिए उटज प्रदान करती हुई तापसियाँ उसमें इङ्गुदी-तेल का दीप जला कर रखती हैं—

ता इङ्गुदीस्नेहकृतप्रदीपमास्तीर्णमेध्याजिनतल्पमन्तः ।
तस्यै सपर्यानुपदं दिनान्ते निवासहेतोरुटजं वितेरुः।। रघुवंश - 14.81

तपस्वियों द्वारा उपयोग में लाए जाने के कारण इसे तापसतरु भी कहते हैं। इसका लेटिन नाम Balanites Gegyptiaca और हिन्दी में व्यवहृत हिंगोट है। इसके फल स्निग्ध-उष्ण होते हैं। स्वाद में मधुर किन्तु कुछ दुर्गन्ध लिए होते हैं। भारत के शुष्क जलवायु वाले, विशेषतः काली मिट्टी वाले क्षेत्रों में पाए जाते हैं।

2. इक्षु

कालिदास ने शिशिर को इक्षु की ऋतु कहा है। इस काल में पृथ्वी शालि और इक्षु से भरी रहती है। शालि और इक्षु शिशिर में पक्व हो जाते हैं। इक्षु को काटकर उसका रस निकालने और उससे गुड़ बनाने की प्रथा बहुत पुरानी है। कवि ने इससे निकट परिचय व्यक्त किया है। शालि और इक्षु दोनों पर्याप्त वर्षा वाले प्रदेशों में ही उत्पन्न होते हैं। शालि की पौध का प्रत्यारोपण किया जाता है। इसे इसी कारण कलम भी कहते हैं। इस पौध के खेत में पानी भरा रहना आवश्यक है। इक्षु को भी अधिक पानी की आवश्यकता होती है। ऋतुसंहार में कालिदास की दृष्टि में ऐसा ही प्रचुर जलवाला प्रदेश रहा है। तभी वह कहते हैं—

प्ररूढशालीक्षुचयावृतक्षितिं . . . वरोरु कालं शिशिराह्वयं शृणु।। ऋतुसंहार - 5.1
प्रचुरगुडविकारः स्वादुशालीक्षुरम्यः . . .
शिशिरसमय एष श्रेयसे वोस्तु नित्यम्।। ऋतुसंहार - 5.16

गावों में शालि के खेतों को पशु पक्षियों से बचाने के लिए प्रायः लड़कियाँ गोफन लेकर इक्षु की मेड़ों पर बैठती हैं। इस समय तक इक्षु इतनी बड़ी हो जाती है कि वे उसकी छाया में बैठ कर धूप से अपनी रक्षा कर सकें—

इक्षुच्छायनिषादिन्यस्तस्य गोप्तुर्गुणोदयम्।
आकुमारकथोद्घातं शालिगोप्यो जगुर्यशः।। रघुवंश - 4. 20

ये दृश्य आज भी गाँवों में देखे जा सकते हैं जहाँ शालिगोपी स्त्रियाँ गाती-गाती अपने खेतों की रखवाली करती हैं।

3. उदुम्बर

कालिदास ने मेघदूत में वर्षा की वायु को उदुम्बरों को पकाने वाली कहा है—**शीतो वायुः परिणमयिता काननोदुम्बराणाम्।** (मेघदूत-1.48)। उदुम्बर को हिन्दी में गूलर कहते हैं। इसके फल शक्तिवर्धक, स्वादिष्ट और भोज्य होते हैं। चिकित्सा की दृष्टि से उदुम्बर का बड़ा महत्त्व है। इसके कच्चे फल शाक के काम आते हैं।

4. एला

ससञ्जुरश्वक्षुण्णानामेलानामुत्पतिष्णवः ।
तुल्यगन्धिषु मत्तेभकटेषु फलरेणवः।। रघुवंश 4. 47

एला छोटी इलायची का नाम है। इसके पौधे छोटे होते हैं और दक्षिण भारत में विशेषतः पाये जाते हैं।

5. असन

असन का उल्लेख रघुवंश में दशरथ के मृगया-प्रसङ्ग में मिलता है जहाँ गुफाओं से निकलकर झपटते हुए व्याघ्रों की उपमा वायु द्वारा जोर से झकझोरे या उखाड़े जाते हुए असन वृक्षों से दी है—**व्याघ्रानभीरभिमुखोत्पतितान् गुहाभ्यः फुल्लासनाग्रविटपानिव वायुरुग्णान्।** (रघुवंश - 9.63)। कालिदास के अतिरिक्त भारवि और माघ ने भी असन की चर्चा की है।

असन उत्तर, पश्चिम, विशेषतः मध्यप्रदेश के विन्ध्यक्षेत्र में पाया जाता था। वनों के अतिरिक्त राज-प्रमद-वनों में भी यह आरोपित किया जाता था। इसके पुष्प भी होते हैं। तभी इनकी उपमा व्याघ्र के पीले धब्बोंदार चर्म से दी गयी है। इसके पुष्प और मञ्जरियाँ देखने में सुन्दर, मधुरगन्ध वाले तथा मधु-स्रावी होते हैं। शरद् ऋतु में फूलते हैं। असन का एक नाम वीजासार भी है। यह रस-निर्यास तथा भवनोपयोगी लकड़ी के लिए प्रसिद्ध है।

6. अगुरु • कालागुरु

ऋतुसंहार में अनेक बार अगुरु और कालागुरु का उल्लेख हुआ है—

प्रकामकालागुरुधूपवासितं विशन्ति शय्यागृहमुत्सुकाः स्त्रियः।

ऋतुसंहार - 5.5

अगुरुसुरभिधूपामोदितं केशपाशं गलितकुसुममालं केशपाशं वहन्ती।

ऋतुसंहार - 5.12

शिरांसि कालागुरुधूपितानि कुर्वन्ति नार्यः सुरतोत्सवाय।।

ऋतुसंहार - 4.5

अगुरु के वृक्ष हिमालय पर पाए जाते हैं। इसकी लकड़ियाँ और छाल सब सुगन्धित होते हैं। अगुरु और तगुरु का काष्ठ-चूर्ण अग्नि में डालने पर सुगन्धित धुआँ निकलता है। धूपदान तथा होम में इसका उपयोग होता है। प्राचीन काल में स्त्रियाँ इसके धूम से अपने केशों को वासित करती थीं। शयनकक्षादि को सुगन्धित बनाने में भी इसका उपयोग होता था।

7. ककुभ

ऋतुसंहार 2. 21 में कवि ने ककुभद्रुम का उल्लेख करते हुए कहा है कि इसकी मञ्जरियों से स्त्रियाँ अपने कर्णों को अलंक्त करती हैं। इतना ही नहीं वे उनसे इच्छानुकूल अन्य अवतंसों की भी रचना करती हैं। ककुभ

सीधा, बड़ा ऊँचा वृक्ष होता है जो वर्षा ऋतु में फूलता है। इसके पुष्प-गुच्छ मसृण और सुगन्धित होते हैं। यह औषधि वृक्ष है। इसकी छाल बहुत गुणकारी होती है। इससे आसव और अरिष्ट भी बनते हैं।

8. कन्दली

चौड़े बड़े पत्तों वाली और चारों ओर फैलने वाली कन्दली वर्षा के प्रारम्भ में फूलती है। यह जलीय प्रदेश में विपुलता से पायी जाती है- **आविर्भूतप्रथममुकुलाः कन्दलीश्चानुकच्छम्।** (मेघदूत - 1.21)। इसे सुदर्शन भी कहते हैं। श्राद्ध में इसका उपयोग वर्जित है। इसके पुष्प अनेक कोशों में स्फुरित होते हैं। श्वेत, पीत और प्रमुखतः रक्त कन्दल कोशों को दृष्टि में रखकर कवि ने राम के मुख से कहलाया है—

आसारसिक्तक्षितिबाष्पयोगान्मामक्षिणोद्यत्र विभिन्नकोशैः।
विडम्ब्यमाना नवकन्दलैस्ते विवाहधूमारुणलोचनश्रीः।। रघुवंश - 13.29

कन्दली के नीलश्याम पत्र धूम के और नवोदित कन्दल धूम से रक्त नेत्रों के उपमान हैं। ठीक ऐसी ही बात पुरुरवा अपनी प्रिया के विषय में कहते हैं—

आरक्तराजिभिरियं नवकन्दली सलिलगर्भैः।
कोपादन्तर्वाष्पे स्मारयति मां लोचने तस्याः।। विक्रमोर्वशीय - 4.15

उभयत्र कालिदास की दृष्टि रक्त कन्दली पर रही है।

9. कलम

कलम शालि उन धानों को कहते हैं जिनकी पौध प्रत्यारोपित की जाती है। इसके पौधे पानी में बढ़ते हैं और जलपूर के वेग को झुक कर सहन कर लेते हैं। पानी में डूबने पर जल्दी सड़ते नहीं। रघु की विजय-यात्रा के प्रसङ्ग में कवि ने कलम (शालि) के इन गुणों का वर्णन किया है—

आपादपद्मप्रणताः कलमा इव ते रघुम्।
फलैः संवर्धयामासुरुत्खातप्रतिरोपिताः ।। रघुवंश - 4.37

आम्रादि फलों का कलम लगाया जाता है। इससे उसके फलों के आकार और स्वाद में वृद्धि होती है। कलम धान शरद् के अन्त तक पकते हैं। तब सारी भूमि उनकी पीत मञ्जरियों और पीतपत्रों के कारण पीताम्बरा दिखायी देती है—

वप्राश्च पक्वकलमावृतभूमिभागाः
प्रोत्कण्ठयन्ति न मनो भुवि कस्य यूनः। ऋतुसंहार - 3.5

10. कङ्केलि

कालिदास ने केवल एक बार ऋतुसंहार में कङ्केलि का उल्लेख किया है— **दन्तावभासविशदस्मितचन्द्र-कान्तिकङ्केलिपुष्परुचिरा नवमालती च)** (3.18)। इसमें मालती और कङ्केलि दोनों के पुष्पों को कान्ताओं के स्वच्छदाँतों की शुभ्रिमा से मण्डित स्मित की शुभ्रिमा को जीतने वाली बतलाया है। मोनियर विलियम्स के अनुसार यह एक पुष्पी पादप का नाम है। इसके पुष्प मालती के समान श्वेत होते हैं। बालरामायण में इसका उल्लेख है।

11. कालीयक

कालीयक की चर्चा कवि ने शीतकाल में स्त्रियों के शरीर पर किए जाने वाले सुगन्धित लेप के साधन के रूप में की है। स्तन-लेप के उपकरण के रूप में भी इसका उल्लेख हुआ है—

प्रियङ्गुकालीयकचर्चितानि सपत्रलेखानि मुखाम्बुजानि। ऋतुसंहार - 4. 5

तथा—

प्रियङ्गुकालीयककुङ्कुमाक्तं स्तनेषु गौरेषु विलासिनीभिः। ऋतुसंहार - 6.12

चन्दन की एक जाति कालीयक कहलाती है। केसर और विशिष्ट हरिद्रा जाति के रूप में भी इस शब्द का प्रयोग मिलता है। सम्भवतः यह पीली जाति का चन्दन है जिसे केसर के साथ मिला कर लेप तैयार किया जाता है।

12. काश

यह तृण जाति है जो कुशों के काम आती है। आसन तथा पवित्री बनाने एवं अनेक धार्मिक कार्यों में कुशों का उपयोग होता है। काश नामक तृणों का उपयोग छप्पर बनाने में भी होता है। नदियों के किनारे या ग्राम्य क्षेत्रों और वनों में शरद् ऋतु में जब काश फूलते हैं तो दूर-दूर तक पृथ्वी चादर ओढ़े नववधू सी दिखाई देती है।

कालिदास ने शरद् की कल्पना नववधू के रूप में करते हुए काशों को उसका रेशमी दुपट्टा बतलाया है जो सिर से लेकर कटि के नीचे तक शरीर को ढँके रहता है। वह कहते हैं—

काशांशुका विकचपद्ममनोज्ञवक्त्रा . . .
प्राप्ता शरन्नववधूरिव रूपरम्या।। ऋतुसंहार - 3.1

तथा - **काशैर्मही शिशिरदीधितिना रजन्यः . . .**
शुक्लीकृतान्युपवनानि च मालतीभिः।। ऋतुसंहार - 3.2

इसी बात को उन्होंने सर्ग के अन्त में फिर दोहराया है—

विकसितनवकाशश्वेतवासो दधाना . . .
प्रतिदिशतु शरद्वश्चेतसः प्रीतिमग्रयाम्।। ऋतुसंहार - 3.28

13. कीचक

कीचक वे वेणु या बाँस होते हैं जो भीतर पोले होते हैं और वायु के आघात से बाँसुरी की सी ध्वनि करते हैं। कालिदास ने कई बार इनकी चर्चा की है—

यः पूरयन् कीचकरन्ध्रभागान् दरीमुखोत्थेन समीरणेन।
उद्गास्यतामिच्छति किन्नराणां तानप्रदायित्वमिवोपगन्तुम्।। कुमारसम्भव - 1. 8

तथा —

स कीचकैर्मारुतपूर्णरन्ध्रैः कूजद्भिरापादितवंशकृत्यम्। रघुवंश - 2.13

यहाँ कीचकों को सङ्गीत-क्रिया में बाँसुरी का काम करते हुए बतलाया है। मेघदूत में भी कवि ने इस बात को दोहराया है—

शब्दायन्ते मधुरमनिलैः कीचकाः पूर्णमाणाः। रघुवंश - 1.53

14. कुङ्कुम

काश्मीर देश में उत्पन्न पादप विशेष तथा उसका पराग भी कुङ्कुम कहलाता है। कुंकुम (Saffron) या पीले रङ्ग का होता है। स्त्रियों को शिशिर ऋतु में कवि ने स्तनों पर कुंकुम का लेप किये बतलाया है। उन्होंने उनके स्तनों को भी कुंकुम के समान पीतवर्ण कहा है—**पयोधरैः कुङ्कुमरागपिञ्जरैः।** (ऋतु. 5.9)। इसी बात को उन्होंने 6.14 में भी दोहराया है—**प्रियङ्गुकालीयक-कुङ्कुमाक्तं स्तनेषु गौरेषु** विलासिनीभिरालिप्यते चन्दनमङ्गनाभिः। कुङ्कुम के विस्तृत खेतों में जब अश्व लोट लगाते हैं तो उनके कंधों में कुङ्कुम के पराग-केसर लिपट जाते हैं—

विनीताध्वश्रमास्तस्य सिन्धुतीरविचेष्टनैः।
दुधुवुर्वाजिनः स्कन्धांल्लग्नकुङ्कुमकेसरान्।। रघुवंश - 4. 67

15. कुसुम्भ

कालिदास ने एक बार उपमान के रूप में इस वृक्ष का उल्लेख किया है। दवाग्नि नये खिले कुसुम्भ के फूलों के समान सिन्दूरवर्ण है— **विकचनवकुसुम्भस्वच्छसिन्दूरभासा** · · · दिशि दिशि परिदग्धा भूमयः पावकेन— (ऋतुसंहार 1.24)। कुसुम्भ के फूलों से वस्त्र रँगने का रंग बनाया जाता है। कुसुम्भी रंग के वस्त्र साधु-संन्यासी प्रायः पहनते हैं। इस ललछौहें पीले रंग को कात्यायन-वार्तिक में **'महारजन'** कहा है (4.2.2)। महाभाष्य (4.1.1) में भी इसका उल्लेख है।

16. कर्कन्धु

कर्कन्धु, जिसका उल्लेख शाकुन्तल में मिलता है, बदर या बेर की एक जाति है। सुश्रुत और चरक दोनों ने इसे बदर की चार जातियों में परिगणित किया है। इनमें बड़े आकार का बदर मधुर और आरोपित बदर वृक्ष का फल होता है। कोल लगाए हुए और वन्य दोनों प्रकार के वृक्षों का फल होता है। यह मीठा और खट्टा तथा ग्राम्य और आरण्य दोनों प्रकार का होता है। तीसरा सौवीर बदर से भी बड़ा, पक्व और अपक्व दोनों अवस्थाओं में मधुर होता है। यह रेगिस्तानी क्षेत्र में उत्पन्न होता है। कर्कन्धु आरण्य सबसे छोटे प्रकार का और खट्टा होता है। आरण्य आश्रमों में इसे शाकों में मिलाकर पकाते थे। कर्कन्धु का चूर्ण वैद्यनाथ धाम (बिहार) के शिवमन्दिर में प्रसाद के रूप में वितरित किया जाता है।

17. कल्पतरु

कालिदास ने अलकापुरी में एक ऐसे वृक्ष का उल्लेख किया है जो अकेला ही नारी के समस्त मण्डन-द्रव्यों को उत्पन्न करता है। यथा— सुन्दरवस्त्र, मधु, पल्लव, पुष्प, आभूषण और लाक्षाराग आदि (मेघदूत 2.11)। यह पौराणिक काल की काल्पनिक सृष्टि है किन्तु वे इस सर्वकामपूरक वृक्ष का वर्णन सत्यवत् करते हैं। यह देववृक्ष है। कालिदास ने इनकी स्थिति अलकापुरी में बतलायी है—

लाक्षारागं चरणकमलन्यासयोग्यं च यस्यामेकः सूते सकलमबलामण्डनं यत्र वृक्षः। मेघदूत - 2.11

विक्रमोर्वशीय में अर्धविक्षिप्त सा पुरुरवा कल्पतरु में नृत्य-व्यापार की कल्पना करता है—

गन्धुम्माइअ महुअर गीएहिवज्जन्तेहिं परहुअतूरेहिं।
परिअ पवणुव्वेल्लिअ पल्लवनिअरु
सुलिलअ विविहय आरेंहि णच्चइ कप्पअरु। विक्रमोर्वशीय - 4.12

18. कोविदार

यह शरद् में फूलता है। इसके कोमल पत्ते और फूल शाक के भी काम आते हैं। इसका औषध मूल्य भी है। इसके पुष्प दर्शनीय और मधुस्त्रावी होते हैं जिनके इर्द गिर्द भ्रमर गूँजते रहते हैं। इसीलिए ऋतुसंहार में कहा है—

मत्तद्विरेफपरिपीतमधुप्रसेकश्चित्तं विदारयति कस्य न कोविदारः। ऋतुसंहार - 3. 6

卐 卐 卐

कालिदासप्रणीत रघुवंश में दोहदतरुश्री

सुषमा कुलश्रेष्ठ

जायन्ते कति जज्ञिरे कति जनिष्यन्ते कतीह क्षितौ
स्रष्टारो नितरामिदं तु कविभिर्निर्मत्सरैः कथ्यताम्।
आपूर्वापरदक्षिणोत्तरहरित्साहित्यसिंहासन-
स्वैरारोहपराक्रमं भजतु कः श्रीकालिदासात्परः।।

रघुकुल के नृपतियों की यशोगाथा पर आधारित कालिदासप्रणीत 'रघुवंश' संस्कृत साहित्य का अप्रतिम महाकाव्य है। पिछली शताब्दी में कालिदास एवम् उनके ग्रन्थों पर अनेक दृष्टियों से विविध शोधपरक कार्य किए जा चुके हैं। प्रस्तुत आलेख में दोहदवृक्षों का रघुवंश के आलोक में विवेचन प्रस्तुत है।

संस्कृत साहित्य में अनेक कविसमय प्रचलित हैं। उनमें से एक अतिशय मनोरम कविसमय दोहदवृक्षों से सम्बद्ध है। 'दोहम्' आकर्षं ददाति (दा + क) इति 'दोहदः'। अन्तर्वत्नी (गर्भवती) स्त्री की प्रबल अभिलाषा 'दोहद' कहलाती है यथा—प्रजावती दोहदशंसिनी ते।[1] एक अन्य उदाहरण द्रष्टव्य है—

उपेत्य सा दोहददुःखशीलतां
यदेव वव्रे तदपश्यदाहृतम्।
न हीष्टमस्य त्रिदिवेऽपि भूपते-
रभूदनासाद्यमधिज्यधन्वनः।।[2]

अन्तर्वत्नी रानी सुदक्षिणा का जब जिस वस्तु पर मन चलता था, वह उसी समय उन्हें मिल भी जाती थी क्योंकि धनुर्धारी राजा दिलीप के लिए स्वर्ग की वस्तुएँ भी सुलभ थीं फिर इस लोक की वस्तुओं की तो बात ही क्या!

वृक्षों एवं लताओं की अभिलाषा भी 'दोहद' कहलाती है। दोहद से वृक्ष अकालिकी पुष्पसम्पत्ति प्रदान करते हैं जैसा श्रीहर्ष का अभिमत है—

इष्टेन पूर्तेन नलस्य वश्या-
स्स्वर्भोगमत्रापि सृजन्त्यमर्त्याः।
महीरुहो दोहदसेकशक्ते-
राकालिकं कोरकमुद्गिरन्ति।।[3]

देववाणी संस्कृत के विपुल साहित्य में अनेक दोहदतरुओं का वर्णन प्राप्त होता है। दोहदवृक्षों में अधोलिखित दश वृक्ष प्रमुख हैं—

1. प्रियङ्गु 6. मन्दार

2. बकुल 7. चम्पक

3. अशोक 8. चूत

4. तिलक 9. नमेरु

5. कुरबक 10. कर्णिकार

प्रत्येक वृक्ष का दोहद भिन्न-भिन्न होता है तथा किसी शृङ्गारिणी नायिका से सम्बद्ध होता है। इन दश वृक्षों के दोहद इस प्रकार हैं—

स्त्रीणां स्पर्शात्प्रियङ्गुर्विकसति बकुलः सीधुगण्डूषसेकात्
पादाघातादशोकस्तिलककुरबकौ वीक्षणालिङ्गनाभ्याम्।
मन्दारो नर्मवाक्यात्पटुमृदुहसनाच्चम्पको वक्त्रवाता-
च्चूतो गीतान्नमेरुर्विकसति च पुरोनर्तनात्कर्णिकारः।।[4]

अर्थात् शृङ्गारिणी रमणियों के स्पर्श से प्रियङ्गु विकसित होता है, उनकी मुखमदिरा के सिञ्चन से बकुल खिलता है, उनके चरणाघात, वीक्षण एवं आलिङ्गन से क्रमशः अशोक, तिलक एवं कुरबक विकसित होते हैं। उनके प्रिय वाक्यों से मन्दार खिलता है, मन्द-मन्द स्मित एवं हसित से चम्पक फूलता है, मुखवातप्रदान से आम्र पल्लवित होता है। गीत एवं पुरोनर्तन से क्रमशः नमेरु एवं कर्णिकार विकसित होते हैं। यहाँ ध्यातव्य है कि सभी वृक्षों के दोहद नायिका के किसी न किसी प्रणय-कृत्य से सम्बद्ध हैं। जिस प्रकार रमणी के स्पर्श, वीक्षण, आश्लेषादि द्वारा उसके प्रिय को सुखानुभूति होती है, उसी प्रकार उसके द्वारा वृक्षों के दोहद-सम्पादन से वृक्ष भी हर्षातिरेक से प्रफुल्लित हो अकालिकी पुष्पसम्पत्ति प्रदान करते हैं। यह बात कविसमयसिद्ध तो है ही, वस्तुतः भी सिद्ध ही है। जिस वृक्ष का जितना अधिक ध्यान रखा जाएगा, सेवा की जाएगी, पुष्पसम्पत्ति एवं फलसम्पत्ति अधिक प्राप्त होगी, यह वनस्पतिविज्ञानसम्मत भी है। अब इन दश दोहदवृक्षों का कालिदासप्रणीत रघुवंश के आलोक में विवेचन प्रस्तुत है।

1. प्रियङ्गु (फलिनी)

प्रियङ्गु (प्रिय + गम् + कु) एक लता है जिसके विषय में प्रसिद्धि है कि वह स्त्रियों के स्पर्शमात्र से विकसित हो जाती है। इसके विषय में मातङ्गलीला में कहा गया है—प्रियङ्गुश्यामाङ्गप्रकृतिरपि।[5] प्रियङ्गु के अन्य नाम 'फलिनी' एवं 'श्यामा' हैं। इसे सहकार (आम्र) की प्रिया भी कहा जाता है।

वसन्त ऋतु में प्रियङ्गुलताएं पुष्पभार से लद जाती हैं तथा स्त्रियों के आभूषणयुक्त बाहुओं की कान्ति को भी अपहृत कर लेती हैं।[6] रमणियाँ प्रियङ्गु, कालीयक, केसर एवं मृगनाभि से युक्त चन्दन का अपने पयोधरों पर लेप करती हैं।[7] कभी-कभी सुन्दरी नायिका की शरीरयष्टि की तुलना भी प्रियङ्गुलता अथवा श्यामालता से की जाती है।[8]

निदर्शन :

(1) **मिथुनं परिकल्पितं त्वया**
सहकारः फलिनी च नन्विमौ।
अविधाय विवाहसत्क्रिया-
मनयोर्गम्यत इत्यसाम्प्रतम्।।[9]

इन्दुमती के दिवङ्गत हो जाने पर अज विलाप करते हुए कहते हैं—तुमने इस आम के वृक्ष तथा फलिनी का विवाह करना निश्चित किया था। इन दोनों के विवाह-मङ्गल को सम्पादित किए बिना तुम्हारा चला जाना उचित नहीं है।

कवियों को वृक्ष-लता के मिथुनभाव का निरूपण अतिशय प्रिय है। कालिदास ने यही मिथुनभाव अभिज्ञानशाकुन्तल में आम्र तथा नवमालिका के मध्य स्थापित किया है यथा—

सङ्कल्पितं प्रथममेव मया तवार्थे
भर्तारमात्मसदृशं सुकृतैर्गता त्वम्।
चूतेन संश्रितवती नवमालिकेय-
मस्यामहं त्वयि च संप्रति वीतचिन्तः।।[10]

2. बकुल (केसर)

कविसमयानुसार बकुल (बङ्क् + उरच् + रेफस्य लत्वम्, न लोपः) तरुणियों की मुखमदिरा के गण्डूषसेक से विकसित होता है। इसका अन्य नाम केसर भी है। 'केसर' शब्द का प्रयोग कालिदास ने 'बकुलपुष्प' तथा 'पुष्पपराग' इन दो अर्थों में किया है। बकुल को लोकभाषा में 'मौलश्री' या 'मौलसिरी' कहते हैं। इसके पुष्प धवल वर्ण के तथा सुरभियुक्त होते हैं।

निर्दशन :

(2) **सुवदनावदनासवसम्भृत-**
स्तदनुवादिगुणः कुसुमोद्गमः।
मधुकरैरकरोन्मधु लोलुपै-
र्बकुलमाकुलमायतपङ्क्तिभिः।।[11]

सुमुखी की मुखमदिरा से प्रादुर्भूत और उस मदिरा के अनुरूप सुरभिगुण वाली पुष्पोत्पत्ति ने मधु के लोभी, लम्बी लम्बी कतारों को बाँध कर आते हुए भ्रमरों से बकुल (मौलसिरी) के वृक्ष को सब ओर से व्याकुल अर्थात् व्याप्त कर दिया।

(3) **सातिरेकमदकारणं रह-**
स्तेन दत्तमभिलेषुरङ्गनाः।
ताभिरप्युपहृतं मुखासवं
सोऽपिबद्बकुलतुल्यदोहदः।।[12]

अतिशय विलासी राजा अग्निवर्ण की अङ्गनाएं अपने प्रियतम का जूठा मदकारी आसव बड़े प्रेम से पीती रहती थीं। जिस प्रकार मौलसिरी का वृक्ष रमणियों के मुख के आसव का पान करने के लिए तरसता रहता है, उसी प्रकार उन रमणियों के मुख से आसव पीने की इच्छा करने वाला अग्निवर्ण भी उनके मुख का आसव पीया करता था। प्रस्तुत उद्धरण में बकुल के दोहद का स्पष्ट निर्देश है।

(4) तव निःश्वसितानुकारिभि-
बर्कुलैरर्धचितां समं मया।
असमाप्य विलासमेखलां
किमिदं किन्नरकण्ठि! सुप्यते।।[13]

इन्दुमती के देहावसान पर अज विलाप करते हुए कहते हैं—हे किन्नर के समान मधुर कण्ठ वाली प्रिये! सुगन्धि में तुम्हारे श्वास का अनुकरण करने वाले इन बकुल (मौलसिरी) के पुष्पों से मेरे साथ आधी गूथी हुई विलास-मेखला को बिना पूरा किए क्यों सो रही हो? बकुल पुष्पों से विलास-काञ्ची बनाने की परम्परा थी जिसका यहाँ स्पष्ट सङ्केत है। प्राचीन काल में तथा आधुनिक काल में भी 'माल्यग्रथन' एक सम्पूर्ण विकसित कला थी तथा है। अनुरागी नायक-नायिका संयुक्तरूप में माल्यग्रथन करते थे और उनकी अनेक प्रणय-केलियों में यह भी एक केलि हुआ करती थी। प्रायः नायक अपनी प्रियाओं को पुष्पाभरणों से अलङ्कृत किया करते थे।

3. अशोक

कविसमयानुसार अशोक वृक्ष का दोहद रमणी के सनूपुर चरणों द्वारा ताडन निर्दिष्ट है—

सनूपुररवेण स्त्रीचरणेनाभिताडनम्।
दोहदं यदशोकस्य ततः पुष्पोद्गमो भवेत्।।[14]

\+ \+ \+ \+ \+ \+

नूपुरान्वितपादेन तरुण्या ताडितो भृशम्।
अशोकः केसरो वक्त्रसीधुसिक्तश्च फुल्लति।। प्रयोगरत्नावल्याम्।

सुन्दरी रमणियाँ अपने झंकृत नूपुरों से युक्त चरणों से जैसे ही अशोक वृक्ष पर ताडन करती हैं, वह पुष्प-भार से लद जाता है तथा उसकी अपूर्व शोभा होती है। अपने साहित्य में अशोक का उल्लेख कालिदास ने अनेकशः किया है।

निदर्शन :

(5) हस्तेन हस्तं परिगृह्य वध्वाः
स राजसूनुः सुतरां चकासे।
अनन्तराशोकलताप्रवालं
प्राप्येव चूतः प्रतिपल्लवेन।।[15]

वे राजकुमार अज अपने हाथ से वधू इन्दुमती का हाथ पकड़कर समीपस्थ अशोकलता के नवपल्लव को अपने पल्लव से प्राप्त कर आम्रवृक्ष के समान अत्यन्त शोभित हुए। यहाँ आम्रवृक्ष तथा अशोकलता में बहुत सुन्दर रूप से मिथुनभाव चित्रित है।

(6) कुसुमं कृतदोहदस्त्वया
यदशोकोऽयमुदीरयिष्यति।
अलकाभरणं कथं नु त-
त्तव नेष्यामि निवापमाल्यताम्।।

(7) **स्मरतेव सशब्दनूपुरं**
चरणानुग्रहमन्यदुर्लभम्।
अमुना कुसुमाश्रुवर्षिणा
त्वमशोकेन सुगात्रि! शोच्यसे।[16]

इन्दुमती के देहावसान पर विलाप करते हुए अज कहते हैं—हे प्रिये! तुमसे प्राप्त पादप्रहार-रूप दोहद वाला यह अशोक वृक्ष जिस पुष्प को उत्पन्न करेगा, तुम्हारे केश के अलङ्करणयोग्य उस पुष्प को मैं किस प्रकार दाहसंस्कार के बाद तिलाञ्जलि में प्रदान करूँगा? हे सुन्दर शरीर वाली प्रिये! दूसरे को दुर्लभ, झङ्कार करते हुए नूपुरों वाली चरणताडनरूप कृपा को स्मरण करते हुए के समान पुष्परूप अश्रु को बरसाता हुआ यह अशोक तुम्हारे लिए मानों पश्चात्ताप कर रहा है। इन दोनों निदर्शनों में भी अशोक वृक्ष का दोहद निरूपित है। अशोक पुष्प का प्रयोग केशसज्जा में किया जाता था।

(8) **कुसुममेव न केवलमार्तवं**
नवमशोकतरोः स्मरदीपनम्।
किसलयप्रसवोऽपि विलासिनां
मदयिता दयिताश्रवणार्पितः।।[17]

वसन्त ऋतु में उत्पन्न अशोक वृक्ष का केवल पुष्प ही कामोद्दीपक नहीं हुआ, अपितु विलासिओं को उन्मादित करने वाला, प्रियाओं का कर्णाभूषण बना हुआ नवपल्लव भी कामोद्दीपक हुआ।

(9) **इमां तटाशोकलतां च तन्वीं**
स्तनाभिरामस्तबकाभिनम्राम्।
त्वत्प्राप्तिबुद्ध्या परिरब्धुकामः
सौमित्रिणा साश्रुरहं निषिद्धः।।[18]

लङ्का से लौटते समय श्रीराम सीता से कहते हैं—पयोधरों के समान मनोहर गुच्छों से झुकी हुई और पतली इस तटवर्तिनी अशोकलता को 'तुम्हें मैंने पा लिया' इस विचार से आलिङ्गन करने को इच्छुक तथा रोते हुए मुझको लक्ष्मण ने रोका था। यहाँ भी अशोक वृक्ष के पुष्पभार से अतिशय लदे हुए होने का वर्णन है।

4. तिलक

कविसमयानुसार तरुणियों के वीक्षण द्वारा तिलक वृक्ष पुष्पसम्पत्ति प्रदान करता है। 'तिलक' वृक्ष का अन्य नाम 'श्रीमान्' भी है—तिलकः श्रीमान्नाम वृक्षः। 'तिलकः क्षुरकः श्रीमान्' इत्यमरः।[19]

निदर्शन :

(10) **उपचितावयवा शुचिभिः कणै-**
रलिकदम्बकयोगमुपेयुषी।
सदृशकान्तिरलक्ष्यत मञ्जरी
तिलकजाऽलकजालकमौक्तिकैः।।[20]

श्वेत परागों से व्याप्त अवयवों वाली तथा भ्रमर-समूह से अधिष्ठित तिलकवृक्ष की मञ्जरी नायिकाओं के केशों को बाँधने वाली जालियों में गुथे हुए मोतियों के समान दिखलाई पड़ती थी। तिलकवृक्ष में मञ्जरियाँ होती हैं तथा उनका उपयोग केशसज्जा में किया जाता था। प्रस्तुत निदर्शन में **'तिलकजाऽलकजालकमौक्तिकैः'** में यमक की छटा दर्शनीय है।

(11) अलिभिरञ्जनबिन्दुमनोहरैः
कुसुमपंक्तिनिपातिभिरङ्कितः।
न खलु शोभयति स्म वनस्थलीं
न तिलकस्तिलकः प्रमदामिव।।[21]

तिलक के वृक्ष ने भी वनस्थली की कम शोभा नहीं बढ़ाई। जैसे किसी युवती के शृङ्गार के लिए उसके मुख पर तिलक लगाया जाता है, वैसे ही उस तिलक वृक्ष के फूलों पर मँडराते हुए कज्जलबिन्दुओं के समान सुन्दर भौंरे ऐसे प्रतीत होते थे मानों वनस्थली के मुख को भी तिलक से अङ्कित कर दिया गया है। इस उद्धरण में 'तिलकस्तिलकः' में यमक की शोभा दर्शनीय है।

5. कुरबक

कहा जाता है कि कुरबक सुन्दरी रमणियों के आलिङ्गन से प्रहर्षित हो रक्त वर्ण की पुष्पसम्पत्ति प्रदान करता है। कुरबक (कुरवक) (ईषत् रवो यत्र इति कुरव + कन्)[22] के पुष्प का प्रयोग केशसज्जा में विशेषतः जूड़े की गाँठ को सज्जित करने में किया जाता है। यह वसन्त ऋतु में खिलता है।

निदर्शन :

(12) विरचिता मधुनोपवनश्रिया-
मभिनवा इव पत्रविशेषकाः।
मधुलिहां मधुदानविशारदाः
कुरबका रवकारणतां ययुः।।[23]

वसन्त ऋतु के द्वारा उपवन-लक्ष्मी की बनायी गयी नई-नई पत्ररचना (स्त्रीकपोलस्थ चन्दनादि की पत्राकार-रचना) के समान स्थित, बहुत मधुदान करने वाले लाल फूलों वाले कुरबक (कटसरैया) के वृक्ष भ्रमरों के गुञ्जार के कारण बन गए। भ्रमर कुरबक पुष्पों के रस का पान कर वैसे गुञ्जार करने लगे जैसे दाता से दान प्राप्त कर याचक उनका गुणगान करते हैं।

6. मन्दार

कविसमयानुसार मन्दार शृङ्गारिणी नायिका के मृदु वचनों से विकसित होता है। मन्दार (मन्द् + आरक्) प्रवालवृक्ष या विद्रुमवृक्ष है। इसके दूसरे नाम हैं— रत्नवृक्ष, मन्दट, रक्तकन्द, रक्तकन्दल, रत्नकन्दल, हेमकन्दल एवं लतामणि। मन्दार देवेन्द्र के नन्दन कानन में विद्यमान पाँच देवतरुओं में अन्यतम है। पाँच देवतरु हैं— मन्दार, पारिजात, सन्तानक, कल्पवृक्ष, हरिचन्दन।

निदर्शन :

(13) क्रियाप्रबन्धादयमध्वराणा-
मजस्रमाहूतसहस्रनेत्रः।
शच्याश्चिरं पाण्डुकपोललम्बा-
न्मन्दारशून्यानलकांश्चकार।।[24]

सुनन्दा राजकुमारी इन्दुमती को किसी राजा का परिचय देती हुई कहती है— सदा यज्ञ-सम्पादन करने से इन्द्र को बार-बार बुलाने वाले इस राजा ने इन्द्राणी शची के पतिविरह से पाण्डुर कपोलों पर लटकते हुए केशों को मन्दार

पुष्प से रहित कर दिया है। जब-जब इन्द्र इस राजा के यहाँ यज्ञ-भाग लेने के लिए जाते हैं तब-तब प्रोषितभर्तृका शची का कपोलमण्डल पाण्डुरवर्ण का हो जाता है तथा वह केशों में मन्दारपुष्पों को गूँथकर शृङ्गार करना छोड़ देती हैं। यह पद्य इस तथ्य का परिचय है कि शची को मन्दारपुष्पों से अपनी केशसज्जा करना अतिशय प्रिय है।

7. चम्पक

नायिकाओं के सुमधुर स्मित एवं हसित से चम्पक विकसित होता है—ऐसा कविसमय में प्रसिद्ध है। चम्पक (चम्प + ण्वुल्) चम्पयति चम्प्यते वा अर्थात् जो विषनाशक गुण वाला है। चम्पक के अन्य नाम स्वर्णपुष्प, हेमपुष्प तथा चम्पा हैं। इसका वृक्ष सीधा 10 मीटर से 20 मीटर तक ऊँचा एवं सदाहरित होता है। इसके पुष्प पीतवर्ण के सुगन्धित एवं मनमोहक होते हैं। पुष्प एवं छाल का चिकित्सा में व्यवहार होता है। चम्पकपुष्पों से रमणियाँ अपना केश-शृङ्गार करती हैं। कालिदास ने ऋतुसंहार में केवल एक स्थान पर चम्पक का उल्लेख स्त्रियों द्वारा केशों को सुवासित करने के प्रसङ्ग में किया है—

निदर्शन :

(14) **ईषुत्तुषारैः कृतशीतहर्म्यैः**
सुवासितं चारु शिरश्च चम्पकैः।
कुर्वन्ति नार्योऽपि वसन्तकाले
स्तनं सहारं कुसुमैर्मनोहरैः।।[25]

कालिदास ने इस पुष्प का बहुशः उल्लेख क्यों नहीं किया, यह अन्वेषणीय है।

8. चूत (आम्र • सहकार • रसाल)

चूत अथवा आम्र सभी भारतीय फलों का राजा है। न केवल भारत में अपितु समग्र विश्व में लोग इसका रसास्वादन कर आनन्दित होते हैं। इसके सहस्राधिक भेद-प्रभेद हैं। इसके अन्य नाम कामशर, रसाल, कामवल्लभ, वामाङ्ग, सहकार, कीरेष्ट तथा माधवद्रुम हैं—

आम्रः कामशरश्चूतः रसालः कामवल्लभः।
वामाङ्गः सहकारश्च कीरेष्टो माधवद्रुमः।।

कविकुलगुरु कालिदास ने अपने साहित्य में लगभग 45 बार चूत अथवा आम्र का उल्लेख किया है। आम के रंग-बिरंगे दृश्य कालिदास ने प्रस्तुत किये हैं। अनेक बार उनके आम्रपरक वर्णन किसी अन्य शास्त्र अथवा विद्या का भी उल्लेख करते हैं जिससे वर्णन और अधिक रम्य बन जाता है। कविसमयानुसार आम्र सुन्दरी रमणियों के मुखवात से प्रफुल्लित होता है। पुष्पबाण कामदेव के पाँच बाणों में चूत अन्यतम है। कामदेव के पाँच बाण निम्नाङ्कित हैं—

अरविन्दमशोकश्च चूतश्च नवमल्लिका।
नीलोत्पलञ्च पञ्चैते पुष्पबाणस्य सायकाः।।

निदर्शन :

(15) **हस्तेन हस्तं परिगृह्य वध्वाः**
स राजसूनुः सुतरां चकासे।
अनन्तराशोकलताप्रवालं
प्राप्येव चूतः प्रतिपल्लवेन।।[26]

वे राजकुमार अज अपने हाथ से वधू इन्दुमती का हाथ पकड़कर समीपस्थ अशोकलता के नवपल्लव को अपने पल्लव से प्राप्त कर आम्रवृक्ष के समान अत्यन्त शोभित हुए। यहाँ वधूवर की अशोकलता एवम् आम्र से उपमा हृदयावर्जक है।

(16) **एषा त्वया पेशलमध्ययापि**
घटाम्बुसंवर्धितबालचूता।
आनन्दयत्युन्मुखकृष्णसारा
दृष्टा चिरात्पञ्चवटी मनो मे।।[27]

लङ्का से लौटते हुए श्रीराम अपनी प्रिया सीता से कहते हैं—कृशोदरी (होने से भार ले चलने में असमर्थ) होने पर भी तुमने घड़ों से सींचकर जहाँ के आम के छोटे-छोटे वृक्षों को बढ़ाया है, ऐसी तथा मुझे देखकर सामने आते हुए कृष्णसार मृगों वाली एवं बहुत दिनों के बाद देखी गई यह पञ्चवटी मुझे आनन्दित कर रही है। प्रस्तुत पद्य सीता तथा श्रीराम दोनों के वनस्पतिविषयक प्रेम का परिचायक है।

(17) **दक्षिणेन पवनेन सम्भृतं**
प्रेक्ष्य चूतकुसुमं सपल्लवम्।
अन्वनैषुरवधूतविग्रहा-
स्तं दुरुत्सहवियोगमङ्गनाः।।[28]

वसन्त ऋतु में अग्निवर्ण की अङ्गनाओं ने दक्षिण (अनुकूल पक्षान्तर में दक्षिण दिशा वाली) वायु से उत्पन्न पल्लवसहित आम्रमञ्जरी को देखकर प्रणयकलह को छोड़ती हुई असह्य विरह वाले उन अग्निवर्ण को अनुनीत किया अर्थात् मनाया। वसन्त ऋतु में आम्रवृक्ष पर आम्रमञ्जरी के विकसित होते ही रमणियाँ कामातुर हो अपना प्रणयमान छोड़ अपने प्रियतम को मनाने लगती हैं। यह है आम्रमञ्जरीमहिमा। रघुवंश में सहकार के अनेक सुन्दर निदर्शन उपलब्ध हैं।[29]

9. नमेरु

कविसमयानुसार सुन्दरी रमणियों के सुमधुर गीत को सुनकर नमेरु (नम् + एरु) वृक्ष में सुन्दर पुष्प खिलते हैं। मल्लिनाथ के अनुसार इसका अन्य नाम सुरपुंनाग है। इसके पुष्पों से स्त्रियाँ अपनी केशसज्जा करती हैं। नमेरु वृक्ष की शाखाएँ इतनी सघन होती हैं कि यह वृक्ष पथिकों को अभीष्ट छाया प्रदान करता है।

निदर्शन :

(18) **विशश्रमुर्नमेरूणां छायास्वध्यास्य सैनिकाः।**
दृशदो वासितोत्सङ्गा निषण्णमृगनाभिभिः।।[30]

रघु के सैनिकों ने नमेरु अथवा सुरपुंनाग नामक वृक्षों की छाया में बैठे हुए कस्तूरीमृगों की नाभिस्थित कस्तूरी से जिनके पृष्ठभाग सुगन्धित हो गए हैं, ऐसी शिलाओं पर बैठकर विश्राम किया।

10. कर्णिकार

कविसमयानुसार रमणियों द्वारा पुरोनर्तन किए जाने पर कर्णिकार वृक्ष कुसुमित होता है। इसका अन्य नाम अमलतास है। कर्णिकार के पुष्प पीले रंग के होते हैं तथा उनमें सुगन्धि नहीं होती। रमणियाँ केशसज्जा में इसके पुष्पों का उपयोग करती हैं। रघुवंश में कर्णिकार का उल्लेख उपलब्ध नहीं है।

निदर्शन :

(19) उमापि नीलालकमध्यशोभि
विस्रंसयन्ती नवकर्णिकारम्।
चकार कर्णच्युतपल्लवेन
मूर्ध्ना प्रणामं वृषभध्वजाय।।[31]

पार्वती भी मस्तक को अत्यधिक झुकाने से काले केशों में गुँथे हुए ताज़े कर्णिकार पुष्प को और कान पर रखे हुए अवतंसभूत पल्लव को गिराती हुई शङ्कर को प्रणाम करने लगीं। पार्वती भी केशसज्जा के लिए कर्णिकार पुष्प का उपयोग करती थीं।

इस प्रकार कविकुलगुरु कालिदास ने रघुवंश में दस दोहदवृक्षों में से आठ का अतिशय मनोहर चित्राङ्कन प्रस्तुत किया है। प्रत्येक वृक्ष का दोहद शृङ्गारिणी नायिका के किसी-न-किसी स्नेह-कृत्य से सम्बद्ध है। दोहद-संतुष्टि होने पर वृक्ष सुन्दर पुष्प-सम्पत्ति प्रदान करते हैं। कुसुम-सम्पत्ति से लदे हुए दोहद-वृक्षों के रमणीय उद्यान को देखकर यह तथ्य उभर कर सामने आता है कि जिस प्रकार वृक्ष सुन्दर व्यवहार पाकर सुन्दर पुष्पराशि प्रदान करते हैं, हम मानवों को भी सदा सभी के प्रति अनुकूल व्यवहार करना चाहिए जिससे दूसरों से हमें भी अनुकूल व्यवहार प्राप्त हो। प्रस्तुत आलेख का समापन आदिकवि वाल्मीकि के पद्यत्रय से किया जा रहा है जहाँ कैलास पर्वत के निकटस्थ वन एवम् उद्यान के अनेक वृक्षों का वर्णन है। संयोगतः यहाँ सात दोहदवृक्ष भी वर्णित हैं—

(20) कर्णिकारवनैर्दीप्तैः कदम्बबकुलैस्तथा।
पद्मिनीभिश्च फुल्लाभिर्मन्दाकिन्या जलैरपि।।
चम्पकाशोकपुंनागमन्दारतरुभिस्तथा।
चूतपाटललोध्रैश्च प्रियङ्ग्वर्जुनकेतकैः।।
तगरैर्नारिकेलैश्च प्रियालपनसैरतथा।
एतैरन्यैश्च तरुभिरुद्भासितवनान्तरे।।[23]

सन्दर्भ-सङ्केत

1. रघुवंशम् - 14. 45
2. रघुवंशम् - 3. 7
3. नैषधीयचरितम् - 3. 21
4. कुमारसम्भवम् (काले-सम्पादित) - 3. 26 की टिप्पणी में उद्धृत
5. मातङ्गलीला - 3. 9; संस्कृत-हिन्दी-कोश (आप्टे) में उद्धृत, पृष्ठ 694
6. ऋतुसंहारम् - 3. 18
7. ऋतुसंहारम् - 4. 14
8. मेघदूतम् - 2. 43
9. रघुवंशम् - 8. 61
10. अभिज्ञानशाकुन्तलम् - 4.13
11. रघुवंशम् - 9.30
12. रघुवंशम् - 19. 12

13. रघुवंशम् - 8. 64
14. कुमारसम्भवम् - 3. 26 की मल्लिनाथ-टीका में उद्धृत
15. रघुवंशम् - 7. 21
16. रघुवंशम् - 8. 62, 63
17. रघुवंशम् - 9. 28
18. रघुवंशम् - 13. 32
19. रघुवंशम - 9. 41 की मल्लिनाथ-टीका में उद्धृत; आप्टे संस्कृत-हिन्दी-कोष, पृ. 1037
20. रघुवंशम् - 9. 44
21. रघुवंशम् - 9. 41
22. आप्टे संस्कृत-हिन्दी-कोष - पृ. 286
23. रघुवंशम् - 9. 29
24. रघुवंशम् - 6. 23
25. ऋतुसंहारम् - 3. 6
26. रघुवंशम् - 7. 21
27. रघुवंशम् - 13. 34
28. रघुवंशम् - 19. 43
29. रघुवंशम् - 6. 69; 8. 61; 9. 33; 16. 52; 19. 46
30. रघुवंशम् - 4. 74
31. कुमारसम्भवम् - 3. 62
32. वाल्मीकि-रामायणम् - 7. 26, 4-6

卐 卐 卐

कुमारसम्भव में वृक्षपुष्पश्री

लता विग

वागर्थाविव सम्पृक्तौ वागर्थप्रतिपत्तये।
जगतः पितरौ वन्दे पार्वतीपरमेश्वरौ।।

सत्य ही है कि महाकवि कालिदास संस्कृत साहित्य में उत्कृष्ट कवि हैं। प्रकृति वर्णन में तो वह बहुत ही निपुण हैं ऐसा प्रतीत होता है कि महाकवि कालिदास स्वयं ही प्रकृति रूप हैं। कालिदास के प्राकृतिक वर्णनों में कुछ ऐसी प्रमुख विशेषताएँ हैं, जो अन्यत्र दुर्लभ हैं। यद्यपि उन्होंने अपनी प्रत्येक रचना में प्रकृति को विशेष महत्त्व दिया है किन्तु वनस्पति की दृष्टि से कुमारसम्भव का स्थान सबसे ऊपर है। कालिदास ने कुमारसम्भव में वनस्पति के अन्तर्गत पुष्प, वृक्ष, धान की बालियों आदि का सजीव चित्रण किया है। प्रस्तुत लेख में महाकवि कालिदास द्वारा कुमारसम्भव में वर्णित प्रत्येक पुष्प, वृक्ष आदि की चर्चा की गई है। सर्वप्रथम यहाँ (कुमारसम्भव में) वर्णित पुष्पों का विस्तृत वर्णन प्रस्तुत है।

आम्रपुष्प (कुसुम) का सुन्दर उदाहरण द्रष्टव्य है—

जैसे नाना प्रकार के पुष्पों के होते हुए भी वसन्त ऋतु की भ्रमरपंक्ति आम्र-कुसुम में ही विशेष रुचि रखती है, वैसे ही पुत्रवान् होते हुए भी हिमालय की दृष्टि पार्वती में ही विशेष रुचि रखती थी।

अनन्तपुष्पस्य मधोर्हि चूते द्विरेफमाला सविशेषसङ्गा। 1. 27

इसी प्रकार आम्रमञ्जरी का निम्न उदाहरण भी द्रष्टव्य है—

आम्रमञ्जरियों के खा लेने से कषैले कण्ठवाले कोकिल की मधुर कूक ही मानिनी नायिकाओं का मानभङ्ग कराने में निपुण कामदेव की वाणी जैसी प्रतीत हो रही थी।

चूताङ्कुरास्वादकषायकण्ठः पुंस्कोकिलो यन्मधुरं चुकूज।
मनस्विनीमानविघातदक्षं तदेव जातं वचनं स्मरस्य।। 3. 32

इसी प्रकार कालिदास ने शङ्कर जी के मुख से कुमुद पुष्प का बहुत ही सुन्दर चित्रण प्रस्तुत किया है—देखो, अब कुमुद के फूल खिल रहे हैं और उनके सम्पुटों में गूञ्जने वाले भ्रमरों की गुञ्जार हो रही है। जिससे ऐसा प्रतीत हो रहा है मानो इन्होंने सांस लेकर चाँदनी का इतना रस पी लिया है कि उसे पचा न सकने के कारण इनके पेट ही फटे जा रहे हैं और वे पीड़ा से कराह रहे हों।

मुक्तषट्पदविरावमञ्जसा भिद्यते कुमुदमानिबन्धनात्।। 8. 70

एवमेव कालिदास ने निम्न उदाहरण में पार्वती की बाहुओं की उपमा शिरीष पुष्पों से दी है। उन्होंने पार्वती की बाहुओं को शिरीष के पुष्पों से भी सुकोमल बताया है—

शिरीषपुष्पाऽधिकसौकुमार्यौ बाहू तदीयाविति मे वितर्कः।
पराजितेनाऽपि कृतौ हरस्य यौ कण्ठपाशौ मकरध्वजेन।। 1.41

इसी प्रकार इस निम्न श्लोक में भी पार्वती के कोमल शरीर की उपमा शिरीष पुष्प से की गई है—

मनीषिताः सन्ति गृहेषु देवतास्तपः क्व वत्से क्व च तावकं वपुः।
पदं सहेत भ्रमरस्य पेलवं शिरीषपुष्पं न पुनः पतत्रिणः।। 5.4

इसी प्रकार कालिदास ने देवताओं के मुख से सुनहले कमलों का विवेचन भी किया है—

उसने (तारकासुर ने) मन्दाकिनी के सुनहले कमलों के पौधे उखाड़-उखाड़कर उन्हें अपनी बावलियों में लगा दिया है। जिससे अब उसमें केवल दिग्गजों के मद से मलिन जल ही बाकी रह गया है।

मन्दाकिन्याः पयः शेषं दिग्वारणमदाविलम्।
हेमाम्भोरुहसस्यानां तद्वाप्यो धाम साम्प्रतम्।। 2.44

सुनहले कमलों के अतिरिक्त कालिदास ने कुमारसम्भव में नील कमलों का भी विवेचन किया है—

तत्काल ही आकाश में वर्षा ऋतु के समान दिखाई पड़ने वाले काले-काले बादलों तथा नीलकमलों के झुण्ड के समान काला धुआँ चारों ओर इतने घने रूप में फैल गया कि चारों ओर कहीं भी कुछ नहीं दिखाई पड़ता था।

सद्यः प्रसस्रुरसितोत्पलदामभासो
दृग्गोचरत्वमखिलं न हि सन्नयन्तः।। 17.35

इसी प्रकार कमल के सन्दर्भ में निम्न उदाहरण भी द्रष्टव्य है—

पार्वती की सखी ब्रह्मचारी से कह रही है—हे साधो! यदि कौतूहल है तो सुनो, मैं बता रही हूँ कि किसलिए मेरी सखी ने अपने इस कोमल शरीर को उसी प्रकार तप का साधन बनाया है जैसे कोई धूप रोकने के लिए कमल को छतरी बनाए हो—

यदर्थमम्भोजमिवोष्णवारणं कृतं तपःसाधनमेतया वपुः।। 5.52

एवमेव पारिजात के पुष्पों का वर्णन कुमारसम्भव में यत्र-तत्र प्राप्त होता है—

रति के समय पार्वती जी की चोटी उनके कंधों पर बिखर गई थी जिससे गुथे हुए फूल भी झड़ गए थे। शङ्कर जी ने उन बिखरे हुए बालों को पारिजात के फूलों की माला से बाँध दिया।

रतिश्लथं तत्कबरीकलापमंसावसक्तं विगलत्प्रसूनम्।
स पारिजातोद्भवपुष्पमय्या स्रजा बबन्धामृतमूर्तिमौलिः।। 9.21

तथा जब देवता भगवान् शिव को झुककर प्रणाम करने लगे तो उस समय उनके मुकुट की नोक से झड़कर पारिजात के फूल बिखर गए—

किरीटकोटिच्युतपारिजातपुष्पोत्करेणानमितेन मूर्ध्ना।
स्वर्गैकवन्द्यो जगदेकवन्द्यं तं देवदेवं प्रणनाम देवः।। 12.29

और इस निम्न दृष्टान्त में कुन्दपुष्प की चर्चा करते हुए सुरसैनिकों के छत्र की उपमा श्वेत कुन्दपुष्पों से की गई है—

कुन्दोज्ज्वलानि सकलातपवारणानि
धूतानि तेन मरुता सुरसैनिकानाम्।
उड्डीयमानकलहंसकुलोपमानि
मेघाभधूलिमलिने नभसि प्रसस्रुः।। 17. 27

इनके अतिरिक्त कालिदास ने पलाश के लाल फूलों का भी सुन्दर दृष्टान्त प्रस्तुत किया है—

द्वितीया के चन्द्रमा जैसे टेढ़ी आकृति वाले पलाश के लाल लाल फूल ऐसे प्रतीत होते थे मानों वसन्त रूपी पुरुष से भोगी गई वनस्थली रूपी शरीर पर ताजे-ताजे नख के क्षत दिखाई दे रहे हों। (3.29)

उपर्युक्त पुष्पों के अतिरिक्त कालिदास ने कुमारसम्भव में बहुत से वृक्षों को भी प्रस्तुत किया है।

सर्वप्रथम देवदारु वृक्ष का उदाहरण द्रष्टव्य है—

गजचर्म को धारण कर जितेन्द्रिय शङ्कर भगवान् तपश्चर्या करने के लिए हिमालय के किसी रमणीय शिखर पर रहा करते थे। जहाँ भागीरथी के जल प्रवाह से सिंचे हुए देवदारु के बहुत से पेड़ थे, चारों तरफ कस्तूरी मृगों की सुगन्ध थी तथा किन्नरमिथुन सर्वदा गाया करते थे।

स कृत्तिवासास्तपसे यतात्मा गङ्गाप्रवाहोक्षितदेवदारु।
प्रस्थं हिमाद्रेर्मृगनाभिगन्धि किञ्चित्क्वणत्किन्नरमध्युवास।। 1. 54

इसी प्रकार निम्न उदाहरण में भी देवदारु वृक्ष का सजीव चित्रण दृष्टिगोचर हो रहा है—

गङ्गा के झरने के जलबिन्दुओं को धारण करने वाली, बारबार देवदारु वृक्षों को कँपाने वाली तथा मोरों के पंखों को उल्लासित करने वाली जिस हिमालय की वायु मृगों को ढूँढ़ने वाले किरातों से सेवन की जाती है—

भागीरथीनिर्झरसीकराणां वोढा मुहुः कम्पितदेवदारुः।
यद्वायुरन्विष्टमृगैः किरातैरासेव्यते भिन्नशिखण्डिबर्हः।। 1.15

एवमेव ताड़वृक्ष के उदाहरण भी कुमारसम्भव महाकाव्य में प्राप्त होते हैं—

फूलों की चोरी लग जाने के भय से वायु भी उसके उद्यानों में तो चलता ही नहीं, यहाँ तक कि उसके पास भी वह ताड़ के पंखे की हवा से अधिक गति से चलने का साहस नहीं कर पाता—

व्यावृत्तगतिरुद्याने कुसुमस्तेयसाध्वसात्।
न वाति वायुस्तत्पार्श्वे तालवृन्ताऽनिलाऽधिकम्।। 2. 35

इसी प्रकार ताड़वृक्ष के सन्दर्भ में एक और उदाहरण प्रस्तुत है—

जिस प्रकार प्रलय करने के लिए अपने तटों की मर्यादा भंग करके चारों ओर फैलते हुए तथा सारी दुनियाँ को डुबाते हुए काल का स्वागत करने वाले दो समुद्र एक दूसरे से टकराते हुए भीषण कोलाहल के साथ चढ़ते चले आते हैं, उसी प्रकार ताड़ वृक्षों से भरी पहाड़ों की तलहटी को फाड़ने में समर्थ देवताओं तथा असुरों की भयानक सेना अत्यन्त भीषण ध्वनि करती हुई तथा कालरूपी अतिथि को भोजन का निमन्त्रण देती हुई सारे ब्रह्माण्ड में फैल गई—

सङ्ग्रामं प्रलयाय सन्निपततो वेलामतिक्रामतो
वृन्दारासुरसैन्यसागरयुगस्याशेषदिग्व्यापिनः।
कालातिथ्यभुजो बभूव बहलः कोलाहलः क्रोषणः
शैलोत्तालतटीविघट्टनपटुर्ब्रह्माण्डकुक्षिम्भरिः।। 15.53

इसके अतिरिक्त कल्पवृक्ष के दृष्टान्त भी इसी महाकाव्य में यत्र-तत्र उपलब्ध होते हैं—

उसके (तारकासुर के) अनुग्रह की कामना रखने वाले इन्द्र भी कल्पवृक्ष के पुष्पों के आभूषणों को दूतों द्वारा बार-बार भेज कर उसे अपने अनुकूल बनाए रखने का प्रयत्न करते रहते हैं।

तत्कृताऽनुग्रहापेक्षी तं मुहुर्दूतहारितैः।
अनुकूलयतीन्द्रोऽपि कल्पद्रुमविभूषणैः।। 2.39

तथा शङ्कर जी पार्वती को कहते हैं—देखो, गन्धमादन की यह वनदेवी तुम्हें यहाँ बैठी हुई देखकर लाल सूर्यकान्त-मणि के प्याले में कल्पवृक्ष की मदिरा लिए तुम्हारा स्वागत करने के लिए स्वयं आई हुई है—

लोहितार्कमणिभाजनार्पितं कल्पवृक्षमधु बिभ्रती स्वयम्।
त्वामियं स्थितिमतीमुपागता गन्धमादनवनाधिदेवता।। 8.75

इसी प्रकार कल्पवृक्ष के सन्दर्भ में एक और दृष्टान्त देखने योग्य है—

उन गणों ने स्फटिक मणियों के बने भवनों पर चमकती हुई किरणों से आकाश को चित्रित कर देने वाली तथा कल्पवृक्षों से उत्पन्न पत्तों तथा फूलों से बनी हुई श्रेष्ठ सुनहरी बन्दनवारें लटका दीं।

स्फुरन्मरीचिच्छुरिताम्बराणि सन्तानशाखिप्रसवाञ्चितानि।
उच्चिक्षिपुः काञ्चनतोरणानि गणा वराणि स्फटिकालयेषु।। 11. 32

अशोक वृक्ष का दृष्टान्त भी कालिदास के कुमारसम्भव में दृष्टिगोचर होता है—

असूत सद्यः कुसुमान्यशोकः स्कन्धात्प्रभृत्येव सपल्लवानि।
पादेन नापैक्षत सुन्दरीणां सम्पर्कमासिञ्जितनूपुरेण।। 3. 26

इसी प्रकार चन्दन वृक्ष का भी एक यह निम्न उदाहरण द्रष्टव्य है—

इसके पश्चात् वह इधर-उधर घूमते-घूमाते हुए मलयाचल पर जा पहुँचे। जहाँ चन्दन की लताओं को हिलाने वाला तथा लौंग के फूलों की धूल से भरा हुआ दक्षिणी वायु रतिक्रीड़ा में लगी हुई पार्वती जी की थकान उसी प्रकार दूर कर रहा था, जैसे कोई चाटुकार मीठी-मीठी बातों से किसी को बहला रहा हो—

तस्य जातु मलयस्थलीरते धूतचन्दनलतः प्रियाक्लमम्।
आचचाम सलवङ्गकेसरश्चाटुकार इव दक्षिणानिलः।। 8.25

सलई वृक्ष का उदाहरण भी द्रष्टव्य है—

सलई के टूटे हुए वृक्षों से निकलने वाली गन्ध के कारण सुवासित अपने दिन भर के निवास-स्थान को छोड़कर ये हाथी प्रातःकाल से अब तक पर्याप्त भोजन कर लेने के पश्चात् तालाब के उस जल को पी रहे हैं जहाँ कमलों में भौंरे बन्द हो चुके हैं—

स्थानमाह्निकमपास्य दन्तिनः सल्लकीविटपभङ्गवासितम्।
आविभातचरणाय गृह्णते वारि वारिरुहबद्धषट्पदम्।। 8. 33

तथा एक श्लोक में महाकवि कालिदास ने तमाल वृक्ष का विवेचन किया है—

हे प्रिय देखो, एक ओर से बढ़ते हुए अन्धकार से घिरी हुई यह सन्ध्या ऐसी लग रही है मानो तमाल वृक्षों से एक तरफ घिरी हुई कोई गेरू की धारा हो—

तामिमां तिमिरवृद्धिपीडितां शैलराजतनयेऽधुना स्थिताम्।
एकतस्तटतमालमालिनीं पश्य धातुरसनिम्नगामिव।। 8. 53

और एक श्लोक में शालवृक्ष का दृष्टान्त भी द्रष्टव्य है—

कुमारकार्तिकेय ने इन्द्र के ऐसे क्रीडावन नन्दन को देखा, जिसके शालवृक्ष या तो तोड़ दिए गए थे अथवा काट दिए गए थे—

ततो व्रजन्नन्दननामधेयं लीलावनं जम्भजितः पुरस्तात्।
विभिन्नभग्नोद्धृतशालसङ्घं प्रेक्षाञ्चकार स्मरशत्रुसूनुः।। 13. 33

उपर्युक्त पुष्पवृक्षों के अतिरिक्त कालिदास ने कुमारसम्भव के एक श्लोक में धान की बालियों का भी विवेचन किया है, उन्होंने पीली जटाओं की उपमा धान की बालियों से की है—

उपेक्षते यः श्लथलम्बिनीर्जटाः कपोलदेशे कलमाग्रपिङ्गलाः।। 5. 47

इस प्रकार हम देखते हैं कि महाकवि कालिदास ने अपने महाकाव्य कुमारसम्भव में बहुत ही सुन्दर ढंग से पुष्प तथा वृक्षों का विवेचन किया है तथा इनका वर्णन इतनी सजीवता से किया है कि पढ़ते ही वह दृश्य नेत्रों के सामने उपस्थित हो जाता है।

卐 卐 卐

मेघदूत एवं वनस्पतिवैभवश्री

आनन्द कुमार श्रीवास्तव

मनुष्य का प्रकृति के साथ अविचल सम्बन्ध है। उसका विकास प्रकृति के बीच में ही हुआ है। अतः वह प्रकृति का अंश है। यदि पर्वत, नदी, वन सबके सब मानव जाति के पोषक हैं तो प्राचीन मनुष्य भी इनके रक्षण में सन्नद्ध दिखायी देता है। प्रकृति सदैव मनुष्य जाति को अपनी ओर आकृष्ट करती रही है तो मनुष्य ने उसकी निकटता का लाभ उठाकर उससे अनेकविध शिक्षा ग्रहण की है। प्रायः मनुष्य ने प्रकृति को अपने समान चेतन, सजीव तथा संवेदनशील मान कर उसे अपना सहचर स्वीकार किया है। वह अपने सुख-दुःख का रूप प्रकृति-दर्पण में देखता है। प्रकृति और मनुष्य के इस निकट सम्बन्ध के कारण प्रकृति-चित्रण संस्कृत काव्य का एक अभिन्न अङ्ग बन गया है। बिना प्रकृति-चित्रण के संस्कृत काव्य—चाहे श्रव्य हो अथवा दृश्य—पूर्णत्व को प्राप्त नहीं होता।

प्राचीन काल में प्रकृति का स्वरूप अत्यन्त शुद्ध था। **'माता भूमिः पुत्रोऽहं पृथिव्याः'** (अथर्ववेद – 12.13.27) भाव के कारण मनुष्य ने पृथिवी से छेड़छाड़ नहीं की। यही कारण है कि कवियों ने प्रायः प्रकृति के विशुद्ध रूप का ही चित्रण किया है। सर्वत्र तपोवन का साम्राज्य, यत्किञ्चित् वायु-प्रदूषण का अनवरत अनुष्ठीयमान यज्ञधूम से शुद्धीकरण, पृथिवी का अशोषण, जल में अशुद्धिकारक तत्त्वों के निक्षेप का निषेध-विधान आदि के कारण प्रकृति पूर्णतः विशुद्ध थी और मनुष्य के लिए हितकारिणी भी। दुर्गा-सप्तशती में कहा गया है कि जब तक पृथिवी पर पर्वत, वन, वृक्ष विद्यमान रहेंगे, मानवजाति जीवित रहेगी। कालान्तर में मानव जाति ने भौतिक समृद्धि के वशीभूत होकर स्वार्थवश जब से प्रकृति-दोहन प्रारम्भ किया, प्रकृति क्रमशः अपूर्ण एवं प्रदूषित होती गयी। आज विभिन्न परमाणु-परीक्षणों एवं वाहन आदि से वायु प्रदूषित हो गयी है तो अनेक कल-कारखानों की गन्दगी के नदियों में प्रवाहित होने से जल भी दूषित हो गया है। इसी प्रकार नगरीकरण ने वनसम्पदा को हानि पहुँचाई है। फलस्वरूप पृथिवी का वास्तविक स्वरूप नष्ट हो रहा है। इन सबके कारण ही आज मानव जीवन असहज हो गया है और वैचारिक प्रदूषण से ग्रस्त भी।

हमारे प्राचीन ग्रन्थ मनुष्य जाति को प्रकृति के संरक्षक के रूप में उपस्थापित करते हैं। ऐतरेय उपनिषद् में कहा गया है कि प्रारम्भ में केवल 'आत्मा' था। उसने सृष्टि की रचना की। फिर उसने सोचा कि इस सृष्टि की रक्षा करने वाला बनाना चाहिए—उसने मनुष्य बनाया।[2] इस कथानक से यह स्पष्ट है कि मनुष्य के ऊपर सृष्टि की रक्षा का दायित्व है। इसी प्रकार रामायण, महाभारत एवं पुराण-साहित्य भी हमें प्रकृति-रक्षण का सन्देश देते हैं।

वृक्ष आदि की रक्षा के लिए ऋषियों ने उसमें देवत्व का आधान स्वीकार कर उसके पूजन का विधान किया। विभिन्न भारतीय वाङ्मय में वट, नारिकेल, अशोक, चम्पक आदि का महत्त्व प्रतिपादित किया गया।

पर्यावरण का अर्थ है—'परितः आवृणोति' अर्थात् प्राणिजगत् को चारों ओर से ढँकने वाला प्रकृति तत्त्व-पृथ्वी, जल, अग्नि, वायु एवं आकाश। गीता में इन पाँच तत्त्वों के अतिरिक्त मन, बुद्धि एवं अहंकार को भी प्रकृति-तत्त्व मान कर प्रकृति को अष्टधा कहा गया है।[3]

महाकवि कालिदास को पर्यावरण से पर्याप्त सहानुभूति है। वे न केवल उससे परिचित हैं अपितु निकटता का अनुभव भी करते हैं। उनके काव्यों में पर्यावरण का सहज रूप भी पाया जाता है और कलात्मक रूप भी। उनके

प्रकृति-चित्रण की एक विशेषता यह भी है कि वे रूढितः प्रकृति वर्णन नहीं करते अपितु वह प्रसङ्ग से सम्बद्ध होता है। प्रस्तुत लेख में कालिदासयुगीन पर्यावरण चेतना (मेघदूत के सन्दर्भ में) पर विचार किया गया है।

कालिदास के प्रायः सभी काव्यों में पर्यावरण का चित्रण है किन्तु मेघदूत तो पर्यावरण की दृष्टि से सर्वोपरि है वस्तुतः यहाँ कथानक गौण है और सब कुछ पर्यावरण का चित्रण ही है। महाकवि कालिदास के काव्यों में अकेला मेघदूत ही इस तथ्य का साक्षी है कि वे पर्यावरण संरक्षण के प्रति सचेत हैं। उन्होंने यहाँ प्रकृति के एक उपकरण मेघ को ही दूत बनाया है। मेघदूत खण्डकाव्य की पृष्ठभूमि उनके पर्यावरण-प्रेम की ओर सङ्केत करती है। प्रचलित कथा के अनुसार यक्ष कुबेर के पुष्पोद्यान के संरक्षक के पद पर नियुक्त था। वह उपवन की रक्षा न कर सका, फलस्वरूप उसे शापभाजन बनना पड़ा और सर्वाधिक कष्टकारी पत्नी-वियोग-दुःख भोगना पड़ा। यह कथा, कालिदास की दृष्टि में उपवन-संरक्षण कितना महत्त्वपूर्ण था, इस ओर इंगित करती है।

अन्तःसाक्ष्य भी उनके पर्यावरण-प्रेम को प्रमाणित करता है। वन-सम्पदा नष्ट न होने पाए इसके लिए कालिदास सचेत करते हैं। यक्ष मेघ से कहता है कि यदि हिमालय के वन में चीड़ के वृक्षों के तनों के संघर्ष से दावानल उत्पन्न हो जाए तो उसे असंख्य जलधाराओं से अवश्य बुझा देना। यही उत्तम जनों का कर्त्तव्य है।[4] अन्यत्र भी कवि ने मेघ से मूसलाधार वर्षा के द्वारा वनाग्नि को शान्त करने की अपेक्षा की है जिससे आम्रकूट पर्वत उपकृत रहेगा।[5]

मेघदूत में वानस्पतिक वैभव पर्याप्त रूप से दृष्टिगोचर होता है। कविकुलगुरु ने अनेकत्र वानस्पतिक सुषमा का वर्णन किया है। उनके द्वारा वर्णित वृक्ष एवं लताएँ न केवल सौन्दर्य की चरम अभिव्यक्ति हैं अपितु वे मानव के लिए लाभकारी भी हैं। कुबेर द्वारा शापित यक्ष रामगिरि के वनाश्रमों में रहता है और वन भी ऐसे हैं जो सघन छाया वाले वृक्षों से युक्त हैं।[6] यह उचित भी है क्योंकि यक्ष की शापजनित उष्णता के निवारण के लिए वृक्षों की घनी छाया अपेक्षित है। पर्यावरण-संरक्षण की दृष्टि से भी घनी छाया वाले वृक्ष अधिक उपयोगी हैं। रामगिरि से अलका नगरी तक का मार्ग वनों, नदियों एवं पर्वतों से व्याप्त है। वे ऐसे किसी भी देश की कल्पना नहीं करते जो वृक्षों से हरा-भरा न हो। माल, दशार्ण, विदिशा, अवन्ती, उज्जयिनी—सबके सब वन जगत् की सुषमा से ओतप्रोत हैं। वे अनेक देशों के उद्यान का विशेष रूप से उल्लेख करते हैं। महाकालेश्वर मन्दिर का उद्यान गन्धवती के कमल पराग से सुगन्धित पवनों से आन्दोलित है।[7] इसी प्रकार अलका नगरी के बाहर भी वैभ्राज नामक प्रसिद्ध उपवन है।[8]

महाकवि कालिदास वर्षा ऋतु में प्रचुर मात्रा में स्वतः उगने वाली कन्दलियों की चर्चा करना नहीं भूलते। ये कन्दलियाँ उग कर जमीन को और उपजाऊ बना देती हैं।[9] इसके अतिरिक्त वर्षा ऋतु में प्रथम जल पाकर भूकन्दली मुकुलित हो उठती है, जिसे सारङ्ग (मृग) बड़े चाव से खाते हैं।[10]

कालिदास ने फलदायक वृक्षों में केवल आम, उदुम्बर, कदली एवं जामुन का ही उल्लेख किया है। आम्रकूट (अमरकण्टक) पर्वत के आस-पास का भाग आम्रवृक्षों से व्याप्त है जो पके हुए पीले फलों से चमकता रहता है।[11] इसी प्रकार दशार्ण देश में जामुन के वृक्षों का वन है जो पके हुए श्यामल फलों के कारण दशार्ण देश को रमणीय बना रहा है।[12] यह ध्येय है कि जम्बूपत्र प्रियदर्शन एवं शैत्यदायक होने के साथ-साथ मनोरम सुगन्धि से युक्त होते हैं। मेघ के देवगिरि (देवगढ़) जाने के मार्ग में गूलर के वृक्षों का भी वन पड़ता है। इसके अतिरिक्त महाकवि स्वर्णिम ताड़ वृक्ष, स्थल वेतस, मन्दार, अशोक, केसर, देवदारु, कल्पवृक्ष आदि का वर्णन करते हैं।

उपर्युक्त वृक्षों के अतिरिक्त नीप, केसर, केतकी, जुही, कुवलय, कमल, कुमुद, कुन्द, कुरबक, लोध्र, शिरीष, मालती, श्यामा आदि पुष्पों एवं लताओं का वर्णन हुआ है। कहीं दशार्ण प्रदेश में उपवनों की बाड़ें केतकी से बनी हुई हैं[13] तो कहीं यक्ष के गृह के क्रीड़ा-शैल पर स्थित माधवी कुञ्ज कुरबक की बाड़ों से घिरा हुआ है।[14]

कालिदासयुगीन समाज का वनस्पतियों से घनिष्ठ सम्बन्ध था। मानव पूर्णतः वनस्पतियों पर निर्भर था। सच तो यह है कि मानव मस्तिष्क का विकास वनस्पति जगत् के मध्य ही हुआ। मनुष्य को प्रकृति की अनुपम छटा देखकर

ही सौन्दर्य-बोध हुआ। कालिदास की प्रायः सभी नायिकाएँ प्रकृति-प्राप्त अलङ्करण सामग्री से ही सौन्दर्यवर्धन करती थीं। प्रकृति से स्वाभाविक रूप से ली गयी सौन्दर्य प्रसाधन सामग्री वसारहित होती है। फलस्वरूप वह अधिक उपयोगी होती है। यही कारण है कि अलकापुरी की वधुएँ लोध्र पुष्प के पराग का चूर्ण मुखों पर धारण करती हैं।[15] स्त्रियों को मण्डन हेतु समस्त सामग्री वृक्षों से ही प्राप्त हो जाना, इस तथ्य का द्योतक है कि कालिदास-युग में वृक्ष एवं पुष्प आदि की बहुलता थी।

प्राचीनकाल में पर्यावरण को सुगन्धि से नियन्त्रित किया जाता था। सुगन्धि आन्दोलित मन को शान्ति प्रदान करती है और उसका त्वचा पर असर भी नहीं होता। इसी दृष्टि से यज्ञ में प्रयुज्यमान सुगन्धित सामग्री का विधान किया गया। महाकवि कालिदास अनेक प्रकार की सुगन्धियों का उल्लेख करते हैं। यक्ष मेघ से कहता है कि माल नामक देश पर इतना जल वर्षण करना कि वह देश सुगन्धित हो उठे।[16] इसी प्रकार हिमालय पर्वत की शिलाएँ कस्तूरी मृगों के बैठने से सदैव सुगन्धित रहती हैं।[17] मेघ के मार्ग में पड़ने वाले सभी पर्वत कुटज पुष्पों से सुरभित हैं और इस सुरभि के कारण मेघ को विलम्ब भी हो सकता है।[18] इतना ही नहीं उज्जयिनी नगरी के प्रासाद भी पुष्पों से सुगन्धित रहते हैं।[19] एक स्थल पर कवि ने पृथिवी की स्वाभाविक सुगन्धि की चर्चा की है। हाथी वनों में पृथिवी की सुगन्धित गन्ध सूँघते हैं।[20] कवि कालिदास केवल सुगन्धित भूमि का ही नहीं अपितु अवसर पाते ही सुगन्धित जल का वर्णन करते हैं। रेवा नदी का जल वन्यगजों के मदजल से सुगन्धित हुआ करता है।[21]

प्राचीनकाल में ध्वनि-प्रदूषण से बचने के लिये प्रायशः सङ्गीत का प्रयोग किया जाता था। यह उल्लेखनीय है कि सामगान अथवा अन्य मन्त्र-पाठों का यह भी एक अवान्तर प्रयोजन था। वेदगान से वायुमण्डल का नियन्त्रण हुआ करता था। कालिदास अलकापुरी के प्रासादों में नाच गाने में मृदङ्गों की मधुर ध्वनि का अनेकशः उल्लेख करते हैं। ध्वनि-प्रदूषण से बचने के लिए अन्यत्र वे मृदङ्ग वाद्य यन्त्र के धीरे-धीरे बजाए जाने का उल्लेख करते हैं।[22] इसी प्रकार वे महाकाल मन्दिर में सान्ध्यकालीन आरती के समय मेघ से नगाड़े की ध्वनि का कार्य करने का आग्रह करते हैं।[23] विरहिणी यक्षिणी भी मनोविनोद के लिए वीणा गोद में रखकर गीत गाती है।[24]

जल पर्यावरण का एक प्रमुख घटक है। जल से जीवन समृद्ध होता है और उसकी अनुपस्थिति से समस्त सृष्टि, पौधे आदि नष्ट हो जाते हैं। चूँकि जल जीवन के अतिरिक्त सभी धार्मिक अनुष्ठानों में आवश्यक था, इसलिए उसकी पवित्रता पर बल दिया गया। महाकवि कालिदास जहाँ कहीं जल का वर्णन करते हैं, उसे नीला एवं शुद्ध अवश्य कहते हैं, जो प्रदूषण-राहित्य का बोधक है। सरस्वती नदी का जल अत्यन्त शुद्ध है। इसलिए यक्ष मेघ से अवश्य पान करने का अनुरोध करता है। वह इतना सुस्वादु है कि बलराम ने अपनी अभीष्ट मदिरा को छोड़कर उसे ग्रहण किया था।[25] गङ्गा का जल भी श्वेत स्फटिक मणि के समान स्वच्छ है। इसलिए मेघ उसे भी पान करने का विचार कर सकता है।[26] मेघ के मार्ग में पड़ने वाली गम्भीरा नदी का जल भी निर्मल है।[27] अतः उसमें मेघ की छाया स्पष्ट रूप से पड़ जाएगी। यक्ष मेघ से कहता है कि तुम दशार्ण प्रदेश की राजधानी विदिशा पहुँच कर वेत्रवती नदी के स्वादयुक्त जल का पान अवश्य करना।[28] स्वादिष्ट एवं तरंगित जल प्रदूषण-राहित्य का द्योतक है। ग्रीष्म ऋतु के कारण निर्विन्ध्या नदी की जलधारा पतली पड़ गई और किनारों पर उगे हुए वृक्षों से गिरने वाले सूखे एवं पीले पत्तों से उसका रंग भी पीला पड़ गया है।[29] निस्सन्देह ऐसा जल प्रदूषणयुक्त होगा। ऐसे प्रदूषण को दूर करने के लिए यक्ष मेघ से कहता है कि वहाँ जल अवश्य बरसाना ताकि नदी की कृशता दूर हो जाय और जल बरस जाने के कारण वृक्षों से सूखे पत्ते नहीं गिरेंगे फलस्वरूप जल गँदला नहीं होगा। यक्ष के गृह में स्थित बावली का जल इतना स्वच्छ है कि उसमें निवास करने वाले हंसों को समीपस्थ मानसरोवर का स्मरण तक नहीं आता।[30]

महाकवि कालिदास ने मेघदूत में यत्र-तत्र शुद्ध वायु का भी वर्णन किया है। वे प्रकारान्तर से शिप्रा नदी के ऊपर से बहने वाली वायु की शुद्धता को रेखांकित करते हैं। शिप्रा नदी की वायु शरीर के लिए सुखकर तथा स्त्रियों

की रतिजन्य खिन्नता को दूर करने वाली है क्योंकि वह कमलों की सुगन्धि के संसर्ग से सुगन्धित रहती है।[31] वायु का अङ्गानुकूल होना तथा खिन्नताहारक होना उसकी शुद्धता, शीतलता एवं पोषकता का द्योतक है। देवगिरि की ओर जाने वाले मेघ के नीचे-नीचे भी शीतल वायु बहती है जो जल-वर्षण के कारण श्वास लेने वाली पृथिवी की गन्ध के संसर्ग से सुगन्धित है।[32] इसी प्रकार देवदारु वृक्षों के नव पल्लवों के गुच्छों को भेदकर उनके दुग्ध के प्रवाह से सुगन्धित वायु दक्षिण दिशा की ओर बहती है।[33]

अलका के बाह्य उद्यान में शङ्कर का साक्षात् निवास है। उनके सिर पर स्थित चन्द्रमा की चाँदनी से अलका नगरी के प्रासाद उज्ज्वल दिखायी पड़ते हैं।[34] यह इस तथ्य का द्योतक है कि चन्द्रमा का सम्पूर्ण प्रकाश पृथिवी पर पहुँचता है जो इस बात का प्रतीक है कि तत्कालीन वायुमण्डल सर्वथा प्रदूषणरहित था। यह ध्येय है कि आज वायुमण्डल के मध्य विद्यमान अनेक प्रदूषक तत्त्वों के कारण चन्द्रमा के सम्पूर्ण प्रकाश से पृथिवी वंचित है। एक अन्य स्थल पर भी कालिदास चन्द्रमा की स्वाभाविक शीतलता की चर्चा करते हैं।[35] इसी प्रकार महाकवि कैलास पर्वत की स्वच्छता का वर्णन करते हैं— कैलास पर्वत अपनी स्वच्छता के कारण देवाङ्गनाओं का दर्पण रूप है।[36]

महाकवि कालिदास तेज प्रकाश के भी पक्षपाती नहीं हैं। यक्ष मेघ से अपने घर के अन्दर जुगुनुओं के समान धीरे-धीरे प्रकाश डालने को कहता है।[37] तेज प्रकाश जहाँ एक ओर भयकारक हो सकता है वहीं दूसरी ओर नेत्ररोग का करण भी।

कालिदास आकाशीय सौन्दर्य का वर्णन इन्द्रधनुष के माध्यम से करते हैं। इन्द्रधनुष पर्यावरण की शुद्धता की ओर सङ्केत करता है। यक्ष मेघ को जाने के लिए प्रोत्साहित करता हुआ कहता है कि तुम आगे बढ़ोगे तो बामी के अग्रभाग से रत्नों की कान्तियों के सम्मिश्रण के समान दर्शनीय इन्द्रधनुष से तुम्हारा शरीर और अधिक शोभायमान हो उठेगा।[38]

वन्य जन्तु भी पर्यावरण से सम्बद्ध हैं। पर्यावरण-सन्तुलन में उनका महत्त्वपूर्ण योगदान है। जीव-जन्तुओं से लाभ सुविदित ही है। प्रकृति, जीव-जन्तु एवं मनुष्य का तालमेल ही पर्यावरण के संरक्षण में सहायक होता है। महाकवि कालिदास ने प्रकृति एवं मानव जाति के साथ-साथ पशु-पक्षियों को भी काव्य में समुचित स्थान दिया है। मेघदूत में प्रायः पक्षियों का ही चित्रण किया गया है और उसमें भी प्रमुख रूप से वर्षा ऋतु से सम्बद्ध पक्षियों की ही चर्चा की गयी है। पूर्वमेघ में चातक, बलाका, राजहंस, मयूर, सारस, शरभ आदि का वर्णन है।

उपर्युक्त विवरणों के आधार पर यह कहा जा सकता है कि कालिदासयुगीन पर्यावरण शुद्ध था, समाज प्रदूषण-चिन्ता से सर्वथा मुक्त था। यही कारण है कि कवि कालिदास पर्यावरण-सुषमा के वर्णन में निरत दिखायी देते हैं। मनुष्य पूरी तरह से प्रकृति पर निर्भर था।

सन्दर्भ-सङ्केत

1. यावद् भूमण्डलं धत्ते सशैलवनकाननम्।
   तावत्तिष्ठति मेदिन्यां सन्ततिः पुत्रपौत्रिकी।।

2. ओ३म् आत्मा वा इदमेक एवाग्र आसीत्। नान्यत् किंचन मिषत्। स ईक्षत लोकान्नु सृजा इति। स इमाँल्लोकनसृजत। अम्भो मरीचीर्मरमापोऽदोम्भः परेण दिवं द्यौः प्रतिष्ठान्तरिक्षं मरीचयः पृथिवी मरो या अधस्तात्ता आपः। स ईक्षते मे नु लोका लोकपालान्नु सृजा इति सोऽद्भ्य एव पुरुषं समुद्धृत्यामूर्छयत्। ऐतरेयोपनिषद् - 1.1. 3

3. भूमिरापोऽनलो वायुः खं मनो बुद्धिरेव च।
   अहङ्कार इतीयं मे भिन्ना प्रकृतिरष्टधा।। श्रीमद्भगवद्गीता-7. 4

4. तं चेद् वायौ सरति सरलस्कन्धसंघट्टजन्मा
   बाधेतोल्काक्षपितचमरीबालभारो दवाग्निः।
   अर्हस्येनं शमयितुमलं वारिधारासहस्रै-
   रापन्नार्तिप्रशमनफलाः सम्पदो ह्युत्तमानाम्।। मेघदूत - 1. 56
5. त्वामासारप्रशमितवनोपप्लवं। मेघदूत - 1.17
6. स्निग्धच्छाया तरुषु वसतिं रामगिर्याश्रमेषु। मेघदूत - 1. 1
7. भर्तुः कण्ठच्छविरिति गणैः सादरं वीक्ष्यमाणः
   पुण्यं यायास्त्रिभुवनगुरोर्धाम चण्डीश्वरस्य।
   धूतोद्यानं कुवलयरजोगन्धिहभर्गन्धवत्या-
   स्तोयक्रीडानिरतयुवतिस्नानतिक्तैर्मरुद्भिः ।। मेघदूत - 1. 36
8. वैभ्राजाख्यं विबुधवनितावारमुख्या सहाया
   बद्धालापा बहिरुपवनं कामिनो निर्विशन्ति। मेघदूत - 2. 10
9. कर्तुं यच्च प्रभवति महीमुच्छिलीन्ध्रामवन्ध्यां। मेघदूत - 1. 11
10. आविर्भूतप्रथममुकुलाः कन्दलीश्चानुकच्छम् । मेघदूत - 1. 21
11. छन्नोपान्तः परिणतफलद्योतिभिः काननाम्रैः । मेघदूत - 1. 18
12. त्वय्यासन्ने परिणतफलश्यामजम्बूवनान्ताः। मेघदूत - 1. 24
13. पाण्डुच्छायोपवनवृत्तयः केतकैः सूचिभिन्नैः। मेघदूत - 1. 24
14. रक्ताशोकश्चलकिसलयः केसरश्चात्र कान्तः
    प्रत्यासन्नौ कुरबकवृतेः माधवीमण्डपस्य। मेघदूत - 2. 18
15. नीता लोध्रप्रसवरजसा पाण्डुतामानने श्रीः। मेघदूत - 2. 2
16. सद्यः सीरोत्कषणसुरभि क्षेत्रमारुह्य मालं। मेघदूत - 1. 16
17. आसीनानां सुरभितशिलं नाभिगन्धैर्मृगाणां। मेघदूत - 1. 55
18. उत्पश्यामि द्रुतमपि सखे मत्प्रियार्थं यियासोः
    कालक्षेपं ककुभसुरभौ पर्वते पर्वते ते। मेघदूत - 1. 23
19. हर्म्येष्वस्याः कुसुमसुरभिष्वध्वखेदं नयेथाः। मेघदूत - 1. 35
20. जग्ध्वारण्येष्वधिकसुरभिं गन्धमाघ्राय चोर्व्याः। मेघदूत - 1. 21
21. तस्यास्तिक्तैर्वनगजमदैर्वासितं वान्तवृष्टि-
    र्जम्बूकुञ्जप्रतिहतरयं तोयमादाय गच्छेः। मेघदूत - 1. 20
22. सङ्गीताय प्रहतमुरजाः स्निग्धगम्भीरघोषम्
    त्वद्गम्भीरध्वनिषु शनकैः पुष्करेष्वाहतेषु। मेघदूत - 2. 1,5
23. कुर्वन् सन्ध्यावलिपटहतां शूलिनः श्लाघनीयाम्। मेघदूत - 1. 37
24. मद्गोत्राङ्कं विरचितपदं गेयमुद्गातुकामा। मेघदूत - 2. 26
25. कृत्वा तासामधिगममपां सौम्य सारस्वतीना-
    मन्तःशुद्धस्त्वमपि भविता वर्णमात्रेण कृष्णः। मेघदूत - 1. 52
26. तस्याः पातुं सुरगज इव व्योम्नि पश्चार्धलम्बी
    त्वञ्चेदच्छस्फटिकविशदं तर्कयेस्तिर्यगम्भः। मेघदूत - 1. 54
27. गम्भीरायाः पयसि सरितश्चेतसीव प्रसन्ने। मेघदूत - 1. 43
28. तीरोपान्तस्तनितसुभगं पास्यसि स्वादु यस्मात्
    सभ्रूभङ्गं मुखमिव पयो वेत्रवत्याश्चलोर्मि। मेघदूत - 1. 25

29. वेणीभूतप्रतनुसलिलाऽसावतीतस्य सिन्धुः
पाण्डुच्छाया तटरुहतरुभ्रंशिभिर्जीर्णपर्णैः।
सौभाग्यं ते सुभग विरहावस्थया व्यञ्जयन्ती
कार्श्यं येन त्यजति विधिना स त्वयैवोपपाद्यः।। मेघदूत - 1.30

30. स्यास्तोये कृतवसतयो मानसं सन्निकृष्टं
नाध्यास्यन्ति व्यपगवशुचस्त्वामपि प्रेक्ष्य हंसाः। मेघदूत - 2.16

31. यत्र स्त्रीणां हरति सुरतग्लानिमङ्गानुकूलः
शिप्रावातः प्रियतम इव प्रार्थनाचाटुकारः। मेघदूत - 1.32

32. नीचैर्वास्यत्युपजिगमिषोर्देवपूर्वं गिरिं ते
शीतो वायुः परिणमयिता काननोदुम्बराणाम्। मेघदूत - 1.45

33. भित्त्वा सद्यः किसलयपुटान् देवदारुद्रुमाणां।
ये तत्क्षीरस्रुतिसुरभयो दक्षिणेन प्रवृत्ताः। मेघदूत - 2.47

34. गन्तव्या ते वसतिरलका नाम यक्षेश्वराणां
बाह्योद्यानस्थितहरशिरश्चन्द्रिकाधौतहर्म्या। मेघदूत - 1.7

35. पादानिन्दोरमृतशिशिराञ्जालमार्गप्रविष्टान्। मेघदूत - 2.30

36. गत्वा चोर्ध्वं दशमुखभुजोच्छ्वासितप्रस्थसन्धेः
कैलासस्य त्रिदशवनितादर्पणस्यातिथिः स्याः। मेघदूत - 1.61

37. अर्हस्यन्तर्भवनपतितां कर्तुमल्पाल्पभासं
खद्योतालीविलसितनिभां विद्युदुन्मेषदृष्टिम्। मेघदूत - 2.21

38. रत्नच्छायाव्यतिकर इव प्रेक्ष्यमेतत् पुरस्तात्
वल्मीकाग्रात् प्रभवति धनुःखण्डमाखण्डलस्य। मेघदूत - 1.15

卐 卐 卐

ऋतुसंहारेऽभिराजिता सुमनोमाला

(कदम्बकेसरकेतकीककुभकल्हारकुमुदकमलकाशकन्दलीकर्णिकार- किंशुककोविदारकुन्दकुरबककुसुम्भकुङ्कुमकुटजकुवलयकलिता)

सच्चिदानन्द पाठकः

1. कदम्बः 2. केसरः 3. केतकी 4. ककुभः

(1) मालाः कदम्बनवकेसरकेतकीभि-
रायोजिताः शिरसि बिभ्रति योषितोऽद्य।
कर्णान्तरेषु ककुभद्रुममञ्जरीभिः
श्रोत्रानुकूलरचितानवतंसकांश्च ।।[1]

(2) कदम्बसर्जार्जुननीपकेतकी-
र्विकम्पयंस्तत्कुसुमाधिवासितः ।
ससीकराम्भोधरसङ्गशीतलः
समीरणः कं न करोति सोत्सुकम्।।[2]

(3) मुदित इव कदम्बैर्जातपुष्पैः समन्तात्
पवनचलितशाखैः शाखिभिर्नृत्यतीव।
हसितमिव विधत्ते सूचिभिः केतकीनां
नवसलिलनिषेकोत्खाततापो वनान्तः।।[3]

(4) शिरसि बकुलमालां मालतीभिः समेतां
विकसितनवपुष्पैर्यूथिकाकुड्मलैश्च।
विकचनवकदम्बैः कर्णपूरं वधूनां
रचयति जलदौघः कान्तवत् काल एषः।।[4]

(5) नवजलकणसङ्गाच्छीततामादधानः
कुसुमभरनतानां लासकः पादपानाम्।
जनितरुचिरगन्धः केतकीनां रजोभि-
रपहरति नभस्वान् प्रोषितानां मनांसि।।[5]

5. कल्हारम् 6. कुमुदम् 7. कमलम् 8. काशम्

(6) कल्हारपद्मकुमुदानि मुहुर्विधुन्वं-
स्तत्सङ्गमादधिकशीतलतामुपेतः ।
पत्रानुलग्नतुहिनाम्बु हरंस्तरूणां
सोत्काः करोति वनिताः पवनः प्रभाते।।[6]

(7) विकचकमलवक्त्रा फुल्लनीलोत्पलाक्षी
विकसितनवकाशं श्वेतवासो वसाना।
कुमुदरुचिरहासा कामिनीवोन्मदेय-
मुपदिशतु शरद्वश्चेतसः प्रीतिमग्र्याम्।।[7]

(8) काशैर्मही शिशिरदीधितिना रजन्यो
हंसैर्जलानि सरितां कुमुदैः सरांसि।
सप्तच्छदैः कुसुमभारनतैर्वनान्ताः
शुक्लीकृतान्युपवनानि च मालतीभिः।।[8]

(9) सोन्मादहंसमिथुनैरुपशोभितानि
स्वच्छानि फुल्लकमलोत्पलभूषितानि।
मन्दप्रचारपवनोद्गतवीचिमाला-
न्युत्कम्पयन्ति सहसा हृदयं सरांसि।।[9]

9. कन्दली

(10) प्रभिन्नवैदूर्यनिभैस्तृणाङ्कुरैः
समाचिता प्रोत्थितकन्दलीदलैः।
विभाति शुक्लेतररत्नभूषिता
वराङ्गनेव क्षितिरिन्द्रगोपकैः ।।[10]

10. कर्णिकारम् 11. किंशुकम्

(11) कर्णेषु योग्यं नवकर्णिकारं
स्तनेषु हारा अलकेष्वशोकम्।
शिखासु फुल्ला नवमालिकाश्च
प्रयान्ति कान्तिं प्रमदाजनस्य।। [11]

(12) आदीप्तवह्निसदृशैरपयातपत्रैः
सर्वत्र किंशुकवनैः कुसुमावकीर्णैः।
सद्यो वसन्तसमयेन समागतेयं
रक्तांशुका नववधूरिव भाति भूमिः।।[12]

(13) किं किंशुकैः शुकमुखच्छविभिर्न भिन्नं
किं कर्णिकारकुसुमैर्न कृतं न दग्धम्।
यत्कोकिलः पुनरयं मधुरैर्वचोभि-
र्यूनां मनः सुवदनानिहितं निहन्ति।।[13]

12. कोविदारः

(14) मन्दानिलाकुलितचारुतराग्रशाखः
पुष्पोद्गमप्रचयकोमलपल्लवाग्रः।
मत्तद्विरेफपरिपीतमधुप्रसेक-
श्चित्तं विदारयति कस्य न कोविदारः।।[14]

13. कुन्दम्

(15) कुन्दैः सविभ्रमवधूहसितावदातै-
रुद्योतितान्युपवनानि मनोहराणि।
चित्तं मुनेरपि हरन्ति निवृत्तरागं
प्रागेव रागमलिनानि मनांसि पुंसाम्।।[15]

14. कुरबकम्

(16) कान्तामुखद्युतिजुषामचिरोद्गतानां
शोभां परां कुरबकद्रुममञ्जरीणाम्।
दृष्ट्वा प्रिये सहृदयस्य भवेन्न कस्य
कन्दर्पबाणपतनव्यथितं हि चेतः।।[16]

15. कुसुम्भम् 16. कुङ्कुमम्

(17) विकचनवकुसुम्भस्वच्छसिन्दूरभासा
प्रबलपवनवेगोद्भूतवेगेन तूर्णम्।
तरुविटपलताग्रालिङ्गनव्याकुलेन
दिशि दिशि परिदग्धा भूमयः पावकेन।।[17]

(18) कुसुम्भरागारुणितैर्दुकूलै-
नितम्बबिम्बानि विलासिनीनाम्।
तन्वंशुकैः कुङ्कुमरागगौरै-
रलङ्क्रियन्ते स्तनमण्डलानि।।[18]

17. कुटजः

(19) नृत्तप्रयोगरहिताञ्छिखिनो विहाय
हंसानुपैति मदनो मधुरप्रगीतान्।
मुक्त्वा कदम्बकुटजार्जुनसर्जनीपान्
सप्तच्छदानुपगता कुसुमोद्गमश्रीः।।[19]

17. कुवलयम्

(20) कुवलयदलनीलैरुन्नतैस्तोयनम्रै-
मृदुपवनविशेषान्मन्दमन्दं चलद्भिः।
अपहृतमिव चेतस्तोयदैः सेन्द्रचापैः
पथिकजनवधूनां तद्वियोगक्षतानाम्।।[20]

सन्दर्भ-सङ्केताः

1. ऋतुसंहारम् (प्रो० रेवाप्रसादद्विवेदिसम्पादितम्, साहित्य अकादमी, 1990)-2. 20
2. ऋतुसंहारम्-2. 17
3. ऋतुसंहारम्-2. 23
4. ऋतुसंहारम्-2. 24
5. ऋतुसंहारम्-2. 26
6. ऋतुसंहारग्-3. 15
7. ऋतुसंहारम्-3. 26
8. ऋतुसंहारम्-3. 2
9. ऋतुसंहारम्-3. 11
10. ऋतुसंहारम्-2. 5
11. ऋतुसंहारम्-6. 5
12. ऋतुसंहारम्-6. 19
13. ऋतुसंहारम्-6. 20
14. ऋतुसंहारम्-3. 6
15. ऋतुसंहारम्-6. 23
16. ऋतुसंहारम्-6. 18
17. ऋतुसंहारम्-1. 24
18. ऋतुसंहारम्-6. 4
19. ऋतुसंहारम्-3. 13
20. ऋतुसंहारम्-2.22

卐 卐 卐

कालिदास का कर्णिकार

कौशल गुप्ता

वाल्मीकि[1] की सीता का प्रिय कर्णिकार कालिदास[2] को रुचा, अश्वघोष[3] के गौतम के अन्तःपुर में भी प्रवेश पा गया। किन्तु लगता है, बाद के कवि ही नहीं, सभी वन-विद् भी भूल गए। निर्लेप भाव से बे-मेल का योग[4] कर बनाए पाणिनि के गण-पाठ[5] में संस्कृत-कवियों के अशोक, कदम्ब, ताल, तमाल सब ही स्थान पा गए— तो शायद स्वीकृति के लिए आतुर अन्य अल्प-परिचितों ने कर्णिकार को पीछे कर दिया होगा। केवल इसी के लिए नए सूत्र की रचना कर वे पुत्रोत्सव-सुख[6] से क्यों वञ्चित रहते? कात्यायन[7] के वार्तिक-रचना काल तक, कवि-हृदय से तो अपदस्थ नहीं हुआ था, पर कर्णिकार के लिए उन्हें वार्तिक की आवश्यकता नहीं हुई। पतञ्जलि[8] ने तो पाणिनि की सञ्चित-सामग्री की ही हाट सजायी थी, अतिरिक्त के लिए गुंजाइश ही नहीं थी।

शब्द-कोषकार भी भ्रान्ति में पड़ गए। कर्णिकार के पर्याय मिले ''द्रुमोत्पल'', परिव्याध (अमरकोष)[9]। वनस्पति-शास्त्रियों का[10] (Pterospermum Acerifolium) बड़े-बड़े पत्रों वाला, गन्ध भरे फूलों वाला 'कनकचम्पा' और 'मुचकुन्द' नाम से अभिज्ञात कर्णिकार ही रहा होगा, पर 'कर्णेषु योग्यं नवकर्णिकारम्'[11] वाली कालिदास की मान्यता कैसे पूरी हो? सद्यः-पुष्पित, सौरभ-वितरण में निरालसी और उदार-मना द्रुमोत्पल के 'उत्पल' सुमन-सुकुमार सुखद-स्पर्श की अनुभूति नहीं देते। फिर उनका आकार? कर्णयोग्य तो कदापि नहीं— कालिदास के काव्य-जगत् की भ्रमर-भार से नत-शिरीषसी पुष्प को धारण करने वाली रमणियों के कर्णयोग्य तो निश्चय ही नहीं।[12]

सच तो यह है, कि प्रकृति-कवि कालिदास ने 'द्रुमोत्पल' या 'परिव्याध' नाम के किसी भी वृक्ष से अपने परिचय का आभास नहीं दिया— नाम-मात्र से इंगित भी नहीं किया। वाल्मीकि सम्भवतः अपने परिचित वृक्षों की पंक्ति में उसे बिठा भी सकते थे, बिना उसका रूप-परिचय दिए, पर वह भी उन्होंने नहीं किया।

मन्त्र-रचयिता उन्मुख-नयन ऋषियों के दृष्टि-पथ का अतिथि नहीं बना धरा को सजाने वाला कर्णिकार।[13] धरा के रूप-वैभव के चितेरे वाल्मीकि द्वारा ही इसे काव्य जगत् में प्रवेश की अनुमति मिली।

चैत्रानिल बड़ा दुःख दे रहा था सीता के विरह में, पर कर्णिकार के रमणीय-रूप के प्रति निरासक्त न रह सका राम का मन—[14-15]

पुष्पितांस्तु पश्य कर्णिकारान् समन्ततः।
हाटकप्रतिच्छन्नान् नरान् पीताम्बरानिव।। (रामायण-किष्किन्धाकाण्ड - 1. 21)

(सोने के (आभूषण) और पीले कपड़े पहने मनुष्यों के समान लगने वाले देखो ये फूले कर्णिकार।)

सोने के रंग वाले जैसे धूप सुनहली। पीतकौशेयवासिनी बनी उस दिन सीता कर्णिकार के फूल चुन रही थीं, उसके पीले फूलों से वनोचित शृङ्गार-सज्जा भी कर ली थी। रावण ने देख लिया, ले चला असहाय को। रावण के पाश से मुक्त होने का प्रयत्न करती सीता फूले कर्णिकार से अपना रूप-साम्य देखकर उसी को अपना सन्देश दे गई थीं, ''जन-स्थान के पुष्पित कर्णिकार से विनती करती हूँ, जल्दी ही राम से कह देना कि सीता को रावण ले जा रहा है।''[16]

आमन्त्रये जनस्थाने कर्णिकारान् सुपुष्पितान्।
क्षिप्रं रामाय शंसध्वं सीतां हरति रावणः।। (रामायण-अरण्यकाण्ड - 49.30)

केश-पाश और कानों में पहने कर्णिकार के फूल राह में फेंकतीं चली थीं। पर कर्णिकार ने सीता के विश्वास की रक्षा न की। राम के सबसे अन्त में किए प्रश्न का कुछ भी उत्तर न देकर यह मौन ही बना रहा। तभी तो राम अन्य वृक्ष-लता, पशु-पक्षियों से सीता का पता पूछते वन-वन भटके थे।

तो कर्णिकार के फूल हुए पीले। कनेर पीला है। 'कनेर' बोलने में ध्वनि भी कर्णिकार की सी देता है।[17] किन्तु फूल-भार लिए भी यह बोना पेड़ ''हाटक-प्रतिच्छन्न'' प्रतीत नहीं होता। फिर यह है भारत की धरा पर बसा विदेशी। वाल्मीकि के साथ दण्डकारण्य में नहीं विचरा था, कालिदास के हाथों अलकशोभि हो शिरोवाह्य नहीं हुआ था[18] और कनेर फूलता है लगभग सारा साल, कर्णिकार तो है वसन्त के उत्तरार्द्ध में खिलने वाला।[19] सो साम्य केवल वर्ण का है। वर्ण-साम्य से नाम 'कर्णिकार' मिल भी जाए, किन्तु नाम के साथ लगे अन्य विशेषणों की सार्थकता कैसे सिद्ध हो?

रम्य-तरु कर्णिकार बाण का केवल उच्छिष्ट ही बना, रुचि से ग्राह्य नहीं। इसे उसका दुर्भाग्य कहें या सौभाग्य?[20-21] अङ्ग-राग के भार से क्लान्त हो जाने वाली बाण के गन्धर्व-राज के अन्तःपुर की निवासिनियों को कर्णिकार का भार क्या सह्य होता?[22] कालिदास की मधुमास छवि तो कर्णिकार के बिना सुचारु नहीं बनती।[23] पर वसन्त-श्री का वर्णन करके भी जयदेव ने कर्णिकार की अवहेलना की। राधा ने कृष्ण से रुचिर-चिकुर पर फूल धरने के लिए कहा था?[24] तो पुष्प-विन्यास करते समय पीताम्बर पीत-कुसुम पहनाते। कर्णिकार से ही केश-सज्जा क्यों न करवा दी? प्रश्न मन को चैन नहीं लेने देता।

उत्तम गन्ध की महक पाकर लोग पता लगा लेते हैं कि जैसी गन्ध वह रही है, उससे मालूम होता है कि कहीं वृक्ष पुष्पित अवश्य हुए होंगे। कर्णिकार की गन्ध का परिचय आदि कवि को मिला नहीं, अवगुण बताना उन्हें रुचा नहीं, सो मौन रहे। कालिदास मुखर हो गए—

वर्णप्रकर्षे सति कर्णिकारं दुनोति निर्गन्धतया स्म चेतः।
प्रायेण सामग्र्यविधौ गुणानां पराङ्मुखी विश्वसृजः प्रवृत्तिः।।[25]

(कुमारसम्भव - 3. 28)

रूप से आकृष्ट जन को गुण की भी अपेक्षा होती है। चारु-रूप तरु निर्गन्ध होकर मन को बड़ी पीड़ा पहुँचाता है। गन्ध न देकर इतनी रूप राशि दे टाली विधाता ने कर्णिकार को, तो गुण-साकल्य-दान में अपनी अनुदार प्रकृति के कारण, या अवगुण न हों तो गुण ग्राही कौन होगा, इस कारण?

अवशेष में कर्णिकार का रंग ही प्रधान हो उठा, पीत-वर्ण ही नयनों में समा गया। पीतमाल्याम्बर धरे सिंहस्थ बुध-ग्रह को कर्णिकार-समद्युति बताते हैं। याज्ञवल्क्य के टीकाकार[26] मत्स्य-पुराण का हवाला देकर। भागवत-पुराण में मिलता है कर्णिकार ''हिरण्मयभुजैरिव''।

काव्य-जगत् में अपदस्थ हुए, सुश्रुत[27] की वृक्ष-सूची से बहिष्कृत कर्णिकार को चरक[28] ने बड़ी दया करके जो आरग्वध के पर्यायों में बिठा दिया, तो उसे विस्मृति-विलय से त्राण चाहे नहीं मिला, किन्तु नाम-कल्प के साथ-साथ रूप-कल्प की व्यर्था से तो रक्षित हुआ।

आरग्वधो राजवृक्षः शम्पाकश्चतुरङ्गुलः।
प्रग्रहकृतमालश्च कर्णिकारोऽवघातकः।।

और ये सब नाम तो सब ही कोणों के अनुसार अमलतास के संस्कृत नाम है। एकदम अन्धकार में आलोक-रेखा दिख गई। संशय मिट गए कर्णिकार के व्यक्तित्व के विषय में। वाल्मीकि और कालिदास के दिए सब विशेषण इसमें साध्य हैं। तो हे कर्णिकार, तुम अमलतास हो, तुम 'हेमद्युति' भी हो, 'हाटक-प्रतिछन्न' भी लगते हो, वसन्त-पुष्पी भी हो। हवा में सौरभ न भर पाने के कारण लगभग निर्गन्ध भी हो ।

शीत की बिदा-बेला में सूखी ठंडी बयार जब सहसा ''हा हतास्मि'' कहकर पछाड़ खाकर वृक्षों के पत्र-वैभव पर गिरकर झकझोरने लगी, तो लोभी पतझड़ ने तुरन्त सब पत्ते बटोर लिए। देखते-देखते फिर चलदल[29] अपना नाम सार्थक करने लगा। वर्षा का उल्लास और बूँदों का सङ्गीत अपने स्वर में भरता चुप बैठा पिक, सहकार-मंजरी की गन्ध के साथ अपनी कूक चतुर्दिक में बिखराने लगा। पलाश[30] ने वनों में फाग खेला। मन्दार[31] अङ्गार से फूलों से दहक उठा, नीम[32] पर कोंपल आई और बौर हवा में गन्ध लुटाने लगे साँझ की छाया में, पुराने का मोह छोड़ नए का आमन्त्रण स्वीकार कर पीले फूलों से भर गए— अमलतास। अपात हुए ने फूली सरसों[33] के रंग को चुपचाप पिया था वही फूट पड़ा अङ्ग-अङ्ग से। हर डाल से लटकते अधखिले फूलों के गुच्छों को देखकर, बस यही लगता है कि पीत-रूप की बरखा होते-होते जादू की छड़ी की हल्की छुअन से अचानक अधर में रुक गई हो— जादू टूटे तो फिर झरे सोने की झड़ी— तब ही तो नाम मिले ''स्वर्णभूषण'' स्वर्णाङ्ग, सोन्दाल, सोनाल। स्वर्णवर्षा ''Golden shower'' (नाम है यह Bignonia Venusta का) अधिक सार्थक होता है। सुनहले फूलों से स्कन्ध से शिखा तक सज्जा किए तुम्हारे रूप को एक बार देखकर भी भूल जाने वाले अचिर-स्मृति जन और किस छवि को संजोकर रख सकते हैं? ऐसों का शायद जीवन के विरस-पक्ष के प्रति ही उत्कट आग्रह रहता है, वही उनके निकट अधिक स्थायी और सत्य है।

निर्गन्ध कहकर अवसाद करके भी कालिदास को ज़रा भी अवकाश मिले कि झट से कर्णिकार को पकड़ लेते हैं। पुष्प-वीथियों में घूमने से क्लान्त षट्पद को वसन्त के आतप से निरापद स्थान मिला कर्णिकार-मुकुल में।[34] उमा का रूप परिष्कार कर नील-अलक के बीच में शोभित कर्णिकार को वृषभध्वज के चरणों में नत कर दिया था।[35] किन्तु कालिदास के बाद तो केवल कवि-वर्णना में कहीं-कहीं छूटे रह गए सूने अन्तरालों को भरने के लिए अवांछित कर्णिकार सहमा सा दुबका बैठा लगता है।[36]

फूल भरे गुच्छों के मंजुल भार को लिए कर्णिकार, यूँ ही विशीर्ण-पुष्प होते रहे। गिरी-अनुतटी को फिर किसी ने दीपों से सजा नहीं कहा।[37] कर्णिकार, तुम्हारा कोमल आकार कारुगण तराशने पर भी पर्वत-शिलाओं में नहीं खोज पाए तो क्या वे क्षम्य हैं और रूप-दक्ष की तूलिका से भी क्या तुम्हारा छवि छंकन न किया जा सका?

क्यों विस्मृति में विलीन हुए तुम, कर्णिकार? ताप का सन्देश लेकर जो आते हो क्या इसीलिए? सर्जन-कर्ता ने जो (यथातथ्यतः व्यदधात् शाश्वतीभ्यः समाभ्यः)[38] शाश्वत काल के लिए सबके लिए यथातथ्य कर्म-विधान कर दिया है? फिर आदेश की अवहेलना करने के अपराध को क्षमाकर देने का सामर्थ्य भी क्या है मानव-जगत् में?[39]

रूपसी के कानों में और सँवरी अलकों में झूलने योग्य[40] विकास-घड़ी का तुम्हारा रूप विगत पुष्प-काल के कुछ अपरूप हो जाता है, क्या केवल इसी कारण 'कर्णिकार' की चारु संज्ञा छिटककर दूर हो गई? फूलमाला पहने 'कृतमाल' नाम भी कम अनुरूप नहीं। अङ्ग-अङ्ग बिखेर कर अङ्ग-व्याधि दूर करके 'व्याधिघात' कहलाए। रूप-ऐश्वर्य के कारण 'राजवृक्ष' बने। फलों के दीर्घ-आकार से 'दीर्घफल' कहलाए।

याद आया फलों की बात से। फल को ही प्रमुख मान, रस और ध्वनि का लेखा-जोखा न रखने वाले अरसिकों ने 'बन्दर-लाठी' और pudding pipe नाम भी तो दे डाला। अपने साथ-साथ तुम्हारा नाता भी 'कपि' के साथ जोड़ दिया अकरुण समाज ने, तो इसमें क्या आपत्ति? पर उनका उपद्रव सहने का सामर्थ्य भी खूब है तुममें। 'कपि-प्रिय' कह देते तो भाषा-विज्ञ अवश्य ही साधन जुटा कर 'कपि-प्रिय' कहकर तुम्हें विशेष से निर्विशेष कर देते।[41] किन्तु 'अमलतास' का ताल-मेल तो न रूप से है, न फूल से और न ही फल से। व्याकरण के नाते व्युत्पत्ति की मीमांसा न भी हो तो क्या है?

नाम समीक्षा से होता भी क्या है? कर्णिकार और अमलतास की दूरी तो उसके बिना भी पट जाएगी। पर कल-कारखाने, मेहनत-मजदूरी, कविता-अकविता, नगर-नागर की भीड़-भाड़ से घिरे काव्य-परिवेश में कर्णिकार, तुम्हें तो क्या; अन्य लोकप्रिय फूलों को भी भूले-भटके ही स्थान मिलता है। अतिवैज्ञानिकता और अति-आधुनिकता का दावा करने वाले, गुलाब के फूल[42] को पेड़ पर टाँगने वाले कवियों के हाथ किसी लता पर लटका कर जग में स्वीकृति पाने के आग्रह के कारण पौरुष की मान-हानि होने से तो अच्छा है तुम वर्ण-प्रकर्ष लिए-लिए अस्वीकृत ही झर जाओ। काव्य में नहीं, अन्य स्थानों में तो, कर्णिकार, अमलतास नाम से तुम्हें फिर पदारूढ़ करने का प्रयत्न है। भारत के नगरों में, राजधानी के मार्गों पर और विदेश के अनुकरण से रचे उद्यानों में जन-दृष्टि के सन्मुख फूलने के लिए कोना तो मिला।

सन्दर्भ-सङ्केत

1. रामायण-3.60.20
2. ऋतुसंहार-6.22, 29; विक्रमोर्वशीय-3.3; कुमारसम्भव-3.28
3. बुद्धचरित-5.51
4. कारकसूत्र-4.6.133
5. अष्टाध्यायी-गणपाठ
6. अर्द्धमात्रालाघवे पुत्रोत्सवं मन्यन्ते वैयाकरणाः।
7. पाणिनिव्याकरण के वार्तिककार का सम्भावित काल प्रथम शताब्दी ई. पू. माना जाता है।
8. अष्टाध्यायी के व्याख्याकार का समय प्रथम शताब्दी ई. माना जाता है।
9. अमरकोष-2.4.60
10. (a) M.Monier Williams, *Sanskrit-English,* Delhi, 1963, p. 257
    (b) MacMillan, *Tropical Planting and Gardening*, London, 1962, p. 99
    (c) Randhawa, M.S., *Beautiful Trees and Gardens,* New Delhi, 1961
    (d) Charles McCann, 100 *Beautiful Trees of India*, Bombay, 1959, p. 1
11. ऋतुसंहार-कर्णेषु योग्यं नवकर्णिकारम्। 6.6
12. कुमारसम्भवम्-5.4
13. प्राचीन वैदिक वाङ्मय में पुष्पों अथवा पुष्प-सम्पत्ति युक्त वृक्षों के वर्णन प्रायः दुर्लभ हैं।
14. रामायण-4.1.20-21; 4.1.32 तथा 41
15. रामायण-4.1.10
16. रामायण-3.46.12; 3.52.16, 19; 3.42.31
17. Cowen, D.V., *Flowering Trees and Shrubs in India,* Bombay, 1957, p. 114
18. कुमारसम्भव-3.62
19. ऋतुसंहार-6.22
20. बाणभट्ट ने कादम्बरी एवं हर्षचरित में अशोक, सहकार, बकुल तथा अन्य पुष्पों की भाँति कर्णिकार की प्रशस्ति नहीं की है।
21. हर्षचरित-(कलकत्ता, 1939) II. पृ. 164
22. कादम्बरी (निर्णय सागर प्रेस, बम्बई, 1940), पृ. 380

23. कुमारसम्भव-3.52; ऋतुसंहार-6.22.29; विक्रमोर्वशीय-2.22
24. गीतगोविन्द-12.24.6
25. कुमारसम्भव-3.28
26. याज्ञवल्क्यस्मृति-I.297 पर मिताक्षरा
27. सुश्रुतसंहिता में कर्णिकार को किसी अन्य वृक्ष के नाम अथवा पर्याय के रूप में नहीं दिया गया है।
28. चरकसंहिता - VIII, 2.3.
29. Ficus Religiosa-संस्कृत में इसका एक पर्याय 'चलदल' है। संस्कृतकविसमयानुसार कोकिल वसन्त ऋतु में गाता है तथा अन्य ऋतुओं में मौन रहता है विशेषत: वर्षा ऋतु में।
30. Butea Monosperma
31. Erythrina Indica
32. Azadirachta Indica
33. Mustard Flower, Brassicajuncea
34. विक्रमोर्वशीय - 2. 22
35. कुमारसम्भव - 3. 62
36. काव्यमीमांसा (चौखम्बा विद्याभवन, वाराणसी, 1964)-XVIII, पृ. 262; बृहत्संहिता (बम्बई, 1952)-80.9
37. ईशोपनिषद्-पद्य 8
38. कठोपनिषद्-2.3.2-3
39. Cowen, D.V., *Flowering Trees and Shrubs in India,* p. 52
40. Favourite of Poets' संस्कृत भाषा में 'प' एवं 'ब' ध्वनियाँ कहीं-कहीं परस्पर परिवर्तनीय हैं। कुछ आधुनिक भारतीय भाषाओं के वक्ता 'ब' तथा 'व' वर्णों के उच्चारण में भेद नहीं करते।
41. संस्कृत काव्य साहित्य में वृक्ष एवं लता को क्रमश: पुरुष एवं नारी के प्रतिनिधिरूप में आलङ्कारिक शैली में वर्णित किया जाता है। वृक्षवाचक शब्द प्राय: पुल्लिङ्ग में तथा लतावाचक शब्द प्राय: स्त्रीलिङ्ग में हैं।
42. एक बार मैंने हिन्दी में निबद्ध एक कविता पढ़ी जिसमें गुलाब को एक वृक्ष पर खिलते हुए वर्णित किया गया। प्राय: गुलाब के पौधों एवं बेलों का वर्णन किया जाता है।

Section VIII

FLORA IN DRAMATIC WORKS OF KĀLIDĀSA

कालिदासनाट्यामृतनिर्झरी

मालविकाग्निमित्र में वृक्षपुष्पसौन्दर्य

उर्मि भूषण गुप्ता

संस्कृत साहित्य में प्राकृतिक सौन्दर्य का वर्णन, प्रकृति के विभिन्न रूपों की कल्पना अपने आप में अद्भुत है। यहाँ पेड़, पौधे, पुष्पों के रूप रंग, उनके सौन्दर्य में मानवीय भावों, कार्य-कलापों की जो एकरूपता दिखाई देती है वह संस्कृत कवियों की अनोखी सूझ और उनके संवेदनगुण की परिचायक है। प्रकृति के विभिन्न व्यापार सहज रूप से चलते हैं, ऋतुएं अलग-अलग प्रभाव उत्पन्न करती हैं। पुष्प विकसित होते हैं, मुरझा जाते हैं, पेड़, पौधे वातावरण को मादक या उदास बना देते हैं। पर संस्कृत कवियों को यह सब सीधे कहना रुचिकर नहीं है। वे सभी प्राकृतिक व्यापारों में कुछ विशिष्टता, कुछ आश्चर्यजनक तत्त्व देखते हैं। प्रकृति के सुख-दुःख को वे मानव के साथ जोड़ते हैं। इसमें ही उन्हें आनन्द मिलता है।

इस सन्दर्भ में कवि प्रसिद्धियों का उदाहरण दिया जा सकता है जिनके अनुसार सुन्दरियों के पाद प्रहार, उनके वीक्षण, आलिङ्गन, मदिरा के गण्डूष, नर्मवाक्य, पटुमृदुहास, वक्त्रवात, गीत, नर्तन आदि से (क्रमशः) अशोक, तिलक, कुरबक, प्रियगु, बकुल, मन्दार, चम्पक, आम्र, कर्णिकार आदि पुष्प खिल उठते हैं।[1] उनकी दोहदेच्छा पूरी हो जाती है, और फिर प्रकृति अपनी यौवनावस्था में उन्मत्त हो जाती है। वास्तवित रूप में ऐसा होता है या नहीं, पर कवि कल्पना में प्रकृति का पुलकोद्गम एवं मानव सौन्दर्य का सम्बन्ध जुड़ जाने के कारण कविता मादक और मनोरंजक बन जाती है। विभिन्न प्रसंगों में नये बिम्ब दिखाई देने लगते हैं। उनमें काव्यात्मकता आ जाती है।

कालिदास की कृतिगों में प्रकृति और मानव की यह घनिष्ठता सर्वत्र विद्यमान है। अलग अलग ऋतुओं के अनुसार पुष्पों का खिलना, तद्नुसार उनका मानव पर प्रभाव[2], माधवीलता का पुष्पित होकर शकुन्तला की भाँति अपनी यौवनावस्था में सहकार वृक्ष का सहारा ढूँढना[3], पुष्पों का अलंकरण के रूप में प्रयोग[4], नायिकाओं के कोमल अङ्गों से उनकी तुलना[5] आदि असंख्य प्रसङ्ग प्रस्तुत किये जा सकते हैं।

इस सन्दर्भ में मालविकाग्निमित्र नाटक में पुष्प, पौधों का चित्रण किस प्रकार हुआ है, उनका उपयोग कवि ने किस प्रकार किया है, यह अपने आप में बहुत रोचक है। राजा अग्निमित्र और राजपुत्री मालविका के प्रणय-व्यापार और अन्तःपुर की रानियों के ईर्ष्या-द्वेष की कथा पर आधारित पाँच अंकों के इस नाटक में वनस्पति-जगत् कई प्रकार की भूमिकायें निभाता हुआ दिखाई देता है।

सामान्य रूप में तो इस नाटक के कथानक को देखकर ऐसा प्रतीत होता है कि इसमें प्राकृतिक सौन्दर्य-निरूपण के लिए कम ही अवकाश है। परन्तु बारीकी से देखने पर पेड़, पौधे विशेष रूप से पुष्प-यथा तपनीय-अशोक, कुरबक, तिलक, अपने सौन्दर्य एवं गुणों के कारण कई अभिप्रायों के सूचक बने गये हैं। उनका साहचर्य— नाटक के पात्र उसकी कथावस्तु और रस (भाव) सभी को प्रभावित करता हुआ प्रतीत होता है। इनके रूप, रङ्ग, आकार आदि को अलंकरण

एवं उपमानों के रूप में प्रयुक्त करके कवि ने नायिकाओं के सौन्दर्य, उनकी कोमलता आदि गुण तथा मनःव्यापारों को व्यक्त किया है। कहीं ये पुष्प प्रेममय वातावरण की सृष्टि करने में सहायक हैं, कहीं पात्रों के कार्य-कलापों से जुड़ कर प्रसंगों को नाटकीयता प्रदान करते हैं। नायक-नायिका के मन में आशा-निराशा आदि भावों को जागृत करते हुए ये पुष्प, पौधे बाह्य और आन्तरिक प्रभावों को व्यक्त करने में महत्त्वपूर्ण योगदान करते हैं। नाटक के विभिन्न प्रसंगों को लेकर उपर्युक्त तथ्यों पर प्रकाश डाला जा सकता है।

प्रमदवन के दृश्य में पुष्पों से समता दिखाते हुए मालविका के सौन्दर्य और मनोभावों को कवि ने कई प्रकार से चित्रित किया है। छलिक नृत्य देखने के पश्चात् राजा प्रमदवन में मालविका को देखकर प्रफुल्लित हो जाता है और कह उठता है-इसके कपोल सरकंडे के समान मलिनवर्ण के हैं, अनलंकृत वेश में— यह वसन्त ऋतु में पीले पत्तों और कम फूलों से युक्त कुन्दलता जैसी लग रही है।[6] दूसरी ओर अपुष्पित अशोक मालविका को अपने समान अपूर्ण मनोरथ वाला प्रतीत हो रहा है।[7] इसी प्रसंग में महावर से रंगे उसके पैर 'अरुणशत पत्र' की भांति सुशोभित हो रहे हैं।[8] इसी तरह मालविका की शारीरिक और मानसिक अवस्था की एक और सुन्दर उपमा है 'मालविकाप्येषु दिवसेष्वनुभूतमुक्तेव मालतीमाला म्लाना लक्ष्यते'[9] (चाही हुई वस्तु न मिलने से) इस समय वह ऐसे मुरझा गई है जैसे सद्य विकसित पुष्पों से गुथी हुई, पर पहन कर उतारी हुई कोमल मालतीमाला मुरझा जाती है। राजा के सम्मुख नृत्य करते समय मालविका खिले पुष्पों के समान थी पर अब अपने प्रियतम से अलग होकर वह म्लान और उदास हो गई है। इन सभी उपमानों में नायिका के मुख का वर्ण, उसके अंगों की कोमलता, सुन्दरता, उसका अलंकरण-युक्त होना या न होना तथा मानसिक स्थिति आदि की तुलना कुन्द, कमल, मालती जैसे पुष्पों से करके कवि ने दोनों की ही कोमलता को बहुत सुन्दर ढंग से उभारा है। सुगन्ध युक्त सभी पुष्प अपने कोमलत्व, माधुर्य आदि गुणों के कारण मालविका से सादृश्य रखते हुए उसके गुणों को भी ध्वनित कर रहे हैं।

कुछ सन्दर्भों में किसी स्थिति विशेष को सूचित करने के लिए कटाक्षपूर्ण उक्तियों के रूप में पुष्पों का प्रयोग किया गया है। जैसे प्रमदवन में लतान्तरित होकर राजा और विदूषक मालविका को देख रहे हैं तभी इरावती के आने की सूचना विदूषक आशंकापूर्वक देता है, तब राजा कहता है-'नहि कमलिनीं दृष्ट्वा ग्राहमवेक्षते मतङ्गजः'[10] और वह इरावती की चिन्ता किये बिना मालविका को देखता रहता है।

अन्य प्रसंग में इरावती और निपुणिका राजा को ढूँढती हुई प्रमदवन में पहुँचती हैं पर वहाँ उन्हें राजा की अपेक्षा मालविका चरणालंकार करती हुई दिखाई दे जाती है और निपुणिका कटाक्ष करती है-'आलोकयतु भट्टिनी चूताङ्कुरं विचिन्वत्योः पिपीलिकाभिदष्टम्'[11] बकुलावलिका और मालविका के राजा के प्रति प्रेमविषयक वार्तालाप के प्रसंग में, रानी इरावती से भयभीत मालविका विश्वास नहीं कर पाती कि राजा ने उसके प्रति प्रेम भाव व्यक्त किया होगा अतः बकुलावलिका व्यंग्य करती है 'मुग्धे भ्रमरसंपातो भविष्यतीति वसन्तावतारसर्वस्वं किं न चूतप्रसवोऽवतंसितव्यः'।[12]

समुद्रगृह में मालविका के मुख पर हर्ष, विषाद के भावों में एवं सूर्योदय और सूर्यास्त के समय कमल की अवस्थाओं में राजा समभाव देखता है।[13]

इस प्रकार इस नाटक में पुष्प अपना सौन्दर्य बिखेरने के साथ विभिन्न परिस्थितियों में संसार की गति, तद्नुसार मानव-प्रतिक्रियाओं के लिए प्रभावी दृष्टान्त भी बन गये हैं।

इस समय वसन्त ऋतु का पदार्पण हुआ है। सारी प्रकृति ने अपने आप को सुसज्जित कर लिया है। कामदेव ने अपने पुष्प बाण छोड़ दिये हैं। वनस्पति-जगत् का हर्षातिरेक एक ओर मानव-सौन्दर्य के साथ सम्बद्ध हो गया है, दूसरी ओर प्रिया-समागम न होने के कारण विरहताप से पीड़ित राजा के लिए कष्टदायक बन गया है। आम्रमंजरियों की सुगन्धि से आमोदित कोमल स्पर्श वाला दक्षिण वायु राजा के करतल का स्पर्श करता हुआ कोकिलालाप द्वारा मानों उसकी कामपीड़ा की बात पूछ रहा है। वसन्त ऋतु में कोकिलालाप प्रेम-संताप को अधिक बढ़ा देता है अतः तज्जनित ताप शान्ति के लिए आम्रमंजरी से सुगन्धित मलयानिल मानों अपने हाथ से राजा के शरीर को सहला रहा है,[14] जिससे कि उसका संताप कम हो जाये। जिस प्रकार रुग्ण व्यक्ति के स्वजन उसके पास जाकर उसकी बात पूछते हैं,

ताप-निवारणार्थ उसके अङ्गों पर हाथ फेरते हैं उसी प्रकार कोयलों की कूक और कोमल स्पर्श द्वारा मलय वायु नायक की काम पीड़ा को बाँटना चाहता है। यहाँ वसन्त का सौन्दर्य, नायक की मनस्थिति उसका उपचार, रुग्ण व्यक्ति से साम्य आदि अनेकों अर्थ द्योतित हो रहे हैं।

इस समय वायु से हिलती हुई पल्लव रूपी उंगलियों से प्रमदवन राजा को शीघ्र प्रवेश करने के लिए प्रेरित कर रहा है।[15] क्योंकि खिले हुए अशोक कुरबक, तिलक पुष्प वसन्तागमन की सूचना देने के साथ-साथ हृदय में प्रेम भावों को उदीप्त कर रहे हैं। वास्तव में वसन्त ऋतु ही तो कंदर्प की प्रिय ऋतु है। इस मनोरम वातावरण में पुष्प, पौधे अपने अपने रंग, रूप, गुण, आकार आदि से सभी को आकृष्ट करते हुए मादक प्रभाव उत्पन्न कर देते हैं। इस समय पुष्पों ने आभूषणों का स्थान ले लिया है और वसन्त रूपी नायिका विभिन्न फूलों के रूप में अपने मुख का श्रृंगार करके आई है। वह इतनी सुन्दर लग रही है कि-रक्तिम्। अशोक ने नायिका के बिम्ब सदृश अधरोष्ठ की लालिमा को, कुरबक पुष्प ने मुख की चित्रकारी को, और तिलक पुष्प ने मुख की बिंदी को भी तिरस्कृत कर दिया है।

रक्ताशोकरुचा विशेषितगुणो बिम्बाधरालक्तकः
प्रत्याख्यातविशेषकं कुरबकं श्यामावदातारुणम्।
आक्रान्ता तिलकक्रिया च तिलकैर्लग्नद्विरेफाञ्जनैः
सावज्ञेव मुखप्रसाधनविधौ श्रीर्माधवी योषिताम्।।[16]

मानों प्रकृति नायिका अपने पुष्पों के साज श्रृङ्गार में युवतियों से समता ही केवल नहीं रखना चाहती, उनसे उत्कृष्ट दिखना चाहती है। अतः उसने वासन्ती पुष्पों को युवतियों के मुख के अलंकरणों के रूप में पहन लिया है। सौन्दर्य वृद्धि हेतु युवतियों द्वारा पुष्पों के अलंकार धरण करना, उनकी अलंकार-प्रियता के साथ उनके हर्ष, उल्लास, प्रेम आदि भावों को भी सूचित कर रहा है जैसे कि यहाँ वसन्तु ऋतु खिले हुए पुष्पों द्वारा अपने हर्षोल्लास को व्यक्त करती हुई प्रेम भाव को भी जागृत कर रही है। यहाँ बाह्य और आन्तरिक प्रभाव, प्रकृति और युवतियाँ, पुष्प और अलंकार आदि बिम्बों में अङ्गागिभाव बहुत सुन्दर बन पड़ा है। इस प्रसंग में लुप्तोपमा, व्यतिरेक, उत्प्रेक्षा, काव्यङ्गि आदि अलंकारों का संकर भी कई अर्थों को ध्वनित कर रहा है।

नायक-नायिका के प्रणय-व्यापार से सम्बद्ध तपनीय अशोक का भी विशेष महत्व है। अशोक-दोहद निमित्त मालविका का पाद प्रहार किया जाना इस नाटक की प्रमुख घटना है (नेपथ्ये) 'आश्चर्यम्, आश्चर्यम्, अपूर्ण एव पञ्चरात्रे दोहदस्य मुकुलैः सनद्धस्तपनीयाशोकः।'[17] इसीलिए कवि ने बार-बार अशोक-दोहद, अशोक-वृक्ष का कई रूपों में उल्लेख किया है।[18] रक्ताशोक यहाँ प्रेम का प्रतीक है जो नायक-नायिका के प्रेम भाव को सूचित करने एवं प्रेम में उनकी आशा, निराशा व्यक्त करने का कार्य करता रहता है। प्रथम साक्षात्कार से अंकुरित होने वाले नायक-नायिका के प्रेम-संवर्धन में अशोक का विशेष हाथ है। उनकी इच्छाओं को जागता हुआ वह इच्छा पूर्ति में बिलम्ब भी सूचित करता रहता है। मालविका के पाद प्रहार से अशोक के पुष्पित हो जाने में प्रबल दोहदेच्छा पूरी होने के रूप में उसका नायक-नायिका से सम्बन्ध जुड़ जाता है। वसन्त ऋतु में सामान्यतः पुष्पित होने वाला अशोक साधारण वृक्ष न रहकर एक प्रकार से नाटक का प्रमुख पात्र बन जाता है। मालविका-नायिका के पाद प्रहार रूपी स्पर्श से नायक रूपी अशोक की प्रणयेच्छा पूरी होती है और वह फूलों से लद जाता है। इसी तरह मालविका और राजा का प्रेम भी पूर्णता को प्राप्त करता है। अशोक वृक्ष का फूलों से लद जाना मानों वसन्तु ऋतु की युवावस्था है।[19] प्रेमाभिलाषा पूरी होना है। जो नाट्य कथा का अंत भी है-'देवी विज्ञापयति तपनीयाशोकस्य कुसुम सह दर्शनेन ममारम्भः सफलः क्रियतामिति'।[20]

अशोक-दोहद की इस कवि कल्पना में प्रकृति और मानव की विभिन्न भाव-दशायें अभिव्यक्त होती रहती हैं। श्रृङ्गार प्रधान इस नाटक में तपनीय अशोक कई रूपों में पूरे नाटक पर छाया हुआ है। विभिन्न स्तरों पर वह नाटक के प्रायः सभी पात्र-नायक, नायिका, चेटियाँ, विदूषक आदि सभी को प्रभावित करता रहता है। कहीं वह पल्लवयुक्त

बालाशोक है, कहीं दोहदापेक्षी वृक्ष और कहीं शाखालम्बी पल्लवगुच्छक है जो प्रेम उद्दीप्त करता रहता है। अन्यत्र वह प्रियंगुलतापरिक्षिप्तशिलापट्टक बनकर नायिका का विश्राम स्थान ही नहीं प्रेम-स्थल भी है। इसी की छाया में बैठकर मालविका का चरणालंकार किया जाता है। और उसके महावर की गीली लकीर इस कन्दर्परूपी वृक्ष में फूटी हुई पहली कली है।[21] इसकी शाखा पर लटके पल्लव-गुच्छक सभी को आकर्षित करते रहते हैं। इसका गुच्छा लाने के कारण-(विदूषक को) सर्प काटने वाली महत्त्वपूर्ण घटना घटित होती है। इसका गुच्छा नायिका के लिए कर्णाभूषण है। यह संकेत गृह भी है। वास्तव में दोहद-मुकलों में सन्नद्ध तपनीय अशोक इन नाटक का प्राण स्वरूप है।

प्रमदवन का दृश्य आते ही रक्ताशोक का प्रसंग प्रारम्भ हो जाता है जो नायक-नायिका की प्रेम कथा का भी प्रारम्भ है। अंत तक अनेकों नाटकीय उतार चढ़ाव आते रहते हैं और अशोक के पुष्पित होने पर कथा चरमोत्कर्ष पर पहुँच जाती है। यही प्रेम, का वसन्त ऋतु, का सभी के आनंद का चरमोत्कर्ष है। कालिदास की अन्य कृतियों में भी दोहदापेक्षी अशोक के प्रसंग है[22] परन्तु मालविकाग्निमित्र नाटक में वह बहुत मनोरम और व्यापक रूप में वर्णित हुआ है। उसकी शोभा अनन्यसाधारण है।

प्रेम के अतिरिक्त अन्य मानवीय भावों को दर्शाने के लिए भी रक्ताशोक की उपमायें बहुत सुन्दर हैं। एक स्थान पर अपुष्पित अशोक और प्रेमीजनों की दशा में साम्य दिखाते हुए राजा कहता है कि दोहद की अपेक्षा रखने पर भी न फूलने के कारण यह अशोक प्रेम में अपराध करके सिर झुकाये प्रियतम की भांति है जिस पर नायिका का पाद प्रहार करना ठीक ही है।

नवकिसलयरागेणाग्रपादेन बाला
स्फुरितनखरुचा द्वौ हन्तुमर्हत्यनेन।
अकुसुमितमशोकं दोहदापेक्षया वा
प्रणमितशिरसं वा कान्तमार्द्रापराधम्।।[23]

पुष्पित न होने के रूप में मानों वह अपराधी प्रेमी है जो नायिका द्वारा ताड़न योग्य है। यहाँ प्रेम सम्बन्धों पर सुन्दर कटाक्ष है।

इसी प्रसंग में मालविका समझती हैं कि वह रूठा हुआ है अतः पुष्पित होना नहीं दिखा रहा है परन्तु राजा उसे गुणहीन और कामुक समझ रहा है अतः रमणी-ताड़न रूप दोहद वहन करना उसके लिए व्यर्थ है।[24]

कभी मालविका को न प्राप्त कर पाने के कारण राजा अपने अधैर्य की तुलना अशोक के पुष्प न खिलने की स्थिति से करने लगता है।[25]

इस प्रकार दोहदापेक्षी अशोक के सन्दर्भ में विभिन्न भावों का यह आदान-प्रदान, बाह्य प्रकृति और मानव को एक धरातल पर ले आती है। वृक्षों और कोमल, सुन्दर पुष्पों के साथ यह भाव साम्य अपनी सहजता और संवदेनशीलता के कारण पाठकों के हृदय को बहुत गहराई से छू जाता है।

कालिदास की सभी रचनाओं में यह विशिष्टता विद्यमान है जिसका कुछ अंश मालविकाग्निमित्र नाटक में देखने को मिला। यहाँ कुछ पुष्पों के प्रसंगों से ही प्रकृति के मनोहर रूप उसके सुन्दर रंगों को चित्रित करने का प्रयास किया गया है। इस संदर्भ में यह कहना उपयुक्त होगा कि इस काव्यमय चित्र को पूर्णता देने के लिए यह आवश्यक है कि प्रकृति की इस धरोहर के सौन्दर्य, उसके वैचित्र्य, उसकी सरसता को प्रत्यक्ष रूप में देखें, समझें एवं साहित्य तथा वनस्पति-विज्ञान में दिये गये विवरणों का तुलनात्मक अध्ययन करें।

सन्दर्भ-सङ्केत

1. पादाघातादशोकस्तिलककुरबकौ वीक्षणालिङ्गनाभ्यां
स्त्रीणां स्पर्शात् प्रियङ्गुर्विकसति बकुलः सीधुगण्डूषसेकात्।
मन्दारो नर्मवाक्यात् पटुमृदुहसनाच्चम्पको वक्त्रवातात्
चूतो गीतान्नमेरुर्विकसति च पुरोनर्तनात् कर्णिकारः।। वी. एस. आप्टे संस्कृत - इंग्लिश डिक्शनरी, पृ. 379

2. ऋतुसंहार
3. अभिज्ञानशाकुन्तल - अंक 1, कालिदास-ग्रन्थावली, संपादक रेवाप्रसाद द्विवेदी-पृ. 436
4. अभिज्ञानशाकुन्तल, ऋतुसंहार, मेघदूत, मालविकाग्निमित्र, विक्रमोर्वशीय, कुमारसम्भव
5. कालिदास के सभी काव्य
6. शरकाण्डपाण्डुगण्डस्थलेयमाभाति परिमिताभरणा।
   माधवपरिणतपत्रा कतिपयकुसुमेव कुन्दलता। मालविकाग्निमित्र- 3.8
   कालिदास-ग्रन्थावली, रेवाप्रसाद द्विवेदी-पृ. 287
7. 'ललितसुकुमारदोहदापेक्षी अगृहीतकुसुमनेपथ्यः उत्कण्ठिताया मम अनुकरोत्यशोकः'- मालविकाग्निमित्र - अंक 3, पृ. 287
8. मालविकाग्निमित्र - अंक 3, पृ. 292
9. मालविकाग्निमित्र - अंक. 2, पृ. 282
10. मालविकाग्निमित्र - अंक 3, पृ. 288
11. मालविकाग्निमित्र - अंक 3, पृ. 291
12. मालविकाग्निमित्र - अंक 3, पृ. 293
13. मालविकाग्निमित्र - 4.7
14. उन्मत्तानां श्रवणसुभगैः कूजितैः कोकिलानां
    सानुक्रोशं मनसिजरुजः सह्यतां पृच्छतेव।
    अङ्गे चूतप्रसवसुरभिर्दक्षिणो मारुतो मे।
    सान्द्रः स्पर्शः करतल इव व्यापृतो माधवेन।।
    मालविकाग्निमित्र - 3.4
15. मालविकाग्निमित्र - अंक 3, पृ. 284
16. मालविकाग्निमित्र - अंक 3.5
17. मालविकाग्निमित्र - अंक 4, पृ. 318
18. मालविकाग्निमित्र - अंक 3-5, पृ. 282, 286, 289, 294, 295, 296, 297, 299, 318, 319, 321, 322, 323, 325, 332
19. सर्वाशोकतरूणां प्रथमं सूचितवसन्तविभवानाम्।
    निर्वृत्तदोहदेऽस्मिन् संक्रान्तानीव कुसुमानि।।
    मालविकाग्निमित्र - 5.5
20 (क) मालविकाग्निमित्र - अंक 5, पृ. 322,
   (ख) मालनिकाग्निमित्र - 5.4
21. चरणान्तनिवेशितां प्रियायाः सरसां पश्य वयस्य रागलेखाम्।
    प्रथमामिव पल्लवप्रसूतिं हरदग्धस्य मनोभवद्रुमस्य।।
    मालविकाग्निमित्र -पद्य 4, पृ. 289
22. (क) ऋतुसंहार - 6.18
    (ख) मेघदूत - 2.15
    (ग) कुमारसंभव -3.26
    (घ) रघुवंश - 8.62-63
    (ङ) विक्रमोर्वशीय - 4.34
23. मालविकाग्निमित्र - 3.12
24. (क) वामः खलु एष अशोकः, यः व्यञ्जकं प्रमाणीकृतकुसुमोद्गमं न दर्शयति। मालविकाग्निमित्र - अंक 3, पृ. 295
    (ख) मालविकाग्निमित्र - 3.17
25 मालविकाग्निमित्र - 3.19

卐 卐 卐

अभिज्ञानशाकुन्तल में नायिकाङ्गसौन्दर्य एवं पुष्पसम्पत्ति

कान्ता भाटिया

संस्कृतसाहित्याकाश में सप्तर्षिवत् देदीप्यमान सात ग्रन्थों के रचयिता कालिदास के ग्रन्थों में यह निर्णय कर पाना असम्भव है कि इनकी कौन सी कृति सर्वश्रेष्ठ है परन्तु इनके नाटक अभिज्ञानशाकुन्तल के विषय में यह कहना निर्विवाद है कि उनका यह नाटक न केवल संस्कृत-वाङ्मय में अपितु विश्वसाहित्य में अपने अद्वितीय माहात्म्य के कारण आज भी सर्वश्रेष्ठ माना जाता है। 'तत्र रम्या शकुन्तला' यह उक्ति इस मत की पुष्टि करती है।

अभिज्ञानशाकुन्तल नाटक का नायक राजा दुष्यन्त है तथा नायिका शकुन्तला है जो विधाता की प्रथम अर्थात् सर्वश्रेष्ठ रचना है—'या सृष्टि स्रष्टुराद्या'। उसका निर्माण सामान्य स्त्री की भांति नहीं हुआ अपितु विधाता ने पहले उसे चित्र में चित्रित किया उसके बाद उसमें प्राण संचार कर पुनः मन में कल्पना करके सौन्दर्य सामग्री से बनाया है। इसी लिए उसका सौन्दर्य अद्वितीय है—

चित्रे निवेश्य परिकल्पितसत्वयोगा
रूपोच्चयेन मनसा विधिना कृता नु।
स्त्रीरत्नसृष्टिरपरा प्रतिभाति सा मे
धातुर्विभुत्वमनुचिन्त्य वपुश्च तस्याः। अभिज्ञानशाकुन्तल 2.9

वह आश्रम में पली बड़ी है और आश्रम का वातावरण नगर के प्रदूषण से रहित पुष्पों एवं वृक्षों की सुगन्ध से परिपूर्ण होता है। अतः नायिका शकुन्तला एवं पुष्पसम्पत्ति में अन्योग्य घनिष्ठ सम्बन्ध स्वाभाविक ही है। शकुन्तला एक फूल है जिसकी सुगन्ध को अभी तक किसी ने नहीं सूंघा तथा ऐसा किसलय है जिस पर किसी के नखों का स्पर्श नहीं हुआ है इसीलिए दुष्यन्त का हृदय उसे पाने के लिए लालायित हो उठता है—

अनाघ्रातं पुष्पं किसलयमलूनं कररुहैः। 2.10

शकुन्तला मेनका नाम्नी अप्सरा की सन्तान है परन्तु कण्वाश्रम में पली है इसलिए उसकी तुलना आंक पर गिरे हुए चमेली के पुष्प से करना बड़ा ही स्वाभाविक है—

सुरयुवतिसम्भवं किल मुनेरपत्यं तदुज्झितमधिगतम्।
अर्कस्योपरि शिथिलं च्युतमिव नवमालिकाकुसुमम्।। 2.8

नाटक में पुष्पसम्पत्ति का प्रयोग अनेक रूपों में उपलब्ध होता है परन्तु सर्वाधिक प्रयोग नायिका के अङ्गों के सौन्दर्य वर्णन में उपमानों के रूप में किया गया है। नाटक के प्रारम्भ में राजा दुष्यन्त आश्रम में प्रवेश करते ही सखियों सहित पौधों को सींचती हुई शकुन्तला के अङ्गलावण्य को देखकर स्तब्ध रह जाते हैं और उन पादपों के बीच मुनिकन्याओं को देखकर कह उठते हैं कि ऐसा लावण्यमय शरीर अन्तःपुर में मिलना दुर्लभ है। कहाँ कृत्रिम सौन्दर्य से युक्त अन्तःपुर की उद्यानलतासदृश स्त्रियाँ तथा कहाँ प्राकृतिक सम्पदाओं के बीच पली बढ़ी वनलताओं जैसी स्वाभाविक सौन्दर्य से युक्त ये मुनिकन्याएँ—

शुद्धान्तदुर्लभमिदं वपुराश्रमवासिनो यदि जनस्य।
दूरीकृता खलु गुणैरुद्यानलता वनलताभिः।। 1.17

नायिका के अलङ्कारों का वर्णन करते हुए साहित्यदर्पणकार ने 'माधुर्य' का लक्षण देते हुए कहा है—'सर्वास्ववस्थाविशेषेषु माधुर्यं रमणीयता'। अर्थात् विशेष अवस्थाओं में रमणीयता माधुर्य कहलाता है। कालिदास शकुन्तला में माधुर्य का वर्णन करते हुए कहते हैं कि शकुन्तला सुन्दर वस्त्राभूषणों के बिना केवल वल्कल वस्त्र में भी उसी प्रकार सुन्दर दिखाई देती है जैसे शैवाल से घिरा होने पर भी कमल तथा काले कलङ्क के कारण चन्द्रमा। इसका कारण यह है कि शकुन्तला की आकृति मधुर है जिसे किसी आभूषण विशेष की आवश्यकता नहीं है—

सरसिजमनुविद्धं शैवलेनापि रम्यं
मलिनमपि हिमांशोर्लक्ष्म लक्ष्मीं तनोति।
इयमधिकमनोज्ञा वल्कलेनापि तन्वी
किमिव हि मधुराणां मण्डनं नाकृतीनाम्।। 1. 20

एक स्थल पर कवि ने शकुन्तला के कोमल शरीर की तुलना नीलकमल के पत्ते की नोक से की है—

ध्रुवं स नीलोत्पलपत्रधारया
शमीलतां छेत्तुमृषिर्व्यवस्यति।। 1.18

शकुन्तला एक लता के समान है उसका प्रत्येक अङ्ग लता के अङ्गों से तुलनीय है। उसका अधर किसलय के समान लाल, भुजाएँ शाखाओं का अनुकरण करने वाली तथा अङ्गों में विद्यमान यौवन पुष्प के समान लुभाने वाला है—

अधरः किसलयरागः कोमलविटपानुकारिणौ बाहू।
कुसुममिव लोभनीयं यौवनमङ्गेःषु सन्नद्धम्।। 1. 21

नवमालिका का उपमान के रूप में अनेक बार प्रयोग किया गया है। शकुन्तला की सखी उसे छेड़ते हुए कहती है ऐसा लगता है कि तात कण्व को आश्रमवृक्ष तुमसे भी अधिक प्रिय हैं तभी तो नवमालिका (चमेली) के पुष्प के समान कोमल तुम्हें वृक्षों को सींचने के काम में नियुक्त किया है— **हला शकुन्तले! त्वत्तोऽपि तातकण्वस्य आश्रमवृक्षाः प्रियतरा इति तर्कयामि येन नवमालिकाकुसुमपरिपेलवापि त्वमेतेषामालवालपरिपूरणे नियुक्ता।**

भ्रमर भी नवमालिका को छोड़कर शकुन्तला के मुख को नवमालिका समझकर उसकी ओर आकर्षित हो जाता है— अम्मो सलिलसेकसम्भ्रमोद्गतो नवमालिकामुज्झित्वा वदनं मे मधुकरोऽभिवर्तते।

कामपीड़िता शकुन्तला की तुलना पत्तों को सुखाने वाली वायु के स्पर्श को प्राप्त करने वाली माधवी लता से करके कवि यह बताते हैं कि यद्यपि कामपीड़ित होने के कारण इसके अङ्गों में कृशता है तथा छवि भी पीली पड़ गई है परन्तु इसका रूप सौन्दर्य अभी-भी उसी प्रकार आकर्षक है जिस प्रकार हवा के थपेड़ों के बीच कुछ-कुछ मुरझाई हुई माधवी लता—

क्षामक्षामकपोलमाननमुरः काठिन्यमुक्तस्तनं
मध्यः क्लान्ततरः प्रकामविनतावंसौ छविः पाण्डुरा।
शोच्या च प्रियदर्शना च मदनग्लानेयमालक्ष्यते
पत्राणामिव शोषणेन मरुता स्पृष्टा लता माधवी।। 3. 8

वल्कलवस्त्रधारी ब्रह्मचारियों के बीच नववधु के रूप में लाल रेशमी वस्त्रों में सजी अवगुण्ठन युक्त तथा कुछ-कुछ दिखाई देते हुए सुन्दर शरीर वाली शकुन्तला की पीले पत्तों के बीच उगे हुए किसलय से तुलना को पढ़कर अनायास ही नेत्रों के सम्मुख दुल्हन की सुन्दर छवि उपस्थित हो जाती है—

केयमवगुण्ठनवती नातिपरिस्फुटशरीरलावण्या।
मध्ये तपोधनानां किसलयमिव पाण्डुपत्राणाम्।। 5.13

गर्भवती शकुन्तला की तुलना अन्दर स्थित अग्नि वाली शमीलता से की गई है। अग्नि के समान तेजस्वी दुष्यन्त की सन्तान तथा शमीलता के समान तेज को धारण करने में समर्थ शकुन्तला कितनी मनोरम दिखाई गई है—

दुष्यन्तेनाहितं तेजो दधानां भूतये भुवः।
अवेहि तनयां ब्रह्मन्नग्निगर्भां शमीमिव।। 4.4

इसी अवस्था में शकुन्तला की तुलना प्रातःकाल में अन्तःस्थित तुषार वाले कुन्द पुष्प से कर उसकी पवित्रता की ओर सङ्केत करते हैं—

इदमुपनतमेवं रूपमक्लिष्टकान्ति
प्रथमपरिगृहीतं स्यान्न वेत्यध्यवस्यन्।
भ्रमर इव विभाते कुन्दमन्तस्तुषारं
न खलु परिभोक्तुं नैव शक्नोमि हातुम्।। 5.19

पुष्पों का शकुन्तला के शृङ्गारप्रसाधन के रूप में भी वर्णन किया गया है। शकुन्तला कान में शिरीष पुष्प धारण करती हैं— बद्धं कर्णशिरीषरोधि वदने धर्मवमनं जालकम्। वक्षस्थल पर कमलनाल के सूत्र की माला धारण करती हैं जिसे राजा दुष्यन्त चित्र में दिखाना भूल जाते हैं।

कृतं न कर्णार्पितबन्धनं सखे
शिरीषमागण्डविलम्बिकेसरम्।
न वा शरच्चन्द्रमरीचिकोमलम्
मृणालसूत्रं रचितं स्तनान्तरे।। 6.18

महर्षि कण्व के प्रभाव से शकुन्तला की विदाई के समय उसके शृङ्गार के लिए विभिन्न वृक्षों द्वारा सौन्दर्य प्रसाधन दिए गए। किसी वृक्ष ने रेशमी वस्त्र, किसी ने हाथों पर लगाने के लिए माङ्गलिक महावर तथा अन्य वृक्षों ने आभूषण दिए—

क्षौमं केनचिदिन्दुपाण्डु तरुणा माङ्गल्यमाविष्कृतं
निष्ठ्यूतश्चरणोपरागसुलभो लाक्षरसः केनचित्।
अन्येभ्यो वनदेवताकरतलैरापर्वभागोत्थितै
र्दत्तान्याभरणानि नः किसलयोद्भेदप्रतिद्वन्द्विभिः।। 4.5

यद्यपि शकुन्तला मण्डनप्रिया हैं किन्तु वह कभी भी वृक्षों से फूलों को तोड़कर शृङ्गार नहीं किया करती थी। वह स्वयं टूटकर गिरे हुए पुष्पों को ही शृङ्गार के लिए प्रयोग करती थीं। यहाँ तक कि जब तक वृक्षों को जल नहीं दे देती थीं वह स्वयं भी जल ग्रहण नहीं करती थीं। वृक्षों पर पुष्प का उगना उसके लिए उत्सव के सम हर्षदायक होता था—

पातुं न प्रथमं व्यवस्यति जलं युष्मास्वपीतेषु या
नादत्ते प्रियमण्डनापि भवतां स्नेहेन या पल्लवम्।
आद्ये वः कुसुमप्रसूतिसमये यस्या भवत्युत्सवः
सेयं याति शकुन्तला पतिगृहं सर्वैरनुज्ञायताम्।। 4.9

शकुन्तला भलिभाँति जानती हैं कि पर्यावरण संरक्षण अत्यन्त अनिवार्य है इसीलिए वह कण्व ऋषि की अनुपस्थिति में प्रतिदिन नियमपूर्वक सभी पेड़ पौधों का सिंचन करती हैं। शकुन्तला का पेड़ पौधों के साथ प्राणियों के समान सम्बन्ध दिखाया गया है। वह उनके साथ सहोदर के समान स्नेह रखती है—**न केवलं तातनियोग एव, अस्ति मे सहोदरस्नेहोऽप्येतेषु।**

शकुन्तला द्वारा स्वयं दिए गए नवज्योत्स्ना नामक नवमालिका लता से विदाई के समय गले मिलने का अनुरोध करना तथा सभी आश्रमवृक्षों से अनुमति लेना यह स्पष्ट करता है कि वे भी जीवन्त प्राणियों के समान मानव के सुख-दुःख में समान रूप से भाग लेते हैं। नवमालिका शकुन्तला के लिए सगी बहन के समान है। उसे भूल जाना शकुन्तला के लिए असम्भव है। प्रथम अङ्क में शकुन्तला एवं सखियों के बीच किए गए वार्तालाप से कहीं भी यह नहीं लगता कि यह जड़ प्रकृति के विषय में वर्णन है। जगदीशचन्द्र बसु का ''पेड़ पौधों में प्राण हैं'' वह अन्वेषण तो हजारों वर्ष पूर्व ही हो चुका था। कालिदास के ग्रन्थ इसका ज्वलन्त प्रमाण हैं।

इस समस्त वर्णन में हमने पाया कि कालिदास की नायिका का अङ्ग सौन्दर्य पुष्प वर्णन के बिना अपूर्ण है। प्रत्येक अवस्था में नायिका का वर्णन पुष्पों के सन्दर्भ में ही किया गया है। उसकी स्वाभाविक सुन्दरता के वर्णन में कामपीड़ित अवस्था के वर्णन में, गर्भावस्था के वर्णन में, विरहावस्था के वर्णन में, विदाई की अवस्था के वर्णन में तथा राजा द्वारा किए गए प्रत्याख्यान की अवस्था के वर्णन में सर्वत्र ही पुष्प सम्पत्ति को ही उपमान के रूप में प्रयुक्त किया गया है। कालिदास ने प्रमुखतः कमल, नीलकमल, माधवी, नवमालिका, कुन्द आदि पुष्पों का चयन किया है। पूरे नाटक में गेंदा एवं गुलाब का अभाव है। सम्भवतः ये पुष्प उस समय भारत में उपलब्ध नहीं थे इस्लाम के साथ ये बाहर से आए थे।

卐 卐 卐

विक्रमोर्वशीयेऽभिवर्णितं वृक्षपुष्पवैभवम्

धर्मा

1. कुरबक : 2. अशोक: 3. आम्र:

(1) अग्रे स्त्रीनखपाटलं कुरबकं श्यामं द्वयोर्भागयो–
बालाशोकमुपोढरागसुभगं भेदोन्मुखं तिष्ठति।
ईषद्बद्धरज:कणाग्रकपिशा चूते नवा वल्लरी
मुग्धत्वस्य च यौवनस्य च सखे मध्ये मधुश्री: स्थिता।।[1]

4. सहकार:

(2) इदमसुलभवस्तुप्रार्थनादुर्निवारं
प्रथममपि मनो मे पञ्चबाण: क्षिणोति।
किमुत मलयवातोन्मूलितापाण्डुपत्रै–
रुपवनसहकारैर्दर्शितेष्वङ्कुरेषु ।।[2]

5. कदम्ब:

(3) रक्तकदम्ब: सोऽयं प्रियया घर्मान्तशंसि यस्येदम्।
कुसुममसमग्रकेसरविषममपि कृतं शिखाभरणम्।।[3]

6. कर्णिकार:

(4) परिजनवनिताकरार्पिताभि:
परिवृत एष विभाति दीपिकाभि:।
गिरिरिव गतिमानपक्षलोपा–
दनुतटपुष्पितकर्णिकारयष्टि: ।।[4]

(5) उष्णालुः शिशिरे निषीदति तरोर्मूलालवाले शिखी
निर्भिद्योपरि कर्णिकारमुकुलान्यालीयते षट्पदः।
तप्तं वारि विहाय तीरनलिनीं कारण्डवः सेवते
क्रीडावेश्मनि चैष पञ्जरशुकः क्लान्तो जलं याचते।।[5]

7. राजजम्बूद्रुमः

(6) महदपि परदुःखं शीतलं सम्यगाहुः
प्रणयमगणयित्वा यन्ममापद्गतस्य।
अधरमिव मदान्धा पातुमेषा प्रवृत्ता
फलमभिनवपाकं राजजम्बूद्रुमस्य।।[6]

8. सल्लकी

(7) अयमचिरोद्गतपल्लावमुपनीतं प्रियतमाग्रहस्तेन।
अभिलषतु तावदासवसुरभिरसं सल्लकीभङ्गम्।।[7]

सन्दर्भ सङ्केताः

1. विक्रमोर्वशीयम् (वेलङ्करसम्पादितम्, साहित्य अकादमी, 1981) - 2. 7
2. विक्रमोर्वशीयम् - 2. 6
3. विक्रमोर्वशीयम् - 4. 61
4. विक्रमोर्वशीयम् - 3. 3
5. विक्रमोर्वशीयम् - 2. 22
6. विक्रमोर्वशीयम् - 4. 27
7. विक्रमोर्वशीयम् - 4. 44

Section IX

FLORA IN BṚHATTRAYĪ & INDIVIDUAL POETS

बृहत्त्रयी-रसझरी

किरातार्जुनीय में ऋतुवर्णन एवं वनविहारवर्णन

सुषमा कुलश्रेष्ठ

ऋतुवर्णन

किरातार्जुनीय में ऋतुवर्णन दो पृथक् स्थलों पर प्राप्त होता है। चतुर्थ सर्ग में केवल शरद् का तथा दशम सर्ग में छः ऋतुओं का वर्णन किया गया है। चतुर्थ सर्ग के ऋतु-वर्णन के आश्रय अर्जुन तथा यक्ष हैं। वैसे इस प्रकार के दृश्य पाठक या श्रोता के भावों के भी आलम्बन होते हैं। दशम सर्ग का ऋतु-वर्णन उद्दीपन रूप में हुआ है।

अर्जुन शरद् ऋतु की शोभा को देखकर बहुत प्रसन्न हुए।[1] ग्राम की सीमा के समीप के भूमि-खण्ड झुके हुए धान की बालों से सुशोभित हो रहे थे। वहाँ कीचड़ नाममात्र को भी नहीं था। जहाँ कहीं जल था भी, वहाँ जल में कमल शोभित हो रहे थे। अर्जुन शरद् ऋतु की सब सम्पत्तियों को अपने प्रति उपहार-रूप में दी गई समझकर अति प्रसन्न हुए।[2] शरद् ऋतु में सरोवर की शोभा का भी सुन्दर वर्णन मिलता है।[3] कहीं-कहीं सरोवरों के जल, जिनमें विकसित कमल शोभित हो रहे थे, फेन और कमल-पराग से आच्छादित थे, जिन्हें देखकर अर्जुन को पृथ्वी पर खिले हुए कमल का भ्रम हो रहा था, किन्तु ऊपर की ओर उल्लुण्ठन करते हुए पाठीन (हज़ार दाँत वाली मछली) से अभिताड़ित होकर पुष्प-पराग और फेन-राशि के हट जाने से जल दिखायी देने लगता था, जिससे अर्जुन का भ्रम दूर हो गया।[4] शस्य-पालिकाओं को देखकर अर्जुन ने शरद् ऋतु को सफल माना।[5] इस ऋतु में मयूर-रुत के श्रुति-कटु तथा हंस-कूजित के कर्ण-प्रिय होने का भी वर्णन है।[6] सरोवर के जल के रङ्ग-बिरङ्गे दिखने पर कवि की सरस उक्ति है—'जल कमलिनी-लता की कान्ति से हरे रङ्ग, कमल-दल से लाल रङ्ग तथा झूमते हुए धान की बालों से पीले रङ्ग को धारण करता है, जिससे वह इन्द्र के धनुष के समान प्रतीत होता है'।[7]

दशम सर्ग में षड्-ऋतु-वर्णन के प्रसङ्ग को अतिकौशल से उपन्यस्त किया गया है। अप्सराओं के इन्द्रकील पर्वत पर आने का प्रमुख उद्देश्य अर्जुन को आकर्षित करना तथा उनके तप में विघ्न उपस्थित करना है। उनके उद्देश्य की सिद्धि के लिए अनुकूल वातावरण अपेक्षित है। पर्वत पर विभिन्न ऋतुओं की शोभा का आविर्भाव उनके उद्देश्य का साधक है। सुर-युवतियों के आदेश पर गन्धर्वों ने मनोरम वीणा और मृदङ्ग-वादन किया। पुनः एक ही काल में छः ऋतुओं को अलग-अलग व्योम तथा वनों में आविष्कृत करके विस्तृत कर दिया।[8] वीणा तथा मृदङ्ग-वादन के साथ ऋतुओं के प्रादुर्भाव का वर्णन कवि के सङ्गीतविषयक ज्ञान का स्पष्ट निदर्शक है। किसी विशिष्ट सङ्गीतज्ञ के गायन अथवा वादन से प्रकृति में होने वाले परिवर्तनों का उल्लेख प्राचीन काल से होता चला आ रहा है। जब बैजू बाबरा तथा तानसेन प्रभृति सङ्गीतज्ञ पत्थर को पिघला सकते थे, दीपक को जला सकते थे, पानी बरसा सकते थे और जब आधुनिक काल के प्रसिद्ध सङ्गीतज्ञ

सङ्गीत-मार्तण्ड पं. ओम्कारनाथ ठाकुर सूरत में घोर सूखा पड़ने पर अपने सङ्गीत के द्वारा मेघों को जल वर्षण के लिए बाध्य कर सके, तब यदि गन्धर्वों ने वीणा और मृदङ्ग-वादन द्वारा सब ऋतुओं को आविष्कृत किया, तो कोई आश्चर्य नहीं।

भारवि ने छः ऋतुओं का पृथक्-पृथक् वर्णन किया है। वर्षा ऋतु में नील नीरद से नभ आच्छन्न हो गया। विद्युल्लता की प्रभा स्पष्ट दिखायी देने लगी। प्रणयिजनों के रति-कालिक कलह को दूर करने वाला गम्भीर मेघगर्जन दिगन्त में गूँज उठा। मालती पुष्प विकसित हो गए। बूँद-बूँद करके जल-वृष्टि ने भूमि की धूलि को शान्त कर दिया। परिपक्व जम्बु-फल के उपभोग से प्रसन्न कोकिला ने कूजन किया, जिसमें नए-नए ढङ्ग से कण्ठ के द्वारा राग का विस्तार किया जा रहा था। कदम्बानिल बह रहा था, मयूर मधुर विरुत कर रहे थे।[9] वर्षा और शरद् की ऋतु-सन्धि को प्रस्तुत करते हुए कवि ने शरद् की वधू तथा वर्षा की वर-रूप में कल्पना की है। मृणाल-तन्तु-रूप कङ्कण को तथा कुमुदिनी के वन-रूप वस्त्र को धारण करती हुई शरद् रूपी वधू के कोमल कर-कमलों का ग्रहण वर्षा रूप वर ने किया।[10] शरद् ऋतु में भ्रमर-समूह, आसपास के कदम्ब-पुष्प-पराग से व्याप्त परागयुक्त केतकी-पुष्प को छोड़कर मकरन्दपूर्ण बन्धूक-पुष्प को मलिन करने लगा।[11] हेमन्त के प्रादुर्भूत होने पर प्रियङ्गुवन के प्रसून विकसित हो उठे। प्रफुल्लित कुन्द के गन्ध से पवन सुरभित हो उठा। लवली-लता के पुष्प तथा लोध्र-पुष्प भी वायु को सुरभित करने में सहायक हुए।[12] अनन्तर कामदेव का एकमात्र सहायक शिशिर प्रादुर्भूत हुआ। इसमें कहीं-कहीं आम्र-मञ्जरियाँ विकसित हो रही थीं। तुषार-कण की न तो बहुलता थी और न ही विरलता।[13] प्रसून-प्रधान पर्वतोपवनों में पहुँचने का अभिलाष किए हुए ऋतुराज ने नव-पल्लव-युक्त आम्रयष्टि का सहारा लेकर सरोजिनी-वन में नूपुरानुकारी भ्रमर-कुल के गुञ्जार के साथ-साथ पदार्पण किया।[14] वसन्त ऋतु में भ्रमर ने काँपती हुई शाल-लता-वधू के पुष्प-रूप मुख का, जिसमें मकरन्द-मद्य की गन्ध व्यक्त हो रही थी, चुम्बन किया। पवन-रूप निश्वास से अधरानुकारी पल्लव हिल रहे थे। वह पुष्प-मुख मानो मानिनी के मुख का अनुकरण कर रहा था।[15] ऋतुराज भी जब अर्जुन से हार मान गए तब निदाघ (ग्रीष्म) ने यह सोचकर कि 'जब अर्जुन के द्वारा सब ऋतुएँ तिरस्कृत कर दी गयीं, तब मेरा सम्मान किस प्रकार हो सकेगा', मनोहर हास के सदृश मल्लिका को विकसित कर, वसन्त पर हँसते हुए से पदार्पण किया।[16]

वनविहारवर्णन

किरातार्जुनीय में अप्सराओं एवं गन्धर्वों की उद्यान-क्रीडा का विस्तार से वर्णन किया गया है। इस उद्यान-क्रीडा-वर्णन के आश्रय वैसे तो अप्सराएँ एवं गन्धर्व हैं, किन्तु इस प्रकार के दृश्य श्रोता या पाठक के भावों के भी आलम्बन होते हैं।

वन-विहार की अभिलाषी सुर-सुन्दरियों ने अपने-अपने प्रिय गन्धर्वों के साथ अपनी कान्तियों से पर्वत और वृक्ष-लताओं को उद्भासित करते हुए जब वन में प्रवेश किया, तब वे विद्युल्लता की सी शोभा को वहन कर रही थीं।[17] वहाँ वन-पथ के वृक्ष प्रचुर पुष्प-सम्पत्ति धारण किए हुए थे।[18] वन के भ्रमरों ने उनके सुगन्धिपूर्ण अङ्गरागों से मुग्ध होकर उन सुराङ्गनाओं की दुर्बल भुजलताओं का सेवन किया जिसमें अलक्तक के लेप से अरुण वर्ण के पल्लव के समान हथेलियाँ थीं और जिनके नखों से किरणें मञ्जरी की तरह निकल रही थीं।[19] भ्रमरपङ्क्ति से डरी हुई किसी अप्सरा को लक्ष्य कर किसी ने कहा—'मानिनि! नूतन-पल्लव-सदृश अपने हाथों के इतस्ततः सञ्चालन से व्यर्थ कष्ट मत उठाओ। यह भ्रमर-पङ्क्ति तो कल्पलताओं के भ्रम से तुम्हारे पास आई है। तुम क्यों डरती हो?[20] कहीं कोई चतुर सखी अपनी मानवती सखी को चतुरतापूर्वक सीख दे रही थी।[21] वन-विहार में अनुरक्त अप्सराओं की मनःस्थिति का कवि ने सुन्दर चित्रण किया है। इन्द्रकील की अधित्यका पर वृक्षों पर सुन्दर-सुन्दर फूल खिले हुए थे। सुराङ्गनाएँ वृक्षों के सुन्दर पुष्पों पर मोहित हो गई थीं। उनके हाथों के लिए वे पुष्प सुलभ थे। किन्तु वे तो उन पुष्पों का स्वयं चयन न कर परिचर्याभिलाषी प्रिय सहचरों के द्वारा चुने हुए पुष्पों को ही ग्रहण करती थीं।[22] मानिनी नायिका का अत्यन्त सरस एवं भावपूर्ण चित्र प्राप्त होता है। किसी गन्धर्व ने किसी अप्सरा को भ्रमवश उसकी सपत्नी के नाम से तार-स्वर में सम्बोधित कर पुष्पों का गुच्छा प्रदान किया। इस पर उस मानिनी ने कुछ नहीं कहा। वह आँखों में आंसू भरकर केवल पैर से भूमि को कुरेदने लगी।[23] कोई अप्सरा

अपने प्रिय के साथ प्रेमालाप में इतनी आसक्त थी कि उसे अपने शरीर और कार्य की भी सुध नहीं रही।[24] किसी अन्य अमराङ्गना ने, नितम्ब-भार से जिसकी नीवी ढीली पड़ गई थी, जिसके स्तन विवस्त्र होकर वक्षःस्थल की शोभा बढ़ा रहे थे और जिसके कृश उदर पर त्रिवली के न रहने से रोमराजि स्पष्ट दिखलाई दे रही थी, अपने प्रियतम के मन को फूल ग्रहण करने के बहाने आकृष्ट कर लिया। उसने पीठ पर कटिपर्यन्त लटकते हुए घुंघराले केशों से तथा अपने बाहु-मूल को दिखाकर भी प्रियतम के मन को आकृष्ट कर लिया।[25] अप्सराओं की शरीर-शोभा को उत्प्रेक्षा द्वारा प्रकट करता हुआ कवि कहता है कि सुराङ्गनाओं के कर-किसलय नए-नए पल्लवों के तोड़ने से रङ्गकर अरुण वर्ण के हो गए थे। पुष्पों के पराग से उनके स्थूल पयोधर पाण्डु-वर्ण के दिखलायी पड़ रहे थे। उनको देखकर ऐसा प्रतीत होता था कि शरीर के गुणों की उत्कृष्टता मानो उन्हें वृक्षों से ही प्राप्त हुई थी।[26] वन-विहार के समय सुराङ्गनाओं के नेत्र और मुख स्वेद से व्याप्त होकर उन कमलों की कान्ति की समानता करते थे जिनकी पंखुड़ियाँ कलियों में सम्पुटित थीं और जिनको नीहारकण चारों ओर से विभूषित कर रहे थे।[27] इन्द्रकील पर्वत के शिखरों के वन-पथ पर विचरण करती हुई सुर-ललनाओं की गति थक जाने से मन्द पड़ गई थी। उनके श्रान्त-क्लान्त अङ्गों को देखकर गन्धर्वगण इतने मुग्ध हो गए, जैसे उन्होंने उन्हें प्रथम बार ही देखा हो। अतः उन अङ्गों को देखने की उत्कट अभिलाषा ने गन्धर्वों पर अपना अधिकार जमा लिया।[28]

सन्दर्भ-सङ्केत

1. किरातार्जुनीय - 4.1-4, 6
2. किरातार्जुनीय— विनम्रशालिप्रसवौघशालिनीरपेतपङ्काः ससरोरुहाम्भसः।
   ननन्द पश्यन्नुपसीम स स्थलीरुपायनीभूतशरद्गुणश्रियः।। 4. 2
3. किरातार्जुनीय— निरीक्ष्यमाणा इव विस्मयाकुलैः पयोभिरुन्मीलितपद्मलोचनैः।
   हतप्रियादृष्टिविलासविभ्रमा मनोऽस्य जह्रुः शफरीविवृत्तयः।।
   नुनोद तस्य स्थलपद्मिनीगतं वितर्कमाविष्कृतफेनसन्तति।
   अवाप्तकिञ्जल्कविभेदमुच्चकैर्विवृत्तपाठीनपराहतं पथः।। 4 .3, 5
4. किरातार्जुनीय - 4.5
5. किरातार्जुनीय— मनोरमं प्रापितमन्तरं भ्रुवोरलङ्कृतं केसररेणुनाऽणुना।
   अलक्तताम्राधरपल्लवश्रिया समानयन्तीमिव बन्धुजीवकम्।।
   नवातपालोहितमाहितं मुहुर्महानिवेशौ परितः पयोधरौ।
   चकासयन्तीमरविन्दजं रजः परिश्रमाम्भःपुलेकन सर्पता।।
   कपोलसंश्लेषि विलोचनत्विषा विभूषयन्तीमवंतसकोत्पलम्।
   सुतेन पाण्डोः कलमस्य गोपिकां निरीक्ष्य मेने शरदः कृतार्थता।। 4. 7-9
6. किरातार्जुनीय— विहाय वाञ्छामुदिते मदात्ययादरक्तकण्ठस्य रुते शिखण्डिनः।
   श्रुतिः श्रयत्युन्मदहंसनिःस्वनं गुणाः प्रियत्वेऽधिकृता न संस्तवः।। 4. 25
7. किरातार्जुनीय— मृणालिनीनामनुरञ्जितं त्विषा विभिन्नमम्भोजपलाशशोभया।
   पयः स्फुरच्छालिशिखापिशङ्गितं द्रुतं धनुष्खण्डमिवाहिविद्विषः।। 4. 27
8. किरातार्जुनीय— सपदि हरिसखैर्वधूनिदेशाद् ध्वनितमनोरमवल्लकीमृदङ्गैः।
   युगपदृतुगणस्य संनिधानं वियति वने च यथायथं वितेने।। 10.18
9. किरातार्जुनीय - 10.19. 23
   परिसुरपतिसूनुधाम सद्यः समुपदधन्मुकुलानि मालतीनाम्।
   विरलमपजहार बद्धबिन्दुः सरजसतामवनेरपां निपातः।।
   व्यथितमपि भृशं मनो हरन्ती परिणतजम्बुफलोपभोगहृष्टा।
   परभृतयुवतिः स्वनं वितेने नवनवयोजितकण्ठरागरम्यम्।।
   अभिभवति मनः कदम्बवायौ मदमधुरे च शिखण्डिनां निनादे।
   जन इव न धृतेश्चचाल जिष्णुर्न हि महतां सुकरः समाधिभङ्गः।। 10. 20, 22, 23

10. किरातार्जुनीय— धृतबिसवलयावलिर्वहन्ती कुमुदवनैकदुकूलमात्तबाणा।
शरदमलतले सरोजपाणौ घनसमयेन वधूरिवावलम्बे।। 10.24

11. किरातार्जुनीय— सरजसमपहाय केतकीनां प्रसवमुपान्तिकनीपरेणुकीर्णम्।
प्रियमधुरसनानि षट्पदाली मलिनयति स्म विनीलबन्धनानि।। 10.26

12. किरातार्जुनीय— अविरलफलिनीवनप्रसूनः कुसुमितकुन्दसुगन्धिगन्धवाहः।
गुणमसमयजं चिराय लेभे विरलतुषारकणस्तुषारकालः।।
निचयिनि लवलीलताविकासे जनयति लोध्रसमीरणे च हर्षम्।
विकृतिमुपययौ न पाण्डुसूनुश्चलति नयान्न जिगीषतां हि चेतः।। 10.28, 29

13. किरातार्जुनीय— कतिपयसहकारपुष्परम्यस्तनुतुहिनोऽल्पविनिद्रसिन्दुवारः ।
सुरभिमुखहिमागमान्तशंसी समुपययौ शिशिरः स्मरैकबन्धुः।।

14. किरातार्जुनीय— कुसुमनगवनान्युपैतुकामा किसलयिनीमलवम्ब्य चूतयष्टिम्।
क्वणदलिकुलनूपुरा निरासे नलिनवनेषु पदं वसन्तलक्ष्मीः।। 10.31

15. किरातार्जुनीय— श्वसनचलितपल्लवाधरोष्ठे नवनिहितेर्ष्यमिवावधूनयन्ती।
मधुसुरभिणि षट्पदेन पुष्पे मुख इव शाललतावधूश्चुचुम्बे।।10.34

16. किरातार्जुनीय— कथमिव तव संमतिर्भवित्री सममृतुभिर्मुनिनावधीरितस्य।
इति विरचितमल्लिकाविकासः स्मयत इव स्म मधुं निदाघकालः।। 10.36

17. किरातार्जुनीय— यथायथं ताः सहिता नभश्चरैः प्रभाभिरुद्भासितशैलवीरुधः।
वनं विशन्त्यो वनजायतेक्षणाः क्षणद्युतीनां दधुरेकरूपताम्।। 8.2

18. किरातार्जुनीय— घनानि कामं कुसुमानि बिभ्रतः करप्रचेयान्यपहाय शाखिनः।
पुरोऽभिसस्रे सुरसुन्दरीजनैर्यथोत्तरेच्छा हि गुणेषु कामिनः।। 8.4

19. किरातार्जुनीय— तनूरलक्तारुणपाणिपल्लवाः स्फुरन्नखांशूत्करमञ्जरीभृतः।
विलासिनीबाहुलता वनालयो विलेपनामोदहृताः सिषेविरे।। 8.5

20. किरातार्जुनीय— करौ धुनाना नवपल्लवाकृती वृथा कृथा मानिनि मा परिश्रमम्।
उपेयुषी कल्पलताभिशङ्कया कथं न्वितस्त्रस्यति षट्पदावलिः।। 8.7

21. किरातार्जुनीय— जहीहि कोपं दयितोऽनुगम्यतां पुराऽनुशेते तव चञ्चलं मनः।
इति प्रियं काञ्चिदुपैतुमिच्छतीं पुराऽनुनिन्ये निपुणः सखीजनः।। 8.8

22. किरातार्जुनीय स्वगोचरे सत्यपि चित्तहारिणा विलोभ्यमाना प्रसवेन शाखिनाम्।
नभश्चराणामुपकर्तुमिच्छतां प्रियाणि चक्रुः प्रणयेन योषितः।। 8.13

23. किरातार्जुनीय— प्रयच्छतोच्चैः कुसुमानि मानिनी विपक्षगोत्रं दयितेन लम्भिता।
न किञ्चिदूचे चरणेन केवलं लिलेख बाष्पाकुललोचना भुवम्।। 8.14

24. किरातार्जुनीय - 8.15

25. किरातार्जुनीय - 8.17-18

26. किरातार्जुनीय - 8.21

27. किरातार्जुनीय - 8.25

28. किरातार्जुनीय - 8.26

卐 卐 卐

माघकाव्य में ऋतुवर्णन एवं वनविहारवर्णन

सुषमा कुलश्रेष्ठ

ऋतुवर्णन

शिशुपालवध के षष्ठ सर्ग में छः ऋतुओं का पहले विस्तार से तथा अन्त में संक्षेप में वर्णन किया गया है। यह वर्णन उद्दीपन रूप में हुआ है। विभिन्न ऋतुओं में भिन्न-भिन्न पुष्पों के विकसित होने आदि के वर्णन के साथ विभिन्न नायक-नायिकाओं की तरह-तरह की क्रीडाओं का भी वर्णन हुआ है। किरातार्जुनीय में शरद् ऋतु से और शिशुपालवध में वसन्त ऋतु से इस वर्णन का आरम्भ किया गया है। किरातार्जुनीय में भी सब ऋतुएँ एक साथ प्रादुर्भूत हुईं। शिशुपालवध में भी श्रीकृष्ण की सेवा करने के लिए सब ऋतुओं ने एक साथ अपने चिह्न प्रकट कर दिए।[1] सब ऋतुएँ किस प्रकार एक साथ प्रादुर्भूत हुईं— इसका भारवि ने अतिसुन्दर कारण दिया है।[2] भारवि के अनुकर्ता माघ यहाँ कोई कारण सुझाना सम्भवतः भूल गए।

वसन्त ऋतु में मृग-नयनियों के ललाट में उत्पन्न श्रम-कणों को सुखाते हुए उनके केश-कलाप को हिलाने वाला, नील-कमलों से युक्त जलाशयों की तरङ्ग-श्रेणि को चपल करता हुआ मलय-पवन बहने लगा।[3] अनेक नूतन-कल्पना-समन्वित वर्णन करने में चतुर माघ ने कहीं-कहीं वर्णन को जुगुप्सा-मय भी बना दिया है— 'शुद्ध सुवर्ण की कान्ति वाले (पीले-पीले) चम्पा पुष्पों से युक्त अशोक का पुष्प विरहियों के विदीर्ण हुए हृदय के, कामाग्नि से कपिशवर्ण किए गए मांस के समान शोभित होता था।'[4] आम्र-वन के पराग मानो कामाग्नि के मुर्मुर-चूर्ण बन गए और सब ओर से ऊपर गिरे हुए वे पथिकों को सन्तप्त करने लगे।[5] पूरे ऋतु वर्णन में भ्रमर पङ्क्ति का अनेक बार उल्लेख हुआ है।[6] मधुर-भाषिणी कोकिला के कूजित को सुनकर मानिनियों ने अपना कोप छोड़ दिया।[7] पर्वत के सब वनों को रक्त-वर्ण करती हुई तथा पथिकों को बार-बार सन्तप्त करती हुई विकसित पलाश पुष्पों की श्रेणि ने दावाग्नि की शोभा को प्राप्त किया।[8]

जिस ऋतु में शिरीष-पुष्प के पराग की कान्ति सूर्य के घोड़ों के हरित-वर्ण वाले रोमों की समानता करती है, नव-मल्लिका के सुगन्ध को स्थायी करता हुआ वह ग्रीष्म आ गया।[9] कोमल पाटल कलिकाओं को विकसित करने वाली तथा अपनी अङ्गनाओं के निःश्वास के सदृश वायु के बहते रहने पर विलासी लोग मद से चञ्चल हो उठे।[10]

श्रावण मास में आकाश में मेघों को देखकर सब स्त्रियाँ सम्भोगार्थ इच्छा करने लगीं।[11] कदम्ब पुष्प के पराग से आकाश को अरुण किए हुए, कदली-पुष्प की सुगन्ध से युक्त पवन ने रागियों के मन में स्त्री-विषयक नूतन राग उत्पन्न किया।[12] मेघों ने थोड़ा ही जल बरसाकर रैवतक को यादव-नृपतियों तथा उनकी रमणियों के आनन्दपूर्वक विहार के योग्य बना दिया।[13] वर्षा ऋतु में मयूर नृत्य करने लगे।[14] इस ऋतु में केतकी, कुटज तथा मालती-पुष्प के विकसित होने का सुन्दर वर्णन किया गया है।[15]

शरद् ऋतु में हंसों के शब्द ने मधुरता को तथा मयूर-रुत ने कर्कशता को प्राप्त किया।[16] हंस-ध्वनि से पराजित ध्वनि वाले मयूरों के पङ्ख मानों ईर्ष्या या क्रोध से झड़ गए।[17] सर्वत्र बाण, जपा तथा सप्तपर्ण पुष्प विकसित होने लगे।[18] आश्विन मास में गोप-वधुएँ धान की रखवाली कर रही थीं और मृग उनके सङ्गीत श्रवण में व्यापृत थे— इस भाव पर कवि की सरस कल्पना देखें— गोप-बधुओं ने उच्च स्वर से गाए गए (उनके) मधुर-गान को सुनते हुए (अतएव) धान खाने

की इच्छा नहीं करने वाले मृगों को नहीं भगाया।[19] मृगों की सङ्गीत-प्रियता लोक-प्रसिद्ध है।

संस्कृत-कवियों ने छः ऋतुओं का वर्णन किया है, "फिर भी कवियों की वृत्ति किसी ऋतु के वर्णन में अधिक रमी है और किसी में कम। वर्षा, शरद् और वसन्त में कवि-वाणी अधिक निमग्न हुई। शिशिर, हेमन्त और निदाघ के वर्णन यदि क्रमानुसार आ भी गए हैं तो उन्हें यों ही चलता कर दिया गया है। हाँ, महाकाव्यों से पृथक् स्वतन्त्र कवियों की उक्तियाँ यत्र-तत्र अवश्य बिखरी हुई हैं। इसका कारण है, किसी भाषा का कवि जीवन की मङ्गलमयी स्थिति का स्पर्श ही प्रायः करता है। शिशिर एवं हेमन्त ऋतुएँ ठहरीं जगत् को जड़ीभूत कर देने वाली। फिर भी वे हमारे कवियों की कल्पनाओं को जड़ न बना सकीं।"[20]

माघ ने भी ग्रीष्म, हेमन्त और शिशिर— ऋतुओं का अपेक्षाकृत संक्षेप में वर्णन किया है। हस्ति-परिमाण वाली नदियों को भी हिम-मय करती हुई हेमन्त की वायु ने पथिकों की स्त्रियों के नेत्रों के अतिशय-संताप-कारक जल-प्रवाह को बढ़ा दिया।[21] इस ऋतु में कामिनियों में स्वेद होता था।[22]

प्रियङ्गु-लताओं को विकसित करता हुआ, मद-कारक भ्रमरियों के ध्वनिरूप हुङ्कारों से युक्त शिशिर ऋतु का पवन विरहिणी युवतियों को कामपीड़ित करने लगा।[23] लवङ्ग तथा कुन्द पुष्प विकसित होने लगे।।[24]

"संस्कृत कवियों ने शिशिर ऋतु के शीत का वर्णन बहुत अधिक किया है और उसके निवारण के उपायों पर भी पर्याप्त चर्चा की है। ऐसे स्थल कहीं न कहीं ऐसी कल्पनाओं से युक्त अवश्य हैं जो आज शिष्ट समाज में अश्लील मानी जाती हैं। यद्यपि ये कल्पनाएँ अनेक स्थानों पर उक्ति-चातुर्य को लिए हुई हैं, फिर भी इनका अधिकांश स्थूल-वासना-प्रधान है।"[25]

वनविहारवर्णन

यादव-जनों तथा यादव-रमणियों के वन-विहार का अतिविस्तृत वर्णन किया गया है। यादव-जनों ने अनेकविध पुष्पों से युक्त वनों में स्त्रियों के साथ जाने की इच्छा की, अन्यथा वे कामदेव के महान् अस्त्रभूत केवल पाँच बाणों को भी सहन करने में समर्थ नहीं थे।[26] 'प्रियों के साथ जाने का शोभन अवसर पाकर रमणियाँ भी पैदल चल पड़ीं और अनेक प्रकार के विलास प्रारम्भ हो गए।'[27] इस प्रसङ्ग में अनेक नायिकाओं की विविध चेष्टाओं का भी सुन्दर वर्णन हुआ है। किसी खण्डिता नायिका को उसकी सखी बड़ी चतुरता से मनाती हुई कहती है—'सखि! यदि मैं तुमको पति के पास नहीं पहुँचा सकी, तो मैं तुमसे बोलना भी छोड़ दूँगी, ऐसा मेरा निश्चय है। इस अवस्था में हम दोनों का विरोध होने पर तुम्हारे शत्रुओं (सपत्नियों) का मनोरथ सफल हो जाएगा (अर्थात् तुम्हारी सपत्नियाँ चाहती ही थीं कि इन दोनों सखियों में विरोध होकर परस्पर सम्भाषण न हो और वह बात भी हो जाएगी)।[28] रमणियों के विविध प्रकार के गमन का भी विस्तृत वर्णन हुआ है।[29] यादवाङ्गनाओं ने, नदियों के पास लोगों के मनोरूप लक्ष्य को वेधने में समर्थ काम-धनुष की टङ्कार का सन्देह उत्पन्न करते हुए सारस पक्षियों की कर्ण-प्रिय ध्वनि को सुना। वन-पवन ने अर्द्धविकसित कलियों से क्षुब्ध भ्रमरों से गिरे हुए विकसित केसरों वाले वृक्षों के पराग को यादव-स्त्रियों के लिए भेंटस्वरूप देते हुए कलियों को विकसित कर दिया।[31] रमणियों की पुष्पावचय-क्रीडा का भी कवि ने सुन्दर दृश्य प्रस्तुत किया है।[32] तोड़े गए नवपल्लव के म्लान होने तथा तरुण विट के तिरस्कृत होकर खिन्न होने का माघ ने सरस वर्णन किया है—'निरन्तर बहते हुए रस वाला। (पक्षान्तर में अविच्छिन्न शृङ्गाररस वाला), राग (लालिमा, पक्षान्तर में अनुराग) से युक्त, नखक्षत से परिचित अर्थात् नाखून से तोड़ा गया (पक्षान्तर में रतिकाल में किए गए नखक्षत वाला), वधू के द्वारा निर्दयतापूर्वक तोड़ा गया (पक्षान्तर में तिरस्कृत किया गया), नवपल्लव (पक्षान्तर में तरुण विट) तत्काल मलिन हो गया (पक्षान्तर में खिन्न हो गया)।[33] सपत्नियों की भी बार-बार चर्चा हुई है।[34] सपत्नी का नाम लेना अङ्गनाओं के लिए मानो अभिचार-मन्त्र ही है क्योंकि इस नाम से बुलाकर कोमल फूल से आहत भी सुतनु मूर्छित हो गई।[35] अन्त में रमणियों के वन-विहार-जन्य श्रम का वर्णन किया गया है।[36]

सन्दर्भ-सङ्केत

1. शिशुपालवध— अथ रिरंसुममुं युगपद्गिरौ कृतयथास्वतरुप्रसवश्रिया।
ऋतुगणेन निषेवितुमादधे भुवि पदं विपदन्तकृतं सताम्।। 6.1
2. किरातार्जुनीय— सपदि हरिसखैर्वधूनिदेशाद् ध्वनितमनोरमवल्लकीमृदङ्गैः।
युगपदृतुगणस्य संनिधानं वियति वने च यथायथं वितेने।। 10.18
3. शिशुपालवध— विलुलितालकसंहतिरामृशन्मृगदृशां श्रमवारि ललाटजम्।
तनुतरङ्गततिं सरसां दलत्कुवलयं वलयन्मरुदाववौ।। 6.3
4. शिशुपालवध— स्फुटमिवोज्ज्वलकाञ्चनकान्तिभिर्युतमशोकमशोभत चम्पकैः।
विरहिणां हृदयस्य भिदाभृतः कपिशितं पिशितं मदनाग्निना।। 6.5
5. शिशुपालवध— स्मरहुताशनमुर्मुरचूर्णतां दधुरिवाम्रवणस्य रजःकणाः।
निपतिताः परितः पथिकव्रजानुपरि ते परितेपुरतो भृशम्।। 6.6
6. शिशुपालवध— रतिपतिप्रहितेव कृतक्रुधः प्रियतमेषु वधूरनुनायिका।
बकुलपुष्परसासवपेशलध्वनिरगान्निरगान्मधुपावलिः ।।
मधुरया मधुबोधितमाधवीमधुसमृद्धिसमेधितमेधया।
मधुकराङ्गनया मुहुरुन्मदध्वनिभृता निभृताक्षरमुज्जगे।। 6.7,20
7. शिशुपालवध— प्रियसखीसदृशं प्रतिबोधिताः किमपि काम्यगिरा परपुष्टया।
प्रियतमाय वपुर्गुरुमत्सरच्छिदुरयाऽदुरयाचितमङ्गनाः।। 6.8
8. शिशुपालवध— अरुणिताखिलशैलवना मुहुर्विदधती पथिकान् परितापिनः।
विकचकिंशुकसंहतिरुच्चकैरुदवहद्दवहव्यवहश्रियम् ।। 6.21
9. शिशुपालवध— रवितुरङ्गतनूरुहतुल्यतां दधति यत्र शिरीषरजोरुचः।
उपययौ विदधन्नवमल्लिकाः शुचिरसौ चिरसौरभसम्पदः।। 6.22
10. शिशुपालवध— दलितकोमलपाटलकुड्मले निजवधूश्वसितानुविधायिनि।
मरुति वाति विलासिभिरुन्मदभ्रमदलौ मदलौल्यमुपाददे।। 6.23
11. शिशुपालवध— गजकदम्बकमेचकमुच्चकैर्नभसि वीक्ष्य नवाम्बुदमम्बरे।
अभिससार न वल्लभमङ्गना न चकमे च कमेकरसं रहः।। 6.26
12. शिशुपालवध— नवकदम्बरजोरुणिताम्बरैरधिपुरन्ध्रि शिलीन्ध्रसुगन्धिभिः।
मनसि रागवतामनुरागिता नवनवा वनवायुभिरादधे।। 6.32
13. शिशुपालवध— शमिततापमपोढमहीरजः प्रथमबिन्दुभिरम्बुमुचोऽम्भसाम्।
प्रविरलैरचलाङ्गनमङ्गनाजनसुगं न सुगन्धि न चक्रिरे।। 6.33
14. शिशुपालवध— जलदपंक्तिरनर्तयदुन्मदं कलविलापि कलापिकदम्बकम्।
कृतसमार्जनमर्दलमण्डलध्वनिजया निजया स्वनसम्पदा।। 6.31
15. शिशुपालवध— द्विरददन्तवलक्षमलक्ष्यत स्फुरितभृङ्गमृगच्छवि केतकम्।
घनघनौघविघट्टनया दिवः कृतशिखं शशिखण्डमिव च्युतम्।।
दलितमौक्तिकचूर्णविपाण्डवः स्फुरितनिर्झरशीकरचारवः।
कुटजपुष्पपरागकणाः स्फुटं विदधिरे दधिरेणुविडम्बनाम्।।
नवपयःकणकोमलमालतीकुसुमसंततिसंततसङ्गिभिः ।
प्रचलितोडुनिभैः परिपाण्डिमा शुभरजोभरजोऽलिभिराददे।। 6.34, 35, 36
16. शिशुपालवध— समय एव करोति बलाबलं प्रणिगदन्त इतीव शरीरिणाम्।
शरदि हंसरवाः परुषीकृतस्वरमयूरमयू रमणीयताम्।। 6.44
17. शिशुपालवध— तनुरुहाणि पुरो विजितध्वनेर्धवलपक्षविहंगमकूजितैः।
जगलुरक्षमयेव शिखण्डिनः परिभवोऽरिभवो हि सुदुःसहः।। 6.45

18. शिशुपालवध— अनुवनं वनराजिवधूमुखे बहलरागजवाधरचारुणि।
विकचबाणदलावलयोऽधिकं रुरुचिरे रुचिरेक्षणविभ्रमाः।।
कृतमदं निगदन्त इवाकुलीकृतजगत्त्रयमूर्जमतङ्गजम्।
ववुरयुक्छदगुच्छसुगन्धयः सततगास्ततगानगिरोऽलिभिः।। 6. 46, 50
19. शिशुपालवध— विगतसस्यजिघत्समघट्टयत्कलमगोपवधूर्न मृगव्रजम्।
श्रुततदीरितकोमलगीतकध्वनिमिषेऽनिमिषेक्षणमग्रतः।। 6. 49
20. डॉ. प्रभुदयालु अग्निहोत्री - 'संस्कृत साहित्य में ऋतुवर्णन - हेमन्त', अजन्ता, दिसम्बर, 1950 ई. पृ. 5-6
21. शिशुपालवध— 6. 55
22. शिशुपालवध— 6. 61
23. शिशुपालवध— कुसुमयन्फलिनीरलिनीरवैर्मदविकासिभिराहितहुंकृतिः ।
उपवनं निरभर्त्सयत प्रियान्वियुवतीर्युवतीः शिशिरानिलः।। 6. 62
24. शिशुपालवध— अधिलवङ्गममी रजसाधिकं मलिनिताः सुमनोदलतालिनः।
स्फुटमिति प्रसवेन पुरोऽहसत्सपदि कुन्दलता दलतालिनः।। 6. 66
25. डॉ. प्रभुदयालु अग्निहोत्री - 'संस्कृत साहित्य में शिशिरवर्णन' - साप्ताहिक परिवर्तन, पृ. 20
26. शिशुपालवध— दधति सुमनसो वनानि बह्वीर्युवतियुता यदवः प्रयातुमीषुः।
मनसिशयमहास्त्रमन्यथामी न कुसुमपञ्चकमप्यलं विसोढुम्।। 7. 2
27. शिशुपालवध— 7. 3-6
28. शिशुपालवध— 7. 9
29. शिशुपालवध— 7. 12-22
30. शिशुपालवध— 7. 24
31. शिशुपालवध— असकलकलिकाकुलीकृतालिस्खलनविकीर्णविकासिकेशराणाम्।
मरुदवनिरुहां रजो वधूभ्यः समुपहरन् विचकार कोरकाणि।। 7. 26
32. शिशुपालवध— 7. 31-38, 49
33. शिशुपालवध— अनवरतरसेन रागभाजा करजपरिक्षतिलब्धसंस्तवेन।
सपदि तरुणपल्लवेन वध्वा विगतदयं खलु खण्डितेन मम्ले।। 7. 31
34. शिशुपालवध— 7. 53, 57, 58, 59
35. शिशुपालवध— स्फुटमिदमभिचारमन्त्र एव प्रतियुवतेरभिधानमङ्गनानाम्।
वरतनुरमुनोपहूय पत्या मृदुकुसुमेन यदाहताप्यमूर्च्छत्।। 7. 58
36. शिशुपालवध— 7. 62-75

卐 卐 卐

नैषधीयचरित में उपवनवर्णन*

चण्डिकाप्रसाद शुक्ल

दमयन्ती के प्रति पूर्वराग-व्यथित नल मन बहलाने के लिए उपवन में जाते हैं। राजोद्यान होने के कारण उपवन हर प्रकार से सम्पन्न दिखाया गया है। आचार्यों ने उद्यान-वर्णन में कुछ वस्तुओं की सूची निर्धारित की है।[1] श्रीहर्ष ने उनका वर्णन यथास्थान किया है, पर इस ढंग से कि वह 'शास्त्र-प्रदर्शन' मात्र नहीं लगता। उन वस्तुओं का वर्णन किसी विशेष सौन्दर्य को बढ़ाने के प्रसंग में हुआ है, अनायास नहीं। कवि उद्यान की प्रत्येक वस्तु को प्रिया-वियुक्त अनुरागी की आँखों से देखता है। सुन्दर फूल फल सभी क्लेश को बढ़ाते ही हैं, घटाते नहीं। आलम्बनों (पुष्प, फल आदि) का चित्रण करते समय कवि ने आश्रय (राजा) के अनुभावों को भी दिखाना चाहा है। ऐसा न होता तो भी पाठक या श्रोता को भावग्रहण में कठिनाई न पड़ती। केतकी को देखकर नल मन-ही-मन झुँझला कर उससे कहते हैं, 'कामदेव अपने पुष्पमय धनुष के मधु से गीले हाथ में तुम्हारे पराग की धूलि लगा कर मुझे अपने बाणों का लक्ष्य बनाता है।'[2]

नल के वियोगी हृदय की प्रतिक्रियाओं का कवि को इतना अधिक ध्यान है कि उसने कहीं-कहीं अतिरम्य फूल-फल का चित्रण अत्यन्त जुगुप्सामय कर दिया है। उदाहरणार्थ-नल ने कामदेव के अर्द्धचन्द्राकार बाणों के समान, वियोगियों के हृदय को विदारने वाले तथा दुर्बल पथिकों का मांस भक्षण करने के कारण (पल अश्) यथार्थ नामवाले पलाश वृक्ष में फूलों का गुच्छा देखा।[3] मानो वह (वियोगियों के हृदय में सम्बद्ध) कालखण्ड (नामक उस काले मांस) से निकला हो (जो दाहिने पार्श्व में रहता है)।

इस उपवन वर्णन में समासोक्ति तथा उत्प्रेक्षा का पूरा प्रयोग हुआ है। 'वायु द्वारा चुम्बित, परागकणों के रूप में रोमाञ्चित, स्मित विकसित कलिकाओं से सुशोभित ईषत्-कम्पित अभिनव लताओं' को नल भय तथा आदर के साथ अपनी आँखों से पी रहे थे।[4] इसी प्रसङ्ग में श्रीहर्ष ने पथिकों का भी उल्लेख किया है। नल को वे चम्पा-कलिकाएँ मदन की बलि-दीप-शिखा ही समझ पड़ीं, जो भ्रमर-रूप (दीपशिखा की) कालिख के बहाने मानो पथिक-पतङ्गों के वध रूप पाप कर्मों का अर्जन कर रही थीं।[5] राजोद्यान में पथिकों की चर्चा कवि-परम्परा-भुक्त ही मानी जायगी। चम्पा पर भ्रमर का बैठना भी एक विशेष परम्परा की प्रेरणा है। उपवन में कोकिल की कूक और भ्रमर की गुंजार भी सुनायी पड़ती है, पर अत्यन्त मधुर कल्पना के परिधान में समावृत। कोकिल अपनी कूक में मानो वियोगियों की करुण कथा कह रहा था और वन उस कोकिल से भ्रमरों की गुंजार-रूप हुंकारों द्वारा उसे सुन-रहा था, तथा करुण-पुष्प करुणरस के समान विकास पा रहे थे।[6] कवि के सूक्ष्म निरीक्षण का एक सुन्दर उदाहरण देखिए, ''नाग-केसर के पुष्प पर भ्रमरों की पङ्क्तियाँ आ-आ कर बैठती थीं तथा उनके भ्रमण की गति से पुष्पों के पराग गिरते थे। नल को ऐसा प्रतीत हुआ, मानो तेजी से चलते हुए श्याम निकष पर मदन-बाण तीक्ष्ण किया जा रहा है, उसके घर्षण से परागरूपी चिनगारियाँ[7] निकल रही हैं। श्लोक का पूर्वार्द्ध प्रस्तुत को बड़ी सूक्ष्मता के साथ वर्णित करता है, उत्तरार्द्ध में कवि ने अप्रस्तुत की योजना नल की दृष्टि से की है। समस्त उद्यानवर्णन में इसी प्रकार प्रस्तुत वस्तु की झाँकी भर मिलती है। तब तक कवि की कल्पना का ऐसा भारी आवरण पड़ जाता है कि पाठक प्रस्तुत को प्रायः भूल ही जाता है। बार-बार पाठक का ध्यान प्रस्तुत से हटा कर दूसरी वस्तुओं की ओर ले जाना कभी-कभी अच्छा नहीं समझ पड़ता। अप्रस्तुत की योजना वस्तु का भावपूर्ण समग्र चित्र उपस्थित करने के लिए की जाती है। बार-बार कामदेव के बाणों तथा पौराणिक कथानकों

की याद मन को उबा देती है। उपवन में वाराङ्गना-कुचोपम पके बिल्व-फल, मदन-तूणीर-सदृश पाटल पुष्प, इन्दुकलानुकारी अगस्त्य पुष्प, मदनशस्त्र-सदृश रक्त पत्तोंवाले अशोक आदि का चमत्कारपूर्ण वर्णन हुआ है। कहीं-कहीं वर्णन अत्यन्त सरस भी हो गया है। वन-पवन का वर्णन करते हुए श्रीहर्ष कहते हैं-'लता-रमणी का नृत्य-कला गुरु, पुष्पसौरभ का चोर, कुसुम-मकरन्द से सुवासित जल में सलील तैरनेवाला वन-पवन नल की सेवा कर रहा था'। पवन के शैत्य, मान्द्य, सौगन्ध्य तीनों गुणों को कवि ने किस निपुणता से व्यञ्जना द्वारा कह दिया है?

इसी उपवन में सरोवर का भी वर्णन है। श्रीहर्ष ने उसे सागर के समान बताया है।[9] उत्प्रेक्षा, रूपक, अपह्नुति आदि के द्वारा सरोवर की प्रत्येक विशेषता सागर की किसी-न-किसी विशेषता से मिलती है। सरोवर के कमलनाल जल-निलीन ऐरावतों के दाँत हैं, जो शेषनाग की पूँछ के समान छविवाले हैं।[10] श्वेत कमल चन्द्रमा है[11] शैवाल वडवाग्नि की धूमराशि है, आदि।[12]

सन्दर्भ- सङ्केत

* सौजन्य : प्रो. चण्डिकाप्रसाद शुक्ल-प्रणीत 'नैषध-परिशीलन' से साभार गृहीत।

1. उद्याने सरणिः सर्वफलपुष्पलताद्रुमाः।
पिकालिकेकिहंसाद्याः क्रीडावाप्यध्वगस्थितिः ।। काव्य-कल्पलता-वृत्तिः 1.5.68

2. धनुर्मधुस्विन्नकरोऽपि भीमजापरं परागैस्तव धूलिहस्तयन्।
प्रसूनधन्वा शरसात्करोति मामिति क्रुधाक्रुश्यत तेन केतकम्।। नैषधीयचरितम् - 1.81

3. स्मरार्धचन्द्रेषुनिभे क्रशीयसां स्फुटं पलाशेऽध्वजुषां पलाशनात्।
स वृन्तमालोकत खण्डमन्वितं वियोगिहृत्खण्डिनि कालखण्डजम्।। नैषधीयचरितम् - 1.84

4. नवा लता गन्धवहेन चुम्बिता करम्बिताङ्गी मकरन्दशीकरैः।
दृशा नृपेण स्मितशोभिकुड्मला दरादराभ्यां दरकम्पिनी पपे।। नैषधीयचरितम् - 1.85

5. विचिन्वतीः पान्थपतङ्गहिंसनैरपुण्यकर्माण्यलिकज्जलच्छलात्।
व्यलोकयच्चम्पककोरकावलीः स शम्बरारेर्बलिदीपिका इव।। नैषधीयचरितम् - 1.86

6. पिकाद्वने शृण्वति भृङ्गहुङ्कृतैर्दशामुदञ्चत्करुणे वियोगिनाम्।। नैषधीयचरितम् - 1.88

7. गलत्पराग भ्रमिभङ्गिभिः पतत्प्रसक्तभृभृङ्गावलि नागकेसरम्।
स मारनाराचनिधर्षणस्खलज्ज्वलत्कणं शाणमिव व्यलोकयत्।। नैषधीयचरितम् - 1.9

8. लताबलालास्यकलागुरुस्तरुप्रसूनगन्धोत्करपश्यतोहरः ।
असेवतामुं मधुगन्धवारिणि प्रणीतलीलाप्लवनो वनानिलः।। नैषधीयचरितम् - 1.106

9. निलीय तस्तिन्निव सन्नपांनिधिर्वने तडाको ददृशेऽवनीभुजो।। नैषधीयचरितम् - 1.107

10. पयोनिलीनाभ्रमुकाभुकावलीरदाननन्तोरगपुच्छसुच्छवीन् ।
जलार्धरुद्धस्य तदान्तभूमिदो मृणालजालस्य मिषाद्बभार यः।। नैषधीयचरितम् - 1.108

11. सिताम्बुजानां निवहस्य यश्छलात् · · ·
· · · कुलं सुधांशोर्बहलं वहन् बहु।। नैषधीयचरितम् - 1.110

12. चलीकृता यत्र तरङ्गरिङ्गणैरबालशैवाललतापरम्पराः।
ध्रुवं दधुर्वाडवहव्यवाडवस्थितिप्ररोहत्तमभूमधूमताम् ।। नैषधीयचरितम् - 1.114

卐 卐 卐

नैषधीयचरितेऽभिराजितं क्रीडाकाननकामनीयकम्

कमलेश कुमारी कुलश्रेष्ठ

1. नवा लता

(1) नवा लता गन्धवहेन चुम्बिता
करम्बिताङ्गी मकरन्दशीकरैः।
दृशा नृपेण स्मितशोभिकुड्मला
दरादराभ्यां दरकम्पिनी पपे।।[1]

2. स्थलपद्मिनी

(2) पिकाद्वने शृण्वति भृङ्गहुंकृतै-
र्दशामुदञ्चत्करुणे वियोगिनाम्।
अनास्थया सूनकरप्रसारिणीं
ददर्श दूनः स्थलपद्मिनीं नलः।।[2]

3. दाडिमी

(3) विदर्भसुभ्रूस्तनतुङ्गताप्तये
घटानिवापश्यदलं तपस्यतः।
फलानि धूमस्य धयानधोमुखा-
न्स दाडिमे दोहदधूपिनि द्रुमे।।[3]

(4) वियोगिनीमैक्षत दाडिमीमसौ
प्रियस्मृतेः स्पष्टमुदीतकण्टकाम्।
फलस्तनस्थानविदीर्णरागिहृ-
द्विशच्छुकास्यस्मरकिंशुकाशुगाम्।।[4]

4. चम्पककोरकावली

(5) विचिन्वतीः पान्थपतङ्गहिंसनै-
रपुण्यकर्माण्यलिकज्जलच्छलात्।
व्यलोकयच्चम्पककोरकावलीः
स शम्बरारेर्बलिदीपिका इव।।[5]

5. पाटला

(6) युवद्वयीचित्तनिमज्जनोचित-
प्रसूनशून्येतरगर्भगह्वरम् ।
स्मरेषुधीकृत्य धिया भयान्धया
स पाटलायाः स्तबकं प्रकम्पितः।।[6]

6. अगस्त्यवृक्षः

(7) मुनिद्रुमः कोरकितः शितिद्युति-
र्वनेऽमुनाऽमन्यत सिंहिकासुतः।
तमिस्रपक्षत्रुटिकूटभक्षितं
कलाकलापं किल वैधवं वमन्।।[7]

7. रसालः

(8) रसालसालः समदृश्यतामुना
स्फुरद्द्विरेफारवरोषहुंकृतिः ।
समीरलोलैर्मुकुलैर्वियोगिने
जनाय दित्सन्निव तर्जनाभियम्।।[8]

8. नागकेसरः

(9) गलत्परागं भ्रमिभङ्गिभिः पत-
त्प्रसक्तभृङ्गावलि नागकेसरम्।
स मारनारीचनिघर्षणस्खल-
ज्ज्वलत्कणं शाणमिव व्यलोकयत्।।[9]

9. बिल्वफलम्

(10) मरुल्लत्पल्लवकण्टकैः क्षतं
समुच्छलच्चन्दनसारसौरभम् ।
स वारनारीकुचसंचितोपमं
ददर्श मालूरफलं पचेलिमम् ।।[10]

10. अशोकः

(11) अशोकमर्थान्वितनामताशया–
गतान् शरण्यं गृहशोचिनोऽध्वगान् ।
अमन्यतावन्तमिवैष पल्लवैः
प्रतीष्टकामज्ज्वलदस्त्रजालकम् ।।[11]

सन्दर्भ-सङ्केताः

1. नैषधीयचरितम् – 1. 85
2. नैषधीयचरितम् – 1. 88
3. नैषधीयचरितम् – 1. 82
4. नैषधीयचरितम् – 1. 83
5. नैषधीयचरितम् – 1.86
6. नैषधीयचरितम् – 1. 95
7. नैषधीयचरितम् – 1. 96
8. नैषधीयचरितम् – 1. 89
9. नैषधीयचरितम् – 1. 92
10. नैषधीयचरितम् – 1. 94
11. नैषधीयचरितम् – 1. 101

卐 卐 卐

भासविरचित रूपकों में वनस्पतिजगत्

उर्मि भूषण गुप्ता

संस्कृत साहित्य के प्रथम नाटककार भास ने तेरह नाटकों की रचना करके भारतीय नाट्य जगत् को गौरवान्वित किया है। भास अकेले ही नाटककार हैं जिनकी कृतियों को रूपक-प्रकारों के अनुसार-नाटक, नाटिका, वीथी, व्यायोग उत्सृष्टिकाङ्क, समवकार आदि की श्रेणी में रखा जा सकता है।[1]

नाटक प्रकार हैं—स्वप्नवासवदत्तम्, अविमारकम्, प्रतिमा, अभिषेक, बालचरितम्। नाटिका की कोटि में चारुदत्तम्, प्रतिज्ञायौगन्धरायणम् हैं और समवकार की कोटि में पञ्चरात्रम्। इनके अतिरिक्त अन्य प्रकारों में मध्यमव्यायोग-व्यायोग, दूतवाक्यम्-वीथी, ऊरुभङ्गम्-उत्सृष्टिकाङ्क, दूतघटोत्कच तथा कर्णभारम् आदि सभी एकांकी अभिनेयता की दृष्टि से अपने आप में महत्त्वपूर्ण हैं।

प्राचीन संस्कृत नाट्य-परम्परा को मूर्त रूप देने वाले नाटककार भास के विषय में यह उक्ति सर्वविदित ही है :—

सूत्रधारकृतारम्भैर्नाटकैर्बहुभूमिकैः ।
सपताकैर्यशो लेभे भासो देवकुलैरिव।।[2]

संस्कृत नाट्य के सभी तत्त्वों से युक्त भास के इन नाटकों में वनस्पति जगत् का सुन्दर चित्रण हुआ है। विभिन्न प्रसंगों में पेड़, पौधे, लताएँ, पुष्प आदि के उल्लेख हैं जो अपने आप में विशिष्ट हैं और मोटे तौर पर इनके चार-पाँच रूप नाटकों में देखे जा सकते हैं। मुख्यतः वृक्ष, पुष्प, लताएँ आदि प्राकृतिक दृश्यों या ऋतुओं के सूचक रूप में प्रयुक्त हैं। इसके अतिरिक्त कहीं पुष्प या लतामण्डप नायक-नायिकाओं के कार्यकलाप में सहायक बने हुए हैं। अन्य स्थलों पर विभिन्न पुष्प नायिकाओं के नेत्र आदि अङ्ग-उपाङ्गों के सौन्दर्य-सूचन में उपमान का कार्य करते हैं और अलङ्कार के रूप में उनका महत्त्व है। कुछ प्रसंगों में लोक-व्यवहार या नैतिकता सूचित करते हुए पुष्पित-पादपों एवं वृक्षों के सुन्दर उदाहरण प्रस्तुत हुए हैं। इन सभी का विस्तार में परिचय देना उपयुक्त होगा।

भास के विभिन्न नाटकों में जिन पुष्पों का उल्लेख है उनमें बन्धुजीवीकुसुम शेफालिकागुच्छ, काशकुसुम, जपापुष्प, असनकुसुम, कनकचम्पक, पद्मिनी, नीलोत्पल, नलिनी पत्र, कोकनद एवं प्रफुल्लित वन्य कुसुम आदि हैं। इनके अतिरिक्त कई पुष्पित, सुगन्धित वृक्ष एवं पौधे भी प्रसङ्गानुसार सूचित हैं—यथा परुषपलाश, बकुल, सरलसर्जा, अर्जुन, कदम्ब, निचुल, अशोक, चम्पक, न्यग्रोध, शालवृक्ष आदि।

सामान्य रूप में ये पुष्प, लताएँ, वृक्ष प्राकृतिक सौन्दर्य प्रस्फुटित करते हुए उपस्थित वातावरण के मधुर, सौम्य, सुगन्धमय रूप को दर्शाते हैं। कहीं-कहीं ये विशिष्ट ऋतु की सूचना भी देते हैं। जैसे स्वप्नवासवदत्तम् नाटक के चतुर्थ अङ्क में हरसिङ्गार से लदे पौधों का वर्णन और चारों ओर क्यारियों का उनसे भर जाना, प्रमदवन के प्राकृतिक सौन्दर्य एवं शरद् ऋतु की रमणीयता को सूचित करता है। यही कारण है पद्मावती अपनी चेटियों को उन्हें चुनने से मना करती

है। यह कुसुम-समृद्धि सभी के हृदय को आनन्द विभोर करने वाली है अतः वह चाहती है कि उन पुष्पों का सौन्दर्य देर तक चारों ओर विद्यमान रहे।[3]

उन बन्धुजीवी कुसुमों की तुलना कवि कई उपमानों से कर देता है—'प्रवालान्तरितैरिव मौक्तिकालम्बकैराचिताकुसुमैः'[24] या फिर 'अर्धमनःशिलापट्टकैरिवशेफालिकाकुसुमपूरितं मेऽञ्जलिम्'[5] वे मोती के गुच्छों में जड़े प्रवाल की भांति हैं। या फिर अर्धमैनसिल पत्थर के टुकड़े की कल्पना इन पुष्पों के रंग रूप को साकार कर रही है। नाटक के कथानक के अनुसार यह शरद् काल का समय है, जब हरसिङ्गार के फूल अपनी सुगन्धि और शोभा चारों ओर बिखेर देते हैं। ऋतु के अनुसार पुष्पों, वृक्षों का वर्णन प्राकृतिक सौन्दर्य को द्विगुणित कर देता है।

इसी प्रकार अविमारकम् पञ्चम अङ्क में[6] कई पुष्पित-पादपों का नाम आया है। वर्षाकाल में फूलों से लदे पौधे चारों ओर सुगन्धि फैलाते हुए नायिका के विरहोन्माद को बढ़ा रहे हैं। अन्तःपुर-प्रासाद के बकुल, सरलसर्जा, अर्जुन, कदम्ब, नीप, निचुल आदि सुरभित पौधे वर्षा ऋतु के पदार्पण से जुड़े हुए हैं। सामान्यतः ये सभी के हृदय को प्रफुल्लित कर देते हैं परन्तु नायक के बिना नायिका कुरङ्गी के लिए ये दुःखदायी हैं।

प्रतिमानाटक प्रथम अङ्क में अशोक वृक्ष के किसलय के बदले चेटी का वल्कल लाना नाट्य-कथा का महत्वपूर्ण सङ्केत है कि परिहास में लाया हुआ वल्कल राम वनवास और सीता के लिए वास्तव में वल्कल वस्त्र बन जाता है। इसी नाटक में रावण के प्रमदवन की समृद्धि का वर्णन है जो सुरेन्द्र-विहार-भूमि-सदृश है। जहाँ रत्न एवं बहुमूल्य धातुओं से जड़ित कृत्रिम पर्वत है, दीर्घिकायें हैं। पुष्प-फलाढ्य पादप हैं, राक्षसियों से घिरी सीता वहाँ बैठी हुई हैं और हनुमान अशोक पादप पर चढ़कर कोटरान्तरित उनका वृत्तान्त जानना चाहते हैं। यहाँ अन्य संस्कृत नाटकों की भाँति अशोक वसन्त ऋतु या दोहद से जुड़ा हुआ नहीं है बल्कि उसके कारण यह वाटिका अशोक वाटिका के नाम से विख्यात हुई है।

कुछ अन्य प्रसंगों में माधवीलतामण्डप प्रमदवन का महत्त्वपूर्ण भाग बनकर नायक नायिका के नाट्य-व्यापार में बहुत उपयोगी सिद्ध होता है। वह नायक-नायिका के एक दूसरे से छिपने का माध्यम बन जाता है और कभी धूप से बचने या थोड़ी देर विश्राम करने का स्थान भी। स्वप्नवासवदत्तम् में[7] माधवीलतामण्डप यही सब प्रयोजन पूरा करता हुआ इस प्रसंग को बहुत मनोरम बना देता है और नाटकीय कथा की आवश्यकतानुसार उदयन, पद्मावती, वासवदत्ता को एक दूसरे के सामने आने से बचाता है। यहाँ पुष्पों के कारण मधुकरों से लदी हुई लटकती लता को हिलाकर पद्मावती और उसकी सखियाँ राजा को माधवीलतामण्डप में आने से रोक पाती हैं अन्यथा वासवदत्ता के सामने पड़ जाने से यौगन्धरायण की योजना ही पूरी नहीं हो पाती। इसी प्रसङ्ग में काशकुसुम की रेणु आँख में पड़ने को अश्रुपात का कारण बताकर[8] एक ओर वासवदत्ता, दूसरी ओर उदयन अपने धर्मसङ्कट से बच जाते हैं। नलिनीपत्र में लाया हुआ जल राजा के लिए मुखोदक बन जाता है। यह पूरा प्रसङ्ग बहुत ही नाटकीय प्रभाव उत्पन्न करता है।

इस प्रकार पुष्प, लता-वृक्ष आदि भास के नाटकों में महत्वपूर्ण भूमिका निभाते हैं। कुर्चगुल्मलग्नावीणा का नाट्य-कथा की दृष्टि से महत्व है। शाल वृक्ष[9]-न्यग्रोध वृक्ष[10] की छाया में विश्राम करके पात्र अपने अग्रिम कार्य के लिए तैयार हो जाते हैं। न्यग्रोध वृक्ष के देवता उनकी रक्षा भी करते हैं। पञ्चरात्रम् में[11] सूखे पेड़ पर कौवे का विस्वर विलाप एक भिन्न प्रकार का नाट्य बिम्ब है। यहाँ भविष्य में होने वाले अनिष्ट की सूचना दी गई है और वृक्ष के सरस रूप की अपेक्षा नाट्य-कथा की आवश्यकतानुसार कठोर रूप को प्रस्तुत किया गया है।

उपमानों के रूप में पुष्पों का प्रयोग संस्कृत साहित्य की विशिष्टता है इस रूप में भास के नाटकों के कुछ उदाहरण द्रष्टव्य हैं यथा पद्मिनीहिमहतामिव पद्मावती[12]; कनकचम्पकपुष्पगौराः प्रफुल्लकमलोत्पन्नवक्त्रनेत्राः, पङ्कजनेत्रवदनाः,

वन्यकुसुमाकुलकेशहस्ताः गोपाङ्गनाः[13]; जपापुष्पमिव रक्तलोचनः गात्रसेवकः[14], नीलोत्पलदामवर्चसा रावणः[15]; स्फुटितकमलपत्रस्पष्टविस्तीर्णदृष्टी अश्वत्थामा[16]; नीलोत्पलाञ्जननिभा भयदाः श्वपाक्यः।[17]

यहाँ उपमा अलङ्कार के माध्यम से पात्रों के अङ्ग-उपाङ्गों के वर्णन में, विशेष रूप से नेत्रों के सौन्दर्य-निरूपण में नीलोत्पल को कवि ने प्राथमिकता दी है। गोपाङ्गनाओं का गौर वर्ण यदि कनकचम्पक पुष्प जैसा है तो उनके नेत्र और वक्त्र प्रफुल्ल-कमलोत्पल या पङ्कज के समान हैं। अश्वत्थामा स्फुटित पत्र के समान स्पष्ट विस्तीर्ण दृष्टि वाले हैं तो श्वपाकियाँ भय उत्पन्न करने वाली और नीलोत्पलाञ्जननिभा हैं। प्रतिज्ञायौगधरायणम् में मदिरापान से उन्मत्त गात्रसेवक के आरक्त लोचन जपापुष्प के समान हैं। कमल की उपमा सर्वत्र मिलती है परन्तु जपाकुसुम का उदाहरण अपने आप में भिन्न है। हिम से हत पद्मिनी के समान वासवदत्ता की उपमा में वासवदत्ता की दशा का पूरा चित्र ही खिंच जाता है।

पुष्प विषयक भास के उल्लेखों में एक विशेषता यह है कि उन्होंने रङ्ग को महत्त्व दिया है। शेफालिका पुष्पों का सफेद और नारङ्गी रङ्ग मोती और प्रवाल या मैनसिल धातु जैसा है। जपापुष्प का उपयोग रक्तिम नेत्रों के लिए किया गया है। नायिकाओं के नेत्र नीलोत्पल जैसे रङ्ग के हैं। गोपाङ्गनाएँ चम्पक पुष्प जैसे गौर वर्ण की हैं। प्रसङ्गानुसार प्रयुक्त पुष्पों के रङ्गों के अनुसार उपमानों का वर्णन एक विशेष प्रभाव उत्पन्न करने में सहायक हुआ है जो भास की विशिष्टता कही जा सकती है।

कहीं-कहीं लोक-व्यवहार-विषयक उक्तियों के रूप में पुष्पित-पादपों या वृक्षों का प्रसङ्ग बहुत प्रभावोत्पादक है—

शुष्केणैकेन वृक्षेण वनं पुष्पितपादपम्।
कुलं चरित्रहीनेन पुरुषेणैव दह्यते।।[18]

यहाँ हविअग्नि द्वारा सब जला दिये जाने के सन्दर्भ में पुष्पित-पादप युक्त वन का उल्लेख है।

मध्यमव्यायोग में ब्राह्मण के द्वितीय (मध्यम) पुत्र को हिडिम्बा के लिए आहार स्वरूप दे देने पर पिता अपने पुत्र के लिए विलाप करता हुआ कहता है—'गजराज दन्त भग्न पुष्पित तरु' की भांति मेरा पुत्र विनाश को प्राप्त हो रहा है।[19] यहाँ पुष्पित-पादप वृक्षों की समृद्धि और ब्राह्मण-पुत्र की यौवनावस्था का सूचक है। दोनों ही प्रसङ्गों में पुष्पित-पादप-अन्तर्भावों को बहुत सुन्दर ढंग से व्यक्त करता हुआ एक नए नाट्यबिम्ब की सृष्टि करता है। पुष्पित-पादप का इस प्रकार का प्रयोग सम्भवतः अन्यत्र कहीं दिखाई नहीं देता।

इनके अतिरिक्त विभिन्न नाटकों में असनकुसुम, कोकनदमाला, पुष्पावचयन, दर्भ, समिधा, वन्यफल, पुष्पमाला-गुम्फन आदि के उल्लेख प्रसङ्गानुसार ही हैं।

इस प्रकार भास के नाटकों में वनस्पति-जगत् के विभिन्न प्रसंग अन्य संस्कृत नाटकों की भाँति सामान्य रूप से प्राकृतिक सौन्दर्य एवं नायक-नायिकाओं के शारीरिक सौन्दर्य वर्णन तथा मानवीय भावों से सम्बद्ध हैं। वृक्ष, पुष्प आदि के चित्रण से विभिन्न दृश्यों या वातावरण की रमणीयता सामने आ जाती है तथा उस सौन्दर्य की झलक पात्रों में भी दिखाई देने लगती है और कभी-कभी उनके सन्दर्भ में पात्रों के सुख, दुःख भी अभिव्यक्त हो जाते हैं।

वास्तव में भास से ही संस्कृत नाट्य-लेखन-परम्परा का सूत्रपात हुआ जिसका कालान्तर में विकास होता गया। जहाँ तक वनस्पति या प्राकृतिक चित्रण का प्रश्न है उपर्युक्त विश्लेषण से सिद्ध हो जाता है कि भास की अपनी कई विशेषताएँ हैं और वनस्पति-जगत् से सम्बद्ध सभी पक्षों को उन्होंने लिया है। फिर भी यदि बारीकी से देखें तो

कहीं-कहीं कुछ कमी का आभास होता है जैसे प्राय: उनके पेड़, पौधों, पुष्पों के प्रसङ्ग अत्यन्त संक्षिप्त या उल्लेख मात्र जैसे रह जाते हैं। नाट्य-कथा एवं पात्रों के साथ उनका भावनात्मक सम्बन्ध नहीं बन पाता यथा प्रमदवन का माधवीलतामण्डप केवल नायक-नायिकाओं के एक दूसरे से छिपने का माध्यम बन गया है, नायक-नायिका के प्रणय-व्यापार में उद्दीपन का कार्य नहीं करता। इसी प्रकार नलिनीपत्र में जल-ग्रहण करने या काशकुसुम रेणु को अश्रुपात का कारण बनाने में (स्वप्नवासवदत्तम्) पुनरुक्ति दिखाई देती है, कोई नया अर्थ ध्वनित नहीं होता। वसन्तसेना की पक्षद्वार वाटिका (चारुदत्तम्) तथा अन्य प्रमदवन आदि के दृश्यों में प्रकृति विषयक सूक्ष्म निरीक्षण या मानव के साथ उसका सम्बन्ध आदि विशिष्ट तत्त्व उभर कर नहीं आ पाए हैं। इनमें वर्णन का अवकाश होने पर भी प्राकृतिक सौन्दर्य पूरी तरह प्रस्फुरित नहीं हो पाया है। न ही एक विशिष्ट वातावरण की सृष्टि हो पाई है।

इसी प्रकार जहाँ नायिकाओं के सौन्दर्य-वर्णन में पुष्पों से तुलना की गई है या उनके नेत्रों आदि के सौन्दर्य का वर्णन है, वहाँ भी यह संक्षिप्तता सूचित होती है। पुष्पों की उपमाओं द्वारा[20] नायिकाओं के अङ्ग-उपाङ्गों की विशेषता सामने तो आ जाती है पर ये विभिन्न बिम्ब एक वाक्य तक सीमित रह जाते हैं। उनसे 'अधर किसलय राग:' की भाँति सम्पूर्णता का बोध नहीं होता और उनमें प्रकृति के साथ तादात्म्य या भावात्मक सौन्दर्य स्थापित नहीं हो पाता है।

अन्त में यह कहा जा सकता है कि भास के वनस्पति-जगत् के इस प्रकार वर्णन के प्रति निश्चय ही कोई विशिष्ट कारण होगा या उनके समय दृष्टिकोण कुछ भिन्न रहा होगा जिसकी बारीकी न समझ पाना हमारी ही कमी है। वास्तव में प्रकृति- चित्रण विषयक उनकी अवधारणा, उनकी शैली, एकदम भिन्न है; उसे परवर्ती कवियों के सन्दर्भ में नहीं देखना चाहिए। हो सकता है कि प्रकृतिचित्रण उनकी प्राथमिकता नहीं थी। उनकी दृष्टि में प्रकृति की अपेक्षा मानव प्रमुख था और मानव-जीवन के विभिन्न पक्षों, उसकी समस्याओं को उन्होंने पूरी तरह उभारा है। भास ने जो नाटक लिखे हैं वे अभिनेय गुण-युक्त हैं, पात्रप्रधान हैं, उनकी भाषा सरल है, संवाद बोधगम्य हैं, कथानक संक्षिप्त, सरस और नाटकीय व्यापार से युक्त हैं। इनमें मानवोचित अच्छाइयों-बुराइयों को बड़ी सहजता से प्रस्तुत किया गया है। उनकी नाट्य शैली में विस्तृत वर्णनों के लिए सम्भवत: कम ही अवकाश है फिर भी उनका वनस्पति-जगत्-निरीक्षण अपने संक्षिप्त रूप में ही सब कुछ व्यक्त कर देता है।

सन्दर्भ-सङ्केत

1. विश्वनाथ भट्टाचार्य— संस्कृत ड्रामा एण्ड ड्रामेटर्जी-अ० VII, पृ० 193-194
2. भासनाटकचक्र-सम्पादक— प्रो० देवधर
3. भासनाटकचक्र-सम्पादक— प्रो० देवधर, स्वप्न० अंक 4
4. स्वप्नवासवदत्ता - अङ्क 4, पृ० 32
5. स्वप्नवासवदत्ता - पृ० 33
6. अविमारक - पृ० 163
7. स्वप्नवासवदत्ता - अङ्क 4, पृ० 26-27
8. स्वप्नवासवदत्ता - अङ्क 4, पृ० 28, 32-33
9. प्रतिज्ञायौगन्धरायण - अङ्क 1, पृ० 63

10. बालचरित - अङ्क 1, पृ० 516
11. पञ्चरात्र - अङ्क 1, पृ० 389
12. स्वप्नवासवदत्ता - अङ्क 5, पृ० 37
13. बालचरित - अङ्क 3, पृ० 539
14. प्रतिज्ञायौगन्धरायण अङ्क 4, पृ० 95
15. प्रतिमा - अङ्क 6, पृ० 300
16. ऊरुभङ्ग - पृ० 504
17. बालचरित - अङ्क 2, पृ० 526
18. पञ्चरात्र - अङ्क 1, पृ० 375, पद्य 12
19. मध्यमव्यायोग - पृ० 428, पद्य 24
20. द्रष्टव्य यही लेख, पृ० 4

卐 卐 卐

जयदेवप्रणीत गीतगोविन्द में कमलविनियोग

सरोज खन्ना

लगभग 800 वर्ष पूर्व जन्मे जयदेव बंगाल के राजा लक्ष्मणसेन के दरबारी कवि थे। कवि जयदेव की सुप्रसिद्ध गीतिरचना गीतगोविन्द वैष्णव-भक्ति की एक अनुपम धार्मिक कृति है। दक्षिण-भारत, बंगाल, उड़ीसा, असम, बिहार-प्रदेशों में गीतगोविन्द के पदों का अभिनय एवं गायन आज भी देखा-सुना जा सकता है। वैष्णव तीर्थों में अब भी लोग जयदेव के पदों को गुनगुनाते रहते हैं।

जयदेव की ललित पदावली का निदर्शन :

ललितलवङ्गलतापरिशीलनकोमलमलयसमीरे ।
मधुकरनिकरकरम्बित कोकिल कूजितकुञ्जकुटीरे।।[1]

शृङ्गाररस के स्थायिभाव रतिभाव का प्रतीक गीतगोविन्द अति-सरस होने से कई विद्वानों की आलोचना का विषय रहा है परन्तु अंग्रेजी में क्या सॉलोमन के गीत कामोत्तेजक नहीं? यूरोप के वेबर एवं कीथ आदि संस्कृत विद्वानों ने इसके रचना कौशल, माधुर्य एवं गेयता की मुक्त-कण्ठ से प्रशंसा की है। डॉ० राजेन्द्र मिश्र के शब्दों में :

गीतगोविन्द के और सॉलोमन के गीतों की समता से डॉ० आदम क्लार्क अत्यन्त मुग्ध हो गए, बाइबिल की अपनी टीका तक में उन्होंने इस बात की चर्चा की है।[2] सन्त सॉलोमन का यह अनूदित गीत इस सम्बन्ध में द्रष्टव्य है :

प्राप्त करूँ मैं
अपने प्रिय के अगणित चुम्बन
कुच-युगलों के बीच लेटकर
पड़ा-पड़ा वह रात बिताये
इस छाती पर
इस ग्रीवा के नीचे उसका वाम बाहु हो
अन्य बाहु हो आलिंगनरत।[3]

राधा-कृष्ण की विशुद्ध काम-केलि-क्रीडा पर आधारित इस सङ्गीत रचना में नायक-नायिका की तीव्र रागात्मक अनुभूतियों का सजीव चित्रण करने में जयदेव ने प्राकृतिक उपादानों का भरपूर प्रयोग किया है। विभिन्न सन्दर्भों में, वनस्पति-जगत् में उपलब्ध लगभग 30 फूलों, फलों एवं वृक्षों का सटीक उल्लेख जयदेव ने अपने गीतगोविन्द काव्य में इन नामों से किया है :

तमाल	कमल	बकुल (केसर)
किंशुक	नाककेसर	पाटलि (गुलाब)
केतकी	इन्दीवर (नीलकमल)	माधविका/चमेली
नवमालिका	जूही/चमेली	सहकार वृक्ष
आम्रमञ्जरियाँ	बन्धुजीव	अशोक
रक्तकमल/कोकनद	मृणाल	कदम्ब
कुरबक	पारिजात	ताड़-फल
अरविन्द	महुआ	तिल
कुन्द	कदली	मन्दार
दाख	बन्धूक	

सचमुच वनस्पति-जगत् के अभाव में मानवीय जीवन असहाय-सा प्रतीत होता है। गीतगोविन्द में इस पुष्पराशि की चर्चा कवि ने कहीं तो नायिका वृषभानुकुमारी राधा एवं नायक यदुकुलनन्दन भगवान् कृष्ण के रूपसौन्दर्य की श्रीवृद्धि के लिए की है और कहीं मानवीय-संवेदना की अभिव्यक्ति का माध्यम इन पेड़-पौधों को बनाया है। प्रस्तुत शोधपत्र में कवि जयदेव की इस वनस्पति-विज्ञान-विषयक रचनाधर्मिता को अभिव्यक्ति देने का प्रयास किया गया है।

इस अलौकिक सङ्गीत-रचना के अध्ययन के समय एक विशेष पक्ष जिसने मेरा ध्यान आकर्षित किया, वह यह है कि यद्यपि जयदेव ने लगभग तीस प्रकार के तरुवर, फल, पुष्पों को अपने काव्य में स्थान दिया है तथापि 'कमल' के प्रति कवि का विशेषानुराग, इसके निर्विकार आकार के प्रति कवि की निष्ठा, कमल की कोमलता एवं कमनीयता ने कहीं सहृदय कवि की हृद्तन्त्रियों को विशेष छू लिया है, तभी तो कवि ने लगभग तीस बार प्रकारान्तर से इसी पुष्प का अपने काव्य में प्रयोग किया है।

कमल को एक ठोस उपमान के रूप में प्रयोग करते समय जयदेव ने इसके विभिन्न पर्यायों/प्रभेदों जैसे अम्बुज, अरविन्द, इन्दीवर, कुवलय, सरसिज, सरोज आदि का यथावत् उपयोग किया है।

द्रष्टव्य हैं कतिपय उद्धरण :

(1) तव करकमलवरे[4] ···

(2) अमल कमलदललोचन[5] ···

(3) तद्वक्त्राम्बुजसौरभं[6] ···

(4) रतिसुखसमयरसालसया दरमुकुलितनयनसरोजम्।
निःसहनिपतिततनुलतया मधुसूदनमुदितमनोजम्।।[7]

'सम्भोग सुख की चरम अनुभूति से मेरा अंग-अंग शिथिल हो जाएगा। उनके भी नयनकमल तृप्ति से मुकुलित हो उठेंगे।' —उत्सुक राधा श्रीकृष्ण के साथ रति-लीला को आतुर है। उसका निराशा से आपूरित मन प्रकृति का सम्बल पा आशावान् हो उठा है।

(5) चिन्तयामि तदाननं कुटिलभ्रू कोपभरेण।
शोणपद्ममिवोपरि भ्रमताऽऽकुलं भ्रमरेण।।[8]

'रह-रह कर मुझे उसका मुख याद आता है · · · क्रोध से तमतमाता चेहरा-तनी हुई भौंहें! लाल कमल पर मानों बेचैन भ्रमर मँडरा रहा हो।'—गोपियों से घिरे कृष्ण को देख वृषभानुजा रूठ कर कहीं चली गई है। किन्तु जाते-जाते वह अपने प्रियतम को अपने मुखारविन्द की याद में बेचैन छोड़ गई है। सचमुच कृष्ण की दशा उस भ्रमर सी तो है।

(6) दिशि-दिशि किरति सजलकणजालम्।
नयननलिनमिव विगलितनालम्।।
राधिका विरहे तव केशव।[9]

'हे केशव! तुम्हारे विरह में राधिका जगह-जगह अश्रुबिन्दु टपकाया करती है, मानो उसके लोचन-कमल को वृन्त (मृणाल) से किसी ने तोड़ लिया हो।'—जिस प्रकार नाल से विलग हुए कमल से देर तक जल कण गिरते ही जाते हैं उसी प्रकार विरहिणी नायिका के अश्रु थमते ही नहीं। प्रकृति चित्र प्रस्तुत करते हुए पेड़-पौधों के साथ कवि जयदेव का, मानवीय-संवेगों का चित्रण वैज्ञानिकता से परिपूर्ण है।

(7) अनिलतरलकुवलयनयनेन[10] · · ·

(8) विकसितसरसिजललितमुखेन[11] · · ·

(9) स्थलजलरुहरुचिकरचरणेन।
लुठति न सा हिमकरकिरणेन।।[12]

(10) हरि हरि याहि माधव याहि मा वद कैतववादम्।
तामनुसर सरसीरुहलोचन या तव हरति विषादम्।।[13]

'जाओ माधव, जाओ! यहाँ क्या है तुम्हारा? क्यों झूठमूठ को गिड़गिड़ाते हो? हे कमलनेत्र, तुम उसी के पास लौट जाओ जो तुम्हारी ग्लानि मिटाया करती है, खण्डित मनोरथा राधा का अपराधी कृष्ण के प्रति 'कमलनयन' सम्बोधन दर्शाता है कि सुख-दुःख की समस्त अनुभूतियों के सम्प्रेषण का माध्यम प्रकृति ही रही है।

(11) नीलनलिनाभमपि तन्वि! तव लोचनं
धारयति कोकनदरूपम्।[14]

कुसुमशरबाणभावेन यदि रञ्जयसि
कृष्णमिदमेतदनुरूपम्।।[15]

'हे तन्वि! नील-कमल सदृश तुम्हारे नेत्र (कोप के कारण) लाल-कमल के सदृश हो रहे हैं। यदि अपने नेत्र को कामदेव का बाण समझकर मुझ 'कृष्ण' को (राग से) रंग रही हो, तो ठीक है।'—मानव फूलों एवं फलों के साथ सनातन रूप से संपृक्त है और अपनी भावनाओं का अभिसार केन्द्र भी इन्हीं को स्वीकारता आया है।

(12) अक्ष्णोर्निक्षिप कज्जलं श्रवणयोस्तापिच्छगुच्छावलीं
मूर्ध्नि श्यामसरोजदाम कुचयोः कस्तूरिकापत्रकम्।[16]

'हे सखि राधे! आंखों में अञ्जन, कानों में मोरपंख के गुच्छे, सिर पर नील-कमलों की माला और कुचों को

कस्तूरी के रस से चित्रित कर अपने प्रिय के पास चलो।'—यहाँ सखि रूठी राधा को प्राकृतिक उपादानों से सजकर, कुञ्ज में माधव के पास चलने को मना रही है। (मानव संवेदनशील प्राणी है, वह अपनी भावनाओं को प्रकृति के साथ जोड़कर अनिर्वचनीय आनन्द में विभोर हो जाना चाहता है।)

गीतगोविन्द में जहाँ कवि जयदेव की पद्मपुष्प के प्रति आस्था, काव्य में इसके भरपूर प्रयोग से स्वतः सिद्ध है, वहीं गुलाब के प्रति कवि की उदासीनता भी स्पष्ट परिलक्षित है। पूरे काव्य में केवल एक ही स्थल पर गुलाब का वर्णन है। किन्तु वसन्त ऋतु के वर्णन में इस पुष्प का एकमात्र सशक्त प्रयोग ही कवि जयदेव की सूक्ष्म-प्रज्ञा का परिचायक बन गया है—

मदनमहीपतिकनकदण्डरुचिकेसरकुसुमविकासे।
मिलितशिलीमुखपाटलपटलकृतस्मरतूणविलासे।।[17]

—'वसन्त के प्रकृति-राज्य में कामदेव राजा की भाँति हैं। विकसित नागकेसर उनका स्वर्णछत्र है और भ्रमर-मण्डित गुलाब तीरों से पूर्ण तरकश का काम कर रहे हैं।'—पाटल-पुष्पों (गुलाब) पर भ्रमरों का मँडराना कवि को बाणों से भरे कामदेव के तूणीर की याद दिलाता है। निःसंदेह यह उपमा कवि के मन में गुलाब के सुडौल आकार और ग्रथित पंखुड़ियों के कारण उपजी है। संस्कृत ग्रन्थों में गुलाब का उल्लेख शतपत्री के नाम से भी पाया जाता है—

शतपत्री तु गन्धाढ्या सौम्यगन्धा शिवप्रिया।
सुशीता च सुवृत्ता च सुमना शतपत्रिका।।[18]

उर्दू, अरबी, फारसी की शेरो-शायरी में जिस रूप में गुलाब की सुन्दरता का बखान मिलता है, उस रूप में हमारे संस्कृत ग्रंथों में गुलाब की चर्चा यद्यपि नहीं है। यत्र-तत्र सुगन्धि के सन्दर्भ में इसका उल्लेख मिलता है—

पाटलसंसर्गसुरभिवनवाताः[19]

विश्व शब्दकोश के अनुसार—

The spread of the rose throughout the Western and Europe owes much to the advance of Islam. As the Arabs moved from Persia, which they conquered in the 7th century, the flowers of Middle-East, including the rose, followed them, eventually to Spain in the west (8th century) and to India in the East (10th century).[20]

इसके विपरीत कमल-पुष्प का साहित्य में अतिशय उपयोग इसके धार्मिक पक्ष को भी उजागर करता है। विश्व के अनेक धार्मिक सम्प्रदायों (e.g. Bahai) ने इसके महत्त्व को स्वीकारा है। हिन्दू-धर्म में कमल, धन की अधिष्ठात्री देवी लक्ष्मी के साथ पहचाना जाता है। बौद्धधर्म के अनुयायी देशों में यह पवित्रता एवं दैवी उत्पत्ति का प्रतीक माना जाता है।

"Like the lotus which germinates under the water and arises to the surface to unfold! So too the 'Buddha' is born in the impure world, but through his enlightenment rises above it. In Buddhism, the fully open lotus preserves a strong solar character, its leaves being obviously identifiable with the rays of the sun, its stem being a kind of Sacred Cosmic-Pivot."[21]

सूर्यांशुभिर्भिन्नमिवारविन्दम्।[22]

सन्दर्भ-सङ्केत

1. गीतगोविन्द - 3.1
2. नागार्जुन-गीतगोविन्द (भू०)
3. Let him kiss me with the kisses of his mouth, he shall be all night betwixt my breast; his left hand is under my head and right hand doth embrace me. Songs of Soloman
4. M.R. Deshmukh, *Gītagovindam* - 1.4
5. M.R. Deshmukh, *Gītagovindam* - 1.2.5.
6. M.R. Deshmukh, *Gītagovindam*
7. गीतगोविन्द, वाणी प्रकाशन - पृ० 28
8. गीतगोविन्द, वाणी प्रकाशन - पृ० 31
9. गीतगोविन्द, वाणी प्रकाशन - पृ० 38
10. गीतगोविन्द, वाणी प्रकाशन - पृ० 55
11. गीतगोविन्द, वाणी प्रकाशन - पृ० 55
12. गीतगोविन्द, वाणी प्रकाशन - पृ० 56
13. गीतगोविन्द, वाणी प्रकाशन - पृ० 59
14. गीतगोविन्द, वाणी प्रकाशन - पृ० 66
15. गीतगोविन्द, वाणी प्रकाशन - पृ० 66
16. M.R. Deshmukh, *Gītagovindam* - 11.2.3.
17. M.R. Deshmukh, *Gītagovindam* - 1.3.4.
18. आत्रेयसंहिता
19. अभिज्ञानशाकुन्तल
20. Encyclopaedia Britanica
21. Encyclopaedia Britanica
22. कुमारसम्भव - 1.32

卐 卐 卐

पण्डितराज-रसाल-रसझरी

सुषमा कुलश्रेष्ठ • अरुणा मोहन

पण्डितराज जगन्नाथ साहित्यशास्त्र के उद्भट पण्डित थे। साथ ही वे अद्भुत प्रतिभाशाली कवि भी थे। कविता की अधिष्ठात्री देवी सरस्वती उनके जिह्वाग्र पर सतत नर्तन किया करती थीं। पण्डितराज ने अनेक काव्यग्रन्थों तथा शास्त्रग्रन्थों का प्रणयन किया। उनके उपलब्ध ग्रन्थ इस प्रकार हैं—

(I) काव्यग्रन्थ

1. पीयूषलहरी (गङ्गालहरी)
2. अमृतलहरी (यमुनालहरी)
3. करुणालहरी (विष्णुलहरी)
4. लक्ष्मीलहरी
5. सुधालहरी
6. प्रास्ताविकविलासः (अन्योक्तिविलासः)
7. शृङ्गारविलासः
8. करुणविलासः
9. शान्तविलासः
10. आसफविलासः
11. प्राणाभरणम् (जगदाभरणम्)
12. प्रस्फुटितान्योक्तयः
13. प्रस्फुटितपद्यानि।

(II) शास्त्रग्रन्थ

1. रसगङ्गाधरः
2. चित्रमीमांसाखण्डनम्
3. काव्यप्रकाशटीका
4. मनोरमाकुचमर्दनम्
5. शब्दकौस्तुभशाणोत्तेजनम्।

पण्डितराज जगन्नाथ को अनेक राजाओं और बादशाहों से सम्मान प्राप्त हुआ। उनका अधिकाधिक समय

बादशाह शाहजहाँ के सान्निध्य में व्यतीत हुआ। शाहजहाँ उनके आश्रयदाता के साथ ही उनके अभिन्न सुहद् भी थे। पण्डितराज की उपाधि भी उन्हें शाहजहाँ ने ही प्रदान की थी। जगन्नाथ के मनोरथों को पूर्ण करने में एकमात्र शाहजहाँ ही समर्थ थे तभी तो कविवर ने कहा था–

दिल्लीश्वरो वा जगदीश्वरो वा
मनोरथं पूरयितुं समर्थः।
अन्यैर्नृपालैः परिदीयमानं
शाकाय वा स्याल्लवणाय वा स्यात्।।[1]

अपनी मनोरथप्रियतमा लवङ्गी भी जगन्नाथ को बादशाह शाहजहाँ से ही प्राप्त हुई थी। एक बार प्रसन्न हुए बादशाह ने जब कुछ माँगने के लिए कहा तो कविवर ने यवनकन्या लवङ्गी को ही माँग लिया। उस समय जो पद्य उन्होंने कहे थे उनमें से निम्नलिखित द्रष्टव्य हैं–

1. **न याचे गजालिं न वा वाजिराशिं**
न वित्तेषु चित्तं मदीयं कदाचित्।
इयं सुस्तनी हस्तविन्यस्तकुम्भा
लवङ्गी कुरङ्गीदृगङ्गीकरोतु।।

2. **यवनी नवनीतकोमलाङ्गी**
शयनीयं यदि नीयते कदाचित्।
अवनीतलमेव साधु मन्ये
न वनी माघवनी विनोदहेतुः।।

3. **यवनी रमणी विपदःशमनी**
कमनीयतमा नवनीतसमा।
'उहि'-'ऊहि' वचोऽमृतपूर्णमुखी
स सुखी जगतीह यदङ्कगता।।[2]

बादशाह शाहजहाँ के समय से लेकर आज तक सहृदयजन पण्डितराज के काव्य की रसमाधुरी का पान कर रहे हैं। संस्कृतभाषा में अच्छी गति रखने वाले तो उनके काव्य का रसास्वाद प्राप्त कर ही लेते हैं किन्तु जिनकी ऐसी गति नहीं, वे अब तक उस आनन्द से वञ्चित रहे हैं। यह कहते हुए मुझे हार्दिक हर्ष है कि साहित्यशास्त्रज्ञ एवं स्वयं एक उत्तम कवि प्रो० हरिनारायण दीक्षित ने पण्डितराज के सभी काव्यग्रन्थों को एक स्थान पर सङ्कलित, सम्पादित एवं राष्ट्रभाषा हिन्दी में अनूदित कर **'पण्डितराजजगन्नाथ-काव्यग्रन्थावली'**[3] नामक ग्रन्थ में प्रस्तुत कर विद्वानों एवं सहृदयों का समान उपकार किया है। पण्डितराज जगन्नाथ की कविता की मिठास तो गज़ब की है पर प्रो० दीक्षित ने जो अनुवाद प्रस्तुत किया है वह भी काबिलेतारीफ़ है, गज़ब का है।

संस्कृत साहित्य रसराज शृङ्गार से मण्डित है। शृङ्गार के उद्दीपन-रूप में छहों ऋतुओं, उन ऋतुओं में फूलने-फलने वाले वृक्षों, पुष्पों एवं फलों के सुन्दर वर्णन साहित्य को अलङ्कृत करते हैं। ऋतुराज वसन्त में फलराज आम्र की अद्भुत शोभा होती है। आम्रवृक्ष, आम्रमञ्जरी, पुंस्कोकिल द्वारा आम्रमञ्जरी-रसपान, रसपान से उसके कण्ठ के कषायमधुर होने, पुंस्कोकिलकूजित आदि का प्रकृष्ट वर्णन संस्कृत साहित्य में उपलब्ध है। आम्र को लक्ष्य कर

अन्योक्तिपरक पद्य भी बहुत रचे गए हैं। कविवर पण्डितराज जगन्नाथ के काव्यग्रन्थों में आम्र को लक्ष्यकर विरचित 40 से अधिक पद्य उपलब्ध हैं। इन पद्यों में कहीं आम्र की अद्‌भुत प्रशस्ति है, तो कहीं उसका गुणगान है, कोकिल के साथ तथा भ्रमर के साथ उसके सम्बन्धों की भी चर्चा है। आम्र तरुण नायक-नायिकाओं के लिए किस प्रकार कोमोद्दीपक है, विरहियों को किस प्रकार संतप्त करता है आदि को भी कवि ने वर्णित किया है। आम्र को लक्ष्यकर उन्होंने अनेक अन्योक्तियों की भी रचना की है। कहीं आम्र की निन्दा भी की है और कहीं आम्र को सभी प्रकार के सुखों का प्रदाता बताकर उसका धन्यवाद ज्ञापन भी किया है। इस प्रकार आम्र के विविध रंगबिरंगे दृश्य जो उनके काव्यग्रन्थों में मिलते हैं, उन दृश्यों से युक्त चुने हुए कतिपय पद्यरत्न यहाँ सहृदयों के आस्वादनार्थ सविवेचन प्रस्तुत हैं। आम के लिए संस्कृत साहित्य में निम्नलिखित पद प्रयुक्त हैं—

आम्रः कामशरश्चूतः रसालः कामवल्लभः।
वामाङ्गः सहकारश्च कीरेष्टो माधवद्रुमः।।

पण्डितराज जगन्नाथ ने आम के लिए आम्र, चूत, रसाल, सहकार, माकन्द, फलराज तथा फलवर्य आदि पदों का प्रयोग किया है। इन सभी पदों के प्रयोग से युक्त पण्डितराज के पद्यों में वर्णित आम्ररसमाधुरी के पान द्वारा आम्रकल्प कर जीवन को सरस बनाया जा सकता है। तो प्रस्तुत हैं आम्रवर्णनपरक पद्य—

1. **आकर्ण्याम्रफलस्तुतिं जलमभूत्तन्नारिकेलान्तरं**
प्रायः कण्टकितस्तथैव पनसः जातं द्विधोर्वारुकम्।
आस्तेऽधोमुखमेव कादलफलं द्राक्षाफलं क्षुद्रतां
श्यामत्वं बत जाम्बवं गतमहो मात्सर्यदोषादिह।।[4]

प्रसङ्ग-उत्तम की प्रशस्ति सुनकर मध्यम एवम् अधम कोटि के लोग ईर्ष्याकषायित हो ही जाते हैं।

यहाँ रसराज आम्र फल की स्तुति सुनकर मात्सर्य के वशीभूत हो जल नारिकेल के भीतर छिप गया, पनस (कटहल) प्रायः काँटों से युक्त हो गया, तर्बूज़ फटकर दो भागों में विभक्त हो गया, केले ने अपना मुँह लटका लिया, अंगूर सूखकर छोटा हो गया और अद्‌भुत आश्चर्य तो यह है कि जामुन का फल काला पड़ गया। नारिकेल, पनस, तर्बूज़, कदली, द्राक्षा एवं जामुन-ये सभी सुस्वादु एवं मीठे फल हैं। इन सबकी मिठास अलग-अलग नमूने की है किन्तु पण्डितराज को तो फलराज आम्र की मिठास ने ही मोहित कर रखा है।

2. **अधिश्रीरुद्याने त्वमसि भवतः पल्लवचयो**
धुरीणः कल्याणे तव जगति शाखा श्रमहरा।
मुदे पुष्पोल्लेखः फलमपि च तुष्ट्यै तनुभृतां
रसाल! त्वां तस्माच्छ्रयति शतशः कोकिलकुलम्।।[5]

प्रसङ्ग-गुणवान् का आश्रयण सभी को प्रिय होता है।

हे रसाल (आम्र) वृक्ष! तुम उद्यान की सर्वातिशायिनी शोभा हो, तुम्हारे पल्लव सर्वाधिक कल्याणप्रद हैं, तुम्हारी शाखाएँ लोगों की क्लान्ति का हरण करती हैं, तुम्हारी मञ्जरियों के सम्पर्क से मन आह्लादित होता है और तुम्हारे फलों के सेवन से लोग संतुष्ट होते हैं। इन्हीं सब कारणों से हे रसाल! सैकड़ों कोकिल तुम्हारे पास आते रहते हैं।

3. रसाल! तव माधुरीप्रथितसत्फलं पक्षिणः
चरन्ति नहि ते यशः प्रकटयन्ति काष्ठासु ते।
पिकस्तु नवपल्लवग्रसनमेव कुर्वन् स्वरैः
प्रकाशयति दिक्षु ते मृदुलपञ्चमाख्यैर्यशः।।[6]

प्रसङ्ग-इस संसार में किसी का लाभ तो बहुत लोग उठाते हैं किन्तु लाभ-प्राप्ति के अनुरूप उसका यशोगान विरले ही करते हैं।

हे रसाल (आम्र) वृक्ष! माधुर्य के लिए प्रसिद्ध तुम्हारे फलों को तो ये सभी पक्षी खाते ही रहते हैं किन्तु तुम्हारे इस गुण को ये संसार के सामने प्रकट नहीं करते हैं। यह तो पुंस्कोकिल ही है जो तुम्हारे नूतन पल्लव का रसास्वाद लेकर अपने सुमधुर पञ्चम स्वर से तुम्हारे इस माहात्म्य को जगत् पर प्रकट कर देता है।

आम्रपल्लव तथा आम्र-मञ्जरी के रसपान से पुंस्कोकिल का कण्ठ कषाय होकर मधुर हो जाता है और तब वह पञ्चम स्वर में अपना कूजित प्रारम्भ करता है। यहाँ ध्यातव्य है कि सुमधुर गान के लिए जो प्रसिद्ध है, वह पिक है, पुंस्कोकिल है, कोकिला नहीं। कोकिल से सङ्गीत के पञ्चम स्वर की उत्पत्ति मानी जाती है।

4. उन्मीलद्रसबिन्दुगन्धकुसुमावल्ल्यो वसन्तोदये
कान्ताः कोमलपल्लवाः कति कति क्रीडावने सन्ति नो।
सौभाग्यैकनिधे! रसाल! तदपि श्रीमञ्जरीशालिनः
त्वत्तोऽन्यत्र च कुत्रचिन्मधुकरश्रेणी न विश्राम्यति।।[7]

प्रसङ्ग-आम्रमञ्जरी की प्रशस्ति।

वसन्त ऋतु, में क्रीडावनों में नूतन सुकुमार किसलयों से युक्त, मनोहर तथा उठते हुए ताज़े पराग की सुरभि से पूर्ण न जाने कितने पुष्प खिले रहते हैं किन्तु फिर भी, सौन्दर्य के निधान, हे रसाल! भ्रमरों का समूह सुन्दर मञ्जरियों से शोभायमान तुम्हारे अतिरिक्त अन्यत्र कहीं भी विश्राम नहीं करता है।

5. त्रपाश्यामा जम्बूर्दलितहृदयं दाडिमफलं
सशूलं संधत्ते हृदयमभिमानेन पनसः।
भयादन्तस्तोयं तरुशिखरजं लाङ्गलिफलं
समुद्भूते चूते जगति फलराजे प्रसरति।।[8]

प्रसङ्ग-आम का फलराजत्व यहाँ वर्णित है।

जगत् में फलों के राजा आम के उत्पन्न होते और प्रसार पाते ही जामुन के फल हीनभावना के वशीभूत हो लज्जा से कृष्णवर्ण हो गए, अनार के फलों का हृदय विदीर्ण हो गया, पनस (कटहल) के फलों के हृदय में काँटे चुभ गए तथा वृक्ष के शिखर पर उत्पन्न होने वाले नारिकेलफलों के अन्दर भयवशात् जल उत्पन्न हो गया। कहने का भाव यह है कि यद्यपि जामुन, दाडिम, पनस एवं नारिकेल—ये सभी सुस्वादु तथा उत्तम फल हैं किन्तु फलराज आम्र के सम्मुख ये कहीं टिकते नहीं। आम केवल हमारे भारत देश का ही फलराज नहीं है प्रत्युत समग्र जगत् में लोग इस फल का रसास्वाद कर आनन्दलाभ करते हैं।

6. उत्फुल्लरम्य! सहकार! रसाल! बन्धो!
कूजत्पिकावलिनिवास! तथा विधेहि।
गुञ्जद्भ्रमद्भ्रमरकस्त्वयि बद्धतृष्णो
नान्यान्प्रयाति पिचुमन्दकरीरवृक्षान्।।[9]

प्रसङ्ग–उत्तम लोगों से सम्बन्ध रहने पर भी अनेक बार लोग मध्यम और अधम की ओर चले जाते हैं। ऐसी स्थिति से रक्षा के लिए अन्योपदेश द्वारा बताया जा रहा है।

विकसित मञ्जरियों से सुन्दर दिखने वाले, कूजन करते हुए कोकिलों का निवास स्थान बने हुए तथा बन्धु–सदृश व्यवहार करने वाले, हे रसाल, हे सहकार, आम्रवृक्ष! तुम कुछ ऐसा विलक्षण कार्य करो जिससे गुञ्जनपूर्वक भटकता हुआ तथा तुम पर आशा लगाए हुए यह भ्रमर नीम, करीर आदि वृक्षों की ओर न चला जाए।

7. त्वं सामान्यतरुभ्रमेण सकलक्षोणीरुहक्ष्मापतौ
माकन्देऽपि किरात! पातय मुधा मास्मिन्कुठारं हठात्।
एष श्लाघ्यजनस्य जीवितमलिव्यूहस्य बन्धुर्मधोः
सर्वस्वं मकरध्वजस्य विजयामात्यः पिकानां गुरुः।।[10]

प्रसङ्ग–मूर्ख लोग उत्तम तथा अधम का अन्तर नहीं समझते। उन्हीं के लिए किरात एवं आम्र के माध्यम से यह अन्योक्ति है।

अरे ओ किरात! तू साधारण वृक्ष समझ कर इस वृक्षराज आम्रवृक्ष पर भी हठात् अपनी कुल्हाड़ी मत चला। यह वृक्ष तो सज्जनों का जीवन है, भँवरों का बन्धु है, ऋतुराज वसन्त का सर्वस्व है, कामदेव का विजय दिलाने वाला अमात्य है तथा पुंस्कोकिलों का सङ्गीतगुरु है।

8. सतां धनं साधुभिरेव भुज्यते
दुरात्मभिर्दुश्चरितात्मनां धनम्।
शुकादयश्चूतफलानि भुञ्जते
भवन्ति निम्बानि च काकभोजनम्।।[11]

प्रसङ्ग–सज्जनों के धन की प्रशस्ति तथा दुर्जनों के धन की निन्दा।

सज्जनों के धन का उपभोग सज्जनों द्वारा ही किया जाता है और दुर्जनों के धन का उपभोग दुर्जनों द्वारा ही किया जाता है तभी तो आम्र के फलों को तोते तथा नीम के फलों को कौवे खाते हैं।

9. कति कति न वसन्ते वल्लयः शाखिनो वा
किसलयसुमनोभिः शोभमाना बभूवुः।
तदपि युवजनानां प्रीतये केवलोऽभू-
दभिनवकलिकालीभारशाली रसालः।।[12]

प्रसङ्ग–आम्र की कामोद्दीपकता का वर्णन।

वसन्त ऋतु में न मालूम कितनी लताएँ और न मालूम कितने वृक्ष नूतन किसलयों तथा पुष्पों से सुशोभित हुए किन्तु फिर भी युवकजनों के मन को नई कलियों से लदे हुए, केवल आम्रवृक्ष ने ही आनन्दित किया। आम्रमञ्जरियों

से लदे हुए आम्रवृक्ष को देखकर तथा आम्रमञ्जरी की सुरभि का पानकर निश्चय ही नेत्रों तथा नासिका को अद्‌भुत तृप्ति का अनुभव होता है।

10. पाटीरद्रुभुजङ्गपुङ्गवमुखायाता इवातापिनो
वाता वान्ति दहन्ति लोचनममी ताम्रा रसालद्रुमाः।
एते हन्त किरन्ति कूजितमयं हालाहलं कोकिला
बाला बालमृणालकोमलतनुः प्राणान् कथं रक्षतु।।[13]

प्रसङ्ग–वसन्त ऋतु में कोई विरही नायक अपनी विरहिणी प्रियतमा का स्मरण कर रहा है। सबको आनन्दित करने वाला आम्रवृक्ष विरहियों के लिए तो सन्तापदायक ही होता है।

वसन्त के इन दिनों में मेरे सदृश विरही जनों को सन्तप्त करने वाली मादक हवाएँ चल रही हैं मानो वे चन्दनवृक्षों में लिपटे हुए बड़े-बड़े सर्पों के मुखों से निकली हों, नूतन किसलयों से लदे हुए अतएव लाल हुए ये आम्रवृक्ष विरहियों के नेत्रों को झुलसा रहे हैं और ऊपर से हाय! ये कोकिल भी अपने कूजित का हालाहल सब ओर बिखेर रहे हैं। ऐसी विषम स्थिति में हाय! कोमल मृणाल के समान सुकुमार शरीर वाली मेरी प्रियतमा अपने प्राणों की रक्षा कैसे कर सकेगी? वसन्त ऋतु में श्रृङ्गाररस का उद्दीपनरूप आम्रवृक्ष विरहियों के संताप को बढ़ा रहा है।

11. दिङ्‌मण्डलं परिमलैः सुरभीकरोषि
सौन्दर्यमावहसि लोचनलोभनीयम्।
हंहो रसाल! फलवर्य! तथापि दूये
यद् ग्रन्थिलं च कठिनं हृदयं बिभर्षि।।[14]

प्रसङ्ग–आम्र की प्रशस्ति और निन्दा दोनों वर्णित हैं।

फलों में श्रेष्ठ हे रसाल! तुम अपनी सुरभि से सम्पूर्ण वातावरण को सुरभित करते हो और नेत्रों को सुख पहुँचाने वाला तुम्हारा सौन्दर्य है किन्तु बड़े दुःख के साथ मुझे कहना पड़ रहा है कि तुम्हारा हृदय अतिशय जटिल और कठोर है।

12. येऽमी आमुकुलोद्गमात् प्रतिदिनं त्वामाश्रिताः षट्पदाः
ते भ्राम्यन्ति फलाद् बहिः कथमहो दृष्ट्वा न सम्भाषसे।
ये कीटास्तव दृक्पथं न च गतास्ते त्वत्फलाभ्यन्तरे
धिक् त्वां चूततरो! परापरपरिज्ञानानभिज्ञो भवान्।।[15]

प्रसङ्ग–आम्रवृक्ष की निन्दा वर्णित है।

हे आम्रवृक्ष! तुम्हें अपने और पराए का ज्ञान नहीं है, अतः तुम्हें धिक्कार है। क्योंकि जो भ्रमर तुम्हारी मञ्जरियों के अङ्कुर निकलने के समय से ही हर दिन तुम्हारा आश्रय लिए रहे, वे तो तुममें फल आने के बाद आज उन फलों के बाहर ही भटक रहे हैं। तुम उन्हें देखकर भी उनसे सम्भाषण नहीं कर रहे हो किन्तु जो कीट तुम्हारे सामने कभी नहीं आए वे आज तुम्हारे फलों के अन्दर विद्यमान हैं।

13. शान्ता घर्मकणाः श्रमः शिथिलितस्तीर्णस्तृषामुद्‌गमो
वारंवारमुदारकोकिलरवैरानन्दितं मानसम्।
सर्वं प्राप्तमभीप्सितं तव तले चूत! प्रसन्नद्विज-
श्रेणीगुञ्जित! रञ्जिताखिलमनो यामो वयं स्वस्ति ते।।[16]

प्रसङ्ग-किसी से सभी प्रकार से सन्तुष्ट व्यक्ति की सदुक्ति।

प्रसन्न हुए पक्षियों के कलरव-गुञ्जन-सङ्गीत से गुञ्जित होते रहने वाले तथा सबके मन को आह्लादित करने वाले, हे आम्रवृक्ष! तुम्हारे आश्रय में मुझे मेरा मनोवाञ्छित सब कुछ मिल गया है, श्रमकण सूख गए हैं, क्लान्ति दूर हो गई है, तृषा शान्त हो गई है और पुंस्कोकिलों के बारंबार सुमधुर कूजन से मेरा मन भी प्रसन्न हो गया है। मैं अब जा रहा हूँ, प्रभु तुम्हारा कल्याण करें।

निष्कर्षतः कहा जा सकता है कि पण्डितराजजगन्नाथ-वर्णित आम्ररसमाधुरी सुधा से भी अधिक आनन्ददायिनी है। संस्कृत-साहित्य तथा जगन्नाथ-साहित्य में उपलब्ध आम्रवर्णनपरक पद्यों का यदि शोधपरक तुलनात्मक अध्ययन किया जाए तो अनेक नूतन तथ्य उद्घाटित होंगे।

सन्दर्भ-सङ्केत

1. पण्डितराजजगन्नाथ-काव्यग्रन्थावली (प्रो० हरिनारायण दीक्षित-सम्पादिता)- प्रस्फुटितपद्यानि 50
2. पण्डितराजजगन्नाथ-काव्यग्रन्थावली - प्रस्फुटितपद्यानि, 53, 56, 57
3. पण्डितराजजगन्नाथ-काव्यग्रन्थावली (प्रो० हरिनारायण दीक्षित-सम्पादिता), ईस्टर्न बुक लिंकर्स, दिल्ली, 1996 ई०।
4. पण्डितराजजगन्नाथ-काव्यग्रन्थावली - प्रस्फुटितान्योक्तयः 252
5. पण्डितराजजगन्नाथ-काव्यग्रन्थावली - प्रस्फुटितान्योक्तयः 249
6. पण्डितराजजगन्नाथ-काव्यग्रन्थावली - प्रस्फुटितान्योक्तयः 128
7. पण्डितराजजगन्नाथ-काव्यग्रन्थावली - प्रस्फुटितान्योक्तयः 256
8. पण्डितराजजगन्नाथ-काव्यग्रन्थावली - प्रस्फुटितान्योक्तयः 260
9. पण्डितराजजगन्नाथ-काव्यग्रन्थावली - प्रस्फुटितान्योक्तयः 255
10. पण्डितराजजगन्नाथ-काव्यग्रन्थावली - प्रस्फुटितान्योक्तयः 261
11. पण्डितराजजगन्नाथ-काव्यग्रन्थावली - प्रस्फुटितान्योक्तयः 17
12. पण्डितराजजगन्नाथ-काव्यग्रन्थावली - प्रस्फुटितान्योक्तयः 257
13. पण्डितराजजगन्नाथ-काव्यग्रन्थावली शृङ्गारविलासः 57
14. पण्डितराजजगन्नाथ-काव्यग्रन्थावली - प्रस्फुटितान्योक्तयः 262
15. पण्डितराजजगन्नाथ-काव्यग्रन्थावली - प्रस्फुटितान्योक्तयः 266
16. पण्डितराजजगन्नाथ-काव्यग्रन्थावली - प्रस्फुटितान्योक्तयः 268

卐 卐 卐

Section X

PLANT SCIENCE & EROTOLOGY

वृक्षायुर्वेदकामशास्त्रनिर्झरी

तुलस्या रक्षितं सर्वं जगदेतच्चराचरम्

कमल आनन्द

इस पञ्चभूतात्मक सृष्टि में अपरिमित द्रव्य हैं। पृथ्वी, जल, तेज, वायु एवं आकाश आदि के मूलभूत तत्त्वों के मेल से सभी द्रव्यों की उत्पत्ति होती है अतः सभी द्रव्य पाञ्चभौतिक हैं। परन्तु प्रत्येक द्रव्य की उत्पत्ति का अधिष्ठान पृथ्वी है और जल इसके अवयवों के अणुओं को मिलाने वाला है। इस प्रकार सृष्टि के सभी द्रव्य औषधमय हैं।

औषधि-ज्ञान एक महत्वपूर्ण ज्ञानशृंखला है और इसका इतिहास अत्यधिक प्राचीन है। ऋग्वेद में इस का स्पष्ट उल्लेख है कि वेदों की उत्पत्ति से पूर्व औषधियां दिव्य ज्ञान द्वारा ही जानी जाती थीं—**'या औषधी पूर्वाजाता देवेभ्यस्त्रियुगं पुरा'।**

धन्वन्तरि ने मनुष्य की उत्पत्ति से पूर्व वनौषधियों की उत्पत्ति का विवरण दिया है। सुश्रुत ने भी इस तथ्य का संकेत अपने ग्रन्थ के प्रारम्भ में ही किया है। सामान्य रूप से चरक संहिता में 1200 औषधियों का और सुश्रुत संहिता में लगभग 550 औषधियों का वर्णन मिलता है। धन्वन्तरि और राजनिघण्टु में लगभग 450 द्रव्यों का वर्णन है। 1550 ईस्वी में रचित भावप्रकाशनिघण्टु 950 उद्भिज औषध द्रव्यों का उल्लेख करता है। कैय्यदेव निघण्टु में 450 द्रव्यों का विवरण है।[1] इन सभी ग्रन्थों में द्रव्यों के विवरण, उनकी आकृति, रचना, रस, गुण तथा प्रयोग के आधार पर किए गए हैं।

चरक के अनुसार औषधमय द्रव्यों के दो भेद माने गए हैं, चेतन और अचेतन। चेतन द्रव्यों के पुनः दो भेद हैं: अन्तश्चेतन तथा बहिरन्तश्चेतन। अन्तश्चेतन वे द्रव्य हैं जिनकी चेतनाभिव्यक्ति बाहर से दृष्टिगोचर नहीं होती जैसे स्थावर, उद्भिद द्रव्य। बहिरन्तश्चेतन वे द्रव्य जिनकी चेतनाभिव्यक्ति बाह्य और आभ्यन्तर दोनों प्रकार से होती है, जैसे मनुष्य, पशु, पक्षी आदि।[2]

स्वरूप भेद से द्रव्य चार प्रकार के होते है; उद्भिज, प्राणिज, जान्तव, पार्थिव। उद्भिद्य पृथिवीं जायते इति अर्थात् पृथ्वी को भेदकर जो बाहर आते हैं वे उद्भिज कहलाते हैं जैसे वृक्ष, लता, वनस्पति आदि। उद्भिज द्रव्य आयुष्य भेद से मुख्यतः तीन प्रकार के होते हैं—एक वर्षायु, द्विवर्षायु तथा बहुवर्षायु और आकृति भेद से ये चार प्रकार के होते हैं—वृक्ष, क्षुप, शाक तथा लता।[3]

वानस्पतिक दृष्टि से तुलसी एक सुपरिचित क्षुप (झाड़) है जिसमें एक ही मूल से अनेक काण्ड निकालकर झाड़ सा बन जाता है। यह स्वावलम्बी होता है और बिना किसी सहारे के खड़े रहने वाला होता है। इसकी शाखाएँ तथा मूल भी छोटे होते हैं। इसका पुष्पकाल अगस्त-सितम्बर होता है। इसके बीज, पत्ते, टहनियाँ सभी प्रयोज्य हैं। यह सर्वत्र सुलभ भी है। आयुर्वेदीय दृष्टि से उद्भिज औषधियों में इसका महत्वपूर्ण स्थान है। सुश्रुत संहिता में इसका उल्लेख 'सुरसा' सुखेन रस्यते आस्वाद्यते इति इस व्याख्या से सुरसादिगण में किया गया है। औषधीय दृष्टि से भी यह एक अतुलनीय क्षुप है।

आयुर्वेदीय निघण्टुकारों ने तुलसी के छः भेद किए हैं परन्तु उसके पर्यायों में कुछ विभिन्नता है। कुछ के अनुसार तुलसी के छः भेद लघुतुलसी, गन्धतुलसी, कृष्णतुलसी, रामतुलसी, बिल्वगन्धतुलसी और वनतुलसी है। वैद्यकशब्दसिन्धु और शब्दकल्पद्रुम के अनुसार तुलसी के छः भेद क्षुद्रपत्रतुलसी, गन्धतुलसी, कृष्णतुलसी, बिल्वगन्धतुलसी, श्वेत-तुलसी और वर्वरीतुलसी है। राजनिघण्टु ने तुलसी के पाँच भेदों का उल्लेख किया है और उनके नाम तुलसी, मरुबक, अर्जक, वर्वर और वनवर्वरिका है जबकि भावप्रकाश ने कुल तीन भेद ही बताए हैं तुलसी, मरुबक और वर्वरी (वनतुलसी)।[4]

भारतीय जीवन में तुलसी अत्यन्त महत्वपूर्ण है। जन्म से लेकर मृत्यु तक सभी कर्मकाण्डों में इस की मुख्य भूमिका रहती है। इसके चमत्कारिक औषधीय गुणों के कारण इसे तुलसी माता तथा तुलसी माँ कहकर पुकारा जाता है। इस आदर-सम्मान व गौरव के कारण ही तुलसी हिन्दु मानव आस्था का केन्द्र बिन्दु बन, धर्म का अंग बन गई है। इसके गुणों से सुपरिचित हमारे ऋषि-मुनि इसे पवित्र व पूज्य मानते रहे हैं। तुलसी-दल का चरणामृत, तुलसी-दल से देव-पूजन, तुलसी-दल का प्रसाद तथा इसके पत्तों के रोग निवारक गुणों के कारण नवजात शिशु पर तुलसीदल मिश्रित जल का छिड़काव और मृत्यु के समय भी मृतक के मुंह में इस के पत्तों का रख दिया जाना यही प्रमाणित करते हैं कि तुलसी बेजोड़ है—

(i) **तुलां सादृश्यं स्यति नाशयतीति तुलसी**

(ii) **नरा नार्यश्च तां दृष्ट्वा तुलनां दातुमक्षमाः।**
तेन नाम्ना च तुलसीं तां विदन्ति पुराविदः।।[5]

(iii) **तकारो मरणं प्रोक्तं तद्योगः स्यादुकारतः।**
मृता लसति सेत्येवं तुलसीत्येव गीयते।।[6]

भारत में ही नहीं, विदेशों में भी यह पौधा पवित्र तथा पूजनीय माना जाता है। पाश्चात्य भाषाओं में तुलसी के पर्याय-नाम ही इस भावना से ओत-प्रोत है। अंग्रेजी का Basil, प्राचीन फ्रैंच का Besile, आधुनिक फ्रैंच का Basilic, इटालियन का Basilico, लैटिन का Baslicum तथा न्यू लैटिन का Ocimum ओष्ठपुष्पी पौधों एवं झाड़ियों के विविध पर्याय है जो पवित्रता के द्योतक है। इन के साथ Holy, Sacred आदि पवित्रता वाचक विशेषण इस की पूजनीयता के प्रमाण है। Holy Basil, Sacred Basil, Monk's Basil, Basilic Saint, Ocimum-Sanctum आदि सभी पर्याय विदेशों में इस अनुपमेय पौधे की महत्ता के ज्वलन्त उदाहरण हैं।[7]

तुलसी का पौधा उपयोगिता की दृष्टि से यथा नाम तथा गुण है। इसीलिए संसार के प्रायः सभी देशों में बहुत प्राचीन काल से इसकी प्रतिष्ठा चली आ रही है। भूमध्यसागर के तटवर्ती प्रदेशों में तुलसी बहुत पाई जाती है और स्वास्थ्यप्रद समझी जाती है। यूनान के गिरजों में भी इसे पवित्र माना जाता है। यह आस्था है कि महात्मा यीशु की कब्र पर तुलसी उग आई थी अतः यूनान के पूर्वीय प्रार्थनाघरों में इसकी पूजा की जाती है और यह पूजा एक विशेष दिन होती है जिसे St. Basil's Day (तुलसी उत्सव) कहते हैं इस दिन महिलाएं तुलसी के पौधे की शाखाएं लेकर मङ्गल-कल्याण के लिए प्रार्थनाघरों में जाती हैं।[8]

आश्चर्य की बात है कि इस क्षुप का 'तुलसी' नाम केवल मध्यकालीन और उत्तरकालीन ग्रन्थों में ही मिलता है। भावप्रकाश में इसे **तुलसी सुरसा ग्राम्या सुलभा बहुमञ्जरी।**
अपेतराक्षसी गौरी शूलघ्नी देवदुन्दुभिः।।[9]

राजनिघण्टु में

तुलसी सुभगा तीव्रा पावनी विष्णुवल्लभा।
सुरेज्या सुरसा ज्ञेया तुलसी कायस्था सुरदुन्दुभिः।।[10]

और कैय्यदेवनिघण्टु में

तुलसी सुरसा गौरी पापघ्नी विष्णुवल्लभा।
मयूरा सरला कृष्णा भूतेष्टा देवदुन्दुभिः।।[11]

कह कर वर्णन किया गया है। परन्तु प्राक्कालीन किसी भी ग्रन्थ में इस का यह पर्याय नहीं मिलता। चरक (700–1000 ई० पूर्व) सुश्रुत (1000 ई० पूर्व से भी पहले) तथा वाग्भट (700–900 शती) में भी तुलसी शब्द नहीं आता। इस क्षुप के भेदों का वर्णन करते समय अवश्य सुरसा-सुमुख, फणिज्जक, कुठेरक, अर्जक आदि नाम दिए गए हैं। परन्तु 12वीं शताब्दी के डल्हणाचार्य (सुश्रुत के टीकाकार) ने 'सुरसा' की व्याख्या करते हुए उस के लोकप्रचलित नाम तुलसी का परिचय दिया है; सुरसा सुरभिपर्णी तुलसीतिलोके। यह उल्लेखनीय है कि 16वीं शताब्दी के भावप्रकाश आदि ग्रन्थों में इस क्षुप को दिए गए विष्णुवल्लभा हरिप्रिया, माधवी, अमृता, पुण्या, पावनी आदि नामों का उल्लेख डल्हण ने नहीं किया। अतः निष्कर्ष रूप में हम कह सकते हैं कि यह क्षुप तो अवश्य सुदूर प्राचीनकाल में उपयोग में आता रहा है। परन्तु इसकी बेजोड़ उपयोगिता को देखकर इस में 'तुलसी' (तुलां सादृश्यं स्यति नाशयतीति तुलसी) नाम पुराणकारों ने भावप्रकाश तथा डल्हण से पूर्व दिया और इसे धार्मिक महत्त्व भी प्रदान किया। वनस्पतियों के विष्णु (विष्लृ व्याप्तौ) अधिष्ठित होने के कारण, इस का सम्बन्ध विष्णु के साथ जोड़ दिया गया।[12]

पुराणों में इसे कृष्णप्रिया, हरिप्रिया, विष्णुवल्लभा, वृन्दा, मञ्जरी तथा बहुमञ्जरी आदि कई नामों से पुकारा गया है। स्कन्दपुराण में इसे 'सर्वलक्षणसम्पन्ना' व 'सर्वाभरणभूषिता' कहा गया है। तुलसी की उत्पत्ति के विषय में कई कथाएं प्रचलित हैं। इन में सबसे प्रसिद्ध कथा तो इस की विष्णुप्रिया होने की ही है। अमरत्व प्रदान करने वाले अमृत कलश को हाथों में लिए श्री विष्णु अत्यन्त प्रसन्न हुए। उनके आनन्द-अश्रुओं की कुछ बूंदें उस अमृत कलश में गिरीं। उसी में से तत्काल मण्डलाकार तुलसी उत्पन्न हुई। इस प्रकार वहाँ प्रकट हुई लक्ष्मी और तुलसी को देवताओं ने विष्णु को समर्पित किया। विष्णु ने उन्हें स्वीकार किया। तभी से यह तुलसी विष्णु की प्रिया हो गई। यह सभी पापों से मुक्त करने वाली, पुण्य प्रदान करने वाली तथा सभी इच्छाओं को पूर्ण करने वाली है सर्वपापहरं पूतं कामदं तुलसीवनम्। तुलसी-वनों का पालन करना हिन्दुओं के नित्य कर्मों में प्रतिपादित है। तुलसी का गौरव व माहात्म्य इस तथ्य से भी प्रतिष्ठित होता है कि तुलसी के रोपण, पालन, सिञ्चन, दर्शन और स्पर्श से ही विविध पाप (वाणी-मन-शरीर के पाप) दग्ध हो जाते हैं :—

रोपणात्पालनात्सेकाद्दर्शनात्स्पर्शनान्नृणाम् ।
तुलसी दहते पापं वाङ्मनःकायसंचितम्।।[13]

तुलसी गङ्गा की तरह पवित्र, पुण्य प्रदान करने वाली और स्वर्गदायिनी मानी गयी है।

यथागङ्गा पवित्राङ्गी सुरलोके विमोक्षदा
यथा भगीरथी पुण्या तथेयं तुलसी शिवा।।[14]

सैकड़ों स्वर्णमुद्राओं के दान का पुण्य तुलसी के एक पत्ते के दान से प्राप्त होने की भी बात शास्त्रों में कही गई है— तुलसीपत्रमेकं तु शतहेमफलप्रदम्।[15]

मणिकाञ्चनपुष्पाणि तथा मुक्ताफलानि तु।
तुलसीपत्रदानस्य कलां नार्हन्ति षोडशीम्।।[16]

सुधाघटसहस्त्रेण या तुष्टिर्न भवेत्समा।
सा च तुष्टिर्भवेन्नृणां तुलसीपत्रदानतः।।[17]

गवामयुतदानेन यत्फलं लभते नरः।
तुलसीपत्रदानेन तत्फलं कार्तिके सति।।[18]

इतना ही नहीं अकेला तुलसीपत्र सभी देवताओं का अधिष्ठान माना गया है। पुष्कर इत्यादि तीर्थ, गङ्गा आदि नदियाँ और ब्रह्मा-विष्णु-महेश आदि देवता सभी तुसली दल में निवास करते हैं :-

पुष्कराद्यानि तीर्थानि गंगाद्याः सरितस्तथा।
वासुदेवादयो देवास्तिष्ठन्ति तुलसीदले।।[19]

पुराणों में तुलसीदल को पूजा के लिए चुनने वाले हाथों को धन्य माना गया है :

तुलसीं ये विचिन्वन्ति धन्यास्ते करपल्लवाः।

पुराणों में तुलसी को तोड़ने की विधि पर भी विशेष ध्यान दिया गया है। जो कदाचित् वैज्ञानिक होने के कारण धर्म व कर्म के साथ जोड़ दी गई है। तुलसी का एक-एक पत्ता न तोड़कर पत्तियों के साथ अग्रभाग को तोड़ना चाहिए। तुलसी की मञ्जरी सब फूलों में उत्तम मानी गई है। मञ्जरी तोड़ते समय उसमें पत्तियों का होना भी आवश्यक माना गया है। पूरे पौधे को हिलाएं बिना, पूज्यभाव से तुलसी दल तोड़कर प्रभु को अर्पण करना चाहिए।

यन्नातिकम्पते शाखा न भङ्गां याति वा तथा।
चिनुयात्तुलसीपत्राण्येवं विष्णुप्रियो भवेत।।[20]

तुलसी को जगतधात्री, कल्याणी, मोक्षप्रदायिनी, सम्पतदायिनी और चराचर की सरंक्षिका माना जाता है। इसके स्मरण मात्र से ही मानव पवित्र हो जाता है। अनेकों ऋषि-मुनि इस कल्याणी के सहारे बैकुण्ठ पहुंच गए बताए गए हैं।

भक्तिमुक्तिप्रदा मुख्या सर्वलोकपरा शुभा।
यामाश्रित्य गताः स्वर्गमक्षयं मुनिसत्तमाः।।[21]

लक्ष्मी, सरस्वती और गङ्गा के समान तुलसी भी नारायण की प्रेमभाजन मानी जाती है।

लक्ष्मी सरस्वती गङ्गा तुलसी लोकपावनी।
एता नारायणस्यैव चतस्त्रश्च प्रिया इति।।[22]

श्राद्ध, दान, तप, होम, सन्ध्योपासन, पूजन, पुराण-पाठादि सत्कृत्य तुलसी के पास ही करने चाहिए।

श्राद्धं दानं तपो होमः सन्ध्योपासनपूजने।
पुराणपठनं चापि तुलसीसन्निधौ चरेत्।।[23]

वस्तुतः तुलसी के पत्ते-फूल-फल-मूल-शाखा-छाल-तना-मिट्टी आदि सभी पवित्र होते हैं। जिस घर में तुलसीमूल की मृत्तिका (तुलसीपदरज) रहती है वहाँ विष्णु, शिव आदि देवता सदा निवास करते हैं-

पत्रं पुष्पं फलं मूलं शाखा त्वक् स्कन्ध संज्ञितम्।
तुलसीसम्भवं सर्वं पावनं मृत्तिकादिकम्।।[24]

यस्मिन्गृहे मुनिश्रेष्ठ तुलसीमूलमृत्तिका।
सर्वदा तत्र तिष्ठन्ति देवताश्च शिवो हरिः।।[25]

जिस घर, गांव या वन में तुलसी उगी होती है वहां दरिद्रता, रोग, बन्धु–वियोग आदि किसी का भय नहीं होता—

गृहे तस्मिन्न दारिद्र्यं नायोगो बन्धुसम्भवः।
न दुःखं न भयं रोगास्तुलसी यत्र तिष्ठति।।[26]

इस के विविध पर्याय उस के गुण–कर्म के आधार पर ही रखे गए है। उनमें से कुछ का विवरण निम्नाङ्कित है जो कदाचित् रोचक तथा ज्ञानवर्धक है।[27]

अपेतराक्षसी	–	अपेतो राक्षस इव पातकं यस्याः अथवा राक्षस रूप ज्वरादि रोग नाशक कीटों को भगा देने वाली।
अमृता	–	न मृता तुलसी। रोग निवारकत्वेन तथात्वम् अमृततुल्यास्वादवत्त्वात्।
ग्राम्या	–	ग्रामे भवा, अतिसुलभत्वात्तथात्वम्।
तुंगी	–	तुञ्जति कृमिकीटादीनिति (तृजि हिंसायाम्)।
देवदुन्दुभिः	–	देवानां दुन्दुभिरिव हर्षप्रदत्वात्।
दोषाक्लेशी	–	दोषानाक्लिश्नाति इति।
नागनामा	–	नागान् नामयति नम्रीकरोति।
पापध्नी	–	पापानि (रोगरूपपापानि) हन्तीति।
पुण्या	–	पुनाति या पूयतेऽनयेति वा।
प्रेतराक्षसी	–	प्रेतस्य भूतभेदस्य राक्षसीव दूरतोऽपसर्पणकारित्वात्।
भूतघ्नी	–	भूतान् (राक्षसरूपकृमीन्) हन्तीति।
भूतप्रिया	–	भूतानां प्रिया प्राणीनां हितकरत्वात्।
भूतेष्टा	–	भूतानां प्राणीनां इष्टा अभिलषिता हितकरत्वात्।
भूरीमञ्जरी	–	भूरयो मञ्जर्योऽस्या इति।
मयूरा	–	मीनाति रोगम् (मीञ् हिंसायाम्) मिनोति प्रक्षिपत्यग्निमान्द्यमिति।
विष्णुवल्लभा	–	विष्णोर्वल्लभा प्रिया।
वैष्णवी	–	विष्णोरियम्।
वृन्दा	–	वृत्यते वृणुते वा।
वैकुण्ठा	–	विगता कुण्ठा नाशो यस्मात्।

शूलघ्नी - शूलं हन्तीति।

सरला - सरतीति (सृ गतौ)।

सुभगा - सुष्ठु भगो माहात्म्यादिर्यस्याः सा।

सुमञ्जरी - सुष्ठुशोभना पुष्पमञ्जरी यस्याः सा।

सुरेज्या - सुष्ठु यथा स्यात्तथा सुरैर्वा इज्यते पूज्यते।

सुलभा - सुखेन लभ्यते यत्रतत्रसर्वत्रापीति।

इस प्रकार धार्मिक व सांस्कृतिक पक्ष के अतिरिक्त तुलसी का सर्वगुणसम्पन्न औषधीय पक्ष भी अत्यन्त महत्त्वपूर्ण है। इस का यह पक्ष पूर्णरूपेण वैज्ञानिक है। देश-विदेश में हुए अनुसन्धानों से यह सिद्ध हुआ है कि तुलसी में उड़नशील तेल है जो हवा में मिलकर कीटाणुओं को नष्ट कर देता है। तुलसी की गन्ध को लेकर वायु दसों दिशाओं में जहां-जहां जाता है, वहां-वहां सभी प्राणियों को पवित्र कर देता है और इस प्रकार लोक कल्याण करता है—

तुलसीगन्धमाघ्राय यत्र गच्छति मारुतः।
दिशो दश च ताः पूता भूतग्रामश्चतुर्विधः।।[28]

इस में वायु शुद्ध करने की विलक्षण क्षमता है। आज के प्रदूषित पर्यावरण में आंगन अथवा फ्लैट में तुलसी का पौधा पूरे परिवार के स्वास्थ्य के लिए उत्तम है। आयुर्वेद तथा होमियोपैथी की 300 से भी अधिक दवाइयों में तुलसी का प्रयोग होता है। यह श्वास रोग, क्षय रोग तथा कुष्ट रोग निवारक है।

तुलसी के परिवेश में रखी गई खाद्य सामग्री व पेय पदार्थ काफी समय तक सुरक्षित रहते हैं। यही कारण है कि सूर्य-ग्रहण तथा चन्द्र-ग्रहण के समय सभी खाद्य व पेय पदार्थों में तुलसी-दल डाल दिए जाते हैं। ग्रहण के समय वातावरण में उपस्थित हानिकारक तत्त्वों के लिए तुलसी का प्रयोग अत्यन्त लाभदायक होता है।

प्रातः स्नानादि के उपरान्त कुछ क्षण तुलसी के पौधे के पास बैठकर, उसके स्पर्श वाली गन्ध से फेफड़ों को भरना चाहिए। कुछ समय तक लम्बे-लम्बे श्वास लेकर, उसे अन्दर रखकर धीरे-धीरे छोड़ने से व्यक्ति का तन-मन पुलकित हो उठता है। माना जाता है कि तुलसी में आध्यात्मिक ऊर्जा भी विद्यमान रहती है, जो व्यक्ति के चिन्तन व मनन में उदार भाव लाती है। शायद यही कारण है कि प्राचीन काल में सभी ऋषि-मुनि अपने आश्रमों में तुलसी के पौधों का प्रचुर आरोपण करते थे। आज के भौतिक युग में भी सात्त्विक आहार-व्यवहार वाले लोगों के घर में तुलसी का पौधा उन के गृहों का विशेष चिह्न है। अतः पर्यावरण तथा विचारों की शुद्धि के लिए तुलसी का पौधा सब से उत्तम माना गया है

सर्वेभ्यः पत्रपुष्पेभ्यः सत्तमा तुलसी शिवा।
सर्वकामप्रदा शुद्धा वैष्णवी विष्णुसुप्रिया।।[29]

इसका सर्वाङ्ग सुगन्धित होता है। तुलसी का रस तीखा (कटु), कड़वा (तिक्त) और कसैला (कषाय) भी होता है। इस की गन्ध तीव्र, रोचक तथा आह्लादक होती है। इस का प्रभाव वात-कफ नाशक, तीक्ष्ण, दाहपित्तकारक और हृदय के लिए लाभकारी होता है। यह श्वास, कास, हिचकी और कृमियों को समाप्त करने की क्षमता रखती है। वमन, दुर्गन्ध, कुण्ठ, पार्श्वशूल (पसली का दर्द), विष, मूत्रकृच्छ्र, रक्तदोष, भूतबाधा, धनुवात (टेटनेस) व्यामोह (हिस्टीरिया), पेट-दर्द, कान दर्द, मलेरिया, टाइफाइड आदि रोगों को नष्ट करती है। इस के उपर्युक्त गुण-प्रभाव का विवेचन सुश्रुत, चरक, धन्वन्तरि, कैय्यदेव, भावप्रकाश आदि आयुर्वेदीय ग्रन्थों में निम्नलिखित प्रकार से दिया गया है—

कफानिलविषश्वासकासदौर्गन्ध्यनाशनः।
पित्तकृत् पार्श्वशूलघ्नः सुरससमुदाहृतः।।[30]

हिक्काकासविषश्वासपार्श्वशूलविनाशनः ।
पित्तकृत् पार्श्वशूलघ्नः सुरसः पूतिगन्धहा।।[31]

तुलसी लघुरुष्णा च रुक्षा कफविनाशिनी।
कृमिदोषं निहन्त्येषा रुचिकृद् वह्निदीपनी।।[32]

तुलसी तु वरा तिक्ता तीक्ष्णोष्णा कटुपाकिनी।
रुक्षा हृद्या लघुः कट्वी दाहपित्ताग्निवर्धनी।।[33]

तुलसी कटुका तिक्ता हृद्योष्णा दाहपित्तकृत्।
दीपनी कुष्ठकृच्छ्रास्त्रपार्श्वरुक्कफवातजित्।।[34]

आयुर्वेदीय उपचारों में तो तुलसी की उपयोगिता उस की अतुलनीयता की प्रमाण है। यह मस्तिष्क के अवरोध को खोलती है। शोथ को शान्त करती है, वायु को दूर करती है, आमाशय की मन्दता को हटाती है और हृदय की व्याकुलता को दूर करती है। यह रक्तविकारजनित रोगों में बहुत लाभकारी है। यह महामारी की वायु से भी रक्षा करती है। शीतप्रधान रोगों में तुलसी विशेषरूप से उपयोग में लायी जाती है। जोड़ों के दर्द और ज्वर में तुलसी बहुत लाभकारी है।

तुलसी के अधिकांश उपचार बहुत सहज हैं, जिनमें से कुछ निम्नाङ्कित हैं—

1. तुलसी के नियमित सेवन से भारी व्यक्ति का वजन घटता है और दुर्बल व्यक्ति का वजन बढ़ता है।
2. दूषित पानी में तुलसी की ताजी पत्तियाँ डालने से पानी शुद्ध हो जाता है।
3. प्रातःकाल खालीपेट दो चम्मच तुलसी के रस का सेवन करने से स्मरण शक्ति बढ़ती है और साथ ही साथ रक्त में शुद्धता हो जाने से मुखमण्डल पर भी विशेष आभा आ जाती है।
4. तुलसी-रस की कुछ बूंदों में थोड़ा सा नमक मिलाकर बेहोश व्यक्ति के नाक में डालने से उसे होश आ जाता है।
5. तुलसी के पत्ते व काली मिर्च के सेवन से मलेरिया तथा टायफाइड बुखार ठीक हो जाता है।
6. चाय में तुलसी के कुछ पत्ते उबाल लेने से सर्दी, जुकाम तथा मांसपेशियों का दर्द ठीक हो जाता है।
7. भोजन के पश्चात् तुलसी की चार-पाँच पत्तियाँ चबाने से पाचन शक्ति बढ़ जाती है।
8. तुलसी दल, सैंधा नमक तथा पिसी सौंठ का काढ़ा पीने से कब्ज दूर हो जाती है।
9. किसी भी प्रकार के चर्मरोग पर तुलसी रस लगाने से लाभ होता है।
10. तुलसी-रस को गर्म करके, उसकी कुछ बूंदें कान में डालने से कान का दर्द ठीक हो जाता है।
11. तुलसी की पत्तियों को पीसकर उनमें नींबू रस मिलाकर लगाने से दाद, खुजली, एग्जीमा ठीक हो जाते हैं।

12. दो-तीन भुने लौंगों के साथ तुलसी की पत्ती चूसने से खांसी में लाभ होता है।

13. प्रतिदिन सवेरे तुलसी की पांच पत्तियां निगलने से कई संक्रामक बीमारियों से सुरक्षा हो जाती है।

तुलसी की उपर्युक्त सर्वगुणसम्पन्नता को ध्यान में रखते हुए यदि हम अपने घरों में तुलसी के पौधों का आरोपण करें, तो इण्डस्ट्री और ट्रेफ़िक के प्रदूषण से प्रभावित पर्यावरण को सहज ही शुद्ध किया जा सकता है। तुलसी वस्तुतः 'तुलसी माँ' है जो सर्वदा अपनी सन्तति की सुरक्षा व स्वास्थ्य के लिए उपस्थित है। आज अशान्ति, कलुषता और भौतिकता के युग में भी यदि हम विष्णुवल्लभा, हरिप्रिया तुलसी को आदर भाव से माँ रूप में स्वीकार करें और तुलसी वनों को आरोपित करें तो निश्चितरूपेण यह तुलसी हमारी ढाल बन रक्षा करने में समर्थ है।

यह कल्याणी-मञ्जरी आबाल-वृद्ध, सभी के स्नेह व आदर की भाजन है। बस एक बार यह घर के आंगन की शोभा बन गई, तो चहुँ ओर इसकी सुरभि से सारा प्रदूषित पर्यावरण स्वच्छ व शुद्ध हो उठेगा।

वस्तुतः तुलसी की पौराणिक महत्ता, उसकी रोगनिवारण क्षमता तथा उसकी औषधीय गुणवत्ता को समग्र दृष्टिकोण (Holistic approach) से अपनाना और उनका यथा-शक्ति जीवन में निर्वाह करना आज के युग की अनिवार्यता है। यह पर्यावरण संरक्षण और आरोग्य जीवन यापन की आधार शिला है। यह कहना अतिशयोक्ति नहीं होगा कि तुलसी सामाजिक, धार्मिक, शारीरिक व मानसिक रूप से पूर्ण स्वस्थ रहने की तालिका है। मानव समाज एवं संस्कृति को वनस्पति से जोड़ने का स्नेहिल कृत्य करने वाली मानवकल्याण में संलग्न, एकनिष्ठ स्वास्थ्य-संवाहिका यह तुलसी वस्तुतः बेजोड़ है।

तुलसी उगाकर प्रदूषण हटाएं।
पर्यावरण-शुद्धि में हम भी हाथ बटाएं।।

सन्दर्भ-सङ्केत

1. प्रयोगात्मक अभिनवद्रव्यगुणविज्ञानम्, डॉ॰ मायाराम उनियाल।
2. प्रयोगात्मक अभिनवद्रव्यगुणविज्ञानम्, डॉ॰ मायाराम उनियाल।
3. प्रयोगात्मक अभिनवद्रव्यगुणविज्ञानम्, डॉ॰ मायाराम उनियाल।
4. तुलसी, कृष्णदास अकादमी वाराणसी, आचार्य ब्रह्मदत्त शर्मा।
5. ब्रह्मवैवर्तपुराण - 2 15, 14
6. बृहद्धर्मपुराण - प्रथम खण्ट 7, 63
7. तुलसी, कृष्णदास अकादमी वाराणसी, आचार्य ब्रह्मदत्त शर्मा।
8. तुलसी, कृष्णदास अकादमी वाराणसी, आचार्य ब्रह्मदत्त शर्मा।
9. भावप्रकाश-पुष्पवर्ग; 61
10. राजनिघण्टु - 10; 150
11. कैय्यदेवनिघण्टु - 1124
12. तुलसी, कृष्णदास अकादमी वाराणसी, आचार्य ब्रह्मदत्त शर्मा।
13. पद्मपुराण - 6; 244, 6

14. पद्मपुराण – 5; 58, 118

15. पद्मपुराण – 5; 58, 113

16. पद्मपुराण – 6; 244, 8

17. ब्रह्मवैवर्तपुराण – 2; 21, 41

18. ब्रह्मवैवर्तपुराण – 2; 21, 42

19. पद्मपुराण – 6; 107, 14

20. बृहद्धर्मपुराण – प्रथम खण्ड, 8, 49

21. पद्मपुराण – 5; 58, 110

22. ब्रह्मवैवर्त पुराण – 2; 12,1

23. बृहद्धर्मपुराण – प्रथम खण्ड, 8. 54

24. पद्मपुराण – 6; 24, 2

25. पद्मपुराण – 6; 25, 36

26. पद्मपुराण – 6; 24, 32

27. तुलसी, कृष्णदास अकादमी वाराणसी, आचार्य ब्रह्मदत्त शर्मा।

28. पद्मपुराण – 6; 25, 35

29. पद्मपुराण – 5; 58, 109

30. सुश्रुतसंहिता, निर्णयसागर प्रेस।

31. चरकसंहिता, निर्णयसागर प्रेस।

32. धन्वन्तरिनिघण्टु, निर्णयसागर प्रेस।

33. कैय्यदेवनिघण्टु, निर्णयसागर प्रेस।

34. भावप्रकाशनिघण्टु – मोतीलाल बनारसीदास।

卐 卐 卐

अश्वत्थश्री

प्रवेश सक्सेना

सृष्टि अनादि है, अनन्त है, वृक्ष भी अनादि है, अनन्त है। सृष्टि की तुलना प्रायः वृक्ष से की जाती है। वृक्ष और बीज में कौन पहले यह रहस्य सृष्टि के रहस्य की तरह ही गुह्य है। जैसे एक बीज में एक विशाल वृक्ष की सम्भावना निहित रहती है वैसे ही प्रलय में सम्पूर्ण सृष्टि के बीज छिपे रहते हैं। 'संसरति इति संसारः'-हर क्षण संसार बदलता रहता है, वैसे ही वृक्ष भी परिवर्तित होता रहता है। सृष्टि-प्रलय, जन्म-मरण, सर्जन-विध्वंस निरन्तर विश्व में चलता रहता है। व्यक्तिगत स्तर पर हमारे शरीर के कोषों में भी चयापचय की प्रक्रिया चलती रहती है। एक वृक्ष अपने ही बीज से (मिट्टी में घुलमिल कर) उगता है। अपने तने, शाखाओं, प्रशाखाओं का विस्तार करता हुआ लाल कोंपलों, हरी पत्तियों का संसार रचता रहता है। इन्हीं से फूल, फिर फल उगते हैं जो फिर क्रम से नए बीजों को उत्पन्न करते हैं जिनसे नए-नए वृक्षों का सर्जन सम्भव होता है। प्रकृति का यह सहज स्वाभाविक नियम है—

एवं लोकस्तुल्यधर्मो वनानाम्।
काले काले छिद्यते रुह्यते च।। (स्वप्नवासवदत्तम्)

सृष्टि के रहस्य को जानने के लिए वैदिक ऋषि ने वेद में अनेक प्रकार से प्रश्न किए हैं और उनके उत्तर भी दिए हैं। ऋग्वेद X 31.10 में पूछा गया है—

किंस्विद्विनं क उ स वृक्ष आस
यतो द्यावापृथिवी निष्टतक्षुः।।

अर्थात् वह कौन-सा वन था? कौन-सा वृक्ष था जिससे द्यावापृथिवी बनाए गए?

सृष्टि की इन जिज्ञासाओं के समाधान जिस वृक्ष में ढूंढे गए वह अश्वत्थ था। वैदिकसाहित्य में ही कठोपनिषद् (2.3.1) में कहा गया है—

ऊर्ध्वमूलोऽवाक्शाख
एषोऽश्वत्थः सनातनः।

ऊपर की ओर मूल वाला, नीचे की ओर शाखा वाला, यह सनातन 'अश्वत्थ' है, गीता में भी इस संसारवृक्ष का रूपक विस्तार से वर्णित है—

ऊर्ध्वमूलमधःशाखमश्वत्थं प्राहुरव्ययम्।

प्रत्येक मानवसंस्कृति में जीवन-वृक्ष की बात कही गई है, इसी सादृश्य पर वंश-वृक्ष की बात भी कही जाती है। संस्कृति की निरन्तरता वृक्ष की निरन्तरता से जुड़ी हुई है। मानव एवं वनस्पति का सम्बन्ध चिरन्तन है। कठोपनिषद्

(2-3-1) में जहाँ अश्वत्थ को सृष्टि-वृक्ष के रूप में कल्पित किया गया है, वहाँ ऊर्ध्व मूल होने का तथ्य अवश्य ही स्वाभाविक नियम के विरुद्ध है, परन्तु यहाँ परमात्मा व सृष्टि के सम्बन्ध को बताने के लिए ही यह कहा गया है, क्योंकि परमात्मा को पाने के लिए व्यक्ति को ऊर्ध्वगामी होना होता है तथा यों भी सृष्टि के नियन्ता का मूल ऊपर की ओर ही माना जाता है। उस परमेश्वर के लिए वहाँ शुक्र, ब्रह्म और अमृत तीन शब्दों का प्रयोग किया गया है।

तदेव शुक्रं तद् ब्रह्म तदेवामृतमुच्यते
तस्मिँल्लोकाः श्रिताः सर्वे तदुनात्येति कश्चन।

अश्वत्थ अर्थात् पीपल के वृक्ष में भी तीनों विशेषताएँ हैं। वनस्पति शास्त्र की दृष्टि से 'अश्वत्थ' सूर्य की रश्मियों से प्रातःकाल अत्यधिक प्रकाशित होता है इसीलिए शुक्र है, ब्रह्म है (बृह् वर्धने) क्योंकि उसे जहाँ स्थान मिलता है वह बढने लगता है, अमृतमय है क्योंकि निरन्तर प्राणवायु (ऑक्सीजन) का उत्सर्जन करता है। सृष्टि के विकास की तरह वृक्ष का विकास भी हर दिशा में होता है। वृक्ष की वृद्धि उसमें निहित आवश्यक तत्वों पर निर्भर है, तब भी अनुकूल परिस्थितियाँ मिलने पर कोई वृक्ष किस दिशा में, किस रूप में फैलेगा यह कोई नहीं बता सकता? यह भी ध्यातव्य है कि प्रकृति कभी आवृत्ति नहीं करती, इसीलिए किन्हीं दो वृक्षों का रूप एक सा नहीं होता। शाखाओं प्रशाखाओं का बहुत्व सृष्टि के रहस्यों एवं सृष्टि के अनन्तत्व का द्योतक है। 'अश्वत्थ' वृक्ष का रूपक हमें प्रकृति व उसके तत्त्वों के प्रति नम्र बनाता है। हमारे अहं को मिटाता है। हम सभी वृक्ष पर लगे पत्तों के समान हैं, पत्ते उगते हैं, समय होने पर झड़ जाते हैं, नयों को स्थान देने के लिए। सर्जन की प्रक्रिया शाश्वत है इसीलिए वृक्ष को अव्यय और अक्षय कहा गया है। यह तो हुई संसाररूपी वृक्ष की बात। शरीररूपी वृक्ष का रूपक भी अथर्ववेद (9.9.20) में हमें मिलता है। और आश्चर्यजनक बात यह है कि यहाँ भी अश्वत्थ अर्थात् पीपल और उसके फल की ओर ही सङ्केत है—

द्वा सुपर्णा सयुजा सखाया समानं वृक्षं परिषस्वजाते।
तयोरन्यः पिप्पलं स्वाद्वत्त्यनश्नन्नन्यो अभिचाकशीति।।

'स्वादुपिप्पल' कर्मफल का द्योतक है। वनस्पति-शास्त्र की दृष्टि से भी पीपल के पेड़ का फल मीठा होता है। पिप्पल अश्वत्थ को भी कहते हैं तथा उसके फल को भी। अथर्ववेद (9.9.21) में पिप्पलम्, पालनीयम् भी इसका अर्थ माना गया है। यहीं कहा गया है—'यस्मिन् वृक्षे मध्वदः सुपर्णा निविशन्ते' अर्थात् जिस वृक्ष में मधु का संचय है वहाँ सुपर्ण पक्षी निवास करते हैं मधु की अभिलाषा से।

अब यहाँ प्रश्न उठता है कि सृष्टि में अनेकों वनस्पतियाँ हैं फिर अश्वत्थ को ही वैदिक ऋषियों ने सृष्टि या शरीर के रूप के लिए ही क्यों चुना? स्पष्ट है अश्वत्थ महान् ओषधि के रूप में श्रेष्ठ वृक्ष के रूप में वैदिक ऋषियों के लिए पूज्य व पवित्र था, इसकी विशेषताओं से वे परिचित थे, इसीलिए अश्वत्थ को यह सम्मान उन्होंने दिया।

ऋग्वेद में अश्वत्थ का उल्लेख इस प्रकार से हुआ है—

अश्वत्थे वो निषदनं
पर्णे वो वसतिष्कृता
गोभाज इत्किलासथ
यत्सनवथ पूरुषम्। (X.97.5)

'तुम्हारा आश्रय अश्वत्थ पर है, पत्र-समूह पर है, तुम भूमि सूर्य व रश्मि का सेवन करने वाली हो, जिससे तुम पुरुष देह का पोषण करती, उसे बल देती हो'। यहाँ अश्वत्थ के ओषधीय गुणों का ज्ञान है वैदिक ऋषि को। यह

ओषधि पोषण, पालन करने के कारण ही पिप्पल या लोक में पीपल कहलाती है। सायणाचार्य ने अश्वत्थ की लकड़ी से बने पात्र में सोमरस की बात भी कही है। ऋग्वेद में ही अश्वत्थ के साथ जय-विजय तथा मधु की बात के द्वारा वास्तव में उसके ओषधीय गुणों की ओर ही सङ्केत किया गया है।

अथर्ववेद में तो अश्वत्थ का नाम सात-आठ बार आया है। इसके अतिरिक्त दो सूक्त ऐसे हैं जिनकी देवता अश्वत्थ (III. 6) तथा पिप्पली (II. 109) है। अथर्ववेद लोकधर्म का प्रतिनिधित्व करता है यहाँ पर अश्वत्थ की विशेषताएं उसके ओषधीय गुणों के रूप में मुख्य रूप से वर्णित हैं। अश्वत्थ वृक्ष का वानस्पतिक व आकृतिमूलक या प्राकृतिक सौन्दर्य तो यहाँ नहीं मिलता परन्तु प्रदूषणरोधीक्षमता एवं रोगनिवारकशक्ति के बारे में हमें स्पष्ट सङ्केत मिलता है।

यहाँ सूक्त के ऋषि का 'जग-बीजम् पुरुषः' नाम भी सार्थक है। सृष्टि का प्रतीक वृक्ष है अश्वत्थ। कौशिक-सूत्र के अनुसार अश्वत्थ के काष्ठ से बनी अश्वमणि को सम्बोधित है यह मन्त्र। शत्रुओं के नाश एवं पराजय की कामना से अश्वत्थमणि का प्रयोग किया जाता था। अश्वत्थमणि को धारण करने का विधान है। आयुर्वेद में मणि का तात्पर्य औषधि की बटी या गोली से भी होता है। कौटिल्य के अर्थशास्त्र (14.179) में कहा गया है—

जातस्याश्वत्थस्य मणिः सर्पविषहरः।

सम्भवतः अथर्ववेद के इस सूक्त के मन्त्रों में इन्हीं ओषधीय गुणों की महत्ता बताई गई है। प्रथम मन्त्र में कहा गया है—

पुमान् पुंसः परिजातोऽश्वत्थः खदिरादधि।
स हन्तु शत्रून् मामकान् यानहं द्वेष्मि ये च माम्।।

यहाँ खदिर वृक्ष पर उत्पन्न पीपल के पेड़ के बारे में बताया गया है। वानस्पतिक दृष्टि से अश्वत्थ एक दुर्निवार पेड़ है इसे कोई लगाए या न लगाए, पुराने मकानों की सन्धियों में दीवार पर, छत पर जहाँ कहीं पीपल का फल (जिसे गोदा भी कहते हैं) खाकर चिड़ियां बीज बिखेर देती हैं वहीं पर यह उग आता है। किसी पेड़ की डाल या खोखल में यदि बीज पड़ जाए तो यह उग आता है। वैदिक साहित्य इतना प्राचीन साहित्य है अश्वत्थ जैसे वृक्ष की विशेषताएं वैदिक ऋषि से छिपी न रह सकीं। आधुनिक वनस्पति-विज्ञानविद् इस विशेषता के कारण इसे परोपजीवी (अंग्रेजी में epiphyte) कहते हैं। कुछ लोग इसे परजीवी मानते हैं परन्तु वास्तव में यह परोपजीवी है अपने आश्रयदाता वृक्ष का नाश नहीं करता प्रत्युत अपना भोजन मजबूत जड़ों से स्वयं ग्रहण करता है। खदिर पर उगे अश्वत्थ को 'पुमान्' अर्थात् अतिशय बल वाला कहा गया है। ग्रिफिथ ने इस पंक्ति का अनुवाद करते हुए कहा है—

'masculine springs from the masculine means the names of both the trees are words of that gender.'

तैत्तिरीयब्राह्मण में अश्वत्थ में अग्नि का निवास माना गया है तथा खदिर वृक्ष भी शक्ति और ऊर्जा का वृक्ष है, शतपथब्राह्मण में भी उर्वशी-पुरुरवस् पर आधरित आख्यायिका के अन्तर्गत अग्निदेवता द्वारा अश्वत्थ के रूप में प्रकट होने की अलौकिक घटना का उल्लेख किया गया है। अग्निदेवता का वास होने के कारण ही यज्ञ की समिधा हेतु अश्वत्थ की लड़की सर्वोपयुक्त मानी जाती है। वनस्पतिविज्ञान की दृष्टि से अश्वत्थ का नाम Ficus Riligiose है तथा खदिर Acacia Catechu है।

खदिर पर उगने से पीपल और अधिक गुणकारी हो जाता है। इस मन्त्र की दूसरी पंक्ति में शत्रुओं के नाश की

बात कही है रोग, दूषित वायु सब मनुष्य के शत्रु हैं, उनको दूर करने का बल पीपल में है। अश्वत्थ का अर्थ ही अश्व अर्थात् बल में स्थित। अश्वत्थ प्राणवायु का मुख्य स्रोत है। निरन्तर प्राणवायु अर्थात् ओषजन विसर्जन करने के कारण यह मिथ भी प्रचलित हो गई कि रात में भी अश्वत्थ आक्सीजन छोड़ता है परन्तु वानस्पतिक शास्त्र की दृष्टि से यह सम्भव नहीं है। प्रकाश-संश्लेषण की क्रिया सौर-प्रकाश में ही सम्भव है। अश्वत्थ अपनी प्राणवायु के बल से प्रदूषण का नाश करे, यही प्रार्थना की गयी है।

इसी सूक्त के दूसरे मन्त्र में अश्वत्थ के लिए विशेषण है—'वैबाध'। सायण ने कहा है-'विविधं बाधते कण्टकैरिति विवाधः खदिरः तत्रोत्पन्नः वैबाधः अश्वत्थः'-अर्थात् कण्टकों से युक्त खदिर पर उत्पन्न अश्वत्थ। ग्रिफिथ ने कहा है वैबाध का अर्थ है-'Burster because it splits asunder the wood'.

इस मन्त्र में कहा गया है कि वह अन्धकार मिटाने वाले (इन्द्र) सूर्य से, मित्र (प्रेरणा देने वाले) वायु से तथा स्वीकार करने योग्य जल (मेदी सन्) स्नेही होकर उन बार-बार भयभीत करने वाले या क्रोधी शत्रुओं को सर्वथा मार डाले—

तानश्वत्थ निः शृणीहि शत्रून् वैबाध दोधतः
इन्द्रेण वृत्रघ्ना मेदी मित्रेण वरुणेन च।।

डॉ० दिनेशचन्द्र अग्रवाल ने वैबाध के कारण इसे विनाशकारी प्रवृत्ति का माना है तथा कहा है कि शत्रुओं के विनाश के लिए पीपल को विशेष आराध्य सम्भवतः आर्यजाति ने इसीलिए माना होगा।

तीसरे मंत्र में कहा गया है कि हे (अश्वत्थमणि के कारणभूत) पीपल के वृक्ष तुम इस विस्तीर्ण अन्तरिक्ष में खदिर के अन्तर्भाग को विदीर्ण कर उत्पन्न हुए हो, ठीक इसी प्रकार तुम शत्रुओं को भी विदीर्ण कर डालो—

यथाश्वत्थ निरभनोऽन्तर्महत्यर्णवे।
एवा तान्त्सर्वान्निर्भङ्ग्धि यानहं द्वेष्मि ये च माम्।।

अथर्ववेद III. 6.4 में अश्वत्थ को 'सासहान' तथा 'ऋषभ' कहा गया है अर्थात् पीपल महाबली और श्रेष्ठ है। ऋषभ एक औषधि का भी नाम है। शब्दकल्पद्रुम में से मीठा, शीतल रक्तपित्त विरेकनाशक आदि कहा गया है। इसी सूक्त के पांचवें मंत्र में पीपल से प्रार्थना की गयी है कि शत्रुओं को अमोक्य (कभी न खुल सकने वाले) मृत्यु के पाशों से बांध डाले। छठे मंत्र में कहा गया है 'हे अश्वत्थ जिस प्रकार तुम वनस्पतियों पर चढ़कर उन्हें 'अधरान् कृणुषे'— नीचा कर देते हो, वैसे ही हमारे शत्रुओं को पराजित करो कि वे लौटकर प्रहार न कर सकें। जैसे तट से बंधी रस्सी के कट जाने पर नौका जल में वह जाती है वैसे ही वे दूर बहकर चले जाएं—

तेऽधराञ्चः प्र प्लवन्तां छिन्ना नौरिव बन्धनात्।
न वैबाधप्रणुत्तानां पुनरस्ति निवर्तनम्।। (अथर्ववेद - III. 6.7)

अन्तिम मन्त्र में सायणाचार्य के अनुसार मन, चित्त तथा मंत्र के द्वारा अधिमन्त्रित अश्वत्थ की शाखा के द्वारा भी सभी शत्रुओं का उच्चाटन करने की बात कही गई है—

प्रैणान् नुदे मनसा चित्तेनोत ब्रह्मणा।
प्रैणान् वृक्षस्य शाखयाश्वत्थस्य नुदामहे।। (अथर्ववेद - III. 6.8)

अथर्ववेद में ही VI.II सूक्त है जिसका प्रयोग 'पुंसवन कर्म' में किया जाता है। प्रजापति इसके ऋषि हैं। यहाँ प्रथम मन्त्र में पुंसवन कर्म की बात की गई है—

शमीमश्वत्थ आरूढस्तत्र पुंसवनं कृतम्
तद्वै पुत्रस्य वेदनं तत् स्त्रीष्वाभरामसि।।

श्री दयानन्द ने भी 'संस्कार-विधि' में इस मन्त्र का उल्लेख किया है। ग्रिफिथ ने कहा है—

'The production of fire by means of the drill, the upperpart of which is made of Aśvattha and the lower part or receptacle of *śamī* wood represents the union of man and wife.'

अर्थात् अरणिमन्थन से अग्नि का उत्पन्न होना पुरुष व स्त्री के संयोग से संतान पैदा होने का प्रतीक है। श्रीकेशवदेव शास्त्री ने 'अर्थवेदीय कर्मज-व्याधि-निरोध' नामक ग्रन्थ में अश्वत्थ के प्रतीकात्मक प्रयोग के कई वर्णन दिए हैं—

'जिस शमीवृक्ष पर पीपल उगा हो उसके नीचे पश्चात् स्त्री-पुरुष अपनी मनोकामना व्यक्त करते हुए वृक्ष का स्पर्श करते हुए यह संकल्प करें कि गर्भाधान तथा पुंसवन के पश्चात् जब पुत्र होगा तो मुण्डन संस्कार यहीं आपकी छाया के नीचे करेंगे। ऐसा करने से वंध्या भी पुत्रवती होती है' (पृ. 389)। श्री देवशास्त्री ने भी इस वृक्ष के नीचे बैठकर 41 दिन इसी का 1100 बार जप करने या कराने से 'पुत्रप्राप्ति' की बात कही है। आचार्य प्रियव्रतवेदवाचस्पति ने वेद और उसकी वैज्ञानिकता (भारतीय मनीषा के परिपेक्ष्य में) नामक ग्रन्थ में इस मन्त्र की वैज्ञानिकता के सम्बन्ध में प्रमाण दिया है। पीपल की जटाएँ, छाल और बारीक जड़ें छाया में सुखाकर चूर्ण बनाकर गर्भाधान से एक मास पूर्व और बाद में भी दो तीन मास तक एक-एक चम्मच गो-दुग्ध के साथ खिलाने से पुत्र की प्राप्ति हुई। (उनके मित्र के सेवक की पत्नी को जिसके कई वर्ष से संतान थी ही नहीं) यह गोदुग्ध भी यदि उन गायों का हो जो शमीवृक्ष पीपल के नीचे निवास करती हों तो और भी अच्छा। दीर्घायु के लिए भी पीपल या खदिर (खैर) की लकड़ियों को अभिमन्त्रित किया जाता है तथा सोए हुए भाग्य को जगाने के लिए अश्वत्थमूल के समीप सन्ध्या करने का विधान कौशिक-सूत्रों में उपलब्ध ा होता है।

शमीवृक्ष लोक में देंकुर नाम से प्रसिद्ध है। इसका वानस्पतिक नाम 'प्रेस्पोय्स स्पीशिगेरा' (Prospois spicigera) है। आयुर्वेद में इसे कड़वा, चरपरा प्रशीतक, कसैला व रेचक कहा गया है तथा यह कफ, खांसी, श्वास, कुष्ठ, भ्रम, बवासीर तथा कृमि रोगों का नाशक है। उभर अश्वत्थ भी आयुर्वेद की दृष्टि से प्रशीतक, भारी करौला, रूखा, वर्ण उत्तम करने वाला, रक्त विकार को नष्ट करने वाला है। बच्चों के होंठ, जीभ, तालु, मुख पकने या आने में शहद के साथ पीपल चूर्ण का लेप हितकर है। व्रण धोने के लिए इसके क्वाथ (Decoction) का प्रयोग किया जाता है।

अश्वत्थ का प्राकृतिक सौन्दर्य भी अद्वितीय है। इसके पत्ते कोमल चिकने और हरे पीले रंग के होते हैं। पत्तों की आकृति पान के पत्तों के समान परन्तु विशेष नोकदार शिरा से पूर्ण होती है। इसके बीज बहुत छोटे होते हैं, हवा से उड़कर या पक्षियों की विष्ठा (बीट) के साथ जहां तहां उग आते हैं। इसके फूल इतने छोटे होते हैं कि दिखाई नहीं देते इसीलिए पीपल का एक नाम गुह्यपुष्पक भी है। इसके पुष्प गूलर, बरगद तथा अञ्जीर के फूलों से मिलते जुलते हैं। इसके परागण की विधि भी विशिष्ट है। चैत्र मास में पतझड़ में इसके पत्ते झड़ जाते हैं। वर्षा से पूर्व ही यह कोमल पत्तों से फिर शोभित हो जाता है। पीपल के पेड़ की जड़ें बहुत मजबूती से, बलपूर्वक जल को खींचती हैं और दिन में, दोपहर में भी इस पेड़ के नीचे जाने पर फुहार सी गिरती महसूस होती है इसीलिए इस पेड़ की छाया बहुत ही सुखद और शीतल होती है। छाया देने वाले वृक्षों में अश्वत्थ को सर्वश्रेष्ठ माना जाता है। अथर्ववेद में इसीलिए इसे

देवसदनः (II. 4.3) कहा गया है अर्थात् अश्वत्थ की छाया में देवता निवास करते हैं। भावार्थ यही है कि पीपल की छाया आरोग्यकारी है। अश्वत्थ का हिन्दी में नाम पीपल है। बंगला में संस्कृत की तरह अश्वत्थ ही कहा जाता है। मराठी में पिपल, कन्नड में अरली, गुजराती में पीपलो कहा जाता है।

पीपल के फल को भी पिप्पल या पिप्पली कहा जाता है। कुछ लोगों के अनुसार पिप्पल या पिप्पली अलग औषधि है परन्तु अथर्ववेद (VI. 109) में व्रण-उपचार संबंधी सूक्त में पिप्पली ओषधी की जिन विशेषताओं का उल्लेख मिलता है इससे तो पीपल के फल का ही बोध होता है। यहां पिप्पली को पालन करने वाली, विक्षिप्तता की, अतिघाव वाले की ओषधी बताया गया है। देवता उसे संजीवनी (जीवितवे अलम्) कहते हैं। आयुर्वेद के अनुसार भी पिप्पली के गुण ज्वर, कुष्ठ, प्रमेह, प्लीह, शूल, आम आदि रोगों के नाश करने वाले हैं। यहां भी (अथर्ववेद VI. 109.3) उसे गठिया के रोगी की, उन्मत्त की ओषधी बताते हुए कहा है—

असुरास्त्वा न्यखनन् देवास्त्वोदवपन् पुनः।
वातीकृतस्य भेषजीमथो क्षिप्तस्य भेषजीम्।।

भारतीय संस्कृति की विशेष उपलब्धि है प्रकृति की उपासना जो अपरोक्ष रूप से मानव को प्रकृति का विनाश करने से रोकती है। आजकल मनुष्य अपने भौतिक स्वार्थवश वृक्षों का तेजी से विनाश कर रहा है उससे वृक्षविहीन धरा आज विनाश के कगार पर खड़ी है। परन्तु वृक्ष हारे नहीं हैं अश्वत्थ तो अपनी पूर्ण जिजीविषा के साथ विद्यमान है। प्रदूषण-रोधी वृक्ष के नाते यूकिलिप्टस, पोपलर व अन्य सजावटी पौधों के स्थान पर 'अश्वत्थ-रोपण' करना पर्यावरण सुरक्षा के लिए बहुत आवश्यक है।

卐 卐 卐

संस्कृत साहित्य में कुश

राजेन्द्र कुमार

संस्कृत साहित्य में चेतन एवम् अचेतन तथा सूक्ष्म एवं विशाल दोनों ही प्रकार की प्रकृति का चित्रण, तात्त्विक, उपयोगी एवं प्रामाणिक रूप से किया गया है। प्रकृति में व्याप्त लघु तत्त्व भी कदाचित् अत्यन्त महत्त्वपूर्ण कार्य सम्पादन करने में समर्थ होता है। भगवान् विष्णु का वामन रूप भी इसी क्रम में एक सुन्दर उदाहरण है। हिन्दी भाषा में एक कवि ने इसी तथ्य की ओर सङ्केत करते हुए कहा है कि—

तिनका कबहुँ नहि निन्दये जों पायनतर होए।
ऊरिन परे जब आँखि में पीर घनेरी होय।।

छोटी-से-छोटी वस्तु भी उपेक्षित नहीं होती। यही कारण है कि विशालकाय प्राणी हाथी भी अत्यन्त लघु जीव चींटी से भयभीत रहता है तथा उसका सतत ध्यान रखता है।

संसार में व्याप्त वनस्पतियों में कुश एक लघु घास है जो अनायास ही उगता रहता है। प्रायः सभी वनस्पतियों का न्यूनाधिक भाव से महत्त्व तो है ही, परन्तु आकृति एवम् आयु से कृश कुश का महत्त्व अत्यन्त श्रेष्ठ एवं पवित्र माना जाता है। यह गुणवान् है, इसके बिना यज्ञ-विधान का सञ्चालन सम्भव नहीं होता है। संस्कृत साहित्य के स्मृति ग्रन्थों में दस प्रकार के दर्भ बताए गए हैं।[1] कुश, काश, शर, दूर्वा, भव, गोधूम, बाल्वज, सुवर्ण, रजत और ताम्र। इनमें से कुश श्रेष्ठ एवं प्रथम है। कुश के अभाव में काश तथा उसके अभाव में क्रमशः अन्य दर्भों का प्रयोग किया जा सकता है। कुश को वनस्पतिशास्त्र में वैज्ञानिक डेस्मोस्टेकिया बाइपिनेटा (Desmostacliya Bipinata) के नाम से जानते हैं। नवम्बर के महीने में इस घास में फूल आता है। कुश का उपयोग प्रायः स्नान, हवन, दान, स्वाध्याय, पितृतर्पण एवं प्रायश्चित्तादि कर्मों में किया जाता है। कुश का प्रयोग शुद्ध एवं रक्षा करने के लिए किया जाता है। यही कारण है कि महर्षि वाल्मीकि ने श्रीरामपुत्र के तेजस्विता एवं सुरक्षा के उद्देश्य से ही एक मुट्ठी कुश प्रदान किया तथा ज्येष्ठ बालक को कुश नाम दिया।[2] वरदातन्त्र में कहा गया है कि कुश से रहित पूजा सफल नहीं हो पाती।[3] यज्ञ में कई रूपों में कुश का प्रयोग किया जाता है। यथा—

कुशासन : संस्कृत साहित्य में कुश का उपयोग आसन के लिए बहुधा किया जाता रहा है। सभी प्रकार के यज्ञ-यागादि विधानों को सम्पन्न करने हेतु कुश के आसन का प्रयोग ही श्रेष्ठ एवम् उचित माना गया है। इसके पीछे दो तर्क विशिष्ट रूप से दिए जा सकते हैं। प्रथम तो यह कि यज्ञ-स्थल यज्ञ से पूर्व क्लिन्न रहता है जिससे अन्य किसी प्रकार का आसन उपयोगी नहीं हो सकता। परन्तु कुश का आसन जल की क्लिन्नता को आसानी से ग्रहण कर लेता है, साथ ही अपने ऊपर विराजमान याज्ञिक को क्लिन्न भी नहीं करता है। दूसरा यह कि यज्ञ, पूजा आदि में बैठे हुए व्यक्ति का मन सदा चञ्चल बना रहता है। शारीरिक रूप से तो वह पूजास्थल पर होता है परन्तु मानसिक स्थिति से वह एकाग्र नहीं हो पाता है। कुश के आसन पर बैठने से उनके पैरों में सदा ही चुभन जैसी अनुभूतियाँ होती रहती हैं। जिसके कारण उसका भटकता हुआ मन सतत उसके आसन पर विराजमान पूजास्थल का स्मरण दिलाता रहता है

और इस रूप में वह आसन अपरोक्ष रूप से व्यक्ति के ऊपर अङ्कुश का कार्य करता है। सम्भवतः इसी प्रकृति के कारण अङ्कुश शब्द का प्रयोग प्रचलन में आया है अतएव कुश का आसन बैठने से अधिक अङ्कुश का कार्य करता है। शिष्य एवं गुरु को भी कुश के आसन पर ही बैठने को कहा गया है क्योंकि कुश का आसन आरामदायक नहीं होने के कारण आलस्य निद्रादि को दूर करता है तथा कार्य के प्रति सजग बनाए रखता है। मनु ने ब्राह्मणों के लिए कुशासन का ही विधान वर्णित किया है—उनका कहना है कि किसी भी यज्ञ–यागादि में ब्राह्मणों को कुश के आसन पर ही बैठना चाहिए।[4] महाकवि कालिदास ने भी रघुवंश में कुश के आसन का वर्णन किया है। प्रथम सर्ग में राजा दिलीप एवं सुदक्षिणा को कुलपति वशिष्ठ के आश्रम में शयन के लिए कुश का आसन ही दिया गया है।[5] इसके अनन्तर रघुवंश के आठवें सर्ग में महाकवि ने कुश के आसन का उल्लेख किया है जिसमें यह कहा गया है कि युवराज अज न्याय के आसन पर बैठकर प्रजाओं के कार्यों को देखते हैं तथा रघु ने कुश का आसन धारण किया है अपने मन को साधने का अभ्यास करने के लिए।[6]

यहाँ महाकवि का सङ्केत सम्भवतः इस ओर प्रतीत होता है कि राज्य सञ्चालन के लिए मन को एकाग्र करने की आवश्यकता नहीं होती है। राजा यदि मन को एकाग्र करता है तो वह सत्ता का सञ्चालन नहीं कर सकता। यही कारण है कि रघु ने जब राज्यभार को अज के ऊपर छोड़ा तभी मन की शुद्धि के लिए कुश का आसन ग्रहण किया अर्थात् व्यावहारिक क्रियाओं के सम्पादन हेतु मन का सर्वाधिक चञ्चल होना आवश्यक होता है।

हस्त में धारण : यज्ञादि सम्पादन के लिए कुश की अँगूठी बनाकर दाहिने हाथ की अनामिका में पहनी जाती है[7] तथा उसके लिए विशेष रूप से एक मन्त्र भी पढ़ा जाता है जिसका उल्लेख शङ्खस्मृति में किया गया है।[8] इस अँगूठी के अतिरिक्त भी कुश को हाथ में रखा जाता है। रघुवंश में ऐसा उल्लेख किया गया है कि वन में रहने वाले तपस्वियों के लिए कुश का संग्रह करना अनिवार्य कार्यों में गिना जाता था।[9] कुश के बिना कोई भी यज्ञ पूर्ण नहीं हो सकता और न ही किसी संस्कार को ही कुश के बिना मान्यता दी जा सकती है।[10] कुश को धारण करने के पीछे विशेष तथ्य यह है कि इसमें पाप एवं कालुष्य को नष्ट करने की शक्ति होती है। 'कुं पापं श्यति।' मनुष्य के शरीर के बाहर एक अदृश्य आवरण होता है जो कदाचित् दुष्ट होने से अनेक रोगों का जनक बनता है। कुश के द्वारा इस आवरण की शुद्धि भी की जाती है। यही कारण है कि बाणभट्ट ने भी कुश को एक सम्मार्जनी की संज्ञा दी है। शुकनास चन्द्रापीड से कहता है कि राज्याभिषेक के समय पुरोहित के हाथ में कुश रहता है, जिसके अग्रभाग से मानो राजा की सहनशीलता हटा दी जाती है।[11] बाणभट्ट के इस व्यङ्ग्य से यह स्पष्ट होता है कि कुश के द्वारा शुद्ध करने की प्रक्रिया प्रचलित थी। साथ ही राजा में सहनशीलता का आधिक्य होना प्रशासन में बाधा उत्पन्न करता है। अतएव उन्होंने सम्मार्जनी की संज्ञा दी है।

बुद्धि के साथ कुश : बुद्धि की उपमा एवं विशेषता के लिए भी कुश के अग्रभाग को श्रेष्ठ माना जाता है क्योंकि कुश के अग्रभाग के समान बुद्धि की तीक्ष्णता अपेक्षित है। अतएव महाकवि कालिदास ने कौत्स की विलक्षण बुद्धि के कारण उन्हें कुशाग्रबुद्धि कहा है।[12] विश्वामित्र को कौशिक कहा जाता है। बहुत सम्भव है कि इसके पीछे भी कुश की तीक्ष्णता एवं तीव्रता का आधार रहा हो। कुमारसम्भवम् में कालिदास ने कुश का उल्लेख किया है। इनके अनुसार हिरण का प्रिय खाद्य कुश है। अतएव वह पार्वती के हाथ से कुश को छीनकर खा जाता है।[13] कदाचित् कुश खाने के कारण हिरणों में भी तत्तुल्य तीव्रता आ जाती है।

कुश के प्रयोग का निषेध : हारीत के अनुसार छः (स्थानों) अवस्थाओं में दर्भ का प्रयोग नहीं करना चाहिए। 'वर्ज्यकुशानाह हारीतः—'चिते दर्भाः पथि दर्भाः ये दर्भा यज्ञभूमिषु। स्तरणासनपिण्डेषु षड् दर्भान् परिवर्जयेत्'।[14]

इसके साथ ही ऐसा भी उल्लेख प्राप्त होता है कि सधवा स्त्रियों को कुश धारण नहीं करना चाहिए।[15]

इसके अतिरिक्त साहित्यशास्त्र में भी यदि लक्षणा में कुशल शब्द का प्रयोग किया गया है, वहाँ कुश की

तीक्ष्णता के स्थान पर दक्षता अर्थ रूढ हो गया है। सम्प्रति कुशलराष्ट्र शब्द अपने अर्थविस्तार से समाचार का द्योतक बन चुका है।

इस प्रकार यदि देखा जाए तो कुश का व्यक्तित्व अत्यन्त ही पवित्र जान पड़ता, परन्तु इसकी प्रकृति का अनुकरण करना इतना सहज नहीं होता। क्योंकि जिस प्रकार यह उपयोगी है उसी प्रकार प्रतिरोधी भी। यह किसी भी रूप में अशिष्ट आचरण को सहन नहीं करता। यही कारण है कि उसके ऊपर पैर रखना तो दूर की बात है, हाथ लगाते हुए भी मनुष्य सदैव सावधान रहता है। इसकी इसी विलक्षणता के कारण प्राचीन संस्कृतज्ञ इसे स्वीकार करते थे परन्तु आज इस प्रकार का आचरण प्रायः समाज में लुप्त-सा हो गया है। यदि कुश की प्रकृति को स्वीकार किया जाए तो सभ्यजन कतई उपेक्षित नहीं हो सकेगा और साथ ही भ्रष्टाचार की व्याधि भी दूर हो सकेगी। बहुत सम्भव है कि यदि विज्ञान ने तकनीक से कुश के रस की औषधि बनाई तो यह बुद्धिवर्धन में अत्यधिक उपयोगी हो सकेगी। इस तरह से कुश को केवल एक घास रूप में नहीं अपितु उसके चारित्रिक गुणों को स्वीकार कर व्यक्ति अपने चरित्र का निर्माण कर सकता है।

सन्दर्भ-सङ्केत

1. कुशकाशशरा दूर्वायवगोधूमबाल्वजाः। सुर्णं रजतं ताम्रं दशदर्भाः प्रकीर्तिताः। स्मृतौ कुशाभावे तु काशाः स्युः काशाः कुशन्समाः स्मृताः। काशाभावे ग्रहीतव्या अन्ये दर्भा यथोचिताः। वाचस्पत्यम् - पृ० 2144
2. कुशमुष्टिमुपादाय लवञ्चैव तु स द्विजः। वाल्मीकिः प्रददौ ताभ्यां रक्षां भूतविनाशिनीम्। वाचस्पत्यम् - पृ० 2145
3. कुशेन रहिता पूजा विफला कथिता मया। वाचस्पत्यम् - पृ० 2145
4. आसनेषूपक्लृप्तेषु बर्हिष्मत्सु पृथक्पृथक्।
उपस्पृष्टोदकान्सम्यग्विप्रांस्तानुपवेशयेत्।। मनुस्मृतिः - 3, 208
5. निर्दिष्टां कुलपतिना स पर्णशालामध्यास्य प्रयतपरिग्रहद्वितीयः।
तच्छिष्याध्ययननिवेदितावसानां संविष्टः कुशशयने निशां निनाय।। 1/95
6. नृपतिः प्रकृतीखेक्षितुं व्यवहारासनमाददे युवा।
परिचेतुमुपांशु धारणां कुशपूतं प्रवयास्तु निष्टरम्।। 8.18
7. द्वाभ्यामनामिकाभ्यां तु धार्ये दर्पपवित्रके पवित्राभावे तु तत्रैव सुमन्तुः ''समूलाग्रौ विगर्भौ तु कुशौ द्वौ दक्षिणे करे। वाचस्पत्यम - पृ० 2144
8. दर्भग्रहणे मन्त्रमाह— विरिञ्चिना सहोत्पन्न। परमेष्ठिन्निसर्गज।।
नुद् सर्वाणि पापानि दर्भ! स्वास्तिकरो भव।। वाचस्पत्यम - 2144
9. वनान्तरादुपावृतैः समित्कुशफलाहरैः।
पूर्यमाणमदृश्याग्निप्रत्युद्यातैस्तपस्विभिः।। 1.49
10. प्रयोजनं बर्हिषि माञ्चयुदञ्चि च प्रास्यतीत्यादौ संस्कारा न कर्त्तव्याः। वाचस्पत्यम् - 2144
11. पुरोहितकुशाग्र-सम्मार्जनीभिरिवापह्रियते क्षान्तिः। कादम्बरी-शुकनासोपदेशः
12. अप्यग्रणीमन्त्रकृतामृषीणां कुशाग्रबुद्धे। कुशली गुरुस्ते।
यतस्त्वया ज्ञानमशेषमाप्तं लोकेन चैतन्यमिवोष्णरश्मेः।। रघुवंशम् - 5.4
13. अपि प्रसन्नं हरिणेषु ते मनः करस्थदर्भप्रणयापहारिषु। कुमारसम्भवम् - 5.35
14. वाचस्पत्यम् - पृष्ठ 2144
15. न स्पृशेत् तिलदर्भाञ्च सधवा तु कथञ्चन। वाचस्पत्यम् - पृ० 2145

卐 卐 卐

वर्षर्तुकालीन वनस्पतिवैभव

अञ्जु बाला

कविकुलगुरुकालिदास की प्रथमकृति ऋतुसंहार में छः ऋतुओं का काव्यात्मक चित्रण मिलता है। ग्रीष्म, वर्षा, शरत्, हेमन्त, शिशिर और वसन्त— इनमें प्रत्येक ऋतु की अपनी विशेषता है। ये ऋतुएँ भारत में ही उपलब्ध हैं अन्यत्र ऐसी विविधता दुर्लभ है। यह ऋतुचक्र सम्पूर्ण मानवजीवन को प्रभावित करने वाला और अत्यन्तोपयोगी है। न केवल मानवजीवन प्रत्युत प्राणिजगत् तथा समस्त प्रकृति इससे प्रभावित होती है। प्रस्तुत शोधलेख में वर्षा ऋतु में उपलब्ध वनस्पति (फल, फूल, वृक्षादि) का विवेचन किया गया है। कवि ने वर्षा, शरत् और वसन्त[1]— इन तीन ऋतुओं में वनस्पति विशेष का मनोरम वर्णन किया है वस्तुतः अन्य ऋतुओं (ग्रीष्म, हेमन्त, शिशिर) में वनस्पति अपेक्षाकृत न्यून पाई जाती है।

समस्त प्राणिजगत् का आधार वर्षा है। भारतवर्ष में वर्षाजल की उपादेयता (कृषिप्रधानतया) निर्विवाद है। वर्षर्तु नदी, पर्वत, वायु, मेघ, मयूर, मेंढक, चातक, नायक-नायिका सभी को प्रभावित करती है। कविकृत कल्पना का सुन्दर निदर्शन निम्नाङ्कित है—

वहन्ति वर्षन्ति नदन्ति भान्ति व्यायन्ति नृत्यन्ति समाश्रयन्ति।
नद्यो घना मत्तगजा वनान्ताः प्रियाविहीनाः शिखिनः प्लवङ्गाः।।[2]

नदियाँ प्रवाहित हो रही हैं, बादल बरस रहे हैं, मत्तगजदल निनाद कर रहे हैं, वनप्रान्तों में हरियाली प्रसृत है और मयूर नृत्य कर रहे हैं।

यह वर्षाजल सर्वत्र प्रशमनकारक, सुखप्रदायक और हरीतिमा का सञ्चालक है। तापनाशक जल के गिरते ही यहाँ वहाँ आनन्द, औत्सुक्य और उन्माद का सा दृश्य उपस्थित हो जाता है।[3] यह पृथ्वी जीवनजल पाकर सस्यश्यामला हो जाती है। कवि ने यहाँ सुन्दरी नायिका से इसकी तुलना की है जो घास के अंकुर कन्दली पत्र और रक्त इन्द्रगोप (वीरबहूटियों) रूपी विविध— रत्नालङ्करणों से शोभायमान है—

प्रभिन्नवैदूर्यनिभैस्तृणाङ्कुरैः समाचिता प्रोत्थितकन्दलीदलैः।
विभाति शुक्लेतररत्नभूषिता वराङ्गनेव क्षितिरिन्द्रगोपकैः।।[4]

वर्षर्तु में सर्वत्र हरियाली है। नवीन किसलयों ने वृक्षों को अलङ्कृत कर दिया है। ऐसे सुशोभित वृक्षों से युक्त यह वन भला किसके चित्त को चलायमान नहीं कर देगा?[5] इस ऋतु में कवि ने उन विरहिणी स्त्रियों की दशा का उल्लेख किया है जो अपने कमल रूपी नेत्रों से अश्रुधारा गिराती हुई मानो बिम्बाफल सदृश अपने कोमल ओठों को सींच रही हों—

विलोचनेन्दीवरवारिबिन्दुभिर्निषिक्तबिम्बाधरचारुपल्लवाः ।
निरस्तमाल्याभरणानुलेपनाः स्थिताः निराशाः प्रमदाः प्रवासिनाम्।।[6]

यहाँ बिम्ब का उल्लेख साभिप्राय है। बिम्ब नामक फल पक जाने पर लाल वर्ण का हो जाता है।[7] कवि ने अनेकत्र[8] तरुण स्त्रियों के ओठों की तुलना बिम्बनामक फल से ही की है। वर्षर्तु में मन्द-मन्द बहती हुई वायु कदम्ब, सर्ज, अर्जुन, केतकी के पुष्पों की सुगन्ध से सुवासित हो रही है। ऐसी वायु किसको उत्सुक न कर देगी—

कदम्बसर्जार्जुनकेतकीवनं विकम्पयंस्तत्कुसुमाधिवासितः।
ससीकराम्भोधरसङ्गशीतलः समीरणः कं न करोति सोत्सुकम्।।[9]

1. कदम्ब (कदम्बक) (NEUCLEA CADAMBA)

(कद्+अम्बच्) कदम्ब मध्यमाकार वर्षाकालीन वृक्ष है। इसके लिए प्रसिद्ध है कि बादलों की गरज के साथ इसकी कलियाँ खिल जाती हैं। यह स्त्रियों द्वारा सिर पर धारण किया जाता है। इसके लिए कवि ने नीप शब्द का प्रयोग किया है।[10] कदम्ब और नीप एक ही पुष्प की भिन्न जातियाँ है। यह भारत और सिंहल में होता है। इसकी ऊँचाई 70 से 80 फुट होती है। नित्य हरित इस वृक्ष के पत्ते महुए के पत्तों की भाँति होते हैं। इसका फूल गेंद के समान गोल होता है। इससे जब पीली केसर झड़ जाती है तब यह फूल ही पककर फल बन जाता है जो खटमिट्ठा होता है। इसी से कादम्ब मदिरा बनाई जाती।[11]

कवि ने इसका उल्लेख ऋतुसंहार में सर्वाधिकार 5 बार किया है।[12] इसके अतिरिक्त अन्य ग्रन्थों में भी द्रष्टव्य है।[13] कुमारसम्भव के अनुसार शिव की सेवा में संलग्न पार्वती उन्हें माल्यार्पण करती हैं तभी कामदेव ने सम्मोहन नामक अपना बाण चढाया इससे पार्वती कदम्बवत् पुलकिताङ्गी, रत्याख्य भाव को प्रकाशित करती हुई लजाने लगीं—

विवृण्वती शैलसुताऽपि भावमङ्गैः स्फुरद्बालकदम्बकल्पैः।
साचीकृता चारुतरेण तस्थौ मुखेन पर्यस्तविलोचनेन।।[14]

रघुवंश के अनुसार सीतासहित विमानारूढ श्रीराम अयोध्या लौट रहे हैं तब वे उनके वियोग में बिताए वर्षाकालीन दिनों को याद करते हुए कहते हैं—नवीन जल के गिरने से उठी हुई भीनी सुगन्ध, अधखिले मञ्जरियों वाले कदम्बपुष्प तथा मयूरों की मधुर केका भी वियोगी (विरही) उनके लिए अरुचिकर थी।

गन्धश्च धाराहतपल्वलानां कादम्बमर्धोद्गतकेसरं च।
स्निग्धाश्च केकाः शिखिनां बभूवुर्यस्मिन्नसह्यानि विना त्वया मे।।[15]

यहाँ कदम्ब के पुष्प का वर्षाकाल में खिलना कवि का अभिप्राय है तभी कवि ने उत्प्रेक्षा की है कि मेघ से सम्पर्क होने के कारण खिले हुए कदम्ब पुष्पों वाला पर्वत प्रफुल्लित हो उठा हो। मेघदूत में नैसर्गिक कदम्ब-शोभा दर्शनीय है।

नीचैराख्यं गिरिमधिवसेस्तत्र विश्रामहेतो-
स्त्वत्सम्पर्कात् पुलकितमिव प्रौढपुष्पैः कदम्बैः।[16]

2. बकुल (MINMUSOPS ELENGI LINN)

(बङ्क् + उरच्) बकुल मौलसिरी या केसर का वृक्ष है, जो भारत के प्रायः सभी स्थानों पर उपलब्ध है। श्वेतवर्णीय, सघन एवं सदाबहार इस वृक्ष को दोहदवृक्षों में परिगणित किया गया है। कविसमयानुसार स्त्रियों द्वारा मदिरा का गण्डूष छिड़कने पर यह पुष्पित हो जाता है—

स्त्रीणां स्पर्शात्प्रियङ्गुर्विकसति बकुलः सीधुगण्डूषसेकात्
पादाघातादशोकस्तिलककुरबकौ वीक्षणालिङ्गनाभ्याम्।
मन्दारो नर्मवाक्यात्पटुमृदुहसनाच्चम्पको वक्त्रवाता-
च्चूतो गीतान्नमेरुर्विकसति च पुरोनर्तनात्कर्णिकारः।।[17]

कवि ने रघुवंश में अग्निवर्ण की अहर्निश विलासप्रियता के प्रसङ्ग में स्पष्ट किया है कि जिस प्रकार बकुल

स्त्रियों के आसव की अपेक्षा करता है, उसी प्रकार अग्निवर्ण ने भी स्त्रियों के मुखासव की इच्छा की—

सातिरेकमदकारणं रहस्तेन दत्तमभिलेषुरङ्गनाः।
ताभिरप्युपहृतं मुखासवं सोऽपिबद्बकुलतुल्यदोहदः।।[18]

कवि ने शृङ्गारोपयोगी उपर्युक्त वृक्ष का अनेकत्र उल्लेख किया है।[19] इसे 'केसर' नाम से भी कवि ने अभिहित किया है।[20] इसके अतिरिक्त अनेकत्र यह पुष्पपराग (केशर) के रूप में भी प्रयुक्त हुआ है यथा कामदेव की भस्म को देखकर प्रलाप करती हुई रति पूछ रही है कहीं वह उसके पूर्वकृत अपराधों से रुष्ट तो नहीं है—

स्मरामि स्मर! मेखलागुणैरुत गोत्रस्खलितेषु बन्धनम्।
च्युतकेशरदूषितेक्षणान्यवतंसोत्पलताडनानि च ।।[21]

अन्यत्र द्रष्टव्य - रघुवंश - 3.27

3. मालती (JASMINUM GRANDIFLORUM)

यह श्वेत पंखड़ियों वाला सुगन्धित पुष्प है, जिसकी डण्ठल लगभग एक इञ्च की होती है। जब मालती के फूल झड़ते हैं तो वृक्ष के नीचे मानों फूलों का-सा बिछौना बिछ जाता है। पद्मपुराण के अनुसार गौरी, लक्ष्मी और श्रद्धा— ये तीन देवियाँ ही धात्री, मालती और तुलसी वृक्षों के रूप में अवतरित हुई हैं।[22]

यह एक प्रकार की चमेली है जो उद्यानों में लगाई जाती है और किसी बड़े पेड़ या मण्डप पर चढ़ा दी जाती है। वन एवं सड़क के आसपास भी प्राकृतिक रूप में उपलब्ध होती है। अमरकोष में सुमना, मालती, नवमल्लिका और जाति— ये चमेली के पर्याय रूप माने गए हैं। यह पुष्प वर्षर्तु से शरद्काल तक होता है। कवि ने ऋतुसंहार और मेघदूत— इन ग्रन्थों में इसका वर्णन किया है।[23] यथा—

शिरसि बकुलमालां मालतीभिः समेतां
विकसितनवपुष्पैर्यूथिका कुड्मलैश्च।
विकचनवकदम्बैः कर्णपूरं वधूनां
रचयति जलदौघः कान्तवत्काल एषः।।[23]

उपर्युक्त श्लोक में अलङ्करणोपयोगिपुष्पों—बकुल, मालती आदि का सुन्दर वर्णन है। इसमें वर्षर्तु को नायक की भांति पुष्पमालाएँ ग्रथित करता हुआ चित्रित किया है।

स्त्रियाँ अलङ्कारप्रिय होती हैं फिर भले ही वे सुवर्णालङ्कार हो, रजतालङ्कार या पुष्पों के ही क्यों न हो। कवि ने अनेकशः स्त्रियों द्वारा पुष्पसम्पत्ति रूपी अलङ्करणधारण का मनोरम चित्रण किया है। ये स्त्रियाँ केसर, केतकी, कदम्ब, मालती और कमलादि पुष्पों से अलङ्कृत हैं। पुष्पों से निर्मित मालाओं, वेणियों तथा कर्णाभूषणों को धारण किए हुए हैं।

केशान्नितान्तघननीलविकुञ्चिताग्रानापूरयन्ति वनिता नवमालतीभिः।
कर्णेषु च प्रवरकाञ्चनकुण्डलेषु नीलोत्पलानि विविधानि निवेशयन्ति।।[25]

मेघ द्वारा संदेश भेजने का इच्छुक यक्ष उससे कहता है कि तुम यक्षिणी को अपने जलबिन्दुओं द्वारा शीतल हुई वायु से उठाना। नवीन जल-बिन्दुओं से वह भी मालती-कलियों की भांति स्वस्थ चैतन्य हो जाएगी—

तामुत्थाप्य स्वजलकणिकाशीतलेनानिलेन
प्रत्याश्वस्तां सममभिनवैर्जालकैर्मालतीनाम्।
विद्युद्गर्भः स्तिमितनयनां त्वत्सनाथे गवाक्षे
वक्तुं धीरः स्तनितवचनैर्मानिनीं प्रक्रमेथाः।।[26]

4. अर्जुन (TERMINALIA ARJUNA)

यह गुणकारी छाल वाला अर्जुन (अर्ज + उनन्, णिलुक् च) नामक वृक्ष है। विशालाकार यह वृक्ष अमरूद के वृक्ष की भाँति होता है। इसके श्वेत, लघु फूलों में बहुत तीखी और मीठी गन्ध होती है। इसे ककुभ और करवीरक भी कहा जाता है। इसकी छाल रक्तवर्णिम तथा अत्यन्त बलवर्धक होती है जो चमड़े को चिकना करने एवं कपड़ा रंगने के काम में प्रयुक्त होती है।[27] गुणधर्म के आधार पर इसकी छाल का प्रयोग चिकित्सा में किया जाता है। यह हृद्य, रक्तस्तम्भक तथा रक्तपित्तशामक है। यह रक्तचाप व हृदयरोग की औषधि है।

कवि ने ऋतुसंहार में दो स्थलों पर इसका उल्लेख किया है।[28] इसके अतिरिक्त अन्यत्र भी प्रतिपादित है।[29]

वर्षाकालीन प्रवहमान वायु के प्रसङ्ग में कवि पूछते हैं कि कदम्ब, सर्ज, अर्जुन तथा केतकी आदि की सुगन्ध से युक्त वायु भला किसे मुग्ध नहीं कर देता—

कदम्बसर्जार्जुनकेतकीवनं विकम्पयंस्तत्कुसुमाधिवासितः।
ससीकराम्भोधरसङ्गशीतलः समीरणः कं न करोति सोत्सुकम्।।[30]

रघुवंशी राजा कुश ने सफलतापूर्वक राज्यशासन चलाया और उनके राज्य में पुष्पवैभव दर्शनीय है—

आपिञ्जरा बद्धरजःकणत्वान्मञ्जर्युदारा शुशुभेऽर्जुनस्य।
दग्ध्वापि देहं गिरिशेन रोषात्खण्डीकृता ज्येव मनोभवस्य।।[31]

5. शाल (सर्ज) (VATICA ROBUSTA)

शाल (शल् + घञ्) का वृक्ष बड़ा लम्बा एवं भव्य (शानदार) होता है। यह सीधा लम्बा बढ़ता है और इसके पत्ते बड़े बड़े होते हैं। इसकी छाल में छेद करने पर गुग्गुल निकलता है तथा इसके वर्षर्तुकालीन छोटे-पुष्पगुच्छों को कोलस्त्रियाँ जूड़े में लगाती हैं।[32] शाल की लकड़ी का प्रयोग गृहनिर्माणादि में किया जाता है। इसका निर्यास चिकित्सा में उपयोगी होता है। साधारण भाषा में इसे शाख कहते हैं और निघण्टुग्रन्थों में इसके लिए अश्वकर्ण, अजकर्ण शब्द प्रयुक्त हुए हैं। कवि कालिदास ने इसका 5 बार उल्लेख किया है।[33]

रघुवंश के अनुसार राजा दिलीप सपत्नीक कुलगुरु वसिष्ठ के आश्रम में जाते हुए मन्द प्रवहित, शालनिर्यास-गन्धयुक्त वायु का सेवन कर रहे हैं—

सेव्यमानौ सुखस्पर्शैः शालनिर्यासगन्धिभिः।
पुष्परेणूत्किरैर्वातैराधूतवनराजिभिः ।।[34]

इसी सर्ग में कवि ने राजा दिलीप को 'शालप्रांशुर्महाभुजः' कहा है।[35] कुमारसम्भव में सेनापतित्व प्राप्त कुमार कार्तिकेय ने देवताओं को आश्वस्त किया और तारकासुर से युद्ध करने के लिए स्वर्ग में प्रविष्ट हुए। वहाँ उन्होंने तारक द्वारा विध्वस्त इन्द्र के उपवन 'नन्दन' को देखा जिसके भव्य शालवृक्ष भग्न कर दिए गए थे—

ततो व्रजन्नन्दननामधेयं लीलावनं जम्भजितः पुरस्तात्।
विभिन्नभग्नोद्धृतशालसंघं प्रेक्षांचकार स्मरशत्रुसूनुः।।[36]

6. केतकी (केवड़ा) (PANDANUS TECTORIUS SOLAND)

केतकी(कित् + ण्वुल्) के लिए केतक पद भी प्रयुक्त हुआ है। सुगन्धित पुष्पों के लिए यह उपवनों में लगाया जाता है। उसके गुल्म खजूर के समान प्रतीत होते हैं। इसके पर्णतटों पर काँटे होते हैं तथा पर्ण बहुत लम्बे होते हैं। इसके गुल्म के मध्य से श्वेत मटमैले वर्ण का गोफा सा निकलता है जो मकई (मक्का) जैसा होता है। केवड़ापुष्प - अर्क तथा शर्बत के लिए उपयोगी होता है। सुगन्धित होने से इससे इत्र भी बनाया जाता है। कवि ने वर्षाकालीन केतकी का अनेकत्र उल्लेख किया है।[37] रघुवंश में इन्दुमती के प्रति प्रगाढ अभिलाषा रखने वाले राजाओं की प्रेम विषयक चेष्टाओं को बताते हुए सुन्दर दृश्य प्रस्तुत किया है यथा—कोई युवा राजा दन्तपत्र एवं श्वेतवर्ण केतकीपुष्प को नखाग्रों से कुरेद रहा है—

विलासिनीविभ्रमदन्तपत्रमापाण्डुरं केतकबर्हमन्यः।
प्रियानितम्बोचितसन्निवेशैर्विपाटयामास युवा नखाग्रैः।।[38]

अन्यत्र महाराजा रघु की शूरवीरता के प्रसङ्ग में कवि कहते हैं—राजाओं को विजय करने में उद्यत रघु की सेना केतकीपुष्परजयुक्त वायु द्वारा बिना किसी प्रयास के ही सुवासित कर दी गई—

मुरलामारुतोद्धूतमगमत्कैतकं रजः।
तद्योधरवारबाणानामयत्नपटवासताम्।।[39]

केतकीपुष्प श्वेतवर्ण के हैं ऐसा कवि ने अनेकत्र प्रतिपादित किया है। कुमारसम्भव में कवि सन्ध्या के पश्चात आने वाली रात्रिकाल में क्रमशः फैलने वाले प्रकाश की उपमा केतकी-पराग से करते हैं—

नूनमुन्नमति यज्वनां पतिः शार्वरस्य तमसो निषिद्धये।
पुण्डरीकमुखि पूर्वदिङ्मुखं केतकैरिव रजोभिराहतम्।।[40]

यक्ष मेघ से कहता है दशार्ण के समीप पहुँचने पर वहाँ पाण्डुवर्ण वाली उपवन सीमाएँ देखोगे।

पाण्डुच्छायोपवनवृतयः केतकैः सूचिभिन्नैः।
नीडारम्भैर्गृहबलिभुजामाकुलग्रामचैत्याः ।।[41]

संक्षेपतः वर्षर्तुकालीन पुष्पसम्पत्ति सर्वत्र व्याप्त है। वायु सम्पर्क से विक्षिप्त वृक्षशाखाएँ, नयनाभिराम नृत्य का दृश्य प्रस्तुत कर रही हैं। यहाँ कदम्ब, सर्ज, अर्जुन, बकुल, केतकी, मालती, यूथिका, केसर, कन्दली, तृण, कुवलय, बिम्बफल आदि का कवि ने मनोहर वर्णन किया है जो उनके पुष्प-पत्र-वृक्षादि वनस्पति-तत्त्वों के सूक्ष्म ज्ञान का द्योतक है।

सन्दर्भ-सङ्केत

1. ऋतुसंहार-2-3, 6 सर्ग
2. ऋतुसंहार-2. 19
3. ऋतुसंहार-2. 24
4. ऋतुसंहार-2. 5
5. ऋतुसंहार-2. 8
6. ऋतुसंहार-2.12

7. संस्कृत-हिन्दी-कोश (आप्टे) - पृ. 717
8. कुमारसम्भव - 3. 67; मालविकाग्निमित्र - 3. 5, 4.14; मेघदूत - 82
9. ऋतुसंहार - 2.17
10. रघु. - 14.37; मेघ. - 21, 71; विक्रम. - 4.42
11. कालिदास-ग्रन्थावली (सीताराम चतुर्वेदी) - अभिधानकोष - पृ. 129
12. ऋतु. - 2.17, 20, 23-24; 3.13
13. कुमार. - 3.68, मेघ. - 25, विक्रम., 13.27, 15-49
14. कुमार. - 3. 68
15. रघु. - 13. 27
16. मेघ. - 1. 25
17. कुमार. - 3.26 के नोट्स में
18. रघु. - 19.12
19. रघु. - 8.64, 9.30, 19.12; कुमार. - 3.55, 4.8, 8.76; ऋतु. - 2.24; मेघ. - 86
20. रघु. - 9.36, 40; कुमार. - 3.55, 8.25; ऋतु. - 2.20; अभिज्ञानशकुन्तल - 1.30, चतुर्थाङ्क
21. कुमार. - 4.8
22. कालिदास-ग्रन्थावली - पृ. 164
23. ऋतुसंहार - 2.24, 3.2, 18-19; मेघ. - 2.37
24. ऋतुसंहार - 2.24
25. ऋतुसंहार - 3.19
26. मेघ. - 2.37
27. कालिदास-ग्रन्थावली - पृ. 125
28. ऋतु. - 2.17; 3.13
29. रघु. - 16.51; 19.37
30. ऋतु. - 2.17
31. रघु. - 16.51
32. कालिदास-ग्रन्थावली - पृ, 172
33. रघु. - 1.13, 38; कुमार - 13-33, ऋतु. - 2.17, 3.13
34. रघु. - 1.38
35. रघु. - 1.13
36. कुमार. - 13.33
37. रघु. - 4.55, 6.17; कुमार. - 8.58; ऋतु. - 2.17, 20, 21, 27; मेघ. - 23; मालविका. - 4, पृ. 74
38. रघु. - 6. 17
39. रघु. - 4. 55
40. कुमार. - 8. 58
41. मेघ. - 1. 23

卐 卐 卐

पञ्चबाणस्य सायकाः

चन्द्रशेखर त्रिपाठी

सृष्टि की सतत प्रवाहमयता के आधारभूत काम नामक तत्त्व की न केवल एक पुरुषार्थ के रूप में अपितु देव रूप में भी कल्पना भारतीय संस्कृति की अद्वितीय विशेषता है। कामदेव को काव्यों में प्रेम का प्रस्फुटन करने वाले देवता के रूप में चित्रित किया गया है। प्रेम के सहज प्रस्फुरण के लिए तदनुकूल परिवेश का होना भी आवश्यक है, अतः वसन्त ऋतु इस कार्य में कामदेव का सहायक हुआ। इस ऋतु को काम का उद्दीपक होने के कारण सत्य ही मधुमास कहा जाता है, जो मधु (आसव) के समान मत्त करने का सामर्थ्य रखता है। परन्तु क्रमशः यह उन्माद किस प्रकार आहत करने वाला हो जाता है कि कामातुर व्यक्ति को इसका परिज्ञान भी नहीं होता। कामभाव के इस क्रमिक विस्तार को काव्यशास्त्र के ग्रन्थों में सुतरां प्रतिपादित किया गया है। परन्तु प्रेम के इस देवता का स्वरूप सदा से ही कोमल भावनाओं का अभिव्यञ्जक माना गया। इसलिए जब इसके द्वारा आहत किए जाने की परिकल्पना बलवती हुई तो भी शस्त्र के रूप में पुष्पसायक की कल्पना कवियों को रुचिकर प्रतीत हुई। जब उसका धनुष पुष्पमय है तो फिर बाण भी उसी प्रकार मृदु होने चाहिएँ। इसलिए कवियों ने प्रकृति से पाँच उद्दीपकों को चुनकर उन्हें काम के बाण होने का गौरव प्रदान किया। फलतः पुष्पधन्वा की एक संज्ञा पञ्चसायक भी हो गई। साहित्य में जहाँ भी कहीं काम से पीड़ित होने का प्रसङ्ग आया, कवियों ने कामदेव के धनुष बाण का उपयोग बड़ा रमकर किया।

कुमारसम्भवम् के तृतीय सर्ग में फूलों के धनुष पर पुष्प का बाण चढ़ाए कामदेव का मनोहारी चित्रण है।[1] वहाँ कामदेव की असली परीक्षा थी। एक ओर समाधि में लीन परमयति भगवान् शङ्कर तो दूसरी ओर देवेन्द्र का श्रेष्ठ अनुचर अपने सम्पूर्ण सामर्थ्य के साथ देवकार्य में संलग्न था। शिव ने काम को भस्म कर दिया परन्तु वह अनङ्ग होकर भी अमर हो गया। नहीं कहा जा सकता कि इस समर में किसकी विजय हुई थी और कौन पराजित हुआ, परन्तु देवकार्य सम्पन्न हो गया। शिव शिवा के प्रेमपाश में आबद्ध हुए, कामदेव अनङ्ग हो गया और रति को अखण्ड सौभाग्यवती होने का वरदान प्राप्त हुआ।

कवि अपने कल्पनालोक का स्वतन्त्र अधिपति है। वह जिस रूप में चाहे, अर्थों को बदल देता है और एक ही बात को भङ्गियाँ बदल-बदल कर प्रतिक्षण नवीन रूप में प्रस्तुत करता है। यही तो सच्चे अर्थों में सौन्दर्य की उपासना है।[2] भास ने उदयन को धनुषबाण रहित कामदेव के रूप में चित्रित किया।[3] वहीं कालिदास ने पार्वती के भौहों के लावण्य के सम्मुख कामदेव के धनुष को व्यर्थ सिद्ध किया।[4] उपमेय को उपमान और उपमान को उपमेय बना देना कवि के लिए सर्वथा सहज है।

कुसुमसायक के ये बाण संख्या में 5 ही हैं, यह कविसमय निर्विवाद रूप से कवियों में मान्य रहा है। भासकृत स्वप्नवासवदत्तम् में अवन्विराजतनया के प्रथम दर्शन के अवसर पर पाँचों बाणों से आहत राजा उदयन पुनः पद्मावती के प्रसङ्ग में कामबिद्ध होकर यह कल्पना करता है कि यदि मदन के बाण पाँच ही हैं तो फिर यह छठा बाण किस प्रकार सक्रिय हुआ।[5] उसका मुग्ध मन यह कल्पना ही नहीं कर पाया कि कामदेव को तो अमर होने का आशीर्वाद मिल चुका है।

परन्तु कामदेव के ये पाँच सायक कौन से हैं, इस बात को लेकर कवि परम्परा में कुछ मतभेद भी दृष्टिगत होता है। सत्य तो यह है कि प्रकृति के जिस सुकुमार और कोमल रूप ने कामभाव का उद्दीपन किया अथवा उसके सहज सौन्दर्य ने कविमन को प्रभावित किया, उसे ही उसने काम के बाण के रूप में मान्यता प्रदान कर दी। तथापि परम्परा से यह एक पद्य प्राप्त होता है, जिसमें अरविन्द, अशोक, आम्र, नवमल्लिका तथा कुरबक को काम के पाँच बाणों के रूप में मान्यता प्रदान की गई है।[6] कहीं-कहीं कुरबक के स्थान पर नीलोत्पल की चर्चा है। नीलोत्पल का अरविन्द जाति का होने से उसे अरविन्द में ही समाहित समझना चाहिए। अधिकांश कवियों ने उपर्युक्त पाँचों को शृङ्गार के उद्दीपक तथा सौन्दर्य के साधन के रूप में स्वीकार कर वर्णित भी किया है, अतः इन्हें ही यहाँ इस पत्र में कुसुमसायक के रूप में स्वीकार कर वर्णित किया जा रहा है। यहाँ विशेषरूप से अवधेय यह भी है कि ये पाँचों रक्तवर्ण के पुष्प हैं। रक्तवर्ण अनुराग एवं कामोद्दीपकता का प्रतीक है, जो कामदेव के धनुष की बाण होने की योग्यता रखता है।

अरविन्द

कमल जाति का एक पादप है, जिसे आंग्ल वनस्पतिशास्त्र में Nelumbium Nucifera Gaertn कहा जाता है। यह सूर्योदयकाल में खिलता है और सूर्यास्त होने पर बन्द हो जाता है।[7] वहीं नीलोत्पल कुमुद के कई पर्यायों में से एक प्रकार है। इसे Blue Nymbhara कहा जाता है।

अशोक

अशोक के वृक्ष सीधे लम्बे होते हैं तथा पत्तियाँ प्रारम्भ में रक्तवर्ण और अनन्तर हरितवर्ण की हो जाती हैं। यह वसन्त ऋतु में पुष्पित होता है।[8] अशोक के सम्बन्ध में कविसमय प्रचलित है कि यह स्त्रियों के चरणाघात से पुष्पित होता है (पादाघातादशोकः)। इस दोहद क्रिया का उल्लेख लगभग सभी कवियों ने यथास्थान अत्यन्त रुचिपूर्वक किया है।[9] इसे Saraca Indica कहा जाता है।

आम्र

इसके कई पर्याय संस्कृत साहित्य में प्राप्त होते हैं। इसे Mangifera Indica कहा जाता है। वसन्त ऋतु में यह मञ्जरित होता है और ग्रीष्म ऋतु में इसके फल प्राप्त होते हैं। कालिदास ने कामदेव के पाँचों बाणों में से आम्र को सर्वाधिक तीक्ष्ण बाण कहा है।[10]

नवमल्लिका

यह चमेली जाति का एक पादप है, जिसे Jasminum Samboc कहा जाता है। बाण ने इसके पुष्पों के कोमल होने का वर्णन किया है।[11]

कुरबक

रक्तवर्ण के इस पुष्प को लालकटसरैया एवं आंग्लभाषा में Barleria Cristatatinn कहा जाता है। अमरकोष में इसे कुरण्टक एवं अम्लातक भी कहा जाता है।[12] इसके सम्बन्ध में यह प्रसिद्धि है कि यह स्त्रियों के आलिङ्गन से पुष्पित होता है। (तिलककुरबकौ वीक्षणालिङ्गनाभ्याम्)।

1. उपमानोपमेय के रूप में

कमल अङ्गों की उपमा के लिए कवियों का सर्वाधिक प्रिय पुष्प रहा है। नेत्र और चरण के साथ इनका साहचर्य उपमा के रूप में अत्यन्त प्रसिद्ध है। हिरणी के चञ्चल नेत्र हों या ललनाओं के चन्द्रमुखों की शोभा कवि कमल से

तुलना के लोभ का संवरण नहीं कर पाए।[13] श्रीहर्ष ने तो नैषध में भ्रमरयुक्त अरविन्द को ही नेत्र कह डाला।[14] कमल की कोमलता और उसकी सुन्दरता कवियों को इतनी रुचिकर लगी कि हस्त की कोमलता को भी कमल की पंखुड़ी जैसा कोमल वर्णित करने से वे अपने को रोक नहीं पाए।[15] चित्रलेखा द्वारा उर्वशी के कामपीड़ित अङ्गों की तुलना मलिन कमलनाल से करना कालिदास के अरविन्द के प्रति विशेष लगाव का द्योतक है।[16] नीलोत्पल भी चपल नेत्रों के उपमानार्थ कवियों द्वारा चर्चा यथास्थान वर्णित हुए। बाण ने एक ओर जहाँ शबरसेनापति के श्यामवर्ण शरीर को नीलकुमुद सदृश बताया[17] तो वहीं कालिदास ने ऋतुसंहार में मेघ को नीलोत्पल कहा।[18] अशोक के रक्तपुष्पों की तुलना पद्मरागमणि से की गई है।[19] जबकि बाण ने एक स्थल पर इन्हें अग्नि के सदृश बताया है। बाण ने स्त्रियों के हृदय की कोमलता की तुलना नवमल्लिका के कोमल पुष्पों से की है।[20] जबकि अशोक के पुष्पों की प्रभा की तुलना कालिदास ने प्रफुल्लित नवमल्लिका के फूलों की प्रभा से की है।[21] कालिदास ने लाल ओष्ठ की तुलना रक्तवर्ण के आम्रपल्लवों तथा नवमल्लिका के लाल-लाल पत्तों से की है।[22] कुरबक की आभा को भी कवियों ने रागाग्नि सदृश ही वर्णित किया।[23]

2. सौन्दर्यप्रसाधन के रूप में

आभरण के रूप में भी इन पुष्पों का प्रयोग बहुलता से प्राप्त होता था। शृङ्गाराभूषण के रूप में युवतियों के द्वारा हस्त तथा कर्ण में कमलपुष्प एवं मृणालधारण करने का प्रचलन था।[24] कमलतन्तुओं की माला भी धारण की जाती थी।[25] कमल को शीतलता प्रदान करने वाला माना गया है। अतः कामज्वर से शान्ति प्रदानार्थ कमल शय्या का वर्णन कवियों ने किया।[26] इनके पत्तों का प्रयोग पंखा तथा पत्र लेखनार्थ भी होता था।[27] अशोक के पल्लव कर्णाभूषण के रूप में सज्जित होते थे।[28] वहीं इसके फूल माला तथा केशसज्जार्थ युवतियों के द्वारा उपयोग में लाए जाते थे।[29] अशोकपल्लवों से मण्डप सज्जा कार्य भी होता था।[30] इस रूप में आज भी इनका उपयोग किया जाता है। आम्र की मञ्जरियाँ भी अङ्गनाओं की कर्णाभूषण बनीं।[31] वहीं उसका उपयोग कामदेव के पूजनार्थ भी किया जाता था।[32] मदन के भस्मसात् होने के अनन्तर रति के द्वारा वसन्त से यह याचना की जाती है कि उसके सती होने के पश्चात् वसन्त आम्रमञ्जरी को ही पितृदान के रूप में प्रयुक्त करे।[33] सुगन्धि के लिए सहकार के तेल का वर्णन बाण ने किया है।[34] कुरबक अपनी रक्त आभा के कारण वनिताओं के केशों की सज्जा का संवर्धन करते थे।[35] माला के रूप में भी इनका प्रयोग किया जाता था।[36]

3. उद्दीपक के रूप में

काम से सम्बन्धित होने से इन पाँच बाण रूपी पुष्पों का उद्दीपक के रूप में वर्णित होना स्वाभाविक ही है। प्रमदवन का वर्णन हो और अशोक, सहकार, कुरबक का वर्णन न हो तो काम की उद्‌भावना हो ही नहीं सकती। रक्तवर्ण शोभित नूतन अशोक वृक्ष काम वृद्धि ही करते थे।[37] मधुमास का वर्णन सहकारवर्णन के बिना पूर्णता को प्राप्त नहीं कर सकता। कामदेव के सहायक पञ्चबाणों में सर्वाधिक उद्दीपक आम्र ही है। अतः उद्दीपक के रूप में सहकार का वर्णन सर्वाधिक हुआ है। वसन्तागमन की सूचना सहकार के अङ्कुर ही देते हैं।[38] लाल-लाल पल्लवों के गुच्छों से नम्र, फूलों से युक्त सुन्दर डालियों वाले पवन के झकोरों से कम्पित आम्र के वृक्ष नारियों के चित्तों को उत्कण्ठित करते हैं।[39] वहीं भौरों के द्वारा आम्र की मञ्जरी को चुम्बित होता देख कामीपुरुषों के मन अपनी प्रियतमाओं से मिलने के लिए उत्कण्ठित हो जाते हैं।[40] कुरबक भी कामाभिलाषा की वृद्धि करते ही प्रस्तुत होते हैं।[41] कालिदास ने कुरबक एवं अशोक को प्रायः एक साथ कामोद्दीपक के रूप में चित्रित किया है।[42] प्रायः सभी कवियों ने सलिल क्रीड़ा वर्णन में कमलाच्छादित सरोवरों का वर्णन किया है।[43] कमल अपनी मदमाती सुगन्ध के कारण कदाचित् कवियों के द्वारा उद्दीपक के रूप में प्रयुक्त हुए हैं।

4. भोज्यपदार्थ के रूप में

अरविन्द, आम्र एवं नीलोत्पल के अवयव भोज्य पदार्थ के रूप में भी वर्णित हुए हैं। कलहंसों को कमल एवं नीलोत्पल के मधुरस प्रिय थे।[44] आम्र के अङ्कुरों का नरकोयल द्वारा रसास्वादन ही उनकी मधुर ध्वनि का कारण बना।[45] कादम्बरी में शबरसेनापति के द्वारा आहार में मृणालिका लेने का उल्लेख बाण ने किया है।[46]

5. माङ्गलिक द्रव्य के रूप में

इनमें से कुछ पुष्प शुभ एवं माङ्गलिक द्रव्य के रूप में भी चित्रित हुए हैं। तलवे में पद्म का चिह्न चक्रवर्ती सम्राट् के लक्षण के रूप में सामुद्रिक शास्त्र में वर्णित है, जो एक अत्यन्त ही शुभ लक्षण माना गया है।[47] माङ्गलिक अवसरों पर आम्रपल्लव का प्रयोग भी शुभ ही है। बाण के द्वारा हर्ष के दरबार में जाने से पहले घर से चलते समय शुभ शकुन के रूप में आम्रपल्लव को मुख में रखा गया।[48] मृणालतन्तुओं से यज्ञोपवीत भी बनाए जाते थे।[49]

सन्दर्भ-सङ्केत

1. तं देशमरोपितपुष्पचापे रतिद्वितीये मदने प्रपन्ने।
   काष्ठागतस्नेहरसानुविद्धं द्वन्द्वानि भावं क्रियया विवव्रुः।। — कुमारसम्भवम् 3/35
2. क्षणे क्षणे यन्नवतामुपैति तदेवरूपं रमणीयतायाः। — शिशुपालवधम्
3. चेटी-शक्यं भणितुं शरचापहीनः कामदेव इति। — स्वप्नवासवदत्तम्-तृतीय अङ्क
4. तस्याः शलाकाञ्जननिर्मितेव कान्तिर्भ्रुवोरायतलेखयोर्या।
   तां वीक्ष्य लीलाचतुरामनङ्गः स्वचापसौन्दर्यमदं मुमोच।। — कुमारसम्भवम् 7/47
5. पञ्चेषुर्मदनों यदा कथमयं षष्ठः शरः पातितः।। — स्वप्नवासवदत्तम् 4/1
6. अरविन्दमशोकं च चूतं च नवमल्लिका।
   कुरबकं चैव पञ्चैते पञ्चबाणस्य सायकाः।। — अज्ञात।
7. सूर्यापाये न खलु कमलं पुष्यति स्वामभिख्याम्। — मेघदूत 2/17
8. मधुमासदिससमिव विकसिताशोकपाटलम्। — कादम्बरी पृ. 157
9. कादम्बरी, 117, 261
10. त्वमसि मया चूताङ्कुर दत्तः कामाय गृहीतधनुषे।
    पथिकजनयुवतिलक्ष्य पञ्चाम्यधिकः शरो भव।। — अभिज्ञानशाकुन्तलम् 6/3
11. नवमल्लिकाकुसुमकोमलानां . . . . — हर्षचरितम् पृ. 446
12. तस्मिन् कुरबकोऽरुण . . . . — अमरकोषः 2/4/73-74
13. ऋतुसंहारम् 3/14, 17, 23, विक्रमोर्वशीयम् 4/16, कुमारसम्भवम् 5/21 इत्यादि
14. नेत्रारविन्दत्वमत्रान्मृगाङ्कः पुरा पुराणस्य यदेष पुंसः।
    अस्याङ्क एवायमगात्तदानीं कनीनिकेन्दिन्दिरसुन्दरत्वम्।। — नैषधीयचरितम् 22/88
15. ऋतुसंहारम् 3/23, अभिज्ञानशाकुन्तलम् 6/18 के अनन्तर विदूषक की उक्ति।
16. म्लानकमलनालोपमैरङ्गैः। — विक्रमोर्वशीयम् 2/13 के अनन्तर चित्रलेखा की उक्ति
17. असितकुवलयश्यामलेन देहप्रभाप्रवाहेण . . . .। — कादम्बरी पृ० 59

18. नीतान्तनीलोत्पलपत्रकान्तिभिः . . . .। ऋतुसंहारम् 2/2, 23

19. (i) अये रक्ताशोकस्तबकसमरागो मणिरयं। विक्रमोर्वशीयम् 4/63

(ii) अशोकनिर्भर्त्सितपद्मरागमाकृष्टहेमद्युतिकर्णिकारम्। कुमारसम्भवम् 3/53

20. हर्षचरितम् पृ० 446 कुमारसम्भवम् 3/53

21. कर्णे सुयोग्यं नवकर्णिकारं चलेषु नीलेष्वलकेष्वशोकम्।

पुष्पं च फुल्लं नवमल्लिकायाः प्रयान्ति कान्तिं प्रमदाजनानाम्।। ऋतुसंहारम् 6/6

22. (i) रागेण बालारुणकोमलेन चूतप्रवालोष्ठमलञ्चकार। कुमारसम्भवम् 3/30

(ii) अमदयन्मधुगन्धसनाथया किसलयाधरसङ्गतया मनः।

कुसुमसम्भृतया नवमल्लिका स्मितरुचा तरुचारुविलासिनी।। रघुवंशम् 9/42

23. नितम्बबिम्बलम्बिविकट कुरण्टक . . . . प्रदीप्त इव रागाग्नि . . . .। हर्षचरितम् पृ० 218

24. (i) कर्णपूरकमल . . . .। तथा विकचकमलकृतकर्णपल्लवावतंस् . . . . कादम्बरी पृ० 334, 183

(ii) स्तनन्यस्तोशीरं शिथिलितमृणालैकवलयं . . . .। अभिज्ञानशाकुन्तलम् 3/7

(iii) शाकु० 3/16, नैषध० 18/21 इत्यादि

25. न वा शरच्चन्द्रमरीचिकोमलं मृणालसूत्रं रचितं स्तनान्तरे।। अभिज्ञानशाकुन्तलम् 6/1

26. कादम्बरी पृ० 291-292

27. (i) हला शाकुन्तले! अपि सुखयति ते नलिनीपत्रवातः?

अभिज्ञानशाकुन्तलम् 3/6 के अनन्तर सखियों की उक्ति

(ii) एतस्मिञ्छुकोदरसुकुमारे नलिनीपत्रे नखैर्निक्षिप्तवर्णं कुरु।

अभिज्ञानशाकुन्तलम् 3/13 के अनन्तर प्रियंवदा की उक्ति

28. कर्णाशोकपल्लवैः . . . .। कादम्बरी पृ० 337

29. (i) ऋतुसंहारम् 2/25

(ii) कुसुमं कृतदोहदस्त्वया यदशोकोऽयमुदीरयिष्यति।

अलकाभरणं कथं नु तत्तव नेष्यामि निवापमाल्यताम्।। रघुवंशम् 8/62

30. हर्षचरितम् पृ० 337

31. नवचूताङ्कुरकर्णपूरया . . . .। कादम्बरी पृ० 273

32. त्वमसि मचा चूताङ्कुर दत्तः कामाय गृहीतधनुषे। अभिज्ञानशाकुन्तलम् 6/3

33. परलोकविधौ च माधव! स्मरमुद्दिश्य विलोलपल्लवाः।

निवपेः सहकारमञ्जरीः प्रियचूतप्रसवो हि ते सखा।। कुमारसम्भवम् 4/38

34. सहकारतैलतिम्यत्तनुखदिरकेसरजालजटिलानि। हर्षचरितम् पृ० 215

35. नवकुरबकपूर्णः केशपाशो मनोज्ञः। ऋतुसंहारम् 6/33

36. नितम्बबिम्बलम्बिविकटकुरण्टकः। हर्षचरितम् पृ० 218

37. (i) असूत सद्यः कुसुमान्यशोकः स्कन्धात्प्रभृत्येव सपल्लवानि। कुमारसम्भवम् 3/26

(ii) विक्रमोर्वशीयम् 2/7

38. प्रफुल्लचूताङ्कुरतीक्ष्णसायको द्विरेफमालाविलसद्धनुर्गुणः।
मनांसि भेत्तुं सुरतप्रसङ्गिनां वसन्तयोद्धा समुपागतः प्रिये।। ऋतुसंहारम् 6/1

39. ताम्रप्रवालस्तबकावनम्राश्चूतद्रुमाः पुष्पितचारुशाखाः।
कुर्वन्ति कामं पवनावधूताः पर्युत्सुकं मानसमङ्गनानाम्।। ऋतुसंहारम् 6/17

40. मत्तद्विरेफपरिचुम्बितचारुपुष्पा मन्दानिलाकुलितनम्रमृदुप्रवालाः।
कुर्वन्ति कामिमनसां सहसोत्सुकत्वं चूताभिरामकलिकाः समवेक्ष्यमाणाः।। ऋतुसंहारम् 6/19

41. कान्तामुखद्युतिजुषामचिरोद्गतानां शोभां परां कुरबकद्रुममञ्जरीणाम्।
दृष्ट्वा प्रिये! सहृदयस्य भवेन्न कस्य कन्दर्पबाणपतनव्यथितं हि चेतः।। ऋतुसंहारम् 6/20

42. रक्ताशोकश्चलकिसलयः केशरश्चात्र कान्तः
प्रत्यासन्नौ कुरबककवृतेर्माधवीमण्डपस्य।
एकः सख्यास्तव सह मया वामपादाभिलाषी
काङ्क्षत्यन्यो वदनमदिरां दोहदच्छद्मनाऽस्याः।। मेघदूतम् 2/18

43. सोन्मादहंसमिथुनैरुपशोभितानि स्वच्छप्रफुल्लकमलोत्पलभूषितानि।
मन्दप्रभातपवनोद्गतवीचिमालान्युत्कण्ठयन्ति सहसा हृदयं सरांसि।। ऋतुसंहारम् 3/11

44. (i) पायय कमलमधुरस भवनकलहंसान्. . . .। कादम्बरी पृ० 335
(ii) हंसाकृष्यमाणनीलोत्पलवनाः . . . .। हर्षचरितम् पृ० 220

45. चूताङ्कुरास्वादकषायकण्ठः पुंस्कोकिलो यन्मधुरं चुकूज।। कुमारसम्भवम् 3/32

46. सेनापतिस्ता मृणालिकाः शशिकला इव . . . .। कादम्बरी पृ० 65

47. जलजशङ्खमीनमकरसनाथतलतया। हर्षचरितम् पृ० 117

48. मुखनिहितनवचूतपल्लवम्. . . .। हर्षचरितम् पृ० 91

49 (i) बिससूत्रयज्ञोपवितम् . . . .। कादम्बरी पृ० 306
(ii) अभिनवबिससूत्रनिर्मितेनेव . . . . यज्ञोपवीतेनोद्भासमानः . . . .। कादम्बरी पृ० 72

卐 卐 卐

Section XI

FLORA IN ASTROLOGY & SMṚTI LITERATURE

ज्योतिषस्मृतिनिर्झरी

ज्योतिषशास्त्र में वनस्पतिविज्ञान

नागेन्द्र पाण्डेय

ऋतु एवं सत्य से संश्लिष्ट त्रिगुणात्मिका सृष्टि की प्रथम उद्भूति वनस्पति है। इसको आलङ्कारिक शब्दों में धरित्री का वसन तथा अँचल कहा गया है। सम्भवतः वनस्पतियों के द्वारा न केवल सौन्दर्यवृद्धि, लज्जा का आवरण अथवा अवगुण्ठन का आच्छादन होता है, अपितु इनसे इस धरित्री के श्वास-प्रश्वास का गहरा सम्बन्ध है। जब हमारे मन्त्रद्रष्टा महर्षि ऋग्वेद 10.97.15 में कहते हैं—

याः फलिनीर्या अपुष्पा या च पुष्पिणी बृहस्पतिप्रसूतस्तानो मुञ्चत्वहंसः।

अर्थात् समस्त वनस्पतियाँ बृहस्पति से निर्मित हैं। वे सभी वनस्पतियाँ जो फलदार हैं, बिना फल की हैं, पुष्परहित हैं अथवा पुष्पों वाली हैं; वे सभी रोगमुक्त करने में समर्थ हैं। इसी प्रकार वैदिक संहिताओं में विभिन्न स्थलों में वनस्पतियों का सप्रयोजन विस्तृत निरूपण किया गया है। उदाहरणार्थ वाजसनेयी संहिता 12.89 तथा तैत्तिरीय संहिता 7.4.17.1 में इसका वर्णन यथोक्त रूप में प्राप्त है। केवल ऋग्वेदसंहिता में वनस्पति मंत्र का उल्लेख छः स्थल पर किया गया है।

ज्योतिष शास्त्र वेद का अङ्गभूत शास्त्र होने के कारण वैदिक संस्कृति से यह सर्वथा अनुस्यूत है। वेदमन्त्र सूत्र रूप में जिन विषयों का निदर्शन करते हैं, ज्योतिष शास्त्र उन विषयों को विस्तृत रूप में व्यवहारिक स्वरूप प्रदान करता है। वनस्पतियों से सम्बन्धित तथ्यपरक ज्ञान ज्योतिष के संहिता ग्रन्थों में समुपलब्ध है। वराहमिहिर (पञ्चम शताब्दी) की बृहत्संहिता और उस पर की गयी भट्टोत्पल की विवृति में वनस्पतियों का सारगर्भित वर्णन किया गया है। प्रस्तुत निबन्ध में संहिताओं के आधार पर वनस्पतिशास्त्र की उपस्थापना अभिप्रेत है।

आचार्य वराहमिहिर ने बृहत्संहिता के कुसुमलताध्याय, सस्सजातकाध्याय, दकार्गलाध्याय, वनसंप्रवेशध्याय और वृक्षायुर्वेदाध्याय में वनस्पतिशास्त्र का सम्यक् विवेचन किया है। आधुनिक काल में वनस्पतियों का महत्त्व पर्यावरण के संरक्षण के लिए माना जा रहा है। मृदा-संरक्षण एवं वृष्टि के लिए वनस्पतियों को आवश्यक माना जा रहा है जबकि वनस्पतियों के माध्यम से भारतीय ज्योतिषशास्त्र में अनेक अनुसन्धानात्मक प्रयोग कर विविध विषयों के परिज्ञान में वनस्पतियों का महत्त्व प्रदर्शित किया गया है।

कुसुमलताध्याय के आरम्भ में ही बताया गया है कि वनस्पतियों के फल एवं पुष्पों की वृद्धि को देखकर द्रव्यों की सुलभता तथा धान्यों की निष्पत्ति जाननी चाहिए। जैसा कि—

फलकुसुमसम्प्रवृद्धिं वनस्पतीनां विलोक्य विज्ञेयम्।
सुलभत्वं द्रव्याणां निष्पत्तिश्चापि सस्यानाम्।।

यह भी कहा गया है कि किस वृक्ष के फलों एवं फूलों की वृद्धि से किन-किन धान्यों की समृद्धि होती है। यथा—

शालेन कलमशाली रक्ताशोकेन रक्तशालिश्च।
पाण्डूकः क्षीरिकया नीलाशोकेन सूकरकः।।

यही नहीं गवादि पशुओं की तथा सुवर्ण एवं रत्नों की भी समृद्धि वनस्पतियों से सम्बन्धित है। जैसा कि कहा गया है— हस्तिकर्ण वृक्ष के फल, पुष्पों से हाथी, अश्वकर्ण वृक्ष से घोड़ा, पाटला से गाय और कदली वृक्ष से बकरी, भेड़ आदि की वृद्धि होती है। इसी प्रकार चम्पा पुष्प की वृद्धि से सोना, बन्धुजीव से मूंगा, कुरवक से वज्र और नन्दिकावर्त से वैदूर्यमणि की वृद्धि होती है। यथा—

करिणश्च हस्तिकर्णैरादेश्या वाजिनोऽश्वकर्णेन।
गावश्च पाटलाभिः कदलीभिरजाविकं भवति।।
चम्पककुसुमैः कनकं विद्रुमसम्पच्च बन्धुजीवेन।
कुरवकवृद्ध्या वज्रं वैडूर्यं नन्दिकावर्तैः।।

यह भी बतलाया गया है कि स्वर्णिम पुष्पों से व्यापारी, कमल से ब्राह्मण, कुमुद से पुरोहित, सुगन्धि से सेनापति और आक (मन्दार) से सोने की वृद्धि का ज्ञान होता है। यथा—

श्रेष्ठी सुवर्णपुष्पात्पद्मैर्विप्राः पुरोहिताः कुमुदैः।
सौगन्धिकेन बलपतिरर्केण हिरण्यपरिवृद्धिः।।

वृक्षों के पत्तों की स्थिति से वर्षा का ज्ञान करना ज्योतिषशास्त्र का सामान्य प्रयोग है। जैसा कि आचार्य वराहमिहिर ने कहा है—

यस्मिन् काले स्निग्धनिश्छिद्रपत्राः सन्दृश्यन्ते वृक्षगुल्मा लताश्च।
तस्मिन्वृष्टिः शोभना सम्प्रदिष्टा रुक्षैश्छिद्रैरल्पमाम्भः प्रदिष्टम्।।

अर्थात् जिस समय वृक्ष गुल्म और लताओं के पत्ते चिकने एवं निश्छिद्र दिखायी दें, उस समय उत्तम वृष्टि होती है। यदि वे पत्ते रुक्ष तथा सछिद्र हों तो अल्पवृष्टि होती है। आचार्य पराशर ने भी इसी आशय को प्रकट करते हुए पराशरसंहिता में लिखा है—

अच्छिद्रपत्राः सुस्निग्धाः फलपुष्पसमन्विताः।
निर्दिशन्ति शुभं वृक्षा विपरीतं विगर्हिताः।।

सस्यों की उत्पत्ति तथा उनका सम्यक् विकास ग्रह-नक्षत्र के योगों से ज्योतिषशास्त्र निर्धारित करता है। सस्यजातकाध्याय में सस्य सम्बन्धी फलादेश उसी प्रकार किए गए हैं, जिस प्रकार से मनुष्य-जातक का फलादेश किया जाता है। उदाहरण के लिए द्रष्टव्य है—

कुम्भे गुरुर्गवि शशी सूर्योऽलिमुखे कुजार्कजौ मकरे।
निष्पत्तिरस्ति महती पश्चात् परचक्रभयरोगम्।।

इसका अभिप्राय यह है कि यदि कुम्भ राशि में गुरु हो, वृष में चन्द्रमा, वृश्चिक के आदि में सूर्य तथा मकर में मंगल और शनि स्थित हों तो धान्यों की अधिक निष्पत्ति होती है। तत्पश्चात् शत्रु का आगमन और रोग का भय होता है।

इसी प्रकार एक और उदाहरण द्रष्टव्य है—

जामित्रकेन्द्रसंस्थौ क्रूरौ सूर्यस्य वृश्चिकस्थस्य।
सस्यविपत्तिं कुरुतः सौम्यैर्दृष्टौ न सर्वत्र।।

अर्थात् वृश्चिकराशि में स्थिति सूर्य से सप्तम में एक और इससे भिन्न केन्द्र (4, 10) में दूसरा पापग्रह (मंगल अथवा शनि) शुभग्रहों से दृष्ट हो तो कुछ स्थानों पर धान्यों का विनाश करते हैं। इसी सन्दर्भ में आचार्य बादरायण ने भी अपना मत उपस्थापित किया है। यथा—

सूर्यात्सप्तमसंस्थः पापोऽन्यः केन्द्रगश्च हानिकरौ।
सौम्यग्रहसन्दृष्टौ न तथा सर्वत्र निर्दिष्टौ।।

विविध प्रकार की वनस्पतियों की मेषादि द्वादश राशियाँ अधिष्ठाता होती हैं। काष्ठौषधियाँ तथा मसूर, गेहूँ, जौ, चना और अरहर का विचार मेष राशि से किया जाता है। इसी प्रकार सभी प्रकार के पुष्प, गेहूँ, कपास तथा शरद और ग्रीष्म इन दोनों ऋतुओं के साथ धान्य वृष राशि से विचारित होते हैं। केला, दूर्वा, सभी प्रकार के फल, कन्द, सुगन्ध पत्र, नारियल और रस पदार्थों का विचार सिंह राशि से किया जाता है। इसी प्रकार मीन पर्यन्त सभी राशियों के अनुसार वनस्पतियों की अनुकूलता और प्रतिकूलता का विचार होता है। सत्ताधारी राजपुरुषों की विपत्ति भी अनेक प्रकार से समुद्भूत होती है। उन्हें राज्य तथा पद की रक्षा हेतु सतत चिन्ता बनी रहती है। राजाओं की दुश्चिन्ता तथा दुर्योग जब दण्ड अथवा शस्त्रबल से शमित नहीं होते हैं तब ज्योतिषीय उपचार का आश्रय लेना पड़ता है। ज्योतिषशास्त्र में पुष्य स्नान के द्वारा राजा की विपत्ति शान्त की जाती है।

पुष्य स्नान के क्रम में वनस्पतियों की महत्ता का बृहत्संहिता के पुष्यस्नानाध्याय में विस्तृत वर्णन किया गया है। पुष्य स्नान के निमित्त उपयुक्त स्थल का रोचक वर्णन करते हुए कहा गया है—

श्लेष्मातकाक्षकण्टकिकटुतिक्तविगन्धिपादपविहीने।
कौशिकगृध्रप्रभृतिभिरनिष्टविहगैः परित्यक्ते।।
तरुणतरुगुल्मवल्लीलताप्रतानान्विते वनोद्देशे।
निरुपहतपत्रपल्लवमनोज्ञमधुरद्रुमप्राये ।।

अर्थात् वन के समीपस्थ क्षेत्र में जहाँ पर लसौड़ा, बहेड़ा, कण्टकी (खैर) आदि कटु, तिक्त (निम्बादि) के साथ ही नूतन वृक्ष, गुल्म, लताओं के समुदाय से युक्त, पत्र पल्लव पुष्पादि सहित मधुर स्वाद वाले वृक्षों से युक्त स्थल पर पुष्य स्नान करना चाहिए। यद्यपि पुष्य स्नान में हवनादि कर्म का तथा मन्त्र पाठों का विशेष महत्त्व है तथापि वनस्पतियों से युक्त परिवेश के साथ ही वनस्पति युक्त जल से स्नान करना मुख्यतया अभिहित किया गया है। जैसा कि स्नानीय द्रव्यों में ज्योतिष्मती, चिरैते का फल, हर्रें, अपराजिता, जीवा, सौंठ, पाठा, समंगा, भंग, सहदेई, नागरमोथा, शतावरी, रीठा, शमी, बला, ब्राह्मी, अजा तथा हल्दी के साथ ही जया, जयन्ती, जीवन्ती, जीवपुत्रिका, पुनर्नवा, विष्णुक्रान्ता, चक्राङ्गा, वाराही, सरसों, दूर्वा, आदि से वनस्पतियों का प्रमुखतया प्रयोग किया जाता है। इन सबसे सम्मिश्रित जल ही 'स्नानीय-जल' के रूप में प्रयुक्त होता है। यथा—

ज्योतिष्मतीं त्रायमाणामभयामपराजिताम्।
जीवां विश्वेश्वरीं पाठां समङ्गां विजयां तथा।।
सहां च सहदेवीं च पूर्णकोशां शतावरीम्।
अरिष्टिकां शिवां भद्रां तेषु कुम्भेषु विन्यसेत्।।

ब्राह्मीं क्षेमामजां चैव सर्वबीजानि काञ्चनीम्।
मङ्गल्यानि यथालाभं सर्वौषध्यो रसास्तथा।।
रत्नानि सर्वगन्धाश्च बिल्वं च सविकङ्कतम्।
प्रशस्तनाम्न्यश्चौषध्यो हिरण्यं मङ्गलानि च।।

सर्वाधिक महत्त्वपूर्ण विषय वृक्षायुर्वेद के नाम से प्रख्यात है। आचार्य वराहमिहिर ने मानव जीवन के लिए वृक्षों की अनिवार्यता को बतलाते हुए उनकी उत्पत्ति, विकास एवं सुरक्षा के साथ ही उत्तम फल-फूल की प्राप्ति के लिए स्पष्ट निर्देश दिया है। एक वृक्ष से दूसरे वृक्ष की दूरी 20 हाथ होना उत्तम, 16 हाथ मध्यम और 12 हाथ का अधम कहा गया है। काश्यपसंहिता में भी इसी अन्तर को स्वीकार करते हुए कहा गया है—

अन्तरं विंशतिर्हस्ता वृक्षाणामुत्तमं स्मृतम्।
मध्यमं षोडशं ज्ञेयमधमं द्वादशं स्मृतम्।।

वृक्षों के रोपने की अति वैज्ञानिक विधि निर्दिष्ट की गई है यथा—

घृतोशीरतिलक्षौद्रविडङ्गक्षीरगोमयैः।
आमूलस्कन्धलिप्तानां सङ्क्रामणविरोपणम्।।

अर्थात् घृत, खश, तिल, शहद, वायबिडंग, दूध और गोबर इन पदार्थों को सम्मिश्रित करके पौधे को मूल से लेकर अग्रपर्यन्त लेप के पश्चात् रोपना चाहिए। इससे पौधे सुरक्षित होकर उत्तम रूप से विकसित होते हैं।

इसी प्रकार वृक्षों में रोगोत्पत्ति का कारण और वृक्षों में फल नहीं लगने का विधान स्पष्ट करते हुए रुग्ण वृक्षों की चिकित्सा भी इस प्रकार कही गयी है—

चिकित्सितमथैतेषां शस्त्रेणादौ विशोधनम्।
विडङ्गघृतपङ्काक्तान् सेचयेत् क्षीरवारिणा।।

इसी क्रम में इमली, तथा कपित्थ के वृक्ष को लता के रूप में उत्पन्न करने के अद्भुत प्रयोग का वर्णन वृक्षायुर्वेदाध्याय में वराहमिहिर के द्वारा किया गया है। इस अध्याय के श्लोक 19 से 30 तक आश्चर्यजनक प्रयोगों का वर्णन मिलता है। अंकोल वृक्ष के बीज को एक ही दिन में फल एवं फूलों से युक्त उत्पन्न कर देने की विधि बतलायी गई है। निश्चित ही आज के कृषि वैज्ञानिकों को इसका परीक्षण करना चाहिए। इसमें किञ्चित् भी आश्चर्य नहीं होगा कि ज्योतिषशास्त्र में वर्णित इन प्रयोगों के आधार पर कृषि क्षेत्र में एक अद्भुत क्रान्ति उत्पन्न की जा सकती है।

जैसा कि प्रारम्भ में ही कहा जा चुका है कि ज्योतिष शास्त्र वनस्पतियों के सम्बन्ध में व्यावहारिक दृष्टिकोण रखता है और इसका लक्ष्य इनके प्रजनन, सुरक्षा एवं संवर्द्धन के साथ ही औषधीय गुणों तथा आनुसंगिक महत्त्व को निर्धारित करना है। वनस्पतियों की उत्पत्ति तथा विकास के लक्षणों से निधि प्राप्ति का निर्धारण, भूमि का शुभाशुभत्व ज्ञात करना एवं जलोद्गम के स्रोतों को निर्दिष्ट करना इस शास्त्र का महत्वपूर्ण उद्देश्य है। आचार्य वराहमिहिर ने ''दकार्गलाध्याय'' में जलोद्गम को ज्ञात करने के लिए विभिन्न लक्षणों को निरूपित किया है। उदाहरणार्थ— यह बतलाया गया है कि श्वेत शमी वृक्ष अत्यधिक काँटों से युक्त जिस स्थान पर स्थित हो उस स्थान से 1 हाथ दक्षिण 75 पुरुष नीचे जल होता है।

श्वेता कण्टकबहुला यत्र शमी दक्षिणेन तत्र पयः।
नरपञ्चकसंयुतया सप्तत्याहिर्नरार्धे च।। 85।।

इसी प्रकार विभिन्न वृक्षों के आधार पर जलोद्गम का निर्धारण किया गया है। इसी अध्याय में यह महत्त्वपूर्ण निर्देश प्राप्त होता है कि जल प्राप्ति के लिए खुदाई करते समय भूमि के नीचे कठोर शिला का प्रस्तर (चट्टान) मिलता है, तब उस शिला का भेदन किस प्रकार किया जाए जिससे उसके अधःस्थित जल का उपयोग किया जा सके।

नैम्बं पत्रं त्वक् च नालं तिलानां सापामार्गं तिन्दुकं स्याद्गुडूची।
गोमूत्रेण स्रावितः क्षार एषां षट्कृत्वोऽतस्तापितो भिद्यतेऽश्मा।। 115।।

अर्थात् निम्ब (नीम) के पत्ते, नीम की छाल, तिलों का नाल, अपामार्ग, तेंदू का फल और गुडूची, इन सभी का भस्म गोमूत्र में मिलाकर तप्त शिला पर इनका छः बार छिड़काव किया जाए तो वह शिला टूट जाती है। इसी क्रम में लोहे की धार को कठोर बनाने की विधि का उल्लेख इसी प्रकार किया गया है।

आर्कं बयो हुडुविषाणमषीसमेतं
पारावताखुशकृता च युतः प्रलेपः।
शास्त्रस्य तैलमथितस्य ततोऽस्य पानं
पश्चाच्छितस्य न शिलासु भवेद्विघातः।। 116।।

अर्थात् लोहे पर तिल का तेल लगाने के पश्चात् उस पर भेड़ के सींग का भस्म तथा कबूतर और चूहे की बीट से मिश्रित मदार (आक) के दूध के मिश्रण का लेप करें। पुनः उसको आग में तपा कर पान देने से वह पत्थर को भी काटने में टूटता नहीं है।

आजकल जल प्रदूषण की भयावह समस्या से जनजीवन संत्रस्त है आधुनिक वैज्ञानिक विविध प्रकार के जलशोधक रसायनों के निर्माण में लगे हुए हैं, तथापि इस समस्या का सम्यक् समाधान नहीं हो पा रहा है। 'दकार्गलाध्याय' में जल शुद्धि के निमित्त अत्यन्त सरल तथा बिना किसी व्यय का सूत्र दिया गया है।

अञ्जनमुस्तोशीरैः शराजकोशातकामलकचूर्णैः
कतकफलसमायुक्तैर्योगः कूपे प्रदातव्यः।। 121।।
कलुषं कटुकं लवणं विरसं सलिलं यदि वाशुभगन्धि भवेत्।
तदनेन भवत्यमलं सुरसं सुसुगन्धि गुणैररपैश्च युतम्।। 122।।

अर्थात् अंजन, मोथा, खस, राजकोशातक, आँवला और कतक का फल, चूर्ण कर कूप, तालाब अथवा जल स्थान (टंकी) में डाल दिया जाए तो जल प्रदूषण रहित होकर सुगन्धित हो जाता है। यहाँ पर यह भी बतलाया गया है। कि इस चूर्ण के प्रभाव से जल का कड़वापन, तिक्तता, खारापन, दुर्गन्ध और गंदगी पूर्णतया समाप्त हो जाती है और वह जल सुगन्ध युक्त होकर स्वास्थ्य तथा रुचि को बढ़ता है।

भूमि के शुभाशुभत्व का भी वनस्पतियों से गहरा सम्बन्ध है। आचार्य वराहमिहिर ने कहा है कि वही भूमि प्रशस्त एवं गृहनिर्माण के योग्य होती है जहाँ पर औषधियाँ वृक्ष तथा लताएँ स्वाभाविक रूप में वृद्धि को प्राप्त करती हों तथा वह भूमि मधुर एवं सुगन्धित वृक्षों से युक्त हो, इस प्रकार की भूमि पर ही वास्तु निर्माण करना चाहिए।

शस्तौषधिद्रुमलता मधुरा सुगन्धा
स्निग्धा समानसुषिराच मही नराणाम्।
अप्यध्वनि श्रमविनोदमुपागतानां
धत्ते श्रियं किमुत शाश्वतमन्दिरेषु।। 78।।

प्रसंगतः यहाँ बता देना समीचीन होगा कि वृक्ष शुभ अथवा अशुभ दोनों प्रकार का परिणाम देते हैं। यदि गृह की पूर्व दिशा में पीपल का वृक्ष, दक्षिण में उदुम्बर (गूलर), पश्चिम में वट वृक्ष (बरगद) तथा उत्तर में पाकड़ का वृक्ष हो तो शुभ होता है इसके विपरीत पूर्व दिशा में बरगद, दक्षिण में पाकड़, पश्चिम में पीपल और उत्तर में गूलर का होना अशुभ माना जाता है। यथा—

अश्वत्थः पूर्वतोधान्यो दक्षिणस्यामुदुम्बरः।
न्यग्रोधः पश्चिमे श्रेष्ठः प्लक्षोऽप्युत्तरतः शुभः।। 79।। (वास्तुमाला)

न्यग्रोधः पूर्वतोवर्ज्यो दक्षिणेप्लक्ष एव च।
अश्वत्थः पश्चिमे भागे उत्तरे चाप्युदुम्बरः।। 72।।

इस प्रकार इस निबन्ध में वनस्पतियों से सम्बन्धित ज्योतिषशास्त्र के दृष्टिकोण को उपस्थापित किया गया है। इस शास्त्र के द्वारा मानवोपयोगी वनस्पतियों का व्यवहारिक पक्ष सूक्ष्मतापूर्वक विश्लेषित है। इस लघु निबन्ध में वनस्पतियों का सम्यक् उपयोग ज्ञात हो सके, यह प्रदर्शित करने का लघु प्रयास किया गया है।

卐 卐 卐

मनुस्मृति में वनस्पतिविज्ञान

उर्मिला रुस्तगी

वनस्पति-विज्ञान शब्द वनस्पति (पेड़-पौधे) तथा विज्ञान (विशेष-ज्ञान) इन दो शब्दों का समूह है जिसका अर्थ है 'पेड़-पौधों का विशेष ज्ञान'। 'वनस्पति' शब्द वनस् तथा पति इन दो शब्दों के योग से बनता है। 'मोनियर विलियम्स' अपने शब्दकोष में वनस् को वन का षष्ठी मानने की सम्भावना करते हैं और इस प्रकार वनानां 'पतिः वनस्पतिः' हुआ अर्थात् 'वनों का संरक्षक'। वनस्पति शब्द का प्रयोग अरण्य के लिए भी होता है तथा पेड़ के लिए भी होता है। भूमि पर उत्पन्न लता, गुल्म, औषधि आदि सभी के लिए वनस्पति शब्द का प्रयोग होता है। अपि च, अकारान्त 'वनस' शब्द का अर्थ है 'तृण आदि' अतः अन्तिम अकार का लोप कर देने पर निष्पन्न हुआ वनस्पति शब्द तृण आदि का संरक्षक अरण्य है अथवा तृण आदि स्वयं हैं।

विज्ञान के अन्तर्गत अध्ययन की जाने वाली तीन शाखाओं[1] में से वनस्पतिविज्ञान 'जीवजन्तुविज्ञान' के अन्तर्गत आता है। जीव जन्तुविज्ञान के अन्दर सुख-दुःख की अनुभूति रखने वाले आन्तरिक चेतना से युक्त जीवों का अध्ययन होता है, अतः स्पष्ट है कि वनस्पतियाँ जीवन तथा अनुभूतियों से युक्त जीव हैं। स्मृतिकार ने भी स्पष्ट यही कुछ व्यक्त किया है कि किसी तमस् गुण से वेष्टित होने के कारण ये जीव इस योनि को प्राप्त करते हैं। इनके अन्दर अन्तः संज्ञा होती है तथा सुख-दुःख की अनुभूति भी।[2] पशु जगत् मूक होता है परन्तु वनस्पतिजगत् मूक एवं गतिहीन होता है[3] अतः मानव जगत् से निम्न-कोटि का है और यही तसस् गुण का आधिक्य है। चैतन्य तथा अनुभूति होते हुए भी ये अपने भावों को व्यक्त करने में असमर्थ हैं।

अनेकानेक पेड़-पौधों, ओषधियों, लताओं, तृण आदि का उल्लेख तो स्मृतिशास्त्रों में हुआ परन्तु क्या हम स्मृतिकारों को वनस्पति जगत् का वैज्ञानिक मान सकते हैं? हमारे समक्ष एक प्रश्न तो अवश्य ही उभरकर आता है कि क्या स्मृतिकारों ने अपने ग्रन्थों में वृक्ष आदि का नामतः उल्लेख यूं ही कर दिया अथवा वे इनके गुणों से अनभिज्ञ थे। पुनश्च, वृक्ष आदि के नामों का ज्ञान अथवा उनका प्रयोग यदि स्मृतिकारों को परम्परा से प्राप्त था तो क्या उसे हम विज्ञान की कोटि में रख सकते हैं? आज हमें अपने पूर्वजों से ओषधियों के प्रयोग विरासत में प्राप्त हैं यथा गुम-चोट में दूध में हल्दी पकाकर पीना, अत्यधिक शौच आने पर गर्म पानी में अदरक का रस मिलाकर पीना, खूनी-बवासीर में पीपल के ताजा-पत्तों के रस का सेवन आदि। इन औषधियों के स्तम्भित कर देने वाले परिणामों को देखकर हम इनके गुणों को अस्वीकार नहीं कर पाते हैं प्रत्युत उन्हें अधिक जानने की तीव्र इच्छा हमारे मन में स्वभाविक रूप से उत्पन्न हो जाती है। किसी भी ओषध के गुणों में विश्वास के भी दो कारण हैं— पहला— हम उस ओषध के गुणों का अध्ययन कर चुके हैं तथा दूसरा— हम उस ओषध के ज्ञानी को आप्त पुरुष मानते हैं। सम्पूर्ण समाज को धर्म का मार्ग बताने वाले स्मृतिकार वृक्ष आदि के विशेष-गुणों से अज्ञ रहकर उनका उल्लेख करें— यह विश्वास के योग्य नहीं है। अतः हम यह मानते हैं कि स्मृतिकार वनस्पति-विज्ञान से केवलमात्र परिचित ही नहीं थे परन्तु वे उनके सूक्ष्म-ज्ञान में सिद्धहस्त थे। एस०सी० बैनर्जी के शब्दों में ''धर्मशास्त्र विभिन्न प्रकार के वृक्ष, पौधों, फल तथा फूलों के विशेष ज्ञान की निधि है।''[4]

स्मृतिशास्त्रों के रचयिता अच्छी प्रकार से जानते हैं कि सम्पूर्ण स्थावर जगत् भूमि अथवा शाखाओं को फोड़कर बाहर आता है। बीजों से उत्पन्न कुछ स्थावर भूमि को फोड़कर बाहर आते हैं तथा शाखा से उत्पन्न कुछ स्थावर शाखाओं को फोड़कर उत्पन्न होते हैं।[5] इन स्थावरों के अन्तर्गत गिनाए जाने वाली विभिन्न जातियों का स्पष्ट उल्लेख स्मृतिकारों के वनस्पति-ज्ञान का प्रत्यक्ष-प्रमाण है। स्मृतियों में स्थावर जगत् की विभिन्न जातियों का उल्लेख इस प्रकार है—

(i) बहुत फूल तथा फलों से लदी हुई तथा फल के पकने पर नष्ट हो जाने वाली 'ओषधियाँ' कहलाती हैं।[6]

(ii) बिना फूलों के फलने वाले 'वनस्पति' जाने जाते हैं।[7]

(iii) फूलों के बाद फलने वाले 'वृक्ष' हैं।[8]

(iv) जड़ से समूह-रूप में उत्पन्न होने वाले शाखारहित 'गुच्छ' हैं[9] यथा मल्लिका।

(v) एक ही जड़ से एकत्रित रूप में उत्पन्न होने वाले बाँस, गन्ना आदि 'गुल्म' हैं।[9]

(vi) उलप आदि 'तृण' की जातियाँ हैं।[10]

(vii) तन्तुओं से युक्त यथा त्रपुष (खीरा) तथा अलाबू (घिया) आदि 'प्रतान' हैं।[11]

(viii) वृक्ष का आरोहण करने वाली गुडूची आदि 'वल्लियाँ' हैं।[12]

स्मृतिकार स्थावर जगत् के विभिन्न भागों यथा मूल, काण्ड, पुष्प, पर्ण, फल, तन्तु आदि से भलीभाँति परिचित थे।[13] वह यह भी जानते थे कि ओषधियाँ तथा वृक्ष यदि प्रयोग में लाई जाने के लिए मूलतः उखाड़ भी लिए जाएँ तो इससे उनकी योनि सुधर जाएगी।[14]

ब्रह्मचारी-दण्ड

स्मृतिशास्त्रों के अनुसार ब्राह्मण ब्रह्मचारी का दण्ड बिल्व या पलाश का हो, क्षत्रिय का वट अथवा खदिर का तथा वैश्य ब्रह्मचारी का पीलु या उदुम्बर वृक्षों का।[15] यद्यपि पलाश आदि प्रत्येक वृक्ष-काष्ठ की अपनी-अपनी विशेषताएँ हैं परन्तु एक ही वृक्ष-काष्ठ का प्रयोग यदि सभी ब्रह्मचारियों के दण्ड के लिए विहित कर दिया जाए तो स्थावर-जगत् तथा पर्यावरण के प्रति अन्याय तथा अत्याचार होगा। अतः अन्य महत्त्वपूर्ण कार्यों तथा ओषधि निर्माण आदि में प्रयुक्त न होने वाले वृक्षों की लकड़ी को दण्ड के रूप में प्रयोग का विधान स्मृतिकारों के वनस्पति-ज्ञान का परिचायक है। हम कहीं भी शाल्मली वृक्ष की लकड़ी का प्रयोग यज्ञ में नहीं पाते क्योंकि यह लकड़ी पक्की तथा चिकनी होती है तथा पानी में खराब नहीं होती। यही कारण है कि धोबी के लिए फलक ऐसी लकड़ी से तैयार किया जाता है।[16]

पेड़-पौधों आदि के महत्त्व को स्मृतिकार तथा तत्कालीन समाज अच्छी प्रकार जानता था। यही कारण है कि स्मृतियों में बगीचे के ऊपर हुए सीमा-विवाद को राजा द्वारा निपटाने तथा बगीचे के हड़पने पर राजा द्वारा 500 या 200 पण से दण्डित करने का विधान प्राप्त है।[17]

सीमा के वृक्ष

स्मृतिकार यह जानते थे कि न्यग्रोध, अश्वत्थ, किंशुक, शाल्मली, साल, ताल, शमी तथा गूलर आदि वृक्ष सैकड़ों वर्षों की आयु वाले तथा पक्की लकड़ी वाले हैं तथा इन्हें संवर्धित करने के लिए किसी प्रकार के मानवीय-श्रम की अथवा कृत्रिम जल की आवश्यकता नहीं है तथा गहरी जड़ों वाले ये वृक्ष उखाड़ने में भी सुलभ नहीं होते। वे यह

भी जानते थे कि बाँस, मुञ्ज तथा कुब्जक तीखे पत्तों वाले स्थावर हैं तथा गुल्म एवं लताएँ पैरों में अटकने वाले स्थावर। ये सभी स्थावर सीमा-सुरक्षा में सहायक सिद्ध होते हैं क्योंकि एक तो दीर्घायु होने से इनसे सीमा की पहचान रहती है तथा तीखे तथा अटकाने वाले पत्ते एवं तन्तुओं से युक्त ये सीमा को आसानी से पार नहीं करने देते। यही कारण है कि देश की सीमाओं पर स्मृतिकारों द्वारा ऐसे ही स्थावरों का उल्लेख किया गया है।[18] इसके अतिरिक्त मुञ्ज, कुश, अश्मन्तक, बल्वज तथा दर्भ का उल्लेख प्रयोगार्ह स्थावर के रूप में मनुस्मृति में प्राप्त है।[19]

शाक

गुरु को प्रीति प्रदान करने वाली वस्तुओं में सोना, गौ आदि के साथ धान्य तथा शाक को भी गिनवाया गया है।[20] शिष्य द्वारा गुरु को शाक आदि देने का नियम तथा अयाचित शाक को दानरूप में स्वीकार करने का विधान[21] शाक के महत्त्व को प्रदर्शित करता है, क्योंकि शाक शरीर में ऊर्जा, स्फूर्ति तथा बल देने वाला अपरिहार्य पदार्थ है। पितरों के तृप्तिदायक भोजन के रूप में 'कालशाक' तथा 'महाशल्क' का उल्लेख प्राप्त है।[22] मनुस्मृति के टीकाकारों में मेधातिथि, गोविन्दराज, सर्वज्ञनारायण, कुल्लूक, राघवानन्द तथा मणिराम की दृष्टि में यह कोई शाकविशेष है, परन्तु नन्दन की दृष्टि में यह कृष्णनिम्ब है तथा रामचन्द्र की दृष्टि में यह चेवक तथा चिञ्चुक है। मोनियर विलियम्स शब्दकोष के अनुसार 'चेवक' चिपिटक है तथा 'चिञ्चिक' इमली है। सम्भवतः चिञ्चुक और चिञ्चिक एक ही पदार्थ हो। मोनियर विलियम्स के शब्दकोष में 'महाशाक' का उल्लेख है जो एक प्रकार का शाक कहा गया है, यहाँ कालशाक कोई शब्द नहीं है। 'महाशल्क' हरगोविन्द शास्त्री के अनुसार काला वथुवा है जबकि सभी टीकाकारों की दृष्टि में यह कोई मत्स्यविशेष है। मोनियर विलियम्स झींगा मछली, केकड़े तथा मीठे-नींबू को 'महाशल्क' बताते हैं।

भूस्तृण शिग्रूक तथा श्लेष्मातक

संन्यासी के लिए भूमि तथा जल में उत्पन्न शाक, मेध्य वृक्षों के पुष्प, मूल तथा फल खाने का विधान है।[23] यह भी कहा गया है कि जो वह खाए वही पञ्चमहायज्ञों में अर्पण करे, भिक्षा में भी वही दे तथा अतिथि-सत्कार भी उन्हीं से करे।[24] पुनश्च, भूस्तृण, शिग्रूक तथा श्लेष्मातक संन्यासी के लिए निषिद्ध कहे गए हैं।[25]

यहाँ यह तो स्पष्ट है कि संन्यास आश्रम में प्रवेश करने वाले व्यक्ति को भक्ष्य पदार्थों की पहचान थी, चाहे ये शाक आदि गाँव में उत्पन्न हो, चाहे गाँव की सीमा के आस-पास अथवा सुदूर अरण्य में। जहाँ तक 'भूस्तृण' तथा 'शिग्रूक' का प्रश्न है, टीकाकार इन्हें शाकविशेष मानते हैं। ये शाक मेधातिथि के अनुसार वाहीक-देश के हैं परन्तु गोविन्दराज, कुल्लूक तथा राघवानन्द के अनुसार 'भूस्तृण' को मालवदेश का कोई प्रसिद्ध शाक है तथा शिग्रूक वाहीक-देश का। मणिराम भी 'भूस्तृण' मालवदेश को विशेष शाक मानते हैं। सर्वज्ञनारायण के अनुसार 'भूस्तृण' कोई शाक है तथा नन्दन के अनुसार यह कोई तृण जातिविशेष है। सर्वज्ञनारायण, मणिराम तथा नन्दन के अनुसार शिग्रूक सोभाञ्जन है। हरगोविन्द शास्त्री भूस्तृण को मालवदेश के जलों में उत्पन्न होने वाला शाक विशेष, शिग्रूक को सहिजन तथा श्लेष्मातक को लसोड़ा मानते हैं। मणिराम ने श्लेष्मातक का अर्थ लहसोण किया है। शेलु (अनु० 5.6) ही श्लेष्मातक है जो मणिराम के अनुसार लहसोरा है तथा अन्य टीकाकारों के अनुसार बहुवार तथा बहुवारक है।

'भूस्तृण', 'शिग्रूक' तथा 'श्लेष्मातक' ये तीनों शाक सर्वदेशीय शाक नहीं हैं तथा इन्हें केवलमात्र उबालकर खाना भी सम्भव नहीं है। स्मृतिकारों द्वारा विहित शाक सर्वमान्य विद्वानों द्वारा जाने जाते हैं अतः यह कहा जा सकता है कि स्मृतिकार केवलमात्र शाक व वृक्षों के नाम से ही अवगत नहीं हैं परन्तु उनके उत्पन्न होने के स्थान तक का उन्हें ज्ञान है। ऐसी स्थिति में स्मृतिकारों को वनस्पति शास्त्र के वैज्ञानिक मानने में कोई शंका नहीं रह जाती है। वनस्पतियों का यही विशिष्टज्ञान उन्हें पदार्थों का भक्ष्य एवम् अभक्ष्य[26] तथा विहित एवम् अविहित घोषित करने में

सहायक होता है। केवलमात्र संन्यासियों के लिए ही नहीं प्रत्युत सभी द्विजों के लिए लहसुन, गुञ्जन (शलजम), प्याज, कवक (छत्राक) तथा अमेध्य स्थानों में उत्पन्न शाक निषिद्ध कहे गए हैं।[27] शेलु अर्थात् लिसोड़ा भी निषिद्ध शाकों में गिनवाया गया है।[28] आज भी बहुत से परिवारों में ऊपरिलिखित शाकों का प्रयोग शास्त्रविरुद्ध माना जाता है। यद्यपि इन शाकों में अपने विशेष गुण हैं परन्तु गन्ध जैसा एक भी दोष चन्द्रमा के कलङ्क की तरह माना जाता है। पुनश्च, मनुस्मृतिकार द्वारा तिल, शण तथा अलसी से निर्मित वस्त्र, फल, मूल, ओषधि, सोम, गुड़, कुश तथा तेल विक्रय के लिए निषिद्ध कहे गए हैं।[29] सम्भवत: इनका विक्रय सामाजिक अव्यवस्था फैलाता हो अथवा जो वस्तु प्रत्येक मनुष्य के प्रयोग की हो यदि उसे बेचने के लिए छूट मिल जाए तो वह प्रत्येक को उपलब्ध नहीं होगी तथा तिल आदि सभी जीवनदायिनी वस्तुएँ हैं अत: इसके इन विशेष गुणों के कारण विक्रय का निषेध आवश्यक था।

यद्यपि पुष्प शब्द का प्रयोग तो स्मृतियों में अनेकश: हुआ है परन्तु पुष्पों के विशेष नाम का उल्लेख पुष्प के रूप में नहीं आया है। पद्म का नाम पद्मव्यूह के रूप में तथा महुए का उल्लेख माध्वी शराब के रूप में आया है। कुछ भी हो, इससे यह तो सिद्ध होता कि स्मृतिशास्त्र रचयिता फूलों के विषय में कुछ जानते ही न थे प्रत्युत वे उनके बाह्य तथा आन्तरिक गुणों का जीवन में प्रयोग करते थे।

वनस्पति की चोरी व दण्ड

स्मृतियों में यत्र-तत्र वनस्पतियों की चोरी के लिए घोषित दण्ड तथा उनके नाश को उपपातक घोषित करना स्थावर-जगत् के महत्त्व को दर्शाता है। यदि फल, वृक्ष, मूल, ओषधि आदि के गुण स्मृतिकारों को ज्ञात न होते तो वे उनके चोर व नाशक को दण्ड क्यों देते? यहाँ कहा गया है कि फूल, हरे धान्य, बिना घेरे वाले गुल्म, वल्ली और वृक्ष तथा साफ न किए धान्य के चुराने पर चोर को पाँच सौ पण का दण्ड तथा साफ किए गए धान्य, शाक, मूल और फलों के चोर को दो सौ पण का दण्ड दिया जाता था।[30] फल, फूल तथा लकड़ी चुराने का काम मलिन-कर्म गिना जाता था।[31] धान्य की चोरी को उपपातक माना गया है।[32] केवल चोरी को ही नहीं, प्रत्युत उद्यानों के बेचने[33] तथा इन्धन के लिए हरे पेड़ों को काटकर गिराने[34] को भी उपपातक कहा गया है। ऐसा करने वालों के लिए प्रायश्चित्तों का विधान यह सिद्ध करता है कि स्मृतिकालीन बुद्धिजीवी व सामान्य नागरिक इनके गुणों तथा महत्त्व से परिचित था। यहाँ बताया गया है कि फल वाले वृक्षों, गुल्म, वल्ली, लता तथा कुसुमित बेलों के काटने पर छेदनकर्त्ता को प्रायश्चित्त रूप में सावित्री आदि सौ ऋचाओं का जाप करना होता था तथा तृण, काष्ठ तथा पेड़ के चुराने पर तीन रात का उपवास रखना होता था।

वन-संरक्षक

प्रायश्चि त्त रूप में कुछेक जड़ी-बूटियों तथा कुश को उबालकर, काढ़ा बनाकर पीने का विधान भी प्राप्त है। सुरापात्र को धोने में प्रयुक्त जल को पीने पर दूध में शंखपुष्पी[35] उबालकर तैयार किए गए काढ़े को पाँच रात पीने का, मदिरा का सौदा करने वाले को तीन दिन तक कुश के काढ़े को पीने का तथा बिल्ली, कौए, चूहे, कुत्ते और नेवले से स्पृष्ट तथा बाल एवं कृमि से दूषित भोजन को खाने पर ब्रह्मसुवर्चला पौधे से तैयार काढ़े को पीने का प्रायश्चित्त रूप में विधान एक ओर स्मृतिकारों के शंखपुष्पी आदि के गुणों के ज्ञान को दर्शाता है तथा दूसरी ओर ऐसे प्रायश्चित्त मनुष्य की मानसिक चिकित्सा करते हैं जिससे कि वे इस तरह के नाशक कार्यों को न करें।[36] स्मृतिकार यह भी मानते हैं कि वनों में घूमने वाले शिकारी, बहेलिए, ग्वाले, मल्लाह, मूल खोदने वाले, सपेरे तथा 'उञ्छ' से जीविकार्जन करने वाले (मनु० 8.260) अप्रत्यक्ष रूप में वनों के संरक्षक हैं। वनों में होने वाली ओषधियों, बहुमूल्य लकड़ियों आदि की चोरी को जानना आसान कार्य नहीं परन्तु शिकारी आदि के माध्यम से तस्करी को जानना तथा तस्करों को पकड़ना सम्भव हो जाता है।

अतः स्मृतियाँ वनस्पति-विज्ञान से युक्त हैं तथा हमारे स्मृतिकार वनस्पतियों की अन्तश्चेतना को समझने वाले तथा उनके गुणों के जौहरी हैं। वनस्पतियों के बाह्य तथा आन्तरिक गुणों को जानने के कारण ही तो उन्होंने प्रायश्चित्त तथा आर्थिक रूप में दण्ड घोषित किए हैं। यदि स्मृतिकार इनके गुणों से अवगत न होते तो किस प्रकार वे कुछ को निषिद्ध भोजन कहते और कुछ को भोज्य। भक्ष्य तथा अभक्ष्य पदार्थों का वर्णन स्मृतिकारों के वनस्पति-विज्ञान का प्रत्यक्ष उदाहरण है। वह यह भी जानते थे कि मानव-जगत् का जीवन वनस्पतिजगत् के जीवन पर आधृत है। मनुष्य, पशु, पक्षी, आदि अपने आहार, विहार, सुख-चैन सभी के लिए वनस्पति-जगत् पर निर्भर करते हैं। स्मृतिशास्त्रों में कुछ वनस्पतियों का व्यापार करना तथा कुछ के व्यापार को निषिद्ध कर देना यह सिद्ध करता है कि कुछ मूल्यवान् (ओषधि आदि गुणों अथवा अन्य प्रयोगों के कारण) वनस्पतियाँ धरा के एक विशेष भाग पर ही होती थीं परन्तु उनकी आवश्यकता धरा के दूसरे भागों पर वास करने वाले निवासियों को भी थी। अतः उनका व्यापार आवश्यक था। आप० (1.2.33, 35; 21.1); बृह० (1.3.14) तथा वसि० (11.5.8) स्मृतियाँ मुञ्ज तथा बल्वज के व्यापार का उल्लेख करती हैं। पुनश्च, तोक्म (अङ्कुरित व्रीहि) तथा मरीच (काली मिर्च) का व्यापार निषिद्ध था क्योंकि एक तो ये लाने ले जाने में ही सड़ जातीं तथा दूसरे इसके लिए विशेष मिट्टी तथा जलवायु की आवश्यकता है। अतः धनलोभ से उन्हें बेचने का बढ़ावा न मिले इनका निषेध ही कर दिया गया क्योंकि दूसरे स्थान पर ले जाने के बाद ये नष्ट ही होते और वनस्पतियों का नाश कदाचित् किसी भी बुद्धिजीवी को सह्य नहीं था। अतः यह कहना अत्युक्ति नहीं कि हमारे स्मृति-शास्त्र-रचयिता वनस्पति-विज्ञान के सूक्ष्मातिसूक्ष्म रहस्यों के ज्ञाता थे। यही कारण है कि साधारण प्रजा को स्थावर-जगत् का संरक्षण सिखाने वाले इन स्मृतिकारों ने वनस्पतियों को देवता का रूप दिया जिससे कि प्रजा इनको नष्ट न करे। यह हमारे धर्म-शास्त्रों की ही देन है कि सामान्य प्राणी केवल मात्र वृक्षों की शुद्ध वायु को ही नहीं प्रत्युत उनकी त्वचा, पत्ते, रस, फूल, फल, मूल सभी को देवगुणों से युक्त बताता है तथा उनके प्रत्येक अङ्ग का संरक्षण भी करता है।

सन्दर्भ-सङ्केत

1. भौतिकी रासायनिक तथा जीवजन्तु विज्ञान।
2. मनु० - 1.49 तमसा बहुरूपेण वेष्टिताः कर्महेतुना।
   अन्तःसंज्ञा भवन्त्येते सुखदुःखसमन्विताः।।
3. वही - 1.46
4. बैनर्जी, सुरेशचन्द्र, धर्मशास्त्र, ए स्टडी इन देअर ओरिजन एण्ड डैवलपमेंट; कलकत्ता, 1962, पृ० 206
5. मनु० - 1.46, 47 उद्भिज्जाः स्थावराः सर्वे बीजकाण्डप्ररोहिणः।
6. मJ० - 1.46 ओषधयः फलपाकान्ता बहुपुष्पफलोपगाः।
   तु०बौ०ध० सू० पर गोविन्दस्वामी की टीका—

   गोविन्दस्वामी दो प्रकार की ओषधियों का वर्णन करते है—(1) वल्ल्यौषधि तथा (2) तृणौषधि।

   येषांवल्लीक्य एव धान्यं गृह्यते वा वल्ल्यौषध्यः ताश्चकुलुद्वादयः तृणौषध्यस्तु तस्माद् उपरिष्टादोषध्यःफलं गृह्णन्ति इत्यत्र या उक्ताः ता वीह्यादयः। तु० बैनर्जी पृ० 211

7. वही - 1.47 अपुष्पाः फलवन्तो ये ते वनस्पतयः स्मृतयः।। तु. बैनर्जी पृ. 211
8. वही - 1.47 पुष्पिणः फलिनश्चैव वृक्षास्तूभयतः स्मृताः।। तु० बैनर्जी पृ० 211
9. वही - 1.48 गुच्छगुल्मं तु विविधं तथैव तृणजातयः।
बीजकाण्डरुहाण्येव प्रताना वल्लय एव च।।

मनु. - 1.48 पर कुल्लूक—

मूलत एव यत्र लतासमूहो भवति न च प्रकाण्डानि ते गुच्छाः मल्लिकादयः। गुल्माः एकमूलाः संघातजाताः शरेक्षुप्रभृतयः। तृणजातयः उलपाद्याः प्रतानाः तन्तुयुक्तास्त्रपुषालाबुप्रभतयः। वल्ल्यः गुडूच्यादयः भूमेर्वृक्षमारोहन्ति।

10. द्र०पा०टि० - 9
11. द्र०पा०टि०
12. द्र०पा०टि०
13. मनु. - 1.46-48, 3.227, 4.73, 5.40
14. वही - 5.40 ओषध्यः पशवो वृक्षास्तिर्यञ्चः पक्षिणस्तथा।
यज्ञार्थं निधनं प्राप्नुवन्त्युत्सृतीः पुनः।।

यहाँ यज्ञार्थम् से तात्पर्य है अच्छे कार्य के लिए प्रयुक्त। क्योंकि यज्ञ भी तो शुभ काम का प्रयोगात्मक रूप ही है।

15. मनु. - 2.45. तु० गौ० स्मृ० 1 इन्होंने ब्राह्मण के दण्ड के लिए मजिष्ठ तथा हरिद्र दण्डों का उल्लेख भी किया है।
16. मनु. - 8.396 शाल्मलीफलके श्लक्ष्णे नेनिज्यान्नेजकः शनैः।
17. वही - 8.262, 264
18. वही - 8.246-247
19. वही - 5.119

दन्तधावन अर्थात् दातुन के लिए विष्णु स्मृति (61) में निम्नलिखित वृक्ष निषिद्ध कहे गए हैं—

नैव श्लेष्मातकारिष्टविभीतकधववधन्वनजम्। न च बन्धूकनिर्गुण्डीशिग्रुतिल्वतिन्दुकजम्। न च कोविदारशमीपीलुपिप्पलेङ्गुदगुग्गुलुजम्। न पारिभद्रकाम्लिकामोचकशाल्मलीशणजम्।। तथा निम्नलिखित वृक्षों का विधान किया गया है— वटासनार्कखदिरकरञ्जवदर-सर्ज्जनिम्बारिभेदापामार्गमालतीककुभबिल्वानामन्यतमम्। कषायं तिक्तं कटुकञ्च।

स्मृतिशास्त्ररचयिता प्रत्येक वृक्ष के गुणों से अवगत थे यही कारण है कि दातुन के लिए जो विशेषताएँ प्रतिपादित की गई हैं यह हैं कि दातुन कषाय, तिक्त तथा कटुक होनी चाहिए। श्लेष्मातक आदि वृक्षों में ये तीनों गुण नहीं होते हैं तथा साथ ही साथ उनकी लकड़ी में अवश्य ही कुछ ऐसे रस होते हैं जो दाँतों के लिए हानिकारक होंगे अतः इनका निषेध तर्कसङ्गत है। पुनश्च वट, असन, निम्ब आदि वृक्षों का दाँतों के लिए नरम, कटु, तिक्त तथा कषाय आदि गुण तथा रसों से युक्त होने के कारण दातुन के रूप में विधान किया गया है।

20. मनु - 3.246
21. वही - 3.246.4.250

22. वही - 3.272

23. वही - 6.13 स्थलजौदकशाकानि पुष्पमूलफलानि च।

मेध्यवृक्षोद्भवान्यद्यात्स्नेहांश्च फलसम्भवान्।।

24. वही - 6.7 यद्भक्ष्यं स्यात्ततो दद्याद्बलिं भिक्षां च शक्तितः।

अम्मूलफलभिक्षाभिरर्चयेदाश्रमागतान् ।।

25 मनु. - 6.14

26. वही - तथा गौ० 17

27. वही - 5.5

28. वही - 5.6, आप० 1.17.26 में परारिक का उल्लेख है तो आप० ध०सू० पर हरदत्त की उज्ज्वला टीकानुसार काली प्याज है।

29. मनु० 19.86.88 तु० बैनर्जी, पृ० 210.211,

तिल का बेचना निषिद्ध रहा है। आप० ध० सू० (1.26.15) के अनुसार तिल को पाप के प्रायश्चित्त रूप में किसी विशेष तिथि पर खाने का विधान प्राप्त है। यह श्राद्ध में प्रयोग किए जाने वाले पदार्थों में से एक है। बृह० स्मृ० (2.3.13) के अनुसार तिल का विधान केवलमात्र खाने, विधियाँ सम्पन्न करने तथा दान देने में किया गया है। काला तिल (बृह० 2.1.18) प्रायश्चित्त रूप में दी जाने वाली गाय पर फेंका जाता था। स्नातक के लिए तण्डुल में तिल मिलाकर खाना निषिद्ध था (बृह० 2.6. 2)। पूर्णिमा के दिनों में पूरे दिन तिल के आहार पर रहना पाप का प्रायश्चित्त रूप माना गया है।

30. मनु०, - 8.330-331

31. वही - 11.70

32. वही - 11.60

33. वही - 11.61

34. वही - 11.64

35. बौ० ध० सू० - 2.1.2 पर गोविन्दस्वामी टीकाकार इसे समुद्र के किनारे उत्पन्न लताविशेष बताते हैं।

वसिष्ठ स्मृ० 27.12 के अनुसार उदुम्बर का काढ़ा भी प्रायश्चित रूप में पीने का विधान है। वसि० (20.25)—

मद्यभाण्डे स्थिता आपो यदि कश्चिद्द्विजः पिबेत्।

पद्मैदुम्बरबिल्वपलाशानामुदकं पीत्वा त्रिरात्रेणैव शुद्धति।।

36. तु०गौ०स्मृ० I. कुत्ते आदि द्वारा स्पर्श किया जाने पर तीन दिन के उपवास, प्रवास, प्राणायाम तथा घृत प्राशन का विधान है।

卐 卐 卐

आङ्गिरस स्मृति में वनस्पतिजगत्

मीना कुमारी

आङ्गिरस स्मृति अपेक्षाकृत अल्पप्रसिद्ध स्मृति है। काणे महोदय ने इसकी गणना गौण स्मृतियों के अन्तर्गत की है। उनका तर्क है कि इसे बहुत कम निबन्धकारों ने उद्धृत किया है अतः इसे गौण स्मृति मानना चाहिए किन्तु इस स्मृति का साङ्गोपाङ्ग विवेचन करने पर अनुभव होता है कि इस ग्रन्थ को अपेक्षित महत्त्व प्राप्त नहीं हुआ है। आठवीं से दसवीं शताब्दी के मध्य में विरचित यह स्मृति पूर्वाङ्गिरस तथा उत्तराङ्गिरस इन दो भागों में विभक्त है। उत्तराङ्गिरस में प्रायश्चित्त का साङ्गोपाङ्ग वर्णन प्राप्त होता है, तो पूर्वाङ्गिरस में श्राद्धकर्म का। 'श्राद्ध' शब्द की व्युत्पत्ति से लेकर तर्पण तक ऐसा कोई भी विषय नहीं है, जो आङ्गिरस की दृष्टि से अगोचर रहा हो।

आङ्गिरस ने श्राद्ध कर्म के लिए उपयोगी डेढ़ सौ से अधिक पेड़-पौधों का वर्णन इस प्रकरण में किया है। उल्लेखनीय यह है कि इसके लिए उन्होंने इनके अप्रचलित नामों का ही प्रयोग किया है यथा हरिलोचन (श्वेत कमल), कामदम् (पान), अक्षिरोध्नः (पठानी लोध), वज्रघ्नः (पाषाण भेद), बारूकः (गौर-सुवर्ण साग), कर्मणः (वटवृक्ष), श्रीकरः (लालकमल), वल्मीकजः (अलाबू अथवा/घिया), कुशलः (महाजलवेतस्), बालपुत्रः (जूही अथवा खदिर), शेखरी (लौंग), मधुरग्रीवः (गन्ना), कुण्डली (गिलोय), खाद्यः (रुद्राक्ष), शतवल्ली (नीली दूर्वा), शातकुम्भ (कनेर), स्थिराकरः (ताड़), नटः (अशोक), मधुरस्त्रावा (पिण्डखजूर)। आङ्गिरस लोक प्रचलित मान्यताओं को अङ्गीकार करने वाले स्मृतिकार हैं, सम्भवतः इसी कारण इन्हें निबन्ध ग्रन्थों में अधिक स्थान नहीं मिला है। यथा मन में जिज्ञासा उत्पन्न होती है कि वटवृक्ष की श्राद्ध में क्या उपयोगिता हो सकती है। इसका उत्तर यह है कि लोक में श्राद्ध के समय वटवृक्ष की पूजा करने का विधान है। इसे यज्ञोपवीत तथा चने की दाल अर्पित की जाती है। इसी प्रकार अलर्क अर्थात् मन्दार वृक्ष है। इसकी जड़ों के रस से भूमि पर विष्णु का चित्र बनाकर पूजा करने का विधान भी लोक-प्रचलित है। ब्रह्मपुराण में अलर्क वृक्ष का सम्बन्ध सूर्य से बतलाया गया है।

अस्तु आङ्गिरस ने ऐसे बहुत से शब्दों का प्रयोग किया है, जिनके अर्थ के लिए अनुमान का आश्रय लेना पड़ता है— यथा 'धान्यद्वेषी' तथा 'करीषकी'। धान्यद्वेषी अर्थात् धान्य से द्वेष करने वाला। यह तो हम सभी जानते हैं कि खेतों में फसलों के साथ-साथ कई शाक स्वयं उग जाते हैं, जो फसलों के पनपने में बाधक होते हैं। इनमें कई शाक प्रयोज्य होते हैं और कई अप्रयोज्य। बथुआ भी ऐसा ही एक शाक है जो गेहूँ तथा जौ के खेतों में स्वभावतः अधिक होता है। यह प्रयोज्य शाक है अतः हम धान्यद्वेषी का अर्थ बथुआ ले सकते हैं। इसी प्रकार का 'करीषकी' शब्द है। 'करीष' का अर्थ होता है 'सूखा गोबर'। बहुत मनन करने पर 'करीषकी' शब्द से 'खुम्बी' अथवा 'मशरूम' ग्राह्य होता है क्योंकि पूर्वी प्रदेशों में इसे 'गोबर छत्ता' कहा जाता है। इसी प्रकार 'कदर्माढ्यः' तथा 'कदर्माधः' शब्द हैं। 'कदर्म' शब्द कीचड़ का वाचक है अतः कदर्माढ्यः का अर्थ हुआ 'कीचड़ से युक्त' तथा 'कदर्माधः' का अर्थ हुआ 'कीचड़ के नीचे'। अतः कल्पना के आधार पर हम इन्हें क्रमशः 'सिंघाड़े' तथा 'कमलककड़ी' के अर्थ में ले सकते है। ऐसे अनेक उदाहरण आङ्गिरस स्मृति में विद्यमान हैं किन्तु उन सभी का वर्णन कर पाना यहाँ सम्भव नहीं है।

आङ्गिरस ने सभी शाकों में सर्वाधिक महत्त्व 'पनस' अर्थात् कटहल को दिया है। उनका कथन है कि यदि सभी

शाकों को एकपात्र में तथा 'पनस' को दूसरे पात्र में रख कर हाथ से तोला जाए तो 'पनस' का महत्त्व कुछ अधिक ही ठहरेगा।[1]

वे कहते हैं कि श्राद्ध के दिन पनस को देखते ही उसे ब्राह्मण को दे दें। इतने मात्र से उसके पितर तृप्त हो जाते हैं। यही नहीं, पनस के फल, पत्र, शाखा से अथवा उसकी छाया में भी किया गया श्राद्ध पितरों को गया क्षेत्र में किए गए हजारों श्राद्धों से अधिक तृप्ति प्रदान करता है किन्तु जो पनस की शाखा, फल, पत्र आदि को देख मौन रहता है, उसके पितर कुपित होकर उसे शाप देते हैं।[2]

आङ्गिरस ने पनस की महिमा का मण्डन करने वाले अनेक प्रसंगों का वर्णन किया है। यथा गालव नामक ऋषि ने कटहल के बीजों को देखकर पाँच-छह बीजों को भक्तिपूर्वक खरीदा और पितरों की तृप्ति के लिए पत्नी सहित उसे भक्तिपूर्वक खाया। इससे उनके पितर नौ वर्ष तक आनन्द सागर में मग्न रहे।[3] पुनः वे माण्डव्य ऋषि का वर्णन करते हैं। कार्तिक मास में महाविन्ध्याटवी के मार्ग में अनायास माण्डव्य ऋषि की दृष्टि भूमि पर पड़ी। कुछ क्षण वे सिर झुकाकर खड़े रहे। फिर उन्होंने भूमि पर गिरे हुए पनस के पत्रों को उठाकर शीघ्रता से एक पात्र बनाया और जल के अभिलाषी किसी विप्रपुत्र को जल पिलाया। इससे उनके पितर बहुत अधिक तृप्त हुए, उन्हें आशीर्वचन दिए और उनके सामने ही बैकुण्ठ को चले गए।[4]

उल्लेखनीय है कि भारत के दक्षिणी प्रदेशों में पनस का बहुत अधिक महत्व है। वहाँ इसके प्रत्येक अंग का किसी न किसी रूप में उपयोग किया जाता है। वहाँ कटहल के बीजों को मिट्टी लगाकर सुखा लिया जाता है और जिन दिनों कटहल उपलब्ध नहीं होता, उन दिनों में इसे खाया जाता है। इसके गूदे को सुखाकर आटा भी बनाया जाता है। आङ्गिरस स्वयं दक्षिणात्य थे अतः कटहल के प्रति उनका पक्षपात स्वाभाविक है।

आगे आङ्गिरस कहते हैं कि एक बार ईश्वर सभी देवों के साथ बैठे हुए थे, तभी कारवेल्ली (करेला), कारूक (कमरख), करुत, कार और कालिका ये पाँच शाक उनके पास पहुँचे। वे उनसे बोले "हमें इस बात का बहुत दुःख है कि काँटे तो हमारे भी हैं किन्तु आपने हमें पनस के समान महत्त्व नहीं दिया। इसका क्या कारण है?" इतना कहकर वे बार-बार रोने लगे। इस पर ईश्वर हँसने लगे और बोले, "पनस के जिस जन्मसिद्ध माहात्म्य को सहन न करते हुए उसकी समकक्षता को प्राप्त करने के उद्देश्य से तुमने मेरे सामने जो रुदन किया है तो आज लोक में दरिद्र होने के कारण 108 श्राद्धों में से किसी एक भी श्राद्ध को करने में असमर्थ कोई भी व्यक्ति काल विशेष में केवल रुदन से ही श्राद्ध के फल को प्राप्त कर लेगा"।[5] यहाँ आङ्गिरस साधनरहित जनसामान्य की पीड़ा का अनुभव करने वाले स्मृतिकार के रूप में उभर कर आते हैं। वैसे भी उनके अनुसार श्राद्ध-सम्पादन के लिए श्रद्धा महत्त्वपूर्ण है। उल्लेखनीय है कि मनु ने श्राद्ध में अश्रुपात का निषेध किया है— नास्त्रमापातयेत् (मनु., 3, 229)।

निष्कलुषता तथा स्पष्टवादिता आङ्गिरस को प्रिय है अतः वह कहते हैं कि कारवेल्ली कारूक आदि की स्पष्टवादिता से ईश्वर प्रसन्न होते हैं क्योंकि उन्होंने पनस को प्राप्त होने वाले महत्त्व से उत्पन्न व्यथा को मन में न रखकर ईश्वर के समक्ष कह दिया अतः ईश्वर ने उन्हें कटहल के समान महत्त्व को प्राप्त कर लेने का आशीर्वाद दिया।[6]

स्पष्टवादिता आङ्गिरस को जितनी प्रिय है, चतुराई अथवा कुटिलता उतनी ही अप्रिय है। बृहती अर्थात् बैंगन की ओर संकेत करते हुए ईश्वर कहते हैं कि कण्टकयुक्त इसकी सभी जाति मन से पनस के तुल्य महत्त्व को चाहती हैं फिर भी इन्होंने चतुराई दिखाई और कारवेल्ली आदि के वृत्तान्त को जानते हुए भी चुप रहीं। इनका हृदय कलुषित है अतः आज से ये केवल तुच्छ प्रेतकर्मों के योग्य रहेंगी।[7]

इसके अनन्तर देवसृष्ट, अतिसुन्दर, पत्र, पुष्प, महावल्ली, शाखाओं और फलों से युक्त ऊर्वारू (ककड़ी अथवा खीरा) अति चंचलता से कैलास पर्वत से आती है। वह हाथ जोड़कर ईश्वर से पूछती है कि मेरी क्या गति है? बृहती

के कपट से खिन्न ईश्वर ऊर्वारू की विनम्रता से प्रसन्न हो जाते हैं। उसे शुद्ध प्रकृतिवाला और गर्वरहित जानकर सभी देवों के समक्ष कहते हैं कि स्वयं शिव ने पार्वती की वाणी से तुम्हारी रचना की है। तुम गुरुप्रिय, विनीत और कलुषता से रहित हो अतः सभी प्रकार के दैव, पितृ, कल्याणकर्म, नित्यनैमित्तिक और अन्य सभी क्रियाओं एवं बालक, वृद्ध और आतुरों के योग्य रहोगी।[8] इस प्रकार के बहुत से आशीर्वाद उसे देते हुए, उसकी सोलह जातियों को सभी श्राद्धकर्मों के योग्य ठहराते हैं।

अन्ततः हम कह सकते हैं कि आङ्गिरस ने वनस्पतिजगत् का वर्णनमात्र नहीं किया है, अपितु उनके व्याज से लोकमान्यताओं, मानवीय संवेदनाओं तथा मूल्यों की स्थापना का प्रयास किया है।

सन्दर्भ-सङ्केत

1. एतत्सर्वं चैकपात्रे निधाय किल पद्मजः।
   अन्यपात्रे च पनसं तुलयासा पाणिना।।
   तदा तु पनसः किंचिद्बभूवाधिक एव वै। (पूर्वाङ्गिरस - 531-32)
2. श्लाटुं पानसं पत्रं फलं दृष्ट्वा तु यो नरः।
   पितृतृप्तिमकृत्वैव तूष्णीं तिष्ठेन्महाजड़ः।।
   तं तस्य पितरः सर्वे शापन्ति किल कोपतः (पूर्वाङ्गिरस - 551-552)
3. गालवस्तु पुरा विप्रो दृष्ट्वा बीजानि भक्तितः।
   त्रयेण पञ्चषड् गृह्य पितृप्रीत्यै बुभुक्षितः।।
   स्वयं पत्न्या भक्षयित्वा पितृतृप्तिं चकार ह।
   तावन्मात्रेण ते चापि परं तृप्ताः शताब्दकात्।।
   आनन्दसागरे मग्ना बभूवुरिति नः श्रुतम्। (पूर्वाङ्गिरस - 556-558)
4. पूर्वाङ्गिरस - 558-567
5. पूर्वाङ्गिरस - 568-575
6. पूर्वाङ्गिरस - 576-580
7. पूर्वाङ्गिरस - 580-585
8. पूर्वाङ्गिरस - 586-603

卐 卐 卐

CASCADE III

(SANSKRIT)

SURABHĀRATĪ - SUMANOJHARĪ

सुरभारती–सुमनोझरी

वागर्थाविव सम्पृक्तौ वागर्थप्रतिपत्तये।
जगतः पितरौ वन्दे पार्वतीपरमेश्वरौ।।

या सृष्टिः सष्टुराद्या वहति विधिहुतं या हविर्या च होत्री
ये द्वे कालं विधत्तः श्रुतिविषयगुणा या स्थिता व्याप्य विश्वम्।
यामाहुः सर्वबीजप्रकृतिरिति यया प्राणिनः प्राणवन्तः
प्रत्यक्षाभिः प्रपन्नस्तनुभिरवतु वस्ताभिरष्टाभिरीशः।।

वेदान्तेषु यमाहुरेकपुरुषं व्याप्य स्थितं रोदसी
यस्मिन्नीश्वर इत्यनन्यविषयः शब्दो यथार्थाक्षरः।
अन्तर्यश्च मुमुक्षुभिर्नियमितप्राणादिभिर्मृग्यते
स स्थाणुः स्थिरभक्तियोगसुलभो निःश्रेयसायास्तु वः।।

Section XII - Plant Kingdom in Vedic Literature

Section XIII - Plant Kingdom in Kālidāsa Literature

Section XIV - Plant Kingdom in Sanskrit Literature & Astrology

Section XII

PLANT KINGDOM IN VEDIC LITERATURE

वेदामृतनिर्झरी

अथर्ववेदे वानस्पतिकं चिन्तनम्

चन्द्रकान्त शुक्लः

विश्वकोशात्मके ज्ञाननिधौ वेदे विविधानां वनस्पतीनामप्युल्लेखः प्राप्यते। तत्र स्थाने-स्थाने एतेषां सूक्ष्मातिसूक्ष्मं विवेचनं वर्गीकरणञ्च लभ्यते। ऋग्वेदे यद्यपि वानस्पतिकानां पदार्थानां कृते विविधानि नामानि दृश्यन्ते, परं वर्गीकरणदृष्ट्या तेषु वनस्पतिः, वनिन्, ओषधि-शब्दाश्चोल्लेख्याः प्रतीयन्ते। अथर्ववेदेऽस्य वर्गीकरणं चतुर्धावलोक्यते-वनस्पतिः, वानस्पत्यः, औषधिः वीरुध् चेति। परिलक्ष्यते यत्प्रारम्भे वनस्पत्योषधिरूपेण भेदद्वयमेवासीत्, परं कालानन्तरं चत्वारः भेदाः स्वीकृताः। सामान्यतया बृहदाकाराः वृक्षाः वनस्पतयः, अपेक्षया लघुवृक्षाः वानस्पत्यनाम्ना कथिताः तथैव पादपाः ओषधयः लतागुल्माश्च वीरुध्नाम्ना परिगणिताः। ध्यातव्यमस्ति यदोषधिशब्दः रोगनिवारकस्यौषधस्य पर्यायभूतः नास्ति। अथर्ववेदे एकस्मिन्नेव मन्त्रे स्पष्टतया चतुर्णामपि भेदानां नामगणनं प्राप्यते—''वनस्पतीन् वानस्पत्यान् ओषधीरुत वीरुधः।''[1]

1. वनस्पतिः

महर्षिः यास्कः वनस्पतिं वनानां पतिः पालयिता वा स्वीकरोति— ''एषः हि वनानां पतिः पालयिता वा।''[2] प्रतीयते यत्सायणाचार्योऽपि यास्केन प्रभावितः सन् कथयति—''वनस्पतिः वनस्य पालयिता वृक्षसमूहः।''[3] सोऽन्यत्र कथयति—''वनस्पतिः वनानां पालयिता · · · वनानां पतिर्वनस्पतिः।''[4] सः वनस्पतौ खदिरपलाशादि वृक्षाणामुल्लेखं करोति—''वनस्पतीन् खदिरपलाशादिलक्षणान् वृक्षान्।''[5] सः वनस्पतिशब्दं वृक्षस्य पर्यायभूतं स्वीकरोति—''वनस्पतिभ्यः सारवद्भ्यो वृक्षेभ्यः।''[6]

शतपथब्राह्मणे यत्र-तत्र वनस्पतिशब्दस्य चर्चा प्राप्यते तस्य विविधानां प्रकृतीनाञ्च विवेचनं लभ्यते। एकस्मिन् स्थाने पूर्वं ''वनस्पतिर्यज्ञियः'' इति कथयित्वा तत्रैवाग्रे कथितमस्ति—''न हि मनुष्या यजेरन् यद् वनस्पतयो न स्युः तस्मादाह वनस्पतिर्यज्ञिय इति।''[7] ''सोमो वै वनस्पतिः।''[8] इति कथयित्वा शतपथे एवोल्लिखितमस्ति यत्सोमः वनस्पतिपर्यायः अस्ति अथवा तस्योत्पादकोऽस्ति।

महर्षिणा पाणिनिनापि ''उभे वनस्पत्यादिषु युगपत्''[9] इति सूत्रे वनस्पति शब्दः उल्लिखितोऽस्ति। वार्तिककारेण कात्यायनेनापि वनस्पतिशब्दस्योल्लेखः कृतोऽस्ति यः महाभाष्ये प्राप्यते।[10]

2. वानस्पत्यः

अथर्ववेदे प्राप्यः वानस्पत्यशब्दः लघुवृक्षाणां वाचकोऽस्ति। अथर्ववेदे एतस्य कृते वृक्षशब्दस्याप्युल्लेखोऽवलोक्यते, परम् ऋग्वेदे एतस्य कृते वनिन् वृक्षशब्दो वा प्राप्यते। शतपथब्राह्मणे वनस्पतेः विकारस्यार्थे वानस्पत्यशब्दोऽस्ति।[11] बृहदारण्यकोपनिषदि वनस्पतिशब्देन सह वानस्पत्यार्थपर्यायः वृक्षशब्दः उल्लिखितोऽस्ति।[12] छान्दोग्योपनिषदि केवलं वृक्षशब्द

एव प्राप्यते।[13] पाणिनिनाऽपि एकस्मिन् सूत्रे वृक्षशब्दस्योल्लेखः कृतोऽस्ति,[14] तत्र काशिकायां[15] दृष्टान्तरूपेण प्लक्षन्यग्रोधावुल्लिखितौ स्तः। पतञ्जल्यनुसारं वनस्पतीनां समूहः वानस्पत्य इत्यस्ति।[16]

3. औषधिः

वेदेष्वोषधिशब्दः स्थाने-स्थाने प्राप्यते। आचार्येण सायणेनास्य शब्दस्य व्याख्या निवेचनञ्च भिन्न-भिन्नस्थानेषु किञ्चित्परिवर्तनपूर्वकं विहितमस्ति। एकत्र सः कथयति–"ओषः पाकः आयु धीयते इति ओषधयः।"[17] तेषां मतानुसारमोषधिः फलपाकान्ता लता, विविधानि अन्नानि, तृणं, गुल्मः, ग्रावा इत्यादिकमस्ति। अथर्ववेदे शताधिकस्थानेषु ओषधिशब्दोऽस्ति। यत्र-तत्र सायणेन तस्य व्याख्याऽपि कृताऽस्ति। द्वित्राप्युदाहरणानि द्रष्टव्यानि सन्ति–"ओषधयः व्रीहियवाद्याः,"[18] "ओषधयः व्रीहियवाद्याः ग्राम्याः आरण्यास्तरुगुल्माद्याः,"[19] तथा "ओषधयः आहारार्थम् उपयुज्यमाना व्रीह्यादयः।"[20] महर्षिणा यास्कानुसारमोषधिः शरीरे शक्तिवर्धिका, शक्तिसंरक्षिका, दोषापकर्षिका वा भवति–"औषधयः औषद्धयन्तीति वा। औषत्येना धयन्तीति वा। दोषं धयन्तीति वा।"[21] शतपथब्राह्मणे विविधस्थानेष्वोषधिशब्दः प्राप्यते। एकत्र सा रसवती कथिताऽस्ति,[22] अपरत्र च सा वस्त्रवदाच्छादिका स्वीकृताऽस्ति यतो हि सा पृथिव्याः आच्छादनं करोति।[23] एकत्र सा मूलिनी कथिताऽस्ति यां पशवः खादित्वा दुग्धोत्पादनं कुर्वन्ति।[24] बृहदारण्यकोपनिषदि वर्णितमस्ति यदोषधिः जले उत्पन्ना भवति पुरुषे क्रमशः वीर्योत्पादनं विदधाति।[25] छान्दोग्योपनिषद्यपि इत्थमेव प्रतिपादितमस्ति।[26] महर्षिणा पाणिनिनाऽपि विविधसूत्रेष्वोषधिशब्दः उल्लिखितोऽस्ति।[27] पतञ्जलिना एकत्रोषधेः उदाहरणरूपेण ब्राह्मी उल्लिखितास्ति।[28] इत्थं प्राचीने संस्कृतसाहित्ये ओषधिशब्दः मौलिकरूपेण लतामयः वनस्पतिरस्ति यस्मिन् आयुर्वेददृष्ट्याऽपि गुणाः भवन्ति।.

4. वीरुध्

ऋग्वेदे स्थाने-स्थाने विरुध् शब्दस्य चर्चा प्राप्यते। आचार्येण सायणेन तस्य व्याख्याक्रमे एकत्र तामोषधिरूपेण,[29] अपरत्र वनस्पतिरूपेण,[30] अन्यत्र लतारूपेण च विवेचितमस्ति।[31] अथर्ववेदे विविधेषु मन्त्रेषु पञ्चाशदधिकस्थानेषु वीरुध्शब्दः उल्लिखितोऽस्ति। "वीरुधो विश्वरूपाः इति मन्त्रांशस्य व्याख्याक्रमे तेन कथितमस्ति–"ओषधीनां स्थाने वीरुध् इति विशेषः। वीरुधः विरोहणशीला आरण्या ओषधिर्वनस्पतयः।"[32] सायणाचार्येण विविधरूपेणास्य शब्दस्य व्याख्या विहिताऽस्ति। दृष्टान्तरूपेण द्वित्राप्युदाहरणानि द्रष्टव्यानि सन्ति–"वीरुधः आरण्या लतारूपाः,"[33] "वीरुत् या तत्तद्रोगभैषज्यप्रस्तावोक्ता ओषधिरस्ति,"[34] "सहस्त्रम् अपरिमिता वीरुधः। विरुन्धन्ति विनाशयन्ति रोगान् इति वीरुधः औषधानि।"[35] इत्थं सायणेन वीरुध् कुत्रापि वनस्पतेः पर्यायरूपेण स्वीकृताऽस्ति, कुत्राप्योषधेः पर्यायरूपेणान्यत्र लतारूपेण च। महर्षिणा पाणिनिना एकस्मिन् सूत्रे वीरुध् शब्दः उल्लिखितोऽस्ति।[36]

इत्थमथर्ववेदे वानस्पत्यपदार्थानां चत्वारोऽपि प्रकाराः लभ्यन्ते येषां विस्तृतं विवेचनं यत्र-तत्र अथर्ववेदे प्राप्यते। अथर्ववेदे प्रकारचतुष्टयातिरिक्तं वानस्पतिकपदार्थानां वर्णदृष्ट्याऽपि वर्गीकरणं विहितमस्ति। वनस्पतयः बभ्रुवर्णाः, श्वेतवर्णाः, रक्तवर्णाः, कृष्णवर्णाः वा भवन्ति।[37] स्वरूपानुरूपं वनस्पतयः लताः वा प्रस्तृणतीः (परितः प्रस्तीर्णाः), स्तम्बिनीः (एकनालिकाः), एकशुङ्गा (एकमूलिन्यः), प्रतन्वतीः (विविधमूलिन्यः), अंशुमतीः (विविधदलयुक्ताः), काण्डिनीः (विविधकाण्डयुक्ताः), विशाखाः (विविधशाखायुक्ताः) च भवन्ति–

प्रस्तृणती स्तम्बिनीरेकशुङ्गाः प्रतन्वतीरोषधीरावदामि ।
अंशुमतीः काण्डिनीर्या विशाखाह्वयामि ते वीरुधो वैश्वदेवीरुग्राः पुरुषजीवनीः।।[38]

गुणदृष्ट्या लताः जीवलाः (जीवनदात्र्यः), नघारिषाः (हानिरहिताः), अरुन्धतीः (शरीरस्थलपूरिण्यः), उन्नयन्तीः (उन्नतकर्त्र्यः), मधुमतीः (मधुररसयुक्ताः), प्रचेतस् (चैतन्यप्रदायित्र्यः), मेदिनीः (स्निग्धताप्रदायित्र्यः), उग्राः (तीव्रगन्धयुक्ताः), विषदूषणीः (विषविनाशिकाः), बलासनाशनीः (कासविनाशिकाः) च सन्ति।[39] तत्रैवौषधीनां फलादिदृष्ट्या विभाजनं कुर्वन् कथितमस्ति यत्ताः फलयुक्ताः, फलरहिताः, पुष्पवत्यः, कन्दलीयुक्ताश्च भवन्ति–"पुष्पवतीः प्रसूमतीः

फलिनीरफला उत।''[40] ऋग्वेदेप्येतादृशं वर्गीकरणं प्राप्यते– ''या फलिनीर्या अफला अपुष्पा याश्च पुष्पिणी।''[41]

इत्थमथर्ववेदे विविधदृष्ट्या वनस्पतीनां वर्गीकरणं प्राप्यते, येन ज्ञायते यत्तस्मिन् काले वानस्पतिकपदार्थाः केन प्रकारेण् समाजे महत्त्वपूर्णाः आसन्।

यद्यप्यथर्ववेदे प्राथम्येन वानस्पतिकपदार्थानां चतुर्धा वर्गीकरणं कृतमस्ति, परं तेषां मध्ये स्पष्टतया पार्थक्यं न परिलक्ष्यते, परं वनस्पत्योषधिभेदावेवोल्लेखनीयौ स्तः। किन्तु तयोर्मध्येऽपि भेदकरणं सुकरं नास्ति। तथापि वृक्षाः वनस्पतयः लतागुल्मश्चोषधयः कथयितुं शक्यन्ते। अथर्ववेदे वनस्पतीनां मध्ये अक्षारुन्धत्यर्जुनाश्वत्थोदुम्बर-कुष्ठखदिरचीयुद्रुतरुणकतलाशातेजनदशवृक्षधवनद्यन्र्याग्रोधपरुषापर्णपर्णधिपूतुद्रुप्रतिसरप्लक्षबिभीतकमधुकशामहा-वृक्षरोहिणीलाक्षारोहितवंशवरणशमीसहदेवीसिलाचीसक्त्यादीनामुल्लेखः प्राप्यते। तथैव अघद्विष्टाऽब्ज-शृङ्ग्यजिरातस्यतिविद्धभेषज्यदृष्टहाऽपराजिताऽपस्म्भापामार्णापाष्ठाभिरोरुदाभिखाताऽराटक्यर्कालसलाऽलाब्वकाऽश्व-वतत्यसिक्न्यस्तृताञ्जनाण्डीकालासुर्यास्रावभेषजेटेन्द्राणीषीकाईर्ष्याभेषजोत्तानपर्णोर्वारुकोलपोर्जस्वत्यौक्षगन्धीकनक्नककब्रुकमल-कर्शफकल्मलिकान्दाविषकिलासनाशनकृतव्यधनीकृष्णाकेराद्ंहणीक्याम्बूक्षप्तभेषजीक्षेत्रियनाशनीखल्व-गुल्गुलुजलाषभेषजजीवन्तजीवन्तीजीवलातस्तुवताबुवतार्ष्टाघतिलतीक्ष्णशृङ्गीतृष्टातौदीतौविलिकात्रायमाणात्रि-वृत्दर्भदशशीर्षदिप्सदूर्वादेवमणिधान्यधानानघारिषानघायनऽनलदनलदीनितत्नीनीलागलसालानीविभार्यपलाल्यापाटापिप्पली-पीलापीलुपुण्डरीकपुनर्नवापुष्करपुष्पापृश्निपर्णीपैद्वप्रमन्दिनीबजबलाबिसभङ्गमण्डूकीमदावतीमदुघमधुजातामाष-मुञ्जयक्ष्मनाशनीयवरजनीरामालिबुजालोहितविश्वभेषजविषदूषणीविषाविषातकीविहह्लवेतसव्रीहिशणशतकाण्डशतपर्वाशतवारशत-शाखाशफशरशिखण्डीशीतिकाशेवालशुकश्यामासंवननीसरूपङ्करणीसहदेवतासहस्रचक्षुसहस्रपर्णीसहस्वतीसुभ-ङ्करणीसोमहरितभेषजहारिद्रवह्लादिकादित्यौषधयः वर्णिताः सन्ति।

अथर्ववेदे उपर्युक्तानां वनस्पतीनामोषधीनां वा यत्र-तत्र केवलं नामोल्लेखोऽस्ति अथवा तेषां विस्तरेण विवेचनमप्यस्ति। अनेके वानस्पतिकाः पदार्थाः एतादृशाः सन्ति येषां विषये अधुनाऽपि ज्ञातव्यमस्ति। सम्प्रत्येते पदार्थाः केन नाम्ना ज्ञायन्ते इत्यूह्यमस्ति।

सन्दर्भ-सङ्केताः

1. अथर्ववेदः (सायणभाष्यसहितः) प्रथमभागतः चतुर्थभागपर्यन्तम् - 8.8.14 कृष्णदास अकादमी, वाराणसी, 1989
2. निरुक्तम् (महर्षिः यास्कः) 8.3 - मोतीलालबनारसीदास, 1967
3. ऋग्वेदः (सायणभाष्यसहितः) - 1.166.5 मन्त्रे सायणः, वैदिक संशोधनमण्डलम् - पूना, 1933
4. ऋग्वेदः (सायणभाष्यसहितः) - 1.91.8 मन्त्रे सायणः
5. ऋग्वेदः (सायणभाष्यसहितः) - 3.34.10 मन्त्रे सायणः
6. अथर्ववेदः - 6.125.2 मन्त्रे सायणः
7. शतपथब्राह्मणम् - 5.4.3.16, राजस्थानपत्रिकाप्रकाशनम्, जयपुरम्, 1967-1970
8. शतपथब्राह्मणम् - 3.8.3.33
9. अष्टाध्यायी (महर्षिः पाणिनिः) - 6.2.140, (काशिकासहिता) - चौखम्बा संस्कृत सीरीज आफिस, वाराणसी, 1972
10. महाभाष्यम् (महर्षिः पतञ्जलिः) - 2.4.12, निर्णयसागरमुद्रणालयः - मुम्बई, 1917
11. शतपथब्रह्मणम् - 5.4.3.16

12. बृहदारण्यकोपनिषद् - 3.9.28.1-6, गीताप्रेस गोरखपुर, सं० 2036
13. छान्दोग्योपनिषद् - 6.9.1-2 तथा 6.11.1 वाणीविलाससंस्कृतपुस्तकालयः, वाराणसी, 1942
14. अष्टाध्यायी - 2.4.12
15. अष्टाध्यायी - 2.4.12 सूत्रे काशिका
16. महाभाष्यम् - 4.1.85
17. ऋग्वेदः - 1.90.6 मन्त्रे सायणः
18. अथर्ववेदः - 4.15.2 मन्त्रे सायणः
19. अथर्ववेदः - 4.16.6 मन्त्रे सायणः
20. अथर्ववेदः - 8.2.15 मन्त्रे सायणः
21. निरुक्तम् - 9.27
22. शतपथब्राह्मणम् - 1.2.2.2
23. शतपथब्राह्मणम् - 1.3.1.14
24. शतपथब्राह्मणम् - 2.3.1.10 तथा 2.6.3.7
25. बृहदारण्यकोपनिषद् - 6.4.1 तथा 5
26. छान्दोग्योपनिषद् - 1.1.2
27. अष्टाध्यायी - 4.3.135, 5.4.37, 6.3.132 तथा 8.4.6
28. महाभाष्यम् - 6.4.171
29. ऋग्वेदः - 1.67.5, 2.35.8, 10.40.9, 10.45.4 मन्त्रेषु सायणः
30. ऋग्वेदः - 9.114.2 मन्त्रे सायणः
31. ऋग्वेदः - 10.145.1 मन्त्रे सायणः
32. अथर्ववेदः - 4.15.3 मन्त्रे सायणः
33. अथर्ववेदः - 11.9.1 मन्त्रे सायणः
34. अथर्ववेदः - 2.9.2 मन्त्रे सायणः
35. अथर्ववेदः - 2.9.3 मन्त्रे सायणः
36. अष्टाध्यायी - 7.3.53
37. अथर्ववेदः - 8.7.1
38. अथर्ववेदः - 8.7.4
39. अथर्ववेदः - 8.7.6-10
40. अथर्ववेदः - 8.7.27
41. ऋग्वेदः - 10.97.15

卐 卐 卐

शुक्लयजुर्वेदे वनस्पतिविचारः

श्रीवत्स शास्त्री

वृक्ष-वनस्पति-ओषधि-तृण-लता-गुल्मादीन् विरहय्य पशु-पक्षी-कीट-पतंग-मनुष्यादीनां जीवनं कियद् भयावहं स्यादिति सम्प्रति सुधीभिः सुतरां कल्पनीयं भवेत् यतोहि वयम् अधुना एतेषाम् अभावे म्रियमाणान् प्राणिणः प्रत्यक्षीकुर्मः मृतांश्च डायनसोरप्रभृतीन् स्थूल- कायान् जन्तून् जानीमः। यद् बिना जीवनमेव न संभवं तद्विषये प्राक्तनपुरुषाः प्रकृतिमात्मसात्कृताः आत्मानं वा प्रकृतिसात्कृता मन्त्रद्रष्टार ऋषयः कथमनभिज्ञाः स्युः? यस्य वैदिकसमाजस्य चतुर्षु त्रयो भागाः वन एव यापनीया अभूवन् तस्य समाजस्य कल्पयितारो वैदिका ऋषयः उद्भिजसृष्टीः कथम् उपैक्षिषत। अतः ऋग्भ्यः आरभ्य अथर्ववेदं यावद् वृक्ष-वनस्पत्यादिविषयः प्रचुरं प्रकीर्णो दरीदृश्यते। सुतरां कर्मकाण्डप्रधानेषु यजुष्षु यज्ञाधारभूतो विषयोऽयं प्रत्यक्षतया प्रकारान्तरेण वा सुस्पष्टमुपबृंहितः। लेखेऽस्मिन् अमुमेव वेदं समाश्रित्य विषयोऽयं सन्नद्धः।

सामान्यं वर्गीकरणम्

ऋषयो मुनयो विद्वांसश्च यथासमयमेषामुद्भिजसृष्टीनां वर्गीकरणायापि प्रयत्नं व्यदधुः। वर्गीकरणं प्रायः पुष्पाणि, पत्राणि, फलानि, कन्दानि वा समाश्रित्य विहितं दृश्यते। ऋग्वेदस्य एकस्मिन् सूक्ते (10/96) फलिनी-अफला-आकृति-रोगाविष्कारक-प्रयोग भेदादिरूपेण महत्त्वपूर्णं वर्गीकरणं क्रियते। यजुर्वेदे (18/14) प्राय भग्राग-औषधी-वनस्पत्यादिरूपेण वर्गीकृतं ज्ञायते। महर्षिणा पाराशरेण वृक्षायुर्वेदे आकारसंरचनामाश्रित्य कुलेषु (गणेषु) पादपाः वर्गीकृताः विद्यन्ते। अथर्ववेदे वनस्पति वानस्पत्य-वीरुध-औषधिरूपेण वर्गीकृतं दृश्यते।[1] सामान्यतया लघुपादपानां कृते औषधिशब्दः बृहतां कृते च वनस्पतिशब्दः दृश्यते।[2] क्वचित्-क्वचित् भाष्यकारैः ओषधिवनस्पतिशब्दौ पर्यायवाचिरूपेणापि प्रयुक्तौ।[3] क्वचित् औषधिवनस्पतिशब्दौ सम्पूर्णोद्‌भिजसृष्ट्यै अपि प्रभुज्येते।[4] वीरध शब्द प्रायः लतागुल्मादिविषये प्रयुक्तः प्रतिभाति। काशिकायामुपलब्धे एकस्मिन् श्लोके पुष्पं बिना फलवान् वनस्पतिः, पुष्पफलवान् वृक्षः, फलपाकान्ते विनाशशीलाः ओषधयः, लताः गुल्माश्च वीरुधः इति वर्णिताः[5]। परमस्मिन् प्रसङ्गे वामनाचार्येण सत्यपि भेदेऽभेदं प्रदर्शितम्।

एतदतिरिक्तं स्थानभेदं, स्वरूपभेदं, गुणभेदं, कर्मभेदम्, अङ्गभेदम्, पत्रभेदं, प्रभावभेदं, विष-विषनाशकभेदम् उररीकृत्यापि वनस्पतिजगत् प्राचीनाचार्यैः स्वयं, संहितासु वा यत्र कुत्रचित्र‌द् विभक्त अवलोक्यते[6]। एवं सामान्यतया वक्तुं शक्यते यत् वृक्ष-वनस्पति-शब्दौ बृहतां पादपानां कृते, विरुधः लतागुल्मानां कृते ओषधिश्च लघु पादपानां कृते, औषधजनकानां कृते वा प्रयुक्तो दृश्यते। सत्यपि अस्मिन् सामान्यं भेदे लेखेऽस्मिन् सामान्योद्भिजसम्बन्धी निखिलोविचारोऽत्र चर्च्यते।

यजुर्वेदे खलु वन-अरण्य-पर्वतादिपादानां विभिन्नविभक्तिषु वचनेषु च पञ्चदशस्थानेषूल्लेखो वर्तते। एषु स्थलेषु वनेषु वानप्रस्थिनां निवास-वनकृत पापविनाशविषये, वनेन ओषधिभिश्च राज्ञः पवित्रीकरणम् उपदिश्यते[7]। वनवासिभ्यः राजा न्यायेन व्यवहरेत्।[8] एवमेव राजा वनानां रक्षकेभ्योऽन्नादि सौविध्यं प्रापयेत्[9]। वनानां रक्षायैः वनपं, दावानलात् रक्षायै च दावपम् अधिकारिणं नियोजयेत्। अर्थात् यदि कश्चित् वनं दाहयेत् तं दूरीकुर्यात्।[10] स्वामी दयानन्दः वनस्य रक्षायै

बहुधा प्रयत्नशीलः परिलक्ष्यते। बहुत्र सः राज्ञः कृते वनरक्षायै उपदिशति। मन्त्राणां भाष्य-माध्यमेन लिखति यत् वनानि चौरदस्युदुष्टादिभिः रहितानि कर्तव्यानि।[11] एकस्मिन् मन्त्रे वरुणस्य वितान विषये वर्णनं लक्ष्यते यस्मिन् वरुणः वनानाम् उपरि वर्षारूपम् आवरणमातनोति।[12] सम्भवतोऽत्र वर्षाभिः वनानां रक्षणं प्रतिभाति। एकस्मिन् मन्त्रे हरितपत्रवन्तो वृक्षाः दुःखाद् त्राणहेतोः नमस्करणीयाः वर्ण्यन्ते।[13]

वनस्पतयः

वनस्पतिर्हि वनस्यान्यतमम् अङ्गम्। शुक्लयजुर्वेदे एकचत्वारिंशद् वारं 'वनस्पति' पदस्योल्लेखो दृश्यते। कोषेषु वनस्पतिशब्दस्य बहवोऽर्था दृश्यन्ते। यथा (1) वनस्वामी, (2) वृक्षः, (3) बृहत्काय आरण्यकोवृक्षः, (4) पुष्पं विना फलदायी वृक्षः (पिप्पलः, वटादयः), (5) वनस्य पालकः, (6) सूर्यः, (7) मेघः इत्यादयः। यजुर्वेदे श्रीमद्दयानन्दादि भाष्यकारैः वनस्पतिपदस्य बहुधा वृक्षः, राजा, विद्वान् आदयोऽर्थाः कृताः।

एकस्मिन् मन्त्रे वनस्पतिं प्रार्थयमानो मन्त्रकारः कथयति यद् अयम् उन्नतिशीलः सन् यज्ञसमाप्तिं यावत् प्रलयं यावत् वा अस्मान् अहंसः रक्षयेत्।[14] एते वनस्पतयः समृद्धिं प्राप्य यथासमयं सिञ्चिताः सन्तः मधुरमन्नमिव नः फलानि ददति।[15] तेजस्विनः सुन्दरफलवन्तो वनस्पतयोऽस्माकमाधारभूताः सन्तोऽस्माकं कृते शक्तिं धारयन्ति।[16] शक्तिदायका वनस्पतय आदरणीया देवा इव सन्ति।[17]

वनस्पतीनां कृपया वयं सहस्रशाखाभिः विविधप्रकारैर्वा समृद्धः भवामः।[18] अथर्ववेदस्यैकस्मिन् मन्त्रखण्डे बिल्व उदुम्बरश्च महान्तौ कल्याणकारिणौ वर्ण्येते।[19] वनस्पतय ओजसां स्रोतांसि सन्ति।[20] अत एव यजुर्वेदे कथितं यत् द्यावापृथिवी-अन्तरिक्ष-वनस्पतयो न सन्तापनीयाः।[21] यज्ञेन यज्ञभावनया वा वनस्पतयः सदा संवर्धनीयाः।[22] राजा एभ्यो वनस्पतिभ्यः शिक्षामाददीत यत् यथा शताधिकैरङ्कुरैः युक्तः वटादि वनस्पतिः भवति तथा राजापि सर्वतः समृद्धो भवेत्। यथा वटः पदं पदमग्रे निदधानः प्रसृतो भवति तथा राजापि अग्रे वर्धेत। समृद्धशाखायुक्तः शाल्यलिखि राजापि समृद्धसाधनैः सेनादिभिः युक्तः सन् प्रजाः रक्षेत्।[23] विश्वरचयितृशक्तिभिः वनस्पतयोऽसृज्यन्त सोमश्च एषां वनस्पतीनामधिपतिर्बभूव।[24] सोमो नः वनस्पतीन् उत्पादयेत इति प्रार्थनापि क्वचित् यजुषि दृश्यते।[25] सोमो वनस्पतीनामाधिपत्ये त्वां सुवताम् इति अत्रैवं महीधरः। अत्रैव स्वामिदयानन्दो लिखति यत् यथा सोमो नाम ओषधिराजोऽन्यौषधीः रोगनाशाय प्रेरयति तथा विद्वांसः राजानं प्रजापालनाय प्रेरयेयुः। एकत्रायं वनस्पतिशब्दस्य वनपालक इति अर्थं कुर्वन् लिखति यत् वनपालकः सुष्ठुविद्यया प्रजानां दुःखनाशनं कुर्यात्।[26] राज्ञा नियुक्तो वनरक्षको यथा दृढबन्धनैः वृक्षान् रक्षति तथा यज्ञकर्ता मधुघृतादिभिः (यज्ञेन) स्वादिष्टं फलमश्नुते। परोक्षतया संभवतः राजैव स्वामित्वेन वनस्य रक्षकत्वादत्रैव वनस्पतिरित्यभिहितः। अत्र उवटमहीधरौ वनस्पतिशब्दस्य भूप इत्यर्थं कृतवन्तौ।[27] एवं विविधैः भाष्यकृद्भिः वनस्पतिशब्दस्य विविधां व्याख्यां कृत्वा विविधं महत्वं प्रदर्शितम्।

ओषधयः

वनस्पतिशब्द इव ओषधिशब्दोऽपि ह्रस्वान्तो दीर्घान्तश्च बहुवारं प्रयुक्तः। विभिन्नविभक्तिवचनेषु यजुर्वेदे षट्षष्ठीवारमयं शब्दो दृश्यते। सामान्यतया तु ''ओषध्यः फल पाकान्ताः इति लक्षणम् ओषधेः निर्दिष्टम्। परन्तु ओषधिषु यवाद्यन्नातिरिक्तमसंख्यं लतागुल्म जातमोषधित्वेन गृह्यते। बहुधा वनस्पतयोऽपि ओषधिरूपेण गृह्यन्ते। पुनरपि यजुर्वेदे एकस्मिन्नेव मन्त्रे वनस्पति-ओषधिशब्दौ द्वित्रिवारं पठितौ।[28] स्वामिदयानन्देन क्वचित्क्वचिदोषधिशब्दस्य उपमानरूपेण राजा-सेनापति-ईश्वरादिकोऽर्थो विहितः।

वनस्पतीनामिव ओषधीनां संरक्षणेऽपि मन्त्रकाराः जागरूका दृश्यन्ते। पृथिव्यां दृढमूला न समूलमुत्पाटनीया ओषधय इति स्पष्टं निर्दिष्यते-''ओषध्यास्ते मूलं न हिंसिषम्''।[29] उत्पाटितश्चोषधिः व्यर्थो न भवेत्, द्विपदां चतुष्पदां च कृते नैरोग्यदायकः स्यात्। ओषधयः स्वबलेन प्रजाः धारयन्ति अतः प्रजा ओषधिभिः प्रसन्ना भवेयुरिति प्रार्थना क्रियते।[30] ओषधय आत्मानं शरीरं च सम्पुष्य मनुष्यं पराक्रमिणं कुर्वन्ति। चौराः यथाव्रजम् उत्क्रम्याक्राम्यन्ति एवमोषधयोऽपि रोगमाक्राम्यन्ति।[31] हस्तगतमोषधिं दृष्ट्वा यक्ष्माया आत्मा पलायते-''ओषधिर्हस्त अदधे। आत्मा यक्ष्यस्य नश्यति''। ओषधयो

मनुष्यं मृत्युमुखात् इन्द्रियविकारेभ्यश्चत्रायन्ते।[32] एते यत्र प्रविशन्ति तत्र पीडा न वसति। एते वैद्यानामादेशं पालयन्ति। एतेषु शक्तिरूपेण परमात्मा व्याप्तो भवति।[33] मेघस्तृतीयसृष्टिरूपस्यास्य ओषधिजगतः जनयिता पालयिताश्च वर्णितः, अग्निश्च जलस्योषधेश्च सारतत्त्वरूपेण व्याख्यातः। ओषधयः फलवत्यः सन्त्यः पच्यन्ते, आसां शाखापत्रादीनि च सर्वाणि सुखप्रदानि भवन्ति। पृथ्वी आसां कामान् पूरयति। सोमः समास्तौषधीनां रसं धारयति। सम्भवतोऽत्र सोमश्चन्द्रः स्यात्, यतोहि सोमरूपश्चन्द्र ओषधीनाम् अधिपतित्वेनापि वर्णितः। वसन्तओषधयः पुष्टा भवन्ति इति प्रतीयते।[34]

ओषधिभिः सुस्थिरं गर्भं धारयितुं शक्यते।[35] सर्वविधरोगप्रशमनाय अस्मभ्यम् ओषधयः सुलभा भवेयुरित्यपि प्रार्थना दृश्यते।[36] दूरस्थाः पार्श्वस्थाश्चोपयुक्ता ओषधीः संकलय्य मिश्रयित्वा च सेवेत बलिष्ठश्च भवेदिति स्पष्टीभूता प्रार्थना।[37] स्त्रीः सौम्यगुणप्रधानौषधिविशेषविज्ञाने प्रवीणा स्यात्।[38] स्त्रियः स्वयमेव स्वात्मनि ओषधय इव शक्तिं धारयन्ति "ओषधीरिति मातरः"।[39] नवाङ्कुरितधान्येषु अद्भुतशक्तिसञ्चयो भवतीति ज्ञायते। शष्पैर्न तेज इन्द्रियम्।[40]

ओषधीनां सन्दर्भे बहूनि उपमानात्मकानि कथनानि प्राप्यन्ते यानि खलु नूतनानि उपादेयानि च सन्ति। अत्र तावत् कानिचिद् दृग्गोचरीक्रियन्ते। राष्ट्ररक्षारूपे यज्ञे विद्वांसः प्रजाश्च ओषधिजलवत् संगत्य वसेयुः। मधुरोषधिषु यथा मधुरोषधयः संगत्य माधुर्यं सुखं चोत्पादयन्ति तथा प्रजाः ज्ञानेन युक्ताः बोभूयुः।[41] औषधं यथा वृक्षवनस्पत्यादिषु गर्भ इव तिष्ठति तथा जीवः गर्भे निहितो वसति।[42] सभायां यथा राजा शोभते तथा ओषधयो यत्र दीव्यन्ति तत्र निवासो विधेय इति—"यत्रौषधीः समग्मत राजानः समिताविव"।[43] राज्ञः सेना ओषधय इव वीर्यवती स्यात्।[44] दुर्वाभिः सह स्त्रिय एवमुपमीयन्ते यत् यथा दुर्वाः पदेपदे दृढाः भूत्वा अन्तरेव स्वकानि काण्डानि वितन्वन्ति तथा स्त्रियः पुत्रपौत्रादिभिः ऐश्वर्यैश्च विस्तारं प्राप्नुयुः।[45] यवाद्योषधयः राष्ट्रपुरुषस्य भ्रुव इव सन्ति—"यवा न बर्हिर्भुवि केसराणि"।[46]

एवं शुक्लयजुर्वेदे वट-पिप्पल-यव-गोधुम-दुर्वा-अश्वत्थादीनां बहूनां वनस्पतीनामोषधीनां नामशः उल्लेखे सत्यपि वनस्पति-ओषधि-शब्दयोः प्रयोगप्राचुर्यं प्राप्यते यत्र एषाम् उपयोगिताविषये, उपमानादिरूपेण शिक्षाप्रदानाय वा विवरणम् उपलभ्यते। भाष्यकारेषु मतवैभिन्ये प्राप्यमाणेऽपि वेदेऽस्मिन् वनस्पतिजगतः महत्ता सुतरां स्पष्टीकृता दरीदृश्यते।

सन्दर्भ-सङ्केताः

1. अथर्ववेदः - 8.8.14. "वनस्पतीन् वानस्पत्यानोषधीरुतवीरुध"।
2. ऋग्वेदः - 10.96.18.
3. दयानन्द० यजुर्वेदः - 6/12
4. ऋग्वेदः - 10.145.1
5. काशिका - 8.4.6., फली वनस्पतिर्ज्ञेयो वृक्षाः पुष्पफलोपगाः। ओषधयः फलपाकान्ता लता-गुल्माश्च वीरुधः।
6. एतत् सर्वं चरकसुश्रुताथर्ववेदादिषु पर्याप्तं विश्लेषितं वर्तते।
7. दयानन्द० यजुर्वेदः - 3/15, 45 तथा 11/27
8. दयानन्द० यजुर्वेदः - 17/12
9. दयानन्द० यजुर्वेदः - 16/19
10. दयानन्द० यजुर्वेदः - वनाय वनपमन्यतोरण्याय दावपम्।
11. दयानन्द० यजुर्वेदः - स्तेनासस्तस्करा वने। · · · · दधाचि जम्भयोः, 11/79
12. दयानन्द० यजुर्वेदः - 4/31, वनेषु व्यन्तरिक्षं ततान · · · वरुणो।
13. दयानन्द० यजुर्वेदः - 16/40, वृक्षेभ्यो हरिकेशेभ्यो नमस्तारायैः।
14. उच्छ्रयस्व वनस्पत ऊर्ध्वो मा पाह्यहंस आस्य यज्ञस्योदृचः, तदेव, 4/10

15. दयानन्द० यजुर्वेदः – 20/65

16. यजुर्वेदः – 21/56 ओजो न · · · वनस्पतिर्नो दधदिन्द्रियाणि · · ·।

17. यजुर्वेदः – 21/58, वनस्पतिः स्विष्टा देवाः।

18. यजुर्वेदः – 5/43 अतस्त्वं देव वनस्पते शतवल्शो विरोह। सहस्रवल्शा विवयं रुहेम।

19. अथर्ववेदः – 20.136.15 महान् वै भद्रो बिल्वः महान् भद्र उदुम्बरः।

20. यजुर्वेदः – 29/53 ओजो उद्भृतं वनस्पतिभ्यः।

21. यजुर्वेदः – 11/45 · · · अभिशोचीर्मान्तरिक्षं मा वनस्पतीन्।

22. यजुर्वेदः – 18/13 · · · वनस्पतयश्च मे · · · यज्ञेन कल्पताम्।

23. यजुर्वेदः – 23/13 न्यग्रोधश्चमसै शाल्मलिर्वृद्ध्या।

24. यजुर्वेदः – 14/31 सातवलेकरः, उव्वटः महीधरश्च।

25. यजुर्वेदः – 9/39 सुवतां · · · सोमो वनस्पतीनाम्।

26. यजुर्वेदः – 21/40 · · · वनानां पालक · · · प्रजादुःख · · ।

27. यजुर्वेदः – 20/45 दयानन्दःउव्वटः महीधरश्च।

28. यजुर्वेदः – 36/17 ओषधयः शान्तिः वनस्पतयः शान्तिः · · · ।

29. यजुर्वेदः – 1/25

30. यजुर्वेदः – 12/95, 4/1, 11/47

31. यजुर्वेदः – 12/82, 84

32. यजुर्वेदः – 12/85, 90

33. यजुर्वेदः – 12/91, 96, 18/73

34. यजुर्वेदः – क्रमशः 17/32, 18/54, 22/22, 28, 12/72, 13/25

35. यजुर्वेदः – 11/43, 48 तथा 12/93

36. यजुर्वेदः – 12/81

37. यजुर्वेदः – 12/94 · · · सर्वाः संगत्य वीरुधोऽस्यै संदत्तवीर्यम्।

38. यजुर्वेदः – 12/92

39. यजुर्वेदः – 12/78 दयानन्दः

40. यजुर्वेदः – 21/29

41. यजुर्वेदः – 1/21 दयानन्दः

42. यजुर्वेदः – 12/36

43. यजुर्वेदः – 12/80

44. यजुर्वेदः – 12/99

45. यजुर्वेदः – 13/20 काण्डात् काण्डात् प्ररोहन्ति · · · ।

46. यजुर्वेदः – 19/91

卐 卐 卐

कृष्णयजुर्वेदे वनस्पतिश्रीः

एन. बालकृष्णन्

तत्र कृष्णयजुर्वेदे चतुर्थकाण्डे ओषधिसूक्तम् इत्येकं प्रसिद्धं सूक्तमस्ति।।

तदित्थमारभ्यते-

या जाता ओषधयो देवेभ्यस्त्रियुगं पुरा।
मन्दामि बभ्रूणामह ँ शतं धामानि सप्त च।।

युग शब्दः कालवाची। देवेभ्यः सकाशात् वर्षाः शरद्वसन्त इति कालत्रयमुद्दिश्य या जाता ओषधयः उत्पन्नाः। बभ्रूणां— प्राणिभरणसमर्थानां तासां धामानि जातिभेदान् दृष्ट्वा अहं हृष्यामि। मदि हर्षे। सप्त च सप्त ग्राम्याः सप्तारण्याः। इति सप्तधान्य भेदांश्चावेक्ष्य अहं हृष्यामि।

I rejoice looking at the plants which are born in the seasons of rain, śarad and spring season and seeing the seven kinds of wild and domestic varieties of grains.

शतं वो अम्ब धामानि सहस्रमुतवो रुहः।
अथा शतक्रत्वो यूथमिमं मे अगदं कृत।।

हे अम्ब! मातृ स्थानी या ओषधयः। वः धामानि-जातिभेदाः शतं सन्ति। उत-अपि च वः रुहः-अङ्कुराः सहस्रं सन्ति। शतं सहस्रमित्याभ्यां अपरिमितत्त्वं उपलक्ष्यते।। हे शतक्रत्वः-शतं क्रतवो (यागविशेषाः) निष्पाद्यन्ते याभिः तादृश्यः। यूयं इमं यजमानं अगदं कुरुत।।

अम्ब इति ऋषिः ओषधीराह्वयति।
अयो आदरातिशयः ऋषेः ओषधीः प्रति।।

O Mother! There are hundreds of varieties of you. And your sprouts are thousands in number. And you enable the performance of hundreds of sacrifices. Make this sacrificer free from diseases.

पुष्पावतीः प्रसूवतीः फलिनी रफला उत।

अश्वा इव सजित्वरीर्वीरुधः पारयिष्णवः।।

ओषधयः प्रशस्यन्तेऽत्र। काश्चित् ओषधयः पुष्पयुक्ताः काश्चित् फलं प्रसुवते। काश्चित् फलरहिताः। काश्चित् वीरुधः लतारूपाः। अश्वा इव जयशीलाः। किञ्च ओषधयः अस्माकं सहायभूताः कर्मफलं प्रापयन्ति।।

ओषधीरिति मातरस्तद्वोदेवीरूपब्रुवे।
रपा ँ सि विघ्नतीरितरयश्चातयमानाः।।

हे मातरः। हे देवीः— हे देव्यः। वः— युष्मान्। उपब्रुवे-प्रार्थये। रपां सि-पापानि विघ्नतीः-विनाशयन्त्यः। रयः-पापफलं

दुःखं चातयमानाः-विनाशयन्त्यः इत-प्राप्नुत।।

अत्रापि ऋषेः सम्बोधनं ''हे मातरः हे देव्यः'' इति यत् तद्विशेषेण ध्यानमर्हति।

अश्वत्थे वो निषदनं पर्णे वो वसतिः कृता।
गो भाज इत्किलासथ यत्सनवथ पूरुषम्।।

हे ओषधिदेवताः। वः निषदनं-वासस्थानं अश्वत्थवृक्षे अस्ति। पर्णे-पलाशवृक्षे वः युष्माकं वसतिः-गृहं कृतम्।। अत एव लोके अश्वत्थवृक्षः प्लाशवृक्षश्च पूज्येते प्रदक्षिणनमस्कारादिभिः। भगवानपि गीतायामाह-अश्वत्थः सर्ववृक्षाणाम्।। इति।। मूलतो ब्रह्मरूपाय अग्रतः शिवरूपिणे। मध्यतो विष्णुरूपाय वृक्षराजाय ते नमः। इति खलु अश्वत्यः प्रार्थ्यते प्रशस्यते च मन्त्रेण।। तथा च अश्वत्थः त्रिमूर्त्यात्मकः इति प्रसिद्धिः। अत एव सर्वेषु देवमन्दिरेषु अश्वथं रोहयन्ति पूजयन्ति च जनाः। एवमेव पलाशवृक्षस्यापि महिमा गीयते। पलाशमधिकृत्य तैत्तिरीयब्राह्मणे श्रूयते—''तृतीयस्थामितो दिवि सोम आसीत्। तं गायत्र्याहरत्। तस्य पर्णमच्छिद्यत। तत्पर्णोऽभवत्। तत्पर्णस्य पर्णत्वम्। इति।। अस्यार्थश्च-इतो भूलोकात् तृतीये स्वर्णलाके पुरा सोमः आसीत्। गायत्री पक्षिरूपं धृत्वा स्वर्गात् सोमं भुवं प्रति आनयति स्म। तस्मिन् समये गायत्र्याः पर्णस्यांशः अल्पीयान् भूमौ पपात। सोऽयमंश एव भूमेः पलाशवृक्षरूपेण पुनः प्ररोहति स्म। अत एव पलाशवृक्षस्य पर्ण इति संज्ञा अभवदिति।।

पलाशवृक्षविषये अन्या अपि कथा तैत्तिरीये श्रूयते। सा चेत्थम्—

देवानां ब्रह्मवादं वदतां यत्।
सुश्रवा वै श्रुतोऽसि।।
देवा वै ब्रह्मन्नवदन्त। तत्पर्ण उपाश्रृणोत्।
सुश्रवा वै नाम।।

अस्यार्थश्च-पुरा कदाचित् पलाशवृक्षस्य छायायामुपविश्य देवाः ब्रह्मविचारमकुर्वन्। परस्परं वादान् कृत्वा बोधयन्ति स्म। तान् ब्रह्मवादान् पलाशवृक्षः सम्यगश्रृणोत्। तदा प्रभृति पलाश वृक्षस्य 'सुश्रवाः' इति नाम सम्पन्नम्।। सु शोभनं श्रवः कीर्तिः यस्य सः सुश्रवाः—शोभन- कीर्तियुक्त इत्यर्थः। अत एव अद्यापि उपनयनसंस्कारसमये ब्रह्मचारी पलाशदण्डं धारयति। तत्र च दण्डधारणे मन्त्रः—

सुश्रवः सुश्रवसं मा कुरु।।
यथात्वं सुश्रवः सुश्रवा अस्येवमहं सुश्रवः सुश्रवा भूयासम् इति।।

किञ्च उदुम्बर-प्लक्ष-न्यग्रोध-बिल्व-विकङ्कत-खदिर-शमीप्रभृतीनां वृक्षाणां उल्लेखोऽस्ति।।

''ऊर्ग्वा उदुम्बरः'', ''विङ्कतं भा आर्च्छत्'', ''ततो बिल्व उदतिष्ठत्'', ''खदिर्यभ्रिर्भवति'', ''शमीगर्भादग्निम्मन्यति'' इत्यादीनि तेषां प्रतिपादकानि वेदवाक्यानि।

एवमेव दर्भ-काश-कुश-दूर्वादिघासाः अपि पठ्यन्ते। दर्भाणां तु महती प्रशंसा कृता। यागेषु दर्भाणां भूयानुपयोगः। परिस्तरणपवित्रकरणकूर्च-रशनाद्यर्थं दर्भा उपयुज्यन्ते। ''पवित्रं वै दर्भाः'' इति वेदवाक्यम्। दर्भाः देशं यजमानं सर्वमपि पुनाति। पवित्री करोति। ''विरिंचिना सहोत्पन्न परमेष्ठिनिसर्गज। नुद सर्वाणि पापानि दर्भ स्वस्तिकरो भव।।'' इति दर्भप्रार्थना पौराणिकी।। ''अग्निवान् वै दर्भस्तम्बः'' इति वेदवाक्यं अग्निदेवतायाः दर्भेषु सान्निध्यं बोधयति।।

सोमः

सोमः ओषधीनां राजत्वेन स्तूयते। ''सोमो वा ओषधीना ँ राजा'' इति। यागेषु सोमलता अभिषूयन्ते। सोमरसः देवताभ्यः समर्प्यते च।। सोमस्य महती स्तुतिः वेदेषु बहुलमुपलभ्यते। 'सोमो धेनु ँ सोमो अर्वन्त माशुं। सोमो वीरं कर्मण्यं ददातु''।

''जातवेदसे सुनवाम सोममरातीयतो निदहाति वेदः।'' ''स्वादिष्ठया मदिष्ठया पवस्व सोमधारया'' इत्यृग्वदीये नवममण्डलं पव्मानाख्यं सोमस्तुतिपरम्।।

खेदस्य विषयः यत् इदानीं भारते सा सोमवल्ली नैव लभ्यते। यागेषु तु याज्ञिकाः प्रतिनिधिकल्पनेन (through substitutes) सोमसदृंशीभिः ओषधीभिः कार्यं सम्पादयन्ति। सोमः जेन्दवेस्थेति विदिते पार्सीनां ग्रन्थे 'होम' शब्देन व्यवह्रियते। श्रूयते पारसीक-ईरान्-अफ्गानिस्तान् आदि देशेषु पर्वतेषु रोहत्ययं सोमः।

तेभ्यो देशेभ्यः पुनरपि सोमः भारते आनेतव्यः, पुन अत्र रोहयितव्यः, प्रचारयितव्यश्च। तथा च याज्ञिकाः पुनरपि यागान् अविकलरूपेण अनुष्ठातुं पारयेयुः। अस्मिन् विषये भारतीयशासन प्रयतितव्यम्।।

''फलिन्यो न ओषधयः पच्यन्तां योगक्षेमो नः कल्पताम्'' इति शिवम्।।

शास्त्रेषु उपलभ्यमानः पुष्पाणां निर्देशः

अस्माकं शास्त्रेषु विशिष्य इतिहास-पुराणेषु, धर्मशास्त्रेषु, आयुर्वेदे, कोशग्रन्थेषु तन्त्रग्रन्थेषु भूयानुपलभ्यते पुष्पाणां निर्देशः।

तत्रादौ अमरकोषे—

स्त्रियः सुमनसः पुष्पं प्रसूनं कुसुमं सुमम्। पुष्प्यति इति पुष्पम्। पुष्पविकसने इति धातोः पचाद्यचि निष्पन्नं रूपम् पुष्पम् इति।।

तत्र पठिताः पुष्पविशेषाश्चेत्थम्-

1. सौगन्धिकं तु कह्लारम्
2. उत्पलं, कुवलयम्=Lily
3. इन्दीवरं=Blue lily
4. कुमुदकैरवे=White lily
5. **पद्मं नलिनमरविन्दं महोत्पलं सहस्रपत्रं कमलं शतपत्रं कुशेशयम्।**
   पङ्केरुहं तामरसं सारसं सरसीरुहं बिसप्रसूनराजीवपुष्कराम्भोरुहाणि च।।

कमल इति हिन्दीभाषायाम्। एतानि कमलपुष्पस्य नामानि। पुण्डरीकं सिताम्भोजम्। श्वेतकमलस्य नाम पुण्डरीकमिति। अथ रक्तसरोरुहे रक्तोत्पलं कोकनदम्। इति द्वे रक्तकमलस्य नामनी। लालकमल।।

शिवस्य प्रियपुष्पाणि धर्मसिन्धौ—

चतुर्णां पुष्पजातीनां गन्धमाघ्राति शंकरः।
अर्कस्य करवीरस्य बिल्वस्य बकुलस्य च ।।

धत्तूरशमीपुष्पद्रोणपुष्पनीलोत्पलानामुतरोत्तरं सहस्त्रगुणत्वम्।।

धत्तूरैर्बृहतीपुष्पैश्च पूजने गोलक्षफलम्। पाटला-मन्दार-अपामार्ग-जाती-चम्पक-उशीर-तगर-नागकेसर-पुन्नाग-जपा-मल्लि-सहकार-कुसुम्भ पुष्पाणि शिवप्रियाणि।।

बकुलः-करवीरः-कनेर। धत्तूरः-धत्तूरा।

केतकीपुष्पं तु शिवपूजायां वर्ज्यम्। कथा तु शिवपुराणे लिङ्गपुराणे स्कान्दे वा द्रष्टव्या।। 'अहं शिवस्य शिरोऽग्रं दृष्टवान्' इति यदा ब्रह्मा मृषा अब्रवीत्, तदा केतकीपुष्पेण मिथ्यासाक्षिवचनप्रयोगात् शिवपूजायां केतकीपुष्पं न गृह्यत इति संक्षेपः।

विष्णोः प्रियपुष्पाणि— मालती-जाती-केतकी-मल्लिका-अशोक-चम्पक-पुन्नाग-बकुल-उत्पल-कुन्द-करवीर-पाटल-तगर-पुष्पाणि विष्णोः प्रियाणि। जातिपुष्पमतीव प्रियम्। आम्रमञ्जर्यपि तथैव।।

गणेशपूजोपयुक्तानि तु-

पुन्नाग-मन्दार-दाडिमी (अनार)-बकुल-अमृणाळ-पाटली-द्रोण-धुत्तूर-चम्पक-रसाल (आमक्तकूल)-केतकी-माधवी-शम्याक-अर्क (आक)-कल्हार-सेवन्तिका-बिल्वपुष्पाणि।। एतानि षोडश पुष्पाणि सिद्धिविनायकपूजायां गणेशाय समर्प्यन्ते।।

''गुलाब्'' इति विख्यातं पुष्पं तु अस्माकं प्राचीनशास्त्रेषु न क्वचिदपि दृश्यते। श्रूयते यत् पंचदशशताब्द्यां महरसीकदेशाद् युगलसंज्ञौ विदेशीयैरानीतं प्रचारितञ्च। इदानीं तु शतपत्र-स्थलकमलादि संज्ञाभिः व्यवह्रियत इदम्पुष्पम् सर्व देवपूजायां प्राचुर्येण गृह्यते उपयुज्यते च।

श्रीमन्महाभारते पर्वणि भीमेन हिमालयपरिसरं गत्वा बह्वायासेन कल्याणसौगन्धिकाख्यं पुष्पमानीतमिति कथा वर्ण्यते।

एवं श्रीमद्भागवतेऽपि दशमस्कन्धे एकोनषष्टितमे अध्याये सत्यभामाप्रेरणया भगवान् श्रीकृष्णः देवलोकात् पारिजाततरुं भूलोकमानिनायेति कथा पठ्यते।।

चोदितो भार्ययोत्पाट्य पारिजातं गरुत्मति।
आरोप्य सेन्द्रान् विबुधान् निर्जित्योपानयत्पुरम्।। इति।।

श्रीमद्रामायणेऽपि बहुषु स्थलेषु पुष्पाणां वर्णनमस्ति। वयं तु अत्र पम्पासरोवर्णने दृश्यमानं वर्णनम् उपस्थापयामः।। तथाहि—

पतितैः पतमानैश्च पादपस्थैश्च मारुतः।
कुसुमैः पश्य सौमित्रे क्रीडतीव समन्ततः।। 13।।

सुपुष्पितांस्तु पश्यैतान्कर्णिकारान्समन्ततः।
हाटकप्रतिसंछन्नान्नरान्पीताम्बरानिव ।। 21।।
कर्णिकारः-कनेर हाटकं-सुवर्णम्।।

कामिनामयमत्यन्तमशोकः शोकवर्धनः।
स्तबकैः पवनोत्क्षिप्तैस्तर्जयन्निव मां स्थितः।।

अमी लक्ष्मण दृश्यन्ते चूताः कुसुमशालिनः।
नलिनानि प्रकाशन्ते जले तरुणसूर्यवत्।।

एषाप्रसन्नसलिला पद्म नीलोत्पलायुता।
हंस कारण्डवाकीर्णा पम्पा सौगन्धिकायुता।।
सौगन्धिकं-सुगन्धिकमलम् ।
गिरिप्रस्थस्तु सौमित्रे सर्वतः सम्प्रपुष्पितैः ।।
निष्पत्रैः सर्वतो रम्यैः प्रदीप्ता इव किंशुकैः।
मालती मल्लिका पद्म करवीराश्च पुष्पिताः ।। 76।।
केतकयः सिन्धुवाराश्च वासन्त्यश्च सुपुष्पिताः।
माधव्यो गन्धपूर्णाश्च कुन्दगुल्माश्च सर्वशः।।
चिरबिल्वा मधूकाश्च वञ्जुला बकुलास्तथा।
चम्पका स्तिलकाश्चैव नागवृक्षाश्च पुष्पिताः।

चिरबिल्वः=चिलबिल। मधूकः=महुआ।
वञ्जुला=बेंत। बकुला=मौलसिरी।
चम्पकाः=चम्पा। नागवृक्षः=नागकेसरः।

पद्मकाश्चैव शोभन्ते नीलाशोकाश्च पुष्पिताः।
लोध्राश्च गिरिपृष्ठेषु सिंहकेसरपिञ्जराः।।

पद्मकः=नीलाशोकः लोध्रः=लोध।

अङ्कोलाश्च कुरण्टाश्च चूर्णकाः पारिभद्रकाः—
चूताः पाटलयश्चापि कोविदाराश्च पुष्पिताः।।
मुचुकुन्दार्जुनाश्चैव दृश्यन्ते गिरिसानुषु।
केतकोद्दालकाश्चैव शिरीषाः शिंशपास्तथा।।
तिनिशा नक्तमालाश्च चन्दनाः स्वन्दनास्तथा।
हिन्तालास्तिलकाश्चैव नागवृक्षाश्च पुष्पिताः।।

चन्दनस्योल्लेखः अस्ति स च विशेषतः ध्यानमर्हति। अद्यापि कर्णाटकदेशे एव चन्दनतरवः भूयिष्ठं प्ररोहन्ति। बाल्मीकि भगवान् चन्दन-मल्लिका-माधवी-कुन्दादीनां निर्देशे पम्पासरः स्थानं कर्णाटकटेशे हम्पी प्रान्तं स्पष्टतया कथयतीव, यतः अद्यापि कर्णाटके एतेषां पुष्पाणां प्रभूतमात्रया उत्पादोऽस्ति। एतानि पुष्पाणि अन्यप्रान्तेभ्यः प्रेष्यन्ते च।। अहो वाल्मीकि भगवतः कीदृशं भौगोलिकं ज्ञानम्, कियत्स्वाभाविकं प्रकृतिसौन्दर्यवर्णनं च।। सहृदया एव स्वयं विभावयन्तु आदिकवेः काव्यमहत्वम्।

भगवद्गीतास्वपि-पत्रं पुष्पं फलं तोयं यो मे भक्त्या प्रयच्छति। तदहं भक्त्युपहृतमश्नामि प्रयतात्मनः।।

तथा च भगवान् शङ्करः बिल्वपत्रसमर्पणेन परां प्रीतिं आप्नोति। महाविष्णुश्च तुलसीपत्रार्पणेन प्रीयते। महागणपतिः दूर्वापत्रैः सुप्रीतो भवति। अम्बिकाऽपि बिल्वतुलसी पत्रैः प्रसीदति।

ऋग्वेदेऽपि—

आयने ते परायणे दूर्वा रोहन्तु पुष्पिणीः।

ह्रदाश्च पुण्डरीकाणि समुद्रस्थ गृहा इमे।।

अस्या अर्थश्च—

एवं तैत्तिरीयारण्यके—"पुष्करदण्डैः पुष्करपर्णैः पुष्करैश्च स ँस्तीर्य" इत्यत्र पुष्करपुष्पनिर्देशोऽस्ति।

किञ्च तत्रैव अनुवाके "योऽपां पुष्पं वेद . . . प्रतितिष्ठति" इति पर्यन्तं मन्त्र पुष्पाभिधं सूक्तं परिपठ्यते। तत्पठनेन देवपूजादिषु मन्त्रपुष्पाञ्जलिः समर्प्यते।। समयाभावात् विस्तरभयाच्च एतावता विरम्यते।

पुष्पाणां विषये किञ्चिद्

दिङ्मात्रमिह वर्णितम्।

विस्तरस्तु यथाशास्त्रं

ग्रन्थेभ्यो ज्ञायतां शुभम्।।

卐 卐 卐

Section XIII

PLANT KINGDOM IN KĀLIDĀSA LITERATURE

कालिदाससाहित्यामृतनिर्झरी

महाकविकालिदासस्य नाट्यकृतिषु उद्दीपनविभावरूपेण चित्रिता वनस्पतयः

अमिता शर्मा

काव्यस्यात्मा स एवार्थस्तथा चादिकवेः पुरा।
क्रौञ्चद्वन्द्ववियोगोत्थः शोकः श्लोकत्वमागतः।।*

काव्ये रस एव मुख्यस्तेनैव सहृदयमनांसि प्रीतिमाप्नुवन्ति स च रसः कथं परिपुष्टो भवतीति वर्णयन् भरताचार्येणोदितम्—

विभावानुभावसंचारिसंयोगाद्रसनिष्पत्तिः।

तस्यैव मतं प्रतिपादयन् दशरूपककारोऽपि भवति।

विभावैरनुभावैश्च सात्त्विकैर्व्यभिचारिभिः
आनीयमानः स्वाद्यत्वं स्थायी भावो रसः स्मृतः।।[1]

रसहीनभावस्य भावहीनरसस्य वा स्थितिरकल्पनीयास्ति। यदि विभावादयः सामाजिकानां सम्मुखं न तिष्ठन्ति तदा तेषु रसानुभूतिरपि न दृश्यते। यथा चोक्तम् भरतमुनिना—

न भावहीनोऽस्ति रसो न भावो रसवर्जितः।
परस्परकृता सिद्धिस्तयोरभिनये भवेत्।।[2]

वस्तुतः कविगतो रस एव काव्ये विभावादीनां वर्णने कारणं भवति। अतएव नाट्यशास्त्रस्य षष्ठाध्यायस्य प्रारम्भे भरतेन भणितम्—

न हि रसादृते कश्चिदर्थो प्रवर्तते।

अत्र 'रस' इति पदेन कविगतो रसः परिलक्ष्यते यथा चोक्तमभिनवगुप्तेन-तदेव मूलबीजस्थानीयः कविगतो रसः। अतएवोक्तमानन्दवर्धनाचार्येणापि-

अपारे काव्यसंसारे कविरेकः प्रजापतिः।
यथास्मै रोचते विश्वं तथेदं परिवर्तते।।
शृङ्गारी चेत् कविः काव्ये जातं रसमयं जगत्।
स एव वीतरागश्चेत् नीरसं सर्वमेव तत्।।[3]

इत्थं स्पष्टं यत् काव्ये वर्णिता विभावादयः कविगतभावानामेव प्रदर्शनं भवन्ति येषां ग्रहणं सहृदयेन काव्यमाध्यमेन क्रियते। यथा चोक्तम् अभिनवगुप्तपादाचार्येण—

अपूर्वं यद्वस्तु प्रथयति विना कारणकलां
जगद्ग्रावप्रख्यं निजरसभरात् सारयति च।
क्रमात् पख्योपाख्याप्रसरसुभगं भासयति तत्
सरस्वत्यास्तत्त्वं कविसहृदयाख्यं विजयते।।[4]

काव्ये विभावाः कविव्यापाराश्रिताः भवन्ति। रामदुष्यन्तादीनां कविनिर्मितं रूपमेव शब्दमाध्यमेन सहृदयानां सम्मुखमायाति। अतएव काव्ये वर्णिताः विभावाः अनपेक्षितबाह्यसत्त्वाः भवन्ति। यथा चोक्तं धनिकेनावलोकटीकायाम्—

अमीषां चानपेक्षितबाह्यसत्त्वानां शब्दोपधानादेवासादिततद्भावानां सामान्यात्मनां स्वस्वसम्बन्धित्वेन विभावितानां साक्षाद्भावकचेतसि विपरिवर्तमानानामालम्बनादिभावः।[5]

रसानुभूतेः कारणं विभाव एव। विभावमेवाश्रित्य वाचिकमाङ्गिकं सात्त्विकञ्चाभिनयस्तिष्ठति। यथा चोक्तं भरतमुनिना—

बहवोऽर्था विभाव्यन्ते वागङ्गाभिनयाश्रयाः।
अनेन यस्मात्तेनायं विभाव इति संज्ञितः।।[6]

विभाव एव काव्ये परिज्ञातो भवति। तेनैव स्थायिसञ्चार्यादिभावानां परिपुष्टिर्भवति। अतएव धनञ्जयेन विभावस्य लक्षणमित्थं कृतम्—

ज्ञायमानतया तत्र विभावो भावपोषकृत्।
आलम्बनोद्दीपनत्वप्रभेदेन स च द्विधा।।[7]

कविः स्वीये काव्ये रसस्य परिपुष्ट्यर्थं रामदुष्यन्तादीनामालम्बनविभावानां स्वरूपं विविधचेष्टावर्णनपूर्वकं प्रदर्शयति। परं तेनैव तस्य कार्यं न परिसमाप्यते यतो हि यावत्पर्यन्तं तत् तत् रसपुष्टये अनुकूलवातावरणस्य सृष्टिर्न भवति तावत्पर्यन्तं कवेः कार्यमपूर्णमेव सहैव च तस्य काव्यमपि। अतएव काव्ये विशिष्टरूपेण दृश्यकाव्ये प्रकृतेः विभिन्नानि तत्त्वानि उद्दीपनरूपेण प्रयोक्तव्यानि भवन्ति यथा चोक्तमानन्दवर्धनाचार्येण—

तस्मान्नास्त्येव तद्वस्तु यत् सर्वात्मना रसतात्पर्यवतः कवेस्तदिच्छया तदभिमतरसाङ्गतां न धत्ते। तथोपनिबध्यमानं वा न चारुत्वातिशयं पुष्णाति। सर्वमेतच्च महाकवीनां काव्येषु दृश्यते।[8]

महाकविकालिदासेनापि सुष्ठुरूपेण स्वनाट्येषु प्रकृतेरेतानि तत्त्वानि क्वचित् चेतनवत् क्वचिच्चाचेतनवत् वर्णितानि, विशिष्टरूपेण वनस्पतयोऽतीवचारुतयाभिमतरसपुष्टये वर्णिताः सन्ति। अभिज्ञानशाकुन्तलस्य प्रथमाङ्के अङ्गीरसस्य शृङ्गारस्य परिपुष्टिरेव कवेरभिमता वर्तते। प्रारम्भादेव कविरनुकूलवातावरणस्य सृष्टौ संलग्नो दृश्यते। राजा दुष्यन्तः आश्रमपदमागतो वर्तते शकुन्तला च पादपान् सिञ्चती यदा नवमालिकालतां वनज्योत्स्नां सहकारवृक्षेणालिङ्गितां पश्यति तदा कथयति—

हला! रमणीये खलु काले एतस्य लतापादपमिथुनस्य व्यतिकरः संवृत्तः। नवकुसुमयौवना वनज्योत्स्ना, बद्धपल्लवतयोपभोगक्षमः सहकारः।[9]

नवमालिकासहकारवृक्षयोरनेन वर्णनेन कविः सहृदयेषु शृङ्गारस्योद्दीपनार्थमनुकूलमावरणं रचयति तथा च

शकुन्तलादुष्यन्तयोः विवाहस्य पूर्वसूचनामपि प्रददाति। तस्मिन्नेव स्थले प्रियंवदाया कथनमपि कवेरभिमतं साधयति—

हला शकुन्तले अत्रैव तावन्मुहूर्तं तिष्ठ, यावत् त्वयोपगतया लतासनाथ इवायं केसरवृक्षकः प्रतिभाति।[10]

एतच्छ्रुत्वां दुष्यन्तस्य हृदये कोऽप्यलौकिको विचारः परिस्फुरति येन प्रेरितः सोऽपि शकुन्तलां लतेव पश्यति—

अधरः किसलयरागः कोमलविटपानुसारिणी बाहू।
कुसुममिव लोभनीयं यौवनमङ्गेषु संनद्धम्।।[11]

चतुर्थाङ्कात् प्राक् विष्कम्भके शकुन्तलाया विरहावस्थाजनितं दुःखं सहृदयेषु संप्रेषणीयं वर्तते। अतएव तत्र कुमुद्वती अपि स्वचेष्ट्या तमेव भावं संपोष्यति—

अन्तर्हिते शशिनि सैव कुमुद्वती मे
दृष्टिं न नन्दयति संस्मरणीयशोभा।
इष्टप्रवासजनितान्यबला जनस्य
दुःखानि नूनमतिमात्रसुदुःसहानि।।[12]

चतुर्थाङ्के शकुन्तलां पतिगृहप्रेषणाय समुत्सुकं आश्रमपदं बन्धुजनविरहेण जनितकरुणयाप्लावितं दृश्यते। तत्र तु वनस्पतिदेवताः किमप्यलौकिकमाचरन्ती गम्यमानायाः शकुन्तलायाः कृते मातृवत् वस्त्राभरणं प्रयच्छति—

क्षौमं केनचिदिन्दुपाण्डुतरुणा माङ्गल्यमाविष्कृतं।
निष्ठ्यूतश्चरणोपभोगसुलभो लाक्षारसः केनचित्।।
अन्येभ्यो वनदेवताकरतलैशपर्वभागोत्थितै-
र्दतान्याभरणानि तत्किसलयोद्भेदप्रतिद्वन्द्विभिः।।[13]

प्रथमाङ्के पादपान् प्रति शकुन्तलाया यः स्नेहः नर्महासस्य कारणमासीत्. सः स्नेहः चतुर्थाङ्के कारुण्यमेव जनयति यथा च—

पातुं न प्रथमं व्यवस्यति जलं युष्मास्वपीतेषु या।
नादत्ते प्रियमण्डनापि भवतां स्नेहेन या पल्लवम्।।
आद्ये वः कुसुमप्रसूतिसमये यस्या भवत्युत्सवः।
सेयं याति शकुन्तला पतिगृहं सर्वैरनुज्ञायताम्।।[14]

शकुन्तलया प्ररूढा नीवारा अपि ऋषेः कण्वस्य दुःखं वर्धयन्ति—

शममेष्यति मम शोकः कथं नु वत्से! त्वया रचितपूर्वम्।
उटजद्वारविरूढं नीवारबलिं विलोकयतः।।[15]

षष्ठाङ्के तु पादपा चेतनवदाचरन्तः दुष्यन्तगतं विरहं सम्यकरूपेण सामाजिकेषु संचारयन्ति यथा—

चूतानां चिरनिर्गतापि कलिका बध्नाति न स्वं रजः।
सन्नद्धं यदपि स्थितं कुरबकं तत्कोरकावस्थया।।
कण्ठेषु स्खलितं गतेऽपि शिशिरे पुंस्कोकिलानां रुतं
शङ्के संहरति स्मरोऽति चकितस्तूर्णार्धकृष्टं शरम्।।[16]

आगतेऽपि वसन्ते आम्रमञ्जरी पुष्पाणि चापि दुष्यन्तस्य विरहावस्थया दुःखितानि विकसितुं नेच्छन्ति। इत्थं कण्वस्याश्रमपदात् प्रारभ्य मारीचस्याश्रमपदं यावत् सर्वत्रैव वनस्पतयः कवेरभिमतं भावमेवानुसरन्ति। निर्हेतुकतया लतापुष्पपादपानां वर्णनस्य अभाव एव दृश्यते कालिदासस्य नाट्येषु।

विक्रमोर्वशीयस्य प्रारम्भे एव लता मित्रवदाचरन्ती राज्ञे अभीष्टसुखं प्रयच्छति—

प्रियमाचरितं लते त्वया मे रामनेऽस्याः क्षणविघ्नमाचस्त्या।
यदियं पुनरप्यपाङ्गनेत्रा परिवृत्तार्धमुखी मया हि दृष्टा।।[18]

द्वितीयाङ्के वसन्तस्य प्रारम्भे पुरुरवसा कृतं पुष्पमञ्जरीणां वर्णनमेतत् उर्वशीमुद्दिश्य तस्यानुरागमेव प्रदर्शयति सामाजिकान् च अनुरागयुक्तान् करोति—

अग्रे स्त्रीनखपाटलं कुरबकं श्यामं द्वयोर्भागयो
रक्ताशोकमुपोढरागसुभगं भेदोन्मुखं तिष्ठति।
ईषद्बद्धरजःकणाग्र कपिशा चूते नवा मञ्जरी
मुग्धत्वस्य च यौवनस्य च सखे! मध्ये मधुश्रीः स्थिता।।[18]

प्रतीयते यत् वनस्पतिवर्णनं व्याजेन उर्वश्या मुग्धावस्था एव वर्णिता वर्ततेऽत्र।

विक्रमोर्वशीस्य चतुर्थाङ्के उपवने भ्रमन् विरहविधुरो राजा लतासु पुष्पेषु वृक्षेषु च सर्वत्र उर्वशीसाम्यं उर्वश्याः स्मृतिचिह्नं वाऽवलोकयति—

आरक्तराजिभिरियं कुसुमैर्नवकन्दली सलिलगर्भैः
कोपादन्तर्वाष्पे स्मरयति मां लोचने तस्याः।[19]

पुष्पैराच्छादितमशोकवृक्षं दृष्ट्वा स मम प्रिया कुत्र गतेति पृच्छति परं पवनधूयमानमूर्धानमवलोक्य राजा कुपितो भवति—

रक्ताशोक! कृशोदरी क्व नु गता त्यक्त्वानुरक्तं जनं
नो दृष्टेति मुधैव चालयसि किं वातावधूतं शिरः।
उत्कण्ठाघटमानषट्पदघटासङ्घट्टदष्टच्छदस्
तत्पादाहतिमन्तरेण भवतः पुष्पोद्गमोऽयं कुतः।।[20]

कुपितोर्वशीसाम्यात् कुसुमरहिता अपि लता मनोहरा प्रतिभाति—

तन्वी मेघजलार्द्रपल्लवतया धौताधरेवाश्रुभिः
शून्येवाभरणैः स्वकालविरहाद् विश्रान्तपुष्पोद्गमा।
चिन्तामौनपमिवास्थिता मधुलिहां शब्दैर्विना लक्ष्यते
चण्डी मामवधूय पादपतितं जालानुतापेव सा।।[21]

मालविकाग्निमित्रस्य तृतीयाङ्के उपवने भ्रमन् राजा मालविकायां स्वानुरागकारणात् वनस्पतिष्वपि योषिच्छविरेवावलोकयति—

रक्ताशोकरुचा विशेषितगुणो बिम्बाधरालक्तकः
प्रत्याख्यातविशेषकं कुरबकं श्यामावदातारुगणम्।
आक्रान्ता तिलकक्रिया च तिलकैर्लग्नद्विरेफाञ्जनैः
सावज्ञेव मुखप्रसाधनविधौ श्रीर्माधवी योषिताम्।।[22]

अपरतश्च अपूर्णमनोरथा मालविका यदा पुष्पविहीनमशोकवृक्षं पश्यति तदा तस्मिन् स्वीयां प्रतिच्छायामेव प्राप्नोति। यथा च—

अयं स ललितसुकुमारदोहदापेक्षी अगृहीतकुसुमनेपथ्यः उत्कण्ठिताया मम अनुकरोत्यशोकः।[23]

मालविका यदा अशोकविकासयितृकं देव्या नियोगमनुतिष्ठति, अशोकवृक्षञ्च स्वपादेन ताडयति तदा कामिजनमिव राजा आत्मानं वञ्चितं मन्यमानः अशोकवृक्षमुपालभ्यते—

अनेन तनुमध्यया मुखरनूपुराराविणा
नवाम्बुरुहकोमलेन चरणेन सम्भावितः।
अशोक यदि सद्य एव मुकुलैर्न सम्पत्स्यसे
वृथा वहसि दोहदं ललितकामिसाधारणम्।।[25]

अत्र स्वोत्कण्ठावशात् अशोकवृक्षमपि कामिजनमिव पश्यति राजा। एतैरुदाहरणैः स्पष्टं यत् कालिदासेन स्वकीयेषु नाट्येषु स्वरचितपात्रानुवृत्त्यनुरूपायेव पादपलतापुष्पाणि विरचितानि अथवा कथयितुं शक्यते यत् प्रकृतिरपि पात्राणां मनोवृतिमनुसरति। अतएव एतेषु नाट्येषु उद्दीपनविभावानां चित्रणगतीव साफल्येन कृतं वर्तते।

यद्यपि नाट्यानां प्रयोगावसरे ध्वनिप्रकाशनाद्यगन्त्रादीनां प्रयोगेन तत्तद्भावानामुद्दीपनं सम्भवं भवति परं कविकृतमिदं वर्णनं तत्र साहाय्यं विदधाति। अन्यच्च पठनसमयेऽपि सहृदयानां हृदयेषु तत्तद्भावानां सञ्चरणं सहजतयैव भवति। अतएवानन्दवर्धनाचार्येण यदुक्तम्—

अपारे काव्यसंसारे कविरेकः प्रजापतिः।
यथाऽस्मै रोचते विश्वं तथेदं परिवर्तते।।

तत् कालिदासप्रसङ्गेऽतीव युक्तियुक्तं प्रतिभाति।

सन्दर्भ-सङ्केताः

* ध्वन्यालोकः - 1.51

1. दशरूपकम् - 4.1
2. नाट्यशास्त्रम् - 6.37
3. ध्वन्यालोकः - 3.42
4. ध्वन्यालोकलोचनस्य मङ्गलाचरणम्
5. दशरूपकस्यावलोकटीका-चतुर्थप्रकाशः
6. नाट्यशास्त्रम् - 7.4
7. दशकरूपकम् - 4.2
8. ध्वन्यालोकः - 3.42
9. अभिज्ञानशाकुन्तलम् - प्रथमोऽङ्कः
10. अभिज्ञानशाकुन्तलम्
11. अभिज्ञानशाकुन्तलम् - 1.19
12. अभिज्ञानशाकुन्तलम् - 4.3
13. अभिज्ञानशाकुन्तलम् - 4.5
14. अभिज्ञानशाकुन्तलम् - 4.9
15. अभिज्ञानशाकुन्तलम् - 4.21
16. अभिज्ञानशाकुन्तलम् - 6.4
17. विक्रमोर्वशीयम् - 1.18
18. विक्रमोर्वशीयम् - 2.7
19. विक्रमोर्वशीयम् - 4.5
20. विक्रमोर्वशीयम् - 4.34
21. विक्रमोर्वशीयम् - 4.39
22. मालविकाग्निमित्रम् - 3.5
23. मालविकाग्निमित्रम् - तृतीयाङ्के
24. मालविकाग्निमित्रम् - 3.17

卐 卐 卐

कालिदासनाट्यकृतिषु वनस्पतिवैभवम्

शशि तिवारी

महाकविं कालिदासं वन्दे वाग्देवतागुरुम्।
यज्ज्ञाने विश्वमाभाति दर्पणे प्रतिबिम्बवत्।।

महाकविकालिदासो यथा संस्कृतस्य सर्वश्रेष्ठः कविर्गण्यते तथैव स सर्वश्रेष्ठनाटककारोऽपि मन्यते। तस्य महाकवेस्त्रीणि नाटकान्युपलभ्यन्ते-मालविकाग्निमित्रम्, विक्रमोर्वशीयम्, अभिज्ञानशाकुन्तलं चेति। कालिदासस्य प्रकृतिप्रेम, पर्यावरणानुरागः, वनस्पतिप्रेम च तस्य कृतिषु सुव्यक्तः वर्तते। महाकवेः समग्रं साहित्यं पर्यावरणसंरक्षणस्य प्रकृतिरक्षणस्य भावनया आप्यायितमस्ति। कालिदासस्य काव्यप्रतिभा प्रकृतिवर्णनेनैव मुखरिता भवति। प्राकृतिकसौन्दर्ये तस्य मानसं रमते। स तं प्रति नितराम् जागरूकः प्रतीयते। कालिदासः प्रकृतेः माङ्गलिकरूपस्योपासकोऽस्ति। रम्यशान्ततपोवननदीतटपवन-भ्रमरमृगकोकिलादीनां वर्णने तस्य प्रतिभा सहजसुन्दरा अतिविशिष्टा दृश्यते। दृश्यकाव्ये श्रव्यकाव्यवत्प्रकृतिचित्रणस्य बृहदवकाशो न सम्भवति, तथापि सत्स्वपि कालिदासस्य नाट्यकृतिषु प्रकृतिचित्रणस्य समावेशः नातिस्वल्पः इति तु सुनिश्चितरूपेण कथयितुं शक्यते। अत्रास्मिन् पत्रे मया तस्य नाट्यकृतिषु विशेषतया वनस्पतिचित्रणस्य संक्षिप्तसमीक्षणमुपनिबद्धमस्ति।

प्राकृतिकसम्पदां प्रति जागरूकस्य महाकवेः कालिदासस्य संवेदनशीला कविप्रतिभा वृक्षेषु लतासु च चेतनभावनायाः अनुभवं करोति। अचेतनेषु चेतनधर्मारोपाणां मानवीकरणप्रक्रियायाः एव रूपान्तरमस्ति। कालिदासदृष्ट्या वृक्षाः पुत्रवत् स्नेहेन परिपालनीयाः वर्तन्ते। निसर्गकन्याशकुन्तला लतासु वृक्षेषु सोदरस्नेहं धत्ते। सा प्रथमपुष्पोद्भवं पुत्रोत्सव इव मन्यते-आद्ये वः कुसुमप्रसूतिसमये यस्याः भवत्युत्सवः।[1] कुमारसम्भवे पार्वती वृक्षकान् स्वयमेव सेचनघटैः सिञ्चति।[2] रघुवंशे देवदारुवृक्षेण प्रति शंकरस्य पुत्रवत् स्नेहः वर्तते।[3] परम् अभिज्ञानशाकुन्तले शकुन्तलायाः प्रकृत्या सह सौहार्दपूर्णो व्यवहारस्तु संस्कृतसाहित्ये अनुपमोऽस्ति। सा प्रियमण्डनापि वृक्षस्य किसलयं न गृह्णाति, अकृतजलसेकेषु तेषु पानीयं ग्रहीतुं न यतते।[4] वृक्षाः तस्या वनवासबन्धवः सन्ति यैरनुमतगमना सा पतिगृहं गच्छति।[5] सा वनस्पतिभ्यः वनदेवताकरतलैः आभरणानि प्राप्नोति।[6] वृक्षेषु देवभावनयाः आरोपणं खलु तेषाम् मानवीयजीवने माहात्म्येव प्रदर्शयति। कविः अनुभवति-यत् केसरवृक्षकः वातेरितपल्लवाङ्गुलीभिः शकुन्तलां त्वरयतीव।[7] अपि च तस्याः वियोगेऽपसृतपाण्डुपत्राः लताः अश्रूणि मुञ्चन्ति इव।[8] एवं वनस्पतिषु मानवीयसंवेगानामभिव्यक्तिः कालिदासस्य वैशिष्ट्यमुपस्थापयति।

वृक्षाणां समुचितविकाराः, तेषु यथाकालं पुष्पोत्पत्तिश्च वनस्पतिजगतः सुसमृद्धिं दृश्येते। अभिज्ञानशाकुन्तले दुष्यन्तः चिन्तां प्रकटयति-'किम् मयापचरितैः वीरुधां प्रसवो विष्टम्भिता':।[9] मालविकाग्निमित्रे चिरायमाणं कुसुमोद्गमं प्रति चिन्ता उत्सुकता च तृतीयाङ्कस्य मुख्या वार्ता विद्यते। राजपरिवारे कुसुमदर्शनं महतीं प्रीतिं जनयति। देवीधारिणी अशोक-कुसुमवृत्तान्तेनप्रसादसुमुखी भवति। सा आर्यपुत्रेण सह अशोकवृक्षस्य प्रसूनलक्ष्मी प्रत्यक्षीकर्तुमिच्छति। अशोकदोहदप्रसङ्गेन कालिदासः वनस्पतीनां समुचितविकासाय यथाकालं समुचितां सजगतां संसूचयति। महाकविमते तु उचितवेलातिक्रमणं खलु महद् दोषो भवति।[10] वृक्षसंरक्षणाय मूलस्य दृढता अतीवानिर्वाया भवति, यतो हि अमात्यमुखेन कविः कथयति-दुर्बलः तरुः समुद्धर्तुं सुकरो भवति।[11]

वृक्षेषु लतासु च परस्परसम्बन्धस्य परिकल्पना अपूर्वा विद्यते कालिदासनाट्यकृतिषु। अभिज्ञाने वनज्योत्स्ना इति कृतनामधेया नवमालिका बालसहकारवृक्षस्य स्वयंवधूः अस्ति, यस्याः रमणीये काले पादपेन सह दाम्पत्यं संवृत्तम्। मालविका अशोकवृक्षं नायकमिव पश्यति—'अयं स ललितसुकुमारदोहदापेक्षी अगृहीतकुसुमनेपथ्योऽशोकः।' प्रतीयते यत् अशोकवृक्षं प्रति परामनुरागभावनां मनसि विधाय एव कालिदासेन मालविकाग्निमित्रं नाटकं निबद्धम्।

कालिदासनाट्यकृतिषु वनस्पतिचित्रणस्य त्रयः पक्षाः सन्ति—वृक्षाः, लताः, पुष्पसम्पद् च। वृक्षेषु प्रमुखाः विद्यन्ते-अशोकः, रक्ताशोकः[12] रक्तकदम्बः,[13] सहकारः,[14] आम्रः,[15] नीपवृक्षः,[16] शल्लकीवृक्षः,[17] बीजपूरकम्,[18] चन्दनवृक्षः,[19] कल्पतरुः[20]। लतासु उल्लेख्याः सन्ति—शमीलता[21], माधवीलता,[22] कौन्दीलता,[23] कुन्दलता,[24] वासन्तीलता।[25] महाकविः उद्यानलतानां वनलताभिः सह सुष्ठु तुलनां अलङ्कारमाध्यमेन निरूपयति।[26]

कालिदासनाट्यकृतिषु यथास्थानं पुष्पाणां चर्चापि दरीदृश्यते, येषु मुख्यानि नामानि सन्ति—सरसिजम्,[27] नवमालिकाकुसुमम्,[28] कुमुदम्,[29] मन्दारपुष्पम्,[30] केसरपुष्पम्,[31] शिरीषकुसुमम्,[32] कुरबकम्,[33] रक्तकुरबकम्,[34] काञ्चनपद्मम्,[35] बकुलम्,[36] बकुलावलिका, कुमुदिनी च धारिण्याः द्वे परिचारिके स्तः। पुष्पाणां स्वरूपं, वर्णं, वैशिष्ट्यं च एतेषां प्रसङ्गेषु सहजतया चर्चितं भवन्ति। बकुलावलिका कथयति—'विमर्दसुरभिर्बकुलावलिका खल्वहम्।[37] मन्दारमाला इन्द्रस्य वक्षस्थले, सुशोभिता भवति, केसरमालिका च शकुन्तलाकृते सुनियोजिता तस्याः सखीद्वयेन। मालतीमालायाः उपमानरूपे वर्णनं मालविकाग्निमित्रनाटके आसीत्।[38] सरसिजस्य पर्यायभूताः कविप्रयुक्ताः शब्दाः सन्ति—नलिनी,[39] कमलिनी,[40] पङ्कजं,[41] पद्मं,[42] कमलम्,[43] पद्मनी,[44] पुण्डरीकम्[45] इत्यादयः। दूर्वाकिसलानि[46], मुस्ताः[47], नीवारवलिः[48] दर्भाः,[49] इत्यपराणि नामानि इतरवनस्पतिं सूचयन्ति।

स्वकीयनाट्यकृतिषु वनस्पतिजगतः सूक्ष्मज्ञानं सम्यक्तया कविना प्रदर्शितम् इत्यस्मिन् विषयेऽस्ति न कोऽपि सन्देहः। पृथिवी-पर्वत-स्वर्गादिकं सम्पूर्णं ब्रह्माण्डं विद्यते तस्य वनस्पतिसंचेतनायाः आधारः। कालिदासस्य वनस्पतिः मानवानां कृते नीतिशिक्षकः इव प्रतिभाति यदा स प्रतिपादयति-''भवन्ति नम्रास्तरवः फलागमैर्नवाम्बुभिर्दूरविलम्बिनो घनाः। अनुद्धता सत्पुरुषाः समृद्धिभिः स्वभाव एवैष परोपकारिणाम्,''[50] एवमेव महाकविः नैसर्गिकनियमानुपालनाय वनस्पतिं प्रशंसति कथयति च—

उदेति पूर्वं कुसुमं ततः फलं
घनोदयः प्राक्तदनन्तरं पयः।
निमित्तनैमित्तिकयोरयं क्रमः।[51]

कालिदासस्य नाट्यकृतिषु वनस्पतिविवरणस्य सन्ति नाना पक्षाः। सर्वे सन्ति विशिष्टमहिमामण्डिताः, स्वाभाविकाः मनोरमाश्च, ये पाठकानां सपक्षं वनस्पतिजगतः साङ्गोपाङ्गसमग्रचित्रमुपस्थापयति। सरस्वतीसमुपासकः कविकालिदासः स्वपीयूषवर्षिन्या लेखन्या यत्किमपि वनस्पतिविषयकं ससर्ज, तत् सर्वं काव्यरसमर्मज्ञैः आस्वादनीयमुपपद्यते-इत्यस्ति मम अध्ययनस्य निष्कर्षः।

सन्दर्भ-सङ्केताः

1. अभिज्ञानशाकुन्तलम् - 4/9
2. अतन्द्रिता सा स्वयमेव वृक्षकान्घटस्तनप्रस्रवणैर्व्यवर्धयत्। कुमारसम्भवम् - 5/14
3. अमुं पुरः पश्यसि देवदारुं पुत्रीकृतोऽसौ वृषभध्वजेन। रघुवंशम् - 2/36

4. पातुं न प्रथगं व्यवस्यति जलं युष्मास्वपीतेषु या।
नादत्ते प्रियमण्डनाऽपि भवतां स्नेहेन या पल्लवम्।। अभिज्ञानशाकुन्तलम् - 4/9
5. अभिज्ञानशाकुन्तलम् - 4/10
6. अभिज्ञानशाकुन्तलम् - 4/5
7. अभिज्ञानशाकुन्तलम् - अङ्कः 1
8. अभिज्ञानशाकुन्तलम् - 4/12
9. अभिज्ञानशाकुन्तलम् - 5/9
10. उचितवेलातिक्रमणे चिकित्सका दोषमुदाहरन्ति। मालविकाग्निमित्रम् - 2/12 अनन्तरम्।
11. नवसंरोपणशिथिलस्तरुरिव सुकरः समुद्धतुम्।। मालविकाग्निमित्रम् - 1/8
12. विक्रमोर्वशीयम् - 2/7, 4/62, 63; मालविकाग्निमित्रम् - 3/5
13. विक्रमोर्वशीयम् - 4/61
14. विक्रमोर्वशीयम् - 2/6
15. विक्रमोर्वशीयम् - 2/7, मालविकाग्निमित्रम् - 3/4
16. विक्रमोर्वशीयम् - 4/42, अनन्तरम् ('कदम्ब' इत्यर्थः)
17. विक्रमोर्वशीयम् - 4/44
18. मालविकाग्निमित्रम् - 3/1 पूर्वम् ('नीबू' इत्यर्थः)
19. अभिज्ञानशाकुन्तलम् - 7/2
20. विक्रमोर्वशीयम् - 4.12
21. अभिज्ञानशाकुन्तलम् - 1/18, 4/4
22. अभिज्ञानशाकुन्तलम् - 3/8, विक्रमोर्वशीयम् - 2/4
23. विक्रमोर्वशीयम् - 2/4
24. मालविकाग्निमित्रम् - 3/8
25. विक्रमोर्वशीयम् - 4/73, पूर्वम्
26. दूरीकृताः खलु गुणैरुद्यानलता वनलताभिः। अभिज्ञानशाकुन्तलम् - 1/17
27. अभिज्ञानशाकुन्तलम् - 1/19
28. अभिज्ञानशाकुन्तलम् - 1/20, अनन्तरम्, 2/8
29. अभिज्ञानशाकुन्तलम् - 5/28, 4/3
30. अभिज्ञानशाकुन्तलम् - 7/2
31. अभिज्ञानशाकुन्तलम् - 4/4 अनन्तरम्
32. अभिज्ञानशाकुन्तलम् - 1/4, 1/28

33. विक्रमोर्वशीयम् - 2/7
34. मालविकाग्निमित्रम् - 3/2 अनन्तरम् - 3/9,
35. अभिज्ञानशाकुन्तलम् - 7/12
36. मालविकाग्निमित्रम् - 3/14 पूर्वम् (मौलसिरी इत्यर्थः)
37. अभिज्ञानशाकुन्तलम् - 3/14 पूर्वम्
38. अभिज्ञानशाकुन्तलम् - 3/1 पूर्वम्
39. अभिज्ञानशाकुन्तलम् - 4/15, अनन्तरम्, विक्रमोर्वशीयम् - 4/39
40. अभिज्ञानशाकुन्तलम् - 4/11
41. अभिज्ञानशाकुन्तलम् - 7/16
42. अभिज्ञानशाकुन्तलम् - 7/12
43. विक्रमोर्वशीयम् - 2/12, अनन्तरम्
44. मालविकाग्निमित्रम् - 2/12
45. मालविकाग्निमित्रम् - 4/7
46. अभिज्ञानशाकुन्तलम् - 4/4 अनन्तरम्
47. अभिज्ञानशाकुन्तलम् - 2/6
48. अभिज्ञानशाकुन्तलम् - 4/21
49. अभिज्ञानशाकुन्तलम् - 2/12
50. अभिज्ञानशाकुन्तलम् - 5/12
51. अभिज्ञानशाकुन्तलम् - 7/30

卐 卐 卐

कालिदासकृतिषु अशोकश्रीः

अञ्जु बाला

कालिदासस्य सर्वेषु ग्रन्थेषु अभिरामं प्रकृतिवर्णनं विलोक्यम् एव। हिमालय-वर्णनप्रसङ्गे रत्नोषधिवनस्पतिकल्पवृक्षादीनाम् उल्लेखाः अनेकशः दृश्यन्ते। महर्षिचरकेणापि उक्तम् — 'ओषधीनां पराभूमिर्हिमवान् शैलसूत्तमः।' एवं हिमालयपर्वतस्तु ओषधीनां वनस्पतीनां कृते सर्वश्रेष्ठः मन्यते।

कालिदासकृतिषु शताधिकाः विभिन्नाः वनस्पतयः वर्णिताः। येषु अगुरु-अपराजिता-अर्क-अर्जुन-अशोक-आम्र-इक्षु-इंगुदी-उत्पल-कमल-कदली-कर्णिकार-कर्कन्धु-कल्पवृक्ष-किंशुक-कीचक-कुटज-कुमुद-कुवलय-कुश-केतकी-केसर-चन्दन- जपा-जम्बू-तमाल-ताल-तिलक-दर्भ-दूर्वा-द्राक्षा-नवमल्लिका-नीवार-पारिजात-प्रियङ्गु-पुण्डरीक-पूग-बकुल-मन्दार-माधवी-मालती-लवङ्ग-लोध्र-वेत्र-शमी-शैवालादयः सन्ति प्रमुखाः। एवं रघुवंश-कुमारसम्भव-ऋतुसंहार-मेघदूत-अभिज्ञानशाकुन्तल-मालविकाग्निमित्र- विक्रमोर्वशीय-एतेषु सप्तग्रन्थेषु भारतीयपुष्प-पादप-वृक्षवनस्पतीनाञ्च सौन्दर्यम् उपवर्णितम्।

अस्मिन् शोधपत्रे अशोवृक्षस्य विवेचनं कृतम्। अत्र विहङ्गमदृष्ट्या पञ्चदशस्थलेषु अशोकवृक्षस्य चर्चा प्राप्ता।

न शोक इति अशोकः अर्थात् शोकनाशक एवाशोकवृक्षः। अमरकोशे अस्याभिधानद्वयम्-वञ्जुलोऽशोके समौ[1] इति। अशोकलता अशोकविटपी च कालिदासकविना प्रयुक्तम्। सदाविकासी एष मध्यमाकृतिवृक्षः। यस्य पर्णानि आम्र इव लम्बाग्रमसृणानि। पुष्पाणि गुच्छरूपेण रक्तवर्णानि वर्तन्ते। हिमालयस्य प्रान्तेषु बङ्गप्रदेशे दक्षिणभारते च दृश्यतेऽयं वृक्षः।

अशोकवृक्षस्य गणना दोहदवृक्षेषु क्रियते। दोहदम् आकर्षं ददाति इति।[2] संस्कृते कविपरम्परानुसारं अशोकबकुलादयः दशवृक्षाः तदैव विकसन्ति यदा तेषां अभिलाषः पूर्णत्वं याति। एते दशदोहदवृक्षा अधोलिखिताः येषु अशोकः अन्यतमः। मल्लिनाथेन वर्णितम्

स्त्रीणां स्पर्शात्प्रियङ्गुर्विकसति बकुलः सीधुगण्डूषसेकात्
पादाघातादशोकस्तिलककुरबकौ वीक्षणालिङ्गनाभ्याम्।
मन्दारो नर्मवाक्यात्पटुमृदुहसनाच्चम्पको वक्त्रवाता-
च्चूतो गीतान्नमेरुर्विकसति च पुरोनर्तनात्कर्णिकारः।।

कविना अनेकशः दोहदवृक्षाणां चर्चा कृता यथा उत्तरमेघानुसारम्—

रक्ताशोकश्चलकिसलयः केसरश्चात्र कान्तः
प्रत्यासन्नौ कुरबककवृतेर्माधवीमण्डपस्य।
एकः सख्यास्तव सह मया वामपादाभिलाषी
काङ्क्षत्यन्यो वदनमदिरां दोहदच्छद्मनाऽस्याः।।[3]

अस्मिन् श्लोके बकुलस्य अशोकस्य च दोहदाभिलाषाः वर्णिताः सन्ति। यथा वदनमदिरागण्डूषेण बकुलः विकसति वामपादाघातेन च अशोकस्य अभिलाषः पूर्णतां गच्छति।

रघुवंशीयाभिरामः श्लोकोऽयम्–

कुसुमं कृतदोहदस्त्वया यदशोकोऽयमुदीरयिष्यति।
अलकाभरणं कथं नु तत्तव नेष्यामि निवापमाल्यताम्।।[4]

अस्मिन् श्लोके रतिविलापप्रसङ्गे महाकविना अशोकस्य पुष्पाणां विकसनं वर्णितम्। दिनकरमतेन 'पादघात एवाशोकस्य दोहदः'।

अस्मिन्नेव प्रसङ्गे प्रकृत्या सह मानवीय-सम्बन्धानाम् अभिव्यक्तिः दृक्पथं प्रयाति।

स्मरतेव सशब्दनूपुरं चरणानुग्रहमन्यदुर्लभम्।
अमुना कुसुमाश्रुवर्षिणा त्वमशोकेन सुगात्रि शोच्यसे।।[5]

एवमेव दोहदवृक्षरूपेण अस्योल्लेखा अन्यत्र द्रष्टव्याः यथा–

मालविकाग्निमित्रनाटके 3/12, 3/16 पूर्वार्द्धः 3/17 उत्तरार्द्धः

अपि च कविना कुमारसम्भवे वर्णितम्।

असूत सद्यः कुसुमान्यशोकः स्कन्धात्प्रभृत्येव सपल्लवानि।
पादेन नापैक्षत सुन्दरीणां सम्पर्कमासिञ्जितनूपुरेण।।[6]

अशोकस्य भेदद्वयं वर्तते 'श्वेतरक्तौ' इति।

प्रसूनकैरशोकस्तु श्वेतो रक्त इति द्विधा।
बहुसिद्धिकरः श्वेतो रक्तोऽत्र स्मरवर्धनः।।

रक्ताशोकः कामोद्दीपकः। कामदेवस्य च पञ्चबाणेषु एष अन्यतमः। ऋतुसंहारगीतिकाव्ये कविना वर्णितं यत् रक्ताशोकस्य पुष्पदर्शनेन प्रमदाः शोकत्वं यान्ति तद्यथा–

आमूलतो विद्रुमरागताम्रं सपल्लवाः पुष्पचयं दधानाः।
कुर्वन्त्यशोका हृदयं सशोकं निरीक्ष्यमाणा नवयौवनानाम्।।[7]

अन्यत्र द्रष्टव्यम् – रघुवंशम् – 9/28

ऋतुराज-वसन्ततौ विकसनशीलः अशोकोऽयं न केवलं स्मरदीपकः अपितु योषित्सु अलङ्करण इव यथा–

कर्णेषु योग्यं नवकर्णिकारं चलेषु नीलेष्वलकेष्वशोकम्।
पुष्पं च फुल्लं च नवमल्लिकायाः प्रयान्ति कान्तिं प्रमदाजनानाम्।।[8]

ऋतुसंहारस्यास्मिन् श्लोके वर्णितमस्ति यत् प्रमदाः अलङ्काररूपेण पुष्पाणि धारयन्ति यथा कर्णेषु नवकर्णिकारपुष्पाणि अलकेषु च नवमल्लिकापुष्पाणि।

सुविज्ञः खलु कालिदासः मानवमनोवृत्तीनां विशेषतः स्त्रीणां विषये। ऋतुसंहारे तेन वर्णितम् यत् अलङ्कारप्रियाः सुन्दर्यः स्वालकेषु कुन्दपुष्पं कर्णेषु शिरीषपुष्पं ललाटे च कदम्बपुष्पं धारयन्ति। तासां मुखानि लोध्रपुष्परजसा च शोभन्ते।

कुमारसम्भवे महाकाव्ये अशोकस्य पुष्पाणां कमनीयता पद्मरागमणिमपि अतिशेते —

अशोकनिर्भर्त्सितपद्मरागमाकृष्टहेमद्युतिकर्णिकारम् ।
मुक्ताकलापीकृतसिन्धुवारं वसन्तपुष्पाभरणं वहन्ती।।[9]

अन्यत्र द्रष्टव्यम्-मालविकाग्निमित्रम् - 3/5

आयुर्वेदशास्त्रे अशोकस्य औषधगुणानां वर्णनम् अनेकधा अनेकशः च कृतं वर्तते यथा शालिग्रामनिघण्टुनाम्नि ग्रन्थे वर्णितम्—

अशोकः शीतलस्तिक्तो ग्राही वर्ण्यकषायकः
दोषापची तृषादाह कृमिशोषविशास्त्रजित्।
अशोकस्य त्वक् रक्तप्रदरस्य विनाशिनी।

अस्योपयोगः रक्तप्रदरगर्भसम्बन्धिषु विकारेषु क्रियते। स्त्रीणां कृते विशेषरूपेण शोकनाशकोऽयमशोकवृक्षः। यथा नाम तथागुणा अशोकश्रीः। इति शम्।

सन्दर्भ-सङ्केताः

1. अमरकोशः (अमरसिंहकृतः) - पृ० 73
2. तरुगुल्मलतादीनामकाले कुशलैः कृतम्।
   पुष्पाद्युत्पादनं द्रव्यं दोहदं स्यात्तु तत्क्रिया।।
3. मेघदूतम् - 2.18
4. रघुवंशम् - 8.62
5. रघुवंशम् - 8.63
6. कुमारसम्भवम् - 3.26
7. ऋतुसंहारम् - 6.18
8. ऋतुसंहारम् - 6.6
9. कुमारसम्भवम् - 3.53

रघुवंशीयं पर्यावरणसौरभम्

सुषमा कुलश्रेष्ठ

जायन्ते कति जज्ञिरे कति जनिष्यन्ते कतीह क्षितौ
स्रष्टारो नितरामिदं तु कविभिर्निर्मत्सरैः कथ्यताम्।
आपूर्वापरदक्षिणोत्तरहरित्साहित्यसिंहासन-
स्वैरारोहपराक्रमं भजतु कः श्रीकालिदासात्परः।।

प्रशस्तिरियं दीपशिखाकालिदासस्य सर्वास्वाशासु साहित्यसाम्राज्यस्य चक्रवर्तित्वं द्योतयति। अस्मान्परितः स्थितं वातावरणं यत् प्रत्यक्षं परोक्षं वास्माभिरुपभुज्यते पर्यावरणमित्यभिधीयते। सामान्यरूपेण हरिता परिपूर्णा प्रकृतिरेवास्ति पर्यावरणम्। सुजला सुफला मलयजशीतला शस्यश्यामला धरेव हरिता प्रकृतिः। पशुपक्षिभिः जीवजन्तुभिः समृद्धा भूरेवास्ति परिपूर्णा प्रकृतिः। पर्यावरणेन सह मानवस्यास्ति कोऽपि अविभाज्यः सम्बन्धः। आदिकालादारभ्य इदमस्ति प्रकृतेरनुशासनम्। अस्मिन् अवाञ्छितं किमपि परिवर्तनं यदि क्रियते तर्हि अनिष्टकरमेव सिद्ध्यति। वर्तमानकाले प्रतिक्षणं महतीं वृद्धिं प्रयान्ती जनसंख्या, कृषीणामौद्योगिकीकरणं, वनानां कर्त्तनं, वन्यजीवानां संहारः, परमाणुपरीक्षणानि च पर्यावरणसन्तुलनं विकुर्वन्ति विसंघटयन्ति विदूषयन्ति च। अनेन न केवलमस्माकं देशः प्रत्युत विश्वमपि जगदस्ति भयाक्रान्तम्।

सकलायाः प्रकृतेर्मनुष्याणाञ्च पारस्परिकसम्बन्धानां माधुर्यं सानुपातिकं सन्तुलनञ्चैव पर्यावरणसंरक्षणसंज्ञकम्। पर्यावरणसंरक्षणस्य सन्ति विभिन्ना आधारा बहूनि साधनानि च। अस्माकं धार्मिकभावनापि पर्यावरणधारणायां केन्द्रीभूता। एवमस्माकं प्राचीनं वैदिकवाङ्मयं पर्यावरणसाहित्यरूपेणैव परिलक्ष्यते। ज्ञानकर्मोपासनात्रिवेण्याप्लाविते वैदिकवाङ्मये यज्ञयागादिकं कर्म भैषज्येण पर्यावरणशुद्धया च सम्बद्धमुपासना च प्राकृतिकोपादानैस्सह सम्बद्धा। ग्निमरुत्पर्जन्य-वरुणसोमसवितृपृथ्वीप्रभृतीनि प्राकृतिकतत्त्वानि वैदिकानां पूजनीयान्यर्चनीयानि च। अस्माकमृषिभिरादिकालत एव प्राकृतिकतत्त्वेषु देवत्वभावना समाहिता। एतेषां देवानां प्रसादाय एभ्यः स्वकल्याणाय सुखसमृद्ध्यै च वेदेषु स्तुतीनां विधानं कृतम्। प्राकृतिकशक्तीनामेषोपासना नासीद् भयपरिणतिरूपा अपितु अभिव्यक्तिरासीदियं श्रद्धासंवलितायाः कृतज्ञतायाः। यद्यपि पर्यावरणप्रदूषणसदृशी काचिन्नासीत्तदानीं समस्या तथापि सन्दर्भेऽस्मिन् प्राचीनानामृषीणां चिन्तनमतिशयेन व्यावहारिकं वैज्ञानिकं चास्ति। पर्यावरणसन्दर्भे ऋषीणां भावनाः निभालनीयाः—

मधु वाता ऋतायते मधु क्षरन्ति सिन्धवः। माध्वीर्नः सन्त्वोषधीः।। मधु नक्तमुतोषसो मधुमत्पार्थिवं रजः।
मधु द्यौरस्तु नः पिता। मधुमान्नो वनस्पतिर्मधुमान् अस्तु सूर्यः। माध्वीर्गावो भवन्तु नः।[1]

कनिष्ठिकाधिष्ठितः दीपशिखाकालिदासः कालजयी कविकुलशिरोमणिर्विजयतेतरां यस्य काव्यानां यया दृष्ट्या विवेचनं क्रियते, प्रतीयते यत् सः तस्यैव क्षेत्रस्य प्रतिनिधिभूतः कविः। तस्य कालजयित्वस्य निकषोपलमस्ति तस्य समाजोपयोगि विलक्षणं कवित्वम्। कालिदासः सर्वेषु कालेषु प्रत्येकं परिवर्तनशीलस्य भारतीयस्य समाजस्य प्रतिनिधित्वं विदधानो दृश्यते प्रासङ्गिकताञ्च धारयति। मूलतः शृङ्गारीकविरसौ परमनयैव सरण्या कान्तासम्मितमुपदेशं प्रदाय त्रिवर्गसन्तुलितं

जीवनं यापयितुं सन्दिशति।

रघुवंशीयानां नृपाणां चरितालङ्कृतं रघुवंशमहाकाव्यमस्ति कालिदासस्य नैसर्गिकप्रतिभायाश्चूडान्तनिदर्शनम्। रघुकारस्य प्रकृतिप्रेम तस्य सर्वासु रचनासु दरीदृश्यते। रघुवंशेऽपि प्रकृतिस्तत्त्वानि विविधेषु रूपेषु वर्णितानि। उपमालङ्कारप्रियोऽसौ स्वकीयानि उपमानानि प्रकृतेतत्त्वेभ्य एव चिनोति। प्रकृतितत्त्वानामुल्लेखदृष्ट्या रघुवंशं पर्यावरणमभिलक्ष्य लिखितं काव्यं प्रतिभाति कथ्यते चेदिदं, नास्ति अत्युक्तिरेषा यतः रघुवंशस्य प्रायः पञ्चशतश्लोकेषु प्रकृतिरूपाः निर्दिष्टाः विविधरूपेषु। एवं यदि कालिदासस्य पर्यावरणचिन्तनमुपलक्ष्य रघुवंशस्य विधिवत् विवेचनं क्रियते तर्हि एकस्य शोधपरकस्य ग्रन्थस्य निर्मितिर्भवेत्। स्थानसीमानं समयसीमानं चाभिलक्ष्यात्र मया रघुवंशस्य त एव प्रसङ्गाः विवेचनीयाः यत्र कविः प्रत्यक्षरूपेण परोक्षरूपेण वा पर्यावरणं सङ्केतयति।

पर्यावरणदृष्ट्या यानि तत्त्वानि प्रामुख्यं भजन्ति तेषु पञ्चमहाभूतानि महत्त्वपूर्णानि। कालिदासानुसारं पञ्चमहाभूतेषु सर्वाणि तत्त्वानि परोपकारीणि। तैस्तत्त्वैर्निर्मिते नृपें दिलीपेऽपि परोपकारितागुणो विराजते—

तं वेधा विदधे नूनं महाभूतसमाधिना।
तथा हि सर्वे तस्यासन्परार्थैकफला गुणाः।।[2]

कालिदासमते पञ्चमहाभूतैस्सह शब्दस्पर्शरूपरसगन्धरूपाणां तत्त्वानामस्ति सम्बन्धः तेषामुत्कर्षेण च प्रकृतेः सकलानि तत्त्वानि नूतनानि जायन्ते —

पञ्चानामपि भूतानामुत्कर्षं पुपुषुर्गुणाः।
नवे तस्मिन्महीपाले सर्वं नवमिवाभवत्।।[3]

पञ्चमहाभूतेषु जलतत्त्वं प्रथमतत्त्वरूपेण प्रतिष्ठितम्। अभिज्ञानशाकुन्तलनामधेयस्य नाटकस्य नान्द्यामपि महाकविः कालिदासः जलतत्त्वं विधातुः आद्या सृष्टिः इतिरूपेण वर्णयति। तन्मते च सर्वे महाभूताः शिवस्य मूर्त्तय एव। रघुवंशे जलतत्त्वस्य निरूपणम् अन्यभूतापेक्षया अधिकं खलु। तन्मतानुसारं जलस्य शुद्धिः आवश्यिकी यतो हि जलेनैव स्नानादिकं सम्पन्नं भवति पितृभ्यः तर्पणं च —

निर्वर्त्यते यैर्नियमाभिषेको येभ्यो निवापाञ्जलयः पितॄणाम्।
तान्युञ्छषष्ठाङ्कितसैकतानि शिवानि वस्तीर्थजलानि कच्चित्।।[4]

यद्यपि प्रकृतौ प्रायशः सर्वत्र जलतत्त्वमुपलभ्यते किन्तु जलधिरेव प्रधानं जलस्रोतः। सूर्यः समुद्रेभ्यः जलं गृहीत्वा मेघं निर्माति, मेघश्च जलमभिवृष्य सर्वं जलमयं करोति। सूर्यः एकतः स्वरश्मिभिः समुद्रेभ्यः जलं गृह्णाति अपरतः समुद्रेषु रत्नानि वर्धन्ते। समुद्रादेव आह्लादकः चन्द्रः जायते —

गर्भं दधत्यर्कमरीचयोऽस्माद्विवृद्धिमत्राश्नुवते वसूनि।
अबिन्धनं वह्निमसौ बिभर्ति प्रह्लादनं ज्योतिरजन्यनेन।।[5]

प्रायशः संस्कृतकवयः सरोवर्णनम् अवश्यं कुर्वन्ति। कालिदासमतानुसारं जलपूर्णं सरः न केवलं सुखदं भवति अपितु श्रान्तिमपि अपनयति। एवमेव कुल्याम्भोभिः उपवनपादपाः हर्षिताः भवन्ति—

सा पौरान्पौरकान्तस्य रामस्याभ्युदयश्रुतिः।
प्रत्येकं ह्लादयाञ्चक्रे कुल्येवोद्यानपादपान्।।[6]

मेघं प्रति कालिदासस्य प्रेम तु मेघदूतकाव्येनैव स्पष्टम्। तथापि यथावसरं स यत्र–तत्र मेघं निरूपयति। रघुवंशे वर्षाजलस्य माहात्म्यं निरूपयन् महाकविः कथयति यत् दिव्यं वर्षोदकं यद्यपि मधुरैकरसं भवति किन्तु ऊषरादिदेशे रसान्तराणि लवणादीनि प्राप्नोति –

रसान्तराण्येकरसं यथा दिव्यं पयोऽश्नुते।
देशे देशे गुणेष्वेवमवस्थास्त्वमविक्रियः।।[7]

मेघः सर्वस्वत्यागी भवन्ति। यत्किञ्चित् स आददाति तत्तु त्यागायैव –

आदानं हि विसर्गाय सतां वारिमुचामिव।।[8]

मेघः जलसेकात् ग्रीष्मतप्ताम् ऊर्वीं नवीकरोति –

पुरं नवीचक्रुरपां विसर्गान्मेघा निदाघग्लपितामिवोर्वीम्।[9]

महाकविकालिदासस्य दृष्टिः न केवलं मेघस्य उपयोगित्वं प्रति गच्छति अपितु तस्य सौन्दर्यविधानेऽपि महाकवेः मनो रमते –

केवलोऽपि सुभगो नवाम्बुदः किं पुनस्त्रिदशचापलाञ्छितः।[10]

नूतनः मेघस्तु रिक्तोऽपि शोभावान् भवति, इन्द्रधनुषा चेत् चिह्नितः स्यात् तर्हि किं कथनम्।

रामरावणयुद्धप्रसङ्गे महाकविः रामस्य उपरि मेघम् आरोप्य रूपकालङ्कारमाध्यमेन मेघं वर्णयति–

रावणावग्रहक्लान्तमिति वागमृतेन सः।
अभिवृष्य मरुत्सस्यं कृष्णमेघस्तिरोदधे।।[11]

नीलमेघः वर्षप्रतिबन्धेन म्लानं सस्यं सलिलेन अभिषिच्य अन्तर्दधे।

रघुकारः नैकेषु स्थलेषु नदीनां सागराणाञ्च सविस्तरं वर्णनं करोति। त्रयोदशसर्गस्य प्रारम्भिकेषु पद्येषु रामः सीतां सागरस्य माहात्म्यम् उपादेयत्वञ्च निवेदयति। प्रथमेऽपि सर्गे महाराजेन दिलीपेन सह सागरस्य तुलनां कुर्वन् महाकविः सागरस्य उभयगुणत्वं दर्शयति। सागरस्तु जलजन्तुभिः अनभिभवनीयः भवति रत्नैश्च आश्रयणीयः भवति –

अधृष्यश्चाभिगम्यश्च यादोरत्नैरिवार्णवः।[12]

महाकविः कालिदासः वायुतत्त्वमपि यत्र–तत्र निरूपयति। स मन्यते यत् धूलिरहितेन वायुना यदि श्वासः गृह्यते तर्ह्यपि सुखकरः। अत्र वायोः शुद्धत्वं प्रति निर्दिशति महाकविः यतो हि तेनैव अस्माकं जीवनं चलति –

विरजस्कैर्नभस्वद्भिर्दिश उच्छ्वसिता इव।।[13]

शीतलवायुः क्लान्तिमपि परिहरति –

अत्रानुगोदं मृगयानिवृत्तस्तरङ्गवातेन विनीतखेदः।[14]

महाकविः यज्ञं वातावरणशोधकं मनुते। हविषा अनिलः शुद्धीभवति तेन अनिलेन च यदि श्वासः गृह्यते तर्हि अन्तःकरणं रजोगुणाद् विमुक्तं जायते –

त्रेताऽग्निधूमाग्रमनिन्द्यकीर्तेस्तस्येदमाक्रान्तविमानमार्गम्।
घ्रात्वा हविर्गन्धिरजोविमुक्तः समश्नुते मे लघिमानमात्मा।।[15]

यज्ञः न केवलं पर्यावरणं शोधयति अपितु वृष्टिं प्रत्यपि कारणतां भजते –

हविरावर्जितं होतस्त्वया विधिवदग्निषु।
वृष्टिर्भवति सस्यानामवग्रहविशोषिणाम्।।[16]

सूर्यचन्द्रमसौ तेजसः प्रतिनिधिभूतौ। सूर्यचन्द्रौ तमसः जनान् रक्षतः –

तत्र दीक्षितमृषिं ररक्षतुर्विघ्नतो दशरथात्मजौ शरैः।
लोकमन्धतमसात्क्रमोदितौ रश्मिभिः शशिदिवाकराविव।।[17]

सूर्यः स्वरश्मिभिः सकलेषु जनेषु चैतन्यं विदधाति –

अप्यग्रणीर्मन्त्रकृतामृषीणां कुशाग्रबुद्धे! कुशली गुरुस्ते।
यतस्त्वया ज्ञानमशेषमाप्तं लोकेन चैतन्यमिवोष्णरश्मेः।।[18]

तस्य कविहृदयं सायंकालीनं सूर्यम् उत्तरदक्षिणयोरुभयोः मार्गयोः पवितारं मन्यते –

सञ्चारपूतानि दिगन्तराणि कृत्वा दिनान्ते निलयाय गन्तुम्।
प्रचक्रमे पल्लवरागताम्रा प्रभा पतङ्गस्य मुनेश्च धेनुः।।[20]

स पितुः पितृमान्वंशं मातुश्चानुपमद्युतिः।
अपुनात्सवितेवोभौ मार्गावुत्तरदक्षिणौ।।[20]

तस्य मते क्षपायाः ज्योतिष्मत्त्वं चन्द्रमसैव भवति नान्यैः साधारणैर्ज्योतिर्भिः –

कामं नृपाः सन्ति सहस्रशोऽन्ये राजन्वतीमाहुरनेन भूमिम्।
नक्षत्रताराग्रहसङ्कुलापि ज्योतिष्मती चन्द्रमसैव रात्रिः।।[21]

उष्णत्वप्रदाता सूर्य उष्णत्वापहारकश्चन्द्रमाश्च –

जनस्य तरिगन्रामये विगाढे बभूवतुर्द्वौ सविशेषकान्तौ।
तापापनोदक्षमपादसेवौ स चोदयस्थौ नृपतिः शशी च।।[22]

चन्द्रिका सर्वेषां जनानां श्रमापनोदिनी सुखप्रदायिनी च भवति किन्तु शृङ्गारिणां विलासिनां कृते तु तस्या माहात्म्यं द्विगुणितं जायते। शृङ्गारी नृपोऽग्निवर्णः कार्तिकीषु शरद्रात्रिषु रमणीभिस्सह रतिकेलिश्रमापहां ज्योत्स्नां भुक्तवान् –

कार्तिकीषु सवितानहर्म्यभाग्यामिनीषु ललिताङ्गनासखः।
अन्वभुङ्क्त सुरतश्रमापहां मेघमुक्तविशदां स चन्द्रिकाम्।।[23]

पञ्चमहाभूतेषु पृथिवीतत्त्वस्योपयोगितापरिहार्यता च प्रत्यक्षं परोक्षं चापि वर्णिता कविकुलगुरुणा। पृथ्वेव जगदिदं धारयति। अतः सा सततं रक्षणीया –

निवर्त्य राजा दयितां दयालुस्तां सौरभेयीं सुरभिर्यशोभिः।
पयोधरीभूतचतुःसमुद्रां जुगोप गोरूपधरामिवोर्वीम्।।[24]

पद्येऽस्मिन् दीपशिखाकवेरुपमाचातुरी निभालनीया। पृथिवीतत्त्वान्तर्गतमेव परिगण्यन्ते पर्वताः वृक्षाः लताः वनस्पतयश्च। सम्पूर्णे कालिदासवाङ्मये विंशत्यधिकशतवनस्पतीनां वर्णनं कृतम्। केवलं रघुवंश एव प्रायशः पञ्चषष्टिवनस्पतीनामुल्लेखः विविधेषु प्रसङ्गेषु समुपलभ्यते। वृक्षलतावनस्पतीनामेते उल्लेखास्तस्य विलक्षणं वैदुष्यं हठात् दृष्टिपथमानयन्ति। यदा वयं तस्य वृक्षलतावनस्पतिपरकान् श्लोकानास्वादयामः। महदाश्चर्यं मनसि सञ्जायते कालिदासः कविः उत वनस्पतिशास्त्रज्ञः उत आयुर्वेदज्ञः उत वृक्षायुर्वेदज्ञः कश्चासौ? रघुवंशे ये पुष्पवृक्षाः फलवृक्षाः अन्यवनस्पतयश्चोल्लिखिताः समयाभावात् स्थानाभावाच्च नामग्रहणमात्रेणैव तेषां माहात्म्यं प्रकटीक्रियते। ते सन्ति अगुरु-अक्ष-अरविन्द-अर्जुन-अशोक-आम्र-इक्षु-इङ्गुदी-इन्दीवर-उत्पल-एला-कदम्ब-कमल-कदली-कल्पवृक्ष-कीचक-कुटज-कुमुद-कुरबक-कुश-कूटशाल्मलि-केसर-खर्जूरी-चन्दन-तमाल-ताम्बूल-ताल-तिलक-दर्भ-दूर्वा-देवदारु-द्राक्षा-नक्तमाल-नमेरु-नारिकेल-नीवार-पङ्कज-पाटला-पारिजात-पुंनाग-प्लक्ष-पुण्डरीक- पूग-बकुल-भूर्ज-मधूक-मन्दार-मलयवृक्ष-मुस्ता-मृणाल-यव-रक्तपाटला-रम्भा-लवङ्ग-लोध्र-वानीर-वेत्र-वेतस-शमी-शाल-शिरीष-शैलेय-शैवाल-सप्तपर्ण-सरलसहकार- हरिचन्दनप्रभृतयः। एतेषां वृक्षाणां सन्दर्भे पर्यावरणविषयिकी चर्चा यदि क्रियते तर्हिनिर्मीयते एकः पृथग् ग्रन्थः।

सम्पूर्णे रघुवंशे वृक्षाणामुपादेयता अनेकत्र वर्णिता। तेषां पालनं पुत्रवत् करणीयमिति सन्दिष्टं महाकविना—

अमुं पुरः पश्यसि देवदारुं पुत्रीकृतोऽसौ वृषभध्वजेन।
यो हेमकुम्भस्तननिःसृतानां स्कन्दस्य मातुः पयसां रसज्ञः।।[25]

आधारबन्धप्रमुखैः प्रयत्नैः संवर्धितानां सुतनिर्विशेषम्।
कच्चिन्न वाय्वादिरुपप्लवो वः श्रमच्छिदामाश्रमपादपानाम्।।[26]

पयोघटैराश्रमबालवृक्षान् संवर्धयन्ती स्वबलानुरूपैः।
असंशयं प्राक्तनयोपपत्तेः स्तनन्धयप्रीतिमवाप्स्यसि त्वम्।।[27]

प्रकारान्तरेण कालिदाससन्देशोऽयं यदा वृक्षाः पुत्रवत् पालितास्तदा तेऽपि आतपपीडितानामाश्रयप्रदातारः भविष्यन्ति। तेषां छायायां शयानानां निद्रा सुखकरी भविष्यति।[28] एते वृक्षाः स्वमधुरैः फलैरतिथीनां स्वागतमपि विदधति—

छायाविनीताध्वपरिश्रमेषु भूयिष्ठसम्भाव्यफलेष्वमीषु।
तस्यातिथीनामधुना सपर्या स्थिता सुपुत्रेष्विव पादपेषु।।[29]

लताः विटपाश्रिता एव शोभन्ते जीवन्ति च। वृक्षाः यदि कृन्त्यन्ते तर्हि लतानां दशा शोचनीया एव भवति। विषयोऽयं इन्दुमत्याः देहावसाने अजविलापे प्रकर्षेणोद्घाटितः —

अथवा मम भाग्यविप्लवादशनिः कल्पित एष वेधसा।
यदनेन तरुर्न पातितः क्षपिता तद्विटपाश्रिता लता।।[30]

मिथुनं परिकल्पितं त्वया सहकारः फलिनी च नन्विमौ।
अविधाय विवाहसत्क्रियामनयोर्गम्यत इत्यसाम्प्रतम्।।[31]

रघुवंशे कविना अनेके पशवः पक्षिणश्चापि विविधप्रसङ्गेषु वर्णितास्तेषामुपादेयता चाभिव्यञ्जिता। पर्यावरणप्रसङ्गे पशुपक्षिणां चर्चायै पुनः पृथग् ग्रन्थोऽपेक्ष्यते। नन्दिनी- माहात्म्यव्यञ्जकं केवलमेकं पद्यमुद्धृत्य मानवेतरजीवप्रसङ्गोऽत्र समाप्तिं नीयते—

भुवं कोष्णेन कुण्डोध्नी मेध्येनावभृथादपि।
प्रस्नवेनाभिवर्षन्ती वत्सालोकप्रवर्तिना।।[32]

रघुवंशे अनेकेषां शास्त्राणां प्रसङ्गाः उल्लिखिताः कविकुलगुरुणा। तेषु अनेकानि शास्त्राणि यथा धर्मशास्त्रम्, कामशास्त्रम्, सङ्गीतशास्त्रञ्च कविना प्रकर्षरूपेण प्रयुक्तानि स्वाभिप्रायप्रकटनार्थम्। एतानि शास्त्राण्यपि अनेकशः पर्यावरणसम्बद्धानि। केवलं सङ्गीतशास्त्रं यदि गृह्यते तदापि दृश्यते कियद् विलक्षणमासीदस्माकं कवेर्मतिवैभवम्। उदाहरणद्वयमेव केवलं प्रस्तूयेदमुद्घोष्यते यत् रघुवंशे प्रकृतेः विविधतत्त्वानां वर्णनेन सिद्धमिदं यत् तेषां तत्त्वानां जीवने महती उपयोगितास्ति, पर्यावरणदृशा तेषामुपादेयता सततं प्रशस्ता—

मनोऽभिरामाः शृण्वन्तौ रथनेमिस्वनोन्मुखैः।
षड्जसंवादिनीः केका द्विधा भिन्नाः शिखण्डिभिः।।[33]

स कीचकैर्मारुतपूर्णरन्ध्रैः कूजद्भिरापादितवंशकृत्यम्।
शुश्राव कुञ्जेषु यशः स्वमुच्चैरुद्गीयमानं वनदेवताभिः।।[34]

सन्दर्भ-सङ्केताः

1. यजुर्वेदः - 13.27-29
2. रघुवंशम् - 1.29
3. रघुवंशम् - 4.11
4. रघुवंशम् - 5.8
5. रघुवंशम् - 13.4
6. रघुवंशम् - 12.3
7. रघुवंशम् - 10.17
8. रघुवंशम् - 4.86
9. रघुवंशम् - 16.38
10. रघुवंशम् - 11.80
11. रघुवंशम् - 10.48
12. रघुवंशम् - 1.16
13. रघुवंशम् - 10.73

14. रघुवंशम् - 13.35
15. रघुवंशम् - 13.37
16. रघुवंशम् - 1.62
17. रघुवंशम् - 11.24
18. रघुवंशम् - 5.4
19. रघुवंशम् - 2.15
20. रघुवंशम् - 17.2
21. रघुवंशम् - 6.22
22. रघुवंशम् - 16.53
23. रघुवंशम् - 19.39
24. रघुवंशम् - 2.3
25. रघुवंशम् - 2.36
26. रघुवंशम् - 5.6
27. रघुवंशम् - 14.78
28. रघुवंशम् - 12.21
29. रघुवंशम् - 13.46
30. रघुवंशम् - 8.47
31. रघुवंशम् - 8.61
32. रघुवंशम् - 1.84
33. रघुवंशम् - 1.39
34. रघुवंशम् - 2.12

卐 卐 卐

Section XIV

PLANT KINGDOM IN SANSKRIT LITERATURE & ASTROLOGY

संस्कृतसाहित्यज्योतिषनिर्झरी

संस्कृतकाव्येषु वनस्पतिरामणीयकम्

चन्द्रधर बिजल्वाणः

अस्ति तावत् संस्कृतकाव्यानां वनस्पतिसमाश्रितम् अनतिसाधारणं किमपि वैशिष्ट्यमिति नास्त्यविदितं संस्कृतसाहित्यरसास्वादितवतां सहृदहृदयानां विदुषाम्। 'सौन्दर्यमलङ्कारः' इत्येवंवादिन एव न अपितु 'काव्यस्यात्मा ध्वनिः', 'वाक्यं रसात्मकं काव्यम्' तथा 'रमणीयार्थप्रतिपादकः शब्दः काव्यम्'— इत्यादि प्रकारेण काव्यं परिभाषयन्तः काव्यात्मतत्त्वज्ञा आचार्या अपि नास्वीकुर्वन्ति कमलकेतककुरवाकादीनां ताम्बूलवल्लीपरिणद्धपूगादीनाञ्च रसाध्याकत्वं काव्यश्रियोऽङ्ग-प्रत्यङ्गविन्यासविधानकविश्लेषणप्रसङ्गेषु।

ऋग्वेदस्य 'अरण्यानीसूक्तम्' भवतु वाल्मीकिरामायणस्य 'अरण्यकाण्डम्' वा भवतु। महाभारतस्य 'अनुशासनपर्व' अस्तु उपनिषदाम् 'आख्यानानि' वा सन्तु, सर्वत्र दृश्यते पादपैः सह प्राणधारिणां सहावस्थानं पारस्परिकं परिष्वजनं पारस्परिकम् उपजीवित्वञ्च। अतः कथं व्यवसिता स्यात् काऽपि शकुन्तला पादपानां सेचनात् पूर्वं जलपानाय? कथं वा न पाययेत पयः भगवती गौरी पुत्रीकृतम् कमपि देवदारुम्?

नास्ति कश्चन विवादः पादपानां प्राणधारिणां च स्वारस्ये, तथापि प्रावर्तन्त नैकाः जिज्ञासाः पादपप्रकारादि विषयेषु बहोकालात् पूर्वमपि जनमानसेषु, येषां समाधानाय विश्लेषणाय वा प्रयतितं चरक-सुश्रुत-प्रभृतिराचार्यैः आयुर्वेदाधारभूतेषु स्वकीयग्रन्थेषु, उपक्रमितं च प्रशस्तपादसदृशैस्तत्त्वविद्भिः-वैशेषिक दर्शनाख्यायकेषु पदार्थधर्मसंग्रहसदृशेषु, वैशेषिकभाष्येषु।

पादपानां वर्गीकरणम्

1. आकारस्य उद्भवस्य च दृष्टया विभिन्नेषु शास्त्रेषु यथा आयुर्वेदे वैशेषिकदर्शने तथा अमरकोषप्रभृतिषु नैकेषु ग्रन्थेषु पादनां वर्गीकरणं दृश्यते। यद्यथा —

(क) चरक-सुश्रुतानुसारं पादपवर्गाः

(1) वनस्पतयः, (2) वानस्पत्याः, (3) औषधयः, (4) वीरुधः, अथवा

(1) अन्तःसंज्ञाः, (2) असंज्ञाः

(ख) वैशेषिकाणामनुसारं पादपवर्गा

(1) तृणानि, (2) औषधयः, (3) लताः, (4) अवतानाः, (5) वृक्षाः, (6) वनस्पतयः

(ग) अगरकोषानुसारं पादपवर्गाः

(1) वृक्षाः, (2) क्षुपाः, (3) लताः, (4) औषधयः, (5) तृणानि, (6) दुमाः।

2. गतानुगतिकरूपेण प्रचलितावधारणासमाश्रयणप्रवणलोकव्यवहारानुरमपि पादपानां वर्गाः प्रायः पञ्चपल्लवत्वेन पञ्चपुष्पत्वेन वृक्षपञ्चत्वेन च भारतस्य विभिन्नेषु क्षेत्रेषु देवपूजनमाश्रित्य किञ्चित्वैषम्यपूर्वकं प्रथिताः सन्ति, तेषु केषाञ्चन उल्लेखो वर्तते सुप्रसिद्धेषु ग्रन्थेष्वपि केषाञ्चन च तु केवलं जनश्रुतिषु। तद्यथा—

(क) पञ्चदेवतरवः

पञ्चैते देवतरवो मन्दारः पारिजातकः।
सन्तानः कल्पवृक्षश्च पुंसि वा हरिचन्दनम्।।[1]

(ख) पञ्चक्षीरिणो वृक्षाः

न्यग्रोधोदुम्बराश्वत्थपारीषप्लक्षपादपाः ।
पञ्चैते क्षीरिणो वृक्षास्तेषां त्वक् पञ्चवल्कलम् ।।[2]

(ग) पञ्चपल्लवाः

आम्रः, जम्बू, कपित्थः, वटः, बिल्वः।

(घ) पञ्चपुष्पाणि • पुष्पपञ्चकम्

(1) चम्पा, (2) आम्रः, (3) शमी, (4) कमलम्, (5) करवीरः।

(ङ) कामस्य बाणपञ्चकम्

(1) अरविन्दः, (2) अशोकः, (3) आम्रः, (4) नवमल्लिकाः, (5) नीलोत्पलम्।

अन्यैरपि बहुभिः प्रकारैः पादपानां वर्गीकरणं दृश्यते।

पादपोत्पादकानां वनोपवनोद्यानादीनां स्वरूपम्

संस्कृतसाहित्ये समुपवर्णितानां वनोपवनोद्यानादीनां संख्या विस्तृतास्ति। स्वतोद्भवस्य तथा जनसमाजद्वारा उत्पादनस्य दृष्ट्या पादपोद्भवस्थलानामपि नैकधा वर्गीकरणं कर्तुं शक्यते। तद्यथा—

(1) अरण्यानी (वानप्रस्थिनिवासपरकं सुविशालं वनम्)।

(2) वनम् (यथा खाण्डववनम्, कुरुजाङ्गलं कुमारवनम्)।

(3) अरण्यम् (यथा नैमिषारण्यम्, दण्डकारण्यम्)।

(4) नागरोद्यानम् (यथा-पुष्पकरण्डकोद्यानम् (मृच्छकटिके), कुसुमाकरोद्यानम् मदनोद्यानम् (मालतीमाधवे), विलासकाननम् (नैषधीयचरिते))।

(5) तपोवनवाटिका (यथा कण्वाश्रमवाटिका)।

(6) प्रमदवनं गृहोद्यानम् वा—राजमहिषीणां कृते निर्मितम् उद्यानं प्रासादानां नातिदूरे संवर्धितम्।

(7) गृहमध्योद्यानम् अथवा माध्यक उद्देशम्-गृहस्य अभ्यन्तरभागे प्रवर्धिताः केचन पूजोपयोगिनः पादपाः सामूहिकरूपेण माध्यक उद्देश्यमित्त्यभिधीयन्ते स्म।

उपरिनिर्दिष्टानां पादपप्ररोहक्षेत्राणां मध्ये सर्वाधिकरूपेण प्रायः प्रमदवनानि संस्कृत-काव्येषु विशेषतश्च नाटकेषु चर्चितानि सन्ति। कालिदासेन मालविकाग्निमित्रे तथा अभिज्ञानशाकुन्तले प्रमदवनानामुल्लेखः कृतः। प्रमदवनेषु प्रायः चत्वारः खण्डाः भवन्ति स्म।

तत्र वृक्षाः क्षुपाः लताश्च—(1) वृक्षखण्डे, (2) हरितखण्डे, (3) फलखण्डे तथा (4) माल्यखण्डे यथायथं स्वीयस्वीयवर्गेषु समारोप्यन्ते स्म। प्रमदवनानामाभ्यन्तरभागेषु दारुनिर्मिताः कृत्रिमाः पर्वताः लतागृहाणि च निर्मीयन्ते स्म। वृक्षपालीनामपि उल्लेखा उपलभ्यन्ते, यथा सागरिकया सह सम्पर्कं साधयितुम् उदयनः क्रमशः एकैकां वृक्षवीथिम् अनुसृत्यैव गच्छति इति सङ्केतयति रत्नवल्यां नाटककारः हर्षः—

पालीयं चम्पकानां नियतमयमसौ सुन्दरः सिन्दुवारः।
सान्द्रा वीथी तथेयं बकुलविटपिनां पाटला पंक्तिरेषा।।[3]

संस्कृतसाहित्ये चर्चिताः प्रमुखाः वनस्पतयः

आदिकविः महर्षिः वाल्मीकिः न केवलं लौकिकसंस्कृतसाहित्यस्य प्रवर्तकः अपितु लौकिकभारतीयपादपानां प्रथमः निर्देष्टा परिज्ञाता तथा परिगणयिता अपि आसीदिति सुस्पष्टं भवति रामायणस्य अवलोकनात्। वाल्मीकिना गोदावरीतटवर्तिनः पम्पासरसमीपस्था ऋष्यमूकपर्वतस्थाः तथा प्रश्रवणगिरिवर्तिनो ये वनस्पतयः परिगणिताः तथा कालिदास-भारवि-माघ-श्रीहर्षः प्रभृतिभिः काव्यकृद्भिः भास-भवभूति प्रभृतिभिः नाटककारै अन्यैश्च संस्कृतकाव्यकारैः ये पादपाः समुल्लिखिताः समुपवर्णिताश्च तेषां नामकीर्तनमपि अस्माकं श्रेयसे स्यादिति कृत्वा तेषां परिगणनमात्रमप्यत्रौचित्याय न स्यात् इति निर्दिशामि तान् अधोलिखितरूपेण —

अगुरुः कर्पू. 1.14; अपराजिता-अभि.; अर्क (मन्दारः)-अभि. 2.8; अर्जुनः (धवलः) ऋतु. 2.2; अश्वत्थः-गीता, आमलकी (धात्री तिष्यफला)-नैष. 1.98; आम्रः (रसालः सहकारः माकन्दः)-पूर्वमेघः 18. कु.सं. 1.27; इङ्गुदी-अभि. 1.14; इक्षुः-रघु. 4.20; उदुम्बरः (गूलर)-पूर्वमेघः 46; उशीरः (खस)-अभि. 3.6; एला (स्थूला-बड़ी इलायची, सूक्ष्मा-छोटी इलायची इति)-रघु.-ऐरण्ड-अनेकत्र; कदम्बः हनुमन्नाटकं, मा.मा. 9.16; कदली-अनेकत्र; कपित्थः-हनू., कमलम्-अनेकत्र; कुमुदम्-अनेकत्र; करवीरः (शातकुम्भः, कनेर; कशेशयः) अभि. 4.11; कर्णिकारः-कुमा. 3.28; काञ्चनारः (कचनार)-अनेकत्र; कापासी (तुण्डकेशी, कर्पासः)-वा.रा., (कुङ्कुमम्)-मृच्छ., रत्ना; कुन्दः (मोगरा)-अभि. 5.19; कुटजः (कालिङ्ग) मा.मा. हनू.; कुरबकः-उत्तरमेघः 2; कूष्माण्डः (कूष्माण्डी, कुम्हडा)-मृच्छ. 1.51; केतकी (केवड़ा)-पूर्वमेघः 25; कोविदारः उ.रा. 5.1; इक्ष्वाकुवंशीयानां राज्ञां ध्वजचिह्नम्-कोविदारकेतुः); कुमुष्कः (पूगः घौरण्ट)-मा.मा. 6.19; खदिरः (कत्था)-वा.रा. 1054; खर्जूरः-अभि; गुग्गुलुः-हनू. 14.87; चन्दनम् (अनेकत्र); हरिचन्दनम् कु.सं. 5-69; चम्पकम्-नैष. 1.91; जपा (जवाकुसुमम्)-पूर्वमेघः 40; जम्बीरः (नीबू)-हनू.; जम्बू-पूर्वमेघः 24; जातिः (जाती, चमेली)-मृच्छ. जीरकः (जीरा)-मृच्छ. 8.13; तमालः (तापिच्छः)-मृच्छ. 5.20; तालः (ताड़, ताड़ी, लेख्यपत्रम्-पूर्वमेघः 35; ताम्बूलः-रघु. 6.64; नैष.; तितिण्डी (चिञ्चा. इमली)-अभि., तिलकः (पुष्पकः)-कु.सं. 6.30; त्रपुषम् (खीरा)-दाडिमः (दाडिमी, दन्तबीजः करकः, अनार)-नैष. 1.83; देवदारुः (सुरभूरुहः)-रघु. 2.36; द्रुघणः (शीशम)-वा.रा. 7-99; नवमालिका (नेवारी)-रत्ना. अभि.; नागकेसरः-नैष. 9.92; नारङ्ग-वा.रा. 2.50; नारिकेलः-अनेकत्र; निचुलः-पूर्वमेघः 14; नीवारः (तृणान्नं वनधान्यम्)-अनेकत्रः निम्बः (पिचुमर्दः, निक्तकः, अरिष्टः,)-अनेकत्र, पनसः कण्टकिफलम् (कटहल)-मृच्छ. 8.8; (पलाण्डुः मुखदूषकः)-अनर्घ. 2.2; पलाशः (किंशुकः ब्रह्मवृक्षः ढाक)-माघः पाटला (पाटलिःमोधा)-नैष. 1.65; बकुलः (मधुगन्धः सिंहकेसरकः मौलसिरी)-बदरी (ककन्धू बेर)-अनेकत्र; बन्धूकः (दोपहरिया), बिल्वः (मालूरफलम्, बेल)-हनू.; भूर्ज (भूर्जपत्राग्); मधूकः (महुआ) उ.भं. 1.11; माधवी (पुण्ड्रकम्)-अभि. 3.7; मालती-मा.मा.; मुस्ता (नागरमोथा)-अभि. 2.6; यवः (शितशूकः)-कु.सं. 7.17; लवङ्ग (देवकुसुमम्, लौंग) हनू; लशुनः (उग्रगन्धः)-मा.माः लोध्रः-उ. मेघ.-2; वञ्जुल-उ.रा. 2.23; वटः-रघु. 11.53; वानीरः (वेतस्)-पूर्वमेघ. 45; शमी-अभि. 1.18; शाल्मलिः-हनु,. शिरीषम्-अभि. 6.18; शेफालिका (हरसिंगार) विदुशा, 2.16; हरिद्रा-कर्पू. 3.1; हरीतकी-हनूमन्नाटकम् अत्रपरिगणिताः।

वनस्पतीनां जीवधारित्वम् अन्तःसंज्ञावत्त्वञ्च

पादपा जीवधारिणस्तथा अन्तः संज्ञावन्तो भवन्तीति विषये समुपलभ्यन्ते नैके समुल्लेखा विभिन्नेषु ग्रन्थेषु। किरणावल्याम् उदयनाचार्यः पृथ्वीनिरूपणप्रसंगे पादपानां जीवधारित्वं निश्चिनोति तद्यथा —

(क) वृक्षादयः प्रतिनियतभोक्त्र्यधिष्ठिताः
जीवनमरणस्वप्नजागरणरोगभेषज-
प्रयोगबोधसजातीयानुबन्धानुकूलोपगम-
प्रतिकूलोपगमादिभ्यः प्रसिद्धशरीरवत्।

(ख) आचार्योदयनस्य 'अतिमन्दान्तः संज्ञितया'-इत्येतत् कथनम् इदं मतं पोषयति यत् —

अन्तः संज्ञा भवन्त्येते सुखदुःखसमन्विताः।

न्यायबिन्दुटीकाकारो धर्मोत्तर एवं कथयति यत् रात्रौ पत्रसङ्कोचः पादपानां स्वापं सङ्केतयति-'स्वापः रात्रौ पत्रसङ्कोचः' षड्दर्शनसमुच्चयस्य भाष्यकारो गुणरत्नः पादपेषु बाल्य-यौवन-वृद्धि-क्षयादीनां समुल्लेखं कुर्वन् कथयति-

विशिष्टं दौहृदादिमत्त्वं विशिष्टस्त्रीशरीवत्
यथा स्त्रोशरीरस्य तथाविधदौहृदपूरणात्।
पुत्रादिप्रसवनं तथा वनस्पतिशरीरस्यापि
तत्पूरणात् पुष्पफलादिप्रसवनम्।।

महाभारतस्य शान्तिपर्वणि तु पादपानां न केवलं संज्ञावत्त्वं सजीवत्त्वं वा अपितु तेषां पञ्चेन्द्रियवत्त्वमपि सम्यग् रूपेण सन्दर्भितमस्ति। तद्यथा—

ऊष्मतो म्लायते पर्णं त्वक् फलं पुष्पमेव च।
म्लायते शीर्यते चापि स्पर्शस्तेनात्र विद्यते।।
वाटवग्न्यशनि निर्घोषैः फलं पुष्पं विशीर्यते।
श्रोत्रेण गृह्यते शब्दस्तस्मात् शृण्वन्ति पादपाः।।
वल्ली वेष्ट्यते वृक्षं सर्वतश्चैव गच्छति।
नह्यद्रष्टुश्च मार्गोऽस्ति तस्मात्पश्यन्ति पादपाः।।
पुण्यापुण्यैस्तथा गन्धैर्धूपैश्च विविधैरपि।
अरोगाः पुष्पिताः सन्ति तस्मात् जिघ्रन्ति पादपाः।।
पदैः सलिलपानाच्च व्याधीनाञ्चापि दर्शनात्।
व्याधिप्रति क्रियत्वाच्च विद्यते रसनं द्रुमे।।
वक्त्रेणोत्पलनालेन यथोर्द्ध जलमाददेत्।
तथा पवनसंयुक्तः पादैः पिबति पादपः।।
सुखदुःखयोश्च ग्रहणात् छिन्नस्य च विरोहणात्।
जीवं पश्यामि वृक्षाणाम् अचैतन्यं न विद्यते।।[4]

पादपानां जीवधारित्वं संज्ञावत्त्वञ्च उदनया दृष्ट्यापि संसिध्यति यत् ते धर्मशास्त्रानुसारं न केवलं प्रियकारिणः अपितु परिस्थित्यनुरूपं जनानाम् अनिष्टमपि कर्तुं क्षमन्ते। अत एव वनस्पतीनां वेधाधायकत्वमपि नैकेषु धर्मशास्त्रीयग्रन्थेषु निरूपितं दृश्यते। गढ़वालक्षेत्रे लब्धजनिः नौटियालोपाह्वः हरिदत्त शर्मा स्वीये धर्मवल्लीग्रन्थे स्पष्टमुद्घोषयति यत् गृहाणि समीपस्थवनस्पतीनां कोणास्थितिं विचार्य निर्मेयानि, अन्यथा वृक्षाणां दुष्प्रभावो भवनेषु आपतति। तद्यथा —

(क) अश्वत्थ प्लक्ष भूर्यघ्रि कनक पयसः प्राप्त उक्ता निषिद्धा।
छाया गेहोपरिष्टाद्यदि पतति तरोः कस्यचिद् वा तदासत्।।

(ख) चारुण्यां कूपवृक्षौ द्रुशमथ दुरगोलूखले शाल्मली च।
दण्डं सौम्यं मखाङ्गः शिवदिशि कदली रक्तपुष्पं न शस्तम्।।

(ग) पूर्वस्यां क्रोशतोश्वत्थ विटपि कदली मन्दिरौच्यं न शस्तम्।
सार्धं क्रोशं तु याम्या मलघुगृहदूषच्चम्पकं प्लक्ष जम्बू।
जाती खर्जूर दाडिम्य सदगमटस्तोरणारिष्ट पूराः।।

हरिदत्तशर्मणावेधानां परिहारोऽपि संकेतितोऽस्ति धर्मवल्याम्। तद्यथा—वेधोऽयं राजधान्यां मनुजपतिपथेऽप्यन्तरा नैवचिन्त्यः।[5]

प्रमुखसंस्कृतकाव्येषु निरूपितं पादपान्तस्तत्त्वम्

रामायणमहाभारतप्रभृति-इतिहासपुराणानाम् अतिरिक्तं संस्कृतस्य सुविशालं वाङ्मयं वर्तते। गौतमबुद्धस्य जन्मकालादारभ्य अद्यावधि यानि ऐतिहासिकानि तथ्यानि व्यावहारिकरूपेण वैज्ञानिकपद्धत्या च परीक्षणीयानि सन्ति तानि अनुसृत्य स्थूलतया संस्कृतकाव्यस्य त्रयः प्रमुखाः काला निर्धारयितुं शक्यन्ते तद्यथा (1) प्राचीनकालः (600 पूर्वख्रिष्टीय शती पर्यन्तम्), मध्यकालः (13 ख्रिष्टीय शतीतः 16 ख्रिष्टीय शती पर्यन्तम्) तथा अर्वाचीनकालः (20 ख्रिष्टीय शतीतः अद्यपर्यन्तम्) एतेषु सर्वेषु कालेषु संस्कृते नैकानि काव्यानि नाटकानि च विरचितानि बहुभिः सुविख्यातैः कविभिः। पूर्वोल्लिखितायाः सूच्याः माध्यमेन एतदवधारयितुं शक्यते यत् पादपैः सह काव्यस्य अविनाभावत्वं वर्तते। एवं प्रकारेण यद्यपि अस्मिन् सन्दर्भे सर्वाणि काव्यानि अवधेयानि सन्ति तथापि स्थानाभाववशात् अत्र कालिदास-भारवि-माघ-श्रीहर्ष द्वारा निर्मितानि काव्यान्याश्रित्यैव एतेषां प्रमुखकवीनां पादपतत्त्वविषयिण्य काश्चन धारणाः स्थालीपुलाकवत् अत्र सन्दर्भ्यन्ते—

(1) कालिदासनिर्दिष्टं पादपान्तस्तत्त्वम्

कालिदासः स्वीये-ऋतुसंहारे, मेघदूते, रघुवंशे च प्रायः समस्तभारतीय-पादपानाम् अवस्थितिम् आकारप्रकारं तथा सौष्ठवमेव न अपितु तेषु अन्तर्निहितं सत्यं शिवं सुन्दरमपि निरूपयति, अतएव कविगणनाप्रसंगेषु पादपतत्त्वानुभूतेः दृष्ट्यापि कालिदासस्य कनिष्ठिकाधिष्ठितत्वं सिध्यति। कालिदासः कथयति यत् पादपेषु मानवीयता, शिवत्वं तथा अर्थत्वमपि भवति, अन्यैरनेकैः सद्गुणैः सह। उदाहरणतया —

(क) पादपा मानववद् व्यवहरन्ति, मानववच्च ते सम्भावनीयाः भवन्ति सहृदगैर्जनैः अर्थात् पादपेषु देवत्वाधिष्ठिता मानवता वर्तते। तद्यथा —

अमुं पुरः पश्यसि देवदारुं पुत्रीकृतोऽसौ वृषभध्वजेन।
यो हेमकुम्भस्तननिःसृतानां स्कन्दस्य मातुः पयसां रसज्ञः।।[6]

(ख) पादपानां सौन्दर्यं सर्वदैव शिवमनुसरति तद्यथा—

त्वया पुरस्तादुपयाचितो यः सो ऽयं वटः श्याम इति प्रतीतः।
राशिर्मणीनामिव गारुडानां सपद्मरागः फलितो विभाति।।[7]

(ग) विवाहसदृशाणि पवित्रबन्धनान्यपि नैकेष्ववसरेषु समीहितपादपपौष्कल्यानुसारणि भवन्ति। प्रकारान्तरेण जीवनमर्थमूलकम् अस्ति। तत्र च पादपानां महती भूमिका वर्तते अर्थात् पादपाः अर्थव्यवस्थायाः स्रोतस्वरूपाः सन्तीति निदर्शयति कविकुलगुरुः सुनन्दाया वचनेषु —

ताम्बूलवल्ली परिणद्धपूगास्वेलालतालिङ्गितचन्दनासु।
तमालपत्रास्तरणासु रन्तुं प्रसीद शाश्वन्मलयस्थलीषु।।[8]

(घ) प्रमदाजनेन शरीरशोभार्थ संधार्यमाणानि विविधानि पुष्पाणि सौन्दर्यवर्धकानि भवन्ति, इति तु सर्वैरेव कविभिर्निर्दिष्टम् किन्तु कालिदासेन शरीरावयवानामनुरूपं पादपसत्यस्य मानवीयसौन्दर्येण सह तथा मानवीयसत्यस्य

पादपीयसौन्दर्येण सह पारस्परिकः समन्वयः कृतः। तद्यथा—

हस्ते लीला कमलमलके बालकुन्दानुविद्धम्
नीता लोध्रप्रसवरजसा पाण्डुतामानने श्रीः।
चूडापाशे नवकुरवकं चारुकर्णे शिरीषम्
सीमन्ते च त्वदुपगमजं यत्र नीपं वधूनाम्।।[9]

प्रकारान्तरेण कालिदासस्यैतत् कथनं सौन्दर्यस्य पादपोत्पादितप्रसाधनेषु प्रयोगौचित्यं वर्तितव्यम् इति संदिशति। एतादृशीमेव भावनां परिपोषयति ऋतुसंहारस्यैतत् पद्यमपि —

कर्णे सुयोग्यं नवकर्णिकारं चलेषु नीलेष्वलकेष्वशोकम्।
पुष्पं च फुल्लं नवमल्लिकायाः प्रयान्ति कान्तिं प्रमदाजनानाम्।।[10]

(ङ) प्रकृतेः रमणीयत्वे पादपानां च सश्रीकत्वे-अस्ति तावत् महान् अनुबन्धः कालिदासस्य। तथापि पूर्णत्वं तु केवलम् ईश्वरे एव भवति, अतः यथा प्राणिषु नैके संसारसुलभाः दोषाः भवन्ति, तथैव सन्ति अनेके दोषाः पादपेष्वपि। प्रकारान्तरेण एतद् वक्तुं शक्यते यत् कालिदासेन एतदपि निर्दिष्टं यत् पादपेष्वपि अपूर्णता विद्यते।

वर्णप्रकर्षे सति कर्णिकारं दुनोति निर्गन्धतया स्म चेतः।
प्रायेण सामग्र्यविधौ गुणानां पराङ्मुखी विश्वसृजः प्रवृत्तिः।।

अत्र कर्णिकारस्य माध्यमेन कालिदासः संसारस्य अपूर्णतायाः तथा एकस्यैव केवलस्य ईश्वरस्य पूर्णत्वं प्रतिपादयति।

(2) भारविनिर्दिष्टं पादपान्तस्तत्त्वम्

भारविः स्वीये 'किरातार्जुनीयम्' इत्याख्ये महाकाव्ये व्यासस्य निर्देशानुसारं तपसा भगवन्तं भूतभावनं शङ्करं प्रीणयित्वा पाशुपतास्त्रमधिगन्तुं द्वैतवनात् हिमालयस्थ इन्द्रकीलपर्वतं यियासोरर्जुनस्य यात्रामार्गमनुसृत्य तत्प्रसङ्गेन हिमालयीयपादपान् अनुवर्णयन् तेषाम् अनितरसाधारणं वैशिष्ट्यं प्रति समादरम् औत्सुक्यञ्च सामाजिकानां हृदयेषु समुत्पादयति। भारवेः पादपवर्णने सन्ति नैकानि वैशिष्ट्यानि तथापि विस्तरभयात् तेष्वत्र केवलं द्वित्रिणामेव समुल्लेखः क्रियते।

(क) हिमालये नैका औषधयः दीपवत् प्रकाशं विकिरन्ति अतः हिमालयस्य नैकेषु पादपेषु दीप्तिमत्त्वम् वर्तते। तद्यथा विवृणोति भारविरस्मिन् पद्ये —

श्रीमल्लता भवनमौषधयः प्रदीपाः शय्या नवानि हरिचन्दनपल्लवानि।
अस्मिन्रतिश्रमनुदश्च सरोजवाताः स्मर्तुं दिशन्ति न दिवः सुरसुन्दरीभ्यः।[12]

(ख) भारविना नैकेषां हिमालयीयपादपानामेतद् वैशिष्ट्यमपि समुद्घाटितं यत् तेषां पत्राणि परिणतानि न भवन्ति। तद्यथा —

रम्या नवद्युतिमपैति न शाद्वलेभ्यः श्याभी भवन्त्यनुदिनं नलिनी वनानि।
अस्मिन् विचित्र कुसुमस्तवकाचितानां शाखाभृतं परिणमन्ति न पल्लवानि।।[13]

(ग) भवभूतिः हिमालयीयपादपानां परागस्य कनकमयातपत्रलक्ष्मीत्वं परिभाव्य पर्यावरणपरिशोधत्वमपि सङ्केतयति। तद्यथा —

उत्फुल्लस्थलनलिनी वनादमुष्मादुद्धूतः सरसिजसम्भवः परागः।
वात्याभिर्वियति निवर्तितः समन्तादाधत्ते कनकमयातपत्रलक्ष्मीम्।।[14]

(3) माघनिर्दिष्टं पादपान्तस्तत्त्वम्

महाकविर्माघः शिशुपालवधमहाकाव्यस्य षष्ठे सर्गे ऋतुवर्णनप्रसङ्गेन रैवतकगिरौ समुपलभ्यमानानां वनस्पतीनां हृदयहारि चित्रणं करोति। सेनानिवेशानन्तरं रेवतके गिरौ रिरंसुं हरिं निषेवितुं सर्वोऽपि ऋतुगणः युगपदेव स्व-स्वनियतवनस्पतीनां सश्रीकतायाः माध्यमेन तत्र समुपास्थोऽभूत्। तदवसरे माघेन पादपानामन्तस्तत्त्वमित्थं समुद्घाटितम् —

(क) वृक्षाः जीवधारिण इव नर्तितुं क्षमाः। तद्यथा —

विगतरागगुणोऽपि जनो न कश्चलनिवाति पयोद्नभस्वति।
अभिहितेऽलिभिरेवमिवोच्चकैरननृते ननृते नवपल्लवैः।।[15]

अस्यायमाशयो यत् वृक्षेषु नृत्यक्षमता वर्तत इति।

(ख) 'वृक्षेषु पुंस्त्वं भवति न वा?—अस्य प्रश्नस्य सङ्केतः माघेन कृतः। अस्योत्तरमपि तेन निषेधात्मकरूपेण निदर्शितम्। तद्यथा —

समभिसृत्य रसादवलम्बितः प्रमदया कुसुमावचिकीर्षया।
अविनमन्न रराज वृथोच्चकैरनृतया नृतया वनपादपः।।[16]

यद्यपि कविसमयप्रसिद्धिः पादपानां पुंस्त्वं वर्तते, तथापि सम्भवतः माघस्य एष भाव अस्ति यत् कविसमयप्रसिद्धिरविश्वसनीया वर्तते। यतः अङ्गनानां पादाघातादिभिः सम्प्रति अशोकेषु विकासो न दृश्यते अपरञ्च माघेनात्र वनपादपस्य उल्लेख कृतः न तु विलासकाननीयस्य कस्यचन पादपस्य।

(ग) पादपानां स्पृहणीयता प्राणिनां स्वभावानुसारं भिद्यते उदाहरणतया क्रमेलकः निम्बपत्राणि प्रेम्णा भक्षयति। किन्तु निम्बपत्रेषु यदि अकस्मात् किञ्चित् आम्रपत्रं मिश्रितं स्यात् तर्हि ग्रासमेव निर्गिरति। तद्यथा —

सार्धं कथञ्चिदुचितैः पिचुमर्दपत्रैरास्यान्तरालमाम्रदलं मदीयः।
दासेरकः सपदि संवलितं निषादै विप्रं पुरा पतकरादिव निर्जगार।।[17]

(4) श्रीहर्षनिर्दिष्टं पादपान्तस्तत्त्वम्

श्रीहर्षः स्वीये नैषधीयचरिते नलदमयन्त्योः प्रणयगाथायाः अङ्गत्वेन, तत्रापि प्रमुखतः नलस्य विरहपीडापनयन प्रसङ्गेन, केतक-दाडिम-पलाश-लता-चम्पक-रथल पद्मिनी-रसाल-चाम्पेय-नागकेसर-मालूरफल-पाटला-अगस्त्यवृक्ष-अशोक-प्रभृति पादपानाम् उल्लेखं करोति। नैषधीयचरितस्य प्रथमे सर्गे भैमी रूपगुण श्रवणोद्भूताभिलाषजन्य-वेदनामपनेतुमेव नलो विलासकानने गच्छति। अतः अत्र नलेन ये पादपाः दृष्टाः तेषु तदानीं विरहावस्थानुरूपं तैक्ष्ण्यं तेनानुभूतम्। एतदेव कारणं यत् येषु पादपेषु कालिदासः प्रायः सौम्यं पश्यति, तेष्वपि प्रायः श्रीहर्षेण तैक्ष्ण्यं निर्दिष्टम्। तद्यथा —

अशोकमर्थान्वितनामताशयागतान् शरण्यं गृहशोचिनोऽध्वगान्।
अमन्यतावन्तमिवैष पल्लवैः प्रतीष्टकामज्वलदस्त्र जालकम्।।[18]

पादपवर्णने हास्यरसस्यानुविधानं कुर्वन् श्रीहर्षः पादपानां तपः शीलत्वमपि सङ्केतयति। तद्यथा —

विदभ्रसुभ्रूस्तनतुङ्गताप्तये घटानिवापश्यदलं तपस्यतः।
फलानि धूमस्य धयानधोमुखान् स दाडिमे दोहदधूपिनि द्रुमे।।[19]

उच्चपदस्य प्राप्त्यर्थं किं किं न करणीयं भवतीत्यपि संदिशत्यत्र श्रीहर्षः। केषाञ्चन पुष्पाणां (वृक्षाणां) देवपूजनामर्हत्वमपि श्रीहर्षेण सङ्केतितम्। तद्यथा–

विनिद्रपत्रालिगतालिकैतवात् मृगाङ्कचूडामणिवर्जनार्जितम्।
दधानमाशासु चरिष्णु दुर्यशः स कौतुकी तत्र ददर्श केतकम्।।[20]

वियोगभाजां हृदि कण्टकैः कटुर्निधीयसे कर्णिशरः स्मरेण यत्।
ततो दुराकर्षतया तदन्तकृत् विगीयसे मन्मथदेहदाहिना।।[21]

वनस्पतीनां पर्यावरणसंशुद्धिपरकं जगत्संरक्षणपरकञ्च महत्त्वम्

संस्कृतकाव्येषु वनस्पतयः सत्यस्य शिवस्य तथा सुन्दरस्य दृश्यमाणाः मूर्तयः निरूपिताः प्रायः सर्वैरेव कविभिः। पादपानां ब्रह्मत्वम् आत्मरूपत्वं देवत्वं दायादत्वं जगत्संरक्षकत्वञ्चसम्यक् स्फुटीभवति संस्कृतकाव्येषु। ध्यातव्यानि सन्त्यस्मिन् सन्दर्भे कानिचन शाश्वतसत्यसमानि अधोनिर्दिष्टानि कथनानि –

(क) पादपानां ब्रह्मरूपत्वम् आत्मरूपत्वं देवरूपत्वञ्च –

ऊर्ध्वमूलमधः शाखमश्वत्थं प्राहुरव्ययम्।
छन्दांसि यस्य पर्णानि यस्तं वेद स वेदवित्।।[22]

(ख) पादापानां पर्यावरणसंशोधकत्वं सुखदायकत्वञ्च –

धत्ते भरं कुसुमपत्रफलावलीनां घर्मव्यथां वहति शीतभवा रुजश्च।
यो देहमर्पयति चान्यसुखस्यहेतोस्तस्मै वदान्यगुरवे तरवे नमोऽस्तु।।[23]

(ग) वृक्षारोपणस्यामुष्मिकसुखदायकत्वम् –

अश्वत्थमेकं पिचुमर्दमेकं न्यग्रोधमेकं दशचिञ्चिणीकम्।
कपित्थबिल्वामलकं त्रयञ्च पञ्चाम्रवापी नरकं न गच्छेत्।।[24]

(घ) वृक्षारोपणस्यैहिकसुखसमृद्धिदायकत्वम् –

ऊँ आदित्यवर्णे तपसोऽधिजातो वनस्पतिस्तव वृक्षोऽथ बिल्वः।
तस्य फलानि तपसा नुदन्तु याः अन्तराः याश्च बाह्याः अलक्ष्मीः।।[25]

(ङ) वृक्षाणां दायादवत्त्वम् वृक्षारोपणस्य पुण्यजनकत्वञ्च –

(i) दशकूपसमा वापी दशवापीसमो ह्रदः।
दश ह्रदसमः पुत्रो दशपुत्रसमो द्रुमः।।[26]

(ii) मानवं पुत्रवद् वृक्षास्तारयन्ति परत्र च।
पुत्रवत्परिपाल्यास्ते पुत्रास्ते धर्मतः स्मृताः।।[27]

एवं प्रकारेण संस्कृतकाव्येषु वनस्पतीनां यन्निरूपणं वर्तते, तदद्यापि अवधेयमस्ति।

सन्दर्भ-सङ्केताः

1. अमरकोषः - 1.1.50
2. अमरकोषः
3. रत्नावली - 3. 8
4. महाभारतम् - शान्तिपर्व
5. धर्मवल्ली - पृ० 134
6. रघुवंशम् - 2.
7. रघुवंशम् - 13.53
8. रघुवंशम् - 6.64
9. मेघदूतम् - 2.2
10. ऋतुसंहारम् - 6.6
11. कुमारसम्भवम् - 3.28
12. किरातार्जुनीयम् - 5.28
13. किरातार्जुनीयम् - 5.37
14. किरातार्जुनीयम् - 5.39
15. शिशुपालवधम् - 6.36
16. शिशुपालवधम् - 6.10
17. शिशुपालवधम् - 5.66
18. नैषधीयचरितम् - 1-101
19. नैषधीयचरितम् - 1.82
20. नैषधीयचरितम् - 1.78
21. नैषधीयचरितम् - 1.79
22. श्रीमद्भगवद्गीता
23. भामिनीविलासः
24. भविष्यपुराणम
25. श्रीसूक्तम् - 6
26. मत्स्यपुराणम्
27. महाभारतम् - अनुशासनपर्व 5. 8.30

卐 卐 卐

संस्कृतसाहित्ये निसर्गसुषमा

मंजु रावल

प्रकृतिः मानवस्य चिरन्तनी सहचरी, अथ च तस्य स्वस्थाय, सरसाय, सफलाय, लौकिकाय आध्यात्मिकाय च जीवनाय अपरिहार्या अस्ति भविष्यति च।

संस्कृतसाहित्यस्य विभिन्नासु कृतिषु समुपलब्धेन प्रकृतिवर्णनेन एतत् स्पष्टतम् अस्ति, यत् कवीनां हृदयेषु प्रकृतिम् प्रति अगाधः प्रेमः आसीत्। ते प्रकृतिसौन्दर्यस्य अन्वेषणम् अकुर्वन्। पदे-पदे प्रकृतिच्छटायाः दर्शनम् भवति। प्रकृतेः सुन्दरात् सुन्दरतराणि अनेकानि चित्राणि वर्तन्ते यानि कवीनां प्रकृतिं प्रति आकर्षणम् तच्चित्रणकौशलम् प्रकटयन्ति। प्राकृतिकदृश्यानाम् संश्लिष्टे, सजीवे, स्वाभाविके च रूपे चित्रणेन तेषाम् स्वरूपस्य अनुभूत्यै तत्सदृशानाम् अप्रस्तुतानाम् मौलिकरूपेण विधानम् कृत्वा तेषाम् चित्रणम् अधिकतरम् सरसम् सुन्दरम् च सम्पादितम्।

वेदे प्रकृतेः चित्रणं आह्लादकारि अस्ति[1]। उषःसूक्ते उषसो वर्णने सुन्दरी युवतिः स्ववस्त्राणीय स्वीयं सौन्दर्यं विस्तारयति[2]। उषा पतिदर्शनं गन्तुम् उद्यता-प्रेमिकामिव वर्णिता[3]। उपनिषत्सु अपि प्रकृत्या गम्भीरं ब्रह्मज्ञानं प्रतिपाद्यते।[4] पुराणेषु प्रकृतौ आधारिताः श्लोकाः दार्शनिकभावोपेताः सन्ति।[5]

आदिकाव्ये रामायणेऽपि प्रकृतिचित्राणि विकीर्णानि वर्तन्ते।[6] स्फुरन्ती विद्युत् रावणस्याङ्के स्फुरन्ती सीतेरिव प्रतिभाति।[7] एकस्मिन् स्थाने चन्द्रोदयवर्णनं भव्यम् अस्ति।[8] कवये सरसि सुप्तः हंसः चन्द्रतुल्यः प्रतीयते।[9] अहो कीदृशं प्रकृतिप्रेम संस्कृतकवीनां हृदयेषु। प्रकृतेः अङ्के एव दर्शनसारसंग्रहम् शिक्षयति गीता।[10]

एवं महाकाव्येषु अपि प्रकृतिः अनेकेषु रूपेषु वर्णिता। कविकुलशिरोमणिः कालिदासः 'प्रकृतेः कविः' कथ्यते। रघुवंशमहाकाव्ये इन्दुमतिः दीपशिखा इव वर्णिता।[11] कियती यथार्था, ललिता च उपमा अस्ति। अत्र एकस्मिन् चित्रे बाललताः पुष्पवर्षणम् कुर्वत्यः दृश्यन्ते।[12] अन्यत्र श्यामलानाम् वनानाम् अतीव स्वाभाविकम् चित्रणम् कृतम् वर्तते।[13]

रघुवंशस्य त्रयोदशः सर्गस्तु भव्यैः प्राकृतिकचित्रैः परिपूर्णः वर्तते। श्रीरामेण दृश्यानाम् वर्णनेन एका चित्रावली उपस्थिता भवति। यमुनातरङ्गैः संसृष्टा गङ्गा विभिन्नरूपेषु दृष्टा अस्ति।[14] श्रीरामः सरयू-नदीं 'माता' इति सम्बोधयन् भावविभोरः भवति। इदम् प्रकृतेः मानवीकरणस्य, तया सह तादात्म्यस्य अनुपमं निदर्शनम् अस्ति।[15] समुद्रः तत्पत्न्यः सरिताश्च प्रेमाविह्वलतया परस्परम् अधरदाने व्यापृताः भवन्त्यः अस्मान् अपि विह्वलाः कारयन्ति।[16]

अपि च सन्ध्याकाले सूर्यास्तवर्णनं तु अति मनोरमं वर्तते।[17] कुमारसम्भवस्य वसन्तवर्णनम् अपि प्रकृतिचित्रणस्य सुन्दरम् निदर्शनम् अस्ति। वसन्तागमने प्रकृतौ अपूर्वः उल्लासः आसीत्। प्रकृतौ ऋतुराजस्य मादकता व्याप्ता आसीत्। वृक्षपुरुषाः लतावधुभिः शाखाभुजाभिः आलिङ्गम् प्राप्तवन्तः।[18] चन्द्रः स्वप्रियां रजनीम् चुम्बति।[19]

बुद्धचरिते अश्वघोषेन प्रकृतेः स्वाभाविकं स्वरूपं प्रस्तुतं कृतम्। गौतमबुद्धस्य जन्मसमये प्रकृतिः आह्लादिता आसीत्।[20] 'किरातार्जुनीयम्' इति महाकाव्ये महाकविः भारविः अपि प्रकृतेः सुषमां अवर्णयत्। सुवर्णछत्रस्य काल्पनिकं रूपं, रमणीयं श्लाघनीयं चास्ति।[21] अनेन भारविः 'आतपत्रभारविः' इति नाम्ना प्रसिद्धः अभवत्। वसन्तवर्णने भारविः

सिद्धस्तः दृश्यते।[22] शरदः नैसर्गिकम् वर्णनम्[23] एवं जलक्रीडायाः सुन्दरं[24] वर्णनम् दर्शनीयम्। कीदृशं संश्लिष्टम् अथ च अलङ्कृतम् प्रकृतिचित्रणम्!

माघेऽपि अपूर्वम् प्रकृतिचित्रणकौशलम् अस्ति। रैवतकपर्वतस्य चित्रस्य रूपे एकं सुन्दरं वस्तुचित्रं प्रकृतिचित्रं द्रष्टव्यमस्ति।[25]

वसन्तस्य वैभवं दर्शनीयम् अस्ति यमकालङ्कारेण।[26] कविना रात्रिः माता, प्रातःकालीनसन्ध्या च पुत्रीरूपेण कथिता या मातरमनुगच्छति।[27] नारदश्रीकृष्णयोः सितासिते कान्ती तथैवारोचयतां यथा रात्रौ पत्रान्तरगोचराः सुधांशोर्मरीचयः।[28] सङ्गीतात्मकं प्राकृतिकं वर्णनं पदे-पदे प्राप्यते।[29] कृष्णं दिदृक्षमाणायाः रमण्याः वदनकमलम् उदयाद्रिकन्दरास्थित-सुधांशुमण्डलमिव व्यराजत।[30]

वर्णने अपूर्वक्षमः श्रीहर्षः विराजते संस्कृतसाहित्यनक्षत्रमण्डले। नलस्य उद्यानवर्णने एतत् स्पष्टम् अस्ति।[31] सायंकालस्य वर्णनं दर्शनीयं अस्ति।[32]

कवेः कल्पना द्रष्टव्या यत्र कालकिरातः दिनद्विपस्य वधम् अकरोत् यस्य रक्तेन सन्ध्या अपि रुचिरा कुम्भस्थलस्य मौक्तिकानि एव ताराश्च सन्ति।[33]

एवम् भट्टिकाव्ये कविना भट्टिना अपि पर्यावरणं सुचित्रितम्। प्रातःकालवर्णनं सरलं सरसं च विद्यते।[34]

न केवलं महाकाव्याः प्रकृतिचित्रणैः सुशोभिताः अपितु नाटकेषु अपि पात्राः यत्र तत्र प्रकृतिप्राङ्गणे एव दृश्यन्ते। भासस्य प्रकृतिचित्रणे दाक्षिण्यं दृश्यते पदे-पदे। 'स्वप्नवासवदत्तम्' इति नाटके सूर्यास्तस्य सजीवं वर्णनं प्राप्यते।[35]

अत्रैव शरत्कालीनगगने सारस-पंक्त्या अंतरिक्षः विभक्तः दृश्यते।[36] शूद्रकस्य प्रकृति-वर्णनम् अपि पाठकानां चित्तं हरति। वर्षाकालवर्णने शूद्रकः निस्संदेहः श्लाघनीयः।[37] मेघाः पुरुषाः इव विद्युच्च स्त्रियः इव कथिताः।[38] प्रकृतिकविः अतिशेते सर्वान् कवीन् प्रकृतिचित्रणे। नृपः दुष्यन्तः वल्कलधारी शकुन्तलायाः नैसर्गिकसौन्दर्ये मुग्धः भवति।[39] प्रकृतिः अपि रोदिति।[40] प्रकृतिः अपि शोकाकुला चित्रिता।[41]

कविताकामिनीकान्तः कालिदासः कस्य नावर्जयति चेतः सचेतसः। कालिदासेन प्रकृतिः अनेकेषु रूपेषु-चित्रिता। तेन अस्याः उपासनात्मिका साधना स्वकीये सम्पूर्णे साहित्यिकजीवने कृता अस्ति। गेटे महोदयेन शाकुन्तलं प्रशंसितम्।[42] स्वकाव्य-सौन्दर्येण भारतीयकवीन्द्राणां गणनाप्रसङ्गे अद्यापि कविकुलगुरुः कालिदास एव कनिष्ठिकामधितिष्ठति।[43] कालिदासः अभिनन्दनीयः सर्वैः कविभिः।[44] तस्य कीर्तिरजराऽमरा च, निश्चयेन तस्य यशः काये जरामरणजं भयं नास्ति।

प्रकृतेः सजीववर्णने कालिदासः असाधरणः कुशलः। दुष्यन्तेन अनुपततः मृगस्य वर्णनं कियत् स्वाभाविकं मनोरमं च।[45] प्रातःकालस्य वर्णनं रोचकं वर्तते। उदयास्तं मनुष्यस्य उत्थानपतनं सूचयति।[46] कालिदासेन अन्तःप्रकृतेः बाह्य-प्रकृतेः च सुन्दरः समन्वयः कृतः।

एवमेव समन्वयः दृश्यते विशाखदत्तस्य मुद्राराक्षसनाटके। जीर्णोपवनस्य वर्णनं दर्शनीयम्। जीर्णोद्यानं सन्तप्त-हृदयमिव लक्ष्यते।[47]

प्रियदर्शिकानाटके हर्षः अपि प्रकृतेः स्वाभाविकं चित्रणम् अकरोत्।[48] भट्टनारायेण वेणीसंहारे प्रकृतेः कठोररूपं[49] सुकुमाररूपं[50] च वर्णितम्।

संवेदनशीलः नाटककारः भवभूतिः नाट्यसाहित्ये सदैव स्मरणीयः भविष्यति। अनेन कविना अश्माः अपि रोदिताः, वज्रहृदयं अपि दलितम्।[51] गौडी-रीत्या कृतं प्रकृतिवर्णनं मनोरमम्।[52] प्रकृतिवर्णनाः ओजगुणोपेताः सन्ति। महावन-वर्णनं क्रौंचपर्वतवर्णनं च अस्य उदाहरणौ स्तः।[53] प्रकृतेः सुकुमाररूपवर्णनं सुकुमारशब्देषु एव कृतम्।[54] प्रकृत्या तादात्म्यं अपि भवभूतिनाटकेषु दरीदृश्यते।[55]

मुरारिकृत-अनर्घराघवनाटकेऽपि प्रकृतिसौषम्यं सुन्दरम्।[56] दण्डीकृतदशकुमारचरिते वसन्तवर्णनं परम्परागतमपि कवेः काव्यकौशलस्य परिचायकं वर्तते।[57] सुबन्धुकृतवासवदत्तायां प्रभातवर्णनं, सन्ध्यावर्णनं वर्षावर्णनं च उल्लेखनीयम् अस्ति।[58] सुबन्धोः रचनायाम् सङ्गीतात्मकता, लयात्मकता नादसौन्दर्यम् चास्ति। एकतः पाण्डित्य-प्रदर्शनम् अस्ति अपरतश्च सरसा प्रसादमाधुर्ययुक्ता च पदावली। एवं वासवदत्तायां मणिकाञ्चनसंयोगम् प्राप्यते। वासवदत्ता प्रौढ-पाण्डित्यस्य निकषः अस्ति। नूनं, वासवदत्ता मालतीमाला इव हृदयं हरति।[59]

बाणभट्टस्य प्रकृतिविवृत्तौ वर्णने चापूर्वं वैशारद्यं वीक्ष्य मन्त्रमुग्धत्वमनुभवन्ति मनीषिणः। सन्ध्या-वर्णने[60], सरोवर-वर्णने,[61] विंध्याटवी-वर्णने[62] वसन्तवर्णने[63] च बाणस्य चातुरी, सूक्ष्मदृष्टिः सर्वांगीणता च विद्यन्ते। कादम्बरी सरस-मधुर-पदावलीयुक्ता रुचिरभावाभिरम्या, सरसा सालङ्कृतिः तरुणीव विद्ग्धमनोमोहिनी गद्यकाव्यसर्वस्वभूता च। सितामधुरं व्यञ्जनमिव सर्वथा मधुरात्मिकैव कादम्बरी। अतएवोच्यते 'कादम्बरीरसज्ञानाम् आहारोऽपि न रोचते'।

परवर्तिगद्यकाव्येषु अम्बिकादत्तव्यासस्य शिवराजविजयः, विश्वेश्वरपाण्डेयस्य मन्दारमञ्जरी, पण्डिता क्षमारावकृता कथामुक्तावली अपि प्रकृतिसौन्दर्येण परिपूर्णाः वर्तन्ते।

गीतिकाव्येऽपि प्रकृतिः मनोहरा उद्दीपिका च दृष्टा। कालिदासकृत—ऋतुसंहारे जीवनः विभिन्नैः ऋतुभिः उल्लसितः भवति। शरदर्तुवर्णनं सङ्गीतात्मकं वर्तते।[64] एषा कृतिः कवेः कल्पनायाः मनोरमं प्रसूनम् अस्ति। मेघदूते मन्दं मन्दं पवनं मन्दाक्रान्ताछन्देन चलन् शोभते।[65] प्रकृत्या तादात्म्यानुभूतिः कमनीया पदावली च दर्शनीया।[66] निर्विन्ध्यायाः नद्याः वर्णनं मेघस्य प्रेयसीरूपेणोपस्थापयते। मेघदूते भावानां गरिमा, कल्पनायाः कमनीयता, चेतसो विशदता, अनुभूति-संवेदनशीलत्वम्, अलङ्काराणाम् ऐन्द्रधनुषी प्रभा, नवपरिधानायाः नववध्वा लावण्यमिव प्रस्तौति। सहृदयहृदयताहेतोः मेघदूतं निर्विवादं लोकप्रियम्।

मेघदूते प्रकृतिः मानवीयभावैः अनुभूतिभिश्च सम्पन्ना अभिनेत्री अस्ति या कमनीयतया सर्वान् आकर्षयति। मेघपर्वतयोः सौहार्दं मनोरमम् अस्ति।[67] मेघदूते वाचौ अपि रसिकता अस्ति।[68] अलकाभवनचित्रणं कवेः कल्पनाशक्तेः मनोज्ञं दृष्टान्तं अस्ति।[69] भावानुसारिणी रसानुकूला वर्ण्यविषयानुरूपा च पदावली प्रशस्यते कविभिः। कथावस्तुनः महनीयता, तस्य सुव्यवस्थितम् संग्रथनम्, प्राकृतिकदृश्यानाम् स्वाभाविकम् रोचकम् च संश्लिष्टवर्णनम्, भाषायाः मधुरः प्रवाहः, इत्येतस्य सर्वस्य समन्वयात् हेतोः 'मेघदूतम्' कवीनां कण्ठहारः भूत्वा स्वस्त्रष्टुः कीर्तिपताकां विश्वे सविलासम् प्रसारयत् वर्तते। एवं संलक्ष्यते यत् कालिदासः कविताकामिन्याः विलासरूप एव।

गीतिकाव्ये ऋतुमादकतया सह जगदेवेन वर्णिता पदमाधुरी प्रशंसनीया।[70]

कथासाहित्यः अपि प्रकृतिवर्णनोपेतः। प्रकृत्या धैर्यशिक्षा दीयते।[71] धैर्यं हि मानवस्य नैसर्गिको धर्मः अस्ति। नाग्निशिखाऽधःकृताऽपि अधोमुखत्वं भजते।[72] अत्र कथारूपे नीतिः उपदिष्टा।[73] कथायाः पात्राः पशु-पक्षिणः सन्ति न तु मनुष्याः। अतः एते कथाः सर्वाः संकीर्णताः उल्लंघ्य मानवमात्रस्य सम्पत्तयः भूताः। अनेकभाषासु आसां कथानाम् अनुवादाः कृताः।[74] अपि च लोककथाः अपि प्रकृतेः नैसर्गिकसुषमोपेताः वर्तन्ते। गुणाढ्यकृता बृहत्कथा, वेतालपञ्चविंशतिका, विक्रमचरितं च प्रसिद्धाः कथाः वर्तन्ते। प्रकृतौ अपि सत्सङ्गतिमहत्वं प्रतिपादितम्।[75]

चम्पूकाव्ये अपि अनेकत्र प्रकृतिचित्रणं प्राप्यते।[76] त्रिविक्रमभट्ट-कृत-नलचम्पूकाव्ये रसानुकूला कठोरता कोमलता आम्रफलमिव उपमिता।[77] कवेः आर्यावर्तवर्णनं वस्तुतः प्रशंसनीयम् अस्ति।[78] भाषा-सौष्ठवस्य माधुर्यगुणस्य अद्भुतं समन्वयं दृश्यते।

अपि च धानयुक्तम् क्षेत्रम् कादम्बरी-तुल्यं कथितम्।[79] एतत् कवेः शब्दभण्डारस्य पाण्डित्यस्य सम्यक् निदर्शनमस्ति। फाल्गुनमासे वृक्षाः पल्लवरहिताः भवन्ति परम् कस्मैश्चित् अपि विपत्तिः न भवति।[80] प्रातः कालस्य वर्णनं दर्शनीयम्।[81] वसन्तस्य मनोरमं वर्णन मधुरशब्देषु कृतम्।[82]

ऐतिहासिककाव्यानि यत्र ऐतिहासिकतादृष्ट्या महत्त्वपूर्णानि सन्ति तत्र कवित्वच्छटा अपि यथास्थानं दृष्टिगोचरा भवति। इतिहासस्य कवेः कल्पनायाः च अद्भुतं संमिश्रणं वर्तते। अश्वघोषस्य बुद्धचरितं, बाणभट्टस्य हर्षचरितं, वाक्पतिराजकृतं गौडवधः, बिल्हणकृतं विक्रमाङ्कदेवचरितम्, कल्हणकृता राजतरंगिणी चेत्यादयः ऐतिहासिकग्रन्थाः अस्य प्रमाणः सन्ति। धूमेन नैतिकता उपदिष्टा कविकल्हणेन।[83] अन्यत्र अपि अगत्स्यवर्णने कवेः प्रतिभा दर्शनीया।[84] एतदतिरिक्तं हेमचन्द्राचार्यकृतं कुमारपालचरितं, जल्हणकृतं सोमपालविजयं, जयानककृतं पृथ्वीराजविजयं, वामनभट्टबाणकृतं वेमभूपालचरितं चेत्यादयः ऐतिहासिकाः वृत्ताः यत्र प्रकृतेः सौषम्यं चित्रितं यत्र-तत्र।

एवं संस्कृत-साहित्यस्य विहङ्गमदृष्ट्या ज्ञायते यत् प्रकृति-प्रेम-तरुः संस्कृत-कवीनां हृदये सदैव पुष्पितः पल्लवितः चासीत्, स्थास्यति च भविष्येऽपि। प्रकृतेः प्राङ्गणे एव तैः सूक्ष्मं तत्त्वं (तत्त्वमसि) अन्वेषितम्। प्रकृतेः अनन्योपासकाः कवयः सदैव श्लाघनीयाः, समरणीयाः च भविष्यन्ति। तेषां कीर्त्या मण्डितं अखिलं भूमण्डलम्।

यस्मिन् देशे मननशीलाः मुनयः तत्त्वद्रष्टारः महर्षयः तपोनिरताः तपस्विनः अनुकरणीयचरित्राः[85] जन्म गृहीतवन्तः, यत्र विविधतत्त्वप्रकाशकानि शास्त्राणि विद्यन्ते यस्य सम्पूर्णम् अपि वाङ्मयं विश्ववाङ्मयस्य अपूर्वः निधिः वर्तते, एतादृशं देशं प्रति अस्माकं स्वपितरौ प्रति आत्मीयता इव आत्मीयता अस्ति। देवैरपि स्पृहणीयः अस्माकम् एषः देशः।[86] विजयतां अस्माकं देशः!

सन्दर्भ-सङ्केताः

1. In it we can find the first outpourings of the human mind, the glow of poetry, the rapture at nature's loveliness and mystery.

   The Discovery of India, Pt. J.L. Nehru, 79

2. अवस्यूमेव चिन्वती मघोन्युषा याति स्वसरस्य पत्नी।
   स्वर्जतन्ती सुभागा सुदंसा आन्ताद् दिवः पप्रथ आपृथिव्याः।। — ऋग्वेदः - 3/61/4

3. कन्नेत तन्ना शाशदानां एषि देवि देवगिगक्षागागग्।
   संस्मयमाना युवतिः पुरस्तादाविर्वक्षांसि कृणुते विभाती।। — ऋग्वेदः - 1/123/10

4. (क) द्वा सुपर्णा सयुजा सखाया समानं वृक्षं परिषस्वजाते।
   तयोरन्यः पिप्पलं स्वाद्वत्यनश्नन्नन्योऽपिभिचाकशीति।। — श्वेताश्वतरोपनिषद् - 4/6

   (ख) यस्तूर्णनाभ इव तन्तुभिः प्रधानजैः स्वभावतः।
   देव एकः स्वमावृणोति स नो दधातुब्रह्माव्ययम्।। — श्वेताश्वतरोपनिषद् - 6/10

5. (क) तं क्लेशकर्मपरिपाकगुणप्रवाहैरव्याहतानुभवमीश्वरमद्वितीयम्।
   प्राणादिभिः स्वविभवरूपगूढमन्यो मन्येत सूर्यमिवमेघहिमोपरागैः।।

   भागवतपुराणम् - 10/84/33

   (ख) द्वे अस्य बीजे शतमूलस्त्रिनालः पञ्चस्कन्धः पञ्चरसप्रसूतिः।
   दशैकशाखो द्विसुपर्णनीऽस्त्रिवल्कलो द्विफलोऽर्कं प्रविष्टः।।

   भागवतपुराणम् - 11/12/22

6. पतितैः पतमानैश्च पादपस्थैश्च मारुतः।
   कुसुमैः पश्य सौमित्रे, क्रीडन्निव समस्ततः।। — रामायणम् - 4/1/13

7. रामायणम् – 4/28/12

8. हंसो यथा राजतपञ्जरस्थः सिंहो यथा मन्दरकन्दरस्थः।
वीरो यथा गर्वितकुञ्जरस्थश्चन्द्रोऽपि बभ्राण तथाऽम्बरस्थः।। रामायणम् – 5/5/4

9. सुप्तैकहसं कुमुदैरूपेतं महाह्रदस्थं सलिलं विभाति।
धनैर्विमुक्तं निशि पूर्णचन्द्रं तारागणाकीर्णमिवान्तरिक्षम्।। रामायणम् – 4/30/48

10. उर्ध्वमूलमधः शाखमश्वत्थं प्राहुरव्ययम्।
छन्दांसि यस्य पर्णानि यस्तं वेद स वेदवित्।। गीता – 15/1

11. संचारिणी दीपशिखेव रात्रौ यं यं व्यतीयाय पतिंवरा सा।
नरेन्द्रमार्गाट्ट इव प्रपेदे विवर्णभावं स स भूमिपालः।। रघुवंशम् – 6/67

12. रघुवंशम् – 2/10

13. स पल्वलोत्तीर्णवराहयूथान्यावासवृक्षोन्मुखबर्हिणानि।
ययौ मृगाध्यासितशाद्वलानि श्यामायमानानि वनानि पश्यन्।। रघुवंशम् – 2/17

14. क्वचिच्च कृष्णोरगभूषणेव भस्माङ्गरागा तनुरीश्वरस्य।
पश्यानवद्याङ्गि! विभाति गंगा भिन्नप्रवाहा यमुनातरङ्गैः।। रघुवंशम् – 13/57

15. सेयं मदीया जननीव तेन मान्येन राज्ञा सरयूर्वियुक्ता।
दूरे वसन्तं शिशिरानिलैर्मा तरङ्गहस्तैरुपगूहतीव।। रघुवंशम् – 13/63

16. मुखार्पणेषु प्रकृतिप्रगल्भाः स्वयं तरङ्गाधरदानदक्षः।
अनन्यसामान्यकलत्रवृत्तिः पिबत्यसौ पाययते च सिन्धूः।। रघुवंशम् – 13/9

17. संचारपूतानि दिगन्तराणि कृत्वा दिनान्ते निलयाय गन्तुम्।
प्रचक्रमे पल्लवरागताम्रा प्रभा पतङ्गस्य मुनेश्च धेनुः।। रघुवंशम् – 2/15

18. पर्याप्तपुष्पस्तबकस्तनाभ्यः
स्फुरत्प्रवालोष्ठमनोहराभ्यः।
लतावधूभ्यस्तरवोऽप्यवापु–
र्विनम्रशाखाभुजबन्धनानि।। कुमारसंभवम् – 3/39

19. कुमारसंभवम् – 8/63

20. वाता ववुः स्पर्शसुखा मनोज्ञा दिव्यानि वासांस्यवपातयन्तः।
सूर्यः स एवाभ्यधिकं चकाशे जज्वाल सौम्यार्चिरनीरितोऽग्निः।। बुद्धचरितम् – 1/22

21. उत्फुल्लस्थलनलिनीवनादमुष्मादुद्धूतः सरसिजसम्भवः परागः।
वात्याभिर्वियति विवर्तितः समन्तादाधत्ते कनकमयातपत्रलक्ष्मीम्।। किरातार्जुनीयम् – 5/39

22. विकसितकुसुमाधरं हसन्तीं कुरबकराजिवधूं विलोकयन्तम्।
ददृशुरिव सुराङ्गना निषण्णं सशरमनङ्गमशोकपल्लवेषु।। किरातार्जुनीयम् – 10/32

23. मुखैरसौ विद्रुमभङ्गलोहितैः शिखाः पिशङ्गीकलमस्य बिभ्रती।
शुकावलिर्व्यक्तशिरीषकोमला धनुःश्रियं गोत्रभिदोऽनुगच्छति।। किरातार्जुनीयम् – 4/36

24. तिरोहितान्तानि नितान्तमाकलैरगां विगाहादलकैः प्रसारिभिः।
यगुर्वधूनां वदनानि तुल्यतां द्विरेफवृन्दान्तरितैः सरोरूहैः।। किरातार्जुनीयम् - 8/47

25. उदयति विततोर्ध्वरश्मिरज्जावहिमरुचौ हिमधाम्नि याति चास्तम्।
वहति गिरिरयं विलम्बिघण्टाद्वयपरिवारितवारणेन्द्रलीलाम्।। शिशुपालवधम् - 4/10

26. नवपलाशपलाशवनं पुरः स्फुटपरागपरागतपङ्कजम्।
मृदुलतान्तलतान्तमलोकयत् स सुरभिं सुरभिं सुमनोभरैः।। शिशुपालवधम् - 6/2

27. अनुपतति विरावैः पत्रिणां व्याहरन्ती।
रजनिमचिरजाता पूर्वसन्ध्या सुतेव।। शिशुपालवधम् - 11/40

28. रथाङ्पाणेः पटलेन रोचिषाम् ऋषित्विषः संवलिता विरेजिरे।
चलत्पलाशान्तरगोचरास्तरोस्तुषारमूर्तेरिव नक्तमंशवः।। शिशुपालवधम् - 1/21

29. मधुरया मधुबोधितमाधवी-मधुसमृद्धिसमेधितमेधया।
मधुकराङ्गनया मुहुरुन्मदध्वनिभृता निभृताक्षरमुज्जगे।। शिशुपालवधम् - 6/20

30. अधिरक्ममन्दिरगवाक्षमुल्लसत् सदृशो रराज मुरजिद्दिदृक्षया।
वदनारविन्दमुदयाद्रिकन्दराविवरोदरस्थितमिवेन्दुमण्डलम् ।। शिशुपालवधम् - 13/35

31. विलासवापीतटवीचिवादनात्
पिकालिगीतेः शिखिलास्यलाघवात्।
वनेऽपि तौर्यत्रिकामारराध तं
क्व भोगमाप्नोति न भाग्यभाग् जनः।। नैषधीयचरितम् - 1/102

32. आदाय दण्डं सकलासु दिक्षु
योऽयं परिभ्रमति भानु भिक्षुः।
अब्धौ निमज्जान्नव तापसोऽयं
सन्ध्याभ्रकाषायमधत्त सायम्।। नैषधीयचरितम् - 22/12

33. कालः किरातः स्फुटपद्मकस्य वधं व्यधाद् यस्य दिनद्विपस्य।
तस्येव सन्ध्या रुचिरास्त्रधारा ताराश्च कुम्भस्थलेमौक्तिकानि।। नैषधीयचरितम् - 22/9

34. (क) निशातुषारैर्नयनाम्बुकल्पैः पत्रान्तपर्यागलदच्छबिन्दुः।
उपारूरोदेव नदत्पतङ्ग कुमुदवतीं तीरतरुर्दिनादौ।। भट्टिकाव्यम् - 2/4

(ख) प्रभातवाताहतिकम्पिताकृतिः कुमुद्वतीरेणुपिशङ्गविग्रहम्।
निरास भृङ्गं कुपितेव पद्मिनी न मानिनी संसहतेऽन्यसङ्गमम्।। भट्टिकाव्यम् - 2/6

35. खगाः वासोपेताः सलिलमवगाढो मुनिजनः
प्रदीप्तोऽग्निर्भाति प्रविचरति धूमो मुनिवनम्।
परिभ्रष्टो दूराद् रविरपि च संक्षिप्तकिरणो
रथं व्यावर्त्यासौ प्रविशति शनैस्तशिखरम्।। स्वप्नवासवदत्तम् - 1/16

36. ऋज्वायतां च विरलां च नतोन्नतां च
सप्तर्षिवंशकुटिलां च निवर्तवेषु।
निर्गुयमानभुजगोदरनिर्मलस्य

सीमाभिवाम्बरतलस्य विभज्यमानाम्।। स्वप्नवासवदत्तम् - 4/2

37. (क) गता नाशं तारा उपकृतमसाधाविव जने
विंयुक्ताः कान्तेन स्त्रिय इव न राजन्ति ककुभः।
प्रकामान्तस्तप्तं त्रिदशपतिशस्त्रस्य शिखिना
द्रवीभूतं मन्ये पतति जलरूपेण गगनम्।। मृच्छकटिकम् - 5/25

(ख) तत्रैव - 5/14

(ग) उन्नमति नमति वर्षति गर्जति मेघः करोति तिमिरोधम्।
प्रथमश्रीरिव पुरुषः करोति रूपाण्यनेकानि।। मृच्छकटिकम् - 5/26

38. यदि गर्जति वारिधरो गर्जतु तन्नाम निष्ठुराः पुरुषाः।
अपि विद्युत् प्रमदानां त्वमपि च दुःखं न जानासि।। मृच्छरुटिकम् - 5/32

39. सरसिजमनुविद्धं शैवलेनापि रम्यं
मलिनमपि हिमांशोर्लक्ष्म लक्ष्मीं तनोति।
इयमधिकमनोज्ञा वल्केनापि तन्वी
किमिव हि मधुराणां मण्डनं नाकृतीनाम्।। अभिज्ञानशाकुन्तलम् - 1/20

40. (क) उदगलितदर्भकवला मृग्यः परित्यक्तनर्तना मयूराः।
अपसृतपाण्डुपत्रा मुञ्चन्त्यश्रूणीव लताः।। अभिज्ञानशाकुन्तलम् - 4/12

(ख) अभिज्ञानशाकुन्तलम् - 4, 5

41. चूतानां चिरनिर्गताऽपि कलिका बध्नाति न स्वं रजः। अभिज्ञानशाकुन्तलम् - 6/4

42. प्रशस्तेरनुवादः —

वासन्तं कुसुमं फलं च युगपद् सर्वं च यद्।
यच्चान्यन्मनसो रसायनमतः सन्तर्पणं मोहनम्।।
एकीभूतपूर्वमथवा स्वर्लोक भूलोकयो।
रैश्वर्यं यदि वाञ्छसि प्रियसखे शाकुन्तलं सेव्यताम्।।

43. पुरा कवीनां गणनाप्रसङ्गे कनिष्ठिकाधिष्ठितकालिदासः।
अद्यापि तत्तुल्यकवेरभावादनामिका सार्थवती बभूव।।

44. (क) कविकुलगुरुः कालिदासो विलासः। प्रसन्नराघवम् - 1/22

(ख) निर्गतासु न वा कस्य कालिदासस्य सूक्तिषु।
प्रीतिर्मधुरसान्द्रासु मञ्जरीष्विव जायते।। हर्षचरितम् - 16

45. ग्रीवाभङ्गाभिरामं मुहुरनुपतति स्यन्दने दत्तदृष्टिः
पश्चार्धेन प्रविष्टः शरपतनभयाद् भूयसा पूर्वकायम्।
दर्भैरर्धावलीढैः श्रमविवृतमुखभ्रंशिभिः कीर्णवर्त्मा
पश्योदग्रप्लुत्वाद् वियति बहुतरं स्तोकमुर्व्यां प्रयाति।। अभिज्ञानशाकुन्तलम् - 1/7

46. अभिज्ञानशाकुन्तलम् - 4/2

47. विपर्यस्तं सौधं कुलमिव महारम्भरचनं

सरः शुष्कं साधोर्हृदयमिव नाशेन सुहृदः।
फलैर्हीना वृक्षा विगुणविधियोगादिव नया-
स्तृणैश्छन्ना भूमिर्मतिरिव कुनीत्या ह्यविदुषः।। मुद्राराक्षसम् - 6/11

48. आभात्यकांशुतापक्वथदिव शफरोद्वर्तनैर्दीर्घिकाम्भ-
श्छत्राभं नृत्तलीलाशिथिलमपि शिखी बर्हभारं तनोति।
छायाचक्रं तरुणां हरिणशिशुरूपैत्यालवालाम्बुलुब्धः
सद्यस्त्यक्त्वा कपोलं विशति मधुकरः कर्णपालीं गजस्य।। प्रियदर्शिका - 1/12

49. विक्षु व्यूढाडघ्रिपाङ्गस्तृणजटिलचलत्पांशुदण्डोऽन्तरिक्षेः। वेणीसंहारम् - 2/19

50. जृम्भारम्भप्रविततदलोपान्तजालप्रविष्टै-
र्भाभिर्मानोर्नृपतय इव स्पृश्यमाना विबुद्धाः।
स्त्रीभिः सार्धं घनपरिमलस्तोकलक्ष्याङ्गरागा-
न्मुञ्चन्त्येते विकचनलिनीगर्भशय्यां द्विरेफाः।। वेणीसंहारम् - 2/8

51. ग्रावा रोदित्यपि दलति वज्रस्य हृदयम्। उत्तररामचरितम् - 1/28

52. कण्डूलद्विपगण्डपिण्डकषणाकम्पेन संपातिभि-
र्घर्मस्रंसितबन्धनैश्च कुसुमैरर्चन्ति गोदावरीम्।
छायापस्किरमाणविष्किरमुखव्याकृष्टकीटत्वचः
कूजत्क्लान्तकपोतकुक्कुटकुलाः कूले कुलायद्रुमाः।। उत्तररामचरितम् - 2/9

53. (क) उत्तररामचरितम् - 2/16

(ख) गुञ्जत्कुञ्जकुटीरकौशिकघटाघूत्कारवत्कीचक-
स्तम्बाडाम्बरमूकमौकुलिकुलः क्रौञ्चाभिधोऽयं गिरि।
एतस्मिन् प्रचलाकिनां प्रचलतामुद्वेजिताः कूजितै-
रुद्वेल्लन्ति पुराणरोहिणतरुस्कन्धेषु कुम्भीनसाः।। उत्तररामचरितम् - 2/29

54. एते त एव गिरयो विरुवन्मयूरा-
स्तान्येव मत्तहरिणानि वनस्थलानि।
आमञ्जुवञ्जुललतानि च तान्यमूनि
नीरन्ध्रनीपनिचुलानि सरित्तटानि।। उत्तररामचरितम् - 2/23

55. यत्र द्रुमा अपि मृगा अपि बन्धवो मे
यानि प्रियासहचरश्चिरमध्यवात्सम्।
एतानि तानि बहुकन्दरनिर्झराणि
गोदावरीपरिसरस्य गिरेस्तटानि।।

56. दृश्यन्ते मधुमत्तकोकिलवधूनिर्धूतधूताङ्कुर-
प्राग्भारप्रसरत्परागतिकतादुर्गास्तटीभूमयः ।
याः कृच्छ्रादतिलङ्घ्य लुब्धकभयात् तैरेव रेणूत्करै-
र्धाराबाहिभिरस्ति लुप्तपदवीनिःशङ्कमेणीकुलम्।। अनर्घराघवम् - 5/6

57. अथ कदाचिदायासितजायारहितचेतसि, लालसालिलङ्घनग्लानघनकेसरे . . .शालीनकन्यकान्तःकरणसंक्रान्तरागलङ्घितलज्जे, दुर्दुरगिरितटचन्दनाश्लेषशीतलानिलाचार्यदत्तनानालता नृत्यलीले काले। दशकुमारचरितम् - उ., 7

58. (क) विद्रुमलतेव चरमार्णवस्य, रक्तकमलिनीव गगनतटाकस्य, काञ्चनकेतुरिव कन्दर्परथस्य · · · बभ्रुरिवकपिलतारकाभगवती सन्ध्या समदृश्यत्। वासवदत्ता - पृ., 158-159

(ख) जलददारुणि लोलतडिल्लताकरपत्रदारिते पवनवेगनिर्धूताश्चूर्णनिकरा इव जलकणा बभुः। वासवदत्ता - पृ., 248-249

(ग) कुमारमयूर इव समारूढशरजन्मा, महातपस्वीव प्रशमितरजःप्रसरः · · · मङ्केश्वर इव समेघनादः विन्ध्य इव घनश्यामः, युवतिजन इव पीनपयोधरः, समाजगाम् वर्षासमयः। वासवदत्ता - पृ., 246

59. अविदितगुणाऽपि सत्कविभणितिः कर्णेषु वमति मधुधाराम्।
अनधिगतपरिमलाऽपि हि हरति दृशं मालतीमाला।। वासवदत्ता - श्लोक 11

60. स्वापि विहत्य दिवसावसाने लोहितितारका तपोवनधेनुरिव कपिला परिवर्तमाना सन्ध्या मुनिभिरदृश्यत्। अपराम्भसि पतिते दिनकरे . . अम्भः सीकरनिकरमिव तारागणमम्बरमधारयत्। कादम्बरी - पृ. 81-82

61. निर्गमनमार्गमिव सागराणाम्, निस्यन्दमिव दिशाम्, अंशावतारमिव गगनतलस्य, कैलाशमिव द्रवतामापन्नम्। कादम्बरी - पृ. 197-200

62. प्रेताधिपनगरीव सदासंनिहितमृत्युभीषणा महिषाधिष्ठिता च, · · · क्रूरसत्त्वापि मुनिजनसेविता, पुष्पवत्यपि पवित्रा विन्ध्याटवी नाम्। कादम्बरी - पृ. 37-40

63. कोमलमलयमारुतावतारतरङ्गितानङ्गध्वजांशुकेषु · · · मधुकरकुलकलकलङ्ककाली-कृतकालेयककुसुमकुड्मलेषु · · · मधुमासदिवसेषु। कादम्बरी - पृ. 221-22

64. काशांशुका विकचपद्ममनोज्ञवक्त्रा सोन्मादहंसनूपुरनादरम्या।
आपक्वशालिरुचिरानतगात्रयष्टिः प्राप्ता शरन्नववधूरिव रूपरम्या।। ऋतुसंहारम् - 3/1

65. मन्दं मन्दं नुदति पवनश्चानुकूलो यथा त्वां।
वामश्चायं नदति मधुरं चातकस्ते सगन्धः।। मेघदूतम् - 1/10

66. वीचिक्षोभस्तनितविहगश्रेणिकाञ्चीगुणायाः
संसर्पन्त्याः स्खलितसुलभं दर्शितावर्तनाभेः।
निर्विन्ध्यायाः पथि भव रसाभ्यन्तरः संनिपत्य
स्त्रीणामाद्यं प्रणयवचनं विभ्रमो हि प्रियेषु।। मेघदूतम् - 1/29

67. काले काले भवति भवतो यस्य संयोगमेत्य।
स्नेहव्यक्तिश्चिरविरहनं मुञ्चतो वाष्पमुष्णम्।। मेघदूतम् - 1/12

68. यत्र स्त्रीणां हरति सुरतग्लानिमङ्गानुकूलः।
शिप्रावातः प्रियतम इव प्रार्थनाचाटुकारः।। मेघदूतम् - 1/32

69. विद्युत्वन्तं ललितवनिताः सेन्द्रचापं सचित्राः
सङ्गीताय प्रहतमुरजाः स्निग्धगम्भीरघोषम्।
अन्तस्तोयं मणिमयभुवस्तुङ्गमभ्रंलिहाग्राः
प्रासादास्त्वा तुलयितुमलं यत्र तैस्तैर्विशेषैः।। मेघदूतम् - 2/1

70. ललितलवङ्गलतापरिशीलनकोमलमलयसमीरे ।
मधुकरनिकरकरम्बित कोकिलकूजितकुञ्जकुटीरे।। गीतगोविन्दम् - 1/3

71. (क) संपतौ च विपतौ च महतामेकरूपता।
उदये सविता रक्तो रक्तश्चास्तमये तथा।। पञ्चतन्त्रम् - 2/7

(ख) सुभाषितावलिः - 2270

72. कदर्थितस्यापि हि धैर्यवृत्तेर्न शक्यते धैर्यगुणः प्रमार्ष्टुम्।
अधोमुखस्यापि कृतस्य वह्नेर्नाधः शिखा याति कदाचिदेव।। हितोपदेशः - 2/69

73. कथाच्छलेन बालानां नीतिस्तदिह कथ्यते। हितोपदेशः - प्रस्तावना - 8

74. महत्त्वपूर्णाः अनुवादाः

(क) हकीम-बुर्जोईकृतः पहलवी-भाषायां। (531-579)

(ख) जॉन ऑफ केपुआ कृतः लेटिन-भाषायां (1264-1278 ई.)

(ग) एन्थानियस फॉन फरकृतः जर्मन-भाषायां (1483 ई.)

(घ) सर टमस नार्थकृतः आंग्लभाषायां (1570 ई.)

75. महाजनस्य संसर्गः नोन्नतिकारकः।
पद्मपत्रस्थितं वारि धत्ते मुक्ताफलश्रियम्।। पञ्चतन्त्रम् - 3/59

76. (क) सममसमं च, निम्नगात्रमनिम्नगात्रं च, ग्रावविषमम्।
अग्रावविषमं च, सश्वापदम् अश्वापदं च, सपादपम्
अपादपं च, विन्ध्यस्कन्धम् अल्लंघ्य। नलचम्पू - उ. 6

(ख) आवासाः कुसुमायुधस्य शबरीसङ्केत-लीलागृहाः।
पुष्पामोद-मिलन्मधुव्रत-वधू-झङ्कार-रूदपाध्वागाः।
सुस्निग्धाः प्रियबान्धवा इव दृशो दूरीभवन्तश्चिरात्।
कस्यैते न दहन्ति हन्त हृदयं विन्ध्याचलस्य द्रुमाः। नलचम्पू - 6/61

77. काव्यस्याम्रफलस्येव कोमलस्येतरस्य च।
बन्धच्छायाविशेषेण रसोऽप्यन्यादृशो भवेत्।। नलचम्पू - 1/17

78. शरण्यः पुष्पकारिणाम्, धाम धर्मस्य, . . . आकरः साधुव्यवहाररत्नानाम्, आर्यावर्तो देशः।
नलचम्पूकाव्यम् - उच्छवासः - 1

79. यत्र च मनोहारि-सारसद्वृन्दाः तत्पुरुषेण द्विगुना चाधिष्ठिताः कादम्बरी गद्य बन्धा इव दृश्यमान-बहुव्रीह्यः केदाराः।
नलचम्पूकाव्यम्-उच्छ्वासः - 1

80. भवन्ति फाल्गुने मासि वृक्षशाखा विपल्लवाः।
जायन्ते न तु लोकस्य कदापि च विपल्लवाः।। नलचम्पूकाव्यम् - 1/27

81. उदयगिरि-गतायां प्राक्प्रभापाण्डुतायाम्
अनुसरति निशीथे शृङ्गमस्ताचलस्य।
जयते किमपि तेजः साम्प्रतं व्योममध्ये
सलिलमिव विभिन्नं जाह्नवं यामुनं च।। नलचम्पूकाव्यम् - 6/1

82. किसलयति वनान्ते कोकिलालापरम्ये।

विकसति न वसन्ते मालती केऽत्र हेतुः।। नलचम्पूकाव्यम् - 7/4

83. योऽयं परापकरणाय सृजत्युपायं तेनैव
तस्य नियमेन भवेद् विनाशः।
धूमं प्रसौति नयनान्ध्यकरं
यमग्निर्भूत्वाम्बुदः स शमयेत् सलिलैस्तमेव।। राजतरङ्गिणी - 4/125

84. कुम्भा पयोनिधि-पयोहरण-प्रवृत्ता
नित्यं वहन्ति किल ये विफलश्रमत्वम्।
चित्रं क्षणादिह तदेक समुद्भवेन
संदर्शिता निखिल-वारिधि-पानलीला।। राजतरङ्गिणी - 4/718

85. एतद्देशप्रसूतस्य सकाशादग्रजन्मनः।
स्वं स्वं चरित्रं शिक्षेरन् पृथिव्यां सर्वमानवाः।। मनुस्मृतिः

86. गायन्ति देवाः किल गीतकानि
धन्यास्तु ये भारतभूमिभागे।
स्वर्गापवर्गास्पदहेतुभूते-
र्भवन्ति भूयः पुरुषाः सुरत्वात्।

卐 卐 卐

ज्योतिषशास्त्रे वनस्पतिः

रामदेव झा

प्रस्तुतेऽस्मिन्निबन्धे त्रिस्कन्धात्मकस्य ज्योतिषशास्त्रस्य संहितास्कन्धमवलम्ब्य वनस्पतिविषये किञ्चिल्लिख्यते मया। यतस्तत्र बहुविधं वनस्पतिवर्णनं शुभाशुभफलद्योतकं लभ्यते। अतो लघुकायेऽत्र निबन्धे समासतोऽपि सर्वविधं वनस्पतिविषयकं ज्ञानविवेचनं कर्तुं न शक्यते। अतो हेतोः किञ्चिदेवोल्लिख्यते। गणितस्कन्ध्यस्यापि चर्चा कृतास्ति।

वनस्पतिपदार्थः

वनस्य पतिर्वनस्पतिरिति पारस्करादित्वात्सुटि कृते निष्पद्यते। यो हि विना पुष्पं फलद्रुमः स एव वनस्पतिः कथ्यते। किन्तु वृक्षमात्रं वनस्पतिरिति मेदिनीकोषे उक्तमिति शब्दकल्पद्रुमे दृश्यते। अस्मिन्निबन्धेऽपि उद्भिज्जाः, स्थावराः सर्वे बीजकाण्डप्ररोहिणः, बहुपुष्पफलोपगा ओषधयः, गुल्मगुच्छादयो वल्लयश्च वनस्पतय एव इति मत्वा ज्योतिषशास्त्रे वनस्पतिजातिविषये ये विचाराः प्राप्यन्ते तत्स्पर्शमेवाकुर्वमहम्।

अन्तःसंज्ञा वनस्पतिः[1]

भारतीयाः प्रकृतिरहस्यविदः इति प्रायः सर्वेविज्ञाः स्वीकुर्वन्ति। केचित्सरलप्राणायामेन केचिच्च द्राविडप्राणायामेनेति कथनं नाति शेते। अस्माकं तपःपूता अतीन्द्रियज्ञानसम्पन्ना ऋषयः आधुनिकाः वैज्ञानिकाः वा भवेयुस्ते सर्वेऽभिज्ञातारः आसन्, सन्तिः, कथयन्ति च यत्सर्वप्राणिनाम् आहारनिद्राभयमैथुनानि साहजिकानि सन्ति। अन्तःसंज्ञा वृक्षाः भवन्ति। ते शब्दार्थविदो भयग्रस्ताश्च भवन्ति। यथा मानवसदसद्गुणोचिता व्यापारास्तथैव वनस्पतीनामपि।

ज्योतिषसंहितास्कन्धे चराचरजगच्छुभाशुभज्ञानाय वनस्पतयः कदा, कियत्, कीदृशं परिणामं लोकमङ्गलामङ्गलसूचकं दर्शयन्तीति बहुशः प्रतिपादितं त्रिकालज्ञैः।

तत्प्रयोजनम्

वनस्पतीनां वृक्षाणां फलकुसुमसम्प्रवृद्धिं विलोक्य सर्वेषां द्रव्याणां सुलभत्वं विज्ञायते। तथा च सस्यानामपि आधिक्यमनाधिक्यञ्च सम्यग् ज्ञायते।[2]

केन कस्य वृद्धिर्ज्ञायते इति विषये कथितं यच्छालस्य वृक्षविशेषस्य फलकुसुमसम्प्रवृद्धिं दृष्ट्वा कलमशाल्यादीनां बहूनां बहुदेशजानां षष्टिकादिधान्यानां सुलभत्वं ज्ञेयम्। रक्ताशोकेन रक्तशालिः, क्षीरिकया पाण्डूकशालिविशेषस्तथा च नीलाशोकेन सूकरकः शालिविशेषो ज्ञेयः।

अन्यच्च – न्यग्रोधेन यवकः शालिविशेषः, तिन्दुकवृद्ध्या षष्ठिकः शालिविशेषो भवति। अश्वत्थेन सर्वसस्यानां सुलभत्वं ज्ञेयम्। जम्बूवृक्षविशेषैस्तिलभाषाः ज्ञातव्याः। शिरीषवृक्षवृद्ध्या प्रियङ्गुवृद्धिर्मधूकैर्गोधूमा ज्ञेयाः। सप्तपर्णवृक्षविशेषैः यववृद्धिर्भवति।

अन्यच्च – अतिमुक्तको वृक्षविशेषः कुन्दश्च यत्र कुन्दपुष्पाणि भवन्ति एताभ्यामतिमुक्तकुन्दाभ्यां कर्पासवृद्धिर्ज्ञेया। अशनो वृक्षविशेषस्तै सर्षपान् कथयेत्। बदरीभिश्च कुलत्थान् ब्रूयात्। चिरबिल्वेन (करञ्जेन) मुद्गान्नं निर्दिशेत्।

अन्यदप्याह – वेतसवृक्षविशेषैरतसी ज्ञेया। पलाशवृक्षविशेषकुसुमैः कोद्रवान्नवृद्धिर्ज्ञायते। तिलकवृक्षकुसुमवृद्ध्या शंखमौक्तिकरजतानि विज्ञेयानि। इङ्गुदवृक्षविशेषेण शणा विज्ञेया।

अन्यच्च – हस्तिकर्णैर्वृक्षैर्गजानां तथाऽश्वकर्णैरश्वानां, पाटलैर्गवां, तथा च कदलीभिरजाविकानां वृद्धिर्ज्ञेया। चम्पकपुष्पैः कनकं, बन्धुजीवेन विद्रुमं, कुरवकेण वज्रं, नन्दिकावर्त्तेन वैदूर्यम् सुलभं स्यात्। इत्थमेव सिन्धुवारेण मौक्तिकं जानीयात्। कुसुम्भेन शिल्पिनं, रक्तोत्पलवृद्ध्या नृपं तथा च नीलोत्पलेन सचिवं विन्द्यात्।

अथान्यत् – आम्रैः क्षेमं, भल्लातकैर्भयं, पीलुभिरारोग्यं तथा खदिरशमीभ्यां प्रवृद्धाभ्यां दुर्भिक्षं भवति। अर्जुनैः सुवृष्टिर्जायते। निम्बवृक्षनागकेसरयोः पुष्पैः सुभिक्षं ज्ञेयम्। कपित्थेन वायुवृद्धिस्तथा च निचुलवृक्षविशेषेणाऽवृष्टिभयं भवति। कुटजेन व्याधिभयं ज्ञेयम्। अथ च दूर्वाकुशकुसुमाभ्यामिक्षुवृद्धिर्जायते। कोविदारेण वह्निभयं तथा च श्यामलतावृद्ध्या वेश्याः वृद्धिं प्राप्नुवन्ति।

एभिर्वृष्टिलक्षणमाह —

यदा वृक्षाः, एकमूलो गुल्मो लताश्चैते यस्मिन् काले निर्मलाः, छिद्ररहितैः पत्रैः संदृश्यन्ते तस्मिन् काले सुवृष्टिः प्रोक्ता। तैरेव रुक्षैश्छिद्रसहितैश्च पत्रैः परिमितं जलवर्षणं प्रदिष्टम्।

यथोक्तम् – **यस्मिन् काले स्निग्धनिश्छिद्रपत्राः**
संदृश्यन्ते वृक्षगुल्मालताश्च।
तस्मिन् वृष्टिः शोभना सम्प्रदिष्टा
रुक्षैश्छिद्रैरल्पमम्भः प्रदिष्टम्।।[3]

पराशरेणाप्येवमेवोक्तम्–

अच्छिद्रपत्राः सुस्निग्धाः फलपुष्पसमन्विताः।
निर्दिशन्ति शुभं वृक्षा विपरीतं विगर्हिताः।।

धर्मार्थकामप्रदगेहनिर्माणोचितभूमिलक्षणबोधको वनस्पतिः[4]

कुशोपेता भूमिर्ब्राह्मणी ज्ञेया, शर (मूञ्ज) युताभूः क्षत्रिया कुशकाशाकुला वैश्या तथा च सर्वतृणाकुला शूद्रेति कथ्यते।[3]

निर्मितवासस्थानात्पूर्वस्यां दिशि अश्वत्थवृक्षः, दक्षिणस्यामुदुम्बरः पश्चिमे न्याग्रोधः, उत्तरे तु पर्कटीवृक्षः श्रेष्ठः कथितः।[4]

निषिद्धासु दिक्षु स्थितेषु वृक्षेषु अश्वत्थोऽग्निभयं सूचयति पर्कटीवृक्षः प्रमादं जनयति, वटवृक्षः शस्त्रभयं करोति, उदुम्बरस्तूदररोगकारको भवति।

अन्यदप्याह – यत्र वृक्षाः प्ररोहन्ति सस्यानि च प्रवर्द्धन्ते सा भूमिर्जीविता कथ्यते अर्थाद् गृहनिर्माणयोग्या वाच्या।

गृहार्थं छिन्द्यवृक्षाः

यस्मिन् वृक्षे खगनिलयो भवेत्, यश्च वृक्षो भग्नर्दग्धो वा स्यात्, यश्च देवालयपरिसरस्थः श्मशाने स्थितो वा स्यात् तथा पिप्लादिक्षीरवृक्षः, धवः विभीतिकः, निम्बः, अरणिः—एतान् वृक्षान् विहाय अन्यान् छिन्द्यात्।[5] तरुच्छेदनलक्षणं पतितस्य च शुभाशुभज्ञानमति प्रोक्तं तत्रैव। रात्रौ कृतवलिपूजं तरुं दिवसे प्रादक्षिण्येन छेदयेत्। तत्र यदि छिन्नो वृक्ष ऐशान्यां पूर्वस्यां वा पतेत् तदा शुभं ज्ञेयम्। अनेन ज्ञातं भवति यदन्यासु दिक्षु पतितो न ग्राह्यः।

जलान्वेषणे सहायको वनस्पतिः[5]

जलवर्जितेदेशे (यत्र स्वभावत एव जलं न विद्यते) जङ्गले यदि वेतसवृक्षो दृश्यते ततस्त्रिभिर्हस्तैः पश्चिमायां दिशि भूम्यधस्तोयं वक्तव्यम्।

एवमेवाम्बुरहितेदेशे यदि जम्बूवृक्षो दृश्यते तदा तस्मादुत्तरस्यां दिशि त्रिभिर्हस्तैरन्तरं सप्तहस्तमितेऽधः खाते जलं प्राप्यते। तथा च यदि जम्बूवृक्षस्य पूर्वस्यां दिशि समीपस्थो वल्मीको भवेत् ततो दक्षिणपार्श्वे स्वादु सलिलं स्यात्।

अन्यच्च - यदि जल वर्जिते देशे वल्मीकयुतो वियुतो वा उदुम्बरस्य वृक्षो दृश्यते तदा तत्र पश्चिमायां दिशि त्रिभिरेवहस्तैरनन्तरमधः स्वादु पेयं जलं प्राप्यते। अर्जुनवृक्षस्य चोत्तरस्यां दिशि वल्मीकः स्यात्तदा ततः पश्चिमायां दिशि त्रिभिर्हस्तैरतीतैरधोऽम्बु भवति।

निर्गुण्डीतिवृक्षविशेषस्तत्र यदि वल्मीककृता मृत्स्तूपाकृतिः स्यात् तदा तस्माद् दक्षिणस्यां दिशि त्रिभिर्हस्तैरन्तरमध ाोऽशोष्यमुदकं भवति। तथा च जलरहिते देशे बदरीवृक्षस्य पूर्वभागे वल्मीककृतो मृत्स्तूपोऽवलोक्यते तदा तस्मात्पश्चिमायां दिशि त्रिभिः करैरधो जलं वक्व्यम्।

अन्यदप्याह - यदि जलरहिते देशे पलाशवृक्षसहिता बदरी दृश्यते सवल्मीका वल्मीकविमुखा वा तदा ततः पश्चिमभागे त्रिभिरेवहस्तैः परतोऽधः सलिलं प्राप्यते। इत्थं विल्वोदुम्बरयोगे हस्तत्रये याम्ये, वल्मीकसमीपस्थफल्गुवृक्षात् दशभिः करैः पश्चिमे, कम्पिल्लवृक्षात् पूर्वभागे करत्रयान् परतोऽधः स्वादु जलं भवति। एवमेव विभीतकवृक्षस्य दक्षिणपार्श्वे हस्तद्वयात् परतः पूर्वस्यां दिशि, कोविदारवृक्षस्येशान्यां दर्भयुक्ते वल्मीके सति कोविदारवल्मीकयोर्मध्ये जलं भवति।

यदि वल्मीकसहितः सप्तपर्णो वृक्षोविशेषो भवेत् तदा तत उत्तरे भागे हस्तात् परतोधः जलं प्राप्यते। तथा च यदि सर्वेषां वृक्षाणामधो मण्डूको दृश्यते तदा तत उत्तरस्यां दिशि हस्तात् परत एवाधः जलं स्यात्।

एवमेव मधूकवृक्षात् कपित्थवृक्षात् तिलकवृक्षात् क्रमशः उत्तरभागे वल्मीकः स्यात्, याम्यभागे कुशैः शाद्वलैश्च सहितो वल्मीको भवेत्तदा मधूकात् पश्चिमे भागे पञ्चहस्तान् परिहृत्याधो जलं भवति तिलकवृक्षादपि पश्चिमे भागे पञ्चभिरेवहस्तैः परतोऽधः जलं भवति तथा च। कपित्थादुत्तरे भागे सप्तकरान् विहायाधः जलं भवतीति ज्ञेयम्।

अन्यच्च - यदि कदम्बवृक्षस्य पश्चिमे भागे वल्मीको दृश्यते तदा दक्षिणस्यां दिशि हस्तत्रितयात् परतोऽधो जलं प्राप्यते। अश्मन्तकवृक्षस्य उत्तरे वदरीवृक्षो वल्मीको वा दृश्यते तदाऽश्मन्तकस्योत्तरे एव षड्भिः करैः परतोऽधः जलं तथा हरिद्रतरोरुत्तरे वल्मीके दृश्ये सति तस्य तदोरेव पूर्वस्यां दिशि हस्तत्रितये परतो जलं प्राप्यते।

अन्यदप्याह - यद् यत्र जलरहिते देशे बहूतकस्थानजातानि यानि लक्षणानि भवन्ति तानि यदि तत्र दृश्यन्ते अथ च वीरणस्तृणविशेषः, शाद्वलम् एते च यत्रातिकोमला दृश्यन्ते तत्र जलं भवतीति ज्ञेयम्।

अपरञ्च - शार्ङ्गी त्रिवृता-दन्ती-सूकरपादी-लक्ष्मणा-नवमालिका, एताः सर्वा एव लताविशेषाः स्वनामभिः प्रसिद्धाः ओषधयो यत्र सन्ति तत्र याम्ये हस्तद्वये त्यक्तेऽधो जलं भवति। तथा च ये द्रुमाः स्निग्धाः, दीर्घलताः, अतिहृस्वाः, विस्तीर्णाः एते सर्व एव सन्निकृष्टोदकाः भवन्ति। तथा ये द्रुमा अन्तरसाराः, जर्जरपत्राः ये च रूक्षास्ते सर्वे जलेन वर्जिताः स्युस्तत्र जलं न भवतीत्यर्थः।

अन्यच्च - यत्र तृणवर्जिते स्थाने तृणसंयुता मही दृश्यते अथ च यत्र सतृणा मही तृणवर्जिता भवति तस्मिन् स्थाने जलं भवति। यत्राकण्टकानां पलासादीनां मध्ये कण्टकिनो वृक्षाः भवन्ति तथा सकण्टकानां मध्येऽकण्टकिनो वृक्षाः स्युस्तत्र पश्चिमायां दिशि त्रिभिर्हस्तैः परतोऽधः जलं भवति। यदि तरोरेका शाखा विनता स्यात् विवर्णा वा भवेत् तत्र तस्याः शाखायास्तले एव जलं ज्ञातव्यम्। यदि कण्टकारिका कण्टकैर्विना दृश्यतेऽथ च एतन्नामके वृक्षे श्वेतपुष्पाणि जायन्ते तदा तदधोऽम्भः जानीयात्। यस्मिन् जलवर्जिते देशे द्विशीर्षा खर्जूरी भवेत् तत्पश्चिमे भागे जलं (भूमेरधः) भवेत्। कर्णिकारवृक्षो यदि श्वेतकुसुमः स्यादथवा सितकुसुमः पलाशवृक्षः स्यात्तत्र कर्णिकारपलाशयोर्हस्तद्वयान्तरे दक्षिणे भागे जलं प्राप्यते। यत्र भूमावुष्मा स्यात् तत्राधो महत्तोयप्रवाहसहितं जलं प्राप्यते इत्थं जाङ्गलानूपभूम्योर्जलपरिज्ञानायाऽस्माकं कृते वनस्पतयः सहायका भवन्ति।

मरुभूमौ जलज्ञानाय सहायको वनस्पतिः[6]

जलवर्जिते मरुभूमिभागे यदि पीलुवृक्षस्य ऐशान्यां दिशि वल्मीककृतो मृत्स्तूपो भवति तदा तद्वृक्षादेव पश्चिमस्यां दिशि सार्धैश्चतुर्भिर्हस्तैः परतोऽधः जलं ज्ञेयम्।

अन्यदप्याह—पीलुवृक्षस्यैव पूर्वभागे यदि वल्मीको दृश्यते तदा तद्वृक्षाद् दक्षिणे भागे सार्धचतुर्भिर्हस्तैः परतोऽधः भागे जलं वाच्यम्। एवमेव यदि करीरवृक्षस्योत्तरस्यां दिशि वल्मीको दृश्यते तदा तस्माद् वृक्षाद्दक्षिणे भागे सार्धचतुर्भिर्हस्तैः परतोऽधः जलं ज्ञेयम्। रोहीतकवृक्षस्य याम्ये वल्मीके सति तस्यामेव दिशि त्रिभिः करैः परतोऽधः जलं भवति।

अन्यच्च-इन्द्रवृक्षस्य प्राक् वल्मीकः स्यात् तदा तत् पश्चिमे भागे, सुवर्णवृक्षस्य वामत उत्तरे भागे वल्मीको भवेत् तदा तद्दक्षिणस्यां दिशि, तथा यदि वदरीरोहीतकवृक्षौ संश्लिष्टौ स्यातां तदा तत्र वल्मीको भवतु न वा, बदरीरोहीतकवृक्षाभ्यां पश्चिमे भागे हस्तत्रयपरतो जलमधो भवति। इत्थमन्येऽपि बहवो जलज्ञानप्रकाराः संहिताग्रन्थेषु दृश्यन्तेऽत्राति- समासेन वर्णिताः वनस्पतिसाहाय्येन तज्ज्ञानोपायाः।

मुहूर्त्तग्रन्थेषु वनस्पतिमहत्त्वम्[7]

वापीखननात् पूर्वं करणीयेषु कार्येषु मुहूर्त्तविचारः प्रथमः कर्त्तव्यः। ततोऽपि प्राथम्यं भजते वाप्यास्तीरनिर्माणम् ककुभः, वटः, आम्रः, प्लक्षः, कदम्बः, एतैः, निचुलेन जम्ब्वा वेतसेन, नीपेन, एभिः सहितैः तथा कुरबकः, तालः, अशोकः, मधूकः, एतैरपि बकुलसंयुतैरावृतस्तीरो यस्या वाप्यास्तथाभूतां कारयेत्।

वनस्पतयरोषधयश्च पूज्या नमस्याः सन्तीति भारतीया मन्यन्ते। ज्योतिषशास्त्रे वृक्षादिरोपण- मुहूर्त्ताः कथिताः सन्ति। तत्र कदलीरोपणम्, बीजवपनम्, धान्यरोपणम्, धान्यच्छेदनम्- इत्यादिकर्मणां कृते विहिताः मुहूर्त्ताः प्रतिपादिताः सन्ति।

गृहसमीपे ग्राह्यवृक्षाः[8]

सदुग्धाः, सकण्टकाः, अफलिनो वृक्षाश्च गृहाद् दूरतस्त्याज्याः कथिताः। तथा चम्पकपाटले प्रशस्ते स्तः। कदली, जाती, केतकी च प्रशस्ताः स्युः। एवं दिवा, प्रहरादूर्ध्वमशेषवृक्षजनिता छाया गृहे न शुभप्रदा स्यात्।

गृहसन्निकटे दुग्धवृक्षा धननाशका भवन्ति। कण्टकिनोऽरिभीतिमुत्पादयन्ति। फलिनः सन्ततिहानिकरा भवन्ति। सुवर्णवर्णा अपि पुष्पवृक्षा न शुभदाः स्युः।

प्रकारान्तरेण दुष्टा वृक्षा अपि न कदाऽपि उच्छेद्या भवन्ति विल्व शमी-अशोक- कुल-पुन्नाग-चम्पक-द्राक्षा- चन्दन-पिप्पली-दाडिमादयो पादपलतादयश्च शुभप्रदा भवन्ति। दिग्वशेन नानापादपलतादीनामारोपणविषये मुहूर्त्तग्रन्थेषु तिथि-वार-नक्षत्रादिसहिता मुहूर्त्तविचाराः कृताः सन्ति।[9]

ज्योतिषगणितस्कन्धे वनस्पतिः[10]

सिद्धान्त (गणित) स्कन्धे भुवनकोशे बहुविधान् वृक्षान् आचार्या व्यावर्णयन्। अत्राऽहं भास्करोक्तोदाहरणबलेन वनस्पतिपरिचायकज्ञानपुरस्सरं गणितसदृशमपि शुष्कज्ञानं कथं सरसं हृदयग्राहि च जातं, तत्प्रस्तौमि।

विश्लेषजात्युदाहरणं यथा —

पञ्चांशोऽलिकुलात् कदम्बमगमत् त्र्यंशः शिलीन्ध्रं तयोर्विश्लेषस्त्रिगुणोमृगाक्षि! कुटजं दोलायमानोऽपरः।

कान्ते! केतकमालतीपरिमलप्राप्तैककालप्रिया दूताहूत इतस्ततो भ्रमति रवे भृङ्गोऽलिसंख्यां वद।। अत्रोदाहरणे कदम्ब-शिलीन्ध्र-कुटज-केतकी-मालतीनां वृक्षलतानां वर्णनं बालबोधाय कृतं वर्त्तते।

अपरञ्च —

षड्भागः पाटलासु भ्रमरनिकरतः स्वत्रिभागः कदम्बे
पादश्चूतद्रुमे च प्रदलितकुसुमे चम्पके पञ्चमांशः।
प्रोत्फुल्लाम्भोजखण्डे रविकरदलिते त्रिंशदंशोऽभिरेमे
तत्रैको मत्तभृङ्गो भ्रमति नभसि चेत् का भवेद् भृङ्गसंख्या।।

अनेनोदाहरणद्वयेन सिद्ध्यति यद् ज्योतिषत्रिस्कन्धेषु वनस्पतीनां महत्त्वं कियद् वर्त्तते।

सारांशः[11]

पञ्चेन्द्रियसमायुक्तास्तथा शयनाहारगमनभाषणश्रवणाघ्राणचेष्टादियुक्ता एव यथा जीविनस्तथैव वनस्पतयोऽपि जायन्ते, वर्द्धन्ते म्रियन्ते सर्वाणि जीवनकर्माणि क्रियन्ते च। ब्रह्माण्डे न कोऽपि पदार्थो लघुतमो बृहत्तमो वा स्यान्निरर्थकोऽस्ति। बहुपदार्थसमन्वितेऽस्मिन् विश्वे पञ्चभ्यो भूतेभ्यः ऋतेऽन्यत् किमपि नास्ति। प्राचीनानामेतदेवज्ञातमर्वाचीनैः श्रीमद्भिराचार्यैर्जगदीशचन्द्रवसुमहोदयैर्दृढप्रमाणपदवीमानीतमाधुनिकैस्तत् सुविज्ञातमेव। संहिताशास्त्रे वृक्षायुर्वेदोऽन्यतमः। अस्मिन् खलु निर्जीवानां चिकित्सा आयुर्वा। यतो जीवनकाल एव आयुः। चिकित्सा च जीवनस्यैव दैर्घ्यसम्पादनाय भवति। विस्तृतिभयान्नात्र मया तदुल्लेखः कृतः। इदानीमहं कियद्वनस्पतिजीवनमहत्त्वं मानवादीनां वा तदुक्त्वा पुनरिदं वाक्यं कथयामि यद् यदेव मानवानां तदेव वनस्पतीनां जीवनमिति शम्।

सन्दर्भ-सङ्केताः

1. मनुस्मृति - प्रथमोऽध्यायः
2. बृहत्संहिता - कुसुमलताध्यायः
3. बृहत्संहिता
4. बृहद्वास्तुमाला - भूमिलक्षणज्ञानप्रकरणम्
5. बृहत्संहिता दकार्गलाध्यायः
6. बृहत्संहिता
7. मुहूर्तचिन्तामणिः— नक्षत्रप्रकरणम्
8. वास्तुराजवल्लभः
9. मुहूर्तचिन्तामणिः नक्षत्रप्रकरणम्
10. लीलावती - भिन्नपरिकर्माष्टम्
11. संस्कृतसाहित्यपरिषत् पत्रिका - प्र.व. प्रथमाङ्कः

卐 卐 卐

CASCADE IV

FLORILEGIUM

सुमनोमाला

माला: कदम्बनवकेसरकेतकीभि-
रायोजिता: शिरसि बिभ्रति योषितोऽद्य।
कर्णान्तरेषु ककुभद्रुममञ्जरीभि:
श्रोत्रानुकूलरचितानवतंसकांश्च ।।

किं किंशुकै: शुकमुखच्छविभिर्न भिन्नं
किं कर्णिकारकुसुमैर्न कृतं न दग्धम्।
यत्कोकिल: पुनरयं मधुरैर्वचोभि-
र्यूनां मन: सुवदनानिहितं निहन्ति।।

जन्माभूदुदधौ विधौ सहजता वृन्दारकैर्वन्द्यता
तत्तत्कामफलाय शक्तिरतुला यस्यास्ति वश्यानिशम्।
विश्रामाय चिराय कल्पलतिका भूयो यमालम्बते
कस्त्वां स्तोतुमपि क्षमोऽस्ति तदपि त्वं जल्प कल्पद्रुम।।

Section XV (i) - Panegyricon
Section XV (ii) - Modern Hindi Literature

CASCADE IV

FLORILEGIUM

सुमनोमाला

एकेन चेत्परिहृतासि महेश्वरेण
किं तेन केतकि! विषादमुरीकरोषि।
अन्ये न किं जगति सन्ति महागुणज्ञाः
ये त्वां वहन्ति शिरसा नरदेवदेवाः।।

श्रीमच्चन्दनवृक्ष! सन्ति बहवस्ते शाखिनः कानने
येषां सौरभमात्रकं निवसति प्रायेण पुष्पश्रियाम्।
प्रत्यङ्गं सुकृतेन तेन शुचिना ख्यातः प्रसिद्धात्मना
यः सौगन्ध्यगुणस्त्वया प्रकटितः क्वासाविह प्रेक्ष्यते?।।

माकन्दे मकरन्दशीधुमधुरे पुन्नागयूनि भ्रमद्-
भृङ्गीनादविनोदभाजि बकुले पुष्पोद्गमामोदिनि।
अन्येष्वत्र महीरुहेषु परितः प्राप्तेषु काचिल्लता
बाला कण्टकितं तरुं शिव! शिव!! स्वैरं समालिङ्गति।।

Section XVI—Flora in Anyokti Literature

Section XV (i)

PANEGYRICON
प्रशस्तिपुष्पनिर्झरी

शुभाशंसितिः

(शब्दार्थसौन्दर्यसहस्त्रचन्द्री-ग्रन्थमभिलक्ष्य)

शब्दार्थसौन्दर्यसहस्त्रचन्द्री
चान्द्रीव दीव्यत्सुमनोमनोज्ञा।
स्वर्गस्य लोकस्य च सुन्दरत्व-
प्रकाशनश्रीसुषमां बिभर्ति।।

जगज्जयद्धा जगदीशधीश-
यशःश्रिये भाति विभूतिभूषा।
ग्रन्थेऽतुलेऽस्मिन् सुषमाकुलस्य
श्रेष्ठत्वमुच्चैः सुचिरप्रतिष्ठम्।।

दरभङ्गातः ❄ शिवजी उपाध्यायः

22.3.2002

卐 卐 卐

शुभाशंसनम्

(सुषमाकलाश्रीः-ग्रन्थमभिलक्ष्य)

साहित्यकेलिकलिताः सकलाः कलाश्च
सौन्दर्यसारसहिताः सुषमाश्रिताश्च।
एकत्र गुम्फितसुरम्यसुमस्रजस्ता
ग्रन्थेऽत्र सन्ति विलसन्ति च भावभव्याः।।

विद्वत्प्रशस्तिपरिभाषितभूरिभूति-
भास्वत्प्रभं किमपि रत्नमिदं महार्घम्।
ग्रन्थाभिधानमनिशं विदुषां समेषां
नूनं शिरोमुकुटभूषणतां दधाति।।

वाराणसीतः
22.3.2002

❄ शिवजी उपाध्यायः

卐 卐 卐

प्रशस्तिः

सुषमामङ्गलजन्मदिनम्

(13.3.2000)

सुषमितं सुरभितं तव व्यक्तित्वम्।
वाग्देवी त्वां खलु दत्तवती वरम्।।
जन्मदिवसेऽद्य ते मङ्गलं कामये।
कृतार्थं यशोऽर्थं भवेज्जीवितं ते।।

सुदीर्घं समृद्धं भवेज्जीवितं ते।।

।। इति शम्।।

सुषमाकलाश्रीः-ग्रन्थलोकार्पणावसरे शुभाशीः

सुषमा सुषमां प्राप्ता
सरस्वत्याः प्रसादतः।
काव्यं शास्त्रञ्च सङ्गीतं
तस्या वैदुष्यभाजनम्।।
श्रेष्ठकुले हि जातेयम्
अरुणाभासमन्विता।
प्राप्नुयात्सा यशः सिद्धिं
प्रतिष्ठां चिरजीवितम्।।

❄ पद्मश्री सुमति मुटाटकर

इन्द्रप्रस्थतः
वैकुण्ठ-चतुर्दशी
13.11.1997

卐 卐 卐

ज्योत्स्नामयश्रीः

ज्योत्स्नामयो गौरवर्णो
मधुरमन्द्रस्वरस्त्वम्।
हृदयं तेऽतिनिर्मलं
स्वच्छमुकुरतुलितम्।।

सर्वेषां सर्वकार्येषु
साहाय्ये तत्परस्सदा।
सहामहे कथं नु ते
भीषणं निर्वाणदुःखम्।।

इन्द्रप्रस्थतः
2.9.2001

❉ पद्मश्री सुमति मुटाटकर

卐 卐 卐

Section XV (ii)

MODERN HINDI LITERATURE

आधुनिकहिन्दीकाव्यामृतनिर्झरी

जीवनसार

जीव पूछता कोऽहं कोऽहम्।
आत्मा कहती सोऽहं सोऽहम्।।
आया कहाँ से जायेगा कहाँ।
बार-बार यह होती पृच्छा।।
आया हूँ ईश्वर के घर से।
जाना है फिर वहीं लौट के।।
जीव जगत जंजाल भरम का।
बूझो रहस मरम क्या इसका।।
श्रद्धा भक्ति भाव से पूरित।
प्यार और सच्चाई से गुञ्जित।।
ईश्वर की आभा से रञ्जित।
प्रभु का नाम जीवनसार।।

❈ सुमति मुटाटकर

अनन्त-चतुर्दशी
20.9.2002

卐 卐 卐

शतवसन्त-सुषमा

शत वसन्त सुषमा मङ्गल घट
लेकर आगे आये।
जीवन उपवन को सिञ्चित कर
सुरभित सफल बनाये।।

❈ रामदेव झा

होलिकोत्सव
29.3.2002

卐 卐 卐

सीखो तरुओं से शीश नवाना

सीखो तरुओं से शीश नवाना
सीखो इनसे सदा मुसकाना!!
ये देखो छाया देते
ये देखो फल देते
बदले में ये कुछ न लेते!! 1 !!

ओषधियों के ये हैं स्त्रोत
इनसे है जीवन में ज्योत!!
नीम पीपल और बबूल
हैं उपचारों से भरपूर
दूर करें रोगों के शूल!! 2 !!

सूरज की किरणों को तरु अपने में समाते
इस तरह सूर्य-ऊर्जा को आगे बढ़ाते!!
कभी न देखा इन को क्रुद्ध
हर पल करते वायु शुद्ध!! 3 !!

लकड़ी आग देवदार और चीड़ की
जान है समस्त ठोस फरनीचर की
सज्जा बनती घर दफ़तर की!!
जब पल्लवियों पर ओसबिन्दु करते किलकारी
स्तब्ध रह जाती पल्लवी देख यह छटा निराली!! 4 !!

लदी फलों से झुकी डालियाँ
नम्रता की यही प्रणालियाँ!!
पूजनीय है वनस्पति-जगत्
हम हृदय से हैं नतमस्तक!!
इन पर चिड़ियों का बसेरा
मिले चहकता हमें सवेरा!! 5 !!

हे मानव! तुम मत काटो
मत काटो मत काटो इन तरुओं को
न जन्म दो रेगिस्तानों को
हासिल कर लो मुसकानों को!! 6 !!

न्यूयॉर्क (अमेरिका)

4.11.2002

❉ पल्लवी मोहन

卐 卐 卐

वन जीवन है जनजीवन का

वन जीवन है जनजीवन का
जन-जन को इन्हें बचाना है,
वन से सरसा संसार यह सारा
सुन्दर और सुहाना है।
जन जीवन है · · · ·

(1)

यही वन थे जहाँ पर ऋषियों ने
सत्-चित्-आनन्द को पाया था,
आत्मबोध के शोध में सबने
वानप्रस्थ अपनाया था।
कभी इन्हीं वनों की महिमा से
भारत स्वर्णिम कहलाया था,
बीते कल की यह धरोहर है
आते कल का यही खज़ाना है।
वन जीवन है · · · ·

(2)

इन वनवासी संग राम-कृष्ण
गौतम ने वर्षों वास किया,
वनदेव-सा उनने पूजा, हमने
'जंगली' कह उपहास किया,

खुद अपनी जड़ों को काट के हम
कहते हैं हमने विकास किया,
फिर जंगल में मंगल कर के
उनका गौरव लौटाना है।
वन जीवन है · · · ·

(3)

सभी वन थे अभय, जहाँ निर्भय
सब वन के जीव विचरते थे,
कहीं सिंह-शावक, कहीं शुक-सारिका,
कहीं वेद के शब्द उभरते थे।
कहीं भरत कहीं एकलव्य कहीं
लव-कुश क्रीड़ा करते थे,
मन के दुष्यन्त में बोध जगा
फिर शाकुन्तलम् सजाना है।
वन जीवन है · · · · ।

नई दिल्ली

6.11.2002

❀ प्रदीप शर्मा

卐 卐 卐

काव्यसुरभि

चन्दनधूलि

एक है चन्दन-धूलि—
अंग-अंग महका दे;
एक है सुमन-धूलि—
सृजन का गीत रच जाए,
एक उड़ी गो-धूलि—
युगों की कथा कह जाए;
देखी है धरा-धूलि—
महक, सृष्टि, युग-कथा
उसी से उद्ग्रीव।
समवेत पावन चरण-धूलि—
ले, ललाट का तिलक सजाऊँ।

कली

कली को आचार्य बना लिया है।
उसकी मैं शिष्या पाद-नत। दक्षिणा देनी है,
सिखाया सीख जाने पर— छोटे से छोटे बक्से में
छोटी से छोटी तह में पोशाक रखने की कला।
कि, निकाल कर खोलने पर
शिकन न पड़े हल्की भी वन-रूपसी की पोशाक में।
फिर, उसी में वापिस रखना सिखा दूँगी,
किसी और से सीखकर—
बिना दक्षिणा ही सुरभि को।

मौलसिरी

मौलसिरी के फूल बिछावन,
सोती बुँदियाँ, महका सावन।

आख़िरी पत्ते

झर गए आख़िरी पत्ते— सूने खड़े पेड़,
रीतेपन की लाज छिपाए नहीं छिपती,
नम्र थे कल, आज बने हीन।
छाया कैसा आतङ्क? मूक मेघों की खामोशी
सहम कर ठहर गई, पेड़ों की परछाईं
चुप जा छिपी ताल के जल में।
भागती गाड़ी चुप्पी के चैन को चौंकाती
दौड़ी जा रही है, और मैं उसके साथ।

मधुर रस

चाय की प्याली में क्या सिमट आया है?
कामदेव के मन्मथ इक्षु-शर-चाप का मधुर रस—
ईख के खेतों में झूमते, कोल्हू में पोर-पोर पिरकर,
गन्ने के रस की संज्ञा से उभर कर,
शक्कर बन मिठास घोल पाया है।
दारज़िलिंग की पहाड़ियों की गोद में
उगी, लता सी लचीली किशोरी।
रूप-रस भीगी या पार्वती,
या जीवन-स्रोत सूखी विगत-रूपा पके बाल—
पटु हाथों चुनती चाय की पत्ती दो कली संग।
आग में उबलकर पानी में डूबकर सुनहरा रंग कहाँ से पाया?
उस रंग में समायी है तालों में नभ को निहार-निहार
थककर सोई पहाड़ों की परछाईं।
कामधेनु वंशजा धरा की धेनु से
तप की साधना की तुष्टि से वर पाये—
दूध के जीवन-बिन्दु छलके हैं प्याली में
चाय चीनी दूध मिल
प्याली को भरते कैसे प्याली के बिना?

स्थितप्रज्ञ

ताल के किनारे पर
खड़ा पेड़, स्थित-प्रज्ञ पेड़
झुकी हुई डाल पानी को छाया से
हिलाती है इधर-उधर, कौन कलश भरने को?'
मन्दिर की सीढ़ियाँ पीपल की छाया बुहारती है
धूप चाँदनी सकेरती कैसे पुण्य सञ्चय को?

चाँदनी

चाँदनी सकेरती रही सारी रात
पीपल की छाया नदी के किनारे
घाट की सीढ़ियों पर— सारी रात।

पवन

ओ पवन तू तुषग्राही पल्लववाही
भटकती फिरती है, पुकारती है।
अस्थिर-गति करती फिरती है अरण्य रोदन।
तुषज तो कुछ नहीं,
पल्लवज होना सम्भव है, पर सदा नहीं।
बीज फेंक इधर-उधर
बनती फिरती कभी सृजन-दर्पी।
पर मूलग्राही जब बनी प्रलय-स्पर्श लेकर चली।
हरित तरुवर विशाख, विक्षत धराशायी।
शिथिल-वृन्त पल्लव उड़े निर्लक्ष्य तुझ सङ्ग।
ढो न सकेगी भार तू दूर तक, ओ आग्रही,
तू सिर धुने या पटके विकटशून्य में।

रूपश्री

तीर धनुरंगी छुटे हैं
तरुवरों के गगन-उन्मुख
फूटते नव-किसलयों पर।
सलिल पर मोती भरे से
थाल से कुवलय दलों पर;
पँखुड़ी की कोर से पँखुड़ी को खोलती
पँखुड़ी की रूपश्री पर तीर धनुरंगी छुटे हैं।

बकुल

तरु बकुल से झरा
बोला बकुल हुआ आकुल—
''नया हूँ बस्ती में— परिचय दे आया हूँ।
अभी सभा होने वाली है—
सबको अपनी कहानी पढ़कर सुनानी है।
तुम तो कवि हो।
मुझे लिखना नहीं आता, पढ़ना भी नहीं आता।
कर दो तुम मेरा काम।
सुनो, मैं सुनाता हूँ।''
'अरे, बस बन्द करो। पन्ने सब भर गए,
माँगे भी चुक गए परिचय ही लिखते लिखते ।
हो तो तुम ऐसे लघुकाय,
मृदुल रम्य कोमल-काय सद्यःजात से।
हुआ कैसे अतीत महाकाय?
हो क्या मृत्युञ्जयी? कालजयी?
तुम्हारी कथा तुम्हारे मुँह सुन, लिखने में
चाहे बने काव्य, या महाकाव्य,
लिखे जाएं इतिहास या उपन्यास,
नहीं लिखूँगा। मैं हूँ अल्पजीवी।
मानो तो, लिख सकता हूँ एक गीत—
स्वर भी दे सकता हूँ।
तुम गाओ, और, चाहो, फिर सुनाओ
जहाँ हों अलि-कुल विहग-कुल
या वीचि-कूल, ओ आकुल-बकुल।

काग़ज़ के फूल

काग़ज़ के फूल सजे थे गुलदान में—
बड़े सजीले थे—
कुशल शिल्पी की कला के नमूने;
पानी की बूँद भी छू ले तो रूप बिगड़ जाए।
बागों में बेल चढ़ी— फूल खिले, गन्ध बही
भ्रमर आए, तान छिड़ी, फूल झड़े, मिट गए।
काग़ज़ के फूल सजे ही रहे
धूल भरे गुलदान में।

मुक्तावली

नगीनों से जड़ी फूलों की छड़ी में
उलझ गई मोती की लड़ी,
सूरज की किरणें जब, हँस-हँस गिरती बिखर पड़ीं।

लाजवन्ती

छुई-मुई का पौधा था छोटा सा— छोटी थी मैं भी।
विस्मय भरा था मेरे लिये छुई-मुई के पौधे में।
छूने से पहले ही उँगली के पास आते ही
लजीली झुक जाती थीं नन्हीं पत्तियाँ दोहरी होकर।

"कोई भय-बाधा तो नहीं" देखने को ज्यों ही
ज़रा नयन उठाती थीं मैं फिर छू देती थी।
दोनों हाथ फैलाकर पौधे को घेर लेती थी,
रखे रहती थी पत्तियों पर। सोचती थी,
'हाथ ही न हटाऊँ तो क्या हो?'

बार-बार छूने से बन्द हो झुक गई लाजवन्ती पत्ती—
लाज-भरी, या छुई-मुई, भय-भरी,
पता नहीं था तब तो, बस कुतूहल था,
जादू सा लगता था जादूगर मैं थी।

कितनी-कितनी देर—पत्तियों के बन्द होने और खुलने पर
चकित होती थी, पर विस्मय में कमी न होती थी।
वह बाल-खेल कर रहा है कौन आज?
छुई-मुई सी मेरी मन पँखुड़ी को
बार-बार छूकर सुलाता है जगाता है?
सुलाता है कौन-बार-बार छूकर जगाता है
कौन प्राणों को घेरे?

❋ कौशल्या गुप्ता

卐 卐 卐

कमलेश-वैजयन्तीमाला

श्रीमती कमलेश कुमारी कुलश्रेष्ठ-प्रणीत गीतियाँ

शकुन्तला मलिक • मीना चन्द्रा

1. ध्रुपद-राग आसावरी-चौताल

प्रथम पूज्य देवन में गणपति गणनायक।
सिद्धिसदन विघ्नहरण मङ्गलसुखदायक।।
वक्रतुण्ड एकदन्त चतुरभुज दयावन्त।
पूरित सब मोरे काज सुन्दर साधक।।[1]

2. गीत-राग यमन-त्रिताल

जय जय जन्म भूमि अरु जननी।
पावन उच्च हो भारत अवनी।।
शान्ति ऐक्य की शक्ति दो प्रभुवर!
पार लगे तब भारत तरनी।।[2]

3. गीत-राग बिलावल-त्रिताल

अनुपम सुखद प्रभात भयो री।
श्याम दरश भये शीतल नयना।।
सुन्दर वदन कमल दल लोचन।
कोटि मदन छवि लाजै सखी री।।[3]

4. गीत-राग काफी-त्रिताल

बहुत दिन बीते आये न मुरारी।
दिखादे मधुर मूरत तोरी प्यारी-प्यारी कल परत नाहीं।।
कुँज गलिन जमुना तट मधुवन।
ढूँढत भटकत डोलत निशदिन।।
दरश दिखादे वेणु बजादे।
रूठ गए क्यों बिहारी।।[4]

5. **गीत-राग भैरव-त्रिताल**

अरुणशिखा धुन सुन प्रभु जागे।
रतनारे अलसाने नयना।
अर्थ खुले निद्रा त्यागे।।
मुख ऊपर घुँघराली अलकें।
अधरन धरी श्याम मुरली।
धुन सुन सुर नर मुनि हैं धाये।
प्रभु चरनन सब लागे।।[5]

6. **गीत-राग भैरवी-त्रिताल**

बँसिया बजाई है कन्हाई
डगर चलत सब रहीं अकुलाई सुध बिसराई।
कर पकरत अरु खींचत सारी
लाज नहीं आई भयो निडर कन्हाई करत ढिठाई।।[6]

7. **गीत-राग आसावरी-त्रिताल**

चलत चाल अलबेली कान्हा।
मधु मुसकान माधुरी चितवन।।
शीश मुकुट श्रुति कुण्डल भ्राजत।
गल बैजंती माल विराजत।
अधर मुरली धर राखी कान्हा।।[7]

8. **गीत-राग देश-त्रिताल**

सखी कारे-कारे बदरा घिर आए।
लरजत गरजत झिरत औ बरसत।।
दादुर मोर पपीहा बोलत।
दामिनी दमकत जिया है डोलत
श्याम सुन्दर मथुरा छाये।।[8]

9. **गीत-राग वृन्दावनी सारंग-त्रिताल**

सज रहीं अलबेली नवेली। स्वर्ण मुकुट फूलन गल माला।।
वसन वासित भूषण भूषित। खेलत संग अति उमंग सब मिल।।
चम्पाकली के सेहरा बनाला। बनी बने के साज सजाला।।
आये कान्हा बाँधो कंगना सब मिल।। रहीं . . .।[9]

10. **गीत–राग देस–त्रिताल**
देखो सखी बरसन को आये बदरा।
रूम--झूम बरसे मोरे अँगना।
बिजली चमक–चमक डरपावे।
पपीहा पी–पी शोर मचावे।।
चैन न आये पिया घर ना।।[10]

11. **गीत–राग काफी–ताल दीपचन्दी**
कैसी ये होरी मचाई। आज मोसों कुँवर कन्हाई।।
अबीर गुलाल मलत मुख ऊपर मारत रङ्ग पिचकारी।
खेलत नवल किशोरी सों होली।।
शोभा वरणी न जाई सो मेरी आली
धूम मचाई! कैसी ये होरी मचाई।।[11]

12. **गीत–राग यमन–एकताल**
चलो हटो जाओ बनवारी, छाँड़ो बैंया मोरी ढीट लँगर।
लाज न आवत तुम कँह, हँसतीं सखियाँ सारी।।
छीनत दधि, मग रोकत, बाट चलत, नित टोकत।
करकि गईं सब चुरियाँ, बिगरि गई सब सारी।।[12]

13. **गीत–राग खमाज–त्रिताल**
नूपुर की झनकार मधुर मृदु।
मन हरणी मतवारी प्यारी।।
संग में सखियाँ बीच कन्हैया।
भूले धुनि सुन सब नर–नारी।।[13]

14. **गीत–राग बहार–त्रिताल**
सघन बन कुंजन बेलरियाँ।
फूल रहीं फुल बगियन भीतर।
डारन डारन नव कलियाँ।।
ऋतु बसंत ऋतुराज है आयो।
मादक भीनी सुगन्ध लायो।
कूक सुनावत कोयलिया।।[14]

15. **गीत-राग भूपाली-ख्याल-त्रिताल**
पार करो मेरी नैया भँवर से।
निशदिन तुमको सुमिरत मन में।।
गहरी नदिया नाव पुरानी।
केवट है मतवाला।।[15]

16. **गीत-राग बागेश्री-ख्याल-त्रिताल**
कटत नहीं रजनी अब सजनी।
प्रभु बिन मोसे रहो न जाय।।
घरि पल छिन-छिन जुग सम बीतत।
बिरहा सतावत चैन न आवत।
कासे जिया की व्यथा कहूँ अपनी।।[16]

17. **गीत-राग भीमपलासी-ख्याल-त्रिताल**
अनुपम जोड़ी की बलिहारी।
मनहर सुन्दर लागत प्यारी।।
इत राजत हैं कृष्ण मुरारी।
उत शोभतीं राधा प्यारी।
कुञ्ज गलिन की उपमा न्यारी।।[17]

18. **गीत-राग केदार-ख्याल-त्रिताल**
देखो री श्याम सुन्दर।
परम मनोहर मुरली अधर घर।।
लसत कण्ठ बैजन्ती माला।
लख-लख मुदित भई ब्रज बाला।।[18]

19. गीत-राग तिलककामोद-त्रिताल
झूमन लागी वन-वन की डाली-डाली।
ऋतु बसन्त में अपनी उमंग सों।।
आई बहार सकल वन फूले।
देख जिया हरषित मुदित आली।।[19]

20. **गीत-राग मालकोश-त्रिताल**
सुकुमारी प्यारी अति छबीली नार।
मनहर शुभ पूरित श्रृङ्गार।।
रतनारे नयना पिकबयनी।
गजगामिनी लाजत मराल।।[20]

सन्दर्भ-सङ्केत

1. संगीत-कौमुदी (श्रीमती कमलेश कुमारी कुलश्रेष्ठ) - अग्रवाल ब्रदर्स, इलाहाबाद, 1947, पृ. 139
2. संगीत-कौमुदी - पृ० 63
3. संगीत-कौमुदी - पृ० 66
4. संगीत-कौमुदी - पृ० 72
5. संगीत-कौमुदी - पृ० 76
6. संगीत-कौमुदी - पृ० 80
7. संगीत-कौमुदी - पृ० 83
8. संगीत-कौमुदी - पृ० 96
9. संगीत-कौमुदी - पृ० 103
10. संगीत-किशोर (श्री जगदीश सहाय कुलश्रेष्ठ), संगीत कार्यालय, हाथरस, पञ्चम संस्करण, 1958, पृ० 67
11. संगीत-किशोर - पृ० 26
12. संगीत-किशोर - पृ० 9
13. संगीत-किशोर - पृ० 17
14. संगीत-सुधा (श्री जगदीश सहाय कुलश्रेष्ठ), पीताम्बर बुक डिपो, नई दिल्ली, तृतीय संस्करण, 1984, पृ० 187
15. संगीत-सुधा - पृ० 101
16. संगीत-सुधा - पृ० 129
17. संगीत-सुधा - पृ० 137
18. संगीत-सुधा - पृ० 144
19. संगीत-सुधा - पृ० 101
20. संगीत-सुधा - पृ० 196

卐 卐 卐

Section XVI

FLORA IN ANYOKTI LITERATURE

अन्योक्ति-सुमनोझरी

पण्डितराजजगन्नाथीया पुष्पान्योक्तिमधुसुरभिः

(मालतीमल्लिकायूथीकेतकीकैरविणीपद्मिनीनलिनीलवङ्गलताकलिता)

रवीन्द्र किशोर सिन्हा • ऋता सिन्हा

1. मालती

(1) अयि मालति! सौरभसारविनि-
जितसंविकसत्कमलानिलये!
मधुपानविधौ मधुपस्य पुनः
भुवने भवतीमहमाकलये।।

(2) किं मालति! म्लायसि मां विहाय
चुचुम्ब तुम्बीकुसुमं षडङ्घ्रिः।
लोकश्चतुर्भिश्चरणैः पशुः स्यात्
स षड्भिरत्यर्थपशुर्न किं स्यात्?।।[1]

2. मल्लिका

(3) न च गन्धवहेन चुम्बिता न च पीता मधुपेन मल्लिका।
निहतैव कठोरशाखया परिणामस्य जगाम गोचरम्।।[2]

3. यूथी

(4) यूथि! यथोचितविधिना विधेयमातिथ्यमेतस्मिन्।
मालतिकाप्राणेशः प्राघुणिकस्ते घुणाक्षरन्यायात्।।[3]

4. केतकी

(5) एकेन चेत्परिहृतासि महेश्वरेण
किं तेन केतकि! विषादमुरीकरोषि।
अन्ये न किं जगति सन्ति महागुणज्ञाः
ये त्वां वहन्ति शिरसा नरदेवदेवाः।।

(6) हे हेमकेताकि! कथं बहुगर्वितासि
संसेव्यसे मधुकरैरखिलैरितीव।
नैषा रसातिशयता नलिनीवियोगा-
त्तैर्दीयते विकटकण्टकशूलझम्पः।।[4]

5. कैरविणी

(7) अयि त्वया कैरविणि व्यधायि
मुधा सुधाबन्धुसुबन्धुभावः।
जनापवादः परितः प्रयातः
समागमो हन्त न जातु जातः।।[5]

6. पद्मिनी

(8) अयि मकरन्दस्यन्दिनि पद्मिनि! मन्ये तवैव सुभगत्वम्।
पुष्पवतीमपि भवतीं त्यजति न वृद्धः शुचिर्हंसः।।

(9) पद्मिनि! किमिति क्रीडसि मधुपैर्लज्जालवोऽपि न हि किं ते?।
हर! हर!! विस्मृत्योक्तं क्व नु लज्जा सवितृरक्तायाः।।[6]

7. मल्ली • मालती • लवङ्गी

(10) हे मल्लि! हे मालति! हे लवङ्गि!
न तादृशी क्वापि भवादृशीनाम्।
क्षणं समाधाय मधुव्रतं या
विस्मारयेदम्बुजिनीवियोगम् ।।[7]

8. नलिनी

(11) कति कति न लताः कलिताः सञ्चरता चञ्चरीकरसिकेन।
नलिनि! भवन्मधु मधुरं यत्पीतं तत्तदेव परिपीतम्।।[8]

9. लवङ्गलता

(12) अयि दुष्कृतकेन केन वत्से!
हालिकद्वारि लवङ्गि! पुष्पितासि।
स्तबकास्तव पांसुभिः परीताः
परितः प्राङ्गणसीम्नि यल्लुठन्ति।।[9]

10. लता

(13) चित्रं कनकलतायां पल्लव एवामृतं सूते।
कुसुमसमुद्गमसमये नो जाने किं फलं भावि।।

(14) माकन्दे मकरन्दशीधुमधुरे पुन्नागयूनि भ्रमद्-
भृङ्गीनादविनोदभाजि बकुले पुष्पोद्गमामोदिनि।
अन्येष्वत्र महीरुहेषु परितः प्राप्तेषु काचिल्लता
बाला कण्टकितं तरुं शिव! शिव!! स्वैरं समालिङ्गति।।[10]

सन्दर्भ-सङ्केताः

1. पण्डितराजजगन्नाथकाव्यग्रन्थावली (डॉ० हरिनारायणदीक्षितसम्पादिता) - प्रस्फुटितान्योक्तयः - 232-233
2. पण्डितराजजगन्नाथकाव्यग्रन्थावली - प्रस्फुटितान्योक्तयः - 229
3. पण्डितराजजगन्नाथकाव्यग्रन्थावली - प्रस्फुटितान्योक्तयः - 241
4. पण्डितराजजगन्नाथकाव्यग्रन्थावली - प्रस्फुटितान्योक्तयः - 111, 113
5. पण्डितराजजगन्नाथकाव्यग्रन्थावली - प्रस्फुटितान्योक्तयः - 52
6. पण्डितराजजगन्नाथकाव्यग्रन्थावली - प्रस्फुटितान्योक्तयः - 53, 59
7. पण्डितराजजगन्नाथकाव्यग्रन्थावली - प्रस्फुटितान्योक्तयः - 63
8. पण्डितराजजगन्नाथकाव्यग्रन्थावली - प्रस्फुटितान्योक्तयः - 8
9. पण्डितराजजगन्नाथकाव्यग्रन्थावली - प्रस्फुटितान्योक्तयः - 274
10. पण्डितराजजगन्नाथकाव्यग्रन्थावली - प्रस्फुटितान्योक्तयः - 272-273

卐 卐 卐

पण्डितराजीया वृक्षान्योक्तिराजी

(कल्पद्रुमचन्दनागुर्वश्वत्थचम्पकजबीरशाल्मलिबर्बूरतालपलाशधुत्तूरेक्षुराजिता)

सुमति मुटाटकर • चन्द्रकान्त द्विवेदी

1. कल्पद्रुमः

(1) जन्माभूदुदधौ विधौ सहजता वृन्दारकैर्वन्द्यता
तत्तत्कामफलाय शक्तिरतुला यस्यास्ति वश्यानिशम्।
विश्रामाय चिराय कल्पलतिका भूयो यमालम्बते
कस्त्वां स्तोतुमपि क्षमोऽस्ति तदपि त्वं जल्पकल्पद्रुम।।[1]

2. चन्दनः

(2) श्रीमच्चन्दनवृक्ष! सन्ति बहवस्ते शाखिनः कानने
येषां सौरभमात्रकं निवसति प्रायेण पुष्पश्रियाम्।
प्रत्यङ्गं सुकृतेन तेन शुचिना ख्यातः प्रसिद्धात्मना
यः सौगन्ध्यगुणस्त्वया प्रकटितः क्वासाविह प्रेक्ष्यते?।।[2]

3. अगुरुः

(3) एणाद्याः पशवः किरातपरिषत् स्नेहेऽगुणग्राहिणी
सञ्चारोऽत्र न नागरस्य विषयोच्छिन्नं मुनीनां मनः।
धूमेनातिसुगन्धिनात्र विपिने दिक्चक्रमामोदयन्
आमूलं परिदह्यतेऽगुरुतरुः कस्मै किमाचक्ष्महे।।[3]

4. अश्वत्थः

(4) अस्ति स्वादु फलं किमत्तुमथवा घ्रातुं पुनः कोरकः
तद् विश्राम्यतु नाम भोक्तुममलं पत्रं किमस्त्यन्ततः।
सेव्यो हन्त यदीदृशोऽपि मनुजैर्वृक्षाधमः पिप्पलो
दुःस्वातन्त्र्यमिदं विधेः कथय तत्कस्याग्रतो रुद्यताम्।।[4]

5. चम्पकः

(5) कोपं चम्पक! मुञ्च याचकजनैरायासितस्त्वं सखे!
मा म्लासीः परितो विलोकय तरुः कस्तेऽधिरूढस्तुलाम्।
कोपश्चेन्नियतस्तवास्ति हृदये धात्रे तदा कुप्यतां
येन त्वं हि सुवर्णवर्णकुसुमामोदोऽद्वितीयः कृतः।।[5]

6. जम्बीरम्

(6) कान्तिस्ते कनकाचलप्रतिनिधिः कान्ताकुचस्पर्द्धि ते
सौभाग्यं क्षितिपालदर्शनविधौ त्वत्पूर्वकं दर्शनम्।
सौरभ्यं सकलातिशायि भवतो जम्बीर! किं ब्रूमहे!
कर्पूरप्रतिकूलता यदि न ते त्वय्येव सर्वे गुणाः।।[6]

7. शाल्मलिः

(7) दूरे मार्गान्निवससि पुनः कण्टकैरावृतोऽसि
च्छायाशून्यः फलमपि च ते वानरैरप्यभक्ष्यम्।
निर्गन्धस्त्वं मधुपरहितः शाल्मले! सारशून्यः
सेवास्माकं भवति विफला तिष्ठ निःश्वस्य यामः।।[7]

8. बर्बूरः

(8) आमूलाग्रनिबद्धकण्टकतनुर्निगन्धपुष्पोद्गमः
छाया न श्रमहारिणी न च फलं क्षुत्क्षामसन्तर्पणम्।
बर्बूरद्रुम! साधुसङ्गरहितः पन्थानमाक्रामसि
त्वन्येषां फलशाखिनां फलवतां गुर्वी वृतिर्जायसे।।[8]

9. तालः

(9) अये ताल! व्रीडां व्रज गुरुतया भाति न भवान्
फलं न च्छाया नो कठिनपरिवारो हि भवतः।
इयं धन्या धन्या सरलकदली सुन्दरदला
परात्मानं मन्ये सुखयति फलेनामृतवता।।[9]

10. पलाशः

(10) किंशुक! किं शुकमुखवत् कुसुमानि विकासयस्यनिशम्।
यस्यां जनोऽनुरागी सा गीरेतैः कदापि नोच्चार्या।।

(11) त्यज किंशुक! पुष्पिताभिमानं निजशीर्षे भ्रमरोपसेवनेन।
विकसन्नवमालिकावियोगात् कुरुते वह्निधिया त्वयि प्रवेशम्।।[10]

11. धुत्तूरः

(12) धुत्तूर! धूर्त! तरुणेन्दुनिवासयोग्य-
स्थाने पिशाचपतिना विनिवेशितोऽसि।
किं कैरवाणि विकसन्ति तमः प्रयाति
चन्द्रोपलः स्रवति वार्धिरुपैति वृद्धिम्?।।[11]

12. इक्षुः

(13) कान्तोऽसि नित्यमधुरोऽसि रसाकुलोऽसि
किं चासि पञ्चशरकार्मुकमद्वितीयम्।
इक्षो! तवास्ति सकलं परमेकमूनं
यत्सेवितो भजसि नीरसतां क्रमेण।।[12]

सन्दर्भ-सङ्केताः

1. पण्डितराजजगन्नाथकाव्यग्रन्थावली (डॉ० हरिनारायण दीक्षितसम्पादिता)-प्रस्फुटितान्योक्तयः -68
2. पण्डितराजजगन्नाथकाव्यग्रन्थावली - प्रस्फुटितान्योक्तयः - 160
3. पण्डितराजजगन्नाथकाव्यग्रन्थावली - प्रस्फुटितान्योक्तयः - 2
4. पण्डितराजजगन्नाथकाव्यग्रन्थावली - प्रस्फुटितान्योक्तयः - 44
5. पण्डितराजजगन्नाथकाव्यग्रन्थावली - प्रस्फुटितान्योक्तयः - 181
6. पण्डितराजजगन्नाथकाव्यग्रन्थावली - प्रस्फुटितान्योक्तयः - 198
7. पण्डितराजजगन्नाथकाव्यग्रन्थावली - प्रस्फुटितान्योक्तयः - 343
8. पण्डितराजजगन्नाथकाव्यग्रन्थावली - प्रस्फुटितान्योक्तयः - 219
9. पण्डितराजजगन्नाथकाव्यग्रन्थावली - प्रस्फुटितान्योक्तयः - 206
10. पण्डितराजजगन्नाथकाव्यग्रन्थावली - प्रस्फुटितान्योक्तयः - 215-216
11. पण्डितराजजगन्नाथकाव्यग्रन्थावली - प्रस्फुटितान्योक्तयः - 210
12. पण्डितराजजगन्नाथकाव्यग्रन्थावली - प्रस्फुटितान्योक्तयः - 48

卐 卐 卐

सुभाषितरत्नभाण्डागारे वृक्षान्योक्तिशशिकला

(हरिचन्दनकल्पद्रुमपारिजातबकुलाशोकसहकाररसालाम्रमाकन्दपनसनालिकेर-खदिरपीलुबिल्वमालूरश्रीफलाढ्या)

ज्योत्स्नामय चैटर्जी • रमण कुमार शर्मा

1. हरिचन्दनः

(1) केचिल्लोचनहारिणः कतिपये सौरभ्यसंभारिणः
केऽप्यन्ये फलधारिणः प्रतिदिनं ते सन्तु हन्त द्रुमाः।
धन्योऽयं हरिचन्दनः परिसरे यस्य स्थितैः शाखिभिः
शाखोटादिभिरप्यहो मृगदृशामङ्गेषु लीलायितम्।।[1]

2. चन्दनः

(2) मूलं भुजङ्गैः शिखरं प्लवङ्गैः शाखा विहङ्गैः कुसुमानि भृङ्गैः।
नास्त्येव तच्चन्दनपादपस्य यन्नाश्रितं सत्त्वभरैः समन्तात्।।

(3) सौरभ्यं भुवनत्रयेऽपि विदितं शैत्यं नु लोकोत्तरं
कीर्तिः किं च दिगङ्गनाङ्गनगता किं त्वेतदेकं शृणु।
सर्वानेव गुणानियं निगिरति श्रीखण्ड ते सुन्दरा-
नुज्झन्ती खलु कोटरेषु गरलज्वालां द्विजिह्वावली।।[2]

3. कल्पद्रुमः

(4) जन्माभूदुदधौ विधौ सहजता वृन्दारकैर्वन्द्यता
तत्तत्कामफलाय शक्तिरतुला यस्यास्ति वश्यानिशम्।
विश्रामाय चिराय कल्पलतिका भूयोऽयमालम्बते
कस्त्वां स्तोतुमपि क्षमोऽस्ति तदपि त्वं जल्प कल्पद्रुम।।[3]

4. पारिजातः

(5) परिमलसुरभितनभसो बहवः कनकाद्रिपरिसरे तरवः।
तदपि सुराणां चेतसि निवसितमिव पारिजातेन।।[4]

5. बकुलः

(6) निसर्गादारामे तरुकुलसमारोपसुकृती
कृती मालाकारो बकुलमपि कुत्रापि निदधे।
इदं को जानीते यदयमिह कोणान्तरगतो
जगज्जालं कर्ता कुसुमभरसौरभ्यभरितम्।।[5]

6. अशोकः

(7) किं ते नम्रतया किमुन्नततया किं वा घनच्छायया
किं वा पल्लवलीलया किमनया वाशोक पुष्पश्रिया।
यत्त्वन्मूलनिषण्णखिन्नपथिकस्तोमः स्तुवन्नन्वहं
न स्वादूनि मृदूनि खादति फलान्याकण्ठमुत्कण्ठितः।।[6]

7. सहकारः • रसालः • आम्रः • माकन्दः

(8) कति पल्लविता न पुष्पिता वा तरवः सन्ति समन्ततो वसन्ते।
जगतीविजये तु पुष्पकेतोः सहकारी सहकार एक एव।।

(9) न तादृक्कर्पूरे न च मलयजे नो मृगमदे
फले वा पुष्पे वा तव मिलति यादृक्परिमलः।
परं त्वेको दोषस्त्वयि खलु रसाले यदधिकः
पिके वा काके वा लघुगुरुविशेषं न मनुषे।।

(10) कूष्माण्डीफलवत्फलं न यदपि न्यग्रोधवन्नोच्चता
रम्भापत्रनिभं दलं न कुसुमं नो केतकीपुष्पवत्।
सौरभ्यं कुसुमे फले तदपि तत्किंचित्समुज्जृम्भते
लोको येन रसाल शालनिकरांस्त्यक्त्वा गुणान्स्तौति ते।।

(11) गर्वं मा कुरु शर्करे तव गुणाञ्जानन्ति राज्ञां गृहे
ये दीना धनवर्जिताश्च कृपणाः स्वप्नेऽपि पश्यन्ति नो।
आम्रोऽहं मधुकूपकैर्मम फलैस्तृप्ता हि सर्वे जना
हे रण्डे तव किं गुणा मम फलैस्तुल्यं न किंचित्फलम्।।

(12) स्निग्धाग्राः फलिनो वृताः परिमलैः पौष्पैर्मधुस्यन्दिनो
नानन्दाय भवन्ति किं वनभुवां भूमीरुहो भूरिशः।
माधुर्यं मधुनस्तवैव परमं माकन्द मन्यामहे
माध्वीमर्मविदो दृढं मधुलिहः स्यूता यतो मर्मणि।।

(13) त्वं सामान्यतरुभ्रमेण सकलक्षोणीरुहक्ष्मापतौ
माकन्देऽपि किरात पातय मुधा मास्मिन्कुठारं हठात्।
एष श्लाघ्यजनस्य जीवितमलिव्यूहस्य बन्धुर्मधोः
सर्वस्वं कुसुमायुधस्य विजयामात्यः पिकानां गुरुः।।[7]

8. पनसः

(14) गरीयः सौरभ्यं रसपरिचये नार्हति सुधा
सिता मृद्वीकापि प्रथिमनि निमग्नः फलभरः।
परार्थे कोशश्रीरिति पुलकितं कण्टकमिषा-
दहो ते चारित्रं पनस मनसः कस्य न मुदे।।[8]

9. नालिकेरः

(15) उच्चैरेष तरुः फलं च विपुलं दृष्ट्वैव हृष्टः शुकः
पक्वं शालिवनं विहाय जडधीस्तं नालिकेरं गतः।
तत्रारुह्य बुभुक्षितेन मनसा यत्नः कृतो भेदने
वाञ्छा तस्य न केवलं विगलिता चञ्चूर्गता चूर्णताम्।।[9]

10. खदिरः

(16) विना खदिरसारेण हारेण हरिणीदृशाम्।
नाधरे जायते रागो नानुरागः पयोधरे।।[10]

11. पीलुः

(17) धन्याः सूक्ष्मफला अपि प्रियतमास्ते पीलुवृक्षाः क्षितौ
क्षुत्क्षीणेन जनेन हि प्रतिदिनं येषां फलं भुज्यते।
किं तैस्तत्र महाफलैरपि पुनः कल्पद्रुमाद्यैर्द्रुमै-
र्येषां नाम मनागपि श्रमनुदे छायापि न प्राप्यते।।[11]

12. बिल्वः · मालूरः · श्रीफलम्

(18) आमोदीनि सुमेदुराणि च मृदुस्वादूनि च क्ष्मारुहा-
मुद्यानेषु वनेषु लब्धजनुषां सन्तीतरेषामपि।
किं तु श्रीफलता तवैव जयिनी मालूर दिङ्मण्डले
यस्यैतानि फलानि यौवनवतीवक्षोजलक्ष्मीगृहाः।।[12]

सन्दर्भ-सङ्केताः

1. सुभाषितरत्नभाण्डागारम् (काशीनाथपाण्डुरंगपरबसङ्कलितम्)-(ईस्टर्न बुक लिंकर्स, दिल्ली, 1991)-प्रकरणम् 5, वृक्षान्योक्तयः, 53
2. सुभाषितरत्नभाण्डागारम् - प्रकरणम् 5, वृक्षान्योक्तयः, 46, 58
3. सुभाषितरत्नभाण्डागारम् - प्रकरणम् 5, वृक्षान्योक्तयः, 37
4. सुभाषितरत्नभाण्डागारम् - प्रकरणम् 5, वृक्षान्योक्तयः, 39
5. सुभाषितरत्नभाण्डागारम् - प्रकरणम् 5, वृक्षान्योक्तयः, 72
6. सुभाषितरत्नभाण्डागारम् - प्रकरणम् 5, वृक्षान्योक्तयः, 77
7. सुभाषितरत्नभाण्डागारम् - प्रकरणम् 5, वृक्षान्योक्तयः, 106, 119, 126, 127, 129, 131
8. सुभाषितरत्नभाण्डागारम् - प्रकरणम् 5, वृक्षान्योक्तयः, 133
9. सुभाषितरत्नभाण्डागारम् - प्रकरणम् 5, वृक्षान्योक्तयः, 140
10. सुभाषितरत्नभाण्डागारम् - प्रकरणम् 5, वृक्षान्योक्तयः, 164
11. सुभाषितरत्नभाण्डागारम् - प्रकरणम् 5, वृक्षान्योक्तयः, 172
12. सुभाषितरत्नभाण्डागारम् - प्रकरणम् 5, वृक्षान्योक्तयः, 175

卐 卐 卐

CASCADE V

MISCELLANEOUS

प्रकीर्णरसझरी

जीवन-रसझरी

जीवनसङ्गीत-रसझरी

कतिपय झलकियाँ

आचार्य डॉ० (प्रो०) जगदीश सहाय कुलश्रेष्ठ

उपाध्यक्ष

कालिदास संस्कृत संगीत कला एकेडमी, दिल्ली

- जन्म-तिथि एवं जन्म-स्थान : प्रथम श्रावण कृष्ण षष्ठी, 1977 विक्रम संवत् तदनुसार 7 जुलाई, 1920 में झाँसी (उ०प्र०) में जन्म। आयु-82 वर्ष।
- स्थायी सङ्केत : मणिका-धवल, के. सी./12बी, अशोक विहार, दिल्ली-110052 दूरभाष : 7143377, 7466139, 7120287
- उत्तर प्रदेश में निवास : जन्म से लेकर 1961 तक : 41 वर्षों तक उत्तर प्रदेश में निवास। अनन्तर 1967-1972 तक नैनीताल (उ०प्र०) में, तदनन्तर 2001 से अद्यावधि देहरादून, उत्तराञ्चल में निवास।
- ग्रन्थ-प्रणयन : अद्यावधि 120 ग्रन्थ प्रकाशित तथा 5 ग्रन्थ प्रकाशनाधीन।
  - लिमका बुक ऑफ़ रिकाड्र्स-2002 में सर्वाधिक ग्रन्थ प्रणयन हेतु नामालंकरण द्वारा विभूषित।

संस्कृत से सम्बद्ध कुछ विशिष्ट ग्रन्थ निम्नलिखित हैं-

1. कालिदास-संगीत-मञ्जरी I : मेघदूत-संगीत-पल्लवी : ईस्टर्न बुक लिंकर्स, दिल्ली, 1990
2. कालिदास-संगीत-मञ्जरी II: ऋतुसंहार-संगीत-सुरभि : ईस्टर्न बुक लिंकर्स, दिल्ली, 1992
3. सुमति-संगीताभरणम् : पद्मश्री सुमतिमुटाटकरभिनन्दनग्रन्थः : प्रतिभा प्रकाशन, दिल्ली, 1994
4. संस्कृत-संगीत-रत्नशती : ईस्टर्न बुक लिंकर्स, दिल्ली, 1996
5. कालिदास-संगीत-वैजयन्ती : संस्कृत संगीत कला प्रकाशन, दिल्ली, 1999
6. देवस्तोत्र-ज्योत्स्नामृतम् : संस्कृत संगीत कला प्रकाशन, दिल्ली, 2000
7. ऋतुराज-निर्झरी : शृङ्गारदीक्षागुरुर्वसन्तः : संस्कृत संगीत कला प्रकाशन, दिल्ली, 2001
8. Flora & Plant Kingdom in Sanskrit Literature वनज्योत्स्ना-सहस्रसौमनसी : ईस्टर्न बुक लिंकर्स, दिल्ली, 2003
9. Fauna : Animal & Bird Kingdom in Sanskrit Literature : संस्कृत-वाङ्मय एवं पशुपक्षिजगत् : ईस्टर्न बुक लिंकर्स, दिल्ली द्वारा प्रकाशनाधीन।
10. स्तोत्र-निर्झरिणी : संस्कृत संगीत कला प्रकाशन, दिल्ली द्वारा प्रकाशनाधीन।

(विस्तृत ग्रन्थ-सूची (मुद्रण वर्ष तथा प्रकाशक के नाम सहित) 'शब्दार्थसौन्दर्य-सहस्रचन्द्री' ग्रन्थ में द्रष्टव्य।

- अभिनन्दन-ग्रन्थों द्वारा सम्मान एवम् अभिनन्दन : विभिन्न विशिष्ट अवसरों पर विशिष्ट समारोहों में निम्नलिखित तीन अभिनन्दन-ग्रन्थों द्वारा सम्मानित एवम् अभिनन्दित :
  1. संस्कृत-संगीत-जगदीश्वरी : Jewels in Sanskrit & Musicology : प्रो० जगदीश सहाय कुलश्रेष्ठ अभिनन्दनग्रन्थ, ईस्टर्न बुक लिंकर्स, दिल्ली, 1995
  2. कवयित्री-कण्ठाभरणम् : Contribution of Women Writers to Sanskrit & Allied Literature : प्रो० जगदीश सहाय कुलश्रेष्ठ शताभिषेकाभिनन्दनग्रन्थ विद्यानिधि प्रकाशन, दिल्ली, 2000
  3. शब्दार्थसौन्दर्य-सहस्रचन्द्री : Beauty of Word & Meaning in Sanskrit & English Literature प्रो० जगदीश सहाय कुलश्रेष्ठ सहस्रचन्द्राभिनन्दनग्रन्थ, संस्कृत संगीत कला प्रकाशन दिल्ली, 2001
- संस्कृत के प्रचार प्रसार एवं विकास के क्षेत्र में योगदान : संस्कृत के प्रचार, प्रसार एवं विकास में पिछले 40 वर्षों से विशेषतः संगीतविधा माध्यम द्वार सतत रत। संस्कृत-सम्बद्ध अनेक ग्रन्थ प्रणीत। मेघदूत का अद्यावधि सबसे लम्बा संगीतमय कैसेट निर्देशित एवं दिल्ली संस्कृत अकादमी द्वारा 1993 में निर्मित।
- शैक्षिक योग्यता :
  (i) आनुवंशिक पद्धति से-आचार्य एवम् अनेक उपाधियाँ प्राप्त। अनेक लब्धप्रतिष्ठ गुरुओं से विधिवत् विद्याध्ययन सम्पन्न।
  (ii) विद्यालयीय पद्धति से-डॉक्टरेट (डी.म्यूज़.-पीएच.डी.) प्रभृति अनेक उपाधियाँ प्राप्त।
- शैक्षणिक अनुभव (अध्यापन तथा अन्य क्षेत्रों में) : 1939 से लेकर आज तक विभिन्न गरिमामण्डित पदों पर सवेतन आसीन रहते हुए सतत विधिवत् सेवारत। अध्यापन क्षेत्र तथा सांस्कृतिक क्षेत्र में अनवरत सेवा का 64वाँ वर्ष। सम्प्रति निदेशक, संस्कृति विभाग, द इण्डियन पब्लिक स्कूल, राजावाला, देहरादून (उत्तराञ्चल)। (विशेष विवरणार्थ द्रष्टव्य विस्तृत जीवन-परिचय)
- संस्कृत भाषा एवं साहित्य से सम्बन्धित तथा सांस्कृतिक संस्थाओं से सम्बन्धित धारित पद : 1. संस्कृत भाषा एवं साहित्य तथा संस्कृति से सम्बद्ध निम्नलिखित संस्थाएं संस्थापित एवं पद धारित :
  (i) कालिदास संस्कृत संगीत कला एकेडमी, दिल्ली, 1994; उपाध्यक्ष, 1994-अद्यावधि।
  (ii) एकेडमी ऑफ़ म्यूज़िक एण्ड फ़ाइन आर्ट्स, दिल्ली, 1994; निदेशक, 1994-अद्यावधि।
  (iii) संस्कृत संगीत कला प्रकाशन, दिल्ली, 1997; अध्यक्ष, 1997-अद्यावधि। इस प्रकाशन द्वारा अद्यावधि 50 ग्रन्थ प्रकाशित।

2. प्रति वर्ष कालिदास संस्कृत संगीत कला एकेडमी के तत्त्वावधान में दिल्ली में त्रिदिवसीय कालिदास-महोत्सव का समायोजन, ग्रन्थों का विधिवत् लोकार्पण, राष्ट्रिय शोध-संगोष्ठियों का आयोजन, विभिन्न शोध-परियोजनाओं का सञ्चालन, ग्रन्थों का प्रकाशन, विद्वानों के अभिनन्दन-ग्रन्थों का निर्माण तथा विद्वानों का अभिनन्दन एवं सम्मान।
3. देश की अनेक संस्थानों से सम्बद्ध तथा अन्य अनेक पद धारित। विस्तृत विवरणार्थ द्रष्टव्य विस्तृत जीवन-परिचय।

- सम्मान एवं पुरस्कार : अनेक सम्मान एवं पुरस्कार प्राप्त यथा -

1. राष्ट्रिय सम्मान : **लिमका बुक ऑफ़ रिकाड्र्स-2002** में सर्वाधिक ग्रन्थ प्रणयन हेतु नामालंकरण से विभूषित।

सन् 2001 तक 16 प्रकाशकों के द्वारा 106 ग्रन्थ प्रकाशित जिनकी लक्षाधिक प्रतियों का विक्रय हुआ। ये ग्रन्थ संस्कृत, हिन्दी, अंग्रेज़ी, उर्दू एवं पंजाबी भाषाओं में प्रकाशित हैं। आचार्य कुलश्रेष्ठ द्वारा कालिदास-प्रणीत मेघदूत के संगीतमय कैसेट के निर्देशन का भी उल्लेख **लिमका बुक ऑफ़ रिकाड्र्स-2002** में है।

2. संगीतकुलमुकुटमणि सम्मान : महर्षि प्रेमाच्युत पूर्ण भक्ति धर्म सभा, श्री साकेत धाम, सोलन, हिमाचल प्रदेश द्वारा **संगीतकुलमुकुटमणि सम्मान** से 1981 में अलंकृत।
3. अमृतमहोत्सव सम्मान : श्रावण कृष्ण षष्ठी तदनसार 17 जुलाई, 1995 को फ़ेडरेशन हाऊस, दिल्ली में आयोजित भव्य समारोह में अमृतमहोत्सव सम्पन्न तथा 'संस्कृत-संगीत-जगदीश्वरी' नामक अमृतमहोत्सवाभिनन्दनग्रन्थ से अभिनन्दित।
4. शताभिषेक सम्मान : श्रावण कृष्ण षष्ठी तदनुसार 22 जुलाई, 2000 को इंडियन मैडिकल एसोसियेशन हाउस, दिल्ली, में आयोजित भव्य समारोह में शताभिषेकमहोत्सव सम्पन्न तथा 'कवयित्री-कण्ठाभरणम्' नामक शताभिषेकाभिनन्दनग्रन्थ से अभिनन्दित।
5. सहस्रचन्द्री सम्मान : श्रावण कृष्ण षष्ठी तदनुसार 11 जुलाई, 2001 को इंडियन मैडिकल एसोसियेशन हाउस, दिल्ली में आयोजित भव्य समारोह में सहस्रचन्द्री महोत्सव सम्पन्न तथा 'शब्दार्थसौन्दर्य-सहस्रचन्द्री' नामक सहस्रचन्द्राभिनन्दनग्रन्थ से अभिनन्दित।
6. उ०प्र० संस्कृत संस्थान पुरस्कार : 'देवस्तोत्र-ज्योत्स्नामृतम्' ग्रन्थ पर वर्ष 2000 के लिए पुरस्कृत।
7. राष्ट्रिय सम्मान : **लिमका बुक ऑफ़ रिकाड्र्स-2003** में सर्वाधिक ग्रन्थ प्रणयन हेतु नामालंकरण स्वीकृत।

- **अन्य विशिष्ट उपलब्धियाँ**

(i) कालिदास-प्रणीत मेघदूत का संगीतमय कैसेट निर्देशित तथा दिल्ली संस्कृत अकादमी द्वारा 1993 में निर्मित एवं लोकार्पित। यह किसी भी संस्कृत ग्रन्थ का अद्यावधि सबसे लम्बा तीन घण्टे की अवधि वाला कैसेट है।

(ii) दस वर्ष की अल्पायु में प्रसिद्ध रिकॉर्डिंग कम्पनी एच.एम.वी. (हिज़ मास्टर्स वॉइस) द्वारा शास्त्रीय संगीत का रिकॉर्ड निर्मित। रिकॉर्ड की परिचय-पत्रिका में बाल कलाकार श्री जगदीश सहाय की प्रशस्ति अङ्कित। द्रष्टव्य विस्तृत जीवन-परिचय।

(iii) 19 वर्ष की आयु से आज 82 वर्ष की आयु तक किसी न किसी सम्मानित संस्था के किसी न किसी गरिमामय पद पर अनवरत सवेतन नियुक्त एवं कार्यरत।

(iv) दस हज़ार से अधिक विद्यार्थियों को प्रशिक्षित किया जिनमें से 500 से अधिक शिष्य देश-विदेश के उच्च पदों पर आसीन।

(v) अद्यावधि 125 ग्रन्थों का प्रणयन एवं प्रकाशन किया जिनकी 2 लाख से अधिक प्रतियाँ देश-विदेश के पुस्तकालयों में सुशोभित तथा सहृदयों के गृहों में उपलब्ध।

- **संस्कृतमय परिवार** : स्वयं तो संस्कृत भाषा एवं साहित्य तथा संगीत के प्रचार-प्रसार एवं विकास के लिए योगदान किया। साथ ही एक ऐसे सुसंस्कृत संस्कृतमय परिवार का निर्माण किया जिसके प्रत्येक सदस्य ने संस्कृत-जगत् में विशिष्ट योगदान किया यथा —

(i) धर्मपत्नी : श्रीमती कमलेश कुमारी कुलश्रेष्ठ : उन्होंने आजीवन साहित्य एवं कलाजगत् में विविध क्रिया कलाप किए।

'संगीत-कौमुदी' नामक प्रसिद्ध ग्रन्थ की लेखिका। श्रीमती कुलश्रेष्ठ के सम्मान में 'संस्कृत-संगीत-वैजयन्ती' नामक स्मृत्यभिनन्दनग्रन्थ 23 नवम्बर, 1991 को इण्डिया इण्टरनेशनल सैन्टर, दिल्ली में एक भव्य समारोह में लोकार्पित।

(ii) ज्येष्ठा पुत्री : प्रो० सुषमा कुलश्रेष्ठ : विगत 36 वर्षों से देश-विदेश में संस्कृत साहित्य एवं कलाजगत् के विभिन कार्यों में सतत संलग्न। उनके अद्यावधि 50 ग्रन्थ प्रकाशित। उ० प्रदेश संस्कृत संस्थान के **बाणभट्ट** सम्मान तथा अन्य अनेक पुरस्कार प्राप्त। दिल्ली विश्वविद्यालय में कार्यरत।

(iii) मध्यमा पुत्री : डॉ० अरुणा मोहन : विगत 30 वर्षों से देश-विदेश में संस्कृत वाङ्मय की विशिष्ट विधा-प्राणिविज्ञान के विभिन्न कार्यों में सतत व्यापृत। अनेक ग्रन्थों का प्रणयन एवं प्रकाशन। दिल्ली विश्वविद्यालय में कार्यरत।

(iv) कनिष्ठा पुत्री : सुश्री आभा कुलश्रेष्ठ : विगत 26 वर्षों से देश-विदेश में संस्कृत साहित्य, संगीत, संगीत एवं विधिशास्त्र के क्रियाकलापों में अनवरत संलग्न। प्रसिद्ध एडवोकेट। अनेक संस्कृत विद्वानों एवं संगीतज्ञों के अभिनन्दन ग्रन्थ सम्पादित किए। विधिशास्त्रपरक अनेक ग्रन्थ प्रणीत एवं प्रकाशित। दिल्ली विश्वविद्यालय एवं जामिया मिलिया विश्वविद्यालय में प्राध्यापन। सम्प्रति गुरु गोविन्द सिंह इन्द्रप्रस्थ विश्वविद्यालय में प्राध्यापन।

निदेशिका
कालिदास संस्कृत संगीत
कला एकेडमी, दिल्ली
वैकुण्ठ-चतुर्दशी
18 नवम्बर, 2002

प्रस्तुतकर्त्री
❋ **पारिजातमञ्जरी**
(सुषमा कुलश्रेष्ठ)
सदस्या, कला संकाय
दिल्ली विश्वविद्यालय

卐 卐 卐

SHRI JYOTSNAMOY CHATTERJEE

A PEERLESS PERSONALITY

A child was born on 25.11.1927 in Lilua, Calcutta (now Kolkata) in the morning at 10.30 a.m. Everybody started calling him "Raja" and later on, official name was given to the child as Jyotsnamoy Chatterjee. Cruel hands of destiny started testing him. At the tender age of eight he lost his father who was a Magistrate and belonged to a very rich family of Zamindars. He had a palatial house at Lilua, having all conforts of life, luxury and money. Mr. Chatterjee's father was a strict disciplinarian. At the age of eight years, the young boy used to go to courts for succession case with his mother and see court proceedings. It was really dificult for the widowed mother to take care of eleven children and her mother-in-law. She did share business to maintain the family since all money left by her husband was spent either on court proceedings or for maintaining the house and family.

The child grew up gradually, facing hardships in life and graduated as an engineer from Pune, held various senior positions in different organisations and finally shifted to Delhi and started a small scale business. By this time he was married and later blessed with a son and a daughter. His wife died of Jaundice just after six years of their marriage. He took care of his children both as father and mother, brought them up and both got settled in life. He led a deserted life, faced lot of business problems. Whatever little happiness he had, he shared with all. He was sympathetic to all, ever ready to help anyone even going out of the way.

I came in his contact through a lawyer when he was facing a complete strike in his factory. I was introduced to him as a lawyer and gradually he became a family member, very close to our family. It became almost a routine that we had lunch together on sundays and holidays, eating, gossiping, joking, planning many things for future.

He was very fond of travelling and to most of the places like Rameshwaram, Puri, Badrinath, Kedarnath, Tungnath, Dwarkadheesh, Somnath, Tirumala-Tirupati, Vaishno Devi, Kanyakumari, Trivendrum, Mysore, Ooty, Kodaikanal we went together. We knew all his brothers-sisters and relations and enjoyed time with them.

Mr. Chatterjee was an inspiration for all of us. He was very fond of music and inspite of best efforts to learn singing, he could not do so. Twice a music teacher was engaged but for one reason or the other, he could not learn music. This affinity for music led him to organise musical evenings at his house where he himself took care of tea, snacks, dinner for every visitor. Every morning and evening he will call us on phone just to ensure that everything is well.

He used to spend whatever money he had on himself and on others and never saved anything for future. His mother once asked him as to why he could not save money and the spontaneous reply was 'why you named me Raja'.

He was very fond of photography and caught the nature, rivers, mountains, forests, landscapes, sun-rise, sun-set, flowers, animals and birds in his cameras. He had more than fifty big albums containing thousands of photographs.

A renowned atstrologer and palmist in Calcutta once told him the date of his demise as 10th October, 1995. Mr. Chatterjee told this to us on 8th Oct. 1995. I laughed and laughed and asked him to visit us and spend the whole day with us on 10.10.95 . He was slightly upset believing partially what the astrologer had told him. The whole day passed on well, we all showed him as if we were not at all worried but from inside we all were really disturbed praying God to help us and grant long life to Mr. Chatterjee. God is great. He accepted our prayers and every thing went off well and we all were very happy.. It was learnt later on, that the said astrologer died on 10.10.1995.

Mr. Chatterjee used to eat very little but make every other person to eat much. He had a very fixed routine in life. He spent long hours in Puja and meditation. He himself was a very good palmist and his predictions always came true.

He was very fond of reading and thousands of books on various subjects were in his library. He had a pet 'Mukta' who was really loved by him. He was really distrubed when Mukta suddenly left us on 30th January, 2001. Mukta was like a child in the house having various dresses, caps, jackets, rug, pillow and even after her departure, Mr. Chatterjee kept her belongings with him as a token of her memory. Many photographs of Mukta are still with us. She lived with us only for one and a half year.

The cruel hands of destiny snatched Mr. Chatterjee from us on 28th August, 2001. Even today, we do not accept that he has gone, since anytime and everytime we feel that he is with us inspiring us to work more and more in the right direction honestly and sincerely. Whatever we do, we feel his presence with us as a guiding force. He was like a burning flame who showed path to everybody and I am sure the flame will always lead us. His fond memories are in our hearts, never to fade.

The last wish that we pray the Almighty Lord to fulfil is 'if there is another birth, let him be again with us.'

DELHI
25th November,2002
Shri J. Chatterjee's
Amṛtamahotsava

❄ ABHA KULSHRESHTHA

卐 卐 卐

APPENDIX I

CONTRIBUTORS

1. Agnihotri, Prabhu Dayalu (Prof.)
   Recipient of President's
   Certificate of Honour & Sahitya
   Vachaspati & U.P. Sanskrit Sansthan Award
   Ex. Vice-Chancellor, Jabalpur University;
   Res.: E 2 /73, Mahavir Nagar
   Bhopal-462016 (M.P.)

2. Anand, Kamal (Dr.)
   Reader & Head, Sanskrit Deptt.
   Lakshmi Bai College
   (University of Delhi), Ashok Vihar
   Delhi-110052

3. Anand, Subhash Chandra
   Principal
   D.A.V. Centenary Public School
   Paschim Enclave, Mia Vali
   New Delhi-110087

4. Anju Bala (Dr.)
   Publication Secretary
   Kalidasa Academy of Sanskrit
   Music & Fine Arts, KC/12 B
   Ashok Vihar, Delhi-110052

5. Balakrishnan, N. (Dr.)
   Reader in Mathematics
   Motilal Nehru College
   (University of Delhi South Campus)
   New Delhi.

6. Bhatia, Kanta (Dr.)
   Reader & Head, Sanskrit Deptt.
   Bharati College (University of Delhi)
   C-4, Janakpuri, New Delhi-110058

7. Bijelwan, Chakradhar (Dr.)
   Delhi

8. Biswas, Mukta (Dr.)
   Reader in Sanskrit, Gauhati University
   Guwahati (Assam)

9. Chandra, Meena (Ms.)
   Research Scholar, Department of Sanskrit
   University of Delhi, Delhi-110007

10. Chatterjee, Jyotsnamoy
    Ex. Managing Director, Bildal Electricals
    No. 11, Okhla Industrial Estate
    New Delhi 110020;
    Ex. Advertising Secretary, Kalidasa
    Academy of Sanskrit Music & Fine Arts
    Delhi-110052

11. Clair, D.S. (Dr.)
    Principal
    S.G.T.B. Khalsa College
    University of Delhi, Delhi 110007

12. Darshananand (Dr.)
    Ex. Dy. Director, Horticulture
    Allahabad Division;
    Res.: C-67, Guru Teg Bahadur Nagar
    (Kareli), Allahabad-211016 (U.P.)

13. Desai, Subhadra (Ms.)
    Research Scholar, Deptt. of Sanskrit
    University of Delhi, Delhi-110007

14. Dharma (Dr.)
Reader in Sanskrit, Lakshmi Bai College
(University of Delhi)
Ashok Vihar, Delhi-110052

15. Dhawal Chandra
KC/12 B, Ashok Vihar
Delhi-110052

16. Dwivedi, Chandrakant (Dr.)
Dy. Director, Uttar Pradesh
Sanskrit Sansthan, New Hyderabad
Lucknow (U.P.)

17. Ghosh, Ila (Prof.)
Principal
Govt. Girls Degree College, Sivni (M.P.);
Res.: 21, Aditya Colony
Narmada Road, Jabalpur (M.P)

18. Goel, Shashi Prabha (Ms.)
D E 128, Tagore Garden
New Delhi-110027

19. Gupta, Kaushalya (Kaushal) (Dr.)
Ex. Head of the Sanskrit Deptt.
Miranda House, University of Delhi;
Res.: 20, Amrapali, 56 I. P. Extension
Patparganj, Delhi-110092

20. Gupta, Manish (Sonu)
Dayal Graphics, 1432 Shorakothi
Subzi Mandi, Ghantaghar
Delhi-110007

21. Gupta, Pushpa (Dr.)
Reader in Sanskrit, Lakshmi Bai College
(University of Delhi), Ashok Vihar
Delhi-110052

22. Gupta, Urmi Bhushan (Dr.)
Reader in Sanskrit
Miranda House, University of Delhi
Delhi-110007

23. Gupta, Vandana (Dr.)
M.V. College of Education
(University of Delhi)
Shakurpur, Delhi

24. Jagan Nath (News Editor)
D.A.V. Centenary Public School
Paschim Enclave, New Delhi-110087

25. Jha, Ram Dev (Pt.)
Ex. Head, Deptt. of Jyotisha
S.L.B.S.R. Sanskrit Vidyapeeth
New Delhi; Res.: A - 260, Shivalik
Malvia Nagar, New Delhi-110016

26. Khanna, Saroj (Dr.)
Reader in Sanskrit
Satyawati College (Morning)
(University of Delhi)
Ashok Vihar, Delhi-110052

27. Kulshreshtha, Abha (Ms.)
LL.M., M.B.I.M. (London)
Advocate, Delhi High Court
102-104, Lawyers' Chambers
Western Wing, Tis Hazari Court
Delhi-110054

28. Kulshreshtha, Jagdish Sahai (Dr.)
Saṅgītakulamukuṭamaṇi
Felicitated in Limca Book of Records-2002
Ex.Principal, Institute of Music & Fine
Arts, Jammu (J&K); Res.: Manika-Dhawal
KC/12 B, Ashok Vihar, Delhi-110052

29. Kulshreshtha, Kamlesh Kumari (Smt.)
KC /12 B, Ashok Vihar
Delhi-110052

30. Kulshreshtha, Sushma (Prof.)
D.Litt., F.R.A.S. (London)
Recipient of Banabhatta Award
Felicitated in Limca Book of Records-2002
Ex. Visiting University Professor
Deptt. of Sanskrit, Ranchi University
Ranchi; Hony. Director
Kalidasa Academy of Sanskrit
Music & Fine Arts;
Res.: KC/12B Ashok Vihar, Delhi-110052

31. Kumar, Rajendra (Dr.)
Ex. Research Scholar, Sanskrit Deptt.
University of Delhi
Delhi-110007

32. Malhotra, Ravi
Sham Printing Agency
Vijay Nagar, Delhi-110009

33. Malhotra, Sham Lal
Proprietor, Eastern Book Linkers
5825, New Chandrawal, Jawahar Nagar
Delhi-110007

34 Meena Kumari
Lecturer in Sanskrit
Miranda House, University of Delhi
Delhi-110007

35. Menon, K.P.A. (Dr.), IAS (Retd.)
Recipient of President's Certificate of
Honour Award, Ex. Chancellor
Sri Lal Bahadur Shastri
Rashtriya Sanskrit Vidyapeeth
Shaheed Jeet Singh Marg
New Delhi-110016

36. Mohan, Aruna (Dr.)
Reader in Zoology & Ex. Co-Ordinator
Indira Gandhi National Open
University Study Centre, Gargi College
(University of Delhi)
New Delhi

37. Mohan, Manjari (Dr.)
Research Associate in Toxicology
National Institute of Immunology
New Delhi

38. Mohan, Pallavi (Ms.)
8241, Pocket 11, Sector B
Vasant Kunj, New Delhi;
New York, U.S.A.

39. Monika (Ms.)
KC/12 B, Ashok Vihar, Delhi-110052

40. Mukta (Ms.)
Ankur Vihar, Loni, Ghaziabad, (U.P.)

41. Mullick, Manju (Ms.)
Vice Principal
D.A.V. Centenary Public School
Paschim Enclave, Mia Vali
New Delhi-110087

42. Mullick, Shakuntala (Prof.)
Ex. Prof. & Head, Deptt. of Sanskrit
M.L.B. Arts & Commerce College
Jeewaji University, Gwalior;
Res.: 22 Lalitpur Colony, Lashkar
Gwaliar (M.P.); New York, USA

43. Mutatkar, Sumati (Prof.), Padmashri
Recipient of Kalidasa Sammana
Ex. Professor & Dean, Faculty of Music
& Fine Arts, University of Delhi
Delhi-110007

44. Pande, Asha Lata (Dr.)
Head of the Sanskrit Deptt.
Delhi Public School, Vasant Vihar
New Delhi

45. Pandey, Nagendra (Dr.)
Chairman, Uttar Pradesh Sanskrit Sansthan
New Hyderabad, Lucknow- 226007 (U.P.);
Deptt. of Jyotisha, Sampurnanand Sanskrit
University, Varanasi (U.P.)

46. Parijatamanjari (Ms.)
Manika - Dhawal, KC/12 B
Ashok Vihar, Delhi-110052

47. Pathak, Sachchidanand (Dr.)
Director, Uttar Pradesh
Sanskrit Sansthan, New Hyderabad
Lucknow (U.P.)

48. Rawal, Manju (Dr.)
Department of Sanskrit
V.V.D.A.V. Public School
Vikaspuri, New Delhi-110018

49. Ray, Bidyut Lata (Dr.)
Reader & Head, Deptt. of Sanskrit
Nilamadhava Mahavidyalaya
(Utkal University)
Kantilo, Nayagarh-752078 (Orissa)

50. Rustagi, Urmila (Dr.)
Ex. Principal, Miranda House
University of Delhi, Delhi-110007

51. Saluja, Chand Kiran (Dr.)
Reader in Education
Central Institute of Education
University of Delhi, Delhi-110007

52. Sarvaria, Prabha (Ms.)
33/10, Rajpur Road, Delhi-110054

53. Saxena, Pravesh (Dr.)
Reader in Sanskrit
Zakir Hussain College (Evening)
(University of Delhi), Ajmeri Gate
New Delhi

54. Sharma, Amita (Dr.)
Reader in Sahitya,
S.L.B.S.R. Sanskrit Vidyapeeth
Shaheed Jeet Singh Marg
New Delhi-110016

55. Sharma, Anita (Dr.)
Lecturer in Sanskrit
Lakshmi Bai College
(University of Delhi)
Ashok Vihar, Delhi-110052

56. Sharma, Pradeep (Dr.)
M.D., M.N.A.M.S.
Addl. Professor of Ophthalmology
Dr. Rajendra Prasad Centre for
Ophthalmic Sciences
AIIMS, New Delhi-110029

57. Sharma, Raman Kumar (Dr.)
Ex. Reader in Sanskrit
Motilal Nehru College
(University of Delhi South Campus)
New Delhi

58. Sharma, Ram Karan (Prof.)
Recipient of President's Certificate of
Honour & Sahitya Akademi Award
Ex. Vice-Chancellor, Sanskrit Universities
of Darbhanga & Varanasi ; Visiting
Professor, University of California
Berkelay, USA
Res.: 63, Vigyan Vihar, Delhi-110092

59. Sharma, T.R.(Dr.)
Ex. Convenor, Sanskrit Deptt.
S.G.T.B. Khalsa College
University of Delhi, Delhi-110007

60. Shastri, Shrivatsa (Dr.)
Reader in Sanskrit
Motilal Nehru College
(University of Delhi South Campus)
New Delhi

61. Shukla, Chandikaprasad (Prof.), D. Litt.
Recipient of President's
Certificate of Honour Award
Ex. Professor & Head
University of Allahabad
Allahabad (U.P.)

62. Shukla, Chandrakant (Prof.), D.Litt.
Pro-Vice-Chancellor, K.S.D. Sanskrit
University, Darbhanga (Bihar)

63. Shukla, Poonam (Ms.)
Research Scholar, Deptt. of Sanskrit
University of Delhi, Delhi-110007

64. Singh, Kanwar
Sector 11, Rohini, New Delhi

65. Singh, Mehar
Samboli, Delhi

66. Singhal, S.K.
Deptt. of English
D.A.V. Centenary Public School
Paschim Enclave, Mia Vali
New Delhi-110087

67. Sinha, Ravindra Kishore
President & Director General
International Institute of Security & Safety
Management & Chairman,
The Indian Public School, Dehradun;
Res.: A-1/152, Safdarjang Enclave
New Delhi-110029

68. Sinha, Rita (Ms.)
Vice-Chairperson
The Indian Public School
Rajawala, Dehradun
(Uttaranchal)

69. Srivastava, Anand Kumar (Dr.)
Reader & Head of the Sanskrit
Deptt., C.M.P. Degree College
Allahabad University, Allahabad

70. Tiwari, Shashi (Dr.)
Secretary, World Association for
Vedic Studies, India Branch ;
Reader in Sanskrit, Maitreyi College
(University of Delhi South Campus);
Res.: 54, Sakshara Apartments
A-3, Paschim Vihar, New Delhi-110063

71. Trikha, Nirmal (Dr.)
Reader in Sanskrit, Daulat Ram College
University of Delhi, Delhi-110007

72. Tripathi, Chandrashekhar
Research Scholar, Deptt. of Sanskrit
University of Delhi, Delhi-110007

73. Upadhyay, Shivji (Prof.)
Recipient of Kalidasa Award
Prof. & Head, Deptts. of Sahitya Sangita &
Kala, Sampurnanand Sanskrit University
Varanasi (U.P.)

74. Vasishtha, Shridhar (Prof.)
Ex. Vice-Chancellor, S.L.B.S.R.
Sanskrit Vidyapeeth, New Delhi;
Res.: House No. 429, Sector 7
Urban Estate, Gurgaon-122001
(Haryana)

75. Wig, Lata (Dr.)
Deptt. of Sanskrit
D.A.V. Centenary Public School
Paschim Enclave, Mia Vali
New Delhi-110087

卐 卐 卐

APPENDIX II

PUBLICATION COMMITTEE

1.	Shri Jagan Nath CHAIRMAN	News Editor, World Feature Service (N.D.), Depthnews Asia, N.D. Bureau (Manila, Philippins), D.A.V. Centenary Public School Paschim Enclave, New Delhi-110087
2.	Dr. Kamal Anand	Reader & Head, Department of Sanskrit, Lakshmi Bai College (University of Delhi), Ashok Vihar, Delhi-110052
3	Dr. Pushpa Gupta	Reader in Sanskrit, Lakshmi Bai College (University of Delhi) Ashok Vihar, Delhi-110052.
4.	Dr. Pravesh Saxena	Reader in Sanskrit, Zakir Hussain College (Evening) (University of Delhi), Ajmeri Gate, New Delhi
5.	Dr. Urmi Bhushan Gupta	Reader in Sanskrit, Miranda House, University of Delhi Delhi-110007
6.	Dr. Manju Rawal	Department of Sanskrit, V.V.D.A.V. Public School Vikaspuri, New Delhi-110018
7.	Ms. Meena Chandra	Research Scholar, Deptt. of Sanskrit, University of Delhi Delhi-110007
8.	Dr. Anju Bala SECRETARY	Publication Secretary, Kalidasa Academy of Sanskrit Music & Fine Arts, KC/12 B, Ashok Vihar, Delhi-110052

卐 卐 卐